HISTORY OF RAILWAYS

HISTORY OF RAILWAYS

HAMLYN-NEL

Contents

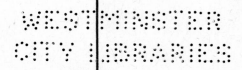

f385.09

DR

Volume Editor: **J. T. Shackleton**
General Editors: **J. H. L. Adams and P. B. Whitehouse**
Picture Editors: **Janice Every, Rosemary Lister and Michele Monk**

First New English Library edition, 1976.
Published by the Hamlyn Publishing Group Limited
London - New York - Sydney - Toronto
Astronaut House, Feltham, Middlesex, England
in association with New English Library,
Barnard's Inn, Holborn, London.
© Text and illustrations copyright New English
Library Ltd., 1974, 1975, 1976
Printed by Fratelli Spada, Ciampino, Rome.
ISBN 0 600 37587 0

7702

Introduction

THE story of railways as we understand them today spans only about a century and half, and yet in that relatively brief period of history the whole pattern of man's social and industrial life has undergone substantial and, indeed, revolutionary changes. It is well known that steam power in the broad sense (and the steam railway in particular) was the principal agent of this transition, and it is perhaps this close link between the railway and so much of our recent history which accounts for the exceptional popular interest which railways have always been capable of generating.

Not surprisingly, the opening days of the earliest railways, the Stockton and Darlington and the Liverpool and Manchester for instance, created scenes of wild enthusiasm and celebration and such was the novelty of this new form of transport that it would be fair to say that many of those early trains would have carried a few passengers who were not going anywhere in particular, but were merely intent upon sampling the pleasurable experience of travel in the abstract. Travelling from town to town had not hitherto been an experience to savour. By horse or on foot, it had been at best an expensive inconvenience and at worst sheer hard work. But now, with the coming of railways, it became an opportunity for relaxation and reflection, for discovery and adventure, a chance to see new ways of life which had not previously been open to most of our forebears, crammed as they were into cities and into exploitative ways of ekeing a living. Robert Louis Stevenson summed up the brave new world which was to be glimpsed through the carriage window in his poem 'From a Railway Carriage' – a century later Colin Gifford succeeded, magnificently and definitively, in expressing it photographically in his books *Each a Glimpse* . . . and its sequel . . . *And Gone For Ever*. It is this sampling of diverse modes of experience through the medium of the railway which, amongst other things, this book sets out to capture; one wonders how much the legendary 'white collar conservative' – the feted Mr Businessman – misses as he is whisked along by Inter-City, poring over cash flows and credit ratings, ignoring the world which flashes by in its infinite variety outside his smoked-glass carriage window.

For those who love them, railways are an endless store of moments – *William Whitelaw* (failed again) limping off its northbound train at Peterborough, to be replaced by a B1 in ruinous condition, Spadina roundhouse, steam-wreathed and darkly mysterious, floating by the frozen window, five General Motors diesels on the front of a hundred cars and flatbeds, bound for Detroit, whining, throbbing and hooting through flashing lights and midnight level-crossing bells, as John Fahey plays on FM radio and the world is – briefly – one. Maybe in these pages there will be a reminder of your own moments of railway magic, diverse, illogical, whatever they may be. Small wonder that as well as the benefits to travel and commerce which the railway gave, it also offered us something worth spending a few moments to watch. In the nineteenth century, no piece of railway art worthy of the name could be complete without a knot of fascinated onlookers standing idly by; no railway terminus today, be it Victoria, Paris Nord or Grand Central, is without its contingent of boys of all ages at the buffer stops. Beside every lineside fence, it seems, there lurks a gricer with his camera.

Undoubtedly, one of the principal factors in this by no means entirely specialist interest in railways has been the steam locomotive, and this book is unashamedly orientated towards this marvellous machine. Although easily the most animated of man's inventions, breathing forth fire and smoke and trumpeting its noisy way across the world, the steam locomotive is a reassuringly manageable beast. Its powerful splendour can be harnessed, but only through discipline, control and organisation. One cannot simply climb into the cab and drive away, as one would with a motor car or even a diesel; several hours of specialised preparation of the locomotive are necessary before it is ready for the road. While it may be technically identical to other locomotives of the same class, each individual locomotive is full of its own handling characteristics and it requires the great skill and attention of its driver to bring out its best performance. The progress of a train requires the painstaking co-operation of signalmen, train reporters and station staff as well as the members of the train crew. This harmony and orderliness of operation must certainly be an influential element in the attraction which the railway has held for so long, offering a sense of stability in a world becoming increasingly chaotic.

Even though the decline of steam is evident throughout the world, it has lost nothing of its appeal; if anything, interest in the steam engine, and in the diesel and electric machines which have replaced it in many parts of the world, is increasing. The steam locomotive is for most people the lead-in to other, equally fascinating aspects of railways: the stations, great and small, the complex web of track and signals, the carriages and wagons, the timetables and above all the personalities behind these things. Because the railway is so visibly present and active, we are led to wonder how and why it all works, where the trains go when they pass out of sight and what means are employed for them to get there.

The fifteen sections of this book do not pretend to answer all the questions which might arise, but they look at many things which may not be immediately obvious and might in turn pose a few questions themselves. The book has been divided basically into two halves. The first part deals with the history and development of railway technology, from the days before the locomotive was even invented to the complicated railway hardware of today. It brings out the significant changes in the development of motive power by detailed studies of principal locomotive types, looks at the changing patterns of freight and passenger services over the years, and emphasises the important role which such matters as signalling and timetabling have played in the evolution of railways. Building on this historical background, the second half of the book moves on to look at the myriad ways in which the railways of the world have established themselves and coped with the particular problems which each country presents for their railway systems. The breadth and variety is exceptional, ranging from the antique narrow-gauge lines of Portugal to the 150mph super railways of Japan, from the big steam engines still to be found in the Andean heights to the modern diesels working across the Nullarbor Plain.

Indeed, the by-ways and sidelines present some of the railway's most fascinating angles: those experimental locomotives which did not quite succeed, the plush interiors of first-class Victorian carriages (and the spartan accommodation in the third class), even the accidents and disasters which have periodically shocked a world accustomed to the exceptional safety record of rail travel. Many people will have seen engravings of the old horse-drawn waggons on eighteenth-century railways, but how many will realise that horses were still being used by railways in various parts of the world until well into the second half of the present century? Do many people know how the American railroad system keeps track of its two million freight vehicles? Or remember the now sadly departed express on which kippers were *de rigueur* for breakfast? It is the careful little details like this which make this book an endless source of new knowledge for even the most dedicated railway enthusiast.

It is a story told in the words of experts, backed up by a superb selection of illustrations, assembled from many different sources all over the world to provide as varied and as comprehensive an account of railway history as one could wish for. There are engravings, paintings, photographs, posters, even cigarette cards and Edwardian picture postcards. For those who have already fallen under the spell cast by the irresistible atmosphere of railways, this book will be a definitive appraisal of railway lore. For those who feel themselves succumbing to the delights of railway history, it will be a guide and companion along the way.

J. T. Shackleton
Brighton
September 1975

1
Early Railways

PRIMITIVE 'RAILWAYS' were in existence well before the appearance of the first steam locomotives. Traces still remain of the flat-topped stone blocks which the Romans laid down to provide a smooth surface for their chariot wheels, which were guided by grooves cut in the blocks. An American investigator interested in the subject, who measured the distance between the grooves on a number of the stoneways unearthed in the ancient city of Herculaneum, discovered the remarkable fact that their average distance apart was 1.445 metres, almost exactly equal to the 4ft 8½in which is now the standard railway gauge in Great Britain, the whole of North America, and various other countries.

In Great Britain the first evidence of anything in the nature of a railway or tramway dates back to 1555, when near Barnard Castle in County Durham parallel baulks of timber were laid down to enable horses to pull heavier loads than they could if the wagons ran only over dirt tracks. By the 1670s such wooden ways had become common, and early in the following century iron plates were being laid over the timber so that it did not wear so quickly under the action of the wagon wheels. By 1776, at the Nunnery Colliery in Sheffield, flat iron plates were being replaced by lengths of angle-iron, laid parallel to one another, to keep the wagons running truly along the track; the flats of the angles still preserved the timber below them. It is of interest that the name 'platelayer', which until quite recent years was applicable to the men who maintained railway permanent way, originated from the gangers who laid down the plates of these early tramways.

The father of the railway track as we know it today was probably William Jessop, who in 1789, on a tramway near Loughborough, tried the experiment of laying down a track with cast-iron rails. These had a broad upper table, to carry the wheels, and a fairly substantial web, beneath which the rail broadened out at the ends to a wide foot. The foot was spiked down to the sleepers to preserve the gauge and also provided a socket into which the end of the next rail fitted. These cast rails, which were of a fish-bellied form for greater strength, were about 3ft long and extended only from one sleeper to the next. By the end of that century such rails were being cast without the feet and sockets at their ends, and in greater lengths, and were being spiked down to the sleepers.

The use of flanged wheels in Britain seems to have originated some time during the 1730s, on the Prior Park tramway in Bath, but over what type of track we have no record. In the change from wagon wheels running on the outside of the angle-irons, which kept them to their prescribed track, to flanges running on the inside of the first rails we probably have the origin of the odd figure of 4ft 8½in which is now our standard gauge. Originally the gauge no doubt was round about

BULL-HEAD to FLAT-BOTTOM
THE HISTORY OF TRACK

5ft, but reduction of the two widths of rail head involved in the change from outside to inside guidance reduced the figure to 4ft 8½in.

Just as the iron plates of the earliest tramways had been laid down to prolong the life of the timber baulks over which the wagons ran, it was found desirable to protect the timber sleepers from indentation by the feet of the early rails. So the practice began of securing the rails in cast-iron chairs, which spread the weight of the moving loads over a bigger area of timber.

Incidentally, one ingenious inventor of this early period was John Blenkinsop, agent of the Middleton Colliery near Leeds, who, like many of his contemporaries, considered that it would be impossible to obtain sufficient adhesion for the movement of heavy loads between the smooth tyres of the locomotive driving wheels and the smooth rail surfaces. He therefore designed a rail on the outside of

which there were cast at regular intervals semi-circular projections, or ears. The cylinders of his locomotives then drove toothed wheels, which engaged with the projections and prevented any possibility of slipping. Such a positive cogwheel was soon proved to be unnecessary, but Blenkinsop undoubtedly was the father of the rack-and-pinion railways of later years, designed to permit working up very steep gradients. Indeed, the Swiss railway up Mount Pilatus, of which the ruling gradient is 1 in 2, is worked precisely on this principle, with a rack which consists of a flat bar of steel with teeth machined out of both its outside edges.

The next development in Great Britain was that cast iron soon proved to be too brittle a material for railway rails, and breakages were frequent. A change then took place to wrought iron, and thus from foundry production to rolling in longer lengths in rolling mills, which produced a much tougher rail. By degrees a rail

Left: A coal wagon serving a Newcastle mine in 1737. The horse hauled the empty wagon up the hill and followed as the loaded wagon was let downhill on the brake.
Science Museum London

Left below: Engraving of the Prior Park Tramway with flanged wheels at Bath.
Science Museum London

Above: William Jessop, civil engineer, who used cast-iron rails on a tramway near Loughborough in 1789. *Science Museum London*

Below: A replica of the cast-iron rack rail and wheel developed by Blenkinsop.
Science Museum London

section was evolved in the shape of a dumbbell, known as the double-head rail, with the head and the foot of equal cross-section, separated by a thinner web; this was secured in the cast-iron chairs by wooden wedges or keys, hammered tightly in and so keeping the rails precisely to gauge. The abrasive action of the wheels gradually wears the rails down in height, and the idea of the double-head rail was that when the head of the rail had been worn down to the safety limit, it could be turned upside down and the wear transferred to the foot, so prolonging its life.

However, it was soon found that this was an unsatisfactory procedure. In course of time the chairs indented the foot of the rail, so that when the rails were turned and the foot became the head, the running over the succession of indentations was extremely rough and noisy. So eventually came the introduction of the bull-head rail, with a head of larger cross-sectional area than the foot, not to be turned but to allow of longer wear before the limit of safety was reached and relaying became necessary.

Another change of the greatest moment began in 1857. Wrought iron might be a tough material, but it had little resistance to abrasive wear, and in locations subject to heavy traffic rail replacement was found to be necessary at uncomfortably frequent intervals. In 1857 the Midland Railway laid down at Derby the first rails rolled from steel, which lasted for 16 years in a location at which replacement every three months had been necessary previously. This was a revolution indeed and steel soon became compulsory in all rail rolling.

Meanwhile in 1836 an engineer named Charles Vignoles had devised a rail section of a quite different type. This had a rounded head to sustain the wear, and then, below a thin web, a flat foot designed to be spiked directly to the sleepers without the interposition of a chair. The attraction of this type of rail was very considerable in countries like the United States, where railways were being extended over great distances through country only sparsely inhabited. Elimination of the chairs meant that it became necessary to transport no more than the rails and the dog-spikes to hold them down to the site of track-laying; sleepers in many cases could be cut down from neighbouring forests.

Be that as it may, while Britain standardised the type of track with bull-head rails keyed in chairs, in almost every other country in the world the flat-bottom rail became the standard. In course of time it was found necessary, for the preservation of the timber of the sleepers, to interpose cast-iron or rolled-steel soleplates between the rails and the sleepers in order to spread the load, but that did nothing to affect the almost universal preference for the flat-bottom form of rail. As traffic weight and density increased, in Great Britain the weight of bull-head rail was gradually increased to 95lb and even 100lb per yard. With the far heavier locomotives and rolling stock in the United States, the weight of flat-bottom rail was increased to 133lb/yd generally and in the case of the Pennsylvania Rail Road to 155lb/yd.

There is one matter connected with steel rails in which Great Britain has always remained well ahead of North America, and that is length. By degrees British rails grew in length from 24ft to 30ft and then to 45ft; the first railway in the country to lay a longer rail was the London & North Western, which rolled 60ft rails in its own mill at Crewe Works and with them proudly claimed 'the finest permanent way in the world'. All this time American steelworks, which had never laid themselves out to handle longer lengths, supplied the railways with no greater length than 39ft. Next the British London & North Eastern Railway experimented with 90ft, and finally with rails no less than 120ft long, although only two steelworks in the country were equipped to handle so awkward a length as this. The aim of increasing length, of course, is to reduce the number of rail joints, which are the weakest points in the track. In recent years, however, much greater lengths have been attained by another method, to which we shall refer later.

By the 1930s British adherence, almost alone in the world, to the bull-head was beginning to be questioned. Was it possible that Britain was the only country to be right, and were all the others wrong? To answer this question, the London Midland & Scottish Railway decided in the middle 1930s to lay a stretch of flat-bottom track, to be soon followed by the London & North Eastern. Success was almost a foregone conclusion; although heavier in weight and thus more expensive to lay, the flat-bottom rail, with its greater depth and broad foot proved stiffer in both vertical and horizontal planes than the bull-head, and therefore more easy to keep strictly in line, so helping to keep down maintenance costs.

But a still greater saving in maintenance was to come later, by the welding of rails into far longer lengths than the 120ft which had been experimented with by the LNER. As previously mentioned, the rail joint is a point of weakness in the track, needing more attention in maintenance than any other part. The pounding of the wheels as they pass over the gaps in the rails sets up high stresses; cracks in the rails necessitating their removal from the track occur more frequently at the rail ends than at any other point and the fish-plates and bolts used to join the rails together break from time to time. Not only that, the vibration and shocks caused by passing over the joints tends to increase the wear and tear of rolling stock. Many different methods of supporting the joints have been tried from time to time, but it is the perfection of rail welding that has solved the problem.

Flash-butt welding is the method generally employed and conveniently situated welding depots with the welding processes automatically controlled to preserve the quality of the welds have been established. At first the process was confined to welding pairs of rails together, but it has been gradually extended until today continuous lengths of rail of 900ft and more are being produced at BR welding depots; they are automatically loaded on to special wagons and run out to the sites at which they are to be laid. Such a procedure is not cheap, but it more than pays for itself by the reduction that it makes possible in the cost of track maintenance. The passenger also benefits in that he has a much quieter ride, with none of the previous 'clickety-clack' from the rail joints.

The question is often asked how expansion of the rails with temperature, which made it necessary to allow gaps between the rails at the joints, is now allowed for. The answer is that experience has proved that if the rails are held sufficiently tightly, the tendency to expand or contract can be confined within the steel as an unrelieved stress, of compression or tension, which disappears when the rails return to the temperature at which they were laid. Possibly a very small measure of expansion or contraction takes place laterally instead of longitudinally, but of that we have no proof. One essential with welded rail is to have substantial ballasting, especially at the sleeper ends, to prevent the rails from buckling in hot weather, which in the past has been the source of a number of derailments. But rail welding has certainly come to stay, and in addition to Great Britain is now a general practice all over Europe and North America.

The soundness of rail steel is a matter of great importance; an undiscovered broken rail can cause disaster, and in the past such casualties have not infrequently occurred. In the course of manufacture rail defects may develop; if they are external, they can be seen during the course of inspection and the rails rejected, but it is a different matter with internal defects. One such which for years gave immense trouble in the United States was a tiny transverse fissure in the rail head, caused by stresses during the cooling of

Above: Remains of flanged track of the Ticknall Tramway with a primitive turnout.
Science Museum London

Below: A German montage depicting various stages in the development of rails, rail fastenings, track bed and track.
DB Film Archiv

Facing page: Lithograph after A B Clayton of Liverpool & Manchester Railway with horsedrawn barge passing under bridge on the Bridgewater canal.
British Transport Museum (B Sharpe)

the rails after rolling in the cold winter temperatures of the USA, which under traffic spread annually, like the rings of a tree-trunk, until some extra stress, like the hammer-blow of a badly balanced locomotive, broke the rail through. Many American rails failed in this way, sometimes with disastrous results.

A partial answer to the problem was provided with the development of the rail flaw detector car, which could be driven slowly along the track and, by passing a series of signals through the rail, could reveal the presence of a hidden fissure, marking its location on a moving paper roll and dropping a splash of paint on the affected rail. So the rail could be replaced before failure occurred.

Some similar trouble with flawed rails was experienced in Great Britain at about the same time with rails which were being treated while still red-hot with a water spray designed to produce a tough skin structure. Eventually a cure was found in the controlled cooling of the rails after rolling, which prevented the development of the internal stresses that produced the initial fissures. Even so, the mobile method of detection has been so successful that something similar has now been evolved in our own country for the patrolling of railway tracks, but able to travel at much higher speed and therefore to check for flaws more frequently.

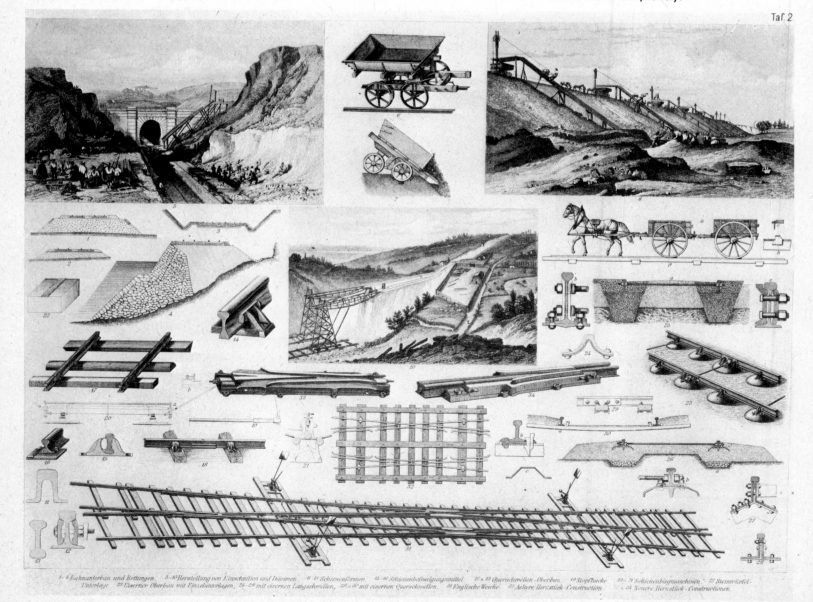

THE START OF LOCOMOTIVE POWER

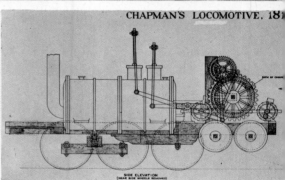

Top: The remains of Richard Trevithick's 1804 locomotive preserved at the Science Museum, London. *Science Museum London*

Above: Chapman's locomotive of 1813 which hauled itself along on a chain. *Science Museum London*

Below: Science Museum's drawing of Blenkinsop's locomotive of 1812 on the rack-drive Middleton railway. *Science Museum London*

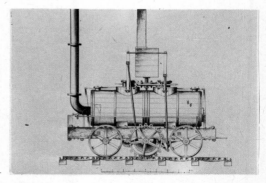

BY THE END of the eighteenth century, steam engines were widely used to drive machinery in factories, and to power lifts and pump water in mines. But they were enormous, bulky, awkward things. They generally had to be contained in a building erected round them. As long as they depended on using steam at only a few pounds pressure, and derived at least part of their power from atmospheric pressure working against a vacuum produced in a condenser, it was impossible to design an engine small enough to move about under its own power and haul a useful load as well. So although James Watt is generally known as the father of the stationary steam engine, it was Richard Trevithick, the apostle of 'strong steam' and the use of pressures as high (by 1805) as 25 pounds per square inch or more, who was the originator of the locomotive.

The first railway locomotive was built by Trevithick in South Wales in 1804, as an experimental modification of one of his high-pressure stationary engines. It ran for long enough to prove the feasibility of the idea, but it was soon taken off its wheels and used in a foundry. Trevithick's second operating locomotive ran for a while on a circular demonstration track in London during 1808, and started much public interest; but the first successful commercial use of locomotives was not until 1812, on the Middleton Railway near Leeds. Four machines of Trevithick's design, but with

two cylinders and other improvements, worked the traffic of this line for over twenty years. But the Middleton engines were untypical in one respect. John Blenkinsop, the manager, believed that the grip of a smooth iron wheel on a smooth iron rail would not suffice to haul a train, and altered Trevithick's design so that the drive was through a toothed wheel engaging with a pinion cast onto the outer edge of one rail.

This problem of adhesion was one which vexed theorists most at that time, perhaps because experience had made people aware of the difficulties of braking wagons in wet weather on steep descents laid with iron rails. The rack-and-pinion solution developed by Blenkinsop and his engineer, Matthew Murray, certainly worked, though at a price. Others tried out locomotives which winched themselves along on a chain (Chapman), or horsed themselves along on mechanical legs (Brunton). Less of a theorist, William Hedley, the engineer of the Wylam Railway near Newcastle, tried experiment instead, and built a wagon whose wheels were turned by cranks operated by a crew of men standing on top. By this means, and with the aid of ballast weights, he proved that in spite of everything an iron wheel had enough frictional bite, without assistance, to allow a locomotive to draw a useful load; and in 1813 he introduced steam locomotion on the Wylam line. Like Blenkinsop, he followed

Trevithick's designs, but with more improvements, and he retained Trevithick's boiler, which was better than Murray's. Hedley's three Wylam locomotives, *Puffing Billy* and its brothers, worked from 1813 to 1862, surviving meanwhile rebuilding from 4 to 8 wheels and back again, and in one case a period powering a tugboat on the Tyne; and they were withdrawn finally because the railway was converted from 5ft to 4ft 8½in gauge. Two of the three still exist, in museums in London and Edinburgh.

Above: A surviving early railway civil engineering construction, The Causey/Tanfield Arch, near Consett, built in 1727 to carry a wagonway.
J B Snell

Below: Hedley's 'Wylam Dilly', which followed 'Puffing Billy' in 1813 at Wylam colliery. *Science Museum London*

Right: Hedley's No 1 'Puffing Billy' which worked at Wylam for nearly 50 years.
Science Museum London

Bottom: A selection of locomotives built for various railways by Vulcan Foundry between 1834 and 1854. *Science Museum London*

Overleaf: Lithographic print of J W Carmichael's drawing entitled 'Haydon Bridge 1838' one of a series commissioned to commemorate the building of the Newcastle & Carlisle Railway.
British Transport Museum (B Sharpe)

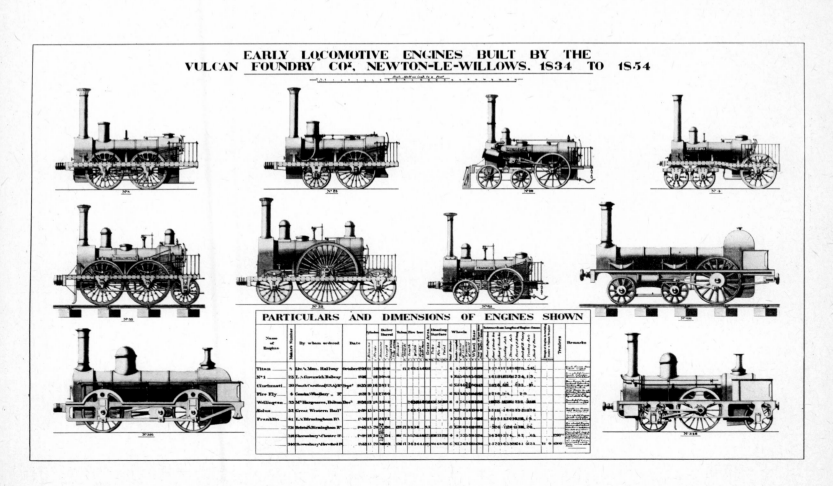

EARLY LOCOMOTIVE ENGINES BUILT BY THE
VULCAN FOUNDRY COᵞ, NEWTON-LE-WILLOWS, 1834 TO 1854

HERE IN 1825
THE STOCKTON AND DARLINGTON
RAILWAY COMPANY
BOOKED THE FIRST PASSENGER
THUS MARKING AN EPOCH
IN THE HISTORY OF MANKIND.

The Stockton & Darlington

Top: Tablet on the building at Stockton on Tees commemorating the place where the first railway passenger in the world was booked. *British Rail NER*

Above left to right: S&D pioneers George Stephenson, Edward Pease and Francis Mewburn. *E D Walker and Wilson*

Below: Plaque commemorating Timothy Hackworth on his birthplace at Shildon. *British Rail NER*

Right: Preserved S&D locomotive 'Locomotion' in Darlington Works in 1960. *John Adams*

STOCKTON &
DARLINGTON
RAILWAY
TIMOTHY HACKWORTH
WHO BUILT THE ROYAL GEORGE
LOCOMOTIVE AT SHILDON
LIVED IN THIS HOUSE FROM
1833 TO 1850

THE SOUTH DURHAM coalfield, near Bishop Auckland, had always suffered from its inaccessibility, and the landowners of the district were by 1815 envious of the riches gained by their brethren owning collieries in the flatter districts nearer the Tyne. The land was too hilly for a canal; their proposal to build a railway from near Bishop Auckland to Darlington and the sea at Stockton was one of the biggest schemes in the air in 1820, though not the biggest, since some horse-worked canal feeder lines building at the same time were even longer. What made the Stockton & Darlington historic was the fact that George Stephenson was appointed its Engineer in 1821, and laid out its main line for 22 miles from Shildon to Stockton for locomotive haulage. Not only was this to be the longest run that locomotives had yet had; the Stockton & Darlington was to be the first railway to use them to handle public traffic.

Following the opening of the line in 1825, and *Locomotion*'s first run with a trainload of coal and several hundred of the company's guests (invited and otherwise), there was a great public interest in the steam experiment. Not all of it was friendly; noise, smoke, and the risk of fires started by hot coals, were all complained of by local landowners, who brought a lawsuit seeking to suppress the nuisance. All this started an 'environmental' protest movement against railways which made life very difficult for

Left top: Opening of the Stockton & Darlington
Railway in 1825 as depicted in a painting
by Terence Cuneo. *British Transport Films*

Left: Share certificate No 535 issued by the
S&D to Thomas Newman in 1823.
Science Museum London

Below: 'Locomotion' as now preserved at
Darlington Station. *Picturepoint*

Above: Advertisement for the S&D's
regular passenger service opened on
October 10, 1825. *E D Walker and Wilson*

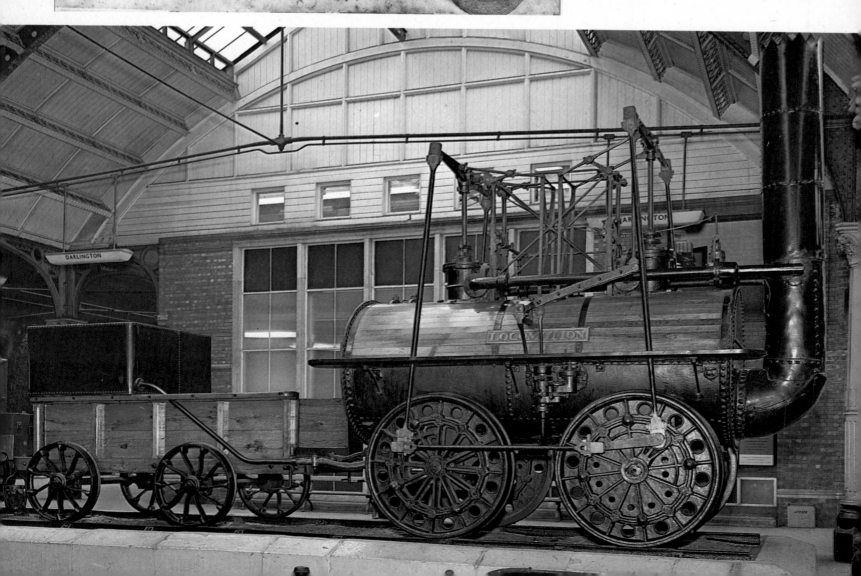

their promoters for ten years or so, until the public benefits they brought had been demonstrated even more widely.

Just as critical was the interest in the technical and economic test. Were locomotives really practical propositions on a public railway? It was several years before the answer to this question was placed beyond all doubt.

At its opening, the S&D was worked by a mixture of steam and horse power. The railway company handled its trains with locomotives, as a rule; but it had been set up on the same legal basis as a canal company or a turnpike trust, and its original main object was simply to provide a road which others might use with their own vehicles, on payment of tolls. So life was made interesting, with the same single line shared by steam goods trains, horse wagons driven by independent and often unruly individuals, and even a rail stagecoach run by another enterprise. There were rules of precedence, as to who should give way to whom when they met on the single track, and horses always had to take to sidings to allow

locomotives to overtake them; marker stones were set up midway between passing loops, and he who passed the marker first could force his opponent to reverse out of the way; policemen were set along the way to enforce the rules (and put out the fires started by the engines), but not infrequently blows resulted. And there was trouble with the engines too. They blew up, rather too often; their cast-iron wheels gave trouble; Timothy Hackworth, the first Locomotive Superintendent of any public railway, had a nerve-wracking job at first, shaking the various bugs out of the system.

At first, the engines proved too short-winded to manage a steady 22-mile upgrade haul; mercilessly thrashed (with much fire-throwing) the Stephenson boiler just about managed, but Hackworth as soon as possible built more powerful machines with more efficient boilers. Right up to the 1840s, the S&D clung to engines with vertical cylinders, which had to be limited to 6-8mph, and so it was a long time before horses disappeared. But as early as 1827 the directors of the railway claimed a saving of 30 per cent on the haulage cost per ton-mile, locomotives compared with horses. Once this cash economy was substantiated, it was clear that locomotives had a future, whatever their opponents might say.

Below: Reconstruction of 1825 Dandy-cart and wrought-iron track laid on stone sleepers, for the Stockton and Darlington Centenary. *Topical Press*

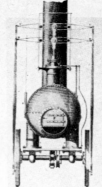

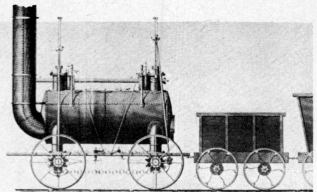

GEORGE STEPHENSON

GEORGE STEPHENSON was born near Wylam, in the Tyne Valley, in 1781. By 1813 he was already an engineer of considerable local reputation, even though he lacked formal education. He had a strong practical bent, and had studied the operation of the pumps and winding engines in the local collieries to such effect that he had often been able to devise improvements to them. One of his achievements had been to produce a miners' safety lamp, following a series of pit explosions, that was in some ways preferable to one invented simultaneously by Sir Humphry Davy. The main consortium of Tyneside coalowners, the 'Grand Allies', had appointed him to have chief responsibility for all their machinery.

Hedley's Wylam locomotives ran on a railway that was near the Grand Allies' territory, but did not belong to them. But the consortium at once took an interest in their possibilities. The price of horse fodder had soared as a result of the war, and they disliked seeing a competitor steal a march on them. They therefore instructed Stephenson to build a locomotive for their Killingworth Railway. Stephenson's first machine, the *Blucher*, took to the rails in 1814. In most ways it was not as advanced as Hedley's, being a very close copy of the Middleton engines, though without the rack drive. But although not an adventurous engineer, Stephenson was a sound one and not averse to small experimental steps; furthermore, he had the immense advantage of working for a richer employer who kept him going. Between 1814 and 1826, during some lean years for business, Stephenson was the only man in Britain who built locomotives.

Stephenson copied Murray's boiler, which had only a single large straight firetube set inside the boiler barrel. The arrangement was very wasteful of heat and fuel and it set a limit on the amount of steam produced by the boiler (and hence its power) because the heating surface was so restricted. Trevithick (and Hedley) used a U-shaped fire tube with vastly more heating surface and greater steam-raising capacity, combining it also with the use of an exhaust steam blast in the chimney to give a forced draught to the fire. The boilers of Stephenson's engines were thus their weak point. Their strength was in the mechanical improvements he brought about.

After a while he dispensed with the noisy, expensive and awkward transmission of power to the wheels by means of a train of gears, which had been used in all previous locomotives, replacing it first of all with a sprocket chain of the familiar modern kind, which he invented for this purpose, and then by coupling and connecting rods. Through his association with the ironmasters William Losh and Michael Longridge, Stephenson was responsible for the develop-

ment of improved cast-iron rails and wheels, as well as the first steel springs strong enough to carry weights of several tons. By experiment with Stephenson's locomotives at Killingworth, Nicholas Wood improved pistons and valves and demonstrated the saving obtained from allowing expansive working of steam in the cylinder, cutting off the admission of live steam from the boiler fairly early in the stroke.

All this while, Stephenson's (and other) locomotives were steaming along, accumulating practical experience of the possibilities and the economics of mechanical traction. By the mid-1820s, the results were beginning to look promising, and there began to be talk of building a network of steam railways throughout Britain.

Top left: Plate showing type of locomotive patented by George Stephenson and William Losh in November 1816; it was used in a patent specification for improved malleable iron rails in 1820 by John Birkinshaw.
Science Museum London

Top right: Engraving of Stephenson's colliery locomotive of 1820, used in the 1825 edition of 'Wood's treatise'.
Science Museum London

Above: Group including (seated) George and (right) Robert Stephenson.
Science Museum London

Below: Engraving of Stephenson's 'Lancashire Witch' with rod couplings for Bolton & Leigh Railway, used in 'Annales des Mines' 1829.
Science Museum, London

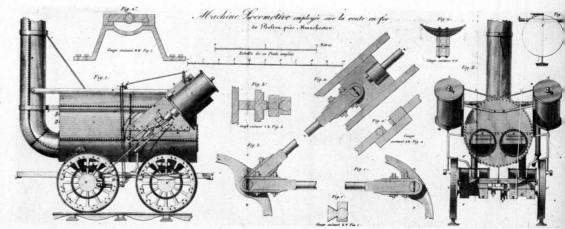

A litho of Hetton Colliery, drawn on stone by
J D Harding. *Science Museum London*

Below: Details of model of Stephenson's
'Planet' of 1830 which set the basic pattern
for steam locomotives for a century.
Science Museum London

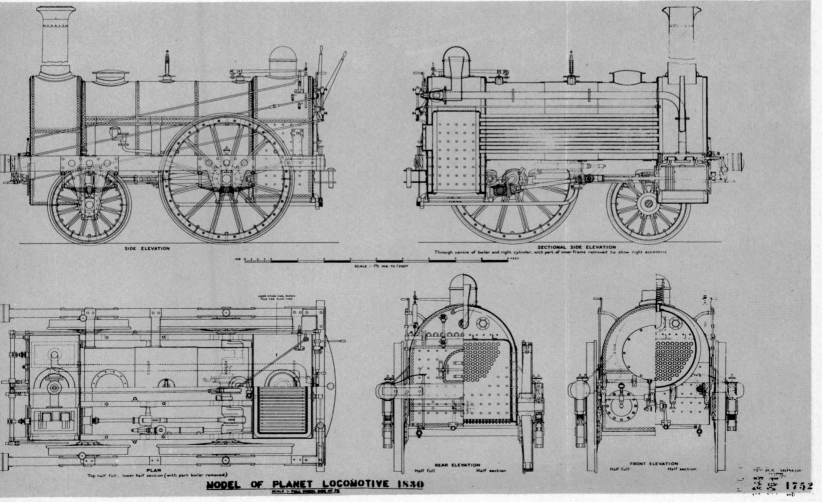

RAINHILL TRIALS

THE LIVERPOOL & MANCHESTER Railway, 30 miles long, was started in 1826, the year after the opening of the Stockton & Darlington. But while the S&D was still basically a colliery railway, whose raison d'etre was the transport of coal from mine to wharf, the L&M was the world's first line intended to form the principal link for all classes of traffic between two large cities. Although about the same length, the L&M was vastly the larger work, with heavier engineering and double track throughout, and there was never any question of using horses to draw the trains. The question was whether steam power should be used in the form of stationary or of locomotive engines. The company decided to try locomotives first, since that experiment would be cheaper.

During 1829 the L&M directors advertised that they would give a prize to the builder of the locomotive which best met their requirements, at a contest to be held that autumn on a completed section of the line at Rainhill. Their conditions were onerous. The engine should not weigh more than $4\frac{1}{2}$ tons (if four-wheeled) or 6 tons (if six-wheeled) excluding tender; it should use steam at not more than 50lb per square inch but the boiler must be tested hydraulically to three times that figure; it had to 'consume its own smoke' (because an Act of Parliament said so); and it had to haul a load of three times its own weight for a total of 30 miles at 10mph.

One determined gentleman entered a horse-powered wagon driven by a treadmill, but this was treated by the judges as rather a jest and it did not have anything like the power required. Many inventors gave notice that they intended to try for the prize, but failed to reach the starting line. There were only three serious contestants. First was Timothy Hackworth's *Sanspareil*, a smaller four-wheeled version of the standard Stockton & Darlington locomotive; second Braithwaite and Ericsson's *Novelty*, a lightweight and unconventional machine based on the boiler and machinery used by Goldsworthy Gurney for his experimental steamdriven coaches of the period on the Bath Road; and finally Robert Stephenson's (George Stephenson's son) *Rocket*.

The *Sanspareil* had been built in a great hurry, and failed to meet the terms of the test. It was rather overweight; it was also very wasteful of fuel, partly because Hackworth still used Trevithick's return-flue boiler, partly because the blast was too strong and threw unburnt fuel out of the chimney, partly also because the boiler was leaky and in an effort to staunch the leaks had 'been fed with more oatmeal than would fatten a pig', and again partly because of a defective cylinder casting. That she ran at all was creditable under the circumstances; with more time the defects might have been alleviated, but they knocked Hackworth out of the ring.

The *Novelty*, like many subsequent machines designed for use on roads, was insufficiently substantial for railway work, and although the favourite of the crowd with its glittering paint and polish, lapping the course at over 30mph, the complex

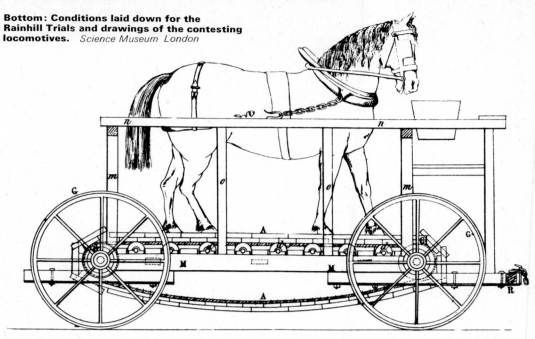

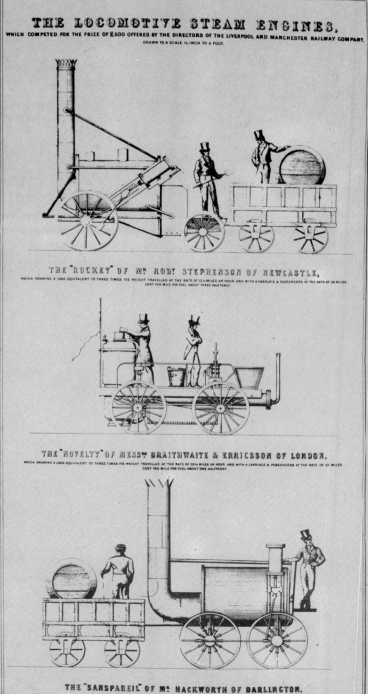

boiler soon gave trouble and so did the bellows which blew the fire. Its progress ended with a bang of an unwelcome sort, and the locomotive had to be pushed clear of the course.

Although also hastily built, the *Rocket* embodied a great deal of careful thought by the younger Stephenson. She had an entirely new design of boiler, using many small tubes to convey heat to the water instead of a single large one. The cylinders were removed from their vertical position, and placed at an inclination; thus they could drive the wheels directly, while still allowing them to move on the springs. And for the first time, weight and expense were saved by using only one pair of driving wheels. The *Rocket* was thus both simpler and more robust than its predecessors, and therefore more efficient, and it romped away with the prize. Having fulfilled the terms of the contest, Stephenson gave his machine its head on the last run and ran nearly as fast as the *Novelty* with the test load; he then gathered a coachload of passengers and steamed them smartly up and down the nearby Whiston incline, of 1 in 96, up which the expert consultants engaged by the Company had declared that no locomotive could ever draw a useful load.

And so the *Rocket* demonstrated the triumph of the steam locomotive. As with so many pioneering machines, it was soon to be overtaken by events and proved too small for the L&M's traffic; but to this day it stands beside the *Sanspareil* in the Science Museum at South Kensington, London.

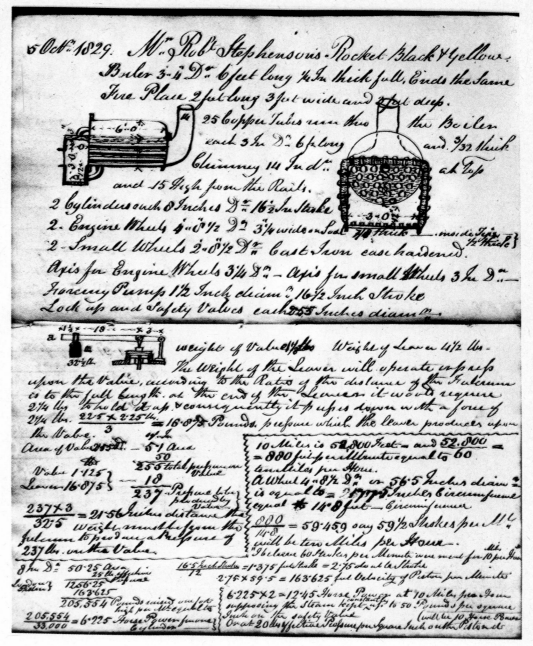

Right: Ackermann print showing the Liverpool & Manchester Railway, one of the Stephenson lines which established the world standard gauge of 4ft 8½in.
British Transport Museum (B Sharpe)

The First Main-Line Locomotives

BETWEEN 1829 AND 1834 the steam locomotive developed out of all recognition. The impetus for this was undoubtedly the Liverpool & Manchester Railway, where for the first time trains were carrying a large quantity of general public traffic, including crowds of passengers. Train weights had grown beyond all forecasts within a few weeks of opening, and there was an advertised timetable which had to be adhered to.

The *Rocket* had been completed in September 1829. By the time the L&M opened, exactly a year later, seven or eight more engines of basically similar type had been built at Robert Stephenson's small works in Newcastle, but with certain changes as

work progressed, since it was soon realised that the 4½-ton *Rocket* was too small. The cylinders were moved downwards to a horizontal position, and the *Rocket* itself was altered to correspond. The firebox was incorporated inside the boiler shell, and its design rapidly evolved to produce the standard Stephenson boiler, fitted to the overwhelming majority of steam locomotives from that day to this. Separate frames began to be used, to relieve the boiler plates of the stresses of running and shunting, and the engines grew successively bigger. The final engines of the Rocket class weigh almost 8 tons, and are pictured in the famous engravings made at the time the line opened.

Top left: Model made in the Science Museum workshops of Stephenson's 2-2-0 'Planet' of 1830.   *Science Museum London*

Above: Remains of Stephenson's 'Rocket' of 1829 preserved at the Science Museum, London.   *Science Museum London*

Above left: Aquatint by S Bourne picturing a commemorative plaque of George Stephenson as engineer and builder of the Liverpool & Manchester Railway.   *British Transport Museum (B Sharpe)*

Below and bottom : Aquatints by J Shaw showing passenger and freight trains at work on the Liverpool and Manchester Railway.   *British Transport Museum (B Sharpe)*

Bottom right: An 1863 print depicting London Kings Cross station of the Metropolitan Railway showing the double-gauge tracks, with GWR broad-gauge locomotive and carriages in occupation.   *London Transport Executive*

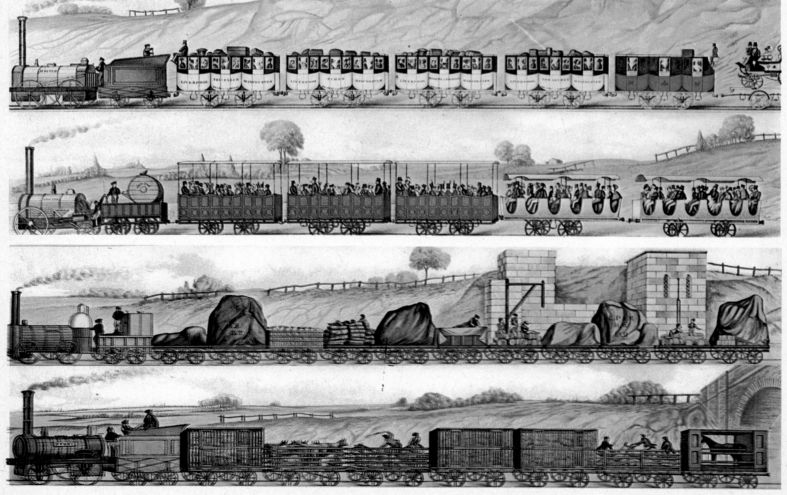

Above: Rocket-type locomotive taking in water at Parkside on the Liverpool and Manchester. *British Transport Museum*

Right: Patentee 2-2-2 locomotive as built from about 1834 to 1850.
Science Museum London (Edito Service)

Overleaf: 'The Depot at Hexham', a Carmichael lithograph of 1836.
British Transport Museum (B Sharpe)

Later in 1830 Stephenson dropped the Rocket design in favour of the Planet type, which foreshadowed later practice even more closely. Retaining all the advances already made, on these engines the cylinders were moved from the rear to the front of the engine, where they have remained ever since (although on the Planets they were situated between the frames, which was to prove a minority taste). Engines broadly similar to the Stephenson Planets were built in great number by many firms; they monopolised the London & Birmingham Railway for some years after its opening in 1838, and were exported to several countries, including the USA. The type was soon varied to produce a version with all four wheels coupled.

A few years more, and it began to be clear that apart from the question of increasing haulage capacity as traffic continued to grow, the cost of maintaining track which was used by hard-working four-wheeled locomotives weighing about ten tons was going to be too high. They rode too roughly, and knocked it out of shape. The remedy was to have larger engines, with six wheels. Hence, in 1833, Stephenson's Patentee class, which was basically a Planet with an additional pair of carrying wheels at the rear. But the opportunities of variation on this theme were not neglected; very soon the L&M had a number of four-coupled Patentees for their growing freight traffic and for assisting trains up hills, naturally given names like *Samson* and *Elephant*. One of them, the *Lion* of 1838, survives as a working museum piece. And one Patentee-type six-coupled engine, built for the Leicester & Swannington Railway in 1834, was a 17-tonner which in every important respect was the forerunner of the standard British goods engine, the inside-cylinder 0-6-0, built in various shapes and sizes and enormous numbers for 110 years. And this had been evolved in the short space of five years, since *Rocket* first steamed out before the crowds at Rainhill, England.

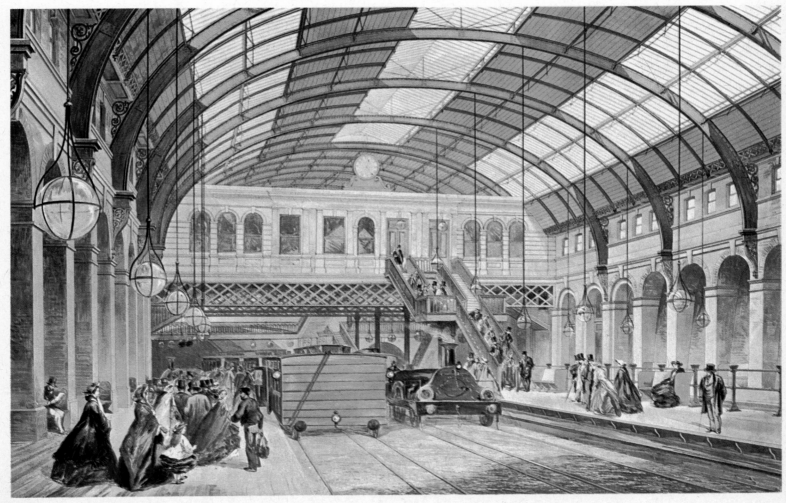

The Lithographs of J.W. Carmichael

This section reproduces several lithographs after paintings of scenes on the Newcastle & Carlisle Railway by the celebrated painter John Wilson Carmichael (1800-1868), a contemporary of Bourne, Bury, Ackermann and other famous early railway artists. His *River Wall at Wylam Scars* was first published in 1836, a year after the first section of the line opened and well before it was completed throughout. It shows one of the two locomotives with which service was opened drawing a train crowded with passengers.

Thanks to Carmichael, and the publishers of the commemorative booklet in which his pictures first appeared, the Newcastle & Carlisle is probably better documented pictorially than any other of the early railways. He produced more than 20 drawings between 1836 and 1838 as various sections of the line were completed which were published first in small groups and then reissued as a complete collection in 1839. Other Carmichael pictures in this book are *Bridge over River Gelt* (facing page), *Haydon Bridge 1838* (p. 16), *Cowran Cutting 1837* (p. 32) and *The Depot at Hexham* (pp. 26-7).

The Newcastle & Carlisle was well worth the attention of an artist of Carmichael's calibre, for there were features in plenty worth recording in the course of its 60-odd miles between east and west sides of the country. Wishaw's *Railways of Great Britain and Ireland*, in its piece of the line opens, 'Whoever is in the habit of travelling on the railway between Newcastle and Carlisle will be forcibly struck with the curiosities of its course throughout.' It adds a nice tribute in, 'Yet, notwithstanding this apparent impediment to speedy locomotion, no railway in the kingdom is better regulated in point of punctuality of the arrivals, especially of the quick trains, nor is there any upon which fewer accidents have occurred.'

Less favourable perhaps was the comment, 'A snakelike motion, however, and frequent jerks, are consequences of this curvilinear course; and unless it had been originally laid out for a railway . . . to be worked by horses, no engineer would have ventured to recommend a plan which exhibits on the face of it almost one continuous series of curves from end to end.' In the event, as was recorded in Part 20, the first section of the line opened with steam traction on March 3, 1835, and apart from a gap of a few weeks in service almost immediately afterwards, used steam continuously thereafter.

Of earthworks in the construction of the line, the Cowran Hill cutting, originally intended to be a tunnel, was the biggest. It had a length of about a mile, an average depth of 43ft and a greatest depth of 110ft,

requiring excavation of around a million cubic yards of spoil. Of the 90 or so original bridges, most notable was the Corby viaduct carrying the railway over the river Eden just outside Carlisle. Five semi-circular arches of 80ft span and the abutments made up a total length of 564ft, with a height above normal river level of 100ft.

The river wall in the picture overleaf is on the south bank of the river Tyne about nine miles from Newcastle. The river formerly ran right up to the base of Wylam Scars, which rise to over 100ft above normal water level, and the railway track bed was built up of rock and rubble quarried from the hillside itself. The wall is about three-quarters of a mile long and carries the track about 26ft above normal river level.

To the left of the view is Wylam colliery, scene of various early railway activity and quite close to the village in which George Stephenson was born. The bridge in the distance was not part of the original railway works, but was a timber construction erected later by subscription, to provide quick communication for foot passengers and vehicles, including railway wagons, between the railway and the Wylam Iron Works also seen in the picture.

Picture Overleaf: River Wall at Wylam Scars.
British Transport Museum (B Sharpe)

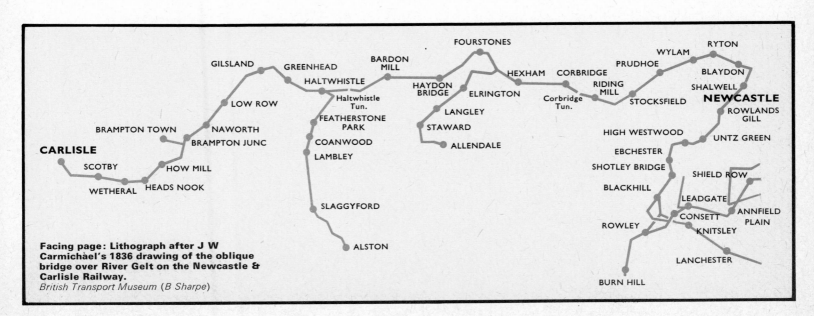

Facing page: Lithograph after J W Carmichael's 1836 drawing of the oblique bridge over River Gelt on the Newcastle & Carlisle Railway.
British Transport Museum (B Sharpe)

THE RAILWAY MANIA

Above: Having laid its track from the beginning in the 1830s to a gauge of 7ft, the GWR had to embark, from the middle 1860s, on the huge task of reducing it to the standard 4ft 8½in, as in this picture; conversion was eventually completed in 1892.
Ian Allan library

Right: Early railway notice to the public on the London Brighton & South Coast Railway of 1899. *British Transport Museum (B Sharpe)*

Below: Lithograph of 1837 after J W Carmichael showing the Cowran cutting on the Newcastle & Carlisle Railway.
British Transport Museum (B Sharpe)

LONDON BRIGHTON AND SOUTH COAST RAILWAY Cᵒʸ
PUBLIC WARNING NOT TO TRESPASS

Persons trespassing upon any Railways belonging or leased to or worked by the London Brighton and South Coast Railway Company solely or in conjunction with any other Company or Companies are under The London Brighton and South Coast Railway [Various Powers] Act, 1899, section 15, liable on conviction to a Penalty of FORTY SHILLINGS in accordance with the provisions of the said Act Public warning is hereby given to all Persons not to trespass upon the said Railways.

LONDON BRIDGE TERMINUS.
OCTOBER 1899.
J. J. Brewer
Secretary

OFTEN ENOUGH an innovator has at first to contend with popular scepticism or even opposition. Then he has his way and the dust settles for a while, and his old opponents and the public at large hold their peace and observe. Then, if the innovation succeeds and especially if it makes money, very often there is a sudden awesome rush as everybody joins the party, the ancient scoffers often leading the field. So it was with railways. During the 1830s the first parts of the main-line inter-city network began to be laid down in Britain, and by 1841 you could travel by train from London to Brighton, Southampton, Bristol, and Birmingham, while branching or extending from the London & Birmingham Railway were lines to Liverpool and Manchester, Leeds, Derby, and York.

These railways had not been in business for more than a few years, but they rapidly proved two things to the whole country. First of all, they gave a very useful and convenient service for passengers and freight, which was of great advantage also to the districts served in opening up new markets for their produce. Secondly, the railway companies were profitable, and paid a very reasonable return on the money invested in them.

By 1841 there were some 1,500 miles of railway in operation in Britain. For the next couple of years there was rapid but fairly steady growth. The government had kept some control over the development of new schemes both by careful debate in Parliament and by requiring them to be approved in draft by a Commission set up for the purpose, which had to consider both the public need for any new railway and also its effect on existing lines. But the Commission was short-lived and was abolished in 1845 out of a feeling that railway promoters knew their own business best, while at the same time a vast rush of new Bills overwhelmed the government machinery. All of a sudden the public caught on to the idea of a national railway grid, which 'Punch' ridiculed by publishing a satirical map of of the future, apparently insanely complex, British railway network which, fifty years later, had come to look fairly accurate. One of the biggest laughs had been the idea of railways in the Isle of Man.

But as so often when politicians' and economists' fashion prompts action, greed appeared also. Many of the schemes of 1845 were ill-considered and not a few were downright fraudulent. For a while it was possible to put one's name down as a subscriber to a railway scheme, receiving shares for a nominal payment, which one could then resell at a substantial profit, so eager was the throng of investors with spare cash; and of course the sharks gathered. A day was named by which all plans for new lines to be considered by the 1845/6 Parliament had to be submitted, and a near-riot followed, with special trains and stage-coaches bringing promoters from all parts with their boxes of papers and rolls of plans. Porters struggled to close the doors of the Board of Trade offices against the pressure of the crowd. It was a brief, mad, spell;

a few weeks later some smooth gentlemen had done extremely well out of it, and rather more had done very badly.

In the usual British manner after things have gone spectacularly wrong, the Government carried on exactly as before. During 1844 and 1845 Parliament had laid down a broad legal framework for the railway system, which remained unaltered for the rest of the century. A department of the Board of Trade was set up with powers to regulate matters of railway safety; certain minimum standards of service were laid down, including a requirement that each line should run at least one train a day, at an average overall speed of at least 12mph, carrying passengers at a fare not above a penny a mile; and the state was given power to control or reduce the charges of any company which paid unreasonably large dividends. As an aid to its efforts, Parliament for the first time codified basic

Company law and laid down standard legal obligations on the railways, avoiding the need to discuss this administrative matter over again with every fresh scheme. But apart from these administrative provisions, 'laissez-faire' ruled. The state did not concern itself with the detail of where railways were to be built, and imposed no plan or strategy. Provided it took its chance, survived the debate, and raised enough money, any project was as good as any other. There was no second Railway Mania because the public had learnt its lesson.

And in spite of the upheaval, railway construction proceeded apace. By 1850 there were some 6,500 miles of line open, and the railway map of Britain looked not unlike today's main-line network. There were some gaps, but not many. The most apparent was the lack of a railway across South Wales, which was not ready until

1852. Twenty years from the opening of the Liverpool & Manchester, therefore, the national railway system was established throughout; later construction was a matter of filling in gaps.

Crests of the Stockton & Darlington, the first public steam railway opened in 1825 and, right, of the Great Western, the first of the four great British railways opened in 1838.

The First Railways in Europe

THE EXPERIMENTS with steam locomotion in England did not go unnoticed on the Continent, although given Britain's head-and-shoulders start in world industrialisation it was several years before much development took place elsewhere. The Prussians built two locomotives of Murray/Blenkinsop pattern at the Royal Iron Foundry in Berlin in 1816 and 1818, which were the first in Europe, but neither saw service outside the works yards. One reason was that there were fewer railways on the Continent; there were indeed lines in the Ruhr, Silesia, south-west of Lyons, and in several other places, but nothing like the networks of Tyneside or South Wales.

The first public steam-worked railway in France was the Lyon & St Etienne, a 38-mile line opened in 1828 which took delivery of its first two engines the following year. They were built by Marc Seguin, a French engineer who had visited England and learnt a great deal from Stephenson's practice. His design solved a number of the problems which had been vexing the Stockton & Darlington, without producing answers as satisfactory as Stephenson came to for the Liverpool & Manchester. For instance, he invented the multi-tubular boiler independently of Stephenson, but combined it with a bricked-in firespace beneath and outside the boiler; and he avoided the fire-throwing problem by substituting fans driven by the wheels for the steam blast (but they blew the fire fiercer when the engine was coasting down than when it was labouring up hills).

Consequently the second and subsequent early French railways, such as the Paris-St Germain (1837) and the two competing lines from Paris to Versailles (1839/40), obtained their earliest locomotives from the Stephenson works at Newcastle. It was some time before native products displaced the imports, partly because so many of the early Continental railways were also built by English engineers. Thus, George Stephenson went to Spain, and Robert to Norway, to lay out their first main lines, and Joseph Locke was responsible, in the mid-1840s, for the main line from Paris to Le Havre, and brought across with him the 'Crewe-type' standard outside-cylinder 2-2-2s designed by Alexander Allan. These multiplied in France, where they were known as 'Buddicoms'.

Similarly with the first public steam railway in Germany, the short line from Nuremberg to Fürth, opened in 1835. This commenced with a Patentee 2-2-2 named *Der Adler*, imported complete with English driver. British machines and men also pioneered railways in Spain, Italy, Switzerland, Austria, Belgium, Holland, Sweden, Russia, and elsewhere.

The importance of this still remains. The Stephenson gauge of 4ft 8½in is the Euro-

Top: A model of 'Der Adler', the first locomotive in Germany built by Robert Stephenson & Co in 1833 for the Nuremberg-Fürth Railway. *DB Film Archiv*

Above: Opening ceremony of the Nuremberg-Fürth line on December 7, 1835. *DB Film Archiv*

Right: William Wilson, a Stephenson pupil, who drove 'Der Adler' on its inaugural run, remained in Germany and eventually became head of the Ludwigs Railway. *DB Film Archiv*

Bottom: First horsedrawn railway carriage in Austria in 1830 on the Budweis-Linz line. *DB Film Archiv*

Facing page top: A model of the first locomotive in Finland 'Ilmarinen' a Crewe-type 4-4-0 built in England in 1861. *Finnish State Railways*

Facing page centre: Opening of the Berlin-Potsdam Railway in September 1838. *DB Film Archiv*

Facing page bottom: French-built 1851 0-6-0T 'Lahore' by J E Cail & Company.

pean standard, and European railways still use the same height and spacing of buffers and couplings as the English originals. On the other hand, the strong legal enforcement of private property and highway rights against the interloping railways in Britain meant that many bridges and tunnels had to be built merely to keep trains out of the way. There was thus an incentive to build them small and tight to save money, and so the British loading gauge has remained relatively cramped from that day to this.

On the Continent matters were otherwise. As a rule, the State itself took on the task of railway building, since private capital was not often available. Governments are always less willing to accept than to impose expense on others; road bridges, etc, were therefore many fewer in Europe, and so Continental engineers took and were given more room around the tracks. It is sometimes said that Britain's smaller trains and tighter clearances are the penalty suffered by the pioneer of railways. On the contrary; the reason for the greater leeway on European lines was originally political and economic.

ie Eifenbahn zwischen Berlin und Potsdam.

THE ESSENTIAL DIFFERENCE between the geographies of Europe and of North America by 1830 was that while in Europe civilisation had existed for centuries, and had established a complex structure of towns, buildings, land ownership, property rights, and other rights-of-way including turnpike roads and canals, through which the railways had to thread themselves, in America a nearly virgin landscape was still being or had only recently been wrested from the red man, and most of the land had no individual owners at all. Turnpike roads and canals had begun to be built, but broad and long the railways could go where they wished without much consideration for other occupiers of the land, since there were none.

Tracks were laid down the main streets of towns—though often enough the tracks were there first and the town later—and they rarely had to build bridges to cross roads. The tendency, especially since money was much scarcer than in Europe, was to build railways quickly and cheaply, and this policy was encouraged by the government, which often granted to the companies large tracts of land in the country to be served by the new line, on condition that trains were running by a given date. The route could always be levelled, straightened, or improved by rebuilding later, and line relocations in the USA are still continuing, although they are quite rare in Europe.

There were a few horse tramways in the Eastern States, built often to act as canal feeders; and it was on one such, the Delaware & Hudson Canal Company's line at Honesdale, Pennsylvania, that the first 'road-service' locomotive in America first ran in 1829. It was the *Stourbridge Lion*, a Killingworth-type engine built in England by Foster & Rastrick of Stourbridge. Unfortunately it was too heavy for the track, and was taken out of service.

Steam locomotion really started in America on the Baltimore & Ohio Railroad, an ambitious project commenced in 1829. During 1831 the railroad company arranged a locomotive contest on similar lines to the one at Rainhill, though with even stricter weight limits, and the main part of the contest consisting of a month's practical service in traffic. Five competitors entered,

all American, and the winner was a watchmaker named Phineas Davis, who entered a vertical-boiler four-wheeler. Although it proved an evolutionary dead end, it was quite a practical design up to a certain size and in fact the last of the 18 similar engines he built for the company stayed at work until 1893. By 1835 steam power ruled the tracks of the B&O to the exclusion of horses, and many other railways were following suit.

Technically, the important difference between American and British railways resulted from the former's lighter and rougher construction, and greater need to save capital outlay. British-type four-wheeled engines and carriages would not stay on the uneven rails, and so they had to be provided with guiding wheels and bogies. This in turn meant that passenger coaches, for instance, had to be built much longer, and the abandonment of compartments in favour of open saloons was then purely a matter of cost saving. On the other hand, the scarcity of bridges and tunnels meant that there was plenty of room to build high and wide, and the steeper gradients put early emphasis on the need to have powerful engines. American locomotive builders, having started by copying Stephenson's Planets, soon developed them greatly, first of all replacing the front carrying wheels by a two-axle bogie, and by the early 1840s had evolved the standard 'Wild West' 4-4-0, a simple, robust and powerful machine which was the commonest motive power unit on American lines until the 1880s.

As early as 1840 the Birmingham & Gloucester Railway in England, faced with the problem of working up the 1 in 37 Lickey Incline and hearing good reports of them from America, ordered 14 typical 4-2-0s from the firm of Norris of Philadelphia. For the rest of the 19th century the development of railways in the world outside Europe and America was, as a rule, in the hands of either British or American engineers and schools of design. British engineers were given a head start by their country's political dominance, but many colonial administrations found the more-basic methods of the Americans better suited to local conditions.

Above: An American Southern Pacific centennial celebration exhibit in 1969 depicting 'Jupiter' (in reality preserved 'Genoa') which hauled the first train from the West to the Golden Spike ceremony in 1869, backed by a modern 3,600hp diesel-electric. *Southern Pacific Transportation Co*

Below: An 1839 locomotive built by Norris in Philadelphia for the Berlin-Potsdam Railway. *DB Film Archiv*

Bottom left: An 1835 locomotive built by Hillingham & Winans, Baltimore, for the Leipzig-Dresden Railway. *DB Film Archiv*

Bottom right: Various productions of the Baldwin Company of Philadelphia in the late 1800s. *Science Museum London*

Facing page: The extraordinary Norris 6-2-0 of 1849, depicted on a Wills cigarette card.

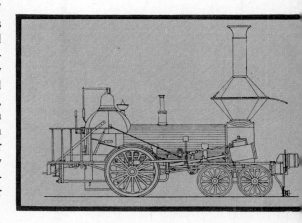

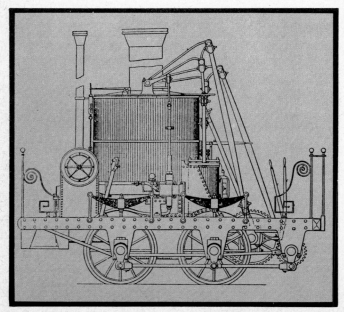

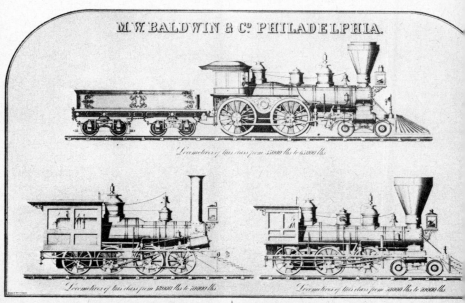

EARLY LOCOMOTIVE, U.S.A.

2
The Development of the Locomotive in the Nineteenth Century

Facing page: Edward Bury's 2-2-0 passenger engine of 1837 for the London & Birmingham Railway, of which 58 were built up to 1841.
Edito Service

Overleaf: This painting of the London Chatham & Dover 2-4-0 locomotive 'Leopard' depicts an example of the type of express engine with coupled wheels that started to replace the big single drivers in the 1860s. Batches of 2-4-0s were produced for several railways by various builders, including Sharp, Stewart and Co, Beyer, Peacock and Co and others.

British Steam Before World War I

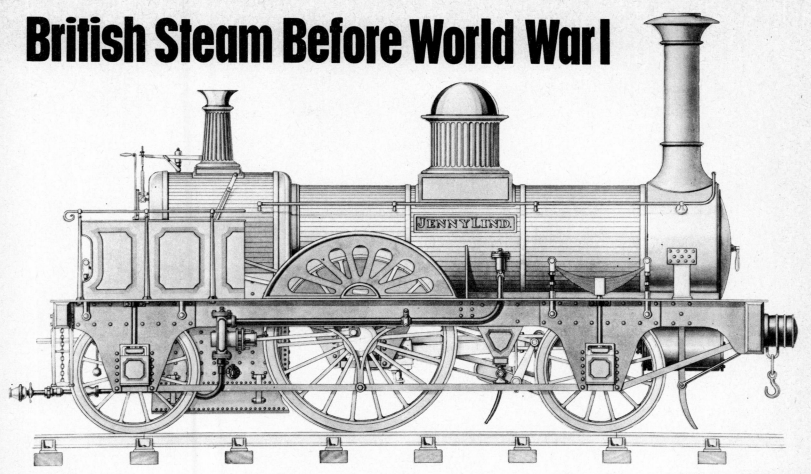

ROCKET BEGAN IT ALL at the Rainhill trials in 1829. Though the 50th, and not the first, steam locomotive, she *was* the first to combine two cylinders at right angles and direct drive, a multi-tubular boiler with separate firebox, and a blast-pipe. These three of the five essentials on which the steam locomotive was based right down to 1959 ensured the success of *Rocket*.

Prior to *Rocket* steam locomotives had been cumbrous machines working on mineral railways at 5 to 10mph. *Rocket* enabled railways to offer speed as a commodity, and was the first express passenger locomotive, topping 30mph.

The magnitude of *Rocket*'s performance was straightaway recognised by Henry Booth, secretary of the Liverpool & Manchester Railway, who referred in 1830 to 'the sudden and marvellous change which has been effected in our ideas of time and space . . . it will pervade society at large.' Here was the real beginning of the British railway system and its 135 years of steam locomotives.

Faster and sounder development over the next decade was hampered by two main causes. First, the generally shocking workmanship, even allowing for the infancy of the machine-tool and mechanical-engineering worlds; secondly, the predominance of civil engineers in railway technics, which led to gifted men such as Brunel and Crampton having too much influence in fields where they were not competent. The constant absence from the Newcastle locomotive manufactory of Robert Stephenson, away on railway construction, was the prime cause of the many complaints of poor workmanship put into the products.

Edward Bury, a business man with an engineering bent, was shrewd enough to engage a good mechanical engineer, Kennedy; they made a better job of locomotive building in the 1830s, and also introduced the bar frame, later favoured in the USA. This, in the 1830s, was at least as successful as the multiplicity of thin plates used by other makers.

Planet followed *Rocket* in the Stephenson list; and with this four-wheel 2-2-0 the firebox, though separate from the tubes, became an integral part of the boiler shell. First Planet frames were baulks of wood; by 1831 they were of iron plate, and this construction was the basis of Stephenson's *Patentee* six-wheeler of 1834, with outside main sandwich frames carrying all axleboxes, and inside secondary frames of plate, a form which lasted until 1870, and was applied to engines five times the weight of the original.

The outside sandwich frame of two iron

Top: 'Jenny Lind' was a 2-2-2 with inside cylinders and outside frames built for several railways from 1847 to 1860. *Science Museum London*

Above: 'Rocket', the first express locomotive as now preserved. *Science Museum London*

Below: 'Lion', a Liverpool & Manchester Railway goods engine of 1838, preserved in Liverpool Museum. *John Adams*

plates separated by oak or ash spacers, was prominent for half a century in Great Western engines of both broad- and narrow-gauge types.

From *Planet* and *Patentee* cylinders were mounted inside the frames and arranged horizontal or nearly so, but were associated with such features as hemispherical, haycock and Gothic fireboxes, until in 1840 came the move towards outside cylinders. Buddicom, originator of the celebrated 'Crewe-type' engine, recorded it was the extreme difficulty of procuring sound crank axles that led him to use outside cylinders with the driving axle bearings in the inside main plate frames, and the carrying-axle boxes in an outside subsidiary plate frame. This combination gave a rigid steady structure.

The London & North Western Railway built Crewe-type engines extensively up to 1857, and its West Coast partner, the Caledonian, up to the 1870s, the Caley rising to 8ft 2in single-drivers and large 2-4-0s. Another line built large Crewe-type singles up to 1883. *Cornwall,* of Crewe build, is still in existence today, and retains the Crewe-type frame in conjunction with 8ft 6in driving wheels.

The Jenny Lind type of 2-2-2 of 1847 kept to the same frame and axlebox layout, but the cylinders were again transferred inside, and so the flimsy crank axle returned; and it *was* flimsy, and so were the frames. The success of many Jennies was due to the higher boiler pressure—120lb per sq in against the then usual 90lb—and to the use of full-expansion valve motion, the fourth of the five fundamental principles 'making' the steam locomotive.

Introduced by the Stephenson works at the end of 1842, the curved link, or shifting link, motion was immediately adopted on a wide spread in place of the fixed cut-off gab gears, because of the great fuel economy and freer running which it brought, and because Robert Stephenson himself would not allow it to be patented. Nevertheless, Daniel Gooch the next year brought out *his* variety, the stationary link type, which he patented. Alexander Allan in 1855 patented the straight link motion, and in 1879 David Joy introduced a radial valve motion. Practically all British locomotives had one or other of these four types until the turn of the 20th century, after which Walschaerts very gradually became the favourite type.

Still further fuel economy was sought by Stephenson through improvement in boiler efficiency, which he attempted by lengthening the tubes and putting firebox and grate entirely behind the rear axle. Better boiler efficiency this gave; but it also produced wretched riding, and the principle did not last long except in slow-speed coal engines, a few of which worked until 1918-20; the last one (No 1275 of the North Eastern Railway) is now in York railway museum.

The 'Battle of the Gauges' in 1844-46 led to increase in size, though not to any real betterment in standard of design. Workmanship gradually improved, but not until around 1857-60 did locomotives appear that had a working life of 40 to 60 years, even if at the end of that time there was nothing left of the originals except the spaces between the wheels.

One initiator of this advance was John Ramsbottom, who took advantage of better shop methods and equipment to introduce wide standardisation, and even a rough measure of interchangeability. Such practices had been tried by Gooch in 1840, when he insisted on outside contractors for Great Western locomotives working to templates for frames; but general methods up and down the country were not then equal to making this efficacious.

The locomotive was still 'emerging' from 1847 to 1860, and to this period belonged such short-lived *incredibilia* as the Cramptons with their fireboxes below the driving axle; the Bristol & Exeter 4-2-4Ts with 9ft flangeless driving wheels; *Mac's Mangle,* an express engine with outside frames, cranks and cylinders that removed platform copings; and the longer-lived and more successful, though primitive, Great Western broad-gauge 4-2-2s that ran until the abolition of the 7ft gauge in 1892.

Except for the novelty of introducing tank engines on many suburban services, the 1860s were perhaps a decade of gestation. In those years materials, fitments, and workshop practices and equipment advanced considerably, often through the contributions of non-railway men such as Joseph Whitworth, Giffard, Krupp and Bessemer. Moreover a new generation of 'chiefs' arose—men who had been properly trained from youth by those whose own youth had been exhausted in steering through the quite uncharted sea of railway and locomotive development from 1812 to 1835, when there were no precedents.

The growth of the railway system and the enormous increase in traffic around that time necessitated a complete revision in permanent-way practice, a mark of which was the introduction of steel rails in 1862. Only with the adoption of heavier rails and much better ballasting and track drainage could larger engines be considered. The fore-shadow was Sturrock's huge 4-2-2 on the Great Northern in 1866, designed to give a time of eight hours between London and Edinburgh, a schedule not bettered in regular service until 1932.

Major advances in British locomotive practice were made in the 1870s. With that decade came a general appearance that lasted until the final steamer was built in 1958. Prominent were the Stirling singles, many of the Stroudley engines, the first express 4-4-0s, and such notable groups as the Tilbury 4-4-2 tanks. The 4-4-0 had come first to the Stockton & Darlington in 1861; but neither this design nor the 4-4-0 export orders from 1852 had any vital effect.

Stirling's great 8ft 4-2-2s with outside cylinders captured the imagination, and in their development became effective express power, with the remarkable propensity of running up the two 12-mile banks on the Great Northern as well as they ran downhill. They were fine all-weather haulers rather than super-speed racers.

Stroudley took workshop practice and sound detail design to a new level, yet his wide influence was through men rather than through things. His engines were designed for the short-run concentrated London, Brighton & South Coast Railway, and included unusual 0-4-2 express types which were not copied elsewhere; but Stroudley-trained men who drifted to other British and overseas railways promoted the country's reputation for careful building and reasoned design.

His 25-ton Terrier 0-6-0 tanks showed how effective a small six-wheel engine could be in passenger traffic, a practice culminating on the Great Eastern Railway, much of whose intense suburban traffic was worked by 0-6-0Ts of 36-40 tons weight until 1921-23. Stroudley's *Grosvenor* 2-2-2 of 1874 was one of the earliest-built locomotives authentically to reach one million miles.

Though the first of the British classic 4-4-0s came in 1871 with the engine that eight years later dived into the Tay when the great bridge collapsed, the type can better be dated to S W Johnson's engines on the Great Eastern in 1874 and on the Midland in 1876. But the wheel arrange-

ment did not at once settle down to inside cylinders, for the Highland-built Crewe-type outside-cylinder models from 1873 to 1892, and the Caledonian, Great Eastern, and London & South Western Railways had large outside-cylinder inside-framed 4-4-0s in 1876-77, and the South-Western built them up to 1892.

As a long-term influence the inside-cylinder 4-4-0s introduced by Drummond on the North British in 1876 were as important as Johnson's efforts, for they brought the Stroudley ideas of construction and details into a size and power range that that engineer never had to attempt; and the reigns of the two Drummond brothers on the North British, Caledonian, LSWR, Highland, and Glasgow & South Western Railways brought the basic engine to ever greater sizes until World War I.

A combination of much heavier (up to 85lb/yd) steel rails and the invention of 'power' (air or steam) sanding in 1884-85 led to a resurgence of the single-driver for express passenger trains for a few years. This brought some of the most beautiful, well-known and short-lived types in English locomotive history; and to this must be ascribed much of the over-importance often attached to this phase, for the total number built was under 250, and represented less than 5 per cent of the fast passenger power of the time.

By the mid-1890s the 4-4-0 of around 44-47 tons weight handled most fast

First 4-6-0 in the British Isles, the 1894 'Jones Goods' of the Highland Railway is now preserved at Glasgow, though it never had such a shade in service. *John Adams*

Top: First Atlantic in England—GNR No 990, the small-boiler type of 1898, preserved at York Railway museum. *Picturepoint*

Above: Zenith of English express passenger locomotives up to 1914—the GWR four-cylinder 4-6-0 Star class 'Lode Star' preserved at Swindon Railway Museum. *John Adams*

Above right: South Eastern & Chatham Railway No 737 originally at Clapham is a clean inside-cylinder 4-4-0 design typical of the early years of the twentieth century. *M Chapman*

trains, and 0-6-0s took nearly all the goods traffic, though many antiquated machines of other axle layouts were to be seen. The growing use of vestibuled bogie coaches, with more and more trains carrying heavier dining and sleeping cars, plus the faster speeds adjudged safe through the then new continuous and fully automatic air and vacuum brakes, led to the emergence of new wheel arrangements and greatly enhanced power by the end of the century.

True, the enhancement was largely by brute force, for only the size was increased; knowledge of the processes of steam generation, steam flow, and steam utilisation did not advance except on one railway. Half-an-inch on to the cylinder bore, 10lb on to the pressure, and 3in on to the boiler diameter was the general order of the day.

The Caledonian *Dunalastair*, a big-boilered development of the basic Drummond 4-4-0, set the pace. It followed the well-known Race to Aberdeen of 1895; but the Dunalastairs of 1896-1904 never had the opportunity of 'racing', yet their performances on fast long non-stop runs in 1896-97 were almost phenomenal judged by the then standards.

From this period dates the 4-4-2 or Atlantic type, on the Great Northern (1898), Lancashire & Yorkshire (1899), Great Northern wide firebox (1902) and North Eastern (1903); and the large-wheel big-boiler 4-6-0 on the NER (1900-01). The sound and forward Highland 'Jones Goods' of 1894 in-

fluenced the other railways not one whit; it was simply substantial increase in train weights and speeds in the late 1890s that forced the adoption of bigger engines, and laying of 90-95lb rails was needed to take the 20-ton axle loads.

In similar fashion eight-coupled engines for heavy mineral traffic came in the 1890s on the LNWR, and then on the Great Northern and North Eastern in 1900-01, and on the Barry Railway in tank engine form in 1896.

In this period the Webb compounds on the LNWR reached their peak. For years too much attention has been attached to them because of peculiarities in their performance and in the character of their designer. Their influence on British practice as a whole was negative. On the LNWR they formed never more than 10 per cent of the locomotive stock. Later compounding in Britain, concentrated almost entirely on the Midland and LMS Railways, apart from two-cylinder compounds in the 1880s and 1890s, owed nothing to Webb. Nor was it ever extensive, for in those days one first-class passenger paid the coal bill.

Around 1906-08 came the last *fundamental* factor in steam locomotive design—superheating, which measurably enhanced the coal and water consumption and, more important, the traffic-moving capacity and the ability to undertake long non-stop runs.

Atlantics and 4-6-0s of 1900-08 had been more effective than 4-4-0s only in simple ratio to their size and adhesion weight, and sometimes not even to that. Application of superheaters increased their capacity further; but only on the Great Western was a revolution quietly being made, the eventual effect of which was perhaps as great as that of any factor since the introduction of *Rocket*. This was the work done under G J Churchward on steam generation and steam utilisation. His higher pressure (225lb) boiler was conceived and developed specifically as a good steam producer which would also

bring the best working conditions for itself, and involve the lowest possible maintenance expense.

His steam utilisation improvements were based on long-lap valves of long travel, which gave a greater range of practicable cut-offs, so that engines could be linked up to 15 per cent cut-off and run with full throttle, contrasted with the minimum of 25 per cent and partial-throttle opening on most other engines. This combination led to coal and water economy, exceptionally free running, and substantial increment in effective power at express speeds. No other British locomotive of 1907-14 could remotely approach the Great Western four-cylinder 4-6-0's ability to haul 480 tons trailing at 62-65mph up faint rising grades for 15 to 20 minutes on end, and with no early assistance from momentum. On other English railways such a standard rarely entered the thoughts of locomotive engineers before 1925.

So the Churchward 4-6-0 four-cylinder engines can be regarded as the peak of British passenger power from *Rocket* to World War I. Yet one further type may be mentioned—the Robinson 2-8-0 of the Great Central introduced in 1911. Just as the Churchward engines were the acme of the practical scientific approach with fine machine construction, so the Great Central Consolidations represented the peak of the British ideals of simplicity and reliability.

With 126 in service on the GCR by August 4, 1914, this freight design was adopted practically *in toto* at the end of 1916 by the Ministry of Munitions for a heavy-service locomotive to be used behind the lines in France. Over the years 1917-19 521 were built; the great majority were on hire to British railways during 1919-21, and then from 1925 to 1927 were bought and put into capital stock by the LNER, GWR, and LMSR. A few lasted until 1966, and were perhaps the last pre-1914 locomotive power to be employed on British main lines.

The British 0-6-0

Above: Representation of the original 0-6-0, 'Royal George', of Hackworth design in the 1830s. *Ian Allan Library*

Below: One of the last surviving Midland Fowler 0-6-0s in October 1965, heading a special train between Nuneaton and Burton-on-Trent in an RCTS 'Midland Locomotives Requiem'. *B Stephenson*

Left: A Barton Wright 0-6-0 built by Beyer Peacock in 1887, preserved on the Keighley & Worth Valley Railway. The improbable livery was applied for film work. *R Bastin*

AS WITH SO MANY wheel arrangements, the first locomotives of the six-coupled type bore no resemblance to the stage of maturity except in the number of wheels and the presence of side rods, for the first six-coupled of all was Timothy Hackworth's *Royal George* on the Stockton & Darlington Railway at the end of 1827. Only with reluctance did Timothy later depart from its vertical cylinders, flue-tube boiler and two-piece cast-iron wheels; his dozen coal engines of 1831-32 were little different from the prototype, and even in Hackworth-type engines of 1846 the cylinders had got down only to a slope of 1 in 3.3.

First approach to what the 0-6-0 eventually became was a Stephenson engine for the Leicester & Swannington Railway in 1834, but being a Patentee it had outside sandwich frames with inside upsloping cylinders and a drawbar pulling on the firebox. But that was merely cutting the first teeth; the form lasted in service until the twentieth century with such big engines as the North Eastern 703 class, and, with the modification of sandwich into plate frames, lasted even longer on the Midland and elsewhere.

Development continued only at a slow pace, for although the L & S acquired two similar engines in 1835 and 1839, not until 1842-44 did the type begin to spread, and then only to a minor (six engines) extent, though with major improvements, for they were the Hull & Selby engines, which were the first

freight power to have expansion valve gear, long-travel valves and a high-pitched boiler. Their frames were a transition stage; the front wheel pair had outside bearings and the other two had inside boxes, and the upward sloping cylinders of the Patentee were retained.

The classic British 0-6-0 with inside cylinders and inside through plate frames needed further transitions before reaching its final form; the next stage was the long-boiler type for freight engines, begun by Stephenson in 1843, with two for the North Midland. For the first time in a goods engine were combined inside downward-sloping cylinders with slide valves between and inside plate frames running from end to end. The firebox being entirely behind the rear axle led to unsteady riding; but such engines were built for large railways until 1875 and were employed on mineral branches to 1920.

Flat valves between the cylinders were a Stephenson patent of 1841, and so general use did not come until the 1850s; that did not apply to the non-patented Stephenson link motion of 1843, applied to a freight engine first in a Midland 0-6-0 of 1844.

Only in 1848 did the 0-6-0 with inside frames, inside cylinders, and firebox between the second and third axles see the light, with Kitson engines for the Leeds & Thirsk and the Midland. Yet still the type was incomplete because the inside frames did not run right through. Rear separate sections were riveted to the forward portions near the throat plate—and by the

This page top and bottom: GWR broad-gauge
0-6-0 locomotive 'Dido' of Gooch design of
the 1850s, *Ian Allan Library*; and one of the
McConnell 0-6-0 engines in original
condition. *Ian Allan Library*

Facing page above: Stephenson long-boiler
short-wheelbase 0-6-0 for the Stockton &
Darlington Railway. *Ian Allan Library*

Facing page below: Preserved SECR
Wainwright P-class engine of 1910 Ashford
build, at Sheffield Park on the Bluebell
Railway in July 1969. *G R Hounsell*

exercise of most ingenuous ingenuity the
rear frames formed the lower portion of
the outer firebox, with hot water at a
pressure around 100lb per square inch
inside them and copper side stays going
through them.

Almost the first standard-gauge 0-6-0s
with the final features combined, and
certainly the first of any note, were the
McConnell fast goods engines on the
Southern Division of the LNWR in 1854;
106 of these 26¾-ton engines were built
until 1863, the last coming after McConnell
had departed from Wolverton. The combination of inside cylinders, inside through
plate frames and all axleboxes inside had
been introduced by McConnell in 1851
with his Bloomer 2-2-2s.

Coincidentally with the LNWR 0-6-0s,
the Manchester, Sheffield & Lincolnshire
introduced equally large engines but with
outside frames. In the MS&L 0-6-0s the
firebox was raised in bridge form to clear
the rear axle, giving in effect two grates
each with its own ashpan and damper.
The forward grate was difficult to fire and
control. They were almost the first of many
special fireboxes over the next decade
intended to burn coal more effectively,
until Markham's adoption of the upsloping brick arch and down-sloping
firedoor deflecting plate brought an end to
all the patents.

Meanwhile for the Great Western Railway's broad gauge, Swindon had been
building since 1846 0-6-0s of substantial
boiler power. In fact, the majority of
Swindon productions over the first 20
years were 0-6-0s, *Premier* being the
first, though with a boiler obtained from
outside. Being broad gauge, the frames
conveniently could be put between the
wheels, and they ran from end to end; but
they were of sandwich type, and so
exemplified yet a further constructional
variation. The fireboxes were of haycock
type, wholly within the wheelbase. GWR
0-6-0s began at 26½ tons weight; by 1851
they scaled 32½ tons, and no succeeding
lot up to 1865 exceeded that figure.

No broad-gauge 0-6-0s were built after
that year; and as the locomotives of
1863-65 were much the same as those
of 1846-49 except for a raised round-top
firebox in place of the haycock, the GW
broad-gauge system had only one basic
type of freight engine throughout its
existence, though in the 1870s and
1880s many engines were rebuilt with
boilers that were standard on the company's narrow-gauge locomotives.

No favourite type of standard-gauge
0-6-0 existed through the 1850s and
1860s. Large numbers of inside-frame
and outside-frame inside-cylinder engines
were constructed in all kinds of combinations, including some Hawthorns with
through inside plate frames and through
outside sandwich frames. Also to be seen

were a few outside-cylinder inside-frame
examples, though two of the earliest, the
Paton and McConnell bankers of 1844-45,
were tank engines. The only notable
tender engines of this type were a couple
of Patrick Stirling's with long wheelbase,
on the Glasgow & South Western in 1855,
and the 39 long-boiler short-wheelbase
Conner engines for the Caledonian in
1874-77.

Long-boiler 0-6-0s became at least as
large as the conventional type in the 1850s,
and were used on trunk routes like the
Southern Division of the LNWR and the
Manchester-Sheffield line of the MS&L,
and came to have 18in cylinders and a
weight above 30 tons; but the MS&L type
continued with outside frames and fly-
cranks.

Fashion for the conventional 0-6-0 was
set with Ramsbottom's DX class. These
engines could deal easily with freights
impossible for the Crewe-type 2-4-0s they
replaced; but their main feature was
standardisation of construction, for Ramsbottom swept away the merely nominal
reference to drawings common under
Trevithick, and the admonition 'dimensions
must be worked to' was put on all Crewe
drawings from 1858.

Ramsbottom's development of the works
and practice at Crewe made possible the
construction of 943 of the DX engines
from 1858 to 1874 coincident with the
production of 60 express singles, hundreds
of 2-4-0 passenger engines, numerous
0-4-0Ts and 0-6-0Ts, and the extensive
rebuilding of old tender engines into
tanks. Among the 943 were 86 for the
Lancashire & Yorkshire Railway, construction of which by the railway company
at Crewe led to a furore in the industry,
with bitter complaint from independent
manufacturers.

The DX engines set the pattern for
goods engines on the Premier Line until

Bowen Cooke's 0-8-0s of 1910, for though
Webb in the last 10 years of his time built
compound eight-coupled locomotives,
their number was as nothing compared to
that of his 'Cauliflower' 18in express goods
engines and the 4ft 3in coal engines,
which were direct derivatives of the DX,
with constant improvement in materials
and constant lowering in costs as Crewe
practice developed. Beyond all, Webb was
a production engineer and organiser.
Cost of an 0-6-0 crank axle fully machined
at Crewe in the mid-1870s was only £20,
and Crewe talk had it that in the 1880s a
standard 0-6-0 coal engine, without
tender, could be built for £500.

Throughout the 1860s the LNWR remained the only major line building inside-
frame 0-6-0s. Other large operators like
the Midland, Great Northern, MS&L and
North Eastern held to outside frames and
flycranks, using both sandwich and iron-
plate frames for mineral engines and for
express goods types with 5ft wheels.
Injected into this period were Sturrock's
steam tenders, whereby he sought to get
the adhesion of double heading with the
boiler of single heading; but though his
boiler was large it was not large enough.
The same decade also saw the last of what
Ahrons called the 'cats up a tree' variety—
inside-frame 0-6-0s with outside cylinders
attached to the smokebox and driving
down on to the rear coupled wheels at a
slope of 1 in 3.7, the last relics of Hackworth
practice.

Outside-frame engines normally were
well and robustly built and had long lives.
But from 1870, with the exception of
Dean's standard-gauge engines on the
GW in 1885-86, a new breed, or rather a
large-scale new brood of DX maternity,
came into being, with Stirling's engines on
the GN, Stroudley's on the LBSC,
Johnson's on the GER and Midland, and
Armstrong's standard-gauge engines on

the GW. Possibly the general change-over was helped by the availability from 1868-70 of single rolled iron plates above 20ft in length, in place of the forge-welded sections of earlier years.

Simplicity was a feature of all, with only the rarest of 'sports' like the Weston wagon-top boiler on a GER Johnson goods, the hinged chimneys for 0-6-0s working over the North Woolwich line, and the simple feedwater heaters on some S & D long-boiler engines. A 28in stroke, helping tractive effort on heavy haulers, was introduced on some of the last-named, but apart from one GW engine in 1882, it was not repeated with inside cylinders until the twentieth century. The 171 Worsdell two-cylinder 42-ton compound 0-6-0s of 1886-92 on the NER could not be called 'sports'; they took an effective part in main line freight traffic. The same applies to the 10 Bromley simples of 1882 for the GER, which had the running plate curved above the wheel tops and so had no splashers.

From the late 1870s the 0-6-0 'just grew'. It grew from 35 tons weight, 48in boilers, 17in by 24in cylinders, 140lb pressure and 15,000lb tractive effort to 59 tons, 66in barrels, 20in by 28in cylinders, 200lb pressure (in one case to 230lb), and to 30,000lb tractive effort. Although from 1911 it started to get a superheater, it retained the essential simplicity—and also the essential inaccessibility, for four eccentrics and two cranks, with rods and curved links and reversing gear, between inside frames could not be called a layout free from encumbrance, and was a waster of man-hours if nothing else.

Moreover, with increasing piston thrusts and axle loads, the double-throw crank axle became a greater problem, whereas after the 1831-60 period it had caused relatively little trouble. Two schools developed. One, with Fowler of the Midland near its head, favoured low-tensile very ductile carbon steels; the other favoured higher-tensile material with small amounts of alloying elements, and sometimes built-up axles. Piston thrusts got up to 65,000lb in conjunction with 19-ton axleloads; in the 1870s they averaged around 32,000lb and $13\frac{1}{2}$ tons.

With the general enlargement as just noted, wheelbase also grew; in fact it became uncomfortably long, getting up to 18ft 10in in GER engines of 1920 (later LNER class J20), which led to track bursting in yards and on certain secondary lines that could take the 18.8-ton axle load. Similar troubles came on occasion with the later LNER J38 and J39 classes which had the heavier weight of 58-59 tons spread over the shorter wheelbase of 17ft, giving a concentrated load of 3.5 tons/ft run of loco wheelbase compared with the GER 3.05 tons, and a general 2.4 tons in the 1870s.

Mineral traffic continued to expand until 1914, and the early years of the present century saw the evolution of some notable haulers, such as the NER classes P2 and P3 and the Midland Fowler 3835 type. The former perpetuated the established NER practice of 55in wheels for mineral engines and 61in wheels for general goods types, the engines otherwise being the same; but the P2 and P3 classes had 66in boilers, with immense steam raising and water storage capacities. One of them is now preserved, having worked on until the late 1960s.

The Fowler was a direct development from the numerous Johnson sub-classes on the Midland. It was a 49-ton 20in by 26in superheated design and was taken as an LMSR standard after the 1923 railway grouping; it was built until 1927. It perpetuated to some small degree on the Western Division the tradition of fast running by 0-6-0s established years earlier on the LNWR. On the Sunday cheap excursions that were a feature of the 1920s, these engines often ran at 60-62mph from Tring down to Watford, perhaps a gentle gambol compared with the 70-73mph attained many times north of Preston with the Special DXs and old Webb Cauliflowers, a rate that meant 410 revolutions per minute.

At grouping in 1923, the LMSR came into possession of approximately 3,500 engines of 0-6-0 tender type, the LNER had about 2,650, the GWR about 520, and the Southern about 360. By far the largest pre-grouping owner was the Midland, whose total above 1,500 was more than that of any other two railways combined. The next largest owner, the NER, at 750 had less than half the Midland total. The only unconventional 0-6-0 coming into the LMSR group was the four-cylinder unit with 135-degree crank arrangement off the North Staffordshire, which had begun life as a four-cylinder 0-6-0T.

On the LNER the J38 (55in wheel) and J39 (62in) were evolved as standard 0-6-0s. Although resembling most closely the largest freight engines of the North British Railway, they were a follow-up in principle to practice on the NER and GNR which had favoured at least two wheel diameters for half a century. In a few engines of the Ivatt-Gresley period the GNR went to a 68in wheel, as did the Midland in Deeley's time, and the NER in the 1880-90 period.

The only 0-6-0s built by the GWR in its post-grouping existence were the $41\frac{1}{2}$-ton $15\frac{3}{4}$-ton axleload 2251 class, intended particularly for South Wales and Cambrian lines, but which spread more widely over the system. The Southern, beginning with a large selection of Jas Stirling, Wainwright, Stroudley, Billinton and Drummond inside-frame 0-6-0s, built no more of the type until the Maunsell Q-class of 1935; and finished up with the well-known Bulleid Q1 'Austerity' engines, which, fittingly as the last-built 0-6-0s for any British railway, had the greatest tractive effort ever found on a home 0-6-0, and the 30,000lb effort involved an adhesion factor of only 3.8.

Far left: A pair of LNWR 'Cauliflower' 0-6-0s
(so nicknamed by a yardman when he first saw
the ornate crest applied to a goods engine,
it is said) at Keswick in May 1950, the one on
the left heading a goods train and the other a
passenger train. *P Ransome-Wallis*

Left: Ugly but effective, one of the SR
Bulleid Q1 Austerity engines entering
Chichester yard with a train from Salisbury.
C R L Coles

Below: Worsdell NER J27 No 2392
(BR 65894), last of the type on BR, crossing
the Wear with a coal train for Sunderland in
August 1967; the engine is now preserved on
the North Yorkshire Moors Railway.
B Stephenson

BRITISH SINGLE DRIVERS

IF INDUSTRIAL archaeology be reckoned to include steam locomotives, then some of the most beautiful examples were among the single-drivers that handled so much of English, and Scottish passenger traffic from 1830 to 1900.

Early development, after the primitive stage to 1830, was handled directly by all three of the premier railway engineers—Robert Stephenson, Joseph Locke and I K Brunel. Later stages were in the hands of many celebrated locomotive engineers, of whom Stirling, Stroudley and Johnson were the cream. Even such later giants as Aspinall and Churchward 'served their time' on singles, which ran through 0-2-2, 2-2-0, 2-2-2, 2-2-2-0, 2-2-2-2, 4-2-0, 4-2-2, 2-2-2T, 2-2-4T and 4-2-4T wheel arrangements.

Robert Stephenson's *Patentee* of 1834 was the first to achieve any symmetry, which came to it naturally when six wheels replaced the four of *Planet* and *Rocket;* and it was the first to have any semblance of beauty, for it had a certain slim elegance compared with all that had gone before. It was not a mechanical engineering success, but many of its descendants were, beginning with the notable Great Western *North Star* of 1837. From that time until around 1875-80 the majority of passenger traffic in England was handled by six-wheel single-drivers of one form or another. From 1887 to 1900 came a sudden revival of the uncoupled engine, this time on eight wheels and 4-2-2 axle notation, though the 230 locomotives of that St Martin's summer handled but an infinitesimal proportion of the total passenger train numbers.

Through half a century from 1834, the enormous variety of single-drivers came mainly within four general types: the Patentee, the Crewe-type, the Jenny Lind, and the Bloomer. Some of the most distinctive and successful singles were outside these categories, but in total numbers did not approach the others. Among the outsiders were the Bury four-wheelers (1830-46), the 60 Ramsbottom 2-2-2 Problems of 1859-65 and, from 1870, the Stirling 8-footers.

Additionally there were the 'sports', such as the Cramptons, the Stephenson long-boiler designs, and the Bristol & Exeter 9ft 4-2-4 tanks; in railway literature they gained far more notice than was warranted by their performance or influence. And of course there were always the Great Western broad-gauge singles of Lord of the Isles and Iron Duke classes that remained an imperfect thing apart.

Patentees had inside cylinders and outside main sandwich-type frames of 3in to 4in oak baulks with $\frac{1}{4}$in to $\frac{3}{8}$in iron flitching plates. These frames carried all axleboxes, whereas the early subsidiary iron inside frames from cylinders to firebox did not carry axleboxes, though they did have supplementary bearings for the driving axle. Jenny Linds (1846-94) had inside cylinders attached to iron-plate inside main frames that, in the early engines, ran only from the front buffer beam to the firebox throat plate, and carried the driving axleboxes; leading and trailing carrying boxes were attached to a shallow outside frame that ran from end to end. The Bloomers (1851-61 in the 'true' variety) had inside cylinders and inside iron-plate

main frames carrying all axleboxes and running from end to end.

The Crewe-type (1841-65 and 1882) had outside cylinders attached to both outside and inside frames, both of which ran the full length of the engine; the inside frames carried the driving axleboxes, and the outside frames housed the leading and trailing carriers. Perhaps the later reputation of the Crewe-type outran its performance, but for its time it was a notable mechanical engineering advance due largely to Locke, though he made no claim for the design—only for the initiation of a type that would better the early Patentees. This is the form widely but quite erroneously known as the Allan type. Alexander Allan was head foreman at Crewe works over a decade when about 260 engines of 2-2-2 and 2-4-0 layouts were built; but he was head foreman, not designer.

Zenith of the Crewe-type was never approached in the place of its origin or on the line of its sponsor and successors. Yet the original thread ran right through from the beginning to the penultimate stage— for it was the Caledonian 8ft 2in and Great Eastern 7ft 2-2-2s that marked the peak of Crewe passenger development in Britain; on both lines the Crewe-type was introduced by Robert Sinclair, one of Locke's 'young men' of the 1830s. The Caley singles were exceeded in weight and size only by the relatively immense Sacré engines for the Manchester, Sheffield & Lincolnshire Railway in 1882, unless one goes to the Crewe-type 4-4-0s built at the Canada works for Finland.

A more curious application of Crewe-type singles was that of 2-2-2 tanks to the short-distance suburban traffic of the London & Blackwall Railway, and the enlargement of that design for semi-express trains on the Eastern Counties Railway, with 78in wheels instead of 66in. There were many small single-driver tank engines of two or three wheel arrangements and types of construction in the 1850s and 1860s, including the George England

lightweight London-built variety; one single-driver tank, *Aerolite*, still exists, though as it stands at York probably none of its parts dates back beyond this century. It remains a two-cylinder compound, but in that form ran only the chief mechanical engineer's saloon on the North Eastern Railway.

Peak of the Bury engine came and went within one decade, 1831-41. The type was then perpetuated beyond its time and power—three, four, and even five having been used at the head of one train on the London & Birmingham Railway in the early 1840s. It was well known for the use of bar frames and haycock fireboxes with a hemispherical top and a grate D-shape in plan. Bury's intention originally had been to get a firebox without stays, but George Stephenson would have none of it, and Bury himself came to realise it was impracticable. Not so well known was Bury's sound workmanship, better than that of almost any other maker in the 1830s. Until 1846 the firm built only 2-2-0 and 0-4-0 wheel arrangements, and the preserved Bury-type at York is of the latter type.

Patentee types included the reputable Sharpies of the 1830s and 1840s, immediately recognisable by the dropped outside frame, the curve down at each end being introduced to get shorter plates for the carrying axleboxes. These plates were a weak point; John Gray, a well-known engineer of the 1840s, and the first man to adopt long valve travel, told the Gauge

Commissioners these plates 'sprung' at speed. In some ways the Cudworth 'mail' engines of the South Eastern Railway, built 1861-66, were the apex of the Patentee in elegance and performance; they worked the Dover boat trains for 20 years.

They were neither the largest nor the most remarkable descendants of Robert Stephenson's 11-tonner of 1834; those attributes were combined in Great Western engines Nos 3021-28. Built in 1891 as broad-gauge Bloomers with inside cylinders, inside frames and inside axleboxes, they were converted in 1892 to standard-gauge Patentees by putting the new wheels and axles inside the frames, which then became of outside type. The only difference from *Patentee* was that the frames were a single plate instead of a sandwich. These engines were the biggest Patentees ever run, and were supplemented by another 22 built new to the 'converted' design; they had the largest cylinders (20in by 24in) ever put on a 2-2-2.

John Gray as much as David Joy can be considered the originator of the Jenny Lind type, both in the frame and general structure and in the use of high pressure. Gray was using 90lb/sq in when others did not go above 70-75lb. David Joy took the Gray basis, and his chief, Fenton, insisted that he went to 120lb pressure; and, as Joy said, that more or less 'made' the engine. Unfortunately the frame structure was not up to the greater force transmitted through the cylinders; nor was his boiler altogether up to the mark, for he retained the old practice of attaching the intermediate drawbar directly to the firebox. He again departed from Gray's lead by using short-travel valves, but he *did* use Stephenson motion from the start, and

Below: Great Western 4-2-2 No 3041 'The Queen' heading a Royal train as used on journeys between London Paddington and Windsor and the West Country.
British Railways

that put him ahead of some of his competitors who were barely giving up the older gab gear. It was more in appearance that the Jennies scored; 'trim and elegant, the *beau ideal* of the single-wheel express', were the words applied to them by one locomotive engineer who had worked on them when he was young.

Another feature of the Jenny Lind type was that the first builder, E B Wilson, made it into a standard engine in the sense of the General Motors diesels a hundred years on—any variation, even an altered clackbox or boiler feed, cost an exorbitant sum. Though standard, the engines could not be built to interchangeable limits. That was for the future, when shop methods and tools were a stage farther advanced.

The principles of the Jenny Lind were taken up by most railways and builders, and engines were made stronger and larger, first by taking the inside frames from end to end and removing the drawbar connection from the firebox. The culmination was found in Patrick Stirling's 7ft 6in 2-2-2s built up to 1894, and which worked in the same links as the better known 8-footers. Jenny Linds were running in daily service well into the 1914-18 war for example on the Great Northern and North British Railways.

Development and improvement in manufacture, as well as progressive ideas, made possible the Bloomer type, though McConnell's first engines of 1851-52 for the Southern Division of the LNWR still had the through main frames made up of two or three plate sections forge-welded end on. Like Gray and Fenton before him, McConnell ensured the traffic-handling success of his engines by high pressure, this time 150lb, at a time when his colleague on the Northern Division, Francis Trevithick, was refusing to go above 90-100lb for his Crewe-type products. For almost 10 years there was in force a big-engine policy down the main line from Euston to Stafford via Birmingham (though not over the Trent Valley line), and a small-engine policy from Stafford and Crewe on to Carlisle over Shap; and the big-engine practice was more notable in that it followed almost at once on the ultra-small four-wheeler era of Bury.

McConnell's deliberate combination of inside cylinders, high-pitched boiler and long wheelbase made his 2-2-2s steady and easy riders. It was a notable contrast to the Northern Division's 2-2-2s 10 years later, for the Problem class of John Ramsbottom had outside cylinders and short wheelbase, and the engines became well known as wobblers. *Their* principal feature, apart from being the first English engines with injectors, was that in an express passenger engine with outside cylinders and 7ft 6in wheels there were many parts standard with those of an inside-cylinder 5ft-wheel goods engine. No more diverse range of standardisation was possible in the next hundred years.

Few Stroudley enthusiasts consider that engineer's simple and effective 2-2-2s as Bloomers, but in essentials they were—with one or two practical differences. Manufacture in 1880 was at quite different levels from what it was in the early 1850s. Stroudley took full advantage of this in raw materials and machining. He also went over every detail with a small-tooth comb; nothing was put on simply because it had been used before, and he insisted on good maintenance and repair. A result was the million-mile lives of his comparatively small 2-2-2s of 1880-82, which incidentally handled a combination of train weights and gradients that still excite wonder.

In fact, these engines, and Stirling's much different and larger 8ft outside-cylinder 4-4-2s and 7ft 6in inside-cylinder 2-2-2s, were the first machines to show that the *métier* of the single-driver had become something different from what was commonly supposed. Free and easy running through absence of side rods, plus the generally great wheel diameter, brought a legend of 'flyers'. Actually, very few single-drivers, or single-wheelers as they were sometimes called, attained super speed. On the contrary, a feature of their operation was steady speed up long gradients of 1 in 150 to 1 in 300 with considerable train loads; Stroudley's even tackled daily the 1 in 80 grades near Haslemere and Rowlands Castle.

Stirling was insistent that his engines could climb the four main uphill stretches on the Great Northern better than any four-coupled engine, but he had no four-coupleds of commensurate size. Nevertheless, his singles became a tradition with the public that was not approached even by the Gresley Pacifics. The preserved Stirling No 1 shows what they were like, though it never ran in just the condition in which it stands at York—a matter of small moment, for no engine of the 53 built was ever exactly the same as any of the other 52.

The spectacular resuscitation of the single-driver from 1886, though in a 4-2-2 inside-cylinder layout seen only once before, in Sturrock's No 215 of 1866, usually is said to have come with the invention of steam sanding by Fred Holt at the Midland's Derby works. In truth, the first of the lot had air sanding, and as might be expected was found on a railway —the Caledonian—that had adopted Westinghouse air brakes. Moreover, the first of the new series, No 123, is still in working condition, whereas all its United Kingdom compeers except one, in non-working order, disappeared 45 years ago, some of the most effective of them after a working life of only 10 years. Extensive introduction of 12-wheel diners and sleepers, and heavy eight-wheel stock up to 70ft in length, early this century, set a term to their practical use.

Following No 123 came more than 230 large single-drivers in 13 years, every one a high-class express passenger engine, every one with inside cylinders, and every one on what in North America would be known as a Class I road. Being singles, the axle load had to be high to get sufficient adhesion; the 10 Great Eastern

engines of 1898 got above 19 tons, not as much as in Stirling's last batch of 8-footers in 1894-95, but enough to get the 270-ton Cromer expresses up the 1 in 70 out of Liverpool Street station, and up the long 1 in 100 to Brentwood, and keep a 49mph non-stop schedule over the 130 miles from London to North Walsham.

Those oil-burners were perhaps the best proven hill climbers of the lot, but were run close by Stirling's 4-2-2 and 2-2-2 classes, and by the Midland 4-2-2s of which 95 were built in five sub-classes from 1887 to 1900, and the last and largest of which yet had tenders heavier than themselves. They were known to take above 300 tons over the southern half of the Midland's main line; and though free runners there is no really authentic record of them exceeding 82mph. That applies almost *in toto* to 11 of the 13 classes of 4-2-2 on seven railways built from 1886 to 1900.

Of all that construction, only the Great Western 3001-80 class and the North Eastern J class were authentically timed above 82mph by more than one competent observer. GWR No 3065 *Duke of Connaught* is reputed to have reached 91.8 mph on slightly easier than level in the record Ocean Mail Special of May 1904; the passing times in the detailed log certainly support a claim for 89-91mph maximum, which must be the highest speed ever attained by a single-driver.

Just as Bury's tiny four-wheelers had been replaced by the immeasurably larger McConnell Bloomers, so the 7ft 8in 4-2-2s on the GWR were replaced by Churchward's four-cylinder 225lb 4-6-0s after only the briefest transition through the Atbara and City 4-4-0s—a jump in about

Facing page top: A LNWR Ramsbottom 2-2-2 'Princess Royal' built in 1859 and rebuilt in 1876. *A Wood*

Facing page centre: A MR Johnson 4-2-2 of 1900, the last single-wheel class built for the Midland. *Colourviews*

Facing page bottom: The one-and-only Caledonian Railway 4-2-2 No 123, seen in 1963 when the engine was on a trip to the Bluebell Railway. *G D King*

Overleaf: Ex-PLM 4 cylinder compound Pacific No 231K 82 about to leave Calais Maritime station with the LCGB La Côte du Nord rail tour for Abbeville on September 29, 1968. *B Stephenson*

Below: Stroudley's standard 6ft 6in 2-2-2 No 329 decorated for the Stephenson centenary commemoration at Newcastle upon Tyne in 1881. *B Reed*

four years from 850 to 1,400 indicated horsepower and from 19 to 56 tons of adhesion.

The North Eastern J-class engines were timed at 83-85mph both in the original two-cylinder compound form and the later two-cylinder simple-expansion rebuilds; and they continued to put up such speeds on the 100-ton Leeds-Scarborough expresses until well on in this century. In their original condition they had the largest cylinders (20in and 28in bore) ever put into a single driver, so large that they had to be staggered, and one sloped upwards and the other downwards; yet the slide valves still had to be outside the frames as there was no room for them inside. They were also the only compound single-drivers to run in regular revenue service.

Some tenacious opinion still holds that the whole Great Central Railway was a mistake. Its forerunner, the Manchester, Sheffield & Lincolnshire Railway was a dividend earner; with the London extension and the change of name dividends ceased. Similarly there must always be question whether the six large GCR inside-cylinder 4-2-2s of 1900 were not an error in judgment, even though they successfully worked the 30-mile Manchester-Liverpool expresses for a couple of decades, and one attained a superheater, probably the only single to get such a fitting. They were also the only singles to be built for English service with a Belpaire firebox, though the four Glasgow-built 4-2-2s for the Shanghai-Nanking Railway in 1910 had them.

Withdrawal in 1927 of the last GCR and last Midland 4-2-2s left only one single driver tender engine running in Britain, the Caley No 123, by that time LMSR No 14010, which continued to run in revenue service for several years in the 1930s, and is still probably in workable condition today, though it has spent the last few years in the Glasgow Transport Museum.

FRENCH compounds

Top: First French main-line compound engine of 1885 by de Glehn, No 701, in its original 2-2-2-0 form. *Ian Allan library*

Above: No 701 after rebuilding in 1892 as a 4-2-2-0, still with uncoupled drivers. *La Vie du Rail*

Left: English Webb compound of 1883-4, of the Compound class, with one inside lp and two outside hp cylinders, built by Sharp Manchester for a French railway. *Ian Allan library*

Below: Decapod tank of 050TQ class of SNCF-N blackening the sky at Calais. *J B Snell*

TIME WAS WHEN no compounds at all existed in France—but that was 99 years ago. There was also a time when there were no main-line compounds in the country; even that was 87 years back. From the early 1890s to the end of steam, compounding and main-line locomotive practice were synonymous in France, even though small numbers of simple-expansion engines were often built, and, near the end, large numbers were in service because of American influence and urgent delivery requirements.

Compounding in practical form was due to Anatole Mallet, by birth a Swiss. Solely to meet the simplicity needed in small locomotives, his first applications were two-cylinder, the tiny 0-4-2T and 0-6-0T types on the Bayonne & Biarritz Railway in 1876-78; but he preferred four cylinders, and invention of the articulated system

that bears his name gave him full scope in that direction from 1884.

Practical compounding for main-line engines was due to Alfred de Glehn, a gifted London-born cosmopolitan with a German-Balt father (von Glehn) and a Scottish mother. He did most of his great work in that no-man's land, Alsace, in its days as the German Reichsland. For certain locomotives in France, Russia and elsewhere, Mallet and de Glehn collaborated at the Société Alsacienne's Mulhouse factory, where de Glehn was chief designer and later chief engineer.

De Glehn's first compound, No 701, began its life in 1885, *à la* Webb, with two uncoupled driving axles preceded by a single carrying axle; but, differing from Webb, it had two high-pressure and two low-pressure cylinders driving different axles. After that inauspicious beginning, de

Glehn never again built an 'uncoupled' locomotive. No 701 itself, a Nord engine, was rebuilt in 1892 with a leading bogie; but strangely its wheels were never coupled, and it became a 4-2-2-0, like Drummond's class on the LSWR.

One further compound system was favoured in France, but only on the PLM; it was devised by Henry, of that railway, as something to differ from what was coming out of Mulhouse. Henry, in 1889, first went to high pressure—218lb against the 156lb of de Glehn's No 701—and adopted only one set of reversing gear for the four sets of motion, resulting in a fixed cut-off in the low-pressure cylinders whatever the cut-offs in the high-pressure pair. Low-pressure reversing was done by a clutch and trip gear connected to the hp reversing screw. In later years this method was developed into a fixed ratio between hp and lp cut-offs. In 1890, when compounds in France were still few, over 400 were running in Germany, but all were of the two-cylinder von Borries type, which was never seriously contemplated in France.

However, from 1890, few simple-expansion engines were constructed, and by 1902 the seven big French railways had between them 1,128 compounds, of which about 90 per cent were de Glehn and de Glehn-du Bousquet types, and the other 10 per cent were Henry type on the PLM. By 1912 there were 5,100 four-cylinder compounds in France and, apart from a few hundred on the PLM and one or two odd-men-out, all were basically de Glehns. Because of the immediate appreciation of de Glehn's early work by du Bousquet, pure de Glehn principles reached their finest form on the Nord, and their peak in the well-known Super-Pacifics.

Chapelon's work was simply an extension of de Glehn's; Chapelon himself wrote of his phenomenal rebuilt Pacifics on the PO Railway: 'they represent the highest development of the four-cylinder compound locomotive of de Glehn-du Bousquet type.' De Glehn realised the importance of free steam flow and reduction in wire-drawing; so did du Bousquet; the latter's successor, Asselin, took those things a stage further. Chapelon recognised that the proportions could, and should, be bettered substantially, and that equal attention was needed to the final lp exhaust flow and its effect on draught. In fact, he set out to improve and co-relate everything from the throttle valve inlet to the top of the chimney outlet, not only in the passages themselves, but in the valve events also. He capped that by a revision of boiler proportions and introduction of thermic syphons, so that boilers of comparatively small overall dimensions could produce and superheat steam enough for 3,000 to 4,000 indicated horsepower, when that output was being obtained at economical steam consumption rates.

Tucked away in Chapelon's researches were figures applicable to simple expansion as well as to compounding; in particular, the value of working at full throttle when the valve motion permitted. A superheated simple-expansion Pacific with a boiler pressure of 185lb, working at full throttle and about 175lb in the steamchest, showed an economy of 6 per cent over working with a partial throttle and 130lb in the steamchest.

In essence, the de Glehn system covered a four-cylinder compound with divided drive, and a valve allowing direct exhaust from the hp cylinders to atmosphere plus a separate regulator admitting live steam at reduced pressure to the lp cylinders. The arrangement thereby permitted: (a) full compound working; (b) compound, but with some live steam at reduced pressure to the lp cylinders in addition to the hp exhaust; (c) four-cylinder simple working; (d) two-cylinder simple with the lp cylinders cut out; and (e) two-cylinder simple with the hp pair cut out and live steam at reduced pressure to the lp cylinders.

Compound working (a above) was normal; (c) was common at starting; (b) was used on certain up-grades with heavy trailing loads, sometimes for 30 to 40 minutes on end; (d) and (e) were useful for emergency working, perhaps after a mechanical failure in one drive or the other. Divided drive was a universal feature of de Glehns, except for a few in Prussia over which Soc Alsacienne had no control. This feature was one which attracted Churchward, and one which he perpetu-

ated in his own four-cylinder simple-expansion engines. De Glehn set out deliberately to get not only the coal and water economy of compounding, but also the good balance, smooth running, and potentially easier conditions in axleboxes of multi-cylinder locomotives with drive on two axles.

Another essential consideration was provision for independent cut-offs in hp and lp cylinders entirely at the discretion of the driver. Mallet considered the facility desirable although he felt few drivers would use it competently. Du Bousquet set out to train his drivers and was followed by other French cmes until main-line driving of both passenger and freight engines

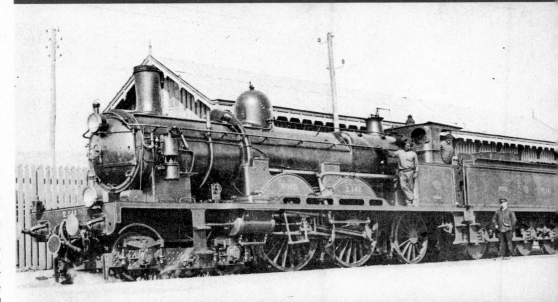

became an accepted science, and not an art as in most other countries.

Though de Glehn had gone over to 4-4-0s by 1889, Henry in that year produced a 2-4-2 four-cylinder compound express engine for the PLM, and his new freight power consisted of equally ugly but more-ruggedly effective four-cylinder compound 0-8-0s, some of which were rebuilt to 4-6-0 after a few years. Through the 1890s, by the influence of de Glehn and du Bousquet and the productive capacity of the Mulhouse and Belfort works of Soc Alsacienne, and to a smaller extent of Schneider, the 4-4-0 with divided drive, and the outside hp cylinders connected to the rear wheel pair, became almost standard throughout France. These engines were real gallopers on railways like the Nord that took advantage of their potentialities to accelerate the schedules, and 54-55mph timings between Paris and Calais were operated.

By the turn of the century, the Atlantic had come in its four-cylinder compound form, with an almost startling power performance and run of development. By the first world war, the 4cc (four-cylinder compound) principle had extended to Pacifics, in 1925 to Mountains, in 1932 to 4-8-0s, and subsequently, experimentally, to a 4-8-4. Du Bousquet initiated the 4-6-4 in 1911, but only two were built throughout France until a small-scale resuscitation in 1939-40, again on the Nord. Up to the late 1920s, those developments were followed on the PLM with the Henry system and developments of it.

For freight work, the 0-8-0s and 2-8-0s gave place to 2-8-2s and 2-10-0s after the 1918 armistice; on the PLM in 1930-31 there appeared one batch of remarkable 120-ton 2-10-2s with 90 tons of adhesion, in which the third side-rod section was inside and worked on double-throw crank axles. Near the end of steam, some highly

Top: Nord No 3.1201, first of the class of the 90 so-called Super Pacifics of 1923-31. *Ian Allan library*

Left: A 2-8-2T at Clermont Ferrand in September 1967. *P-B Whitehouse*

Above: A preserved example of the very powerful Class 241A express compound 4-8-2 engines. *SNCF*

Below: Ex-PLM compound Pacific 231K16 on the Fleche d'Or at Boulogne Tintilleries in September 1968. *B Stephenson*

Right below: Major characteristic of the big French compounds was the huge outside lp cylinders, here seen on 150P104 at Longueau shed, Amiens, in August 1964. *E J Dew*

efficient 4cc 2-8-2s with piston valves provided excellent mixed-traffic power during and after the 1939-45 war; they developed up to 2,800hp at the drawbar at 65mph on the road, and 3,200hp at 45mph on Vitry test bank. Chapelon bowed himself out of active design work on the SNCF with one six-cylinder poppet-valve compound 2-12-0 with superheat, resuperheat, steam jacketing of cylinders, and feedwater heating.

When superheating came to the fore prior to the earlier war, extensive trials were made, notably by Maréchal on the PLM, between generally similar 90-ton 4cc and four-cylinder simple Pacifics, in each case with and without superheating. Other railways simply accepted super-heated compounds as best. The PLM proved it with figures; and thereafter 4cc superheater engines became universal for main-line passenger and freight power, except for urgent-delivery war-time 4-6-0s, 4-6-2s and 2-8-2s from Glasgow and America. Even the Glasgow-built 4-6-2s of 1916 for the Etat were compounds, and were probably the only British-built engines to have trapezoidal grates and fireboxes.

Similar in steam circuits and mechanical arrangements, the de Glehn compound 4-6-2s and 2-8-2s varied in firebox type on the different railways. The PO went early to the trapezoidal form, and kept it for new construction to 1939; the Etat had some of the same type but many more simple wide boxes; the Nord alone kept to the deep long narrow box, with Belpaire top; the other lines adopted normal round-top wide boxes.

Just as the de Glehn 4-4-0s of the 1890s had set quite new standards of express locomotive performance, so did the Atlantics in their turn; and the application of superheaters to those engines around 1911-12 once more increased performance substantially, from about 1,350hp (indicated) maximum with the saturated-steam type to 1,500ihp when superheated. As late as the early 1930s, Nord superheater 4-4-2s of pre-1914

origin could be found on the light Paris-Brussels and Paris-Liége mile-a-minute non-stop trains.

Against the Atlantic background, du Bousquet put in hand two cumbersome 4-6-4s that were completed by his successor; but Asselin believed he could get close to the same output with two wheels fewer and, in collaboration with de Glehn, he developed the first Nord Pacifics, the 3.1151-70 series of 1912, which could develop 2,000ihp when running up 1 in 125 and 1 in 200, and had greater adhesion than the Atlantics. The so-called Super-Pacifics of 1923-31 were developments undertaken by Asselin's successors, Bré-villé and Collin, and the 90 engines of the type set the pace of European passenger-power development until the rise of Chapelon. A common experience was to dawdle late down to Dover on a 400-ton boat train behind a Southern Railway King Arthur 4-6-0, and then travel on a 550/600-tonne train over the 185 miles from Calais to Paris in three hours, and be taken up long 1 in 200 grades at a steady 65mph.

At that time the PLM was using mainly its big Pacifics, but from 1925 it began slowly to introduce lengthy 4-8-2s with a drive on the first axle and wheels scarcely 6ft in diameter. They were developed in the early 1930s into larger-wheel engines with drive on to the second coupled axle; but along the Paris-Lyons-Marseilles main line were to be found a few variations like *les trains aerodynamiques*—four-coach extra-fare sets hauled by rebuilt and stream-lined 4cc 4-4-2s. From the mid-1930s extensive rebuilding of PLM Pacifics on Chapelon lines was undertaken; eventually nearly 270 were converted.

Just at the time Chapelon's first rebuilt Pacifics on the PO were coming out of Tours works in 1930, the Est began to develop from its single prototype 4-8-2 of 1925 a stud of 42 Mountains on de Glehn principles; up to the war they handled all the heaviest expresses from Paris to Strasbourg and Basle. Although they never developed the specific outputs of some of Chapelon's own engines, they were masters of their work. They retained piston valves for all cylinders; so did the numerous Est Pacifics, which had load limits of 600-650 tonnes compared with the 750 tonnes of the 4-8-2s. Increase in capacity of Est de Glehn compounds was shown by the drawbar horsepower at 100km/h (62mph) —1,240 from the 4-6-0s, 1,725 from the 4-6-2s, and 2,425 from the 4-8-2s.

At an earlier stage the Ouest, forerunner of the Etat, had a variety of 4cc and simple-expansion Pacifics, including two of the most remarkable examples to run in France, with hp cylinders inside, and with

two sets of outside Walschaerts motion on each side, and a reach rod in the reversing gear that dwarfed Ivatt's enormity on the Great Northern's big-boiler Atlantics. These machines had been designed by the cme after a visit to the St Louis Exposition in 1904, but they did not get on the rails until 1908.

Chapelon's PO rebuilds began on Pacifics, transformed into what certainly *were* Super Pacifics, and continued on a smaller scale with Pacifics rebuilt into 4-8-0s. The rebuilds, weighing 107 tons loco only, achieved the record of 4,170ihp, or 39.5ihp/ton of weight, and they could sustain 3,500 to 4,000ihp for some time. One of them on test on the Nord took a 635-ton trailing load from Calais to Amiens at 72.9mph start-to-stop and from Amiens to Paris at 68.5mph, maintaining an average of 79.7mph over 46 consecutive miles averaging 1 in 800 up, attaining a peak of 90.7mph (with 73in wheels), and maintaining 2,700 to 3,000dbhp for miles at 50-55mph uphill.

To get the best possible port openings and valve events, Chapelon adopted for his Pacifics and 4-8-0s large-diameter poppet valves, but he kept the Walschaerts motion and oscillating cams because, piston and steam speeds being what they were, he saw no sense in using the rotary-cam type. Many Pacifics on the PO and other systems which were remodelled generally on Chapelon ideas did not get poppet valves, but were given Willoteaux double-ported piston valves, which worked well though they did not permit the peak outputs attained by the true Chapelons.

After a few years revolutionising express working on the non-electrified sections of the PO, Chapelon rebuilds, new engines to the 'rebuilt' design, and modifications following Chapelon's researches according to the ideas of the particular cme concerned, began to spread to the other lines, as already related for the PLM; in the end about 750 engines, nearly all of them Pacifics, were reconstructed or bought new. The Nord got 20 Tours rebuilds, and then 30 new engines from industry. Some 4-8-0 rebuilds appeared after the war on the PLM, and they, along with the earlier Pacific rebuilds, resulted in the disappearance of the old Henry-type compounds on the PLM, or Région du Sud-Est, as it was called from the formation of the SNCF in January 1938.

Glamour of the Chapelons attached solely to the outstanding performance in traffic. There was none in their appearance; nor were miles between heavy repairs, or total miles, outstanding, but the ton-miles per engine-hour in traffic were. The glamorous aspects of the de Glehn-Chapelon leadership crystalised in the Nord's de Caso 4-6-4s in 1940, just 29 years after the first Nord Baltics. Four of those engines (Class 232R) were three-cylinder simple-expansion types and four (Class 232S) were four-cylinder compounds. Mechanically they were a distinct Nord creation, though OCEM participated, but appropriately they were built by Soc Alsacienne. The poppet valves were operated by Cossart gear. After the war, one more 4-6-4, No 232.U.1, was completed in 1949, but it had piston valves for both hp and lp cylinders. Differing from the 1911 Baltics, the later Nord engines had radial trailing trucks.

By many, the 1940 and 1949 Baltics are regarded as the finest French steam power of all, especially by those who knew not the epoch-making years 1932-38 of the Chapelons; fortunately the last of the nine, withdrawn in 1961, is preserved at the Mulhouse museum of transport, adjacent to the first de Glehn of all, No 701.

Ex-Nord compound Pacific 231 E23 at Calais Maritime in October 1966. *J M Cramp*

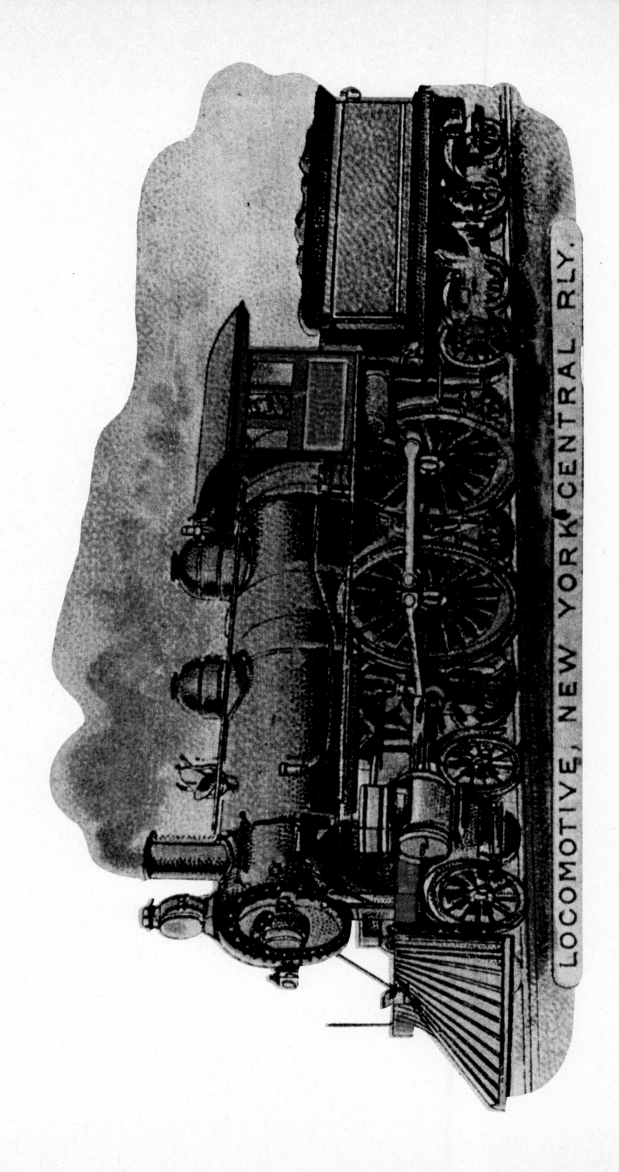

LOCOMOTIVE, NEW YORK CENTRAL RLY.

Left: 4-4-0 No 494 of Boston & Maine RR, a static exhibit at White River pictured in July 1970. *V Goldberg*

Below: Wheeling & Lake Erie Railroad No 32, as running in the 1890s. *B Reed*

Bottom: A distinctive feature of engines on early American railways, which were largely unfenced, and particularly of the 4-4-0s was the cowcatcher (or pilot) shown in this engraving from the 'Graphic' of October 11, 1873.

Facing page: Wills cigarette card depicting an American 4-4-0.

THE AMERICAN 4-4-0

THE FORD MODEL T automobile and the 4-4-0 steam locomotive in North America have fair claims to be considered in the same category. Both became institutions of American life; both spread over the borders and over seas; both became an outer symbol of the USA; and both were built in enormous numbers. The difference was that Model T came mainly from the brain and will of one man, and was built in mass production to interchangeable limits; the 'American-type' 4-4-0 was before the time of limits-and-fits, and although to one general type, it was of infinite variety. Cheapness was an essential of each; so far as the locomotive was concerned, it was 20-22 per cent less in first cost than English machines of the same output and period.

Evolution was through a painful stage of nearly two decades, for only slowly and by many hands was the first 4-4-0 of 1836 wrought into the classic form by the early 1850s. That form was a beautifully pro-portioned long-wheelbase long-truck type with horizontal outside cylinders centred above the front truck, Stephenson link motion, three-point suspension, and a deep round-top firebox dropped between the coupled axles.

It came finally from the efforts of an American builder, Thomas Rogers, and his English-born technical chief, William S Hudson, and the first examples were turned out of the Rogers works at Paterson, NJ, in 1851. By 1855-56 practically every North American builder—and there were three dozen of them at that time—was building nothing else for passenger and mixed working, and little other than the same design extended into a 4-6-0 for freight or steep-grade haulage; the four-coupled outnumbered the latter by at least eight to one.

Gone were all the old close-coupled short-base bogie types with loco wheel-base of 10 to 12ft, steeply inclined out-side cylinders bolted to the smokebox, and haycock or vertical fireboxes, such as the Norris and Baldwin builds, which had grown directly from the popular 4-2-0 layout. The 'New England' type, with inside cylinders and short-base truck far forward, had also disappeared from the new lists; as had the few odd types with rear-axle drive like the *Gowan and Marx* and its brother—the only two steam loco-motives ever to be named after bankers. They went out with the decided develop-ments in general practice and design that began in the late 1840s, and with the progress in shop tooling. Only a handful of small makers, such as Moore & Richardson of Cincinatti, continued the short-base truck type into the mid-1850s.

The perfected design of Rogers came just at the right time, for the route mileage open in the United States exactly doubled

Left: Virginia & Truckee RR No 11, an 1872 Baldwin, which saw service with the M-G-M film unit and was afterwards shown by the Railway and Locomotive Historical Society in America at the 1969 centenary celebration of the first transcontinental link-up at Promontory. *B Reed*

Below: Traditional 4-4-0 'William Mason' of Baltimore & Ohio Railroad, pictured at Baltimore in 1952. *J M Jarvis*

between 1851 and the end of 1855—from 10,880 to 21,450 miles. In the same period, too, the number of active locomotive builders doubled, and the great majority took the Rogers basic design and proportions. Half of the builders went out of business, or out of the locomotive trade, in 1857-58 as a result of the financial panic of the former year; but the loco type remained, and its construction was carried on until the early 1880s, by which time the 4-4-0 was growing so large, so heavy and so sophisticated that no longer could it be called the American-type.

For close on half a century about 60 per cent of all locomotives running in the States and in Canada were true American-type 4-4-0s, and in the time of the American civil war and the decade thereafter the proportion was 80 per cent or more. Laid down in basic dimensions and wheelbase, the range was small, as it also was in certain fundamental features of construction; but the variety in appearance and embellishment was immense, and the American motive power scene was colourful and overflowing with interest. By no means were all locomotives of standard gauge. Of the 350 different roads in the US at the time of the war, 14 were laid to 6ft gauge and 125 were between 4ft $9\frac{1}{4}$in and 5ft 6in; the remaining 210 to standard gauge accounted for only 54 per cent of the total mileage, though probably for 60 per cent of the locomotive stock.

The cloud no bigger than a man's hand that presaged the disappearance, leaving, by the time of the 1914-18 war, scarcely a wrack behind, was the small-scale standardisation introduced by the Pennsylvania Railroad in 1868, for although three classes of 4-4-0 with common constituents formed the first move, they were simplified and devoid of decoration; in consequence they gradually accumulated dirt, a thing tolerated on no road in days when drivers and firemen would spend half their Sunday in cleaning up their own engine, resetting the brasses, and cutting the fat off their Sunday joint to mix with the valve oil. At about the same time the Vanderbilt lines, that later became the New York Central, pooled the locomotives so that no crew had its own engine.

It was also the Pennsylvania that took the lead in another great departure that edged the true American type of history and cinema into the conventional 4-4-0 of later years—the substitution of coal fuel for wood. That, of course, was coming in any case, as wood supplies receded farther and farther from the tracks. The cutting of Sussex oaks for England's wooden walls yielded nothing to the timber felling that went on for years in America to provide daily fuel for 10,000 locomotives and more; and into the half-inch iron fireboxes went many thousand cords of superb wood as well as green wood, hemlock and hornbeam. A good wood could evaporate up to $2\frac{1}{2}$ times its own weight of water.

A cord was 128 cubic feet; that might be anything from 2,000 to 4,000lb in weight according to the wood, but it was the unit of purchase. On only a rough estimate, American-type 4-4-0s in the USA consumed at least 75 million cords in 40 years. Wood-burning was no sinecure for the fireman, for quite ordinary runs with 150-ton passenger trains at 40mph average could mean 160lb of wood fired per mile; and that took some doing.

Apart from roads like the Philadelphia & Reading that had always used anthracite (good stuff, not the culm dust with Wootton firebox of later years), the use of bituminous coals with decreasing wood

Right: No 1 of Stockton Terminal & Eastern Railroad, preserved at Traveltown in Los Angeles, taken in June 1969. *V Goldberg*

Below: New York & New England 4-4-0 at Boston in the 1880s; it was one of the few American-type series to have tenders with water pick-up. *B Reed*

Bottom: A New York Central & Hudson River RR 4-4-0 pictured in the type of severe winter conditions that cracked up the cast-iron wheels. *B Reed*

Facing page: A model in the London Science Museum of a traditional American-type 4-4-0 built by William R Lendrum, Scranton. *Science Museum London*

stocks at economic prices was given a fillip by the steel firebox, which came into trial use in 1861. Boxes built 1861-63 were shown by 1869 to have an unexpired life of seven to eight years, and after a favourable Master Mechanics report of that year a rapid increase was made over the four or five hundred boxes by that time in service.

With the substitution of coal for wood, there disappeared that great symbol of the American-type—the enormous balloon stack containing one or other of the 60-odd forms of spark arrester actually tried, a small percentage of the 1,000 different patents. This fitting was seen to be essential long before the time of the 4-4-0, in fact from 1832 when $60,000 in paper money being carried in an open car on the Newcastle & Frenchtown was fired by sparks from the locomotive. Around 1860, extended smokeboxes began to appear, and eased the spark throwing to some extent.

Keeping at full heat a fire consuming two tons or more of wood in an hour needed a blast pipe nozzle no more than $3\frac{1}{2}$in in diameter, though almost universally from 1855 to 1870 two nozzles of around $2\frac{1}{2}$in diameter were used with 16in cylinders, and two of $1\frac{7}{8}$in with 15in cylinders. Well might a celebrated locomotive engineer write in the 1860s that each exhaust blast went off like a rifle. Distinct from English practice, the nozzles were very low down in the smokebox, and petticoats extended downwards from the stack.

Well on into the coal-burning era the boiler plates were extremely thin for the pressure used, and the factor of safety was below the levels acceptable in Europe. As a result, along with the often rough working and infrequent inspection (this was before the days of the Interstate Commerce Commission's Bureau of Inspection), boiler explosions were comparatively numerous. This was a feature of the American railroad scene until the end of steam; even as late as the years of the 1939-45 war there were between four and eight locomotive boiler explosions a year, compared with 15 to 25 a year in the 1860s. Boiler pressures of 120lb in the 1860s got plates of only $\frac{1}{4}$in iron for 4ft diameter, or $\frac{5}{16}$in when the rear end of the barrel was tapered up wagon-top fashion.

Most boilers had front-end throttles until around 1870, despite the presence of a large dome, usually on the firebox top. Mechanically driven pump feed was obligatory, there being no alternative until 1861, when Sellers got a manufacturing licence from Sharp Stewart in England for the Giffard type of injector, and sold over 2,000 in the first year.

Another great feature of American practice that came with the Rogers 4-4-0 was the bar frame. There had been crude bar frames before, and there were plate frames before and after; but by 1855-56 the bar

frame as understood in later years had become almost universal. Throughout the time of the American-type engine, it gave no trouble, for spliced joints did not loosen much when piston thrusts were only around 26,000lb and axle loads were about 10 tons. Only with the increases to over 50,000lb and 20 tons in the 1890s did the bolted sections of the bar frame require incessant maintenance attention.

Simplicity in the American 4-4-0 came mainly from the iron bar frames, to which were attached two outside cylinders of 15in to 17in diameter, with flat slide valves on top, and three-point suspension gained by equalising the coupled springs down each side and leaving the leading truck springs on their own. The spring arrangement gave easy movement, and maximum possibility for the wheels to follow the numerous irregularities in the lightly laid track, very often without ballast of any kind. A not unknown occurrence was for a pair of wheels to be derailed and then become rerailed before the driver had awoken to the fact and applied the brake and shut the throttle. Fortunately, as the Rogers-type 4-4-0 was coming in and sizes were going up, the old American strap rails were going out, or had already gone on many roads; but the after effects of them and the light track construction lasted many years. Three-point suspension had been patented by Harrison in 1838, with a revision in 1842; but the patents had expired by the time the American-type really got going.

The whole riding was further improved by the long distance between the leading drivers and the front truck, which permitted a connecting-rod length seven or eight times the crank throw, and so minimised the upward thrusts on the slidebars and the side-to-side disturbing forces; the long wheelbase itself contributed to easier riding.

By 1860 another practice was in vogue that lasted until the twilight of steam 70 years later. That was the casting of one cylinder and valve chest with half the saddle supporting the smokebox. A saddle support itself had first been seen in 1848 on a McQueen 4-4-0 of pre-Rogers form, but the incorporation of the cylinder with half the saddle was a Baldwin innovation of 1857. It lasted more or less until the coming of the cast-steel integral locomotive bed in the late 1920s. There was full access to the slide valves simply by removing a dozen bolts and lifting off the cast-iron cover.

The inside Stephenson gear, always with marine-type links, had transverse rocking shafts to transmit the motion outside; again, everything was accessible because of the bar frames. Rogers adopted this gear in 1849, before his first American-type; other builders adopted it only gradually over the next five or six years, and some used the Gooch stationary-link motion as an intermediate stage. After 1855 non-Stephenson gear engines were rare. The long distance from front drivers to truck also permitted long eccentric rods, sometimes up to 6ft, which produced very even valve events.

Not so blatantly visible as the balloon stack and enormous oil-burning head-lamps, the coupled wheels were just as characteristic a detail of the American 4-4-0. Well under one per cent were forged; the remaining 99 per cent until the 1880s were of cast iron, even with tread diameters as great as 78 inches; and from the 1851-52 beginnings until after the civil war the great majority of coupled-wheel tyres also were of cast iron, with

chilled tread. Only with the coming of steel tyres did the cast types disappear; and it was time they did, for in the endeavour to make the cast-iron type stronger the thickness had got up to $3\frac{1}{2}$in and the weight was enormous for the general size of the engines. A 6ft wheel-and-axle pair with cast-iron centres and cast-iron tyres weighed around 7,000lb in an engine of no more than 20,000lb axle load.

The normal severe and long-lasting winter temperatures, which not only affected ferrous materials but also froze the roadbed solid, led to regular annual epidemics of wheel centre and tyre breakages; and a common winter sight was an engine at work with several cracked spokes—not hair cracks, either, but real full splits asunder.

An early development was the one-piece cast-iron truck wheel without separate tyre. The same wheels were used for freight wagons and some passenger cars, so the production was large enough to justify investment of considerable capital in research and plant; prior to 1870 a 33in disc wheel could be made for 20 dollars, including the slow cooling, and its $\frac{1}{2}$in chill on the tread would normally last for well over 50,000 miles. But the unmachined treads were not always perfectly circular, so that the generally smooth movement on good track could still be disturbed by chatter.

However, light tracks, light construction, and general operating requirements prevented any high speeds. It is doubtful whether any true American-type ever topped 65mph before the 1880s, and even a mile a minute was rare. There were few tracks that could take that speed; in the 1860s a schedule of 42mph was something to be written about, for it might involve a peak not far short of 60 mph.

The amount of polished brass, including a 30 to 60lb bell, and polished copper was extensive, and was supplemented by the shining purple of the Russian iron lagging sheets; few, if any, of the American-type 4-4-0s had the polished or painted wood lagging strips of English locomotives, though they had been seen in the States in the 1830s and early 1840s. Additional were numerous ornamental scrolls and devices and two to four brass flagstaffs, and a lavish display of colour painting that put Stroudley's efforts on the Brighton line in England into the Black Five class.

New construction of the real American-type went down sharply in the early 1880s. Although in essence the principles of wheelbase spacing, machinery arrangement and suspension remained, the introduction of steel frames, cast-steel wheel centres, great increase in boiler size and heating surface, and, above all, the suppression of brass, copper and colour, led to a complete change to brute force instead of elegance in appearance.

Deterioration in appearance came first around 1878 when the Philadelphia & Reading introduced camelback 4-4-0s with Wootton grates four times the normal area; but mechanically the Pennsy was again the leader in change, with its K-class of 1882, in which the enlarged boiler was placed 12in to 15in higher than had been known before, and the grate was spread out over the top bars of the frame instead of being dropped between. A few of the true American-type, constructed in the 1870s and early 1880s, continued to run until at least 1948, and a few are preserved, but none restored to the glories of the 1850s and 1860s. One fine example of 1857 construction did remain until 1942, and was then sacrificed in a war-time scrap drive.

3
Progress and Experiment in the Twentieth-century Steam Locomotive

THOUGH GREAT WESTERN 4-6-0s generally are reckoned as two major groups—two-cylinder and four-cylinder; the wheel arrangement actually was built at Swindon over a period of 54 years, under five chief mechanical engineers, and for three different legal entities, namely the old Great Western, the reconstituted Great Western of the 1923 railway grouping, and the nationalised British Railways. About eight years after the very beginning, there was established what became an easy natural flow in development and enlargement that retained the same concept almost throughout.

With technical knowledge, and reasonable imagination, one might think the later Castles, Kings and Halls were out of Churchward's earliest 4-6-0 No 100 of 1902. Not even the imagination of an Edgar Allen Poe could have thought backwards from a Queen of 1910 to the first Dean enormities of 1896 and 1899, Nos 36 and 2601. Nor could anyone have thought forward from them to the first 4-6-0 Star of 1907. Cumbrous in the extreme, the Dean engines had all manner of obsolescences and novelties that could not last the pace. For example, there were Mansell wooden bogie wheel centres, Serve ribbed tubes, and double frames with four boxes on each coupled axle in No 36; and double frames, a complete set of volute springs, and a primitive combustion chamber in No 2601. No 36 had a grate area exceeded in any Great Western engine only by the Pacific *Great Bear*.

The 4-6-0 was inherent in the whole of the wide standardisation programme beginning to take shape in Churchward's mind in 1902, after a few months' running of his own first engine of that wheel layout, No 100, completed in February of that year; and it remained more than the backbone of main-line power to the end of the Great Western on December 31, 1947. It was the be-all and end-all, the only departures being the brief simple-expansion Atlantic phase of 1903-12, the three French compound Atlantics, and the one class of 4-4-0 Counties, for the Cities of 1903 were but a stop-gap carry-over from Dean.

Yet it is doubtful whether Churchward foresaw in 1902 and 1903 the four-cylinder development that formed the real basis of all GWR top-class passenger power for 43 years of new construction and lasted in service until almost the end

Above: Dean's prototype 4-6-0 No 36 of 1896.
British Railways WR

Below: GWR No 6000 'King George V', complete with bell fitted for its visit to the United States and retained in preservation at Bulmers cider works. *J R Woolley*

of steam. That sudden opening out, which turned a good progressive far-seeing idea into something brilliant, came with the trial French four-cylinder compound Atlantics Nos 102-04 in 1903-05. Churchward's competence and 'bigness' were shown by the way he seized on all the good points in those engines and reshaped his own programme to incorporate them. Contrast the shocking handling of the compound question on the Great Northern in 1905-07.

Observe how Churchward calmly took a year or two to try out the new major possibilities, for he desired to establish standards that, with any enlargements, would suffice for new construction over the remainder of his working life. He began by making a simple-expansion four-cylinder equivalent of the French de Glehn compounds, and gave it his standard No 1 short-coned boiler of the time, as fitted to two-cylinder 4-6-0s and 4-4-2s; but he raised the pressure from the standard 200lb to 225lb to give stricter comparison with a compound, and he adopted the French divided drive. Moreover, he did not neglect to install a valve gear that actually did permit in practice a range of steam expansion not far short of what would be found in a compound.

From that four-cylinder 4-4-2, No 40 *North Star,* he developed, while continuing to build improved 4-6-0s derived from No 100, the first of the true Great Western four-cylinder 4-6-0s, the 10 Star-class engines Nos 4001-10 that came out of Swindon in 1907. *North Star* continued to run as an Atlantic until converted to 4-6-0 in 1909; it was renumbered 4000 in 1912, and continued to run with its original Stévart valve motion until 1929, when it was rebuilt into a Castle.

The four-cylinder engines, with two sets of Walschaerts motion actuated by inside eccentrics in place of outside fly-cranks, and with neat rocking shafts operating the American-type piston valves of the outside cylinders, continued to multiply every year, except 1912, up to the beginning of the 1914-18 war. Fortunately the last of a batch of 15 was completed just before August 1914, and so the GWR managed to handle its war-time passenger traffic without having to build more power during the critical years.

Outside appearance of all these 4-6-0s, 61 in number, was enhanced by the adoption of full-cone taper boilers, running plates curved down at each end, the deepening of the cab from its original high perch, and the divided drive. In the vernacular, they were, if not 'streets ahead of their time', at least streets ahead of any other English express engines until 1925-27. Certainly no other English type of pre-1914 vintage could haul 480 tons for 15 to 20 minutes steadily at 63mph against a slight rising grade, or give close on 1,000 drawbar horsepower at 70mph with 20-per cent cut-off. Moreover, those feats were with saturated steam, for not until 1910 did Churchward begin to fit the four-cylinder engines with superheaters as standard, and then they were of low-temperature form.

Coincident with all the aforementioned construction, two-cylinder 4-6-0s derived from the early 4-6-0s and 4-4-2s (converted to 4-6-0 in 1912-13) continued to come out of Swindon works, developed in boiler design and pressure, and in appearance, like the four-cylinder locomotives, and with a final enlargement of cylinder bore from 18in to 18½in. Churchward in essence considered the four-cylinder machines were for the best high-speed services; but although they were retained for crack trains and many of the Plymouth services, the alternative two-cylinder engines were not really restricted in speed, and operated fast timings on the Bristol and new Birmingham-direct lines. They ran as fast, but not so sweetly, as the Stars.

The lesser engines retained one of the cardinal points of the first Churchward standardisation programme—a 30-inch piston stroke, along with Stephenson valve motion designed to give almost negative lead at starting and advancing to full positive lead at about 20-per cent cut-off. From both power and valve-gear aspects the four-cylinder engines could be run easily and adequately at 14 or 15 percent cut-off; the two-cylinder engines could not be linked up with comfort below about 22 per cent, and their riding was not so sweet. In fact, balancing of no GW two-cylinder engine, tender or tank, ever got to just the right pitch; the fact could be well observed by passengers in the leading coaches with a Saint or Court 4-6-0 or a 5ft 8in 2-6-2T at the head.

After the end of the first war, main-line passenger engine construction did not at once get high priority; not until the end of Churchward's time was another order placed, and the engines actually appeared under his successor, Collett, who for long had been Churchward's 'number two'. The new engines were the Abbeys, but essentially they were the last pre-war Princess batch with different crank axles, no bogie brakes, and a few other alterations of which the most visible was the replacement of the large copper-capped chimney by a puerile tapered cast-iron pattern; but the performance was up to standard.

To some extent Churchward was always limited in axle load, and neither his four-cylinder nor two-cylinder 4-6-0s exceeded 19 tons on the axles, or 57 tons of adhesion. Only around the time of Collett's accession did the civil engineer authorise a 20-ton axle load; as train weights were increasing and pre-1914 speed levels were being reinstated, Collett had to take advantage of the increment, and in 1923 produced the four-cylinder Castles, the first of which, No 4073 *Caerphilly Castle,* is now in the Science Museum, South Kensington.

Increased adhesion weight permitted a 12in extension at the back end, which allowed a firebox with 12 per cent more grate area and six per cent more heating surface than the Abbeys; in turn this made

practicable cylinders of 16-inch diameter in place of Churchward's 15 inches. Axle load fell just short of 20 tons and adhesion weight was 59 tons. The advances, along with a 10-per cent increase in evaporative heating surface, changes in steam pipes and so on, brought a substantial power increment. So much so that in 1925 No 4079 *Pendennis Castle* far overshot the LNER Pacific performance in the comparative trials; and in 1926 the easy mastery over LMSR loads and timings between London and Carlisle by No 5000 *Launceston Castle* led directly to the Royal Scots.

The early Castles were even more epoch-making in their time than any of Churchward's own engines, for the benefits of the latter were confined to the Great Western because 'foreign' chief mechanical engineers were insufficiently advanced to realise what GW engines did and why they did it. By 1925-26 the superiority was too obvious to be neglected under the greater financial pressures and widening horizons of grouping; consequently, the Castles had as startling an effect on British locomotive practice as Chapelon had on French practice.

The Castles permitted inauguration of a new speed era, beginning with the acceleration of the Cheltenham Flyer; for

long distances covered at unbroken 85-92mph, they probably still hold the palm among steam locomotives, being approached most closely by the Gresley A4 Pacifics. Whether any Castle or King actually topped 100mph tends to be questionable. One or two observers of some experience claim to have done it. On the other hand Collett once said that he could never really satisfy himself that 100mph *had* been attained, and that was after special attempts were made with a King running light.

In yet another way the Castles were among the most remarkable locomotives of the twentieth century, for new construction did not end until 1950, thus outspanning later and 'improved' Swindon 4-6-0s such as Kings and Counties. This was because their successful performance was allied to wide route availability. That was not a feature of the later Kings, which class arose from the completion in 1926 of a 20-year bridge strengthening programme. Completion of that was realised by the board and by the chief mechanical engineer almost by chance; but it, and the work of the Bridge Stress Committee, indicated that an axle load of 22 tons could be permitted on the West of England, Bristol and Birmingham routes.

So Collett produced the Kings, but

Facing page lower: County-class 4-6-0 No 1009 'County of Carmarthen' at Dawlish in August 1962. *B A Reeves*

Top: Prototype of the Star class, No 4001 'Dog Star' of 1907. *Ian Allan library*

Above: GWR No 40 'North Star', originally a 4-4-2, rebuilt as a 4-6-0 in 1909 and renumbered 4000 in 1912, here seen at Stafford Road in BR days. *P B Whitehouse*

Left: No 6812 'Chesford Grange' of the 4-6-0 class introduced in 1936, just out of Swindon works. *M Pope*

Above: A not-very-serious attempt at streamlining, No 6014 'King Henry VII' of the 1927 King class. *British Railways WR*

Right: Preserved Manor-class 4-6-0 No 7808 'Cookham Manor' at Tyseley in October 1969. *R Bastin*

Below: End of a mighty Castle (unidentified) at Barry scrapyard. *M Pope*

Facing page above: Preserved Castle No 7029 'Clun Castle', at Banbury depot in June 1967. *D Huntriss*

Facing page bottom: One of the numerous Hall class, No 5982 'Harrington Hall' on a goods train in August 1962. *B A Reeves*

because of the restricted route availability and the high day-by-day standard of Castle performance, only 30 were built in 1927, 1928 and 1930, whereas a total of 171 Castles were constructed. The Kings were probably the most powerful 4-6-0s to run anywhere, but their original weight of 89 tons and their final weight of 90 tons might have been exceeded by one or two United States classes of inferior output.

Undoubtedly GWR four-cylinder 4-6-0s cost more to build and to repair than two-cylinder engines, but not necessarily more in normal maintenance; and in pre-1914 years they could run 120,000 miles between general overhauls against the 85,000 miles of two-cylinder Saints and Courts. There were steady improvements in four-cylinder 4-6-0 performance. The Churchward engines of 1907-14 averaged 42,000 to 46,000 miles a year throughout lives of 25 to 44 years, and five of the 61 topped totals of two million miles. The Castles built in the 1920s averaged 45,000 to 52,000 miles a year over 35-37 years, and all built in that period went

above 1½ million miles. The Kings averaged 50,000 to 56,000 miles a year for 30 to 35 years, and though none topped two million miles, 10 got above 1.9 million. With gradually increasing average mileages, ton-mileages went up to an even greater extent.

Churchward four-cylinder Stars cost from £3,000 to £3,300 per engine and tender over the years 1907-14, compared with £2,550 to £2,725 for the two-cylinder Saints and Courts. Under the immensely altered conditions after 1918, the Abbeys cost £7,500 at the most expensive time of all, 1921-22. Engineering prices in general then decreased, and the larger Castles of 1923-24 cost £6,850 apiece, and the Kings, larger again, were charged at £7,420 in 1927-28.

To come from this apogee of power and speed to the more numerous smaller two-cylinder 4-6-0s of later years might seem an anti-climax; but shortly after the accession of Collett, or perhaps more truly after grouping in 1923, the GWR began to build 4-6-0s for heavy, medium and light general-purpose duties in preference to the hundreds of 2-6-0s built under Churchward; they were standard through the three 43XX, 53XX and 63XX classes. One of the engines with 68in wheels reached 75mph on bridge tests, but reputedly the traffic department was the prime mover in the post-1925 changeover to 4-6-0s in new construction. As no 68in-wheel 2-6-0s were scrapped for years, the succession of Halls, Manors and Granges, in that descending order of power, really replaced County and Flower 4-4-0s and Dean 0-6-0s.

All the smaller engines had full incorporation of the best Churchward-Collett principles of design and construction, including the Zeiss optical lining-up of frames in the Swindon erecting shop. They emphasised the theme that even

engines for secondary services can with benefit be given the best of thermo-dynamic and mechanical practice; and it is not really untrue to say that they embodied the best of the two lines that began with Churchward's 80in Saints and 80in Stars, although they had 68in wheels. Their numbers were nearly legion: Halls 330, Granges 80, and Manors 30; and, like the Castles, some Halls and 10 Manors were built by British Railways in 1950, that is, 22 and 12 years after inception of the designs.

The 30 Hawksworth 4-6-0 Counties of 1945-47 had their admirers, but they were an imperfect thing apart, an interlude in a 50-year Great Western 4-6-0 'success story'. With two 18½in by 30in cylinders and 75in wheels they can hardly be classed as the final developments of the Churchward 4-6-0s of 1903-05; and for equal axle loads and weights per foot-run, the Castles were preferred before them when British Railways renewed construction of pure Swindon types in 1948-50.

Yet it was Hawksworth who initiated the measure that was to bring the seeming anti-climax of small general-purpose and large mediocre passenger engines to a St Martin's summer of GW 4-6-0s, in the form of the four-row high-temperature Schmidt-type superheater in place of the Swindon medium-temperature type; this was followed up by the improved draughting arrangements with double exhaust worked out at Swindon in the 1950s. They were the first real breakaways from Churchward principles. The power and economy improvements they gave under the deteriorating general conditions after the 1939-45 war brought the Castles and Kings once again into the front rank of all 4-6-0s, a position they retained until the steady withdrawal over the years 1960-64 to make way for diesel-hydraulic locomotives.

Top: NYC Hudson No 5449 still in steam at Albany, NY, in 1952. *J M Jarvis*

Centre: Chicago & North Western Pacific No 1650 at Milwaukee in mid-1952. *J M Jarvis*

Left: Typical of New York Central's top expresses of the 1940s, drawn by streamlined Hudson 4-6-4s. *Ian Allan library*

Class K4 4-6-2 No 3749 of the
Pennsylvania Railroad pictured on a
westbound passenger train in the
Pennsylvanian mountains in August 1952.
J M Jarvis

Great American Passenger Engines

**Above: Chicago & North Western streamlined
Pacific locomotive No 620 leaving Chicago
with a heavy passenger train in May 1955.**
V Goldberg collection

**Below: Southern Pacific 4-6-2 locomotive
No 2476 leaving San Francisco on an evening
rush-hour local train in the summer
of 1952.** *J M Jarvis*

STEAM RAILROADING in the United
States had a romance all its own. American
locomotives always seemed very much
larger than British—as indeed they were.
As early as 1903 4-6-2s comparable in
size with the British Railways Britannia
Pacifics of 50 years later were already at
work on a few railroads, while the ultimate
4-8-4s of the 1940s were roughly twice as
heavy (taking the engine only) and twice
as powerful as a Stanier LMSR Duchess
Pacific.

At the dawn of the twentieth century the
4-4-2, or Atlantic, dominated the US
motive power scene, having then recently
superseded the 4-4-0 in order to obtain
increased boiler capacity to cope with
increasingly heavy passenger stock. First
truly introduced on the Atlantic Coast Line
in 1894, the 4-4-2 was soon adopted by
many railroads, including some in the
west, but it became particularly associated
with railroads serving the Eastern seaboard, namely, the Pennsylvania Railroad,
the Philadelphia & Reading Central Railroad of New Jersey, and the ACL itself.

Many of the early American 4-4-2s were
not objects of beauty, some being of the
camelback or Mother Hubbard type (see
illustration overleaf), in which the fireman was banished to a vestigial cab at the
rear to stoke the huge Wootten firebox. As
boilers got ever bigger, after about 1905
the driver was reunited with his fireman
and the curious camelback form mercifully
disappeared. Nevertheless, 4-6-0s of that
pattern operated in commuter service until
1954 on the Central Railroad of New
Jersey, which obtained from the Brooks
Locomotive Works in 1902 three camelback Atlantics with 7ft drivers and 82sq ft
of grate.

Quite a large proportion of American
4-4-2s were compounds. Many of the
earlier examples built in the 1890s and
early 1900s operated on the Vauclain
principle with high- and low-pressure
(outside) cylinders one above the other
and cast together in one piece, and having
a common crosshead. Few if any tandem
compounds were built for passenger ser-

vice (as they were for freight) and during
about 1904-6 quite a number of Cole so-
called balanced compounds were built,
both with divided and unified cylinder
drive. The same principle was applied to
some early 4-6-2s, for example, on the
Northern Pacific, but the advent of superheating virtually ousted compounding
overnight as far as concerned new passenger locomotive construction.

Nevertheless, the Atcheson Topeka &
Santa Fe combined compounding and
superheaters in 4-4-2s and 4-6-2s built
as late as 1910 and 1911 respectively.
Initiated in the USA by the same redoubt-
able Cole, in 1905, the superheater was
becoming well-established by about 1910
and from, say, 1912, superheated two-
cylinder simple-expansion locomotives became the almost invariable standard for
new American passenger locomotive construction until the end of the steam era.

The most outstanding American 4-4-2s
were those of the Pennsylvania RR, which,
almost soleley in the USA, designed,
developed and built its own locomotives;
they were further distinguished by the
Belpaire firebox. The first PRR 4-4-2
(Class E1) was built in 1899 and there
followed from its Altoona, Pa, shops
several varieties, including Cole compounds, and a de Glehn compound 4-4-2
was experimentally purchased from France.

Although a 4-6-2 was purchased for
experiment in 1907, PRR 4-4-2 development continued and in 1910 three large-
boilered engines using saturated steam
(Class E6) were built; they eclipsed in
haulage capacity the first PRR-designed
4-6-2s built the following year which
weighed 22 per cent more. Superheating
was in vogue at that time (c 1910) and it
was soon to revolutionise locomotive
practice the world over. As a result, a
superheater 4-4-2(Class E6s) was built in
1914 which put out a phenomenal maximum of 2,448 indicated horsepower,
making it effectively the most powerful
four-coupled locomotive ever built. Eighty
of the PRR E6 class were built and extensively used east of Harrisburg between

New York and Philadelphia. All survived the 1939-45 war, and three lasted until as recently as 1955.

No doubt inspired by the PRR's four-coupled powerpack were four 4-4-4s built by the Philadelphia & Reading in 1914-15. The first American exponent of the trailing four-wheeled truck, the new P&R engines had Wootten fireboxes with grates of a monstrous 108sq ft, scarcely to be excelled even by a 4-8-4. Very unstable in operation, the rare machines were soon rebuilt as 4-4-2s and never matched their Pennsy counterparts.

With the appearance of the Reading 4-4-4s and the last PRR E6s in 1915, four-coupled locomotive development in the USA almost ceased—but not quite. Just 20 years later, after the resurgence from the economic depression of the early 1930s, a pair of gaudy orange-and-red streamlined new 4-4-2s with 300lb boiler pressure appeared on the Chicago Milwaukee & St Paul RR in 1935. They had been evolved to counter the rival Burlington Route's new high-speed diesel train and whisk a lightweight luxury five-car train 400 miles in 400 minutes, with scheduled maxima of 100mph en route. Unlike all previous US non-compound 4-4-2s, cylinder drive was on the leading coupled axle and the wheelbase was well spaced out. Oil firing imposed no limit on sustained maximum output as it did on the hand-fired Pennsy 4-4-2. An experimental 4-4-4 also appeared on the Baltimore & Ohio at the same time and there were several smaller examples of this type on the Canadian Pacific north of the 49th parallel, but the outbreak of war a few years later rendered all those light four-coupled machines white elephants for the rest of their short lives.

The Pennsy E6s set a commendable standard in that its superb boiler could supply any amount of steam the cylinders demanded; but it still had one severe limitation—adhesion. First introduced in the USA as early as 1850, the 4-6-0 type was already rapidly becoming obsolescent except in secondary service by the end of the nineteenth century. In a 4-6-0 it was not readily possible to combine a large wide firebox with large-diameter driving wheels.

During the early 1900s, a number of 2-6-2 tender engines, or Prairies, were built for express passenger service. Probably the most outstanding of them were ten with 79in drivers built by the Brooks works (by then a part of the American Locomotive Company) in 1905 for the Lake Shore & Michigan Southern in 1905. They held the then highly ephemeral distinction of being the largest passenger engines in the world until superseded by even larger 4-6-2s on the same railroad in 1907. A subsequent batch (1906) ranked among the earliest applications of Walschaerts valve gear in passenger service in North America. Having an adhesive factor as high as almost 6.0, they should have been very surefooted machines, but instability at speed because of the leading pony truck led to the rapid fall from favour of the 2-6-2 type in high-speed service, although smaller-wheeled Prairies lasted on the Northern Pacific until the end of steam around 1958. A leading bogie was obviously necessary.

The 4-6-2, or Pacific, made its effective debut on the Missouri Pacific in 1902 and on the Chesapeake & Ohio a few weeks later; it had become very widespread and had increased dramatically in size and capacity by 1910. Large-boilered saturated-steam 4-6-2s with piston valves and Walschaerts valve gear built by American Loco. in 1907 for the NYC and PRR,

systems (for trial) could be said to be the progenitor of the modern American steam passenger locomotive. The earliest 4-6-2s had inside Stephenson valve gear and inboard steamchests, or even slide valves, but external Walschaerts or Baker valve gear and piston valves soon became standard.

Most outstanding of the almost innumerable US 4-6-2 designs was the Pennsylvania K4s first introduced in 1914, of which no fewer than 425 ultimately appeared. It was essentially a six-coupled enlargement of the E6s 4-4-2 and although several latterly were updated with roller bearings, poppet valves and so on, it was basically the rugged piston-valve 4-6-2 of 1914 (with the later addition of a mechanical stoker) that was still handling the backbone of the PRR passenger services 30 years later.

The K4s ran with a variety of tenders of increasing size. Whereas the original engine had a small one with capacity for 7,000 US gallons of water and $12\frac{1}{2}$ short tons of coal, some later engines hauled immense 16-wheelers holding 24,400 gallons and 25 tons of fuel. It was symptomatic of the increasingly heavy trains hauled and the longer ·distances run between engine changes. An attempt to develop the K4s yet one stage further into the K5, with higher boiler pressure but retaining the same 70sq ft of hand-fired grate, met with little success and only two such engines, one with Caprotti poppet valve gear, were built.

By the time the last new 4-6-2 entered

service on the Pennsylvania RR in 1929, a development manifested on the rival New York Central, which had itself progressively developed the 4-6-2 for over 20 years, in many respects rendered obsolete the Pacific in heavy-duty passenger service. In 1927 the NYC placed in service the first of 275 4-6-4 Hudsons on its highly competitive (with the PRR) New York-Chicago run. The trailing four-wheeled truck permitted a larger (mechanically fired) grate and much greater power than in the hand-fired Pennsy 4-6-2.

The NYC 4-6-4s themselves were improved considerably over their eleven-year constructional period. The final examples could develop 25 per cent greater maximum power for a mere five per cent more weight. The improvement was achieved mainly through incorporating a combustion chamber in the firebox and the extensive use of high-tensile nickel alloy steel in the boiler plates and running gear. The earlier engines had Walschaerts valve gear which was later replaced by Baker gear—a peculiarly American derivative more suitable to cope with maximum valve travel lengths of the order of $8\frac{1}{2}$ inches. Later engines also had disc or Boxpok driving wheel centres designed to reduce weight and inflict less punishment on the track. As with the Pennsy 4-6-2s, tender size steadily increased.

Although the best known, the ̂NYC Hudsons were by no means the largest US 4-6-4s. In the late 1930s, streamlined high-speed examples with 84in drivers

Overleaf: Milwaukee Road Pacific No 157 leaving Chicago with an evening commuter train in the summer of 1952.
J M Jarvis

were built for the CM & St P and Chicago and North Western Railroads. When new, the engines regularly exceeded 100mph, and almost mythical tales were told of them. The heaviest and last were five built by the Baldwin Locomotive Works in 1948 for the Chesapeake & Ohio; they had sophisticated Franklin poppet-valve gear and weighed 198 tons apiece without tender.

Many American locomotives of the early 20th century were of decidedly austere appearance, but that was certainly not true of later machines. The visit of the British GWR 4-6-0 *King George V* to the USA in 1927 impressed many US railroad officials and there was thereafter a conscious effort in many quarters to conceal extraneous pipework beneath boiler jackets and to improve appearance generally. Nevertheless, American engines retained a handsome, if essentially functional, appearance to the end. The huge boilers of later years left little room inside loading gauges for them to be so obviously cluttered with such protruberances as feed-water heaters and air pumps, as had been prominent in the early 1920s.

In time, the limitations of six-coupled wheels, even when backed up by adequate boiler capacity, began to make themselves felt. The 4-8-2 featured relatively little in front-rank passenger service, being more of a mixed-traffic/fast-freight type, of which the somewhat conservative NYC and PRR concerns operated huge fleets having drivers of 69in to 72in which were

frequently pressed into passenger service. The Great Northern had some 4-8-2s with cylindrical Vanderbilt tenders (they had some almost identical counterparts on the Canadian National) built by Baldwin in 1923; they handled the crack GNR Oriental Limited for some years.

By the time passenger loadings generally demanded eight-coupled wheels the so-called Super Power concept, with four-wheeled trailing truck, had arrived. The result was the 4-8-4, which epitomised the final heroic period of North American steam railroading, from 1930 to 1950. A passenger 4-8-4 of, say, 1940 represented a tremendous advance over its 4-6-2 counterpart of only 20 years earlier. It would develop about 60,000lb of tractive effort compared to 40,000lb, although its cylinder dimensions could still be much the same because of a rise in boiler pres-

sure from 200lb to 300lb per square inch. In place of the bar frames and separately cast cylinders of the 4-6-2, all those parts would be cast together as a single unit in the 4-8-4, which would also very likely have the refinement of roller bearings in place of plain journals.

The three big American locomotive builders Alco, Baldwin and Lima all built appreciable numbers of 4-8-4s, as did several railroads in their own shops. They were all remarkably uniform as to the bare essentials, having two cylinders (except for one obscure experimental unit on the NYC) and round-topped fireboxes, except for one series with Belpaire on the Great Northern. One of the few major variations was in valve gear—Walschaerts versus Baker, although one 4-8-4 for the NYC in 1946 was given poppet valves. The final series of 4-8-4s on the Union Pacific were

Overleaf: Beyer-Garratts Nos 4088 and 4167 leaving Albert Falls near Pietermaritzburg, South Africa. *GEC Photo Society (E Talbot)*

Far left: South Georgia RR 4-6-0 No 103 at Rewy, Fla, in August 1933. *W Monypeny (C L Andrews)*

Left: Southern Pacific streamlined 4-8-4 No 447 at Los Angeles Union station in 1947. *V Goldberg collection*

Below: Florida East Coast Railway 4-8-2 No 442 at Miami in 1940. *W Monypeny (C L Andrews)*

Bottom: Union Pacific 4-8-4 No 183 leaving Denver in the summer of 1952. *J M Jarvis*

unusually equipped with double blast-pipes and double chimneys.

A few 4-8-4s were streamlined in vogue with their period of construction, almost entirely for publicity purposes rather than to save horsepower at high speed. Among the most striking of the streamliners were the great orange-and-red oil burners of the Southern Pacific, which hauled the SP's Daylights down the California coast well into the 1950s. The black bullet-nosed 4-8-4s of the Norfolk & Western with 70in drivers developed a record 80,000lb tractive effort without booster and could exceed 100mph with ease.

The heavier US 4-8-4s represented probably the largest high-speed steam motive power on rails possible within the generous confines of the US loading gauge. No greater diameter of boiler could be got in, which fixed an upper limit on maximum steaming capacity. The largest 4-8-4s could develop 6,000-7,000 cylinder horsepower, of which 4,000-5,000hp emerged at the drawbar. The massive and robust machines were exploited ruthlessly both in power output and endurance. The oil-burning 4-8-4s of the Atcheson Topeka & Santa Fe, the *heaviest* ever at 231 long tons without tender in the final Baldwin series of 1943-4, regularly ran right through the 1,791 miles between Kansas City and Los Angeles with six refuelling and 16 water stops, and 11 crew changes.

Facilities were developed to achieve long through runs with coal-burning steam power also. Refuelling was carried out by overhead chutes at stops, where the ashpan was emptied and the fire cleaned. The latter-day 4-8-4s of the New York Central, delivered in 1945-6, when new regularly ran the 928 miles throughout between Harmon (33 miles north of New York) and Chicago. With the provision of water pick-up apparatus, rare in the USA, the engines carried no less than 41 long tons of coal, thus necessitating only one coaling stop on the run. Equipped with every modern device, the NYC 4-8-4s were the most intensively utilised steam locomotives ever built. When new, repre-

sentatives were pitted against diesel-electrics to determine future NYC motive power policy and covered over a quarter of a million miles apiece per annum, a truly amazing figure!

One curious departure from the norm at that late stage was the short-lived Pennsylvania Duplex 4-4-4-4. Later 4-8-4s had attained such a size that they were beginning to suffer self-strangulation from their huge cylinders and limited valves, while the corresponding heavy machinery revolving and reciprocating at high speeds was mutually destructive of both the locomotive and the track upon which it ran. The 52 PRR 4-4-4-4s were thus 4-8-4s with four small cylinders and lighter moving parts and two sets of four-coupled wheels. Excessive slipping and high maintenance costs associated with the complicated poppet valve gear only facilitated the rapid influx of diesels while the engines were still new.

A modern American steam passenger locomotive of the 1940s weighed about twice as much as its counterpart of the early 1900s, but such were the technological advances made in the intervening period, particularly superheating but also in metallurgy, that it could develop between three and four times more power. For instance, an early non-superheated NYC 120-ton 4-6-2 of 1907 developed a maximum of 16.7 indicated horsepower per long ton (2,000ihp), which was precisely half that of the 210-ton Niagara 4-8-4 of 1945 when worked all out at 7,000ihp.

American locomotives were almost invariably worked at high power outputs, with attendant colossal firing and combustion rates. Under such conditions, boiler thermal efficiencies often sank to 50 per cent and below. Spectacular to witness and to hear in full eruption, such prodigal consumption of increasingly costly coal was a contributory factor to the rapid supersession of steam by diesel-electric in the USA in the late 1940s and early 1950s, when many still new steam machines were consigned to the scrap-heap.

ARTICULATED LOCOMOTIVES

THE CELEBRATED SEMMERING locomotive competition of 1851 was the practical beginning of articulated engines; in the next 75 years at least 70 different systems were invented, and probably 85 per cent of them had at least one application. If one was to count all variations, the total probably would reach 200. Yet, in the end, something like 90 per cent of all construction must have been made up of Mallets and Garratts, and of the remainder half would be Fairlies of one type or another.

Articulated locomotives in the first half of their history were unlike those of the second half. In the 40 to 50 years from 1851, inventions were legion and construction limited; from the 1890s, new inventions amounted only to a handful, but construction swelled enormously. This was due, first, to the success of the Mallet, and, secondly, to the supplementing of that type by the Garratt. With these two as practical propositions, building of the older forms almost disappeared, and construction of later systems scarcely got above single orders.

Theoretically, an articulated locomotive is one in which one or more driven axles can take up positions not parallel with the others, and can take up angular locations on curves. Rigid-frame engines with leading Krauss or Zara trucks do not come within this definition, because the lateral play of the pivot ensures that the included coupled-axle moves transversely and not radially. Similarly, in Beugniot-lever locomotives, the two groups of axles remain parallel.

In practice, the presence of one or more trucks is the feature that distinguishes the articulated locomotive, but one, or two, may be pivoted. Other defining conditions

Top: East African Railways Class 59 4-8-2 + 2-8-4 Beyer-Garratt locomotive at Nairobi in June 1969. *T B Owen*

Above: One of Festiniog Railway's double Fairlie engines, No 3 'Earl of Merioneth' at Boston Lodge in August 1970. *J Hunt*

Below: A New Zealand Railways double Fairlie by Avonside (Bristol) of the 1870s on the Auckland & Mercer Railway.
New Zealand Railways

as to type are the way in which the boiler is supported, whether the draw-and-buffing gear is carried on the trucks or on a main frame, and the number of driving-engine groups. However, in themselves, those features have nothing to do with articulation.

Strictly there are articulated and semi-articulated principles, and in each can (or could) be found examples of a single engine and a single driving bogie, a single engine and two driven bogies, and two engines and two driven bogies. Full articulateds are two-truck engines, represented mainly by Fairlies, Meyers and Garratts. Within the term can be found both single and double Fairlies, NBL Modified Fairlies, Shays, Kitson-Meyers, Beyer-Garratts, and the few du Bousquet locomotives. Semi-articulated types, with one rigid driving group and one driven truck, are exemplified principally by the Mallet, but include the well-known though little-built Hagans type in Germany, Serbia and Tasmania, and the Hagans-Weidknecht engines in Greece and France.

Historically, the first articulated locomotive of all was Horatio Allen's *South Carolina*, set to work in 1832. This double-boiler single-firebox 2-2-2-2 was not a practical success. The importance of the Semmering contest was that, out of the four competitors, the Wiener Neustadt engine became the prototype of the later Meyer system, and the Cockerill (Seraing) engine became the prototype of the Fairlie group, though the basic principle was that of the *South Carolina*. The practical non-success of the four competitors, plus the absolute need to work the Semmering line when it was completed three years later, led to introduction of the Engerth semi-articulated design, in which use was made of the tender for some of the adhesion weight. This was popular freight and steep-grade power in Austria, Belgium and France from the 1850s to the 1870s; but one of the best-known Austrian engines, the *Steierdorf*, was of the Fink semi-articulated type.

Of reciprocating steam forms with direct drive, the Meyer, dating from 1868, had two driven bogies connected by a rod or bar, the buffing-and-draw gear was on the bogies, the boiler was supported on the front truck through a spherical pivot and on the rear truck through normal expansion brackets. True Meyers had the four cylinders at the centre; the later Kitson-Meyers sometimes had the cylinders at the outer ends, and they had a girder frame carrying the superstructure. Du Bousquet's engines were of Meyer type with a main frame above two trucks, and the main frame carried the boiler and the draw-and-buffing gear. In that respect it was closer to the Wiener Neustadt original than to the Meyer development.

Fairlie's first patent was dated 1863. A double Fairlie had two driven trucks carrying draw-and-buffing gear, a single central firebox with two boiler barrels leading forward and backward with their weights supported above the respective pivots, and with draw and buffing forces transmitted through the boiler. Its apotheosis was seen in the heavy 0-6-6-0s for Mexico, a country that also ran some of the American Mason-Fairlie version in 2-6-6-6 form. The single Fairlie had only one boiler, one driven truck and one carrying truck; examples were the 0-6-4Ts on the North Wales Narrow Gauge Railway.

The Modified Fairlie as built by North British Locomotive Co and Henschel for the South African Railways had pivots at the wheelbase centres of each truck, but the trucks were well apart so that a

Above: NBL Modified Fairlie for South African Railways, with 2-6-2 + 2-6-2 wheel arrangement. *B Jackson*

Below: A 3ft 6in-gauge Beyer-Garratt of the numerous 4-8-2 + 2-8-4 SAR GEA class.

Right top: Latest of the EAR Beyer-Garratts, Class 60 No 6008 at Tararo in July 1969. *T B Owen*

Right Bottom: SAR Class GMA 4-8-2 + 2-8-4 No 4136/70 by North British Loco, near Pietermaritzburg in June 1969. *T B Owen*

Garratt-slung boiler could be used, and the main girder frame carried boiler, cab, front and back tanks, and coal bunker. A derivation of Fairlie principles was the well-known Péchot double-boiler locomotive, of which hundreds ran on the 600mm-gauge tracks behind the Allied lines in France during the 1914-18 war.

The Garratt had two driven trucks carrying the draw-and-buffing gear, and the forces were transmitted between one truck and the other through a girder frame that also carried the boiler and cab; the tanks were mounted on the trucks. The Garratt-Union, built by Maffei, had the main girder frame extended back over the rear truck to support the back water tank and the coal bunker: the practical advantage, shared with the Modified Fairlie, was that a mechanical stoker could be applied without inconvenience. In the Hanomag type of the 1920s, the girder

frame was extended forward to carry the front tanks; the rear tank and coal bunker remained on the rear truck, and the two trucks were separated by a distance just sufficient to get in a big firebox. Thus the engine was shorter, and the inside throw-over on curves less than with a normal Garratt.

In the Mallet, the rear group was a fixed unit carrying the back end of the boiler on expansion brackets; the front truck was pivoted to the forward end of the fixed unit, and carried the front end of the cantilevered boiler on slides; draw-and-buffing gear was on the trucks. In effect, the front truck was a multi-axle engine-driven Bissell. A reversal of the Mallett was the Rimrott, in which the rear truck was the swivelling one; perhaps it is truer to say the Mallet was an inversion of the Rimrott, for the latter was patented in 1878, six years before the Mallet patent,

and it grew out of the Engerth type.

All the forms so far mentioned had both trucks driven by engine groups of their own; sometimes the two were linked thermodynamically by compound propulsion, with the high-pressure cylinders on one truck and the low-pressure pair on the other. This was the normal arrangement with Mallet compounds. There was also the principle of a single engine driving both trucks and the best-known examples were the Shay, Heisler and Climax geared locomotives. The principle of one engine driving two trucks was applied first by the Neath Abbey industrial works in South Wales in 1839, but there the drive was through a combination of countershaft and spur gears.

Only in the last-mentioned group was ability to traverse very sharp curves the prime reason for evolution. Quite powerful Shays could go round 60-65ft curves on narrow gauge. In the other instances, great power (for the time) allied to sharp curves and light track was the motive. In later years certain well-established types were further developed on the basis of sheer power, curves being flat and permissible axle load high; prominent examples were the North American Mallets from 1903 onwards, and a few Garratts such as the Bengal-Nagpur Railway double 4-8-0 and the Russian double 4-8-2.

The Whyte system of wheel notation was long preceded by articulated locomotives, which up to 1900 could be described only by a cumbrous wordy account. In the Whyte system, it became usual to insert the + sign between trucks and give the full notation for each wheel group only with the Garratt; a 2-8-0+ 0-8-2 Garratt, for example, was the equivalent (wheel-wise) of a 2-8-8-2 Mallet or Kitson-Meyer.

Articulated locomotives were never a prominent feature of British steam practice. Apart from the 33 six-coupled LMSR Garratts on the Toton-Brent coal haulage duty, the single LNER 2-8-0+0-8-2 banker, and one or two industrial Garratts, it was the narrow-gauge railways in North Wales that perpetuated the type, with single and double Fairlies, some of which still run. Away from that area, early single Fairlies included the well-known standard-gauge 0-4-4T of the Swindon, Marlborough & Andover Junction Railway in 1881—the first engine to run in England with Walschaerts valve motion; and also two 0-4-4Ts on the Great Southern & Western Railway in Ireland in 1869-70, which were to 5ft 3in gauge. No Mallet ever operated revenue services in Britain, but 94 were built for export between 1907 and 1921, and all but six (from Beardmore) came from NBL. Only one Shay ever ran in England.

On the other hand, articulated locomotives were a very decided feature of operation in certain non-European countries, and on the secondary lines of several countries within that continent. On railways of any size, articulated locomotives were almost entirely of Mallet or Garratt forms, for such principles as the Kitson-Meyer, and even the Fairlie, were used only in small numbers by comparatively small railways, for example in Colombia, Chile, Mexico and New Zealand.

Mallet's invention was specifically to widen the use of his patent compound system; but the two things could be, and were, used independently, and eventually non-compound Mallets formed the greatest number in new construction, and comprised all the largest and most powerful engines. Most of Mallet's early European

Top: American Mallet 2-8-8-2 of Southern Railway System at Appalachia, Va, in January 1935. *C L Andrews*

Above: Chesapeake & Ohio 2-6-6-2 Mallet No 1397 at Beckley roundhouse, W Va, in September 1951. *J M Jarvis*

Right: One of the 2ft-gauge Beyer-Garratts, SAR Class NG 155, at work near Harding in June 1969. *T B Owen*

Below: Beyer-Garratt developed for the 2ft-gauge lines in Africa, as it left the Gorton, Manchester, works in 1958.

engines were compounds for light rails and sharp curves, but notable exceptions were the large 0-6-6-0s on the Gotthard line with its 1 in 37 grades and international passenger and freight traffics. Only after close study of the earlier big engines and their work did Alco decide to take up construction in the USA in 1903. The development of the American engines up to the Big Boy 4-8-8-4s of 1941-44 can be found in the following chapter. The last Mallets of all were a handful in the USSR in the early 1950s.

Mallet construction for Asia and South America continued up to the years of the 1939-45 war, sometimes with powerful machines such as the metre-gauge 2-8-8-4s of 258,000lb loco weight for the Central Railway of Brazil. In at least one case, on the 3ft-gauge Uintah Railway in Colorado, Mallets proved superior to Shays in haulage up grades as steep as 1 in 13-14, though the 66ft curves taken by

the Shays had to be eased to 80ft for the 2-6-6-2T Mallets. Many similar Mallets, both tender and tank, operated in logging service over 1 in 15-20 grades; but in general the Shay was the articulated engine *par excellence* for the logging roads, for the combination of single-engine gear drive with two or more short-base trucks provided best use of the adhesion along with ability to go round extremely tight curves and keep the track.

On steep grades, the Mallet had one disadvantage compared with the Garratt, and one that had a leading effect on the supersession of the Mallet on the South African Railways. That was, the boiler was so long that the firebox crown could easily become uncovered on grades around 1 in 33 or steeper. The shorter and squatter boiler of the Garratt did not have that defect; it also invariably permitted a grate that could burn any class of coal, whereas the Mallet was limited by the loading gauge

Just as two or three triplex Mallets—originated by George Henderson—were built in 2-8-8-8-2 and 2-8-8-8-4 wheel arrangements in 1913-16, so Beyer-Peacock had designs for triplex Garratts, as well as steam turbine Garratts, but they were never built. No Garratt ever got to a 10-coupled layout, though some were proposed and designed. The only 10-coupled Mallets to give successful service were the 10 Virginian 2-10-10-2s of 1918, though the Santa Fe in 1911 rebuilt pairs of 2-10-2s into 2-10-10-2 Mallets with flexible boilers.

One aspect that favoured the Garratt was that even the largest engines built did not reach the development ceiling; whereas the 4-8-8-4 Big Boys and 2-6-6-6s in the USA did represent the high-pressure Mallet's limit in size and weight, though not in output, for no Chapelon features were embodied in North American practice. Had they been, it is probable that the 8,000 indicated horsepower of the Big Boys could have been raised above 10,000ihp, and with a reduction in coal consumption that might have made the surrounding country a little less like the back of a chimney.

Some purists regard steam-tender locomotives as articulated types; certainly they meet the definitions included in the third paragraph. In that case the second and the last forms of articulated engines to be initiated in England were of that form; they were, respectively, the Sturrock steam tenders on the Great Northern Railway in the 1860s, and the Poultney 50-per cent max cut-off 2-8-2+0-8-0 combination *River Esk* on the 15in-gauge Ravenglass & Eskdale Railway in 1928. That year saw also the single application of the last new type of articulated locomotive, the Golwé, applied to Ivory Coast engines on patents granted in Belgium in 1924.

in this respect, for the grate and ashpan had to go above the wheels.

More or less until 1924 at least, 99 per cent of all Mallets built were compounds; but of the total eventual Garratt construction, at least 99 per cent were four-cylinder simples. That in itself overcame most of the sluggishness that characterised Mallet compounds—an inability to run faster than 25 to 30mph. The Garratt did not suffer the same defect, yet its slow-speed performance was just as good as that of the older type. The high-pressure Mallet, after being improved also in riding qualities in the mid-1930s, could run at 60 to 70mph even in the largest sizes. A few Garratts, such as the Algerian and Sao Paulo types, also ran express trains; but in general the Garratt was a low-axleload steep-grade performer.

The phenomenal world application of the Garratt over the 20 years 1925-45 was due largely to Beyer Peacock, and in particular to Sam Jackson (design and construction) and Cyril Williams (sales). No Churchward, Gresley or Stanier engine was more integrated with an individual than were Beyer-Garratts with these two men—one dour and undemonstrative, the other full of life and even of flamboyance. The patentee, Herbert W Garratt, died early and took practically no part in development. After the original patent of 1907 ran its 14 years, Beyer Peacock steadily developed all the details, and it was this later work that gave rise to the name Beyer-Garratt, which was a trade name and not a patent name.

Fortunately the first Garratt of all, the Tasmanian 2ft-gauge double 0-4-0 of 1908, is still preserved on the Festiniog Railway, and some of the largest of all later builds are still in daily service on the South African Railways. New engines for the 2ft-gauge system of the SAR were built as late as the 1960s.

THE AMERICAN MALLETS

Above: Class Y6B 2-8-8-2 compound Mallet of the Norfolk & Western Railway, builder of its own Mallet locomotives, based on USRA designs, until 1952. *Norfolk & Western Railway*

Below: Typical heavy Mallet of the Chesapeake & Ohio Railroad, with imposing array of gear around the smokebox door. *C&O/B&O Railroads*

Facing page: Norfolk and Western Railway Mallet No 2174 on Trace Fork Viaduct, in the Allegheny mountains, in November 1959. *D K Johnson*

FROM THE FIRST 334,000lb 0-6-6-0 in 1903, Mallet articulated locomotives in the USA were 'the biggest locomotive in the world', far surpassing all Garratts, and culminating in the 340-ton (English) Big Boy 4-8-8-4s of the Union Pacific in 1941. That weight was for the engine alone; combined engine and tender total was 535 English tons, or just on 1,200,000lb. Several other classes in the 1930s and 1940s topped the million-pound mark with tender, but apart from the special Erie and Virginian triplex models, only three got above 700,000lb engine weight.

Among notable holders of the 'largest', meaning 'heaviest,' title from 1903 were the Baltimore & Ohio 0-6-6-0 No 2400, the Erie 0-8-8-0s of 1907 (the only three Mallets with Wootten fireboxes), the first Southern Pacific oil-burning 2-8-8-2s of 1909, the Santa Fe's rebuilt 2-10-10-2s with flexible boiler joints in 1911, the Virginian 2-10-10-2s of 1918, and the Northern Pacific's Z5-class 2-8-8-4s of 1929-30 which had the largest grate area ever (182sq ft). These examples exclude the Erie triplex engines of 1913-16 and the one Virginian triplex of 1916, but all four of them were Mallet tank engines, the only standard-gauge examples in the States, though there were narrow-gauge Mallet tanks for some of the Colorado lines.

From the mid-1920s the title holders were no longer four-cylinder compounds but four-cylinder simple expansion; they retained the system of articulation evolved by Anatole Mallet in 1884. His system of compounding dated back to 1874.

Adopted first by the then newly formed Alco combine after close study of the Gotthard-line 0-6-6-0s and other European Mallets of lighter weight, the B & O engine was 17 per cent heavier than the biggest rigid-framed engine of the time, and its adhesion weight was 40 per cent more. For 18 months after its completion the future of the Mallet in North America was dubious; but the continued good behaviour of that 12-wheeler throughout the year following its release from the St Louis Exposition of 1904 led to adoption of the format by other roads for steep-grade pusher service, and then for drag freight work.

The original 0-6-6-0 wheel notation died out for new construction after 80 had been built; the larger 0-8-8-0 went to a total of 150. In a sense that finished the definite banking designs, though in practice engines with leading and trailing trucks often did pusher service. The front trucks gave rather easier riding at 20mph upwards; trailing trucks gave better air-flow and ashpan conditions. And so extension began with 2-6-6-0s, 2-6-6-2s, 2-8-8-0s and

2-8-8-2s, all of which had appeared by 1909.

Few Mallets were ever built specifically for passenger service, perhaps only the Southern Pacific's 2-6-6-2s, soon rebuilt to 4-6-6-2, and a few rebuilds on the Santa Fe; on steep-grade sections normal Mallets often were employed on passenger trains, either as head-end power or as pushers.

General designs settled down with remarkably little trouble, partly because speed in the first few years rarely got as high as 25mph. Only one or two roads, like the Santa Fe, laid up trouble for themselves with flexibly jointed boilers, semi-flexible fireboxes, and rebuilds of two old rigid-frame engines into one Mallet; though for years Baldwin pushed its sectional boiler with smoke chamber and feedwater heater compartment without benefit to users. Reason for the variations was the sudden surge in locomotive length with the incorporation of end trucks, on which designers had not ruminated.

Mallet construction from 1909-10 was extensive, but a further fillip was given after the USA came tardily into the 1914-18 war, for then the United States Railway Administration standardised further wartime construction on half-a-dozen new locomotive types, including light· and heavy 2-8-8-2 Mallets that were quite a success. Later, some railroads, like the Norfolk & Western, based their own Mallets on the USRA designs, and that parentage could be traced even on the last-built N & W 2-8-8-2s of 1948-52.

Until the early 1920s, limits to the application of big Mallets came from the number of freight cars not fitted with the latest pattern of MCB centre coupler, and starting efforts around 100,000lb pulled out too many drawbars with an un-assisted Mallet at the head of the train. On the other hand, those were the days of immense coal trains requiring, say, a couple of 2-10-10-2 bankers at the rear and one 2-8-8-2 at the head to get 15,000

tons up 1 in 50 at around 8mph, with a total coal consumption approximating to 15 tons an hour. Such trains commonly were of high-capacity limited-route wagons.

Nevertheless, by 1922 the locomotive itself, rather than centre couplers, was forming the limitation; the compound system applied to the long articulated layout, with the two steam circuits as part of one system, had reached its peak, not only in mechanical matters such as the size of the low-pressure cylinders, which in the Virginian 2-10-10-2s were 48in bore, but in the sluggishness of steam and exhaust flows, which practically prevented top speeds above 25mph; that meant drag hauls scarcely above 14mph, and little over half that on steep grades, even with pushers.

Compound development reached its peak in size with the 10 Virginian 2-10-10-2s Nos 800-09 of 1918, which weighed 684,000lb engine only and had the largest heating surface ever, 8,606sq ft. Even for Mallets they were pot-bellied, with a boiler barrel 9ft 10in diameter; they were the only ten-coupled Mallets built new as such. Compound Mallets built from 1919 to 1924 were more modest and were mainly 2-8-8-2s. Only the N & W thereafter developed the compound to get advantage from higher pressure; to 1924 few Mallets had above 210lb.

By that time higher effective freight train speeds were becoming essential, partly for quick delivery of perishables, but also for a straight increase in line capacity to take the growing traffic of all types. Mallets had given an increase in capacity over Mikados and 2-10-0s of earlier years, but in the early 1920s there were several instances where more-modern simple-expansion 2-10-2s, when fitted with boosters, increased the line capacity compared with Mallets of nearly twice the size, simply because the higher speed uphill more than counterbalanced the heavier load that could be taken by the Mallets.

Top: One of the 2-6-6-6 Mallets of very high adhesion weight and over 7,000 drawbar hp built by the Chesapeake & Ohio, in this instance, for the Virginia Railroad. *C&O/B&O Railroads*

Above left: First subject of the title 'Biggest in the World', the 334,000lb 0-6-6-0 Mallet No 2400 of Baltimore & Ohio RR of 1905.

Above: At rest in Java in August 1972, a 2-8-8-0 Alco Mallet of 1919 at work until comparatively recently on Indonesian State Railways. *C J Gammell*

Left: First of the Baltimore & Ohio's new fleet of EMI Mallets in June 1945, No 7600 tops a 17-mile grade at Altamont, W Virginia. *H W Pontin*

Next stage was initiated in 1924 with 25 Alco-built four-cylinder simple 2-8-8-2s on the Chesapeake & Ohio. General increase in boiler pressures in the States was another two or three years off, for the 240lb of the USRA designs had not been repeated, and the C & O machines had only 205lb. The increase in practicable speed which they brought was notable, and they could be got up to a maximum of 35mph on suitable sections, which meant that 14-15mph drag freight schedules could be accelerated to 20-22 mph; yet the normal output of those engines was not more than 3,300 indicated horsepower at 20mph.

They were not the first simple-expansion Mallets, for the Pennsylvania built a 50 per cent max cut-off 2-8-8-0 in 1919, and that itself followed eight years after another 'one-off' 2-8-8-2 in 1911. Nothing came of those two prototypes, and otherwise the Pennsy had only a handful of compound 2-8-8-2s. The four-cylinder simple-expansion 2-8-8-2 soon spread to the Great Northern, Rio Grande, Southern and other roads, but only to a total of 86, for it was overtaken by developments that followed Lima's application of a four-wheel trailing truck to rigid–frame locomotives, so that by 1928 the Mallet also was appearing with two-axle trucks.

Strangely, almost the first application was a 'reverse-order' 4-8-8-2—the new breed of cab-in-front SP Mallets for the Sierra section, which began after a 15-year gap since the construction of the last compounds for the route. With that layout, the oil-burning firebox could be carried above the drivers, and so the four-wheel truck was used mainly for better guiding at the leading end. As many as 195 of the 4-8-8-2 cab-in-front engines were acquired between 1928 and 1944, with a gradual increase in weight from 481,000 to 658,000lb.

First of the notable four-wheel trailing truck installations was to the 12 Yellowstone 2-8-8-4s of the Northern Pacific in 1929-30. To burn lignite from the railroad's own mines a grate of 182sq ft was provided; the evaporative heating surface of 7,673sq ft was exceeded only by the old Virginian 2-10-10-2s, which had the A-type superheater, whereas the NP engines had the E-type equipment.

In this second stage of Mallet development, the simple expansion, higher pressures, and greater attention to valves, valve motion, and boiler output increased substantially the effective speed and power compared with the best of the older compounds; moreover, slipping was considerably decreased as the back and front steam systems were separate and had no intersurges. One major failing of the big Mallet still remained; the poor riding and instability. Simple-expansion engines could attain 35 to 40mph and occasionally more, but the riding then was almost dangerous and the imposed track stresses very high. There was a consequential

deleterious effect on the bar frames, despite the size to cope with axle loads of 70,000lb and piston thrusts above 130,000lb.

Integral cast frames, dating from around 1928 for large locomotives, eased the frame position, though not the actual stresses coming on them. The principle of the Mallet articulation was that the rear group was the fixed unit, and the whole front group pivoted about it like a heavily laden multi-axle Bissell truck, with the front end of the boiler resting on curved slides, and with the additional complication that the Bissell was driven. Movement of the whole front group was inherently unstable, but the effects could be tolerated up to 30-35mph.

Simple-expansion Mallets had improved one aspect in that both steam and exhaust pipes attached to the rear cylinder group could be carried on the boiler and so needed no universal or flexible sliding joints; the front engine still needed such joints for live steam and exhaust.

In the early 1930s lateral-motion devices giving up to one inch each way of spring-cushioned side movement were adopted for the leading drivers on all new Mallets, and more engines for fast freight also had four-wheel leading trucks with spring-controlled side movement instead of swing links. But only when precision-machined and precision-fitted flat supports for the front end of the boiler, and articulation joints that prevented 'rock 'n roll', were added in the UP 4-6-6-4 Challengers in 1935 did the Mallet become a safe mile-a-minute proposition, and the third and final stage of American Mallet development begin.

For sheer fast passenger and fast freight work the Challengers themselves were never surpassed, though many similar 4-6-4-4s followed on lines such as the Delaware & Hudson, Western Pacific, and DRGW, and about 215 were built altogether. The N & W got equally satisfactory riding, high speeds, and a drawbar output up to 6,300hp, with a 2-6-6-4 layout, built by the road 1936-50. The design was developed also into the huge 4-8-8-4s of the UP and NP, and they also were no mean performers in speed, having been designed for 70mph top.

Transition from first to second stage in Mallet development had brought the type out of the pure pusher stage and put it into

Top: Southern Pacific's 'reverse-order' 4-8-8-2 Mallet of 1928, of which nearly 200 were built, permitted the mounting of the oil burning firebox over one set of drivers.
Southern Pacific Transportation Company

Above: Among the big post-war Mallets were the 1943 Baldwin-built Yellowstone 2-8-8-4s for Duluth, Missabe & Iron Range Railway, with a total weight of 569 US tons and 140,000lb tractive effort. *B D Whebell*

Right top to bottom: Mallets at work; Norfolk & Western 2-8-8-2 No 2174 at Haperstown, Ma, in August 1952; Norfolk & Western 2-8-8-4 on coal empties in New River Gorge in September 1951; and Milwaukee Road 2-6-6-2 on the Olympic Hiawatha train at Tacoma, Wash, in July 1952. *All J M Jarvis*

the drag-freight long-haul range, and even just into the manifest freight speeds as they were in the early 1920s. In the 1930s those speeds had to go up sharply, and it was the third stage in development which permitted that to be done—and, incidentally, diminished the new construction of large rigid-frame 2-10-4s.

The great adhesion and power of third-stage Mallets could still be used in pusher service over crucial sections where an economic survey showed the great capital investment was warranted. Several were so used to help traffic in the 1939-45 war, including the Big Boys themselves up the 30 miles of average 1 in 85 grade to Sherman summit, working there for a couple of hours or more at full throttle and 65 per cent cut-off, with speed staying between 10 and 15mph.

The C & O, with an allowable axle load of 78,500lb on some routes, adopted the 2-6-6-6 layout to get a grate area of 135sq ft; but the UP and DRGW got larger grates above more heavily laden four-wheel trucks. No other six-coupled Mallet approached the C & O adhesion weight of 471,000lb except the handful built to the same design for the Virginian. The C & O machines were checked at above 7,000 drawbar horsepower.

Strangely, the last Mallets to be built in the USA for home service were compounds. The N & W had never given up compound propulsion or the 2-8-8-2 wheel arrangement for its drag coal trains;

and, being the last Class I railroad to continue at full blast with steam traction, built at its Roanoke shops through 1948-52 a series of 30 locomotives which, though they had practically the same cylinder size and wheel diameter as the engines built in 1918-19, had 300lb boiler pressure, 16 per cent greater weight, and advanced valve motion. The 39in low-pressure cylinders were notable in having 18in piston valves, probably the largest diameter ever put into a steam locomotive.

The last batch of engines brought the N & W total of 2-8-8-2s to 220. The company's charged price of $260,000 per engine and tender (incidentally 2.65 times the cost of the first 2-8-8-2s in 1919) was cheap at a time when Lima was getting from the Louisville & Nashville $255,000 for a 2-8-4 roller-bearing engine and tender.

As the largest steam locomotives ever, the Big Boys deserve a word. They were built in two batches, in 1941 and 1944. The latter weighed 772,000lb and had a 14-wheel tender scaling 437,000lb all on, giving a total of 1,209,000lb. With a total wheelbase of 117ft 7in and an overall length of 127ft, they were given 135ft turntables at the principal points. The pressure of 300lb was the highest ever used in a simple-expansion Mallet, but as the cylinders were only $23\frac{3}{4}$in bore the piston thrust did not rise above 133,000lb, a long way off the maximum of 219,000lb in a rigid-frame locomotive. Next heaviest engine was the C & O 2-6-6-6 at 724,500lb, and then came the NP Class Z5 2-8-8-4 at 723,500lb. Big Boys and Challengers also had the biggest tenders among Mallets, with 21,000 imperial gallons of water and 25 long tons of coal.

In the 49 years from 1903 about 3,100 standard-gauge Mallets in 21 different wheel arrangements were built in the States for home service, plus the two types of triplex engines, and a few Mallet tank and tender engines of 3ft gauge for the Uintah Railway and some logging roads. Just over 40 per cent of all engines were 2-6-6-2s. Of the standard-gauge engines nearly 2,400 were compounds, so that while the later simple-expansion engines made a tremendous difference to fast freight working on a few major railroads, they by no means changed the general picture of main-line freight working throughout the USA.

THE UNION PACIFIC BIG BOYS

Above: Oil-burning 3800-class 4-6-6-4 No 3819 piloting coal-burning Big Boy No 4023, about to leave Cheyenne with a 106-car freight train on the run described in the text.
Lord Garnock

Below: 4000-class Big Boy 4-8-8-4 No 4019 climbing Weber canyon, Utah, with an extra (X in the train number) freight train of refrigerated wagons. *Union Pacific RR*

TO RAILROAD FANS, the initials UP have indeed always stood for Union Pacific, but to students of mechanical engineering those same initials recall the phrase 'unlimited power', and there is no better slogan with which to describe Union Pacific motive power practice.

The Union Pacific was part of the first American transcontinental railroad. Particularly in respect of locomotive policy, its progressive management enjoyed a reputation for research, for innovation and for an ability to operate a stud of locomotives representing the ultimate in technical development and capable performance. Thus it was no accident that UP steam power was invariably ahead of the company's current requirements; that freight trains ran on schedules which were highly satisfactory to shippers; and that the combined tonnage and speeds achieved resulted in an operating ratio which even the most exacting system cost accountant termed efficient.

The Big Boys were no isolated achievement. The research and development that went into their construction came from a wealth of experience and a long line of remarkable locomotives. By 1930, the railroad had in service almost one hundred 4-12-2s designed, in the words of the then chief of motive power, 'to haul mile-long freight trains at passenger train speeds'. That their 4,330hp was capable of pulling at 50mph the same train that the Mallet compounds they replaced could only struggle with at 25mph was never in doubt.

The 4-12-2s were unique on four counts. They represented the high watermark in North America in size of locomotive with rigid frames, being the largest non-articulateds ever built. They were the only 12-coupled locomotives constructed in the States. In an age when built-up crank axles had been superseded by a straight two-cylinder design, the 9000s were given three cylinders. And finally, all but a handful were fitted with the Gresley conjugate valve gear (though I never met anyone who knew the origin of that name).

The next significant development came in 1936, when the Challenger 4-6-6-4 wheel arrangement was introduced. By then the railway had gone right away from the Mallet, or compound articulated, into the realm of simple articulated locomotives. The 3900s were not only remarkable looking engines, they were the first articulateds able to achieve mile-a-minute speeds due to improved front-end boiler support and articulated joints. Indeed, the Challenger was a true dual-purpose or mixed-traffic engine and on 'second sections' and passenger extras, speeds in the seventies have been recorded.

In parallel with the development of the 4-6-6-4s, the 800s, or Northern 4-8-4s, were introduced. At 456 short tons, they were among the heaviest locomotives of that wheel arrangement. The 4-8-4s looked good on the drawing board and were even better in steel and steam at the head end. Until the advent of the 800s, the older Mountain-class 4-8-2s had reached the limit of tonnage and speed. Double-heading was the rule and UP headquarters in Omaha were looking for something to boost speeds, increase tonnage and cut costs. They certainly found it with the 800s. From the very start in 1937, the first 20 engines in the class averaged 15,000 miles per month per locomotive and pushed up the availability from 65.3 per cent in the case of the Mountains to a remarkable figure of 93.4 per cent.

Costwise, the 800s effected the economy required by management. During the first year of operation, savings of $1¼ million were turned in, being attributed to more-efficient operation, and the elimination of double-heading and extra sections (reliefs). The return on investment achieved was slightly over 50 per cent.

Many of the features of the 800s later came to be employed on the Big Boys. The 4-8-4s were the first locomotives on the system to be fitted with roller bearings on all axles and the first to have a boiler of 300lb pressure, which was to play such an important part in the Big Boy story. Other new features were the use of a manually controlled blow-off and sludge-removal system, needle-roller bearings for all valve motion parts and mechanical forced-feed lubrication applied widely throughout the locomotive. The 800s were designed for continuous 90mph operation and early on it was discovered that 3,000 miles could be attained between entering engine terminals for servicing. A typical 1949 diagram of that mileage would be Kansas City – Denver – La Grande – Green River-Ogden – Cheyenne, and in those days it was rare for an 800 to fail to complete its diagram.

Thus was the stage set for the introduction in 1941 of the first of the Big Boys, of which 25 were to be built by Alco at Schenectady, New York, before the end of the war. The huge 4-8-8-4 simple articulateds were the brain-child of the same successful partnership that had directed UP motive power policy throughout the thirties—Jabelman and Jeffers. The former occupied the position of chief of research and development, motive power and machinery; the latter was chief mechanical engineer.

At the close of the nineteen-thirties, the effects of the depression had ended and American industry was firmly established and expanding fast out on the west coast to escape from the over-populated eastern seaboard. Los Angeles and San Francisco, and indeed the whole of California, were expanding at a rate four-and-a-half times the national average. An ever-increasing freight traffic movement was apparent, linking the population growth in the Pacific with the traditional eastern and mid-western markets. By building heavier and more-powerful freight locomotives, the board of the Union Pacific was determined to increase the railway's share of the traffic.

Late in 1940, Otto Jabelman decided that not even the 40 Challengers would eliminate the older Mallets from double-heading and banking on the Wahsatch and Sherman grades, where the main line crosses the two toughest ranges within the Rockies. By tradition, the American Locomotive Company had built the UP's modern power, and Alco was again consulted. This resulted in drawings being prepared under Jabelman's direction for what were the largest steam locomotives in the world, the 4-8-8-4 Big Boys. Such was their size that none ever surpassed them, so the title was retained until the scrapyard cutting torch took its toll in the early nineteen-sixties.

Previous wheel arrangements all carried distinguishing names—Mountain (4-8-2), Union Pacific (4-12-2), Northern (4-8-4) and Challenger (4-6-6-4), and a similarly stirring name was planned for the 4-8-8-4s. However, history does not relate what it was, because events overtook the decision. The first engine was universally known as *Big Boy*, and the name, originally thought to have been coined by a fitter at the Alco plant, stuck and was officially retained.

The first engine, No 4000, was handed over to the railroad at Council Bluffs on September 4, 1941, and immediately went into freight service between Cheyenne and Ogden hauling tonnage trains over the severe mountain grades. The engine arrived on the UP not without incident. Schenectady is in the eastern seaboard state of New York and never previously had anything weighing 605 short tons in working order had to be worked the 1,500 miles from there to the Union Pacific. It proved to be a slow and tedious journey.

One of the more delightful, though possibly apocryphal, stories of those early days with No 4000 occurred during a luncheon the Union Pacific board gave to the Chamber of Trade and business community in Omaha to celebrate the arrival of the first Big Boy, which was by then in freight service west of Cheyenne. There had always been tremendous rivalry between the railway and its competitor, the Northern Pacific, which had an equal reputation for operating large locomotives and immensely long freight trains. At that date the NP had been claiming the largest locomotive, in its Yellowstone 2-8-8-4 Class Z5 engines. The Big Boys surpassed the Yellowstones in size and weight, though not in tractive effort or grate area.

Towards the end of the luncheon the UP president rose to his feet to toast the Big Boy, concluding his speech '. . . so I am now proudly able to say that once again the Union Pacific have the largest locomotive on earth'. His words were particularly apt, because at that moment the first Big Boy had derailed at a place where there was a low fill (what we would call embankment), leaving the divisional master mechanic scratching his head as to precisely how something of that weight should be 'put back on'.

The 4000s had a wheelbase of 117ft 7in and an overall length of 132ft 9¼in, engine and tender. This extreme length necessitated installing 136ft turntables in the roundhouses at Cheyenne, Green River, Laramie and Ogden, all terminals on the main line to the Pacific coast. At other places the engines were 'wyed', or as we would say in Britain, turned on a triangle, while at one or two terminals with only a standard length table the engines were 'jack-knifed'. This was a remarkable process in which the engine was run forward over and past the end of the table to enable lifting frogs to be placed behind the tender wheels. The engine was then backed on to the table, with the rear wheels of the tender elevated enough off the end to allow the table to rotate.

All 25 Big Boys were put into pool service between Cheyenne in the east and Ogden in the west, representing the mountain divisions of the UP main line. The Union Pacific divides into two distinct parts. At the eastern end the railroad starts at Council Bluffs, Iowa/Omaha, Nebraska (two cities facing one another across the Missouri river) and runs for 528 miles across the rolling prairies of Nebraska to Cheyenne in the extreme south-east cor-

This page top: Picture from the fireman's seat of a Big Boy being piloted up the 1 in 69 Sherman grade by a 4-6-6-4 Challenger. *Lord Garnock*

Centre: Train X4023 (in the text) starting off downhill from Sherman after the pilot was detached. *Lord Garnock*

Above: Cheyenne (Wyoming) roundhouse, with 46 stalls and 136ft turntable, and engine repair shops in background. *Lord Garnock*

Above: Prototype three-cylinder 4-12-2 No 9000, forerunner of a class total of 102 engines. *Union Pacific RR*

Right: UP 2-8-8-2 No 3525 climbing a 1 in 50 grade in the Blue mountains with a 75-car train, and No 3613 banking. *R H Kindig*

ner of Wyoming. In that distance, the track, and indeed the whole terrain, gradually climbs at ten feet each mile uniformly, which averages 1 in 500 for 500 miles without a steep ruling grade. Thus Cheyenne, the capital of Wyoming, is reached at an altitude of 6,060 feet above sea level before the Union Pacific starts mountain railroading. Needless to say, Big Boys were never to be found on the Nebraska division, nor indeed east of Cheyenne.

Westward out of Cheyenne, before the so-called new line was built in the 1950s 'to ease the grades and help the diesels', the first 31 miles required westbound trains to be lifted 1,953 feet, to an elevation of 8,013 feet at Sherman summit, on a ruling grade of 1 in $64\frac{1}{2}$ and an average of 1 in 85. The distance over the Wyoming and Utah divisions from Cheyenne to Ogden is somewhat less than so-called level railroading across Nebraska, but it includes the two rugged climbs over Sherman and, west of Green river, through the Wahsatch range with a ruling grade of 1 in 88. The Wahsatch grade was the principal factor in the decision made at an early stage in the design of the 4-8-8-4s that maximum continuous horsepower output should take place at 30mph.

The Big Boys were not often noted in passenger service, although they were designed for speeds of up to 70mph. During the war they were known on troop

trains and in the mid-1940s an occasional passenger extra felt their tremendous force but they were rare birds to be seen heading a 'string of varnish'. On freights they excelled.

While most aspects of railroading in North America are large in the widest sense of the word, nonetheless, one was still not quite prepared for the sheer size and bulk of a Big Boy. In the States, mechanical dimensions tend to be given in small units such as pounds and inches—possibly to make the resultant large figures larger still, or more probably because most formulae and calculation require that form—with an impressive result in the case of the 4000s. The locomotive alone weighed 772,000lb and the total with tender in working order was 1,209,000lb. The sheet length of 132ft $9\frac{1}{4}$in carried on 16 68in drivers and two four-wheel trucks (all fitted with roller bearings) gave the effect of a giant

centipede from the age of the dinosaur.

The four cylinders, admittedly not as impressive in size as their low-pressure counterparts on a true Mallet, but still eye-catching at $23\frac{3}{4}$in bore and a 32in stroke, were fed by a boiler pressed for 300lb to give a tractive effort of 135,375lb. Perhaps the most awe-inspiring statistic was to discover that the two sand boxes astride the boiler had a total capacity of three tons.

The 14-wheel centipede-type tender was no less impressive. The centipede was a development of the cylindrical Vanderbilt tank and was designed to overcome the 60,000lb axle weight restriction by using 10 rigid wheels preceded by a four-wheel truck (known as a 4-10-0 tender arrangement). The 42in wheels were all mounted on roller bearings. Capacities varied slightly on the different marks of centipede tank, but the final arrangement for the tenders running behind Nos 4020-24 took 25,000 US gallons of

Below: Another view of No 4012 at Steamtown. *D K Johnson*

Below centre: Line-up of UP's big steam power at Cheyenne engine house in 1949, with two Big Boys on the nearest track, two Class 800 4-8-4s next, and two Class 3900 engines at extreme right. *Lord Garnock*

Bottom: A typical Mallet, a Denver & Rio Grande Western 2-8-8-2, climbing 1 in 33 Tennessee pass, Colorado, at 15mph with a passenger train in 1949, illustrating how the front drivers 'heel' into the curve before the boiler starts to deviate. *Lord Garnock*

water and 28 short tons of coal. Additional baffle plates were fitted after early experience of surging, particularly when the water was down to half capacity or less. Cheyenne yard and terminal used to abound in stories of head-end brakesmen and firemen arriving back off Sherman hill ashen-faced from what became known as 'centipede sickness'. In common with US practice, the tender contained a worm-wheel stoker.

At one stage in design of the locomotive, boosters were considered, but they were not used. The boiler varied in diameter between 95in and 105in, with a welded firebox 235in by 96½in, and a combustion chamber 112in in length. It is wonderful what can be done with a loading gauge of 15ft 6in height and 10ft 9in width and an axle load of 30 short tons running on 133lb rail! In accordance with normal UP practice at that date, a live-steam injector was fitted on one side and an exhaust-steam and centrifugal pumps on the other. The locomotive was given a double chimney consisting of four-jet exhaust nozzles on a common base.

Experiments in oil-firing were carried out on No 4005 during 1947-48, but the single burner could not get the fire close enough to the crown to generate the required heat. The resultant poor oil combustion necessitated reconversion back to coal in March 1948.

The two engine beds on the 4-8-8-4s were connected by means of a vertical articulated hinge, so arranged that when the boiler was full, a seven-ton load was applied to the tongue of the rear bed unit; consequently, the two engine beds were held rigid in the vertical plane, unlike what had been experienced with their predecessors. A new type of articulated side rod was fitted to eliminate the more-usual knuckle-pin connections. Each set of cylinders and frame was produced in an integral mono-block casting. The live and exhaust steam pipes were larger than anything previously used to permit better utilisation of boiler capacity and obtain maximum power output.

One of the more novel—for 1941—innovations was the running gear arrangement, in which a system of lateral motion control was designed to fit all wheels to the rails, thus to reduce binding on curvature to a minimum. In addition, it adjusted the wheels to vertical track differential with minimum disturbance to the weight distribution of the locomotive. The effect was to produce a stable engine on straight track but with the ability to adjust to curvature. Consequently the Big Boys used to 'heel to the curves' smoothly without the tell-tale violent front-end oscillation or nosing so characteristic of articulateds. From the cab, the impression on curves was totally different from riding on articulateds of other railroads. On the latter in a curve, this writer used to be left with the feeling of the front drivers answering to the curvature while the boiler (rigid to the rear drivers) continued straight on for what seemed an age before suddenly jerking round when the rear drivers hit the curve.

The punishment to which the Big Boys were subjected is beyond anything known in this country, so that a word or two on their performance will not be out of place. One hot July day in 1949, westbound extra freight consisting of ninety-nine loads and seven empties plus caboose (107 cars weighing 5,192 tons) was awaiting the 'high ball' to leave Cheyenne yard behind 4-8-8-4 No 4023 (I was on the footplate), with 4-6-6-4 No 3819 as pilot. One moment the two giants were quietly simmering in the heat, and the

next, a roar like thunder as the engineers opened their throttles and prepared to surmount the 1 in 81 grade immediately they emerged on to the main line.

Engineer Hooker of the Big Boy started by using 65 per cent cut-off and full throttle, but after four miles, in which speed had reached 19mph, there came the ruling grade of 1 in 64½; even though the cut-off was altered to 75 per cent, speed gradually dropped in five miles to 8mph. Another two miles and speed was increased by one mile per hour, but only at the expense of the boiler pressure which had declined (small wonder with full throttle and 75 per cent cut-off) from 295 to 260lb; so, the Elesco pump was temporarily shut off until the pressure increased. By that time all normal sounds were eliminated by the pounding and slipping of 28 driving-wheels; the sun was entirely blotted out by the combined efforts of both exhausts and a black mass resembling a thunder cloud drifted in the otherwise clear atmosphere right the way back to Cheyenne.

Otto water-tower hove into sight and when we stopped with our pilot spotted opposite the column we were 69¾ minutes and 14 miles out of Cheyenne. To save restarting the train twice, the second engine is watered by cutting the locomotives off the train and running them forward. But to start the train once, let alone twice, required considerable ingenuity, as it is impossible for a train of that tonnage to be restarted on a 1 in 64½ grade by only two locomotives. The regular procedure is that a freight train stopped at the water tower is banked by the pilot engine of the following freighter, the pusher dropping off when it comes up to the water-column—thus each train has rear-end assistance for restarting. Freight trains are sent 'over the top' in batches of about four or five during lulls in the passenger service; the fifth or last train is lightly loaded so that it can get away from Otto without rear-end assistance.

My 'extra freight west' restarted 12½ minutes after arriving there and achieved 14mph in six minutes nine seconds, when the 4-6-6-4 pusher dropped off. Speed thereupon began to diminish and was down to 5mph when the grade changed for the better to 1 in 81. I thought that No 4023 would be given some respite there, but still Hooker kept his engine at full throttle and in full forward gear. Back to 5mph for some more ruling grade, but on the final six miles of lighter grades, we hit 16mph for the first time in two hours eleven minutes, and when the train stopped at Sherman to detach the pilot, the 31 miles had taken 162¼ minutes running time. Throughout, the Big Boy had been worked at full throttle and never less than 65 per cent cut-off, spending 109 minutes in full forward gear! It had used about 23 tons of coal and 26,000 gallons of water in 31 miles, all in order to lift 5,000 tons a vertical height of 2,000 feet.

The description of that particular run has been included to illustrate the way in which the 4000s could be operated under arduous conditions. It is not typical of Sherman in that our pilot, No 3819, was not steaming well and therefore contributing less than would normally have been expected.

The Big Boys truly lived up to their name and reputation. Perhaps the most memorable sight of all was the view forward from the cab of a 4-8-8-4 piloted by a 4-6-6-4. The tender of the pilot engine seemed far enough away, but the whole combination appeared to stretch far into the distance . . .

LOCOMOTIVE, BRISTOL & EXETER RLY. 1853.

Great Locomotives That Failed

THROUGHOUT locomotive history there have been designers who have had revolutionary ideas for improvements in locomotive design, and many of them chief mechanical engineers who have been in a position to try those ideas out in actual locomotives. But in many such cases one or two prototypes only have come into existence, and have proved that the designer has been over-optimistic; some experimenters have failed to foresee faults in performance which have outweighed any possible advantages that the new development might have brought about. So many experimental locomotives have remained single examples and had but a brief life, while others have achieved their purpose, but have never been multiplied.

The century opened with the production at Stratford works of the Great Eastern Railway of a most remarkable locomotive,

designed and built to prove that steam could equal the performance to that date of electric power in suburban work. The GER was being threatened at that time with the construction of an electric railway from the City to the north-eastern suburbs of London, in competition with the GER. James Holden, GER locomotive superintendent, was commissioned by his directors to produce a steam locomotive which would be able to accelerate a 300-ton train from rest to 30mph in 30 seconds. The resulting No 20, of 1902, was by far the most massive and powerful locomotive in Great Britain to that date. No 20 was an 0-10-0 tank engine, and its 10 wheels, or 'feet', earned it the nickname of Decapod.

The Great Eastern loading gauge was rather restricted and it was no easy matter to perch a 5ft 3in-diameter boiler above

4ft 6in-diameter coupled wheels; the chimney and dome were almost squeezed out of existence. In many ways the machine established new records. For example, the wide firebox had a grate area of 42sq ft, and there were three cylinders of 18½in diameter and 24in stroke. Two cylinders were outside, driving the middle pair of coupled wheels, and the third between the frames, driving the second pair; the arrangement required a forked connecting-rod that completely enclosed

Facing page: 9ft wheels failed to make a success of this early 4-2-4.

Above: Holden's Great Eastern Railway Decapod tank engine of 1902, claimed in this Knight-series postcard to be the most powerful engine in the world. *A Wood*

Below: Paget's Midland Railway 8-cylinder 2-6-2 engine of 1907. *British Railways LMR*

Right above: Churchward's Great Western Railway 4-6-2 'The Great Bear' of 1908, the first British Pacific, pictured in this F Moore painting leaving London with a Plymouth train. *Locomotive Publishing Co (V Goldberg)*

Right lower: Gresley's London & North Eastern Railway 178-ton double-2-8-0 Garratt of 1924, which banked on the Worsborough incline until 1954 and the Lickey incline for a short while thereafter. *V Goldberg collection*

Below: Another Gresley experiment, 4-6-2-2 No 10000 with high-pressure boiler of 1929, pictured here on a Valentine's postcard heading the Flying Scotsman. *V Goldberg collection*

Facing page: No 10000 after rebuilding in 1937 on streamlined A4 Pacific lines but retaining the two trailing axles covered by longer-than-standard cab. *British Railways ER*

Bottom: Midland Railway Lickey banker 'Big Bertha' of 1919, Britain's first 10-coupled tender engine, which performed its work on Lickey for about 40 years but remained the only one of its class. *British Railways LMR*

the leading axle, which was cranked to give the necessary clearance. For the GER, the working pressure of 200lb/sq in was exceptional, and to be on the safe side the designer provided no fewer than six Ramsbottom safety valves. The weight of the engine in working order, 80 tons, was concentrated on a wheelbase of only 19ft 8in.

To test the accelerative powers of the Decapod, a special plant was laid down at Chadwell Heath. In tests in 1903, No 20 worked a 335-ton train up to 30mph in slightly under 30 seconds from rest, at an acceleration rate of all but 1.50ft per sec per sec. Its triumphant performance was sufficient to defeat the Bill in Parliament for the projected electric competitor, and was felt to have fully justified what had been spent in designing and building the engine. But when it came to introducing No 20 to revenue service it was realised by the GER board that the cost of the bridge strengthening needed to carry locomotives of such concentrated weight could not be justified. So there was a nominal rebuilding of the engine as a rather ungainly 0-8-0 tender freight engine,

although actually it was no more than a number of parts that were worked into the rebuild.

Then there was a curious locomotive that was turned out of Derby works of the Midland Railway in 1907. It was designed by Cecil Paget, who had just previously been promoted from works manager to general superintendent. Over the head of Midland chief mechanical engineer Deeley and, it is reputed, at Paget's own expense, he had built an 8-cylinder 2-6-2 locomotive with cylinders fed through sleeve valves that admitted steam to each pair of cylinders simultaneously, the two trunk pistons moving away from one another; the eight cylinders thus were equivalent to four double-acting cylinders. Exhaust was through ports in the cylinder walls as they were uncovered by the moving pistons.

Externally the engine was unlike normal Midland design. Because of the space taken up between the frames by the eight cylinders, the six-coupled driving wheels, of 5ft 4in diameter, had outside bearings, as also had the leading and trailing wheels of the 2-6-2. One prominent feature was a

firebox extending to the full width of the engine, with the casing enclosing the upper part of the rear coupled wheels. The engine received the running number 2299, but it never entered revenue service. It is reputed to have reached a top speed of 82mph while under trial, but there was trouble with the sleeve valves and other things and eventually No 2299 was broken up. Perhaps a more extended trial would have provided different results, but the circumstances in which it was built caused much bad blood at Derby and resulted eventually in R M Deeley's resignation.

In the same year, 1908, another revolutionary locomotive appeared, this time out of Swindon works of the Great Western Railway. It was Britain's first Pacific express engine, No 111 *The Great Bear*. What prompted the experiment is a mystery, as the GWR Star-class 4-6-0s were handling all heavy Great Western assignments without difficulty, and there were no challenges to GWR prestige at that time from any other British railways. Moreover, for once the eminent GWR chief mechanical engineer, G J Churchward, seems to have produced an under-

designed engine, which in consequence was not a success.

Actually *The Great Bear* was little more than a drawn-out version of a 4-6-0 Star, identical in dimensions save for the wide firebox, with the extension at the rear end of the main frames and the extra pair of wheels to carry it. But the length of the engine gave trouble on curves and its weight precluded its use on the West of England main line; so it was confined to service between Paddington and Bristol, and partly on freight trains. It remained as Britain's only Pacific until the emergence of Gresley's first 4-6-2 *Great Northern* in 1922; two years later *The Great Bear* was rebuilt (actually little more than a paper transaction, as parts only of the original 4-6-2 remained) and became Castle-class 4-6-0 No 111 *Viscount Churchill*. It was the only Pacific locomotive built in Swindon works.

An experiment on the former North Eastern Railway used a similar uniflow system of steam flow to that in Paget's Midland 2-6-2, described earlier. In the uniflow system, cylinders are about twice the normal length and have ports at each end and in the middle; the live steam enters through the end ports alternately, pushing a hollow piston that bridges, in turn, the distance between each end port and the single central exhaust port. Round about 1910, a German engineer named

Stumpf devised a uniflow system for locomotives, which in 1913 was applied by Vincent Raven, NER chief mechanical engineer, to No 825, a mixed-traffic 4-6-0 of the NER Class S2. Shortly afterwards, Atlantic No 2212 of Class Z was dealt with similarly.

In the 4-6-0 the change in external appearance was considerable, with the very large outside cylinders and their valve-chests extending over the full length of the smokebox. In the 4-4-2, the only difference from the other Z-class Atlantics was a box-like casing below the smokebox at the leading end. In service both locomotives could be readily recognised acoustically by the explosive nature of their exhaust, caused by the sudden release of steam from the cylinders. As it turned out, tests did not show any advantage in thermal efficiency of the uniflow engines over other engines of their respective classes, and no further S2s or Zs were equipped similarly.

Another unique locomotive was 0-10-0 No 2290 (BR 58100) turned out of Derby works in 1919 and the only ten-coupled tender locomotive in Great Britain up to then. It was designed and built for the sole purpose of banking northbound trains up the 2-mile 1 in 37¾ Lickey incline from Bromsgrove to Blackwell. It had four cylinders 16¾in by 28in, 4ft 7½in coupled wheels, 31.5sq ft of firegrate area, 180lb pressure and a weight in working order of 73¾ tons, and was by far the biggest and most powerful locomotive built at Derby in Midland days. It could not be described as a failure, as it remained in service for about 40 years, but equally it was not an outstanding success, or more of the type would have been built to replace the pairs of 0-6-0 tanks which shared with No 2290 the banking work up the Lickey.

The year 1924 saw the introduction of the largest and most powerful locomotive ever built for service in Great Britain. On the Great Central section of the LNER, heavy coal trains leaving the marshalling yard at Wath, north of Sheffield, for the Manchester direction had to mount the 1 in 40 Worsborough incline before joining the Sheffield-Manchester main line at Penistone. Trains of 750 to 1,000 tons in weight required the services of two 2-8-0 banking engines as well as their own train engine. H N Gresley, LNER chief mechanical engineer, conceived the idea that two 2-8-0 chassis could be used to support the single boiler of an articulated Garratt locomotive, so reducing two engine-crews to one; as a result, 1924 saw the emergence of 2-8-8-2 No 2395. It was based on two LNER Class 02 chassis and had boasted six 18½in by 26in cylinders, exerting a total tractive effort of 72,940lb. The boiler was no less than 7ft in diameter, with a grate area of 56.5sq ft.

Fortunately the 3-mile Worsborough bank needed no more than a quarter of an hour of hard steaming, otherwise firing would have been beyond the capacity of a single fireman. The overall length of the monster Garratt was 79ft, and its weight in running order of 178 tons was greater than that of any engine and tender that has run on British rails before or since. No 2295 worked between Wath and Penistone until the line was electrified in 1954, after which it was transferred for a time to banking duty on the Lickey incline, but it was so unpopular at Bromsgrove that its stay there before being broken up was only brief.

At the end of 1929, two very remarkable locomotives were designed to investigate the possibility of using steam at a higher pressure than ever previously, in association with compound propulsion. From the LNER Doncaster works there emerged No 10000, the only 4-6-2-2 tender engine ever built for a British railway in which the traditional locomotive boiler was replaced by a water-tube boiler of the kind used in marine work, designed to produce steam at 450lb/sq in. Gresley's problem in mounting such a boiler on a locomotive chassis, was to keep his boiler within the limits of the British loading gauge; it meant building the boiler casing up to the extreme height that the loading gauge permitted. The boiler comprised one upper steam drum of 3ft diameter, two water drums of 1ft 6in diameter on each side of the firebox, and two water drums of 1ft 7in diameter ahead of and at a slightly higher level than the firebox. Connecting the steam drum with the water drums were serried ranks of arched 2½in-diameter tubes, with a screen of tubes at the back of the firebox. Inside the boiler casing the tubes over the firebox were in direct contact with the fire, while the forward tubes were exposed to the hot gases on their way to the chimney.

Under test at the makers' works, the boiler produced 20,000lb of steam per hour for four hours continuously. The purpose of producing high-pressure steam was to use it, as already mentioned, in conjunction with compounding. No 10000 was therefore fitted with two high-pressure cylinders of 12in (later reduced to 10in) diameter and 26in stroke, while the outside low-pressure cylinders were of the normal Gresley Pacific 20in by 26in size. Arrangements were made for admitting hp steam direct to the lp cylinders for a few moments after starting, but a special safety-valve was provided to ensure that the pressure in the lp cylinders could not rise above 200lb/sq in.

In its original form, the experimental engine did a certain amount of revenue service, and worked the non-stop Flying Scotsman to time over the 393 miles between Kings Cross and Edinburgh, though on the easy original timing of 8¼ hours. But many troubles were experienced and despite a large number of design modifications, No 10000 proved uncertain in performance and more costly in fuel and to maintain than the standard Gresley Pacifics. Consequently it was decided in 1937 to rebuild the engine on the same lines as one of the streamlined A4 Pacifics, but retaining a 4-6-2-2 wheel arrangement and providing a firebox with 50sq ft of grate compared with the 41¼sq ft of an A4. On a tractive-effort basis, No 10000 produced 41,440lb at 85 per cent of the working pressure, and was thus nominally the most powerful express passenger locomotive in the country. It was usefully engaged in revenue service until broken up in 1960.

The other 1929 innovation, involving a considerably higher steam pressure, was a London Midland & Scottish Royal Scot-type 4-6-0 equipped with a super-pressure boiler of the German Schmidt type. The three-stage boiler started with a closed circuit generating steam at 1,400 to 1,800lb/sq in (depending on the rate of firing), the tubes surrounding the inner firebox. The tubes were expanded at the top into equalising drums, from which pipes were led to evaporating elements in a high-pressure drum, which generated steam at 900lb/sq in for use in a high-pressure cylinder of the engine. The expanded exhaust from the hp cylinder was mixed with steam generated in the ordinary way at 250lb/sq in and expanded in two outside cylinders of 18in diameter and 26in stroke.

Externally No 6399 did not differ greatly in appearance from a standard Royal Scot, except in the size of the firebox casing, which was built up to the full height permitted by the loading gauge. The engine was named Fury, and unhappily lived up to it by bursting a high-pressure steam tube on an experimental run and killing an inspector who was riding on the footplate. The engine was never taken out again, but after Stanier had become chief mechanical engineer of the LMS it was completely rebuilt, and as No 6170 British Legion became the prototype of the highly successful rebuilt Royal Scot 4-6-0s.

In 1923, Gresley of the LNER became interested in the locomotive booster engine, which was being applied to a great many locomotives in the United States. The booster was a small auxiliary pair of cylinders, usually driving a rear pair of carrying wheels under the cab, which gave assistance to the locomotive on starting, but could be cut out of action as soon as the train had got up to speed. So he fitted Ivatt Atlantic No 4419 with two 10in by 12in cylinders driving the rear wheels, with gearing which automatically cut the booster out of mesh when a speed of 27mph or so had been reached. On test, No 4419 started an 18-coach train of 535 tons out of Kings Cross, and restarted it on a 1 in 105 gradient after being stopped between the tunnels at Copenhagen junction. But in day-to-day running the extra cylinders made too great a drain on steam capacity and after a relatively short time the booster was removed.

Rather the opposite was the case when, in 1925, Gresley built two massive 2-8-2 freight engines with boosters, fitted with boilers identical with those of the Pacifics. The aim was to introduce locomotives capable of handling 100-wagon freight trains, but trains of such length proved so troublesome to the operating authorities that the experiment also was abortive.

The next booster experiment was quite extraordinary. In 1931 two former North Eastern Railway three-cylinder Atlantics, Nos 727 and 2171, were rebuilt in such a way that the locomotives were articulated to their tenders; the rear locomotive and front tender axles were carried in a single bogie frame, and the remaining two tender axles were replaced by a bogie. The three 16½in by 26in engine cylinders were supplemented by two 10½in by 14in booster cylinders driving the front axle of the articulating bogie, and adding 5,000lb to the tractive effort. The booster engines could start trains up to 750 tons in weight on level track, but on the Newcastle-Edinburgh main line, on which they were

intended to work, the four miles at 1 in 96 of Cockburnspath bank required an excessive consumption of steam with a heavy train, and as the boosters could not cut in until speed had dropped below 27mph the booster equipment was not as helpful as had been hoped. The engine-tender articulation proved troublesome also, so this experiment proved unproductive.

Some years were to elapse before anything else of a really revolutionary description was seen in the British locomotive world, but in 1949 all previous records for originality were broken when Brighton locomotive works of the Southern Railway turned out the most sensational tank locomotive in British history. It was a creation of the adventurous mind of SR chief mechanical engineer O V S Bulleid, who had already in 1942 shown originality in the Class Q1 0-6-0s. They were so extraordinary in appearance (in the interest of weight reduction) that when Stanier of the LMS saw a photograph of one, his comment was reported as 'I don't believe it!' Bulleid's Merchant Navy Pacifics also had all kinds of equipment never tried before in Great Britain, such as chain-driven valve motions enclosed in oil-baths, all-welded boilers and so on, but their novelty was put completely in the shade when the *Leader* tank locomotive made its appearance in 1949.

The new engine was of 0-6-6-0 wheel arrangement, with chain drive replacing the normal coupling rods. The whole locomotive body with its box-like casing was perched high above a massive girder frame measuring 67ft over buffers, with the entire 120 tons weight available for adhesion. The all-welded boiler was offset on the main frames, to permit a side corridor connecting the front and rear driving cabs; the lopsided arrangement meant that the corridor side had to be ballast weighted to preserve balance. The six 12¼in by 15in cylinders, three on each bogie, were to be fed with steam at 280lb pressure through sleeve valves, similar to those on Paget's Midland 2-6-2 of 42 years earlier.

Had Bulleid been given the needed time, the many defects in the design that were revealed in over a year of trial running might have been cured, but he was very near retirement, and after his departure British Railways decided to end the very expensive experiment and break up the two engines built. They represented the last attempt in British locomotive history radically to change the traditional form of steam locomotive design.

STEAM STREAMLINERS

THE STEAM LOCOMOTIVE is a machine with many angles and corners in its outline, all of which tend to increase air resistance when the locomotive is travelling at speed. As speeds increased, therefore, it is not surprising that the minds of locomotive engineers should turn towards means of reducing the resistance, especially when designing locomotives for high-speed train services. The obvious and probably cheapest means of reducing drag at the time was to cover up the protruberances and corners by smooth casings, generally referred to as streamlining.

At the beginning of the century the French PLM (Paris-Lyons-Mediterranée) Railway had taken some tentative steps towards streamlining. From 1894 the company introduced both 4-4-0 and 4-6-0 express engines with 'wind-cutter' features, which included conical smoke-box doors, chimneys with a section tapering toward the front and cabs with very pronounced V-shaped fronts. At the moderate speeds of that period the embellishments probably had little measurable result in reducing resistance; in any event, in later designs the conical smokeboxes and tapering chimneys were abandoned, though the V-fronted cabs remained as standard in France for a long time afterwards.

It was not until the 1930s that there was any notable development of steam locomotive streamlining, and then there was a widespread renewal of interest in Europe and the United States. The first diesel streamlined trains were being introduced,

and were demonstrating far higher possibilities of rail speed than had ever previously been thought possible. The new challenge caused steam locomotive engineers to examine afresh ways of improving designs and providing higher speed at economic cost. In 1933 the German State Railways had brought into service the world's first high-speed diesel-powered streamlined train, the Flying Hamburger, which required speeds up to 100mph for timekeeping; it was quite in keeping that the same administration a year later should have produced an extensively streamlined 4-6-4 express steam locomotive.

In appearance nothing like it had ever run on rails before. From the rounded front to the rear of the tender, the whole locomotive was shrouded in a casing which was carried down almost to rail level. Nothing could be seen of the boiler or any of its fittings other than the chimney, and the wheels were all but encased; the result was anything but beautiful, but it was a case of handsome is as handsome does. The new No 05.001 had three cylinders 17¾in by 26in, coupled wheels of the large diameter of 7ft 6in, a boiler designed for 284lb/sq in and a firegrate area of 50 square feet. The weight in working order was 125 tons, but only 56 tons was available for adhesion.

The locomotive was designed to be able to haul 250 tons on the level at 93mph, but its speed capacity proved to be considerably greater than that. On a demonstration run in 1936, for the British Institution of Locomotive Engineers,

between Berlin and Hamburg, on which the writer was present, the second locomotive of the class, No 05.002, worked the test train up to 118mph on the level, though with only a four-coach load of 141 tons gross. In a later test one of the 4-6-4s attained a maximum speed of 124½mph. The class was designed also to have new high rates of braking, from 100mph to rest in 1,100 yards being claimed. To counter the threat of diesel traction, steam protagonists of the day called attention to the fact that whereas the streamlined 4-6-4 and tender cost about 265,000 German marks, the streamlined diesel Flying Hamburger cost 450,000 marks. The diesel train, of course, included passenger accommodation, but it was emphasised that the steam 4-6-4 could handle twice the passenger accommodation of the 820hp diesel engines.

An unusual variant among the first of the 4-6-4s was the third locomotive; it was built reversed, with a glass-fronted cab at the head end and the chimney at the rear. Also in 1936, the German firm of Kassel built for the German State Railways a streamlined 4-6-4 of similar dimensions, but in the form of a 128-ton tank locomotive; it was coupled to a four-coach streamlined train set and worked a high-speed service between Berlin and Dresden.

Meantime, there had been a happening of note in Great Britain. To celebrate the Jubilee of the reign of King George V and Queen Mary in 1935, the London & North Eastern Railway was contemplating a new express train between London and New-

Top: Prototype British (West Coast) LMS streamlined Pacific No 6220 'Coronation'.
Science Museum London

Above: Representative of the East Coast streamlined A4 Pacifics, LNER No 4464 (later 19) 'Bittern,' one of six of the class preserved, at York in September 1972.
C J Gammell

Right: French streamlined 4-6-4 of 1940, at Paris La Chappelle shed in April 1958.
R Shenton

castle in an hour or more less than any existing time between those cities. Estimates were obtained by H N Gresley, the LNER chief mechanical engineer, from the German builders of the Flying Hamburger of the running time of a diesel train of three coaches (the Hamburger had two only) between Kings Cross and Newcastle, taking all speed restrictions into account. The answer was 4¼ hours. Gresley then assured the LNER management that with steam power and a seven-coach train he could cover the distance in four hours, and forthwith he was given instructions to go ahead.

On September 27, 1935, his striking creation of silver grey and steel, Pacific locomotive No 2509 *Silver Link*, was exhibited to the public. Here at last, after exhaustive experiments with models in a wind tunnel, were real effectiveness and elegance in locomotive streamlining. From the buffer-beam a casing in the form of a wedge front rose to the chimney, designed both to cut through the air at speed and to help in lifting the exhaust from the chimney clear of the cab. Then a secondary casing at a lower level, with its upper surface shaped like an aerofoil curve, extended backwards from the cylinders and covered the motion and upper part of the coupled wheels with a deep valance. A canopy extended from the cab to the tender top, and along the train rubber fairings joined coach to coach, with valances between the coach bogies carried almost down to rail level, so giving the train a smooth surface from end to end.

The Gresley A4 Pacifics had three 18½in by 26in cylinders, with the Gresley conjugated motion for the inside cylinder; the coupled wheels were 6ft 8in in diameter and the boilers had a working pressure of 250lb/sq in and firegrates with an area of 41.25sq ft. Weight in working order was 103 tons. Although of considerably less nominal power and weight than the streamlined German 4-6-4s, the maximum achievements of Gresley's A4s beat any of those recorded with the German rivals.

A special run of the Silver Jubilee for members of the press, on September 27, 1935, is never likely to be forgotten by those who, the writer included, participated in it. At the 30th milepost out of Kings Cross, speed passed 100mph; for the next 25 miles the rate was never less than 100mph and twice rose to 112½mph, and an average of 100mph was kept up for 43 miles on end. Nothing approaching such a feat had ever been achieved before in Great Britain. After that there were many occasions on which the streamlined A4 Pacifics exceeded 100mph; they culminated in the historic flight of *Mallard* on

July 3, 1938, when 126mph, the generally acknowledged world record for steam, was attained.

The later locomotive *Mallard* had the advantage over *Silver Link* of a double blastpipe and double chimney, allowing greater freedom of exhaust. Of the A4s generally, it was calculated that the resistance of the Silver Jubilee train worked out at an average of 620hp between London and Newcastle, requiring the locomotives to put out an average of 970hp, compared with the 1,070hp of one of the earlier A3 Pacifics, which were not streamlined; obviously the smoothed-out steam passages of the A4 Pacifics and other design improvements contributed as well as the external streamlining in effecting the economy.

Streamlining, of course, had disadvantages as well as advantages. Attention even to the outside of the boiler of a streamlined locomotive necessitated removal of the streamlined casing, putting up maintenance costs. Gresley's box-like casings over the motion and part of the coupled wheels of the A4 Pacifics made access to the motion difficult. Because of that, his successor, Edward Thompson, had all the valances cut away, which considerably altered the appearance of the engines, but Thompson did not interfere with the rest of the streamlining.

During the 1930s, there was quite a widespread rash of locomotive streamlining. A few months before *Silver Link* appeared, the Great Western Railway, for prestige reasons, decided to do something in the same direction. So 4-6-0 No 6014 *King Henry VII* was fitted with a bullet-shaped nose, triangular pieces of metal tapering downwards back from the chimney and safety valves, a V-shaped cab front and a bulbous casing over the cylinders. A Castle-class 4-6-0 received similar treatment. However, so little money was allocated by the management for the experiment that the GWR'S apology for streamlining could have had little effect other than to make possible some spectacular photographs of the locomotives at speed.

The next British streamlining development was of considerably greater importance. Flushed with the success of the streamlined Silver Jubilee, the LNER decided to celebrate the Coronation of King George VI and Queen Elizabeth in 1937 by introducing another streamlined high-speed train; it was named Coronation and designed to cover the 393 miles between London and Edinburgh in six hours. For prestige reasons, the London Midland & Scottish Railway decided to follow suit, and so planned a similar express, named Coronation Scot, between

Experimental American 6-4-4-6 for express passenger work, forerunner of a production batch of 4-4-4-4 streamlined engines for Pennsylvania Railroad. *C J Allen*

London and Glasgow. Although eventually the 6½-hour run of the LMS train, did not involve such high speeds as those of the Coronation, the LMSR management nevertheless decided, no doubt partly for publicity reasons, to build some streamlined Pacifics for its working.

So, in 1937, there emerged from Crewe works the first of W H Stanier's fine streamlined Pacifics, No 6220 *Coronation*. In appearance, it differed considerably from the Gresley A4. Instead of a wedge front, the LMS 4-6-2 had a bullet-shaped nose, merging at the top with a sloping front to the smokebox, on which the short stovepipe chimney was perched. The boiler casing tapered outwards on both sides to longitudinal casings running the length of the engine, with a lower valance which was raised above the coupled wheels to expose the motion. The tender sides were curved round at the top exactly in line with the curves of the cab roof. Like the train, the locomotive was painted blue, with white lines starting in front of the bulbous nose and rising in curves to be carried round both sides of the engine and down the length of the train. The whole had a very impressive appearance.

The locomotive *Coronation* had four 16½in by 26in cylinders, 6ft 9in coupled wheels, 50sq ft firegrate area and 250lb pressure; the weight in working order was 108 tons. The new engine lost no time in giving a demonstration of its speed capacity; on a press trip on July 5, 1937, a maximum speed of 114mph was attained, 1mph faster than the highest recorded

Left: Third in the German series of streamlined steam locomotives of the middle nineteen-thirties, a fully shrouded 4-6-4 designed to run with driver ahead of boiler. *C J Allen*

Centre right: One of the few Canadian National streamlined steam engines, 4-8-4 No 6402, leaving Toronto in April 1952. *J M Jarvis*

Right: A4 Pacific No 2510 'Quicksilver' in full streamlining with the Silver Jubilee train at Newcastle in May 1936. *H C Casserley*

speed of a Gresley A4 to that date; incidentally, that speed was attained at a point so near to Crewe that it was a miracle that the test train was not derailed on the reverse curves leading into the station.

In the following year, Coronation's 114mph was soundly beaten by the 126 mph of the A4 *Mallard*, and in general the Stanier streamlined Pacifics never reached the high speeds frequently recorded in ordinary service by the Gresley stream-liners. Moreover, in the post-war period high speeds were not in prospect for some time to come, and the streamlining was putting up the cost of maintenance, so in 1946 all the 24 LMS streamlined Pacifics had the casings removed. For a time, until they were reboilered, it had a curious and not very attractive effect on their appear-ance, because of the downward slope of the smokebox top from the chimney forward.

The urge to streamline moved also to the south of Great Britain. In 1937 O V S Bulleid, who had been personal assistant to H N Gresley, the LNER chief mechanical engineer at Doncaster, and had had a close contact with the designers of the stream-lined A4 Pacifics, was himself appointed chief mechanical engineer to the Southern Railway, so it was not surprising that he took streamline ideas with him to his new post. In 1939 he designed a handsome streamlined casing for the SR Schools-class 4-4-0s and applied a mock-up of it to locomotive No 935, but the develop-ment did not go beyond a mock-up.

Not so, however, with his first original design, the controversial Merchant Navy Pacific, the first example of which appeared in 1941. Bulleid never claimed that it was streamlined, but rather that it was 'air-smoothed', and certainly the casing differed considerably from any previous locomo-tive streamlining, especially at the front end. There was no wedge front or bullet nose, but two smoothed side casings that terminated at the leading end in the form of wings on each side of the smokebox;

no fittings could be seen above the boiler, and the sheet steel sides were carried over the boiler top and finished at the front end in the form of an arch joining the two wings together. Soon it was proved that the front end was going to be very troublesome, because it made no provision for lifting the chimney exhaust clear of the cab. Numerous experiments carried out in an attempt to cure the serious defect included making an opening in the casing ahead of the chimney, mounting a kind of inverted dish in front of the chimney connecting the tops of the two wings, and fitting additional flat wind deflectors of various shapes and sizes outside the wings at the front end. Eventually the trouble was greatly reduced, though possibly not completely cured; it was partly due, perhaps, to the relatively soft blast from the multiple-jet exhaust and large-diameter chimneys of the engines.

In all, 30 of the Merchant Navy class were built, followed by 110 of the light Pacifics of the West Country and Battle of Britain classes. The lightweight engines were almost identical in design, and became the most numerous series of streamlined or semi-streamlined locomotives that ever ran on any railway in the world. The Merchant Navy Pacifics had three 18in by 24in cylinders, operated by a unique chain-driven motion of Bulleid's design. The coupled wheels were of 6ft 2in diameter and with free-steaming characteristics they could comfortably attain 100mph on level track; the boilers carried the high pressure of 280lb/sq in and had firegrates with an area of 48.5sq ft. Weight had been held down by every possible means because of Southern track restrictions and amounted to 92½ tons in working order. After nationalisation, because of excessive coal and oil consumption and difficulties with the chain-driven valve-motion, it was decided completely to rebuild the Bulleid Pacifics; all 30 Merchant Navy engines and 60 of the lightweight series were so treated, and in the rebuilding the air-smoothed casings were removed.

Other streamlining experiments of the 1930s were for the most part with individual locomotives; no other railways in the world built large classes of streamliners as the British railways did. In many cases locomotives were streamlined and smartened up in order to work specific trains, and perhaps often more to achieve spectacular appearance than a scientific reduction of head-end resistance. In 1935 the PLM Railway in France completely streamlined an Atlantic locomotive and a train of three coaches; it was designed to compete between Paris and the Riviera with a three-coach petrol-engined train which it was also proposed to build, but little further was heard of the experiment.

In the same year there emerged the striking orange and red Atlantics built by the American Chicago, Milwaukee St Paul & Pacific Railroad to haul the new Hiawatha express between Chicago and Minneapolis, followed in 1938 by the more-powerful Type F7 4-6-4s, some of the fastest and most-handsome locomotives ever seen on rails. In 1936 the New York Central System, after considerable research in the aerodynamic field, applied a complete streamlined casing to one of its famous J3 Hudson 4-6-4s, having calculated that it would reduce air resistance by 35 to 50 per cent. No further J3s were treated similarly, and later experiments were with a semi-streamlining of striking appearance, applied to Hudson-class locomotives for working the Twentieth Century Limited. The Pennsylvania Railroad also produced its spectacular 6-4-4-6 mammoth with bullet nose and almost complete streamlining, and followed it up with a series of 52 semi-streamlined 4-4-4-4s, each with a 16-wheel tender of enormous size. ·

Back in Europe, the French had applied streamlined casings to one of the Nord Pacifics in 1936, but had not apparently carried the development farther. In 1939 the Belgian State Railways built a few streamlined 4-4-2s to work a 60-minute service over the 70.8 miles between Brussels and Ostend; they were probably the last locomotives of the Atlantic wheel arrangement to be built in any country. There appeared to be little interest in the subject anywhere in the immediate post-war years and it was therefore no small surprise when in 1949 the French produced the magnificent De Caso Class U1 streamlined 4-6-4s, designed mainly for the fast Paris-Brussels trains. But by that date steam locomotive history in France, as elsewhere, was nearing its close, and with it the possibilities of further streamlining developments also.

Austerity Locomotives

Above: A preserved War Department 2-10-0 locomotive, No 600 'Gordon' (originally WD No 3651), heading a train on one of the open days at Longmoor Military Railway. *M Pope*

This picture: The heavier of the two basic German Austerity 2-10-0 engines, Class 42 No 976.

Facing page: BR 8F No 90503, an ex-WD Austerity bought by BR in 1948, with a Derby-Sheffield train near Ambergate in 1967. *D Huntriss*

MANY STUDENTS of history fail to note that only when the world is bursting with plenty is the word 'austerity' introduced. Hence, as applied to locomotives, the word came not with the struggles of George and Robert Stephenson, when engines were of necessity austere, built by candle-light and with the use of hand-cut taps and dies, but only about 115 years later, when productive capacity in general was around 3,000 per cent greater than when *Locomotion* first turned its wheels.

How quickly the austerity idea developed is shown by a cast back to the 1914-18 war, when few efforts were made to sim-

plify the Robinson 2-8-0 chosen by the military as the 4ft 8½in-gauge standard locomotive. It was already an unsophisticated engine for the time and that was enough; only one modification was made to suit the conditions of materials shortage in wartime, and that was the substitution of steel for copper in the firebox. Detail changes were largely to cater for working in France and not to save labour time. Nor were the several standard USRA types in 1918 characterised by great savings or simplicity. In fact, the claim of those American engines to notice was that probably they were the first successful

steam locomotives to be designed by a committee.

Once the 1939-45 war began, production engineers had a far greater say in planning, and although basic design of steam locomotives could scarcely be altered, materials and production processes could be revolutionised, and were in cases where large numbers of locomotives were required. Essentially only three countries—Germany, USA and Britain—were involved in large-scale production of standard steam locomotives between 1941 and 1946, though as some of the German production was spread over three or four

115

Above: An ex-USA 0-06-0 tank, originally WD No 1973, then Southern Railway No 72 (BR30072), here pictured on its present home ground, the Keighley & Worth Valley Railway, in 1970. *M Pope*

Left: An ex-WD 2-10-0, BR No 90761, photographed at Motherwell in May 1957. *R K Evans*

occupied territories, and actual operation ranged from the Bosphorus to the Arctic Circle and from White Russia to the Atlantic seaboard, the German machines were really European types.

In no case was a long life postulated for a 1939-45 austerity engine. In fact, the British Minister of Supply at the time, Sir Andrew Duncan, said he was not interested in the state or scrap value five years hence; he wanted quickest possible delivery and up to three years' hard work with indifferent maintenance out of the products. This philosophy applied also to the German productions, but not so brusquely, for there was a well-marked transition stage in which several savings were made before locomotives were moved up to a high priority. In Britain, from a very low priority, locomotives were moved up close to the top at one bound.

A highly standardised locomotive is not necessarily an austerity type, but an austerity is highly standardised, and is constructed of simple materials, having a life expectancy that would give enormous yearly financial charges if accountants attempted to apply conventional methods to wartime finance. However, things did not always turn out in the expected way, and some austerities of 1941-46 are still in daily service.

The number of types actually designated austerity was few, and can be listed easily. They were the German 2-10-0s of Classes 42, 52 and 52KON, plus the earlier transition stage of 50UK; the British Ministry of Supply 2-8-0, 2-10-0 and 0-6-0ST; the US-built 2-8-0 for the British Ministry of Supply; and to some extent the American-built (H K Porter) 46-ton 0-6-0T with the drive on the rear axle, 14 of which were bought by the Southern Railway in 1946 and which later became BR Nos 30061-74. The Bulleid 0-6-0 classified Q1 was an odd man out; it was the only austerity designed and built by a private railway. Its introduction at that time was possible because despite intense production problems, the British Government did not freeze home locomotive designs through the war period, whereas the American Government did. The American proscription resulted in the resuscitation of the Lima super-power 2-8-4 and 2-10-4 types; there was no austerity about them, but no new design work was involved.

It was not until the summer of 1942 that a definite decision to invade Europe as soon as circumstances were propitious moved locomotives right up the priority scale. Hitherto, war needs were confined to the home country and on a small scale to the Near East, and had been met mainly by the construction of Stanier-type 2-8-0s little altered from pre-war construction for the LMSR—though those for abroad had air brakes and oil firing. The new types required by Sir Andrew Duncan would be needed not only to handle intensified home traffic preparatory to any invasion of Europe, but also to deal with traffic on Continental lines as soon as a military breakthrough had been achieved.

Early requirements were based on a copper-firebox 2-8-0 of 15.5 tons axle load to haul 1,000 tons, and an 0-6-0ST of 16.5 tons axle load and 11ft wheelbase for shunting and marshalling trains up to the same weight. To get going on them with all celerity, North British Locomotive Co was taken entirely off tank production temporarily, and Vulcan Foundry partly so over a short period, so that they could handle tender locomotive construction. Hunslet Engine Co was gradually released from armament work to take over design and early construction of the 0-6-0ST and

to arrange contracts with other builders as the demand increased. Eventually 377 were built to MoS orders after R A Riddles, then deputy director of Royal Engineer equipment, had been persuaded against the LMSR standard 3F 0-6-0T of 16ft 6in wheelbase, having been shown that, for equal man-hours, three 0-6-0STs could be produced against two of the LMSR type. These measures ensured that the first MoS engines of both types were ready by the turn of 1942-43.

Two further steps had to be taken. To meet the foreseen demand for 2-8-0s an MoS order was placed for an American version of the same general proportions and capacity, but with detail design left to the US builders; thus the two groups had little in common except approximate performance. The American austerities began to appear at the end of 1942 and delivery continued through 1943. They had wide fireboxes of 41sq ft grate area and a loco wheelbase of 23ft; the British 2-8-0s had narrow grates of 28.6 sq ft area and a loco wheelbase of 24ft 10in. Even the tenders were quite different, the US type running on two trucks and the British type on four fixed axles.

The second step was the evolution of a Ministry of Supply 2-10-0 that could assist with home traffic and then be used on lightly laid Continental tracks likely to be in sub-standard condition as a result of war conditions. This design had a 13.5-ton maximum axle load. It was the first 10-coupled type to run in numbers in Britain, and its success was a direct factor in the adoption of the 2-10-0 layout for the most successful of all the later British Railways standard types.

All three of the austerity tender engines had 19in cylinder bore, but the Americans had 26in stroke against the 28in of the British builds, which were themselves a legacy of their Stanier 2-8-0 origins. The basic American design was used also for 5ft-gauge Consolidations forming part of US war supplies to the Soviet Union of Russia.

Only 25 of the MoS 2-10-0s found their way into the motive power stock of the nationalised railways after January 1, 1948; they were numbered 90750-74, and were acquired with a view to service in the Scottish Region. On the other hand, BR purchased in 1948 a total of 733 of the MoS 2-8-0s and numbered them in the 90xx series. (They had run under 70xx numbers in the latter days of MoS ownership.) They were known generally as WD engines and had the 8F power classification, as had the ex-MoS 2-10-0s. The North British company had built 545 of the type, and No 7029 in the original MoS numbering was the 25,000th locomotive built by NBL and its three predecessors. Over 250 of the Consolidation engines lasted past the mid-1960s, and so had a life almost ten times Sir Andrew Duncan's requirements. Both 2-10-0s and 2-8-0s also found their way into such an unlikely place (for 1942-44) as the Rugby test house, and the 2-8-0 got into the BR interchange trials of 1948.

The LNER bought 75 of the 0-6-0STs before its absorption into British Railways, and classified them J94. All came into BR stock and were numbered 68006-80. In later days one or two drifted to the LMR Cromford-High Peak line for the 1 in 14 gradient. Last of all to go was No 68012, withdrawn in October 1967. Many of those not taken over by BR went into industry, particularly to the National Coal Board, which had 40 returned from overseas; that body adopted the type as a standard and had new locomotives built

to the old design. One of the most controversial points about the engine in 1942 —the use of cast-iron wheel centres—was retained, for no trouble had arisen from that material. On the other hand, the cast-iron coupling-rod bushes tried on a few of the originals in 1943 had been discarded within a few weeks.

All the above-mentioned MoS austerities were just preceded by Bulleid's 0-6-0s, which began to appear in 1942, and of which 40 were built. Numbered originally in the curious Bulleid style of C1 *et seq,* they were renumbered in BR stock as 33001-40. Devoid of running plates, splashers and separate boiler cladding attached to the barrel, they nevertheless had cast-steel disc wheels. Their principal advantage was that they were much more powerful than any other Southern Railway 0-6-0, yet could run over 93 per cent of the company's route mileage. The design was austere in appearance rather than in materials and production technique, and had a taper boiler, copper firebox, 230lb

Facing page: Imposing view of a German Class 42 2-10-0, smart in new paint, possibly for preservation. *DB Film Archiv*

Above: WD 0-6-0ST No 761480, originally built in 1945, nicknamed 'Fred' when it was later in the service of Manchester Collieries, now on the KWVR, here seen at Haworth in June 1970. *R Bastin*

Below: Unusually, a Southern Q1 0-6-0 Austerity (piloting a U1 2-6-0) on a passenger train. *D Cross*

Bottom: Another of the WD 2-10-0s, No 73755 'Longmoor', built in 1945.

pressure (the highest used in an 0-6-0), and many up-to-date and efficacious details in no way stinted. The class did not become extinct until the 1960s.

Development of German austerities was not dissimilar to that of the British types, although it was confined to 2-10-0s; in fact, it began with a simplified version (Class 50UK) of a pre-war standard 2-10-0 (Class 50), and then went to a completely new design (Class 52) as war needs became more urgent and materials and labour scarcer. There the similarity between the two countries' austerity locomotive programmes ended. For one thing, the Germans introduced a further true austerity of heavier axle load (Class 42); they also built 168 of a condensing variety of the 52 (Class 52KON), and always had a few prototype variations on the stocks or running, such as the Brotan boiler units. Even more pronounced was the difference in production totals. The British-built MoS 2-8-0s and 2-10-0s came from only two works and totalled around 1,000 units altogether. German construction of the two main classes (42 and 52) was around 10,000, and the 20 locomotive works participating in erection were aided by almost 1,000 sub-contractors at one time or another between 1942 and 1945.

The Class 52 was the second most numerous steam locomotive class in the 165 years of steam loco building. It was, of course, far exceeded by the Russian E-class 0-10-0 of which 12,000 to 13,000 were built, but construction of the Russian engines was spread over 40 years in five countries, and included several sub-types. The German construction programme produced about 6,050 of Class 52, 168 of Class 52KON and over 800 of Class 42 within two and a half years; the last two years were affected by widespread bombing attacks, one of which stopped all production in one leading works during 1943.

Even the austerity totals did not represent the whole German wartime locomotive effort, for certain Reichsbahn standard types, notably the heavy three-cylinder 2-10-0 Class 44, were also built throughout the war with merely detail changes in design. During 1942 German works produced 1,896 engines of 2-10-0 form and 263 of 2-8-2T type. In the peak year of 1943, with the help of a handful of works in Austria, Czechoslovakia, Poland and Belgium, 4,478 2-10-0s and 57 2-8-2Ts were completed. Despite the ever-increasing scale of bombing, 3,061 2-10-0 tender engines were completed in 1944. Over the five years 1940-44 German locomotive production, excluding industrial and shunting tanks, totalled 12,127, of which 11,414 were 2-10-0s. Nevertheless, output did not reach the production rate visualised in 1942, when Dorpmüller placed a blanket order for 15,000 austerity locomotives of sketchily defined types at a delivery rate of 7,500 a year. Peak rate actually attained was 505 2-10-0 engine-tender combin-

ations of Class 52 in September 1943.

To meet production of such proportions, the greatest possible reduction had to be made in man-hours required for manufacture and in the use of scarce non-ferrous materials. Compared with the pre-war Class 50 engines, the non-ferrous savings could not be high, for the inner firebox already was of steel, but the weight was brought down from 3,150lb to 1,285lb per locomotive in the raw-material state. Partly because of extensive sub-contracting, a reliable estimate of man-hours could hardly be made, but the saving was around 40 per cent of the pre-war Class 50 figure. The tender was of altogether special design evolved by the Westwaggon concern, giving a saving in man-hours said to be 50 per cent and a cost under DM20,000.

Like the USRA types of the 1914-18 war, Class 52 was a fine committee design —and some of the committee members were not locomotive men. Details were never frozen, and tests and experiments were often commissioned and small numbers of variants built. Of major variations of the basic design, the substitution of plate frames for three-inch slab frames was the most important, made solely because of increased demand for thick plates for armaments coincident with decreased supplies. The well-known German all-welded boiler of post-war years actually began in some of the Class 52 engines produced by Skoda in Czechoslovakia.

The 52KON condensing engine was really a production variant, with 240 sanctioned and 168 actually built. They were for the Russian front and could make journeys of over 600 miles without re-watering. Blast was provided by a smoke-box fan driven by an exhaust-steam turbine; three more exhaust-steam turbine-driven fans were installed in the condensing tender. (The turbo-fan equipments came from Switzerland and France.)

No great post-war service was obtained in Western Germany from 52-class engines. Only 150 in working condition plus 650 damaged were in stock in 1949; by 1954 only 100 were left, and in 1960 there were eight. On the other hand, great care was taken of war-time 50UK engines and some are still at work on the Deutsche Bundesbahn today. After the collapse of Germany, 52-class engines were retained all over Central and South-east Europe, and some are still at work on the national systems of Austria, Yugoslavia, and possibly elsewhere, as are some of the 50UK engines. Eastern Germany got about 200 of the 50UKs, and also built a further 88 new ones in 1956-60. Class 42 engines were not so widespread as the others, and did not last so long, though 100 were built new for the Polish State Railways from 1946. Altogether 18 European railway administrations, including the USSR, used one or other of the German austerity types from 1945 onwards, and those taken by the Soviets were converted to 5ft gauge.

THE BR 2~10~0 LOCOMOTIVE

UPON THE FORMATION of British Railways in 1948, the decision was taken to produce a fleet of standard steam locomotives of about twelve types to cover the vast majority of duties on the six railway regions. Most of the types were based upon existing design, but in the case of the larger locomotives, the two-cylinder Pacific designs of Classes 6 and 7 were entirely new, as was the heavy freight locomotive, the Class 9F 2-10-0.

The member of the Railway Executive responsible for mechanical and electrical engineering was Mr R A Riddles CBE and the design of the various types of locomotives was undertaken, under his control, at Derby, Doncaster, Swindon and Brighton. The designs were co-ordinated by a committee under the chairmanship of Mr E S Cox to endeavour to select the best practices of the various BR regions and to ensure a common design policy and a maximum of standardisation. The first BR standard locomotive to emerge from the building works, in this case Crewe, was the Class 7 4-6-2, and the prototype locomotive *Britannia* was exhibited at London Marylebone station on January 30, 1951.

At that time, the heavy freight locomotive was no more than a space on a sheet of engine diagrams. When, several months later, a start was made with schemes for the locomotive, the first intentions were that it should be a 2-8-2, closely following the design of the *Britannia* and using the same boiler and cylinders, but with driving wheels of 5ft 6in diameter instead of 6ft 2in. As such it would, no doubt, have been useful as a mixed-traffic locomotive,

Top: BR Class 9F No 92009 with a fast freight at Dent Head between Long Meg and Blackburn in August 1965. *R Bastin*

Above: Close-up of the motion of 9F No 92203. *B Cross*

Facing page: 2-10-0 No 92205 and V2 2-6-2 No 60886 stand in York roundhouse. *R Bastin*

but would have had the disadvantage of all types having trailing carrying wheels, namely, that under heavy traction conditions, weight is transferred from the leading truck to the trailing truck, whereas if the locomotive was, say, a 4-8-0 or a 2-10-0 the weight transferred would augment the adhesion weight on the coupled wheels and thereby reduced the tendency to slip.

Within the British loading gauge it was not practicable to mount a wide-firebox boiler on top of 5ft 6in-diameter driving wheels; in fact, the largest diameter of driving wheel permitting that important feature, and then only with some difficulty, was 5ft. If the locomotive was to be a

4-8-0, such a wheel arrangement would suggest a mixed-traffic type and 5ft 6in wheels would be reasonable. This however would have necessitated a narrow firebox, hence the choice of the 2-10-0 wheel arrangement for the heavy freight locomotives. It also permitted a very moderate axle load of $15\frac{1}{2}$ tons, giving an almost universal BR route availability.

There was, perhaps, another and more personal reason for the decision to build a 2-10-0. Mr Riddles, as director of Royal Engineer Equipment, Ministry of Supply, during the 1939-45 war, had been responsible for the War Department 'Austerity' 2-10-0s and had a very soft spot for the type. In any case, the decision proved to be the right one. The Class 9F became a best seller with a total of 251 locomotives built—far more than any other of the BR standard classes. It is probably fair to say that they were the most successful type in the fleet.

The scheme for the locomotive was prepared in the development drawing office at Derby and the Brighton drawing office was allotted the work of developing the design and producing the majority of the working drawings. Under the arrangements for the design of the BR standard locomotives, each of the main design offices undertook the detail design of certain parts, and other parts were already catered for as standard items used on other classes. Something of the order of 400 new drawings were required altogether. The work was started in July 1951 and the time required for design was about eighteen months; by close co-operation between design office and building works

Classes 5, 6 & 7. This was done because the then modern steel axlebox, with a pressed-in horseshoe brass bearing, under-feed lubrication from a worsted pad, and manganese steel liners on the guide faces, was a very trouble-free component, was considerably cheaper than a roller-bearing axlebox and did not demand the extreme accuracy of erection where five pairs of wheels were coupled together in a frame.

The two cylinders, steel castings with cast-iron liners to the barrel and steam-chest, were originally intended to be identical to the Class 7 4-6-2, but in order to accommodate the axlebox clearances necessary for a locomotive with a long fixed wheelbase, they had their transverse centres increased by approximately two inches. The coupled-wheel centres were steel castings with rolled-steel tyres, and the middle pair, on to which the connecting rods drove, had no flanges, giving them freedom to move laterally across the rails so as not to restrict excessively the curving of the long-wheelbase locomotives. It enabled them to negotiate a curve of six chains radius without distortion of either locomotive or track.

Another interesting feature of the design was the novel method of balancing the wheels and motion. The rotational masses were balanced in the normal way, with weights in the wheels consisting of steel plates riveted to each side of the spokes and filled in with lead between. The angles at which the weights were applied in each wheel were such as to give static and dynamic balance, again as in normal practice. The reciprocating masses, how-ever, consisting of the piston and rod, crosshead and part of the connecting rod, were statically balanced to the extent of 40 per cent by placing additional lead in the wheels in the same phase on both sides of the locomotive. This left the fore-and-aft balance of the locomotive the same as if the normal procedure had been followed, that is, of making the reciprocating mass balance coincide with the rotating mass balance, but it left a larger unbalanced couple tending to produce a nosing oscillation. However, the additional couple was so small that it had no ill effect in practice and the advantage gained was a considerable reduction in the balance weights required.

The foregoing points have been included to set out the main departures, in this design, from the policies employed on other BR standard classes, and the reasons for their adoption. In other respects the Class 9F 2-10-0s closely followed the general pattern. The 251 locomotives of the class took altogether six years to build; 198 were built at Crewe and the remaining 53 at Swindon. It was one of the Swindon build which had the doubtful honour of being the last steam locomotive to be built by British Railways. To celebrate the occasion the locomotive, No 92220, was painted in fully lined-out passenger green livery and was named *Evening Star*. A small celebration was held at Swindon on March 18, 1960, to mark the event.

The allocation of the locomotives to the regions was; Eastern 85, London Midland 100, North Eastern 10 and Western 56. As heavy freight locomotives, their duties were not, perhaps, spectacular in the same way as those of locomotives used on the named expresses, but they were very effective operating tools and acquitted themselves well.

The first batch went to the Western Region at Newport, Mon, where they were set to work on the heavy iron-ore trains from Rogerstone to Ebbw Vale. It was there that the first trouble was encountered. It was found that in certain situations the

Above: Privately owned 9F No 92203, now named 'Black Prince', one of two of the class preserved, at Cricklewood shed in 1968. *M Pope*

Left and far left: Two views of the first of the BR 9Fs, No 92000, in the erecting shops of Crewe works. *British Railways*

Below left: The other preserved Class 9F, No 92220 'Evening Star', on the Pines Express passenger train at Combe Down in 1962. *J B Snell*

it was possible for the first locomotives to be turned out of Crewe works by December 1953.

The leading dimensions were as follows:

Cylinders (2) dia and stroke	20in x 28in
Wheels, coupled, dia	5ft
Wheelbase, coupled	21ft 8in
Wheelbase, engine	30ft 2in
Heating surface:	
Tubes	1,836sq ft
Firebox	179sq ft
Total evaporation	2015sq ft
Superheater	535sq ft
Grate area	40.2sq ft
Boiler pressure	250lb/sq in
Tractive effort	39,667lb
Weight of engine in working order	86 tons 14cwt
Weight of engine and tender in working order	139 tons 4cwt

The boiler was generally similar to the wide-firebox types fitted to Classes 6 & 7, but as the firebox was placed over the two trailing pairs of wheels, the depth had to be reduced. The boiler thus became a com-promise between the Classes 6 & 7, in that the firebox was made from cut-down pressings from the press-blocks of the former and the front tube plate was made from the press-blocks for the latter. Another component which departed from the practice employed on the 4-6-2s was the regulator. This, instead of being of the multiple-valve type, which tended to be both heavy and expensive, was of the grid type located in the dome. The main and 'jockey' valves operated in a horizontal plane to get them as high as possible above the water level. This was necessary because the pitching of the boiler per-mitted only a very minimal height for the dome.

The main frame was particularly rigid on the 2-10-0s. There were always two schools of thought on the subject of whether frames should be rigid or flexible, and the decision was taken very definitely on this class that they should be as rigid as possible, the necessary flexibility of the wheelbase for negotiating tight curves being achieved by suitable axlebox and wheel clearances. It might be asked why a bar frame, so common in American and Continental practice, was not adopted. It could, for example, have been of the form employing rolled steel slabs four to five inches thick, or considering the quantity of the class ultimately built, a cast bedplate would probably have been an economic proposition. At all events, the bar frame had its advocates among the design personnel, but the traditional plate frame died hard and was adopted.

Plain-bearing axleboxes were employed throughout the engine, in this respect differing from the larger mixed-traffic

locomotive started to slip when pulling hard, and the driver found himself unable to close the regulator, so that slipping became uncontrollable. This phenomenon was by no means unknown on other classes of locomotive, in particular the LMS Duchess class which had a similar type of regulator; in one such occurrence at Watford, the rails were nearly cut through.

The action required in such a case was to apply the brakes and check the spin to allow the steamchest pressure to build up. This tended to equalise the pressure in the steampipe with that in the boiler, so as more nearly to balance the pressures on both sides of the large flat regulator valve and reduce the frictional resistance to closure. This was all very well for a stationary or nearly stationary locomotive, starting a train, but needed a good deal of courage, and also good fortune, when hauling a 780-ton train which was just nicely on the move on a heavy gradient. In this case, by the time the slipping had been checked, the train was likely to have stalled.

The problem was rather baffling, and was complicated by springiness of regulator operating gear and deflection of the valves under pressure. Another feature of the particular type of regulator was that it did not readily permit of any suitable or lasting form of lubrication for its large frictional surfaces. The trouble was overcome by fitting a regulator having valves of smaller area, and tests carried out on the stationary testing plant at Rugby proved that they made no practical difference to the maximum power output of the locomotive, and there was no further complaint of regulators sticking open. The only other complaint concerned the hand brake on the tender, which was a general matter affecting all the tenders of BR standard locomotives and details will not be included here, except to say that the problem was solved very neatly by Swindon drawing office. So much for troubles.

Odd incidents and failures of one kind and another arose from time to time, but in general terms, the Class 9F 2-10-0 could be said to be trouble free after the points mentioned had been disposed of. The class performed very effectively on two of the principal heavy coal services from the Midlands to London, namely, Toton to Brent on the former Midland main line and Annesley to Woodford on the old Great Central. The GC route was notable for the speeds attained by coal trains, which frequently reached the 60mph level.

The riding of the engines was particularly good. As a heavy freight class, it was expected that their maximum speed would not normally exceed 60mph, although with 5ft coupled wheels it was known that they would have no difficulty, should the need arise, in running at 75mph. From the design office point of view, no limit of speed had ever been laid down for the 2-10-0s, and so when, as happened on several occasions, on various regions, they had to stand in for a failed express passenger locomotive, who could complain if they ran at express passenger speeds? In fact they showed a quite remarkable aptitude for a gallop and are reported to have achieved speeds into the nineties!

However, a comparison of dimensions shows that the rotational and piston speeds of a Class 9F at 90mph were much the same as those of the Gresley Pacific *Mallard* at 126mph. Certainly the bursts of speed did cause lifting of eyebrows at headquarters and a learned professor suggested in the technical press that they were unwise. As a result the regions were instructed to desist, but the fact remains,

the locomotives were very free running, their balancing was vindicated and, from a riding point of view, on relatively straight main line track, what could be better than a long fixed wheelbase?

Even so, in spite of the ability to work passenger trains, so amply demonstrated, the class retained the freight and not mixed-traffic classification, for the very simple reason that train heating equipment was not provided and thus passenger trains could not be worked during the heating season. A notable exception was the allocation of 9Fs to the Somerset & Dorset line, a heavily graded and largely single-track route between Bath and Bournemouth, where they were especially useful in hauling the heavy summer-time holiday trains to and from the latter resort. On this line, their ten-coupled arrangement provided the adhesion so valuable to goods and passenger trains alike. It is also worth recording that one Class 9F took the place of the Midland Railway 0-10-0 banking engine, known as 'Big Bertha', assisting trains up the 1 in 39 Lickey incline and continued on that duty until diesel traction took over.

Very few modifications were made to the class as a whole and the only substantial difference between the first and the two hundred and fifty first to be built was the inclusion in the later locomotives of a double blast pipe and chimney. The justification for the additional cost of that equipment had not been proved at the time of the original design, whereas subsequently, as a result of development work carried out at Swindon, it was proved that the overall efficiency of a locomotive could be increased by a reduction in back pressure in the cylinders, made possible by the double blast pipe, at a given rate of steam production, or that a given boiler could produce more steam per hour by increasing draught on the fire and burning more coal.

It is worth remembering that the limitation of steam locomotive power is the amount of coal that a fireman can shovel; it is quite possible, with a locomotive of the size of the 9F, to raise the potential steaming rate to a level which the fireman cannot sustain. For test purposes with both the single and double blast pipe arrangements, the maximum output of the boiler was increased to approximately 28,000lb of steam per hour simply by reducing the blast pipe nozzle diameters by $\frac{1}{8}$-inch. However, this modification was not, thereupon, applied to all the locomotives in service, because the general run of duties called for no such elevated steaming rates, which, in any case, demanded a firing rate beyond that which a fireman could reasonably be expected to maintain continuously.

In order to realise the full potential of the locomotives in service, three Class 9F engines were fitted with mechanical stokers of American origin. One of them tested at Rugby proved that somewhat higher steaming rates than with hand firing could be achieved, but at an uneconomic increase in coal consumption of up to 25 per cent compared with hand firing. Earlier tests on a Merchant Navy-class Pacific had produced similar results, so it might well be asked why American and many other railways relied to a very great extent upon mechanical stokers of the same general type. The facts could only be that the locomotives were so large and the duties so arduous that hand firing was out of the question, but the combustion efficiency must have been well below that which was expected of British locomotives.

Again, if the coal consumption to produce a given steaming rate was consider-

ably increased, where did the extra coal go? The answer was that crushing the coal in the tender to convey it to the firebox tended to produce a lot of dust. The method of distributing the coal in the grate was by steam jet, over the fire, so the dust tended to be carried away unburnt, or only partially burnt, up the chimney. The principle of the locomotive mechanical stoker, laying the fresh coal on top of the firebed was, moreover, an inefficient way of feeding a furnace. Hence the use in power station practice of underfeed stoking, in which the volatile content of the coal passes up through the white-hot firebed, ensuring full combustion. Unfortunately no-one had devised a satisfactory underfeed stoker for a locomotive up to the time that British Railways lost interest in the steam locomotive.

Another approach to the attainment of the full potential of the locomotive was to burn oil. Unless oil could be obtained very cheaply, it was not an economic proposition, because at the time the Class 9Fs were built, gas oil was costing two and a half times as much per therm as coal, and the combustion efficiency would not have been improved appreciably. The suggestion was made that residual oils were available and some thought was given to the provision of oil-burning equipment on these locomotives. It then transpired that no residual oils were going to be available to British Railways at an economic price, and that was that. Today the situation would be entirely different, with oil, if

anything, slightly cheaper per therm than coal.

The story of the Class 9F 2-10-0 would not be complete without reference to two experimental variations on the theme, and one adaptation to meet a special circumstance. Taking the last first, the adaptation applied to ten locomotives built specially for the iron ore traffic between Tyne dock and Consett on the North Eastern Region. These engines had to operate the hopper doors of the wagons and therefore had to have air compressors; they were fitted with two Westinghouse donkey pumps on the right-hand (fireman's) side.

At the same time as the design work started on the 2-10-0, interest was aroused in the Franco-Crosti patents in Italy, and the building of two German Federal Class 52 locomotives with a simplified arrangement of pre-heater. The matter was investigated and there appeared to be a case for making a parallel experiment on British Railways, and what better class to try it on than the Class 9F. Within the limitations of the British loading gauge, it presented the Brighton drawing office with a pretty tough assignment. Ten locomotives were built, basically similar to the Class 9F, but with a modified boiler and a pre-heater to the recommendations of Dr Piero Crosti. Space does not permit a description of the locomotives, nor of all the factors which led, in due course, to their being altered back to the traditional form.

The other experiment applied to one locomotive and covered the provision of a Giesl ejector in place of the standard blast pipe and chimney. This fitting has been found successful on a number of overseas railways, but it never became the policy of the British Transport Commission to adopt it. Only one other BR locomotive was so fitted—one of the Bulleid Battle of Britain class.

As a result of the modernisation programme and the demise of steam on British Railways, the life of the Class 9F 2-10-0 was relatively short and all were withdrawn after only about ten years' service, long before they were worn out. Two of the class are preserved, one of them, *Evening Star*, by the British Railways Board and the other by Mr David Shepherd, the artist.

Above: Forerunner of the BR Class 9F, War Department Austerity 2-10-0 No 600 'Gordon', at a Longmoor Military Railway open day in 1968. *B Stephenson*

Below: No 92030 on an iron ore train south of Harbury tunnel in October 1965. *D Huntriss*

4
Diesel, Electric and Turbine Locomotives

Facing page: End of BR steam, August 1968.
B A Reeves

Overleaf: New Tokaido Line train makes one of its infrequent station stops. The NTL is Japan's only standard-gauge railway, linking Tokyo and Osaka, and it carries only express passenger trains formed of streamlined electric multiple-unit stock. *Picturepoint*

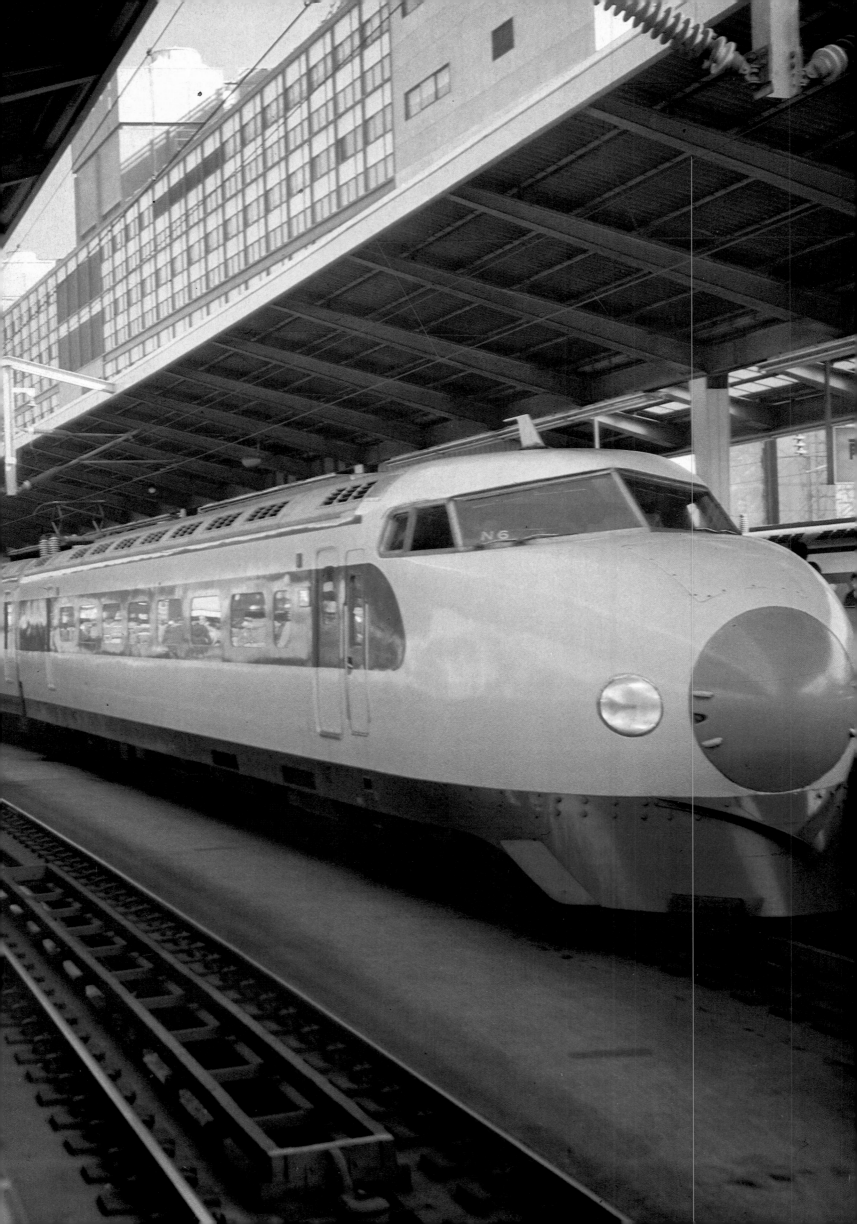

Birth of ELECTRIC TRACTION

WHEN THE Stockton and Darlington Railway was opened in 1825 the power of electricity was already realised, but its harnessing to useful work remained a problem. In the same year William Sturgeon exhibited the first practical electro-magnet in London. At that time, however, its effectiveness was limited by the small power available from the Voltaic pile—then the only source of a continuous current.

By 1830 Sturgeon had improved the Voltaic pile, but the next decisive step towards industrial electricity was the development of the first practical primary cell by J F Daniell, who published his work in 1836. The primary cell or battery provided a stronger and more reliable means of energising electro-magnets, and many inventors turned their attention to methods of driving machinery by electro-magnetic action. Most of them were thinking of alternatives to the stationary steam engine, but as early as 1837 Thomas Davenport, of Vermont, in the United States of America, demonstrated electric propulsion of a small vehicle on a short length of track.

The Science Museum in London has a poster, believed to have been printed about 1843, advertising an 'Electro-Magnetic Exhibition' at the Egyptian Hall, Piccadilly, London, at which a Mr Robert Davidson was to show 'a locomotive engine carrying passengers on a circular railway'. Davidson's locomotive had already been tested on the Edinburgh & Glasgow Railway in 1842 and attracted sufficient notice for some details to have come down to us. The locomotive was driven by the attraction of electro-magnets on iron bars secured to wooden drums on the axles, so that there was already an approach towards the modern traction motor. But the drums were kept rotating by the fluctuating pull of magnets being continuously switched on and off. In the motor as known today rotation is produced by forces exerted continuously by the interaction of magnetic fields. Davidson started and stopped his locomotive by cranking the zinc plates in and out of the primary cells which provided the power.

Apparently Davidson's locomotive met with a violent end, being destroyed by

Top: Liverpool Overhead Railway's No 27 at Seaforth Sands. *John Adams*

Upper Centre: Motor and gear drive of the first Siemens electric locomotive shown at a Berlin exhibition in 1879. *DB Film Archiv*

Above: Siemens & Halske electric coach which ran at 210.2km/h at the Marienfelde-Zossen trials in November 1903. *DB Film Archiv*

Below: Electric locomotive of the City & South London Railway, opened in 1890. *London Transport Executive*

rivals who feared unemployment if electricity supplanted steam. It was, in any case seriously handicapped by the size and weight of the batteries which had to be carried. Serious development of electric traction had to await the first mechanically driven electrical generators, and then the evolution of the electric motor. This was a slow process, and more than a decade after Davidson's locomotive made its brief appearance other inventors were still experimenting with electro-magnetic drives of various kinds.

No doubt Davidson's experiments had been followed in the USA, for in 1850 Congress commissioned Professor Charles G Page to build a locomotive working on the electro-magnetic system. Page's rather cumbersome machine made a demonstration run on the railway from Washington to Bladensburg, 5½ miles away, on April 29, 1851, but its performance did not impress the men from the ministry and no more money was forthcoming to continue the experiments.

The way to the electric generator was pointed by Michael Faraday's discovery of electro-magnetic induction, which he announced in 1831. Faraday stated the principle that when an electrical conductor is moved at right angles to the lines of force of a magnetic field, a voltage is developed between its ends. It took many years of mechanical ingenuity to devise practical systems of rotating conductors and stationary magnets, or vice versa, from which useful power could be drawn. There was less interest in the electric motor at first, although Faraday's arguments had shown that current supplied to a conductor in a magnetic field would cause the conductor to move. A report in an Italian technical journal in 1864 that an engineer called Pacinotti had built a machine which would operate either as a generator or a motor seems to have attracted surprisingly little attention. Its significance was not fully grasped until the

Belgian engineer Gramme demonstrated a generator running as a motor when supplied with current from another machine at an exhibition in Vienna in 1873. Even then the effect is said to have been discovered accidentally when the two machines were inadvertently connected together.

By the end of the 1870s the basic requirements for an electric railway taking power from a stationary generator were available. The first public exhibition of such a railway was given by the firm of Siemens & Halske at the Berlin Exhibition of 1879, where a 3hp locomotive designed by Werner von Siemens hauled trains on a track 300yd long. Power was supplied to a central 'live' rail at 150V, collected by copper brushes on the locomotive, and returned to the generator through the running rails—all the elements, in fact, of a direct-current third-rail system.

It is an interesting fact that the basic electrical generator operating on the principle discovered by Faraday does not produce direct, but alternating current. Automatic switches—commutators—to convert alternating current (ac) into direct current (dc) were quickly developed because of the interest in electric lighting with arc lamps, which need a dc supply. The fitting of commutators also enabled the machines to work interchangeably as generators or motors.

Siemens & Halske soon followed up their electric railway demonstration at the Berlin Exhibition by equipping a short electric line between the railway station and the military academy in Lichterfelde. Opened on May 16, 1881, this line is generally accepted as the first electric railway to provide a regular commercial passenger service. It was soon followed in Britain by Volk's electric railway on the sea front at Brighton, opened on August 13, 1883.

At that period Edison in the United States was also experimenting with electric traction. His first locomotive ran at speeds

up to 40mph on narrow-gauge track specially laid for the purpose in 1880. Like the Siemens locomotive of 1879 it was basically a four-wheel trolley with a motor, but contemporary illustrations show it with a superstructure of steam locomotive shape. A diminutive 'boiler' carried a massive headlamp and was overshadowed by a palatial cab at the other end. In 1883 Edison developed another locomotive, *The Judge*, in collaboration with his partner, Field. Locomotive-style cab, headlamp and cowcatcher appeared again, but the sham boiler which covered the 'works' had changed its outline to look more like a large dog kennel.

Leo Daft, another American pioneer of the same period, was content for his four-wheel locomotives to look like what they were. His first locomotive, *Ampère,* towed a passenger coach on the narrow-gauge Saratoga and Mt McGregor Railway on November 24, 1883, but was derailed and wrecked at the end of the demonstration. Later he electrified and operated with three locomotives—*Morse, Faraday* and *Ohm*—a 3-mile branch line of the Baltimore horse tramways. Daft's biggest locomotive was the 9-ton *Benjamin Franklin* of 1885, built for an electrification experiment on the New York Elevated. Originally it had one pair of driving and one pair of trailing wheels, but it was rebuilt in 1888 with four driving wheels and gave an improved performance, being able to haul eight-car trains at 25mph. The naming of locomotives after electrical pioneers is interesting. Daft also built a *Volta* and a *Pacinotti*, and Robert Davidson had called his first locomotive *Galvani*.

The years from 1890 to 1910 saw very rapid and widespread development in electric traction. On December 18, 1890, the first three miles of the City & South London Railway were opened between Stockwell and King William Street. This was the first underground electric railway in the world. The trains were hauled by four-wheel

Above: Manx Electric Railway's car No 20 at Laxey. *Colourviews*

Facing page: A 7-car electric multiple-unit train with BTH equipment of the type that replaced locomotive-hauled stock on the Central London Railway in 1903. *English Electric-AEI Traction Ltd*

Above: Manx Electric Railway's car No 20 at Laxey. *Colourviews*

Below: A Brown-Boveri locomotive built in 1899 for the Burgdorf-Thun line. *DB Film Archiv*

Bottom left: An AEG electric railcar that took part in the 1903 Marienfelde-Zossen trials. *DB Film Archiv*

Right: One of the original 1900-vintage BTH locomotives supplied to the Central London Railway. *English Electric-AEI Traction Ltd*

Below right: Loco-hauled train of the City & South London Railway in 1922. *London Transport Executive*

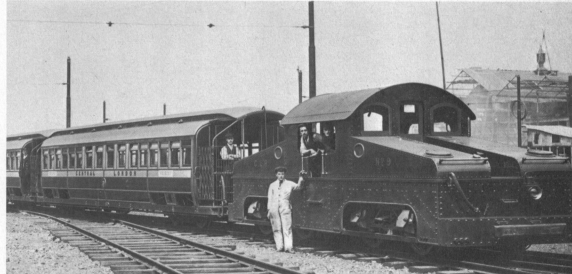

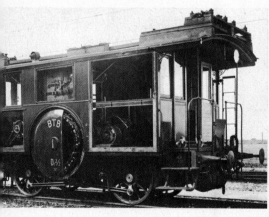

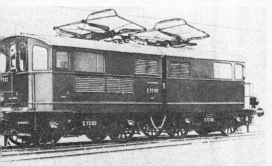

electric locomotives operating on a 500V dc supply, which was generated in the railway's own power station at Stockwell. Up to that time many electrifications had been of tramway-type lines or only short sections of railway lines, and so the City & South London has been claimed as the first complete electric railway in the world, having its own stations, signalling, and rolling stock hauled by electric locomotives.

Five years after the City & South London opening, the first conversion of a section of steam railway to electric working took place. That was in Baltimore, USA, where nearly four miles of the Baltimore & Ohio Railway were electrified where it ran in tunnel under the city; the work was completed in 1895. The locomotives followed a practice begun by the City & South London in that the motors were not geared to the axles but mounted directly on them. Total output of the four motors of a B & O locomotive was 1,080hp, compared with 100hp developed by the two motors of the City & South London locomotives.

One of the advantages of electric traction is that the motive power can be built into passenger-carrying vehicles. On some types of service there is no need to use separate locomotives which must move their own weight as well as that of the train. Early lines were often worked by a single motor coach, later supplemented by trailer cars. If there was a motor coach at both ends of a train, the motors on the rear one had to be connected to the driver's controller in the leading cab by cables running through the train. This was the practice at first on the Liverpool Overhead Railway (opened March 1893), the Waterloo & City Railway (opened August 1898) and the Liverpool-Southport section of the Lancashire & Yorkshire Railway (opened March 1904). The controllers were manually operated drum switches which carried the full motor current. This system enabled a single train unit of two or more coaches to be driven from either end, but it was not practicable to couple units together to form longer trains as is done on electrified suburban lines and some main lines today. The inventor who made this possible was Frank J Sprague in the United States. In his multiple-unit control system the driving cabs were fitted with master controllers which switched a low-voltage supply to operate the power switches in all the motor coaches of the train. The driver no longer had contacts carrying hundreds of amperes almost literally at his finger tips, and the light current control cables could be extended to several train units without difficulty by means of "jumper" cable connections between the end coaches. Sprague's first multiple-unit control was introduced in 1897 on the Chicago elevated railway.

Meanwhile industrial electrification had been following its own path. The distribution of power as alternating current at high voltage was being developed and the first practical ac motors were making their appearance. These machines already used

Top: Two 680hp 1,500V dc locomotives supplied to New Zealand in 1923 by English Electric-AEI, heading a train at Otira-Arthur's Pass. *English Electric-AEI Traction Ltd*

Above: A German 750kW 15,000V ac locomotive of 1914 vintage. *DB Film Archiv*

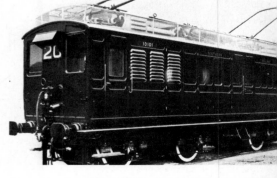

Right: A GEC-equipped 1,000hp 6,700V ac electric locomotive supplied in 1923 for the 'Elevated Electric' lines of London, which after grouping into the Southern Railway adopted a 650V dc third-rail system.
English Electric-AEI Traction Ltd

Right lower: A 1,500V dc locomotive for the EE-AEI designed electrification of the North Eastern Railway's Newport-Shildon section in 1915. *English Electric-AEI Traction Ltd*

Facing page: London Metropolitan Line locomotive No 1 at Baker Street.
D Trevor Rowe

the three-phase form of ac supply which today is the standard for large-scale distribution. Railway engineers followed these developments with interest, because as increasing lengths of line were electrified the low-voltage dc system involved substantial loss of power at points distant from the generating station.

In Switzerland in 1899 the Swiss firm, Brown Boveri, electrified the line from Burgdorf to Thun to demonstrate three-phase traction and built the first three-phase electric locomotives in the world to operate on it. In a three-phase system the motors can only run at a few fixed speeds depending on the frequency of the supply. Compensations for this are the rugged and mechanically simple motors, and the fact that if a train descending a gradient tries to exceed the selected speed, the motors automatically feed power back into the supply and act as brakes. Three-phase traction therefore tended to be used on steeply graded lines, notably in Northern Italy from 1902, where it lasted until after the second world war. The system was also chosen for the electrification through the Simplon Tunnel between Switzerland and Italy in 1906, but this section was converted to the alternative single-phase ac system in 1930 in conformity with the rest of the Swiss Federal Railways network. In the USA the Great Northern Railroad chose three-phase ac for electrifying its mountain section through the Cascade Tunnel in 1909, but this line, too, was later changed to single-phase supply, conversion taking place in 1927-8.

Although the three-phase system has only been used commercially on lines where speed is of secondary importance, it was selected by the German Siemens and AEG companies for experiments between 1902 and 1903 intended to demonstrate the high-speed capabilities of electric traction. The climax of the tests was reached when two railcars each attained a

speed of 130mph. A three-phase locomotive ran at nearly 94mph. Railways at that time, however, showed little interest in the possibilities of travel at such speeds, for which their permanent way, signalling and rolling stock would have been unsuitable, while the challenge of the aeroplane was undreamed of. However, the high-speed runs between Marienfelde and Zossen pointed to the future in a way not then realised, because the speed of the vehicles was not controlled by the drivers but by the power station engineers, who could vary the frequency of the current supplied by their generators. There was a hint here of the centralised supervision of speed which figures in automatic train control proposals today.

Single-phase ac corresponds to the type of current used for domestic lighting, heating and small motor drives. When supplied to a railway, it allows the use of traction motors similar in construction to dc machines, and gives a full range of speed control. Unfortunately the vital switching process that keeps a motor turning — commutation — works less smoothly in an ac traction motor and can cause violent sparking which calls for frequent maintenance. None-the-less, the economy of high-voltage ac distribution right up to the overhead wires on the railway attracted engineers at an early stage and much work on perfecting ac traction motors took place in Switzerland, where the first single-phase locomotives in the world ran on the line between Seebach and Wettingen in 1904. A year earlier trial running of motor coaches had taken place on an experimental single-phase line in Berlin. Commutation difficulties were overcome by using a frequency only one-third that of the normal industrial ac supply. This meant that single-phase railways must either generate their own supplies or install conversion equipment to produce the sub-standard frequency. The result was that the single-phase ac system found

most favour in countries where railways could generate their own electricity cheaply by water power.

By the early 1900s the dc railways had outgrown local generation for individual lines and were taking high-voltage ac supplies and converting them to dc at lineside substations. Trains were operating at higher voltages, too, because this enabled the substations to be farther apart and reduced electrification costs. In Britain five miles of the Lancashire & Yorkshire Railway between Bury and Holcombe Brook were electrified at 3,600V dc in 1912—the world's first high-voltage dc electrification. Later, however, the voltage was reduced to 1,200V to conform with the section between Bury and Manchester. In general, when dc supplies of more than 750V are concerned, overhead wiring is used, but the 1,200V Manchester-Bury line remains an exception with a protected third-rail supply.

The 3,600V Bury-Holcombe Brook experiment foreshadowed the later widespread use of 3,000V dc in other countries, often with British-built equipment. The first main-line electrification at this voltage was in the USA on the Chicago, Milwaukee, St Paul & Pacific Railroad, where 660 route-miles were operating at this voltage by 1920. Other dc main lines at that period and later were electrified at 1,500V.

Over the first half of the present century the dc and ac systems pursued their separate ways, each eventually accounting for about half the total world railway electrified mileage. For about 30 years the merits of each were hotly argued. One or two 'hybrid' schemes appeared, however, which attempted to combine the best features of both, and for some far-sighted engineers this goal was always in view. It was not to be fully attained until science had put at their disposal methods and materials undreamed of when the first railway wheels were turned by electric power.

Above : Last of the British experimental steam turbine locomotives, Stanier's Princess-class Pacific No 6202, heading a Liverpool express at Camden.
Ian Allan library

STEAM TURBINE LOCOMOTIVES

IT IS NO DOUBT to the water-wheels of former days, driving corn mills and performing other useful services, that turbine propulsion in part at least can be traced. From the mill wheel to the water turbine was but a step, and the next step was to drive the turbine wheel by a more powerful agent than by water—that is, by steam. Also the steam turbine can trace its origin back to the windmill, as the principle behind the rotation of both is the same. But the steam turbine had to be something very much more compact than the windmill with its lengthy sails.

Most of the credit is due to Sir Charles Parsons and his associates for the initial development of the steam turbine. In 1884 he introduced his method of 'pressure compounding', which in effect was the mounting of two or more turbines on the one shaft, with the exhaust steam from each turbine being carried on to drive the next until final exhaust of the steam at the end of the series, so obtaining the maximum possible degree of efficiency. Other inventors, such as de Laval in Sweden with his 'steam windmill' of 1887 and Curtis of the United States with his 'velocity compounding' of 1898, played their parts, but the Parsons turbines showed a higher efficiency than others. Even so, 13 years were to elapse before any serious notice was taken in Europe of the pioneering Parsons work.

The next steam turbine development of note was that of the Swedish engineer Ljungström, who in 1912 invented his 'compound reaction' turbine, in which the steam was made to flow radially outwards, and instead of having alternate rows of fixed and moving blades, the guide nozzles themselves were made to rotate, but in the opposite direction. The turbine blades were attached in two concentric rings to two discs, mounted on shafts with a common horizontal axis, revolving in opposite directions, and, in a turbo-electric plant, driving separate dynamos. We shall come later to the adaptation of a Ljungström turbine drive to a British steam locomotive.

It was inevitable that in course of time the idea of turbine propulsion of a locomotive should suggest itself to locomotive designers. It was attractive because, instead of reciprocating motion with its balancing and other problems, the even torque or turning moment of turbine drive would have great advantages, even though other problems would need to be solved before turbine drive was likely to prove reliable and efficient.

The first British experiment with turbine propulsion on rails appears to have been made in 1910 by the North British Locomotive Company, and was designed jointly by Sir Hugh Reid, managing director of that firm, and W M Ramsay. It was known as the Reid-Ramsay electro-turbo locomotive, as the turbines drove electric generators. Little information was released by the firm about its novel product, but it was known that steam, produced and superheated in a locomotive-type boiler at one end of the chassis, was led to a turbine of the impulse type, running at about 3,000rpm. The latter was coupled directly to a continuous-current variable-voltage dynamo, supplying current at pressures varying from 200 to 600 volts to four series-wound traction motors mounted on the locomotive's four driving axles.

The exhaust steam from the turbine passed to an ejector condenser, from which the condensed water was collected in a hot well and pumped back into the boiler. So the locomotive should have been able to run for considerable distances without taking water, the water stored in the tanks being for condensing purposes only. The lengthy frame of the locomotive was carried on two 8-wheel bogies, each with a leading 4-wheel bogie truck followed by two motor-driven axles. The boiler, with a large-diameter chimney, was at the front end; in the centre was the turbo-generator, followed by the cab; and at the rear the condenser unit. Trials of the locomotive took place in Scotland, but nothing more was heard of it.

Left and bottom: A traction motor and wheelset of the first British experiment of 1910, the Reid-Ramsay Electro-Turbo-Loco by North British Locomotive Co Ltd. *Both B Jackson*

Below: Another picture of the London Midland's No 6202 at work, passing Hatch End in 1935. *Ian Allan library*

Eleven years passed before another turbine - powered condensing locomotive emerged from the Newcastle works of the firm of Armstrong - Whitworth, of a different type but also designed by W M Ramsay. It was a machine of extraordinary appearance; at the leading end, housed in a projecting casing, was a circular fan of a diameter equal to the full width of the loading gauge, forming a part of the condensing equipment. The contraption was carried on a chassis with a 2-6-0 wheel arrangement, which was coupled to a similar 0-6-2 chassis carrying a locomotive - type boiler of a height to the maximum limit permitted by the loading gauge.

Steam at 200lb per sq in pressure was supplied to an impulse-pressure compound multi-stage turbine which was directly coupled to a three-phase generator operating at 3,000rpm. The current was used in four 275hp motors, two driving two of the axles of the boiler unit and two those of the condensing unit. The overall length of this monster was 69ft 7in, and its total weight was 130¾ tons, of which 108½ tons was available for adhesion.

Particularly careful attention had been paid to the condensing equipment; the exhaust steam was passed through tubes in a casing which revolved slowly in a tank containing 2,200 gallons of water, and the condensing process was assisted by the large fan. As no exhaust passed through the chimney, forced draught had to be provided for the boiler. Once again, after trials on the North British Railway, this expensive machine passed into obscurity.

The next steam turbine locomotive came a good deal more under public notice by being on show at the 1924 British Empire Exhibition at Wembley. Built by the North British Locomotive Company, in external appearance the new Reid-MacLeod locomotive closely resembled the Reid-Ramsay engine of 1910, but with the essential difference that instead of electrical transmission there was direct mechanical drive from the turbines to the driving wheels. As before, the lengthy chassis was carried on two 8-wheel bogies, each with two driving and two carrying axles. Beneath a sleek casing, extending from end to end of the locomotive and making it look like a glorified side-tank engine, there was the boiler at the leading end, a central cab and the condensing plant at the rear.

Two two-stage turbines were installed, each driving two of the motored axles through the medium of gearing. Although eulogistic claims were made of a high thermal efficency and smooth power output from the new machine, with benefits both in improved acceleration and savings in track maintenance, once again nothing more was heard of it after the exhibition was over. (By contrast the two steam locomotives that were exhibited alongside it—the Great Western 4-6-0 *Caerphilly Castle* and the London & North Eastern 4-6-2 *Flying Scotsman,* were to prove two of the most multiplied and successful locomotive classes in British history!)

Meantime the Swedish engineer Fredrik Ljungström, mentioned earlier, had been busy in his own country, and had produced a turbine - driven locomotive of quite extraordinary appearance and characteristics. The leading end carried only the boiler on a 4-wheel bogie and the firebox on a 6-wheel frame; the turbine power plant and the condenser were at the rear end, carried on a 6-coupled chassis and a rear pair of carrying wheels. The grotesque appearance was increased by a 7-ton coal bunker placed on top of the firebox, with sides sloping down to the running-plate.

The 1,800hp 9,200rpm turbine drove the coupled wheels through double-reduction gearing. The condensate of the exhaust steam from the final turbine stage was pumped as feed water back into the boiler, and helped towards an overall thermal efficiency of 14.7 per cent, roughly twice that obtainable with a steam locomotive of traditional design. As the turbine was uni-directional in action, provision was made in the gearing for reversing the direction of travel. The machine did some successful running on the Swedish State Railways, but only the one example was built at that time. In a second experiment some years later several locomotives were built.

In Great Britain the firm of Beyer Peacock, in conjunction with the London Midland & Scottish Railway, decided to make a trial of the Ljungström patents, and in 1926 built a turbine-driven locomotive which ran about 5,400 miles in revenue service on the Midland main line between Manchester and St Pancras. It also was a machine of odd appearance. The boiler was carried on a leading 4-wheel bogie and three fixed axles with outside bearings under the firebox, with the cab at its rear end. The turbine and condenser were carried on a six-coupled arrangement of 5ft 3in driving wheels and, at the rear end, another 4-wheel bogie.

Transmission from the turbines was by means of triple-reduction gearing. Steam was generated at 300lb per sq in and the maximum drawbar pull was 18 tons; at 75mph the turbine rotated at 10,500rpm. On the St Pancras-Manchester expresses this turbine locomotive is reported to have done excellent work, slightly superior to that of the Midland 4-4-0 compounds. But it was at the cost of a weight in working order of 144 tons, and no lower coal consumption to balance the far higher constructional cost. Once again success had not been achieved, and this locomotive also passed into oblivion.

The next and last British locomotive experiment with steam turbine propulsion attracted most attention of them all. It was made in 1935 by the London Midland & Scottish Railway, whose chief mechanical engineer, W A Stanier, in 1935 had just produced his first two Pacifics of the Princess Royal class, Nos 6200 and 6201. For the third locomotive of the series, No 6202, he decided to substitute turbine drive for the standard four cylinders and reciprocating motion, and to employ a Ljungström-type turbine for the purpose. It also employed mechanical drive but a vital difference between Stanier's creation and its predecessors was that he decided to dispense with the condenser. In appearance, therefore, No 6202 differed little from the standard Pacific, save that casings on both sides of the smokebox enclosing the turbines replaced the usual outside cylinders and Walschaerts motion.

In the cab, instead of a regulator, the driver had six hand-operated valves which, opened in succession, admitted more steam to the turbine and permitted a progressive increase in speed. From the turbine the exhaust steam was led to a double chimney, where a special type of blastpipe compensated for the fact that the average exhaust pressure was less than that from a reciprocating engine's locomotive cylinders, and provided sufficient draught for the fire without additional forced draught.

The turbine shaft was aligned at right-angles to the fore-and-aft axis of the engine and coupled directly to the high-speed pinion of a geartrain. The motion was transmitted to the driving axle through a double-helical reduction gear enclosed in a gearcase. As the main turbine could not be operated in reverse, a smaller turbine on the opposite side of the smokebox provided for reverse working when necessary; a safety device ensured that the reverse turbine could not be engaged unless the locomotive was stationary.

The boiler was practically identical with that of the two other Pacifics; the coupled wheel diameter of 6ft 6in also was identical. Of the 109 tons weight of No 6202, 71 tons was carried over the driving wheels and available for adhesion. The tender, with 4,000 gallons of water and 9 tons of coal, weighed 54¾ tons, making a total for engine and tender of 163¾ tons.

For a considerable period No 6202 handled some of the fastest and heaviest express services from and to Euston; some of its maximum efforts were superior to those of the original Stanier Pacifics. On one occasion a load of 345 tons was worked over the 152.7 miles from Crewe to Willesden Junction in 131min at an average speed of 69.8mph, with a minimum of 72mph up the long 1 in 330 ascent to Tring and a maximum of 90mph on the subsequent descent. On another run, with

Above: Impressive end view of the NBL Co's second steam turbine experiment of 1924. *B Jackson*

Left top to bottom: The first Swedish experimental locomotive using the Ljungström steam turbine; the later Swedish turbine locomotive of rather more conventional appearance, of which three were built; the Beyer Peacock locomotive based on the earlier Swedish design which was run by the LMS for more than 5,000 miles on the Midland main line in 1926. *All Ian Allan library*

362 tons, an average of 75.6mph was maintained over the 67.2 miles from Welton to Willesden.

However, there were several troublesome failures in service, and eventually, as the desired aim of reduced coal consumption was not being achieved, No 6202 was converted to a 4-cylinder Pacific, generally uniform with the other Stanier Pacifics. But it was for a short life only, for *Princess Anne,* as it was named after the conversion, was one of the three locomotives involved in a disastrous collision in October 1952 at Harrow Wealdstone, and was scrapped as a result of heavy damage sustained.

Similar steam turbine experiments in various countries recorded equal lack of success. The main reason has been that, although theoretically the turbine has a considerably higher overall thermal efficiency than a reciprocating engine, any such gain achieved was more than nullified by much higher constructional and maintenance costs, of the turbines in particular. The condensing plants of most of the designs also added considerably to weight and length, though without the vacuum effect produced by condensing one of the major contributions to improved thermal efficiency would have been lost. In retrospect it would seem that without the potential benefits of condensing Stainer's No 6202 could hardly have hoped for any ultimate success. Another form of turbine propulsion, however, the gas turbine, might well have a very different outcome, despite a not-too-promising start, as we shall recount in later parts of this work.

Right above: A Micheline petrol-engined railcar in service with French National Railways in 1933 and, far right above, the same company's type 23 Autorail as it appeared in 1936. *Ian Allan library*

Right centre: The spark that helped to start the railcar development in France was the promotion of the use of rubber tyres, which equipped this 1931 experimental vehicle.

Far right centre: More conventional development in France included this 1935 Lorraine Autorail for French State & Eastern Railway.

Below: Most of the original petrol/diesel railcars were converted buses or lorries, like this Napier 'Captain Cook' in service in Queensland, Australia from 1916 to 1930. *Queensland Railways*

Right below: A German railway internal combustion pioneering effort was this 1000hp 2B2 locomotive with mechanical drive produced in 1912 for the Prussian State Railway.

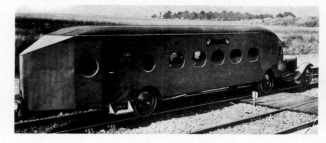

The birth of the DIESEL

IT IS NO SURPRISE that the success on the roads of the internal combustion engine in the early years of the century prompted an enquiry as to why the same type of motive power should not be equally successful on railways. Not surprisingly, also, the first railway vehicles so propelled were capacious passenger motor-coaches, and, like road motorcars, were powered by petrol engines. So far as can be traced, in Great Britain the first such motorcoach was introduced by the North Eastern Railway in 1903. It was 53ft 6in long and seated 52 passengers; a Wolseley four-cylinder petrol motor of 80hp drove an electric generator, which supplied current to four traction motors, for each axle. This car was tried extensively on NER branch lines, but nothing seems to have come of the experiment. In 1905 the Union Pacific Railroad in the USA built a similar car, but with mechanical instead of electric drive, and in 1906 the General Electric Company built for the Delware & Hudson RR a bigger car, with petrol-electric drive, which proved to be the prototype of some 250 similar vehicles introduced in the USA up to 1914.

In effect these vehicles were little more than omnibuses on rails; indeed, after World War I the London & North Eastern Railway experimented round York with a Ford bus with its rubber-tyred wheels replaced by flanged steel wheels. But by now it was being realised that the internal combustion engine offered high speed possibilities that were worth exploitation, and so it was that in 1933 the famous motor-manufacturing firm of Bugatti built for the French State Railways a petrol-engined railcar 76ft long, which with its four 200hp eight-cylinder engines but weight of no more than 23 tons reached a top speed of 107mph on an experimental run. In that year the Bugatti car went into regular service between Paris and Trouville-Deauville, covering the 136.3 miles in 2hr, at 68.2mph. The working was so successful that it soon had to be doubled, and before long both Bugatti and Micheline cars were operating also between Paris and Le Havre, Vichy and Lyons.

But the petrol engine was not destined to survive as a motive power on rails. A highly refined fuel such as petrol was

expensive; and in the event of a derailment or other mishap damaging the fuel tanks, so highly inflammable a fuel as petrol might involve serious fire risks. What was needed was an internal combustion engine which would work efficiently with an oil fuel needing far less refinement and with a low flash-point. The answer was the diesel engine.

The German inventor Dr Rudolf Diesel is generally credited with being the sole originator of the engine which ever since has borne his name, but part of the credit undoubtedly belongs to a British pioneer named Ackroyd Stuart, who from 1886 to 1890 was experimenting with the principles of compression ignition. It was not until 1893, however, that Dr Diesel produced the first diesel engine, in which a spray of atomised oil injected into the cylinder was instantly ignited by air which had been compressed and raised to a high temperature by the previous stroke of the piston. By the resultant explosion the piston was driven back; the principle is known as compression-ignition. It was not until 1898 that the first diesel engine was exhibited publicly, and its success was

such that in 1899 Diesel established a works at Augsburg to be devoted exclusively to diesel production.

Thirteen years were to elapse, however, before the first application of diesel drive to a railway vehicle. In 1912 the Swiss firm of Sulzer, in later years to become famous as the providers of power for diesel locomotives, built a diesel with the 4-4-4 wheel arrangement, rated at 1,000 to 1,200hp and weighing 85 tons. The framing and body were supplied by the German firm of Borsig, in Berlin, and the locomotive intended for the German State Railways, but nothing more seems to have been heard of it.

An early introduction of diesel power on rails was by the Canadian National Railways in 1925. Eight diesel-electric railcars entered service, each powered by a Beardmore diesel engine of 340hp, with the very light weight of 2½ tons, which drove the generator. One striking test of the reliability of the engine was made by working one of these cars across the entire 2,930 miles from Montreal to Vancouver, during which, despite a number of intermediate stops, the engine was never once stopped over a period of 67hr continuously. Three years later the CNR introduced a 2,660hp diesel-electric locomotive, comprising two 2-D-2 units coupled, each with a 12-cylinder engine. But despite this promising start, a good many years still were to elapse before diesel power began seriously to take over from steam on the railways of Canada.

The limelight now moved to Germany.

In 1932 the German State Railways started to operate, between Berlin and Hamburg, a train which probably had a greater influence on the spread of diesel passenger transport than any other in railway history.

This was the two-coach 'Flying Hamburger', an extraordinary name for an extraordinary vehicle. Suffice it to say that the train-set, 137ft 6in long, had 102 seats, a small buffet, two lavatories and a luggage compartment; it was powered by two V-type 12-cylinder Maybach diesel engines of the airless-injection type, using heavy oil and developing 820hp. After some experimental running it soon settled down to a schedule of 138min for the 178.1 miles between Berlin and Hamburg, demanding a start-to-stop average speed of 77.4mph and maximum speeds up to 100mph—the first train in the world to require a three-figure speed for time-keeping. In a very short time similar streamlined diesel train-sets were working on a number of main lines to and from Berlin, and on various German cross-country routes also.

Elsewhere in the world the country which took the most serious notice of this German development was the United States. In the early 1930s the USA was in the depths of a trade depression, and orders on American rolling stock builders by the railways for new passenger rolling stock had practically dried up. Certain enterprising builders realised that something revolutionary was needed both to stimulate the railways to recommence placing rolling stock orders, and the public

to take a renewed interest in rail travel. Streamlined high speed trains with diesel traction and new ideas in internal furnishing and *décor* might provide the ideal solution. A further notable inducement was the vast indigenous USA supplies of oil, and the fact that on the many lengthy railway runs over that great continent it would be possible to use to the maximum advantage the continuous availability of the diesel engine.

Needless to say, the builders of internal combustion engines were just as much interested in the possibilities as the rolling stock builders. As far back as 1923 a company called Electro-Motive had been formed to build petrol-engined railcars, and in 1930 this was acquired by the influential General Motors Corporation, of which it became the Electro-Motive Division. From then on this Division was to concentrate on diesel-driven trains and locomotives, and to become the biggest manufacturer in the world of both types. By 1933 this firm had evolved a two-cycle diesel engine of 600hp which was no more than one-quarter the size and one-fifth the weight of other diesels of comparable power; and the stage was now set for diesel developments on an enormously wide scale.

Two railways, the Chicago, Burlington & Quincy and the Union Pacific, decided to order streamline trains which would incorporate the new Electro-Motive diesel engine. The Edward G Budd Company built the Burlington train, which was 197ft long and weighed 87½ tons; it had

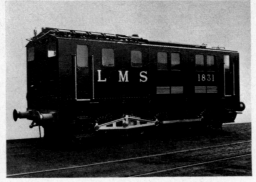

Left: A modern ML-Worthington diesel-electric locomotive of Canadian Pacific heads a passenger train out of Montreal. *D T Rowe*

Left above: One of a batch of diesel railcars produced by the Great Western Railway, introduced in 1940. *British Rail*

Above: London Midland & Scottish Railway's diesel-mechanical locomotive built at Derby in 1932. *British Rail LMR*

Right above: A diesel-electric coach built by English Electric-AEI in trial service coupled with a standard passenger coach on the LMSR in 1933. *English Electric-AEI Traction Ltd*

Right: Among earliest types of British main-line diesel locomotives was this 1,600hp 1Co-Co1 design, with English Electric engine and electrical equipment, built in Southern Region workshops in 1951. *British Rail LMR*

Right below: No 10000 was the first British main-line diesel locomotive, one of two 1,600hp diesel-electric machines produced by the London Midland & Scottish Railway in 1967. *British Rail LMR*

seating for 72 passengers, with buffet and lavatories and the usual American space for postal work. Christened the 'Zephyr', it soon made a name for itself by a run over the 1,017.2 miles from Denver to Chicago without any intermediate stop, at an average speed of 77.7mph. The first Union Pacific train was similar, but the second was of a more ambitious type. It comprised six cars, one housing the power plant, and included sleeping accommodation, and for a time, as the 'City of Portland', it provided a regular service between Chicago and Portland. With lightweight construction, this 376-ft train-set weighed 188 tons, and with its 900hp power plant experimentally covered 60 miles at an average of 102.8mph, with a top speed of 120mph. Its most notable experimental run was one through from the Pacific to the Atlantic coast, a journey of 3,193 miles from Los Angeles to New York completed in a record time of 56hr 55min.

These sensational achievements had a profound effect on American opinion, and from then on diesel building started in earnest. But it was of independent diesel locomotives rather than set trains with the power incorporated, and it proceeded at such a pace that even though slowed down by World War II the USA by 1946 had 4,441 diesels in service, and by 1957 over 27,000, handling 90 per cent of all USA railway operation. Today, apart from the limited mileage of electrified lines, the entire United States rail traffic is handled by diesel-electric power; and certain

stretches of line which had been electrified have since been turned over to diesels. This is probably the greatest revolution in railway motive power that the world has ever known in so short a period.

In Great Britain, with our ample resources of good locomotive coal, it is not surprising that in the early days of diesel rail development this type of traction had little appeal here, as a change to diesels would have involved the use of imported fuel. But one railway, the Great Western, came to the conclusion that branch line passenger work might be carried on economically with diesel railcars having simple mechanical transmissions, and put this idea to the test in 1934. A railcar of this type was built for branch service, and also two 480hp 40-seat cars with small buffets, lavatories and luggage space. The latter were for operating between Birmingham and Cardiff, but soon had to be replaced by steam-hauled trains, owing to insufficient accommodation. After this start branch line cars of 210 to 240hp, with seating for 48 to 70 passengers, were built until their total reached 36 units; while in 1941 and 1942 two 420hp cars were turned out for main line work, capable of hauling between them a 70ft coach with which the three-coach train provided 184 seats.

Meantime the London Midland & Scottish Railway had been experimenting with diesel power for shunting work. In 1931 the chassis of a standard 0-6-0 steam tank was mated to a 400hp diesel engine, with hydraulic transmission; and

four years later ten diesel shunters of 150 to 250hp, with various transmissions, one electric, were being thoroughly tested. It was soon found that a shunter which never needed time off for taking water, and only required to be fuelled every third day or so—that is to say, which could work right round the clock if necessary, and in addition was smarter in handling than its steam counterpart—was going to be a most valuable acquisition. Before World War II the first 350hp diesel-mechanical shunters were at work, and when building was resumed after the war it was at such a pace that by 1955 over 250 diesel shunters were at work in Great Britain.

Then, after the war, with diesel power rapidly sweeping steam off the rails in North America, and in view of the pre-war success of the German streamlined diesel trains, the question began to be raised as to whether we ought not to be experimenting in this country with main line diesels also. There was talk of importing some Electro-Motive units from the United States, but eventually it was the London Midland & Scottish Railway that in 1947 introduced two diesel-electric locomotives of 1,600hp each, marshalling them in a twin formation of 3,200hp. These were followed, in 1952 and 1954, by three Southern diesel-electrics with the 1Co-Co1 wheel arrangement, weighing 135 tons, Nos 10201 and 10202 of 1,750hp and 10203 of 2,000hp. Within two years these three had been transferred to the London Midland Region of

Far left above: Head view of a current German Federal 221 class 2,700hp diesel-hydraulic locomotive. *DB Film Archiv*

Above: Head view of a current British Rail Western class 2,700hp diesel-hydraulic locomotive. *British Rail*

Far left: Unusual arrangement of the power unit of the Lorraine Autorail shown on page 137, with diesel engine and mechanical transmission mounted in the bogie.

Left above: Unusual arrangement of power unit of French National CC70000 experimental locomotive of the 1960s with two SEMT diesel engines back to back, one driving the stator and the other driving the rotor of a single Alsthom alternator. *SNCF*

Left: Articulated two-car diesel-electric set with two 410hp engines of the type used for the Flying Hamburger, built in 1934.

Far left below: Power for the original Flying Hamburger was provided by two of these 12-cylinder Maybach diesel engines mounted directly on the outer bogies. *Ian Allan library*

what had now become British Railways, and No 10203 was showing itself capable of working the heavy 21.10 sleeper from Euston to Glasgow and returning with the Royal Scot—805 miles each day. Such continuous availability made an immediate impression, and the stage was now set for British diesel building in earnest.

By now another reason for a change from steam was becoming urgent; it was the difficulty of recruiting labour for the maintenance and manning of steam locomotives. With other better-paid occupations available, in comfortable shops and with regular hours, the dirty job of locomotive cleaning (often in very poor shed conditions), followed by the labour of locomotive firing as the only approach to the responsibility of driving, the steam locomotive no longer was offering any attraction to British youth. So after British Railways had decided in 1953 to spend £500,000 on two-car diesel-mechanical units for local passenger work, there came the momentous decision, in the modernisation and re-equipment plan of 1955, that all future building of locomotives for other than electrified railways in Britain would be of diesels.

The first mass invasion of main line diesels was the 200 English Electric 1Co-Co1 series, introduced in 1958, of 2,000hp units, based on the Southern No 10203 design, followed a year later by the 193 BR Derby-built Peaks, with the same wheel arrangement. Then from 1958 to 1960 there appeared the 76 Bo-Bo Warship diesels of the Western Region, with hydraulic instead of electric transmissions. What was destined to become the most numerous of the main line diesels was the Co-Co series which began emergence from the Brush works at Loughborough in 1962, finally multiplied to a total of 509 units, of 2,750hp and a weight of 117 tons. The Western Region also produced from 1961 onwards, in collaboration with Crewe, the 74 Western C-C class diesel-hydraulics, of 2,700hp.

Many other diesel types have been introduced in Great Britain for the lighter duties and for shunting, and also the most powerful of all the main line types. This is the English Electric Deltic Co-Co series, 22 in number, for the Kings Cross-Leeds and Edinburgh services. These unique machines derive their distinctive name from the Greek letter *Delta,* which in inverted form represents the Deltic cylinder arrangement. Each engine has

18 cylinders, arranged triangularly in banks of six, and with double-acting pistons working the common crank-shafts at the corner of each triangle. With two complete engines each Deltic therefore has 36 double-acting cylinders, putting out a maximum of 3,300hp and with electrical transmission, and all within a weight of no more than 99 tons. These Deltics have been doing magnificent work over the East Coast main line, and *inter alia* have permitted a reduction in fastest train times to 2hr 40min between London and Leeds, and 5¾hr by the Flying Scotsman between London and Edinburgh, with sustained 100mph speeds *en route.*

At the same time many complete train sets with diesel power have been built for Inter-City services, and the two-car and three-car diesel multiple-units, with their attractive interiors, have kept on the rails and indeed have increased much local passenger traffic that might have been lost to the roads. Of diesel-electric and diesel-hydraulic locomotives some 2,500 have been built for British Railways, with about 4,500 motor-coaches, making Great Britain the greatest rail diesel user in the world relative to the total mileage of its lines.

Top: Prototype BR high-speed train (HST) with diesel-electric power cars at each end, designed for 125mph. *British Transport Films*

Above: Warship-class diesel-hydraulic locomotive No D820 'Grenville' passing Clapham Junction with a Waterloo-Exeter train. *B Stephenson*

Right centre: Class 47 Brush diesel-electric No 1106 at Derby with a York-Poole train. *V Bamford*

Right: A pair of BR-Sulzer Type 2 diesel-electrics on a car-delivery train at Skipton, Yorks. *R Lush*

Overleaf: 6,600 hp Union Pacific diesel built in 1969, the most powerful single-unit diesel in the world. *Union Pacific Railroad Company*

IN THE MID-1940s, when diesel-electric locomotive traction was carrying all before it in the United States, and was just beginning to make an impact in Great Britain, attention became directed towards another potential form of locomotive power—the gas turbine. As we have seen, in earlier years a number of experiments had been made with steam turbines on rails, but for various reasons had not achieved success. Experience with gas turbine propulsion in the air suggested, however, that it might have possibilities for locomotive propulsion.

As in a petrol or diesel (reciprocating) internal-combustion engine, the gas-turbine engine derives its power from the rapid expansion of gases when a combustible mixture is burned in a confined space. But unlike a petrol or diesel engine, in which the expanding gases force a piston along a cylinder and the linear motion has to be converted into a rotary motion through a crank, the gas turbine is an entirely rotary machine. So it is basically a very simple machine, with none of the many sliding, rubbing surfaces of the reciprocating engine that cause lubrication and wear problems.

Also unlike the piston engine, in which the power impulses are in fact a succession of separate controlled explosions, in the gas turbine the burning and expansion take place continuously and evenly, so it is basically a very smooth and quiet engine. It also operates with a high air to fuel ratio, so that there is more complete combustion than in most piston engines and therefore a cleaner exhaust.

In principle, the basic gas turbine engine comprises a shaft running in bearings in a tube. At one end of the shaft is a set of compressor blades, so that when the shaft is rotated air is drawn in, compressed and driven towards the other end of the tube. Into the compressed air atomised fuel (usually oil, though it can be gas or pulverised solids) is forced and ignited. As it burns energy is added to the gases which expand and try to escape from the opposite end of the tube with great speed and force. To leave the chamber they are made to pass another set of blades forming a turbine on the other end of the shaft. Much of the energy put into the shaft by the turbine is required to keep the compressor working, but there is a working balance which forms the power output of the engine and can be used as a propulsive jet, or to drive an electric generator or transmission gear from the single main shaft, or to work a smaller power turbine on a second shaft.

However the gas turbine engine is arranged, its main attractions for any form of vehicle power unit are lower weight and bulk than a piston engine of equal power, and the smoother running, cleaner exhaust and the low maintenance costs arising from simplicity and few moving parts. In practical terms a gas turbine comes out at about half the weight of a similarly powered diesel engine and can be made to occupy about a quarter of the space. Its main disadvantages are higher cost because of the

very precise engineering required in its construction and much higher fuel consumption except in a very narrow band of shaft speed and output power. The useful operating band can be broadened but at the expense of greater complexity, and hence of initial and maintenance costs and proneness to derangement. Like most engineering developments, the story of the gas turbine in rail traction is one of reducing the disadvantages without whittling away too much of the advantages, until one day a balance is reached and it becomes a commercial proposition, or it is overtaken by more-promising developments.

Switzerland was the first country to experiment with rail traction gas turbines, when the firm of Brown Boveri built a 2,200hp gas-turbine-electric locomotive. It was started in 1939 and with the support and co-operation of the Swiss Federal Railways practical testing out on the track was begun about the end of 1940. The gas turbine was designed to burn crude oil and it was mounted in the locomotive with a 110hp diesel-generator set that produced the fairly high power required to motor the turbine into life. The 92-ton locomotive covered about 1,250 miles in the first 12 months or so, developing an output well in advance of its designed 2,200hp, and went on to work for some years over Swiss Federal branches which up till then had not been electrified. It was reported also to have hauled trains up to 700 tons in weight over the French National main line between Basle and Chaumont, making a 300-mile round trip daily on a fuel consumption of 25lb per mile (0.5 to 0.6lb per ton-mile). Though the Swiss Railways co-operated in the Brown Boveri development, with the abundance of hydro-electric power in Switzerland, there was little likelihood of domestic orders for gas-turbine locomotives materialising.

The next significant development came after the then Chief Mechanical Engineer of the Great Western Railway in England, F W Hawksworth, had been to Switzerland to see the locomotive at work. He considered it promising enough to warrant trials on the GWR, which in 1946 ordered from the Swiss firm a similar locomotive and, for purposes of comparison, a second gas-turbine locomotive from the British firm of Metropolitan-Vickers, which at that time was experimenting in the same direction (as also were concerns in Germany and the United States).

Before either of the GWR locomotives had been delivered in 1947, Brown Boveri announced a considerably more powerful gas-turbine-electric locomotive, of 4,000hp, 151 tons weight and 75ft 6in long, carried on two eight-wheel bogies. Only two axles of each bogie were motored. The gas turbine was mounted on an auxiliary frame with the generator to which it was directly coupled. A feature of the new design was a novel rotating pressure-cum-heat exchanger designed to improve fuel efficiency at part load, which has always been the most disadvan-

Top right: In service on British Railways in July 195(the 2,700hp gas-turbine-electric locomotive No 1800(built by Brown Boveri for the GWR in 1946-7
British Railways W

Above: No 18000 outside Swindon works in 1957
Ivo Peter

Right: The Metrovick gas-turbine-electri locomotive No 18100 heading the Merchan Venturer at Bath in 1953. *Ivo Peter*

Below: Another picture of No 18100 taken in 195.
British Railways W

Right: The English Electric gas-turbine-mechanical locomotive GT3 in experimental BR service in 1961 at Ashby Magna on the GC main line.
M Mensing

Below: The GT3 at Leicester in 1961. *G Wheeler*

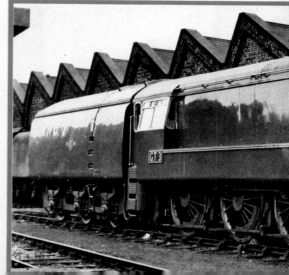

tageous feature of the gas turbine for road and rail traction applications. No record seems to have been published of the performance of the second Swiss locomotive.

The first of the GWR locomotives was delivered by Brown Boveri late in 1949 and became No 18000. It was of the A1A-A1A wheel arrangement (that is, two six-wheel bogies with the four outer axles motored). The industrial-type power plant comprised axial-flow compressor, heat exchanger, combustion chamber and single-stage turbine. Delivery of the Metrovick locomotive soon followed. It was of the Co-Co type and received the number 18100. Metropolitan - Vickers at first fitted the locomotive with a type of marine propulsion gas turbine derived from an aircraft jet, but with a heat exchanger added in the interests of part-load efficiency. However, in 1948 the builder evolved a new type of gas turbine which gave the needed overall efficiency without a heat exchanger and the locomotive was redesigned to include the new piece of equipment, saving in both weight and bulk of the power plant.

The Metrovick No 18100 therefore differed considerably from the Swiss-built No 18000 in internal arrangement. Its three main components were a 15-stage axial-flow compressor, a combustion chamber of the multi-flame-tube type, and a five-stage axial-flow turbine. The turbine output was absorbed by three main generators (with an auxiliary for train services) driven at 1,600rpm at full load through a single-reduction gearbox. Maximum gross power rating of the turbine was 3,500hp at 7,000rpm, reduced to about 2,700hp net at the rails after transmission losses and the demands of the auxiliaries.

The major difference between the two locomotives was that No 18000 incorporated a heat exchanger and No 18100 did not. The latter therefore might have been expected to be the lighter and more compact unit of the two, but actually was not, for the respective weights were $115\frac{1}{4}$ and 120 tons, and the overall lengths were 63ft and 66ft 8in. With A1A-A1A wheel arrangement, the adhesion weight of No 18000 was 77 tons, compared with the 120 tons of the Co-Co example. There is no record, however, that No 18000 suffered from deficient adhesion.

Both locomotives were drafted into the main line services of what had by then become the Western Region of British Railways, turn - and - turn - about with 4-6-0 King and Castle classes of steam locomotive; they are reported to have handled those duties with complete competence, but they were beset with troubles which had nothing to do with the gas turbines. There were difficulties with the traction motors, but far worse was the erratic behaviour of the automatically fired steam-heating boilers, which were then in their infancy, nothing of the kind having been needed previously with steam locomotion. This made the gas-turbine pair unpopular with travellers in cold weather,

when they often had to be replaced by steam power. But apart from some trouble with erosion of turbine blades, the turbines apparently behaved well and it is a great pity that what had been a promising experiment was not carried further. Eventually, as had been the case with the earlier steam turbine locomotive experiments, Nos 18000 and 18100 were withdrawn from service. It is fair to say that no well-founded conclusions had apparently been drawn.

Meantime, however, a gas-turbine locomotive development which can be regarded as having had a moderately successful outcome had been taking place in the United States. In 1948, the American Locomotive Company (Alco) with the General Electric Company, and Baldwin-Westinghouse had both produced experimental gas turbine - electric locomotives, each with the Bo-Bo-Bo-Bo wheel arrangement and had loaned them to various American railways for trial running. Trials of the Baldwin - Westinghouse prototype were confined to the Pittsburgh & Lake Erie RR, hauling 2,000-ton ore trains, and to the Pennsylvania RR, but though said to be quite successful they did not result in any purchases.

However, the Alco-GE locomotive had a much more extensive itinerary, particularly over the Union Pacific RR west of Cheyenne, working freight trains averaging 3,245 tons in weight up the long 1 in 65 climb to the 8,013ft altitude of Sherman summit in Wyoming. In 19 months of testing the locomotive handled 344,950 million gross tons of traffic on a total fuel consumption of 1,448,787 gallons, 95 per cent of which was cheap Bunker C crude oil.

By the end of 1950, the Union Pacific management was sufficiently impressed with the prototype's performance to place an order with Alco-GE for ten locomotives of generally similar design, and then to order another 15 in 1952. The General Electric single-shaft gas turbine produced 4,500hp at 6,000rpm and was arranged to drive four separate traction-current generators through a 6-to-1 reduction gearbox. A 200hp diesel-generator set provided current for starting the gas turbine, by motoring one of the traction generators, and for locomotive services, and the diesel output could be diverted to the traction motors of one bogie to provide power for manoeuvring the locomotive in a yard without starting up the main engine. A steam generator was carried to heat the heavy oil to pumpable liquid consistency.

Apart from the axle arrangement of four two-axle bogies, the experimental gas-turbine locomotive was of similar general appearance to a contemporary diesel-electric unit of double-ended (two-cab) type, but there was a considerably bigger area of air-intake grilles in the sides to cope with the voracious appetite for air of the gas turbine. The prototype was numbered X50 in the UP fleet. The first production batch of the class were generally similar to X50, except that they had a cab at one end only. The second batch had full-width

cabs connected by open walkways along the locomotive sides.

No doubt mainly because of their ability to run on the cheapest of unrefined oil (though they had to be started up on ordinary diesel fuel) and the nature of the long and heavy freight hauls that characterised the work they were put to by Union Pacific, the operation of the gas-turbine locomotives was judged to be highly successful. So much so in fact that in 1955 Union Pacific Railroad ordered a further 15 locomotives, but of even greater power, namely 8,500hp. A later uprating of the engines was reported to have provided 5,000hp and 10,000hp respectively in the two types.

The new locomotives were enormous; they were designed as two close-coupled units, each mounted on two three-axle bogies with all axles motored, giving a Co-Co+Co-Co formation, with a single cab at one end. The locomotives were designed to draw a tender carrying fuel oil, the whole outfit measuring about 180ft overall. The auxiliary diesel engine on the big machines was of 1,000hp to provide sufficient yard manoeuvring power, as well as to power all essential auxiliaries, such as brake compressors and traction motor blowers, so that the gas turbine could be shut down entirely on long downgrades and at lengthy stops to save fuel.

However, qualified success in the specialised type of operation in UP service, that is, in long periods of hauling on full load, only at which is the fuel economy of the gas turbine really acceptable, did not spell success in general rail traction. No other railway ordered gas-turbine locomotives and the UP machines came more and more to be used as boosters, marshalled with diesels on heavy trains and the gas turbines in use only during the demands for lengthy full-power hauls. They have been gradually phased out of service from about the middle 1960s, the last of the high-power machines having been scrapped in 1971.

That is not quite the end of the gas-turbine locomotive story. During the 1950s Union Pacific carried out abortive experiments with a pulverised coal-burning gas turbine, and in England the English Electric Company designed and built a gas-turbine locomotive of great promise, though it also proved abortive in the end.

The English Electric locomotive, named GT3 because it was the third British gas-

turbine railway engine, differed fundamentally from all the others because it replaced the heavy and expensive electric transmission with direct mechanical drive. To do that it employed a two-shaft gas turbine, that is, an engine in which there is a separate power turbine on a shaft separated from the compressor and its turbine. This arrangement allows the compressor and gas generator to run up to full speed and power while the power turbine, which is directly geared to the driving wheels, is still at rest, providing full power for starting and acceleration and acting as an integral torque converter. The engine also worked on the recuperative cycle, which means it had a heat exchanger designed to pass some of the exhaust heat to the ingoing air, so to improve fuel efficiency.

The GT3 type of engine considerably improved the potential economics of gas-turbine traction and probably could, with the right encouragement from users, have been developed to compete effectively with diesel traction, largely through eliminating the weight and the capital and maintenance costs of the electric transmission. The locomotive itself underwent a lengthy period of dynamometer and practical track trials, with the co-operation of British Railways. It showed up very well in normal field service against contemporary steam and diesel locomotives, and demonstrated an overall efficiency of 22 per cent at full load, which is not greatly below that of the average diesel-electric locomotive. It was also a significant improvement over all the gas-turbine-electric results and the fall-off in efficiency away from full load was less drastic than in the turbo-electric designs.

GT3 probably ranks as a classic missed opportunity. Its tiny number of working parts compared with any other machine of equal performance warranted greater persistence, with the goal of decimated maintenance costs and service failures comparable with what the gas turbine did

for air transport. Even in initial undeveloped form its statistics—80 tons weight, 2,700hp, 36,000lb starting effort—looked right for many railways.

Perhaps a factor in the absence of backing for GT3 was the over-cautious approach that led the designers to put their new wine into an old bottle. For they adopted a basic steam locomotive layout with 4-6-0 wheel formation. It perpetuated all the worst features of the steam engine for modern-minded railwaymen — poor visibility from the cab situated behind the 'works', the need for long turntables at locomotive depots and terminal stations, and less than 100 per cent adhesive weight.

But even GT3 is not necessarily the end of the gas-turbine locomotive story. The French, who have achieved the greatest practical success to date with gas turbine-powered multiple-unit trains, as we shall see in the following chapter of this book, are known to be studying designs for a new gas-turbine locomotive. They envisage the use of a modern aircraft jet engine as a high-efficiency gas generator, allied with a new design of power turbine driving through electric transmission. By that means, a locomotive of standard form and weight could be perhaps double the power of the best current diesel locomotive.

The Germans have contented themselves with a halfway stage and have probably found the most practical use for gas turbines in locomotives at present technological levels. They have taken a standard design of four-axle diesel-hydraulic locomotive, capable of development comfortably to about 3,000hp, and added an aircraft-type gas turbine driving directly into the main transmission and boosting output by 1,000hp or so. The turbine is purely a booster, arranged to come in automatically at or near its efficient full-load output only when the locomotive controls are set towards the top end of the power demand to accelerate a heavy train or on long upgrades. With further development of the diesel engine and gas turbine, a combined usable output of 5,000hp or more in an 80-ton locomotive is thought to be possible.

Most motive power engineers, however, now think the gas turbine's most promising role in rail transport is in the high-speed multiple-unit passenger train. That is where most active development is taking place, which will be dealt with in a later part.

THE TURBOTRAIN AT LAST

AFTER FURTHER DEVELOPMENT of locomotives powered by gas turbines was abandoned in the middle and late 1950s, there was a gap of several years before active work was resumed in attempting to apply the gas turbine to rail traction. It was not that the potential advantages of the turbine had been forgotten by railway engineers and operators, only that the type of engine essential for economic railway service did not exist and was likely to be very expensive to develop.

Yet the advantages of the rotary engine with no rubbing or reciprocating parts still attracted railway designers, particularly perhaps to provide on non-electrified lines the faster passenger services that were becoming recognised as an essential ingredient of successful operation. As steam died out, the diesel engine became the established power on non-electric lines and had proved capable of maintaining passenger train speeds up to a maximum of 90 to 100mph, using both normal locomotives and self-powered multiple units.

However, developing the rail-traction diesel engine for even higher performance (quick acceleration with heavy loads as well as top speed) introduced problems. If the engine is merely made bigger it outgrows the limited space available for it in a railway vehicle, and it makes the

Top: First British Railways gas turbine-powered mu, the experimental advanced passenger train about to start track testing in July 1972. *British Railways*

Above: French National Railways ETG turbotrain on the regular Paris-Caen-Cherbourg service. *SNCF*

Right: One of the French ETG turbotrains at Caen station in July 1970. *J Winkley*

vehicle heavier and therefore likely to wear and damage its wheels and the track at high speed. The alternative is to produce more power from a same-sized engine which inevitably will be more sophisticated, more highly stressed and more expensive, and hence probably more prone to mechanical troubles and certainly more costly to maintain.

With circumstances squeezing the balance of advantage of diesel power for the modern passenger railway, thoughts turned actively once more to the gas turbine. In particular, thoughts turned to the small engines which by the early 1960s were being made in several countries in fairly large numbers for helicopters and light aircraft and which, it seemed, would fit well into the general design of multiple-unit passenger trains. The Americans were first to make their intentions known and active development started in

the middle 1960s by United Aircraft Company of its Turbo-Train, to be built in both the United States and Canada. Several other American developments started shortly afterwards, followed by gas-turbine mu projects by French National Railways, Japanese National Railways, British Railways and German Federal Railway.

Of the various systems under development, only the French turbotrain has so far been carried successfully to the stage of regular revenue service. The American UAC design came close to it on Canadian National Railways but it has been dogged by a variety of troubles and no longer runs in Canada (though service might be resumed shortly); two US-built UAC three-car trains have been running since 1969 in America. The Japanese ran an experimental gas turbine-powered railcar and are constructing a multiple-unit set so powered. The Germans have just started trial running with one of the DB ex-TEE diesel motor units converted to gas-turbine power (and have been developing a gas-turbine booster in diesel-hydraulic locomotives for some years). A British Railways experimental four-car turbine-powered advanced passenger train has just started track trials.

There are several different ways in which a gas turbine can be applied to transport. In ordinary turbojet aircraft the power output in the form of the rapid expansion of heated air is used as a propulsive jet, which is quite out of the question for surface transport. But in turboprop aircraft and helicopters the gas is used to drive a shaft in a power turbine or free turbine and the 'free' shaft turns the propeller or rotor.

The second type, or two-shaft engine, is the one generally figuring in rail-traction developments. The output shaft can be used to drive the axles and running wheels directly through a fixed-reduction or two-speed gearbox, or through a mechanical multispeed gearbox or a hydraulic torque converter; or it can drive an electric generator to produce current to power conventional traction motors. There is some variety also in the actual application of gas turbines to rail vehicles; some developers have used comparatively powerful engines of 1,000hp upwards in the power cars of multiple-unit trains, others have used smaller engines of only a few hundred horsepower each in groups.

However the gas turbine is applied, its principal attractions are smaller size and lower weight than a reciprocating engine of

equal power, smoother running and low maintenance cost arising from simplicity and few moving parts. Its main disadvantages compared with diesel for use in surface transport vehicles are higher initial cost, high throughput of air entailing comprehensive intake and exhaust noise suppression equipment, and considerably higher fuel consumption except in a narrow band of shaft speed and full power output.

Without question, the French gas-turbine passenger train project is much farther ahead in practical terms than any of the others. The experiments started in 1964-65, using a French-built Turbomeca two-shaft gas turbine giving a maximum of about 1,500hp for aircraft application, borrowed from the French Air Force.

The engine was de-rated to about 1,100hp for rail traction and fitted into the trailer of a standard SNCF two-car diesel mu, leaving the diesel engine in the normal power car. Much of the early running was concerned with development of efficient silencing and getting the gas turbine to run efficiently on diesel fuel. Development went well and by June 1967 the two-car set, which was mounted on new-style high-speed bogies, had been run successfully at speeds approaching 150mph on straight and level track.

In the original experiment, the gas turbine was coupled to the shafts driving the wheels through a simple reduction gear and, without the help of the diesel engine, accelerating from rest and low-speed performance were not very bright.

Consequently, it was decided to include a hydraulic torque converter in the drive, which provided the necessary improvement and permitted operation over the entire speed range using the gas turbine alone. With that satisfactory development, the SNCF placed orders in July 1968 for 10 four-car gas turbine-hydraulic trainsets (Type ETG) designed for a maximum speed of 112mph.

At the same time it was decided to build two experimental trains of considerably higher power (Type TGV) and with gas turbines driving through electric transmission. The first TGV, which is intended to investigate speed possibilities up to about 200mph, started running trials recently. Since the initial orders and as a result of further developments, the SNCF has ordered a second series of five-car gas-turbo-hydraulic multiple units (Type RTG) capable of 125mph; a prototype has just started running tests. In addition, a further four of the original four-car ETG sets have been ordered.

The French turbotrains have been developed to replace diesel passenger trains

Left and below far left: Two views of the first of the higher-power French RTG turbotrains for cross-country services, on show in Paris in June 1972. *SNCF*

Below left: Restaurant car on the Paris-Cherbourg ETG turbotrain. *SNCF*

Bottom left: Turbomeca Turmo III gas turbine used in the French developments, at present 1,100hp for regular rail traction and being developed for 1,250hp and later over 1,450hp. *SNCF*

Below: French experimental gas turbo-electric advanced passenger train's first appearance at Belfort in April 1972. *La Vie du Rail (Y Broncard)*

on lines where the traffic potential does not justify the high capital cost of electrification but where there is a possibility that faster service will improve passenger receipts. Many such lines are comparatively lightly constructed, with moderate gradients and curvature, on which the higher performance felt to be essential was thought to be obtainable more economically with gas turbine than with diesel power.

The ETG was, in fact, developed particularly for the Paris-Caen-Cherbourg route, on which the full turbotrain service with the initial 10 trains was introduced in September 1970. (First revenue journeys were in March 1970.) It brought an important improvement in journey time, cutting 50 minutes off the best previous time of three hours 49 minutes with diesel traction for the 231-mile run. Non-stop time between Paris and Caen (148 miles) was brought down to 109 minutes —a start-to-stop average speed of 81.4mph. Other benefits have been higher utilisation of the new stock and higher train frequency. In the first full year of operation, the number of passenger journeys on the route showed an increase of 20 per cent.

The ETG is a four-car set with the 1,100hp turbo-hydraulic power car at one end and a diesel-mechanical power car at the other. The RTG five-car sets, which have been designed to provide higher speed and improved passenger comfort on longish non-electric cross-country services, have two of the turbo-hydraulic power cars for traction. They are about to enter revenue service on Lyons-Stras-

bourg, Lyons-Nantes and Lyons-Bordeaux routes. In both types, later versions of the Turmo III gas turbine used can provide up to 1,250hp per engine and a still later development is expected to achieve over 1,450hp.

The ETG and RTG trains are formed of individual bogie vehicles, but the experimental TGV is designed as an articulated train in which the adjacent ends of each coach share bogies. Thus, the five-car prototype TGV has only four two-axle bogies and the proposed seven-car train for revenue service would have six, saving considerable weight and possibly cost over conventional construction. Another fundamental difference is in the power transmission. With hydraulic transmission only the bogies of the power car(s) can be driven (or have dynamic braking applied economically); electric transmission permits all axles of the train to be powered and dynamically braked, which is of major importance for both performance and safety reasons where lightweight rolling stock and high speeds are concerned.

The power unit of the TGV fitted into both end cars of the formation is comprised of a pair of Turmo gas turbines driving a single alternator to generate power to drive the traction motors of each axle. The two power cars provide a total of 5,000hp per train at present levels and up to 5,900hp with projected engine development.

The American turbotrain development by United Aircraft Corporation has had a less satisfactory record of introduction to revenue service, though it has perhaps suffered more troubles with the many other

new-to-railway ideas and equipment in the design than with the gas turbines themselves. For the power equipment, UAC has utilised its own small ST6 two-shaft gas turbine, which is derated to about 400hp for rail traction service, though some have been run experimentally on track at up to 550hp. Two or more of the engines drive into a common simple reduction gearbox, the output of which is taken by mechanical couplings and shafts to the axles of one bogie of the power car.

UAC started to study the possibilities of gas-turbine rail traction in 1963 and in 1965 submitted a project to the responsible US government department (now the Department of Transportation). It resulted in a contract to supply the DOT with two three-car turbotrains for testing, the first by December 1966, an ambitious delivery date that was missed by about six months. The first set ran many thousands of miles on test from May 1966 onwards and, despite financial troubles of the railway selected to start operating turbotrains (the New Haven), it was finally cleared for operation by Penn Central and the second train started revenue service on the Boston-New York route in April 1969. Regular service, generally of one train each way daily, has been maintained on that route and, more recently, one of the two trains has been making demonstration runs under the auspices of the US government-sponsored Amtrak passenger network in various parts of the United States.

The UAC turbotrain early attracted the attention of Canadian National Railways, who considered it for a high-speed high-quality passenger service on the important Montreal-Toronto route. Arrangements were made for the new design to be built in Canada and for CNR to lease five seven-car turbotrains from UAC to operate the service. Delivery and start of service were scheduled to coincide with the opening of the Canadian Centennial celebrations in the summer of 1967, but a succession of troubles delayed the actual start of service until December 1968. After running for only a few weeks the service was withdrawn for various modifications to be made and there was a fresh start in May 1970. Once again, operation was dogged by a variety of mechanical troubles and the turbos were all out of service again by the end of January 1971. But by early 1974 it seemed that these teething troubles had been ironed out and the Turbotrain has been in regular Montreal-Toronto service.

In all the difficulties with the American trains, it is reported that there has been no serious trouble with the power units and, in fact, there were good indications that gas turbines could provide reliable high-quality service at reasonably economical cost. The real trouble with the UAC developments was that there was too much that was new—vehicle structure, engines, transmission, pendular suspension, air conditioning, electric auxiliaries; all were entirely new, generally based on

equipment developed for aircraft use, and in some cases considerable modification has been needed before reliable service in railway operation could be assured. In that particular respect the American turbotrain development was in direct contrast to that of the French, who first took a conventional railway vehicle in which to develop and prove the traction gas turbine in revenue service, and only then proceeded to apply it to a more-advanced vehicle.

The current German passenger turbotrain experiment is generally similar to the French, with a single medium-power gas turbine substituted for the diesel engine in each power car of an established type of diesel-hydraulic passenger motor train—the type, in fact, that has been in use for several years on German Trans Europe Express services.

Below: Standard two-car diesel mu that featured i the first French gas turbine experiments in 1964-! *La Vie du Ra*

Below right: UAC ST-6 aircraft turbine modified fc rail traction use, giving about 400h *United Aircraft Corporatic*

Bottom right: One of the five Canadian-built seven-ca UAC turbotrains used on Montreal-Toronto service for short periods in 1968-69 and 1970-7 *B Jacksc*

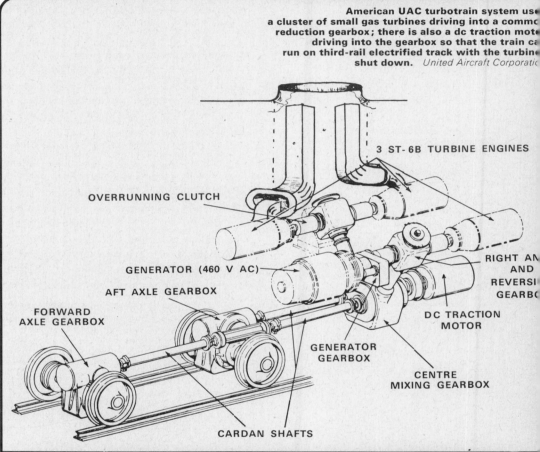

American UAC turbotrain system use a cluster of small gas turbines driving into a commo reduction gearbox; there is also a dc traction motc driving into the gearbox so that the train ca run on third-rail electrified track with the turbine shut down. *United Aircraft Corporatic*

3 ST-6B TURBINE ENGINES

OVERRUNNING CLUTCH

GENERATOR (460 V AC)

AFT AXLE GEARBOX

FORWARD AXLE GEARBOX

RIGHT AN AND REVERSII GEARBC

DC TRACTION MOTOR

GENERATOR GEARBOX

CENTRE MIXING GEARBOX

CARDAN SHAFTS

UAC three-car turbotrain for trial running on American tracks for the US Department of Transportation. *United Aircraft Corporation*

The British development, in contrast, is more akin to the American project, with a great deal of the design, apart from the gas turbines, that is quite new to railway engineering practice. But even the gas turbines of the British turbotrain prototype differ fundamentally from those of all the others. As in the UAC design, several low-power engines, rather than one of medium power, are used in each power car, but the Leyland gas turbine used is one developed for road transport instead of aircraft application. Consequently, the designers have paid particular attention to getting better fuel economy over a broader range of output and a longer life between overhauls than most aircraft engines can be tuned to provide. The improvement is obtained at the expense of greater engine complexity and only service experience

will show whether the development has been worthwhile.

In the British Railways project the gas turbine is incidental and the basic vehicle design, named advanced passenger train or APT, can be powered by any type of on-board engine, provided it is light and powerful enough to fit into the structure and provide the required performance, or by electric power picked up from an overhead wire or extra rail in the normal way. In fact, the first APT for revenue service could be fitted to run under the wire on the London-Glasgow route, the northern part of which is now being equipped to provide electrification throughout by 1974. The basis of APT design is an entirely new approach to wheel/rail interaction and vehicle suspension, aimed at a big improvement in speed (up to

150mph) and passenger comfort on existing track and with savings at the same time in wear and tear of vehicle and track.

However, the first APT to be built and now in the early stage of track testing is a four-car articulated trainset powered by gas turbines and electric transmission. The train is designated APT-E (experimental) and is designed purely as a working test-bed for research and development. A working train would be similar in having power cars at each end, but would have up to eight unpowered passenger coaches in between of similar articulated design.

Each power car is fitted with four traction gas turbines, of about 300hp each initially, directly coupled to individual alternator/rectifier units. The dc outputs from the turbo-alternator sets are fed in parallel pairs through conventional control gear to two traction motors, one driving each axle of the single driving bogie of each power car.

Whatever the outcome of the broader developments represented in the various turbotrain projects—in lightweight structures, body-tilting suspensions, non-wearing stable wheel forms and the rest—it seems that the gas turbine can now be considered seriously as a passenger train power unit. In the past decade or so the gas turbine has revolutionised the speed and comfort of passenger flight; perhaps we now see it poised to bring about a similar transformation in railway passenger service.

MODERN ELECTRIC POWER

A GLANCE AT the smooth and often elegant exterior of an electric locomotive gives little clue to the variety of equipment inside. Here, within the limits set by the railway loading gauge, the designer has to accommodate a complex assembly of switchgear, rotary machines and heavy static items, planning the layout to distribute the weight evenly over the locomotive underframe and carrying driving bogies.

Different types of electrical installation are necessary for alternating current (ac) and direct current (dc) locomotives, although some features are common to both. Among common equipment are the motor-driven blowers which continuously supply cooling air to the traction motors. The cooling requirement—perhaps 3,500 cubic feet of air per minute to each motor, is a reminder of the virtually unlimited power in the supply network on which an electric locomotive can draw.

Electric traction motors are given two horse-power ratings—for continuous and one-hour performance. Both are based on temperature rise, because the electric motor converts electrical into mechanical energy and no conversion process is 100 per cent efficient. Some of the energy appears as heat, which must be carried away by the stream of cooling air or else the temperature of the motors would rise to a level which would damage them.

Motors can be allowed to work harder for one hour than continuously, and so the one-hour rating can be up to about 20 per cent higher than the continuous. Over very short periods the output can be higher still sometimes approaching double the continuous. This advantage is unique to the electric locomotive. It is not shared by any other form of motive power—steam, diesel, or gas turbine, all of which are limited to the capacity of the primary power plant carried on board.

The heating of the motors is related to the current flowing, and this is shown on meters in the driving cab. Often part of the meter scale is coloured red to warn the driver that the pointer must only be allowed to stay there for a short time. Much has been done in recent years to improve the materials used in traction motor construction, particularly in their insulation, so that high temperatures can be tolerated for longer, and maximum use can be made of reserve power from the network for rapid acceleration after speed reductions and recovering lost time.

In early electric locomotives the body between the end cabs was virtually an engine room, the traction motors being mounted on the main frames and occupying much of the interior. The drive was transmitted from the motor shafts to the axles by various rod systems corresponding to the connecting and coupling rods of a steam locomotive. The geometry of the driving systems allowed for relative movement between the motors and the axles due to the springs, but the high motor mountings and heavy rods tended to make the locomotives top-heavy and unstable at speed. Therefore the next step was to transmit the drive through gears, as had been done from the beginning with electric motor coaches. In locomotives, however, much larger motors were involved, because all the power required to

haul a train had to be concentrated in one motive power unit instead of being distributed through the train. The motor coach practice of using small axle-hung motors in the bogies was not practicable and motors continued to be mounted on the main frames of the locomotives.

Designers still had the problem of accommodating changes in the centre-to-centre distance of the drives as the suspension springs flexed. Gearwheels could not be mounted directly on the axles because they would not mesh accurately with the motor pinions. Generally the solution was to mount the gearwheel on a hollow shaft, or quill, running in bearings at a fixed distance from the motor shaft, and to pass the axle through the quill with sufficient clearance for it to move up and down while revolving. The drive from quill to axle was provided by one of many forms of flexible linkage.

As long as traction motors remained on the main frames, the driving wheelbase had to be fixed, as in a steam locomotive, and so electric locomotive wheel arrangements followed steam locomotive patterns, with non-motored carrying axles in bogie or pony trucks fore and aft. Main-line locomotives were being built to this pattern right up to the 1950s. It was seen in the 4,000hp 4-8-4 locomotives built for the Paris to Lyons electrification of the French National Railways opened in 1952. These were descendants of a long line of French locomotives of the same wheel arrangement, and by the time they went into service another form of electric locomotive construction had already emerged, and one which was soon to become universal.

This new concept for main-line electric traction can be dated from four 4,000hp locomotives built for the Berne-Lötschberg Railway in Switzerland in 1945. Here for the first time it had been found possible to accommodate motors of 1,000hp in the bogies, taking advantage of advances in electrical and mechanical design and materials. The improvements were not confined to the motors, but extended to the design of the bogies themselves and the suspension of the body on them, so that the bogies could fill the dual function of driving and guiding the locomotive. Every axle was now a driving axle, and the whole weight of the locomotive was used for adhesion. The pattern for the modern electric locomotive had been set.

In electric locomotive wheel arrangement notation, motored axles are denoted by a letter (B for 2, C for 3 and so on) and non-motored axles by a figure. When an axle is driven by its own motor, a small letter 'o' is written after the letter. The Berne-Lötschberg-Simplon locomotives had two two-axle bogies, every axle driven by its own motor, and so their designation is Bo-Bo. In the French National Railways 4,000hp locomotives mentioned earlier there is a two-axle bogie at front and rear and a fixed four-axle driving wheelbase with independently-driven axles. This is the same as a steam 4-8-4 (steam notation being based on numbers of wheels, not axles). In electric notation it becomes 2-Do-2.

British main-line electrification began in the 1930s on the Southern Railway, and at first services were operated entirely by

motor-coach trains under multiple-unit control, freight continuing to be steam-hauled. At the beginning of the second world war, however, two 1,470hp electric locomotives were introduced on the SR for freight work and passenger services which could not be formed of multiple-unit stock, such as through trains to other parts of the railway system, and boat trains. These locomotives had two three-axle bogies with individual-axle drive (Co-Co). After the war numbers of 1,868hp four-axle (Bo-Bo) and 2,700hp six-axle (Co-Co) locomotives were built for freight and passenger work on the Eastern Region electrification between Sheffield and Manchester.

In all these designs the motors were of under 500hp and were axle-hung in the bogies in the same way as in motor coaches. In axle-hung suspension about half the motor weight rests directly on the axle, the remainder being supported from the bogie frame by some form of resilient mounting which allows the motor to rise and fall with movements of the axle. The more powerful motors in Continental locomotives of the same period, however, were solidly attached to the bogie frames so that the whole of their weight was spring-borne. As in the case of the earlier practice of carrying motors on the main frames, quill drives with flexible linkages were required, but by that time such transmissions were becoming lighter and smaller, and required less maintenance.

With the London Midland Region 25kV ac electrification from Euston to Manchester and Liverpool in the 1960s the need for more-powerful electric loco-

motives arose in Britain, and the first designs were Bo-Bos of about 3,300hp, so that individual motor outputs were around 850hp. All the first 100 new locomotives followed the Continental practice of fully spring-borne motors in the bogies with flexible drives to the axles. Flexible transmissions had long been a source of controversy among traction engineers, and one school of thought held that the modern traction motor could stand up to the shocks it received at speed when axle-hung. The second series of 100 locomotives for the Euston-Manchester-Liverpool routes, rated at first at 3,600hp, but later increased in some cases to 4,000hp, reverted to axle-hung motors. However, since their introduction in 1967 experience has shown that the use of fully spring-borne motors is justified on high-speed routes by the saving in wear and tear of the permanent way. This practice was followed in the new 5,100hp locomotives for the electrification extension to Glasgow.

For most of the 1960s the favoured type of main-line electric locomotive was a Bo-Bo of about 80 tons weight and a rating between 3,000 and 5,000hp. This was true for all systems of electrification. After dropping the 2-Do-2 type in favour of a Co-Co wheel arrangement in the early 1950s, the French National Railways started experimenting with Bo-Bo designs and soon ordered them in large numbers both for its 1,500V dc and 25kV ac lines. South Africa had imported from Britain in the 1950s some 3,030hp 3,000V dc electric locomotives with two three-axle motor bogies and carrying axles fore and

aft (1Co-Co1), but its next order was for a Bo-Bo of 2,020hp, the policy being to double-head trains when more power was needed. In the latest version of the Bo-Bo locomotives the output has been raised to 3,340hp by improvements in motor design. These are remarkable achievements considering the dimensional constraints of the 3ft 6in gauge of South African Railways.

The same trend was seen on railways with low-frequency ac electrification. Switzerland followed its 6,000hp Co-Cos for the Gotthard line with a prototype 5,540hp Bo-Bo equipped for working in pairs when necessary, and later uprated a production series to 6,050hp. After a locomotive standardisation programme in Western Germany the railways were equipped with several Bo-Bo classes, the most powerful of which was rated at 4,850hp.

It is a sign of the vigour of the railway industry that nothing is static. Already the Co-Co locomotive is beginning to re-appear for certain duties which were barely contemplated a decade ago. The need to maintain tractive effort at speeds up to 125mph has brought the demand for still higher horsepower and so the 8,000hp electric locomotive carried on two three-axle bogies is now a reality. Germany has its 103 class for low-frequency ac, and France its 21000, 14500 and 6500 classes, the first covering both standard-frequency ac (50Hz) and 1,500V dc operation, and the other two being for standard-frequency ac and 1,500V dc respectively.

It is still general practice for each axle

of an electric locomotive to be driven by its own motor, but there are some noteworthy exceptions. In several French locomotive classes there is only one large motor in each bogie and this drives all axles through trains of gears. Often two ratios are provided and can be selected from inside the locomotive when it is at a standstill. In this way the range of duties that can be undertaken economically by one locomotive—already wide in electric traction—is still further extended. The coupling of the axles in each bogie through the gears reduces the chance of wheelspin on greasy rail.

The biggest changes in the internal equipment of electric locomotives have taken place on railways using 25kV ac at the standard industrial frequency of 50Hz. As on any ac system, the largest single piece of apparatus is the transformer, with which there is usually associated a motor-driven tap-changer to control the voltage applied to the traction motors. Between the transformer and the motors, however, it is now usual to connect semiconductor rectifiers which convert the ac into dc. There is always a residual 'ripple' in dc produced by rectifying a single-phase supply such as is used on railways and this is minimised by smoothing chokes, which in themselves are quite bulky and heavy items to fit into a locomotive.

A dc supply is also needed to charge the locomotive battery, because certain essential services must be battery-powered if there is no supply for traction. Usually this auxiliary dc is taken from a separate small rectifier instead of from a motor-generator set.

In some ac locomotives the traction rectifiers consist partly of thyristors, which both rectify the ac input and allow the dc output voltage to be controlled electronically without using a tap-changer. It is not practicable for one group of thyristors to cover the whole range from zero to the full traction motor voltage and so the cells are arranged in two or more groups which act in sequence. Some switching may be involved in changing from group to group, but it is much simpler than the conventional tap-changing process and varies the voltage so gradually that the system is often called 'stepless control'. Sudden increases in voltage as the driver increases power when starting a heavy train can start wheelspin, and so the smooth build-up possible with thyristors enables the best use to be made of the adhesive weight of the locomotive.

In dc traction the motor voltage is still usually controlled by resistances and changes of motor grouping. Exceptions are the Southern Region electric and electro-diesel (electric with auxiliary diesel power) locomotives in which power from the third rail drives a motor-generator set. The generator output first opposes and then boosts the third-rail supply, which process enables the voltage applied to the traction motors to be varied from zero to maximum without wasting power in resistances in the main motor circuit.

Another alternative to resistance control for dc locomotives is just coming into the picture. It is called 'chopper' control, and uses thyristors as on/off switches which act in a similar way to the contacts of a vibrating voltage regulator. Installations are working satisfactorily in motor coaches, and a 3,000V dc chopper locomotive is ready for trials in Italy.

Getting an electric locomotive on the move with its train by increasing the power—'notching up'—calls for skill in keeping the current within the safe limits. In most modern locomotives the driver's controller has two main positions. In one position the equipment notches up automatically, but the process can be stopped at any stage by moving the lever back a step. The second position enables the driver to notch up manually by moving the lever up to it and back again. Each to-and-fro action advances the equipment one notch.

In addition to the development of locomotives for the separate ac and dc systems, recent years have seen the emergence of locomotives able to work on both types of supply. The ac locomotive with rectifiers has made this possible, because it is 'half dc' anyway, and so when it reaches dc territory the supply is simply switched directly to the power circuit, bypassing the transformer and rectifiers. Belgium, France and Germany all have locomotives which can work on the two ac systems (low- and standard-frequency) and the two dc voltages (1,500V and 3,000V) used on the main lines of the European Continent. Some countries remain faithful to the systems of electrification they have developed over many years, but the traveller in the international electric expresses of today passes from one system to another without being aware of it.

5
Passenger Vehicles

Facing page: Painting by C Hamilton Ellis of
ex-Caledonian Railway River-class No 14759
at Blair Atholl. *C Hamilton Ellis*

DEVELOPMENT OF PASSENGER SERVICES TO 1900

IN THE LATTER PART of the nineteenth century some of the principal British railway companies had become convinced that speed had no special virtues and that to achieve fast runs required an unwarrantable consumption of locomotive coal. The South Eastern Railway definitely forbade speeds in excess of 60mph in the rule book. Even where companies were in direct rivalry, the one with the longer route very often dictated the time. The small engine policy initiated by Bury on the London & Birmingham and weak underline bridgework that prevented mechanical engineers from building bigger machines made it easy to justify moderate speeds, because thrashing of inadequate locomotives inevitably led to an eruption of live cinders from the chimney and an excessive coal bill.

Pinchpenny restrictions did not apply to the Great Northern, which as a latecomer to London felt its competitive position must be maintained by a reputation for fast travel. This gave edge to its shorter mileage to towns east of the Pennines and even justified expresses over its roundabout route to Manchester over the Manchester, Sheffield & Lincolnshire Railway from Retford. This Manchester service began in 1883, with 100-ton trains which covered the 105½ miles from Grantham to Kings Cross in 124 and later 117 minutes. In 1880 there were also Leeds expresses from London in 3¾ hours. Maxima of over 70mph were common with the Stirling 8ft singles.

On the Great Western, which had been at pains in earlier years to show the speed capabilities of its 7ft gauge, the trains that averaged much more than 40mph were few and far between; dilatory schedules were made worse by the 10-minute compulsory refreshment stop at Swindon, which was eventually eliminated in 1895 by buying out the lessees, whose rights extended to 1940. In the eighteen-eighties there were two trains that averaged nearly 46mph between London and Exeter, but on the South Wales line the Irish boat express to Milford could claim only 35mph. The great awakening came after the retirement of G N Tyrell as superintendent of the line. Whereas in 1887 there were five morning trains from Paddington only one' of which could be called express, by the end of the century there were 11 trains in the same period, of which eight qualified.

High speeds by a few holiday trains began towards the end of the century; the

Above left: Comic cartoon of a German train departure in 1895, in which a ticket collector warns the young lady blowing a kiss to the man on the platform that it is forbidden to throw things from the window. *DB Film Archiv*

Left: The well-known Frith painting of the 1850s 'The Railway Station', depicting London Paddington station, the original of which hung for many years at Hanover station in Germany. *DB Film Archiv*

Below: A rail travel study by Lance Calkin: 'Third Class' from 'The Graphic' of December 4, 1904.

present direct 107½-mile route to Bournemouth opened in 1888 with a train taking 147 minutes; in 1898 a 2hr 5min non-stop became one of the fastest bookings in the country. The Great Eastern Cromer expresses in 1897 ran non-stop from Liverpool Street to North Walsham, 131 miles at 49mph. The North Eastern, which had thought 30mph a good average for its Scarborough trains, called for 50mph running from York to the sea from 1898.

Whereas on the London & North Western in 1889 the train called by popular acclaim the 'Wild Irishman' averaged only just over 40mph to Holyhead, the Midland had a Scottish train which averaged 52mph from St Pancras to Leicester and 48mph through the Pennines from Skipton to Carlisle. In the 'nineties the leaven of the 1888 and 1895 races to Scotland worked on many services, resulting in faster runs, dining cars, corridor trains and some curious through carriage workings. Although Bradshaw was often dubbed a work of fiction, it is safe to say that Britain made a better showing than most of Europe for speed and frequency and certainly better than most of the USA, where 25mph was often about the top average.

RAILWAY TRAVELLING AS IT OUGHT TO BE.

Guard. "Did you Ring, Sir?" Passenger. "Yes. Where are we now?"
Guard. "Just passing Donkeysbridge, Sir. Shan't Stop till we get to Stunnington, Forty Miles further on."
Passenger. "Oh! Ah! Then just Bring me another Sherry-and-Soda, and a Cigar, and Two or Three more Volumes of Punch."
Guard. "Yessir."

Above: Early twentieth-century 'Punch' representation of rail travel as it ought to be.
Punch Library

Right: By the time of the Pearson-designed Rothwell 10-wheel tank engine for passenger work in 1853, the flangeless drivers had grown to 9ft diameter.
Science Museum London

Contrasting standards in British passenger travel in 1854, as depicted in paintings by Abraham Solomon: first-class (below) and third-class (overleaf).

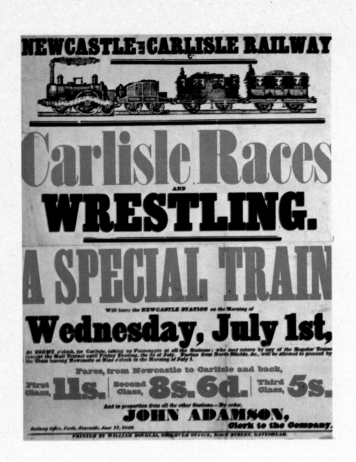

NEWCASTLE AND CARLISLE RAILWAY

Carlisle Races
AND
WRESTLING.

A SPECIAL TRAIN

Will leave the NEWCASTLE STATION on the Morning of

Wednesday, July 1st,

At EIGHT o'clock for Carlisle, taking up Passengers at all the Stations; who may return by any of the Regular Trains (except the Mail Trains) until Friday Evening, the 3d of July. Parties from North Shields, &c., will be allowed to proceed by the Train leaving Newcastle at Nine o'clock in the Morning of July 1.

Fares, from Newcastle to Carlisle and back,

First Class, **11s.** | Second Class, **8s. 6d.** | Third Class, **5s.**

And in proportion from all the other Stations.—By order,

JOHN ADAMSON,
Clerk to the Company.

Railway Office, Forth, Newcastle, June 17, 1846.

PRINTED BY WILLIAM DOUGLAS, OBSERVER OFFICE, High Street, Gateshead.

Midland and North Eastern Railways.
GARIBALDI
DEMONSTRATION
AT THE CRYSTAL PALACE.

On SATURDAY, APRIL 16,
A Cheap Excursion Train will leave
HULL, SELBY, YORK
And the undermentioned Stations for
LONDON
(KING'S CROSS STATION)

FARES THERE AND BACK AND TIMES OF STARTING.

Stations		a.m.	FIRST CLASS	COVERED CARS
Hull	dep.	6. 0		
Howden	"	6.54	25 0	12 6
Selby	"	7.20		
York	"	7.15		
Church Fenton	"	7.43	21 0	10 6
Milford	"	8. 2		

LONDON (KING'S CROSS) ARRIVE ABOUT 4.45 P.M.

Children under Three years of Age Free; above Three and under Twelve, Half-fare.

The Return Train will leave the King's Cross Station, London, on Wednesday, April 20th, at 10.15 a.m.

Tickets are not transferable, and will be available for returning by this Train only.
Luggage must be conveyed under the Passengers' own care, as the Company will not be responsible.
Ten Minutes will be allowed at Trent Station for Refreshments both in going and returning.

Derby, April 1864.

BY ORDER.

Bemrose and Sons, Printers by Steam Power, Derby.

Top left: Early excursion handbill from the Newcastle & Carlisle Railway, 1846.
British Transport Museum (B Sharpe)

Top right: 1864 handbill advertising a cheap excursion to London.
British Transport Museum (B Sharpe)

Left: A Dutch painting of a carriage interior of 1885 by Constant Cap (1842-1915)
Nederlandse Spoorwegen Museum Utrecht

Below: 1930s poster by A R Thomson for the LNER's Flying Scotsman.
British Transport Museum (B Sharpe)

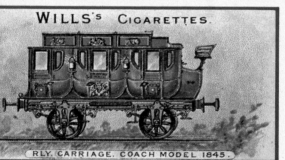

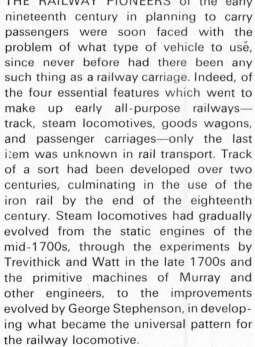

Top left and above left: Passenger coaches of the Liverpool & Manchester Railway, formally opened in 1830, an open-top third-class and a first-class vehicle. Both are replicas at the Birmingham Railway Museum.

Above: Engraving from 'The Illustrated London News' of May 29, 1858, of a 'summer saloon' coach produced at Saltley works, Birmingham, for the Viceroy of Egypt.
Illustrated London News

Left: Artist's impression of a first-class railway carriage based on road coach practice, as used on the London & Birmingham Railway in the early 1840s, from the Wills's cigarette card series.

Development of the Railway Carriage

THE RAILWAY PIONEERS of the early nineteenth century in planning to carry passengers were soon faced with the problem of what type of vehicle to use, since never before had there been any such thing as a railway carriage. Indeed, of the four essential features which went to make up early all-purpose railways—track, steam locomotives, goods wagons, and passenger carriages—only the last item was unknown in rail transport. Track of a sort had been developed over two centuries, culminating in the use of the iron rail by the end of the eighteenth century. Steam locomotives had gradually evolved from the static engines of the mid-1700s, through the experiments by Trevithick and Watt in the late 1700s and the primitive machines of Murray and other engineers, to the improvements evolved by George Stephenson, in developing what became the universal pattern for the railway locomotive.

Wagons running on tracks for the transport of coal, stone and so on had been used for nearly 300 years, but passenger carriages, specifically for railway use, had not been seen before. Thus it was inevitable that the engineers of the first passenger railways, the Swansea & Mumbles in 1807 and the Stockton & Darlington in 1825, should have turned to existing road vehicles for inspiration and the first railway coaches were little more than road coaches on railway wheels. Indeed, with horse traction employed on

the first lines there was hardly any difference between road and rail carriages. With the adoption of steam locomotives which could haul far greater loads, several carriages could be coupled together to form a train. It was soon realised that it was not necessary to provide individual wheels to each single carriage body and two or three bodies were mounted together on one underframe to form a longer carriage with separate compartments. Thus was born, at the dawn of railways, the traditional British compartment carriage which is only now disappearing from the railway scene.

The British class system, with its divisions into the wealthy, the middle class and the poor, immediately made its mark on the railways. Until the coming of the steam railway the horse had been the fastest means of transport, travelling at speeds of 20mph or more singly with a solo rider, between 10 and 15mph in pairs or fours hauling road coaches, and at little more than walking pace hauling the great lumbering goods wagons which usually carried a fair proportion of poorer travellers. In practice, it was largely only the wealthy who travelled around the country, for the average working man was tied to his place of work on the farm or the developing factories of the industrial revolution. The wealthiest had their own private carriages and horses, while merchants and others who needed to travel frequently took the express stage or mail

coaches. Many road carriages had two classes of travel—inside or outside. Inside was the most luxurious with well-padded seats for four or six passengers, but outside passengers were subject to the vagaries of the English climate. Apart from the main passenger compartment, the coach usually had a boot at the back for the carriage of mailbags or valuables, while luggage was carried on the roof between or behind the outside passenger seats.

It was this sort of vehicle that was adapted for railway use, even to the boot, and racks on the roof for luggage. The road coach body was followed almost to the last detail, with the curved panelling and decorative mouldings of the body-sides. However, for obvious reasons passengers did not ride on the roofs of railway coaches; second-class passengers were given separate coaches, more austere in design than the best, sometimes consisting of little more than a wooden box on wheels with seats inside, and a door with a space instead of a glazed window. The equivalent of the slow road wagon used by the poorest travellers was the open carriage, in effect, nothing more than a goods wagon fitted with seats, with holes in the bottom to let out the water when it rained; such was the miserable beginning of the third class. Some railways did not even take third-class passengers; if they did the carriages were often attached to goods trains, or ran only at night. Flat wagons were also run on some railways to

carry private road carriages for those who preferred to travel in their own vehicle—virtually a forerunner of today's Motorail trains.

These primitive railway carriages were very small by today's standards; nearly all were four-wheelers with a length of about 20ft, a width of about 6ft and a body height of 6-7ft. There was little improvement when the first of what became trunk railways—the Liverpool & Manchester (1830), London & Birmingham (1837), and the London & Southampton (1840)—were opened. Only the Great Western, which opened its first section in 1838, brought any marked improvement, largely because the company adopted the broad gauge of 7ft 0¼in compared with the standard Stephenson gauge of 4ft 8½in. From the start, Great Western first- and second-class coaches were carried on six wheels and the bodies were much wider (9-10ft) and longer, (30ft or more). The Great Western also built some saloons of much the same size but with a central entrance and seats arranged around the sides of the coach, facing inwards. These coaches were also distinguished with clerestory roofs, that

is, a roof in which a centre section is raised along its length above the side sections with windows in the sides of the top deck. This form of construction was often used in buildings, churches for example, and it was to be seen in railway use on and off for nearly a century. Other than that carriage roofs at that period were almost flat, with only a slight trace of curvature.

It was not possible to stop a train travelling at speeds higher than 20mph very quickly using the locomotive brakes, certainly not as rapidly as a horse-drawn road carriage, so hand brakes were fitted to railway carriages and were operated by guards or brakesmen riding on the roof of selected coaches of each train. They took their cue from the engine driver or front guard who signalled to apply the brakes. Because of the smoke and cinders from the engine, which might have injured the brakesmen, special brake carriages were fitted with enclosed observation look-out positions above roof level to allow the brakesmen to see over the top of the carriages ahead. This form of vantage point was given the name of a lantern or

birdcage roof and could be found on certain brake vans in Britain until recent times. Other railways provided guards with a side observation window known as a ducket.

Gradually passengers were provided with lights at night, but they consisted of nothing more than an oil lamp which was sometimes shared between two compartments. Lamps were dropped in through the roof by a lampman who walked along the train at a convenient station.

During the 1840s and 50s passenger amenities improved slightly; after the passing of Gladstone's Regulation of Railways Act in 1844—which among other things provided that railways must run at least one train a day conveying third-class passengers in covered carriages, at an average speed of not less than 12mph, for a fare of not more than one penny a mile—the lot of the third-class passenger was better than it had been. Carriages themselves had also improved, they were longer—between 30 and 35ft, wider—between 7 and 8ft (except on the Great Western), and there was usually one light to each compartment. First-class coaches were luxuriously upholstered with padded seats and backs, arm and head rests and carpets. Second-class coaches usually had some form of padding in seats but were more austere, while third-class coaches had wooden seats and plain wooden partitions, if indeed they had partitions at all. Some third-class coaches were arranged in the form of one open saloon with benches across the middle and only one or two external doors. Sometimes there were no windows other than in the doors. If the third-class coaches seemed very poor and spartan to our eyes today it must be remembered that the habits and manners of some travellers were not exactly hygenic and many did not know how to behave in public. Clothing, too, was often dirty.

From the middle of the 19th century private saloon carriages began to make their appearance on railways. They were vehicles equipped for carrying families with servants, and were attached as required to ordinary trains; some even contained a bed for carrying invalids. It is in the private carriages, and the royal saloons of the period built for Queen Victoria, that we see the first signs of real improvement in passenger comfort. Many features now taken for granted as a normal part of rail travel—toilet facilities, heating,

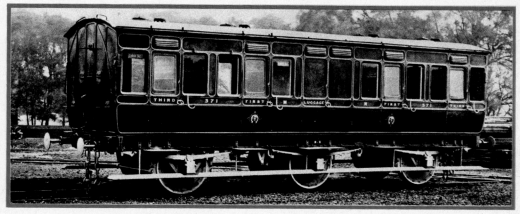

Far left: Magnificent interior of sitting room of Queen Victoria's saloon on the LNWR, built in 1869. *British Transport Museum*

Above left: A mixed-class coach of the Bodmin & Wadebridge Railway (originally all first-class) showing direct descent from road coaches typical of earliest railway carriage practice.

Above: Mixed-class coach of the LNWR of 1862, still retaining traces of road vehicle styling. *Science Museum London*

Above right: Third-class Highland Railway coach of the 1860s; end smoking compartments are enclosed, others are open above seatbacks.

Right: Standard Midland Railway six-wheel mixed-class coach of the 1870s. *British Railways LMR*

refreshments and sleeping berths—first saw the light of day in a primitive form in mid-Victorian saloon carriages. The first sleeping facilities, for example, were in what were known as bed carriages, in which a form of stretcher bridged the gap between facing seats in a compartment to allow the passenger to lie down. This can be seen today in the surviving bed carriage preserved in the collection at Clapham Museum. It was originally used by Queen Adelaide on the London & Birmingham Railway from 1842, but because the compartment provided no more than 5ft between partitions the bed extended into the boot at the end of the coach.

Toilets were provided in some saloons, consisting of simple hoppers opening out on to the track beneath the floor, a primitive and extremely unhygenic system, but one which survives in modified form today. Queen Victoria's pair of six-wheel saloons built in 1869, respectively for day and night travel, had inter-coach gangways to allow the royal passengers to pass from one to the other through the coach ends, and a pantry in which hot drinks could be prepared.

By the 1870s sleeping saloons with proper beds had also been introduced. They were not always arranged in compartments and some beds were in large saloons, respectively for men and women. Nevertheless, the sleeping saloon did not come into wide use for another 20 years or so. During the 1870s railway carriages again increased in size, particularly in length, a development permitted by the introduction of bogies, that is pivoted trucks carrying the wheels, placed at each end of the coach underframe. Bogies gave a much smoother ride than rigid four- or six-wheel types, or indeed the fixed eight-wheel arrangement which had been tried by some companies. Bogies were able to take curves more easily and could ride up

and down track imperfections without transmitting the inequalities to the coach body. They were adopted first in Britain from the early 1870s but had been used in America, particularly, for some years before that.

Indeed, in North America the four- and six-wheel rigid-wheelbase coach was virtually unknown. So, too, were compartments, for American carriages were usually massive clerestory-roofed saloons entered through open balconies at the ends, with the seats arranged on each side of a central passageway. This was the traditional American carriage (or car as it was known) from the start of railways in North America. In Europe many railways followed British practice, inevitably, perhaps, since numerous lines were built or designed by British engineers. Thus the compartment coach was normally used in Europe, although some railways preferred the American-pattern end-balcony type.

The 1870s marked the end of what might be termed first-generation railway carriages, for gradually from that time onwards carriages took on the shape more familiar to our own eyes and looked less like the road coaches of the previous century. The introduction of bogies, while allowing longer coaches to be built, brought a problem. On some lines carriage length was restricted by the need to avoid bridging fouling bars at facing points in the track. Fouling bars consisted of a length of steel angle connected to a bolt which locked point switches one way or the other, depending on which route the train was to take. The bars were made longer than the distance between any two pairs of wheels on a passing train and were located alongside the rail in such a way that the wheels of a train passing over prevented the bar from being lifted and the points unbolted. This was a safety device evolved to prevent points being moved

under a train. On some lines before longer coaches could be built all facing point lock fouling bars had to be lengthened.

Nearly all coaches in ordinary service, whether for main or local lines, were of the non-corridor compartment type and it was not until the 1870s that toilets began to be provided on a few coaches used on long-distance trains. Even then they were at first connected to only one or two compartments and only for first-class passengers. It was not until 1882 that the first side-corridor coach appeared, a six-wheeled vehicle on the Great Northern Railway in which passengers in the compartments could reach toilets at the ends of the coach.

The Midland Railway created a stir in railway circles in the mid-1870s by abolishing second class and conveying first- and third-class coaches by all trains. Moreover, it provided third-class passengers with padded seats. Not content with such a revolutionary move it introduced Pullman cars to Britain. They were massive American-built cars with end balconies and domed clerestory roofs. There were several types of car, including day saloons with open interiors and armchair seats, and convertible saloons for night use. They were equipped with pairs of facing seats, on each side of a central passageway, which could be extended towards each other to form a bed, while a second upper berth, folded away against the roof during the day, could be lowered at night to allow passengers to sleep one above the other. Curtains on each side of the passageway provided privacy between each section.

Despite the Midland's enterprise, Pullmans were not an outstanding success, although the cars survived for many years and spread at times to other railways. A noteworthy user was the London-Brighton line, where daytime Pullman

saloons were a feature of Brighton services for the next 90 years, culminating in the Southern Railway electric Pullmans, including the Brighton Belle, which survived until 1972.

In 1879 the Great Northern Railway introduced the first dining car to Britain, a Pullman vehicle, and during the following decade railway-owned dining cars appeared on a number of long-distance routes, particularly those between London and the North. Apart from Pullman cars there was still no means for passengers to move from one coach to another while the train was running and passengers had to join and leave dining cars at an intermediate station or travel all the way in the diner. It was not until 1892 that the first true corridor train with inter-coach gangways was introduced, on the Great Western Railway. The ordinary coaches were still of the compartment type but with a side corridor extending from one end to the other; dining cars naturally were of the open pattern with a centre passageway and seats on each side.

Other improvements to passenger comfort were taking place with better lighting and heating. Old oil lamps gradually gave way to compressed oil gas, and experiments were being conducted with electricity. Unfortunately electrical equipment of the time was very heavy and cumbersome and gas was the principal means of illumination on trains for some years to come. It was also highly imflammable, which the railways found to their cost in

Top: Preserved corridor-third carriage of East Coast Joint stock, built in 1898 by the North Eastern to Great Northern design, as restored for Kings Cross station centenary.

Above centre: GWR corridor-brake-third of 1892, one of the first side-corridor coaches for full-length corridor trains. *British Railways WR*

Above left and right: Two views of luxurious first-class accommodation in a South Eastern Railway new vestibule train, from 'The Graphic' of November 9, 1897. *Illustrated London News*

Below: GWR carriage for Queen Victoria as restored, now preserved by Dart Valley Railway. *G R Hounsell*

the number of accidents when crashed carriages caught fire. Primitive forms of heating were being tried by using steam from the locomotive passed through a pipe down the train to heat radiators in the coaches. But many companies still pro-

vided no heat at all and passengers had to rely on warm clothing and footwarmers, metal containers filled with hot water and sodium acetate which could be hired by passengers.

By the last decade of the century all trains had to be equipped with continuous power brakes, which had been made compulsory by the Regulation of Railways Act in 1889. They were operated by differences in air pressure in either a compressed-air or vacuum system in such a way that if the train became uncoupled or if a passenger operated the alarm signal the brakes were applied automatically, apart of course from normal brake applications by the driver.

This was a period of considerable contrast in railway carriage design; there were still thousands of four- and six-wheel coaches on local and main-line stopping services and they appeared quite diminutive alongside the newest bogie vehicles. By then the latest of them were massive 12-wheel types on two six-wheel bogies, more than 60ft long and 9ft wide, mostly with clerestory roofs. Indeed, the clerestory roof reached its zenith towards the turn of the century and was used by many railways in an attempt to provide better daytime lighting and ventilation. On the debit side was the higher cost than the otherwise low-arc roof and the fact that it was not always weatherproof, so that rain sometimes seeped through joints in the clerestory deck.

Gradually other companies, particularly those in the north, followed the Midland's example by abolishing second-class accommodation; sleeping cars had become general on overnight services between London, the North of England, Scotland and the West Country, but were still only for first-class passengers. The standard form of sleeping car was a side corridor compartment coach with single berths or beds in each compartment.

The turn of the century marked the start of a period of great opulence in railway carriage design and passenger comfort. The period had also brought a vast increase in train weights, which meant that locomotives had to be larger and more powerful. This was the high-water mark in passenger comfort in everyday service. Speeds may have been comparatively slow, but this, for first-class passengers, was more than adequately compensated by luxurious accommodation.

Top left: Standard GWR third-class corridor coach of the late 1920s. *British Railways WR*

Top right: Saloon and buffet of a GWR twin diesel railcar set of the late 1930s. *British Railways WR*

Above: LMS semi-open first of the early 1930s, the near end of which featured corner seating for every passenger. *British Railways LMR*

Left: Midland and Glasgow & South Western joint stock 12-wheeled dining car with clerestory roof built in 1914 and now preserved. *British Railways*

Top of page: A rare form of Birdcage coach, a corridor brake tri-composite. *G M Kichenside*

The decade between the end of Queen Victoria's reign and the outbreak of the first world war saw the peak of British carriage development; until that time coaches had gradually been getting longer, higher and wider, to reach the maximum dimensions permitted by the British loading gauge. This allowed a width of about 9ft and a height from rail of nearly 13ft, with lengths varying between 50ft and 65ft. On the Great Western, however, the broad gauge had left its mark for the generous clearances provided by Brunel's 7ft gauge, finally abolished in 1892, meant that even after standard gauge had been adopted throughout the GWR the principal former broad-gauge lines could take coaches and locomotives wider and longer

than on other railways. In 1905 the Great Western produced some of the widest and longest coaches seen on a British railway until that time, or indeed since. Nicknamed Dreadnoughts, they were no less than 70ft long and 9ft 7in wide, with high elliptical roofs.

The same period saw the beginning of the decline of the clerestory roof on all railways that had used it, except the Midland, which continued to build clerestory stock until the end of the 1914-18 war, and on London Underground stock, where it was employed more for ventilation purposes than added daylight, until the mid-1930s. A few clerestory-roofed examples survive today on one or two lines of London Transport and on former

underground coaches currently in use on the Isle of Wight. The true clerestory as used on main line stock, however, was employed to improve natural lighting with windows in the roof-deck side. A disadvantage was that after dark, lighting a clerestory coach was a problem; if only one light was provided in each compartment it tended to be suspended high in the clerestory, causing shadows; alternatively two lights (and greater cost) were needed. At that period gas lighting was generally employed and the incandescent burners, reflectors and massive glass globes took up a considerable space below the roof.

There were other disadvantages. The construction of the clerestory roof was complex since the roof itself was in three parts, respectively the two lower side decks and the raised top deck, all of which needed separate framing. Although a wooden-bodied coach did not stand up very well in a serious accident in any case, the clerestory roof weakened the whole coach by virtually breaking the back of the coach down the middle. Until the coming of the clerestory, the normal shape of roof was in the form of a low arc but the new century saw the development of non-clerestory stock with higher roofs, first the semi-ellipse with the sides curving sharply down to meet the body side, and then the high elliptical roof, familiar today. Modern construction in fact gives a much lighter and more spacious effect, despite the loss of natural light through roof glazing.

Although gas continued to be the normal lighting medium for several years to come, and did not disappear finally in Britain until the early 1960s, electricity was gradually adopted for carriage lighting for its greater effectiveness and better safety in an accident. The first experiments in electric lighting had taken place in the 1880s but some railways were slow to adopt it because the method of generation, which had become standardised, by belts from coach axles driving dynamos to charge batteries, added to the friction and rolling resistance of the train, so that more-powerful engines were needed. It was all part of the general trend towards heavier trains brought about by the introduction of corridor stock, which increased the train weight per passenger and was considered a retrograde step by some companies. It took a number of accidents just before the 1914-18 war, culminating in the worst disaster ever on a British railway at Quintinshill in 1915, in which train wreckage caught fire from escaping gas, to convince the pro-gas faction of its dangers.

Edwardian main-line railway carriages also reached a peak in sumptuous appointment, particularly in first-class coaches, with deep well-padded and sprung seats, velvet upholstery, carpets, padded body sides, ornate decoration, including panelled ceilings, curtains and, on electrically-lit stock, ornamental lighting. Second class, although still well in evidence was dying and becoming merged with third class (except in the South of England where second class survived until the 1920s). Third-class compartments had become comfortably appointed, if at times somewhat spartan. From the Midland Railway's revolution of the 1870s by providing the third-class passenger with padded upholstered seats, all railways provided reasonably comfortable third-class accommodation, far superior to anything found on the European mainland.

The movement of commuters by rail (to use the comparatively recent and

Left top to bottom: Stanier corridor third circa 1935, the standard LMS type for the decade before and after the second world war. *G M Kichenside*

Southern Railway Maunsell 1st/3rd corridor coach of the 1930s found all over the system on the SR steam services. *G M Kichenside*

An ex-SECR saloon coach as used on the Isle of Wight during the 1940s and 50s. *G M Kichenside*

Typical BR diesel multiple-unit of the 1950s; this one was built by Wickham of Ware and is seen at Kings Lynn, Norfolk. *G M Kichenside*

Top: Standard 3rd class non-smoking compartment of LMS corridor stock from mid-1930s featuring armrests, a new feature of LMS long-distance third-class stock. *British Railways*

Above: Great Eastern Railway turn-of-the-century device for widening suburban coaches. *British Railways*

convenient American description) by the turn of the century was beginning to reach large proportions, although journeys were generally short and the suburbs around London at least were only five to ten miles out from the city centre. The underground system had hardly begun, the motorbus and private car had yet to be developed, and electric tramways were in their infancy. Thus the railways had a monopoly in taking people to and from work and the new habit of living at a distance from one's workplace was encouraged by a policy of frequent trains and cheap workmen's fares. The trains themselves were almost invariably formed of long rakes of four-wheelers with narrow compartments. The Third-class coaches had low seat backs and no partitions, just like their predecessors 60 years earlier.

The problem was to get as many people on to a train as possible, in the 8ft width of what had become the basic standard suburban carriage, which permitted only five passengers to sit side by side. The Great Eastern Railway, realising that its loading gauge allowed coaches to be another foot wider, and not wishing to scrap its existing stock, carried out a surgical operation by cutting the 8ft-wide coaches down the middle lengthways, splicing in new frames and panelling which increased the width to 9ft, thus allowing 12 passengers to be seated in each third-class compartment instead of the previous ten. Moreover, some of the four-wheel coach bodies were placed in pairs on new bogie underframes, which improved the riding. In fact, bogie coaches were generally built from then on for suburban use, although four- and six-wheelers continued to be built by some companies up to the 1914-18 war, and by the Caledonian as late as 1923 (by which time it had become part of the LMS).

The 1914-18 war marked the end of an era, for it changed the way of life, not only for everyone in Great Britain but throughout Western Europe. It hastened the development of the internal-combustion engine which brought the expansion of private motoring and a resurgence of public road transport which challenged the railways for traffic. The electric tram had eaten into city suburban rail services, many of which closed down, and although another 40 years were to pass before major rail closures began to take effect, life on the railways was never quite the same after the war. In all aspects economy became the watchword and although the railways regained some of their vitality during the 1920s and '30s it was not in the same form as in Victorian and Edwardian days

After 1918 the railways, which had become run down by wartime activities, recovered only slowly and it was clear that the 100 or so companies in existence needed a massive reorganisation. Under a 1921 Act of Parliament, four major companies were set up to take over practically all the companies in existence

until that time. The grouping opened the way to standardisation of equipment, including locomotives and coaches, to bring considerable economy in construction and maintenance.

Although nobody realised it at the time, it was also the start of the decline of the steam locomotive. Pioneer electric railways appeared in the 1880s and the first conversions of main lines to electric traction took place in the Edwardian years with the introduction of electric working in the Newcastle, Liverpool and London areas in 1903-5. All three of those early electric systems employed similar types of coach which were new to passengers used to the traditional compartment carriage. They were based on American designs, and internally were laid out in open saloons with seats each side of a central passageway and entry through end doors or open end balconies. In London, the saloon coach had already been used by the first deep-level tube railways of the 1890s, in which side swing doors were precluded by limited tunnel clearances; it was now adopted on the sub-surface Metropolitan and District railways also. In Liverpool, the Mersey Railway used saloon coaches, as did the Lancashire & Yorkshire on its Liverpool-Southport line. The Liverpool-Southport coaches were distinguished by being the widest in the country, with a body width of 10ft.

During the 1914-18 war, further London suburban lines were converted to electric operation, accelerated by the need to release steam engines for war traffic. The London & North Western adopted saloon coaches with end doors but the London & South Western employed traditional compartment coaches; indeed, its electric trains were rebuilt from steam-hauled vehicles. Conversion was also used extensively on the newly formed Southern Railway after the grouping for its suburban electrifications of the 1920s and 1930s. Often the rebuilding was quite elaborate, with parts from two or even three older carriages being mounted on new bogie underframes. Although the Southern carried heavy commuter traffic, the 8ft-wide coach body surprisingly persisted and there was nothing like the Great Eastern's splicing operation.

For main-line service, new designs soon appeared on the four group companies, some bearing a considerable likeness to previous pre-grouping types. On the LMS, for example, it was the Midland carriage superintendent, R W Reid, who took over the similar post of the newly formed company and it was not surprising that Midland practices became the new standard. Timber bodies on steel underframes were standardised and Derby Works was reorganised to produce wooden bodied coaches on mass-production lines. Although coaches could be built much more quickly by new methods, the demands of the LMS re-equipment outpaced the capacity of the various LMS carriage works and over 200 all-steel coaches were built for the LMS by outside contractors. All were open vehicles with seats on each side of a central passageway and end doors; open coaches had been used for dining purposes from the 1890s, but they were a complete break from the traditional side-corridor compartment coach for ordinary travel.

Yet the time of the all-steel coach had not really arrived and timber construction was still cheaper than steel. On the LNER, Gresley, who had come from the Great Northern Railway, continued to use the teak-bodied coach, unpainted on the outside and simply varnished over the natural wood. The Great Western had begun to use steel body panelling over timber framing, which obviated the need for decorative wooden mouldings covering body panel joints which had characterised railway carriages for nearly a century. On the LMS steel coaches, mentioned above, it was felt that the plain steel sides needed decoration, so an ornate panel lining was painted on to look like wooden mouldings!

On the Southern Railway, Maunsell, the chief mechanical engineer, introduced new designs; until then, apart from a few corridor trains on the London & South Western and for Continental boat train use on the South Eastern & Chatham, corridor trains were a rarity in Southern England. Distances were, of course, fairly short and most runs were under 100 miles in length. The Southern inherited from all three of its principal constituents large quantities of non-gangway lavatory stock, that is compartment coaches with toilet facilities serving only one or two compartments, or with only a short internal corridor linking three compartments. From the outside it was not always possible to determine exactly which compartments had toilet access.

The LMS and LNER also built quantities of this type of stock for longer-distance stopping services.

In contrast, the Southern did not build any locomotive-hauled non-corridor stock throughout its 25-year existence; with its vast electrification programme it did not need to. In 1933 came the first of the various Southern main-line electric conversions for which Maunsell designed corridor electric stock similar to his steam stock for other lines. The newly electrified lines serving Brighton, Hastings, Worthing and other places on the South Coast were served by Pullman cars in the new electric units, and a speciality was the all-electric complete Pullman train for the Brighton Belle, certainly a luxury on a 55-mile outer suburban run. It lasted until mid-1972 when the train was given an honourable retirement; most of the Pullman cars have been sold for continued use as restaurants, mostly far from their native haunts and in some cases far from a railway line.

The other three companies also produced their special trains for particular services; some were no more than special sets of coaches hardly differing in their

This page top to bottom: **Great Western Dreadnought 1st/3rd composite coach dating from 1905.** *G M Kichenside*

British Rail Mk II open second in general use on most Inter-City trains today. The latest version is air-conditioned. *G M Kichenside*

Metro-Cammell Pullman built for East Coast services in the 1960s. *R Bastin*

SECR non-corridor composite formed into three-coach sets and used extensively in Kent. *G M Kichenside*

Facing page top: BR Mk IIC open first coach employed on Inter City services. *British Railways*

Right: Great Western railcar No 4 at Didcot. *C M Whitehouse*

Overleaf: A Brighton Terrier with a Hayling Island-Havant train crosses Langstone Bridge at sunset. *Alison Esau*

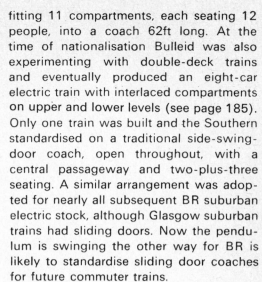

appointments from ordinary stock but for exclusive use on a named train. The LNER specialised in luxury coaches for several of its named expresses; the coaches for the streamlined Coronation and West Riding expresses were formed entirely of open saloon vehicles but the first-class coaches had the seats partitioned off in groups of four or six, with a central passageway.

By the end of the 1930s steel was being used to a far greater extent in coach body construction, usually for side and roof panels, with the timber framing retained. Once again designers turned their attention to all-metal coaches and the LMS built some lightweight electric vehicles using steel and aluminium components for Liverpool area lines. However, the outbreak of war in 1939 interrupted further development. Quite soon after the war ended, the four group companies were again producing new coaches, including all-steel types on the LMS, but individual development was again halted in 1948, this time by nationalisation of the four companies to form British Railways.

One important development did take place during the 1939-45 war, when Bulleid, who had taken over as chief mechanical engineer of the Southern Railway, introduced a new type of suburban electric train for the Southern with 9ft-wide bodies of welded steel construction. Inside, the seats were taken almost up to the outer body skin and the early coaches were very austere and cramped, not surprisingly as Bulleid had succeeded in

fitting 11 compartments, each seating 12 people, into a coach 62ft long. At the time of nationalisation Bulleid was also experimenting with double-deck trains and eventually produced an eight-car electric train with interlaced compartments on upper and lower levels (see page 185). Only one train was built and the Southern standardised on a traditional side-swing-door coach, open throughout, with a central passageway and two-plus-three seating. A similar arrangement was adopted for nearly all subsequent BR suburban electric stock, although Glasgow suburban trains had sliding doors. Now the pendulum is swinging the other way for BR is likely to standardise sliding door coaches for future commuter trains.

From the start, the new British Railways main-line corridor coaches were entirely of steel, but internally they differed little from previous designs, with wood-grain decor and rather dull moquettes for seating. There was little change in design for more than a decade, despite the production of numerous prototypes and the Mark I fleet, as it became known, spread to all main lines throughout the country. From the mid-1960s, big double-glazed windows, better heating, ventilation and soundproofing, wide doors and modern decor, have gradually been introduced, to provide a Mark II standard, and the latest version, which has reverted to small windows, is fully air conditioned. At the other end of the scale, from the mid-1950s BR introduced a large fleet of coaches formed into diesel multiple units. They were built for local and suburban use and some had bus-type seats.

Latest BR development having entered service in a new high-speed train is the Mark III coach, a longer vehicle than has been seen before on British Railways. It has a body length of about 75ft and a width of 9ft, is designed for speeds up to 125mph and is fully air conditioned. A feature is the abolition of individual compartments and all seats for both first- and second-class passengers will be in open saloons. In some proposed layouts for the second-class saloons, some of the seats will not coincide with windows and some passengers will sit alongside solid panels between windows, a retrograde step reminiscent of some of the worst features of 60 years ago.

The other important development for the 1970s is the Advanced Passenger Train, designed for speeds up to 155mph on existing track, and possibly much higher speed on specially prepared tracks. To allow a train to take existing curves at a higher speed than at present the coach bodies will tilt. To keep them within the loading gauge the body sides are inclined inwards so that from the waist upwards coach interiors will be narrower than at present. Although they will have very advanced running gear, the general design of the air-conditioned passenger accommodation of the APT saloons will be little different from the standard Mark III coaches.

THROUGHOUT THE HISTORY of railways, the conveyance of Royalty has always been a major preoccupation for the authorities. In modern times, the motorcar and the aeroplane offer alternative means of transport, and whereas the frequency of Royal journeys has increased, the Royal Family's use of trains has decreased. But from the day, June 13, 1842, on which Queen Victoria first entrusted her Royal person to the Great Western Railway to be carried from Slough to Paddington, only four years after the first section of the GWR had been opened, Royal railway journeys have always been the subject of the most meticulous preparation and supervision. It can be added that on the day of the Queen's first rail journey, the locomotive *Phlegethon* was driven by Daniel Gooch, the GWR Locomotive Superintendent, accompanied on the footplate by none other than Isambard Kingdom Brunel in person, and that Her Majesty was so pleased with the experience that ten days later she returned to Slough in the same manner.

The longest rail journeys of Queen Victoria resulted from her purchase in 1852 of Balmoral House on Deeside (which she had leased from 1848), and which on its enlargement in 1855 became Balmoral Castle. Visits to Osborne House, in the Isle of Wight, also necessitated rail travel to and from Gosport. The first journeys of Queen Victoria between Windsor and Scotland were made over the East Coast main line, which was joined at Finsbury Park after the Royal train had travelled over the London & South Western line to Kew and then by the North & South West Junction line through Willesden to Canonbury, where reversal was necessary. But from 1861 the responsibility was transferred to the West Coast authorities, the Great Western working the train from Windsor by the west curve at Slough and then through Oxford and Banbury to Wolverhampton, where the London & North Western took over. The train continued in LNWR hands to Carlisle, and in those of the Caledonian to Aberdeen and finally the Great North of Scotland to

Above: Royal crest as carried on a plate for attaching to the vehicles of Royal trains.
British Transport Museum (R Kerry)

Below left and right: Interior and general views of Queen Adelaide's London & Birmingham Railway coach of 1842.
British Transport Museum

Ballater, a night journey which was allowed a total of 12 hours.

The undue time taken on the journey is a reminder that Queen Victoria had a great aversion to speed, though not so great as that of the Shah of Persia, who after a rail journey from Dover on arrival at Victoria demanded the instant execution of the driver for having exceeded what the Shah regarded as the safe limit of 10mph. But Queen Victoria's limit of 40mph was troublesome enough, especially as she insisted that if the Royal train was behind time there must be no attempt to exceed the limit in order to recover the arrears. Not infrequently such delays were caused by Her Majesty calling for some unscheduled stop, but the minutes so lost might then be recovered surreptitiously, and often were, during the darkness of the night.

In 1863, the Prince of Wales, later King Edward VII, bought Sandringham House, in Norfolk, which from then on became very popular with the Royal Family. So the Great Eastern Railway had the task of working many special trains to and from Wolferton, the station for Sandringham. In earlier days, when the GER had regular services between St Pancras and the Cambridge main line, as well as those to and from Liverpool Street, St Pancras was usually the starting point for Wolferton specials, which used the Tottenham & Hampstead line between Kentish Town and Tottenham. In later years, and until the present day, Liverpool Street became the normal London terminal, though after the formation of the London & North Eastern Railway in 1923 Kings Cross for a time was used for the purpose, with the route by way of Hitchin and Cambridge. Today the Royal trains have to terminate at Kings Lynn, as the Hunstanton branch is no more, and the station at Wolferton, with its finely appointed Royal waiting rooms, has become a private residence.

In earlier years the regulations governing the working of Royal trains were extremely strict. Ten minutes ahead of the special a 'pilot' locomotive was run, and after its passage any train running on a parallel line, in either direction, had to be stopped. All level crossing gates were locked, and often also all points over which the train would pass. At all switches and bridges platelayers were stationed, armed with flags and detonators, supplemented by policemen on overline bridges, who allowed no one to cross them between the passage of the pilot engine and the train. Tunnels were patrolled shortly before the train was due. Occasionally when foreign Royalties were travelling whose crowns rested less securely on their heads than that of our own Sovereign, the route would be lined from end to end by patrols within sight of one another.

A special bell-code was used to signal both the pilot and the Royal train, and special sheet timetables showed the scheduled passing time at every station on the route. Chief officers of the railways con-

cerned travelled with the train, as well as telegraph linesmen with apparatus for tapping telegraph lines anywhere along the route in the event of a breakdown. At stations, whether those stopped at or passed by the special, stationmasters had to be on duty. Also, needless to say, the trains were composed of luxurious Royal saloons and of special accompanying rolling stock, and were headed by locomotives kept in first-class order and spick-and-span condition.

In modern times, however, rules concerning Royal train travel have been greatly relaxed. There is no longer any running of pilot engines ahead of the Royal train, nor of bringing other trains to a halt, stationing trackmen at switches and the like, although the working of a Royal train is still the subject of special arrangements. It is worth mention that Royal personages do not travel free; first-class fares are paid for every one of them and for every member of their entourage, and also the appropriate rate per mile for special trains, when they are required.

Royal patronage was anticipated before the first Royal journey was made, for as early as 1840 the Great Western Railway built at Swindon Works Britain's first Royal saloon. It was a 21ft-long four-wheeler designed of course for the GWR 7ft broad gauge. Internal furnishing, panelling, hangings of crimson and white silk

and fine paintings, were noteworthy for the period, and among unusual features were wooden tyres, designed to deaden the noise of travel.

Further Royal saloons were built by the GWR in 1848 and 1873; the later vehicle was converted to the standard 4ft 8½in gauge in 1889, and it is reported that Queen Victoria became so attached to it that when a new vestibuled Royal train was being turned out at Swindon in the Queen's Diamond Jubilee year, 1897, she gave strict instructions that her own compartment was on no account to be altered. By a remarkable feat of coach-building Swindon succeeded in incorporating it bodily in a new coach 58ft in length. Another rather troublesome Royal whim was that her coach must continue to be lit by oil lamps, which she considered to give a softer light than the electric lighting which the GWR had installed for the first time throughout the new train.

Of the 1873 GWR saloon a contemporary account read. 'The woodwork is of sycamore, panelled with choice and delicate satinwood, and roofed with an elegantly hand-painted ceiling. The whole interior sparkles with mirrors, silver-plated door mountings, gilded figures and supports and the like. The green-and-white carpet which covers the floor is of enormous thickness, with pile over an inch long. One large lamp hangs from the ceiling,

with candelabra fixed to the sides or walls of the compartment to provide additional illumination.' The interior walls of the saloon were padded with buttoned upholstery, which matched that of the armchairs and the long settee under one of the windows. No wonder Queen Victoria fell in love with this palace on wheels!

With the transfer in 1861 of the Royal journeys to and from Balmoral from the East to the West Coast route, the London & North Western Railway in that year built its first Royal saloons at its Wolverton works. There were two six-wheeled carriages which were close-coupled and vestibuled together, though not to the remainder of the Royal train; even well after the introduction of the first corridor trains the Royal saloons were still isolated, to ensure privacy, from the remaining coaches.

This arrangement had some problems for members of the Royal entourage, for if Her Majesty called capriciously, as she often did, for the Royal train to be stopped at some point in the open country, buxom ladies of the Royal household might have to make the perilous descent from their compartments to the ballast, and though entry to the Royal saloon by its folding steps might not be too difficult, being 'bunked up' on return to their own compartments was a different matter. Once again, when in later years the LNWR

wanted to modernise its Royal train, the Queen refused to contemplate any alterations to her own apartments; so Wolverton took the two six-wheel bodies off their wheels, and mounted them on a single frame carried on two six-wheel bogies. Oil lamps still persisted in the Queen's own rooms, but the rest of the Royal saloon now enjoyed electric lighting. The last journey made by Queen Victoria in this saloon was in 1900.

Meantime other railways had been building Royal saloons for their shorter journeys. The London & South Western Railway did so in 1885, while in 1897 the London Brighton & South Coast Railway turned out a very fine five-coach train, entirely of clerestory-roofed vehicles and with the Royal saloon proper carried, most unusually for the LBSCR, on 12 wheels; this train was used to and from Epsom Downs for race meetings, and to and from Portsmouth on naval occasions.

In 1897 the Great Eastern Railway built a 41ft saloon for the use of the then Prince of Wales, later King Edward VII, on his journeys to and from Sandringham, and four years later a much finer 50ft saloon for Queen Alexandra. One feature of all the early Royal vehicles was padding from floor to ceiling with buttoned upholstery or morocco leather, whether to protect the occupants from possible injury if the Royal train swayed on curves or for what other reason has never been explained. The purpose, however, could hardly have been to confine the Royal personages in 'padded cells'! In 1903 the South Eastern & Chatham Railway built a very fine Royal saloon for journeys between Dover and London, but in modern times Pullman cars are used for such Royal journeys.

With the death of Queen Victoria a complete change came about, and new Royal saloons could now be built fully in line with Twentieth Century ideas. Consequently, in 1903 there emerged from the Wolverton Works of the London & North Western Railway two 65ft 12-wheel saloons which were destined to be the most-used Royal vehicles ever to run on British metals. One saloon was for King Edward VII and the other for Queen Alexandra; but they continued in use through the reign of King George V and Queen Mary and through part also of that of King George VI and Queen Elizabeth. Each saloon included a bedroom, and

during the 1914-18 war, when during their journeys the King and Queen often lived in the train for days at a time (to relieve their subjects from having to entertain Royalty in difficult war conditions) bathrooms also were installed in each vehicle.

In course of time a complete LNWR Royal train was assembled, normally of about 11 clerestory-roofed vehicles, and comprising, in addition to the Royal saloons, two dining cars, and a collection of what were known as 'semi-Royal' saloons with adjustable partitions by which the coaches could be formed into a considerable variety of day saloon and night sleeping car accommodation. The East Coast Companies also in 1908 built two splendid 12-wheel saloons, 67ft long, which in later years have been used chiefly for journeys between London and Wolferton or Kings Lynn, for visits to Sandringham.

Last to be described are the three superb vehicles built at Wolverton by the London Midland & Scottish Railway in 1941, in order primarily to house the Royal Family and their staff in completely self-contained conditions during their journeys during the 1939-45 war. The two Royal saloons, each 69ft long, weigh 57 tons apiece, and are probably the heaviest passenger vehicles ever to run on British metals; attached to them is a 52-ton 'combination

car', with sleeping accommodation for some of the staff, luggage space, and, most important, a diesel-electric plant to supply light and power to the entire train.

The Royal saloons each comprise a bedroom, full-size bathroom, a small sleeping compartment for a servant, and a comfortable lounge. Internally the decoration represents an exceptionally fine example of the coach-builder's art. Everything conceivable has been done to reduce running noises, including acoustic blankets and devices to prevent rattling of the brake gear or creaking of the car structure. Complete air-conditioning and humidity control are installed. There is also a 25-line automatic telephone exchange serving the length of the train. It undoubtedly represents the last word in luxurious rail travel.

Royal preferences have always been consulted in the furnishing and arrangements of Royal trains. The extreme conservatism of Queen Victoria in these matters has been mentioned already, and its effect in the retention of such archaic details as oil lighting. King Edward VII had a strong leaning towards furnishing and *décor* that would remind him of a ship, which resulted in a change in a number of Royal saloons from padded walls to a white enamel finish. In LMSR days King George V expressed a strong objection to

the substitution of Midland red for the typical chocolate-and-white exterior of the Royal train; and during his lifetime chocolate-and-white it remained.

Finally, it is perhaps of interest to recall one or two notable Royal journeys. On March 7, 1902, King Edward VII and Queen Alexandra were taken non-stop by the GWR over the $228\frac{1}{2}$ miles from Paddington to Kingswear (via Bristol) in four hours $22\frac{1}{2}$ minutes, and three days later the Royal couple were carried back to London in the first non-stop run ever made over the $246\frac{1}{2}$ miles from Millbay Junction, Plymouth, in four hours 24 minutes. But this was nothing to what happened on July 14 of the following year, when 4-4-0 No 3433 *City of Bath* whirled the Prince and Princess of Wales from Paddington down to Plymouth via Bristol in three hours $53\frac{1}{2}$ minutes, in 37 minutes *less* than the booked time.

Which is a reminder that the highest speed at which Queen Victoria ever travelled was after her death, which occurred at Osborne, in the Isle of Wight. The body was being brought from Gosport to Victoria in the London Brighton & South Coast Royal train, which was handed over by the LSWR to the LBSCR at Fareham. Due to one or two delays, the train was 10 minutes late away from Fareham, and King Edward VII, who was a stickler for punc-

tuality, gave orders that Driver Cooper was to do his best to make up the lost time. As a result, the body of Queen Victoria was hurried by No 54 *Queen Empress* through Chichester at a speed estimated at 80mph, but the greatest thrills were as *Queen Empress* was given her head down from Ockley and bucketed over the reverse curves into Dorking at a speed far higher than the prescribed maximum. Eventually Victoria was reached two minutes early, Driver Cooper having covered a difficult 88 miles in 110 minutes.

In retrospect it seems almost incredible that such risks could have been taken with a train carrying many of the crowned heads of Europe, some hedged about with far stricter security precautions than our own Royalties, yet so it was. Space does not allow a description of the funeral trains carrying the late King Edward VII, King George V and King George VI, but none could have been more exciting than the one which hurried Queen Victoria's body up to London at a speed twice as high as that which she had permitted in her lifetime.

Top: A Royal train headed by BR Class B2 locomotive No 61671 'Royal Sovereign'.
B Jackson

Left: BR Schools class locomotive No 30926 spick and span ready to head a Royal train at Stewart's Lane in 1962. *D Cobbe*

Below: Bedroom of Queen Elizabeth's coach of 1941, which continues in use today.
Conway Picture Library

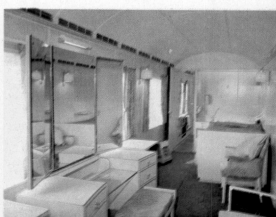

Pullman observation car of Baltimore & Ohio Railroad's George Washington train between Washington, DC, and Cincinatti, Ohio, in the 1930s, the first fully air-conditioned train.
B & O Railroad

THE NORTH AMERICAN RAILWAY CARRIAGE

THE NORTH AMERICAN railway carriage or passenger car (we must not use the term coach for reasons which will be made clear later) has for many years offered the ordinary passenger standards of comfort which he will look for in vain in any other field of public transport. Before looking at the subject in more detail, a few words on its evolution will not be out of place. As in Britain, the earliest carriages on rails were but developments of the highway coach—primitive four-wheelers. The track on which they ran was often cheaply built and of light construction, and the design soon moved to a longer vehicle on two four-wheeled trucks, or bogies, which rode very much more easily. The adoption of an open (or saloon) interior, with seats on each side of a central longitudinal aisle, has been ascribed to the 'democratic' nature of American society.

As the American railroad network grew, journeys of 24 hours or more became commonplace (speeds were not high) and

the need for a vehicle which made provision for both day and night travel became clear. Economy required that such a vehicle should be convertible and from a number of early designs, that of George Mortimer Pullman became most widely adopted. In the Pullman layout, groups of four seats (two facing pairs) on each side of the aisle could, by rearrangement of the cushions and backs, be made into a bed, or lower berth. An upper berth was built into the upper wall and ceiling panelling and could be lowered when required; privacy was achieved by heavy curtains. Toilet facilities were provided at the car ends.

American railways, with little traffic offering in early days, had to be cheaply built and high-level station platforms were an expensive luxury when perhaps only two or three trains a day were involved. Passenger cars were thus provided with open vestibules at each end, with steps down almost to rail level. The final gap to

the ground was bridged by a portable stepping stool, placed in position during stops by a trainman.

Heating was by stove, one or sometimes two to a car, and using wood, coal or occasionally oil as a fuel. Lighting developed from oil, through gas to electricity. Seats in ordinary coaches were often reversible ('walkover') and plush finished, although rattan was sometimes used for shorter journeys. Windows generally were narrow and could be opened upwards, to admit (in summer) a cooling draught—and dust and cinders! Sometimes, a gauze sash was fitted in an attempt to reduce in-blown rubbish, and in the northerly areas, a second glazed window, or storm sash, could be fitted in winter. Early and widespread adoption of the clerestory roof contributed both to ventilation and to lighting; it continued to feature in new construction up to about 1930.

The early car bodies were mainly of wood construction but increasing size of vehicles and emphasis on greater safety led first, in the latter part of the 19th century, to the steel underframe and eventually, in late Edwardian times, to the all-steel car.

As car design developed, meeting the needs of an expanding, prosperous nation, details improved. The open-end platform gave way first to narrow enclosed vestibules, and later to full-width vestibules. Even in later years, with the very few high-level station platforms, it was necessary to provide specially for access from rail level. Doors were invariably at car ends and, outside the trucks, opened inwards. Often they were split, Dutch style, and a hinged flap (with handrail on its underside) lifted to reveal the steps.

A feature of American rail travel (to European eyes) is the door opening ceremony performed by trainmen, who also assist passengers joining or alighting from trains. Both halves of the door are swung inwards while the train is slowing, the trap is lifted and clipped up, the handrail is wiped clean of dust with a paper towel after the trainman has descended to the bottom step, with the stepping stool ready, and finally, as the train stops, the stool is placed on the ground beside the steps.

By late Victorian times, a considerable degree of comfort was provided. Dining cars had replaced station meal stops, so reducing journey time, and both dining and sleeping cars were ornately decorated, in keeping with the times, with a high degree of craftsmanship used in decorative woodwork of various styles. Electric light was coming into use, and the Westinghouse air brake, adopted earlier, improved not only safety but comfort in stopping. Car lengths had increased from the early 50 or 60ft to 70 to 75ft. The larger and heavier cars often rode on two 6-wheeled bogies, which became universal for Pullman's sleepers and dining cars.

The ornate finish was not confined to interiors. Externally, dark green was, perhaps, the most common livery, and 'tuscan' red was used by a number of companies, including, up to the last few years, the Pennsylvania, and Canadian Pacific. The railway's name appeared along the 'letter board' above the windows, commonly in gold leaf and usually in an extended Roman script, with serifs. Car sides prior to adoption of the all-steel body were often matchboarded and could be elaborately lined out, though the last-named feature became a casualty of the 1914-18 war.

With the larger cars, windows of passenger spaces were often arched, with the upper part fitted with stained glass. An essential feature of all American passenger cars (in contrast with British practice) was the handbrake. On open-platform cars, it was applied by a horizontal wheel, but later, vertical wheels or levers with ratchets were provided inside the vestibule. Even after automatic brakes became universal, the handbrake was, and still is, required for parking. Another universal feature

from quite early days was the provision of a supply of drinking water, sometimes iced in summer, in all passenger cars.

Two classes of travel were generally provided, 'coach', that is day-coach, with sitting accommodation for day (and night) use. First class carried a different connotation from Europe. A first-class ticket entitled one to occupy Pullman car sleeping space, which had to be paid for additionally, but there was no ordinary first-class accommodation. First - class day travel could be either in a Parlor car, where a seat supplement was payable, as in a Pullman car in Britain, or by day occupancy (if the train times and journey permitted) of sleeping-car space. 'Pullman' and 'sleeper' are almost synonymous in American practice.

The Parlor car, provided where day-time demand for first-class travel warranted it, was arranged with single armchairs each side of a central longitudinal aisle; it carried a Pullman porter to serve light

refreshments from a pantry or small buffet. Each sleeping car had its own attendant, or porter, traditionally a negro, who stayed with the car for each journey. (He would sleep in an unoccupied berth when available; otherwise he made do in his cubicle seat, or in the smoking room at the car end.)

The Edwardian period witnessed the development of the all-steel car. Initially, constructional details continued to give a visual impression of the later ornate styles of the wooden car. After the 1914-18 war (during which American railways were placed under government control), designs were much simplified; while there was no diminution in comfort, ornate decoration was largely cast aside. In its place came simplicity and standardisation.

This is an appropriate place to make the point that few American railroads had or have sufficient capacity to build all their own rolling stock (or, for that matter, locomotives). There is a very sizeable

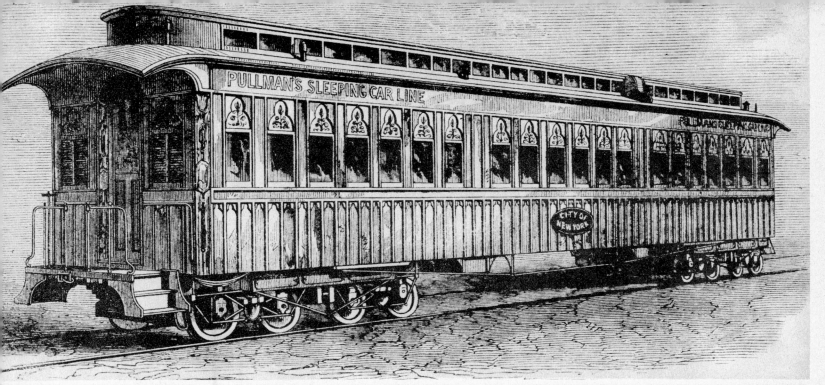

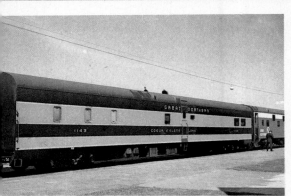

Facing page: Artist's impression of an American Pullman Parlor car interior, from 'The Illustrated London News' of January 13, 1923. *Illustrated London News*

Top: Another drawing from 'The Illustrated London News', of October 10, 1869, of one of the early Pullman sleepers. *Illustrated London News*

Above: Pleasure Dome lounge car introduced in January 1951 by Santa Fe Railway on its Super Chief train.
Atchison, Topeka & Santa Fe Railway

Left upper: Great Northern dormitory and lunch-counter car with the fancy name 'Coer d'Alene Lake' at Whitefish, Mont, in July 1970. *V Goldberg*

Left lower: Budd diesel railcar of the Dominion Atlantic Railway (constituent of CP Rail) in August 1966. *J K Hayward*

industry in the USA manufacturing both freight and passenger vehicles and while some railroads' railway works ('backshops') could, and did, manufacture locomotives or cars (the Pennsylvania built both at its Altoona, Pa, shops), outside purchase was more common.

Interworking in traffic had long made some degree of standardisation essential, and purchasing from common equipment manufacturers carried the process considerably farther, so that the 1920s became known as the Standard Era.

Use of Pullman cars was particularly influential, for the Pullman Company provided sleeping car service under contract to almost every road which required it. The Pullman fleet rose to almost 10,000 cars by 1931, and 4,000 of them were of one basic design. That was the 12-1 type; it contained 12 sections, each with lower and upper berths, plus a drawing room for three persons with its own toilet cubicle. For the 24 possible occupants of the sections, separate men's ('smoking') and women's ('rest') rooms were provided at opposite ends of the car. Each washroom contained two or three wash-basins, a dental bowl, a sofa or lounge chairs for three, and a single WC annexe. Towards the end of a night's journey, these facilities sometimes became heavily taxed.

The day coach, too, might well have smoking/rest room facilities at each end, but the interior was changed only in details of the fittings; seats were still arranged in pairs on each side of the central aisle. Whereas Pullman sleepers had for years been a product of the Pullman - Standard Manufacturing Company, there were other manufacturers of coach and other passenger vehicles; American Car & Foundry was one such, with several plants, including some taken over from previously independent firms. The heavy steel 'Standard' cars weighed 80 tons, or more, and largely rode on six-wheeled trucks. A solid train of such vehicles was an impressive sight, and no mean load for the motive power—then steam, except for a few electrified sections of line.

It is worth looking at the make-up ('consist') of a typical train of the Standard Era. Behind the locomotive came the head-end cars. Leading them would probably be a Railway Post Office car (RPO) carrying mail and with sorting facilities for en route dropping and collection. Behind the RPO would be baggage and express cars, for passengers' luggage and parcels traffic. Baggagemen, express messengers, and postal clerks—the latter two categories often armed with revolvers—had their duties 'up front'.

Next came the coaches; often one would be set aside for local passengers making short journeys, while passengers for major stations might be directed to particular coaches, thus making on-train ticket checking somewhat easier. Between the coaches and the Pullmans came the dining car, kitchen section to rear (so that the train's draught did not blow the heat from the kitchen back on to the diners). Then came the Pullmans and, at the rear of any train worth its salt in the nineteen-twenties, an observation car, at one time with the traditional open rear-end plat-form and brass railings, but later more likely a solarium or enclosed lounge space with large windows. Although Pullmans were convertible for day use, passengers could also sit in the lounge (and, except during the period of Prohibition, enjoy a drink). The lounge car might also have certain other on-train facilities, maybe a library, or a barber shop (with shower), or even a radio.

A long-distance through train of the period might run over the tracks of two or three companies, each of which contri-buted cars for the train, in proportion to their part of the mileage. Often, in such cases, the regular cars for the train would carry the name of the train on the letter board instead of the company owning the car. With many journeys over 24 hours,

Top: Santa Fe commemorated the American transcontinental centennial in 1969 with this Club car finished in 1890s style for its new streamlined Kansas City Chief train.
Atchison, Topeka & Santa Fe Railway

Above: Typical observation/lounge car of the post-war North American prestige passenger trains. *J K Hayward*

Left: Latest in US commuter trains, new Budd electric rolling stock of the Long Island Rail Road, New York. *Long Island Rail Road*

Left, top to bottom: Typical between-the-wars heavyweight passenger coach of Canadian National Railways, interesting in this picture for having an up-to-the-minute ACI (automatic car identification) colour code on its side.
J R Batts

Observation dome car on Norfolk & Western Railway City of St Louis train in August 1961.
J K Hayward

Northern Pacific Railway Slumbercoach 'Loch Katrine' at Mandan in July 1970.
V Goldberg

Denver & Rio Grande Western Railroad traditional (1880) narrow-gauge clerestory-roof coaches, much rebuilt and preserved at Silverton, Colorado, pictured in July 1970.
V Goldberg

limited capacity. The Budd Company of Philadelphia pioneered the production of a much lighter type of locomotive-hauled passenger car. It had load-bearing sides of welded corrugated stainless steel. Gone were the rivetted sides and clerestory roof, replaced by a sleek bright car, 85ft long, with large 'picture' windows, riding once again on two four-wheeled trucks. Weight came down to around 60 tons, despite the fitting of air conditioning, reclining seats, electric ice water coolers and so on.

Air conditioning was also applied, in the nineteen thirties, to existing Standard cars, firstly to diners, then to sleepers, and to a limited extent, to coaches. The financial position of many railways after the depression restricted investment in new stock, hence the refurbishing of older cars, which had then to meet the enormous flood of war-time traffic, without benefit of new construction, while builders were on war production work.

After the war, large orders were placed for passenger cars and in the period from about 1946 to 1957, the principal trains, and many others, on the majority of railroads were re-equipped with entirely new sets of cars. Some lines favoured the stainless-steel finish, others adopted smooth-sided lightweight cars, with distinctive colour schemes. To re-equip a transcontinental train running from Chicago to the Pacific coast might require five or six train-sets with up to 18 vehicles in each; an expensive investment.

The Pullman car changed greatly in the 'streamline' era. The demand was now for accommodation with more privacy. The roomette, with a fold-away bed, was in fact a single room with built-in toilet facilities. Bedrooms and compartments each provided space for two, and drawing rooms for three people. All except roomettes could be obtained *en-suite*, for family use by folding away the common dividing partition.

Each of the vehicle types mentioned earlier was represented in streamline form, although the observation car took on a round-ended rear lounge. The most distinctive new post-war innovation was the Dome car. Used mainly in the west, where clearances were adequate, the vista-dome provided glazing not only at each side, but ahead, to the rear and in the roof. It was an instant success on scenic routes. Generally, a dome was associated with a coach (second-class) configuration, with generously spaced reclining seats at normal floor level and washrooms located beneath the dome. Dome sleepers, and dome-café cars were also built, and today, AMTRAK, the US Government corporation which operates most long-distance passenger trains, includes dome equipment on most of its services, except in the east where clearances are tighter.

AMTRAK today operates its nationwide services with the best of the streamline equipment. Let us hope that these most comfortable of public transport vehicles continue to make it possible to enjoy 'riding the rails' long into the jet-plane era.

several sets of trains were often needed to meet the requirements of a particular service in each direction. Such, then, was railway travel in the Standard Era.

The spread of paved roads and use of private motorcars, the practical development of commercial flying and the depression, from 1930 made heavy inroads into rail passenger business. Contraction was severe, but several developments in the early 1930s brought the internal-combustion engine to main-line passenger service, in conjunction with new lightweight high-speed motorised trains, albeit of rather

THE PULLMAN STORY

APPLIED TO A transport vehicle, 'Pullman' connotes comfort of a high order. Motorcars have been christened Pullman to create just that impression. Autopullman is a name used on the Continent of Europe to attract tourists to motorcoaches that lack what most people think of as Pullman features—comfortable armchairs with tables and plenty of legroom. A Pullman railway carriage is generally one for day travel more comfortable than a standard coach and purchase of a Pullman ticket normally also reserves a numbered seat. Pullman coaches are usually air conditioned and equipped and decorated with special elegance; there is a high standard of service with meals and refreshments at each seat—and mostly a supplementary charge over and above the normal fare is charged.

That is the basic concept; there are variations. Some Pullman parlour (day) cars include a small compartment at one end, or both ends, flanked by a corridor and seating four, providing more privacy than the main saloon for small groups, while retaining Pullman service. In North America until quite recently, and in Britain during the last century, the term Pullman also applied to the type of sleeping car with longitudinal berths invented by the American George Mortimer Pullman and first built by him and the company he founded in the USA; now Pullman as a term for a sleeper has almost disappeared.

What most Europeans and Americans today think of as a Pullman is a parlour car, or in the US or Canada a club car, for which a supplementary fare is charged. Night travel in America is another story, though most sleeping cars there and the world over incorporate several of Pullman's patents or developments of other men's ideas built into modern coaching stock. When George Pullman completed his first sleeping car in Chicago in 1864, he lit a candle that has never been put out. Others have designed and built luxury railway coaches, but only Pullman's name has lasted.

It is rather odd that the only Pullman cars running regularly in the world today and officially so-termed (apart from possible survivors in South or Central America) that provide all the Pullman characteristics, including supplementary fares, are on British Railways. True, the Compagnie Internationale des Wagons-Lits et du Tourisme, operator of the now-defunct regular Pullman car services in Western Europe (the last ran in Italy in June 1971)

hires out Pullmans, mostly in complete trains for travel in connection with special events when meal service is required for large groups; but there are no longer any regular Pullman services on the Continent.

Below: Page from 'The Graphic' of November 21, 1874, illustrating the Pullman facilities just introduced by the Midland.
Illustrated London News

There are now no all-Pullman trains but there are various combinations of first-class Pullman with second-class ordinary coaches. Best known of them—though only a shadow of its one-time all-Pullman splendour—is the Golden Arrow, down in the morning from Victoria to Dover Marine and back in the afternoon in connection with the Dover-Calais packet. The Arrow started in 1926 as a first-class train connecting with a special Golden Arrow steamer, the *Canterbury*, and the French all-Pullman Flèche d'Or between Calais and Paris. War apart, it has had its ups and downs, largely downs. Second-class ordinary coaches were added in recent years by a pessimistic management. The Pullmans on the French side were not replaced when they grew old. The Golden Arrow is no longer a luxury service but the name still evokes a worthy tradition. If there is to be a Channel Tunnel, it is important that the notion of specially comfortable and speedy day travel between London and Paris should survive; with smartened up Golden Arrow and Flèche d'Or, a London-Paris transit through the tunnel could be considerably less than half the present seven hours, and to many thousands of travellers no doubt a welcome alternative to the herding and growing squalor of air travel.

Other BR services combining first-class Pullman with second-class ordinary and restaurant cars for non-Pullman passengers are business trains between London and the North. The London Midland Region's Liverpool Pullman covers the 193 miles between Euston and Liverpool twice each way daily Mondays to Fridays in just over 2½ hours. In the Eastern Region there are three trains which similarly provide first-class Pullman and second-class ordinary coach accommodation; namely, the Hull, Tees-Tyne and Yorkshire Pullmans. They leave Hull, Newcastle and Leeds on workday mornings and make one return trip to

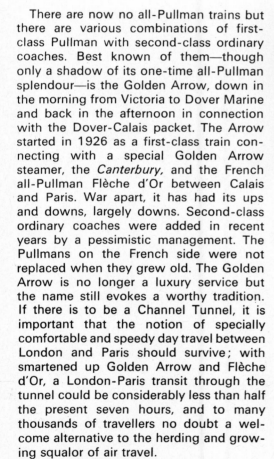

London Kings Cross.

Although British Rail's present Pullman business is considerable in terms of revenue, and most of the prestige business services are popular, the present Pullman trains and coaches—even the relatively new ones of the Manchester and Liverpool trains—are survivors of the past or represent a concept now abandoned. The British Railways Board intends that in principle ordinary first- and second-class air-conditioned vehicles now in full service shall provide the highest standards of travel by Inter-City services. So, like the other major operators, after a century of experimenting with Pullman cars, Britain's railways seem likely to revert to reliance on their own modern passenger vehicles to serve the luxury travel market.

High levels of comfort and personal service were the essential ingredients of the original concept of George Mortimer Pullman, whose experiences of the low standards in American mid-nineteenth century trains convinced him that there was profit to be made from offering something better. His plan was not to build luxury coaches for sale, but to pay the railroads to operate the coaches owned and staffed by the Pullman company, whose profit would come from the supplementary fares passengers would be willing to pay for the superior service. Despite the derision of most established railroad men he per-

sisted, and from his first convertible parlour/sleeping car *Pioneer* of 1864 there rapidly grew a vast fleet of Pullmans operating on every major American railroad.

To European rail travellers, the American-built Pullman did not at first seem to offer so much more. Its armchairs were little if any better than the well-upholstered seats of an ordinary first-class compartment. British travellers to North America had already complained of the lack of privacy in the open saloons of Pullman cars. It was only later in the century that experience of the blessings of steam heating, corridors, lavatories and meals served in the train changed peoples' ideas, and by that time the railways of this and other of the more developed countries were providing them in ordinary trains—in the case of some Continental railways emulating Pullman in part by arranging for train catering by the non-railway Wagons-Lits Company. But the Pullman company showed the way and obtained a firm foothold in this country by the 1880s, while the Continental activities it did establish are only now dying down after fifty years.

The start of the Pullman enterprise in Britain was on the Midland Railway in 1873. An agreement between the Midland General Manager, James Allport, and George Pullman allowed for *inter alia* operation on that line of cars built in the

Pullman works at Detroit and reassembled at the MR Derby works. The first Midland Pullmans were built to the conventional pattern of sleeping car. Most of the berths were longitudinal, the upper berth folding upwards for day travel and the lower formed from a pair of transverse seats; both berths occupied a Pullman 'section' each of which flanked the centre gangway from which they were separated by two curtains. There were also compartments with transverse berths in the same cars opening off a side corridor. The cars were at first used also for day travel over the MR between St Pancras and Bradford.

The forerunner of the basic Pullman parlour car and its variants that became widely familiar in subsequent years in North America, Europe and elsewhere was the MR Pullman *Victoria,* placed in service in 1874. It was a bogie vehicle incorporating a saloon with 17 swivelling armchairs and a coupe at each end. It was heated by hot water pipes and lit by paraffin lamps hung from the ceiling. It was more luxurious than any public day travel vehicle previously seen anywhere in the world.

In 1832 the Pullman Palace Car Company was registered in Britain; thereafter the growth of Pullman car day travel in Britain was rapid. Nevertheless some railways, such as the Great Northern and the London Chatham and Dover, went no farther than experiments with Pullman cars. Even the Midland dropped Pullman services after its contract with the company expired in 1888, while the London Chatham and Dover and the South Eastern operated rival Club Trains between London and Dover with saloon cars supplied by the Wagons-Lits company, and the SER for a short period ran Gilbert cars (American-type cars resembling Pullmans) on internal services. In general, the main-line railways to the North preferred to provide their own rolling stock and restaurant cars, and lines south of the Thames, where the runs were shorter for geographical reasons and provision by railways themselves of costly de luxe carriages would not have been economic, exploited the Pullman parlour car in earnest.

The London Brighton and South Coast's first Pullman car began running in 1875. Its first all-Pullman train began running between London and Brighton in 1881. It was not a commercial success but it engendered a number of individual Pullman-car services on the LB & SCR; a further all-Pullman London-Brighton train in 1888 was progenitor of the famous Southern Belle of 1908, which in turn was succeeded by the Brighton Belle when the line was electrified in 1932, after the Southern Belle had begun to include third-class accommodation during the first world war.

The London and South Western started to run Pullmans in a desultory way from the early 1880s, but replaced them with its own better main-line stock and restaurant cars during the Edwardian period. The South Eastern and Chatham (as it had become in 1899 on the union for operating purposes of the SER and LC&DR) started Pullman services on its Continental boat trains in 1911 and they slowly were extended to ordinary services. There were negotiations between the Pullman Car Company and the Great Central in 1909 but without result. The following year saw the beginning of the unique Pullman services over the Metropolitan Railway between Aldgate or Liverpool Street and Buckinghamshire which lasted until 1939, after the Metropolitan had become part of London Transport. The Caledonian Railway joined the Pullman-operating lines in 1914; among several CR Pullman services were the famous observation cars on the Oban line.

After 1918 there began a second Pullman boom. In the early 1920s before Grouping, the Great Eastern lavishly instituted several services between London and seaside resorts including to nearby Southend; none survived long except the London and North Eastern Railway's Eastern Belle, which ran in summer to destinations that differed on different days. The Pullman cars in the Liverpool Street-Harwich boat trains survived until the second world war. In 1923 the newly formed London and North Eastern Railway initiated the Harrogate Pullman, first of a series of Pullman trains from and to Kings Cross that have continued to this day. The Great Western experimented with Pullmans unsuccessfully in 1929-30.

Undoubtedly the biggest expansion was on the Southern Railway, more particularly when certain ex-LB & SCR lines were electrified to the South Coast and the frequent electric multiple-unit services included Pullman cars. The Southern also originated other services such as the Golden Arrow and the Bournemouth Belle. The London Midland and Scottish Railway was not Pullman-minded, preferring, like the GWR, to reply on the comfort of its own stock and on the merits of its own catering. Ireland's only Pullman cars ran as such for a decade from 1926, in fulfilment of a contract between the then Great Southern Railway and the Pullman subsidiary company Irish Pullman Limited; the contract was not renewed and the GSR bought the cars and worked them as its own.

Since 1945, and more particularly since nationalisation, there have been both expansion and contraction. The Southern Railway revived the Golden Arrow and instituted the unsuccessful Devon Belle between Waterloo and Plymouth and Ilfracombe. British Rail thereafter introduced the Western Region diesel Pullmans early in 1960 and the Manchester Pullman between St Pancras and Manchester over the Midland route (now withdrawn).

The early history of saloon cars on the Continent is involved. Generally, it is true to say that until 1925 almost all saloon cars running on the Continent were operated by the Wagons-Lits Company and other bodies, and were not Pullman cars. An important exception was the Canadian Pacific Railway's venture of running Pullman - designed cars in 1911-14 over various lines in the then Austrian Empire; war ended what might have proved a successful series of services. The Pullman cars that ran in Southern Italy in the 1880s seem to have been Pullman sleepers, though there is mention of purchase by the Wagons-Lits Company in 1884 of a Pullman parlour car that ran in Italy.

Continental Europe's first real Pullman day service was the Milan-San Remo-Nice-Cannes all-Pullman train of 1925. It was quickly followed by others, including the Flèche d'Or, the Sud Express between Paris and Biarritz and the Spanish frontier (replacing Wagons-Lits saloons), the Paris-Brussels Etoile du Nord and many other services of all-Pullman trains or individual cars. All these were operated by the Wagons-Lits Company.

Eventually Wagons-Lits trains, or individual coaches, ran in many countries in Europe, and even in Egypt. They included a complete train—the Andaluces Express—in Southern Spain, two shortlived services in Switzerland—the Gotthard Pullman and the Golden Mountain Express over the metre-gauge Montreux-Oberland Bernois line, and many other services in France, Belgium and Italy, to health resorts and spas, and even a coach between Amsterdam and Flushing. There were no services within Germany, which was outside Wagons-Lits territory, or in Scandinavia. The European Pullman heyday was 1929. Thereafter economic depression and road and air competition caused the withdrawal of many services.

The process has continued since the last war, in which many Pullman and other coaches were destroyed. Moreover, travel habits have changed; this and the high capital cost of new cars have made the Wagons-Lits Company reluctant to renew time - expired vehicles. The railway administrations, as in Britain, tend to rely on their own vehicles to afford high standards of comfort combined with the high speeds looked for by the travellers of today and tomorrow. Hence the new Trans-Europe Expresses and plans for high-speed luxury trains. But however grand the new concepts, all in some degree owe something to George Pullman, who foresaw the demand for luxury rail travel.

**Left: Preserved Pullman car 'Topaz'
pictured at Brighton. It was a 31-seater built
in 1914 by Birmingham RCW Co and continued
in service until 1960.** *British Transport Museum*

DEUTSCHE REICHSBAHN

50 50 26-25 113-0
DBv

Above: East-German-built double-deck coach of the Deutsche Reichsbahn; many of similar design have been built for suburban services in other East European countries.
D R Stopher

Left: A decorative old two-class double-deck coach of the French Est Railway network in pre-SNCF days, now preserved at the transport museum in Mulhouse.
Jean-Claude Roca

Below: BR Southern Region experimental double-deck train used on Dartford and Bexleyheath services between 1949 and 1971.
A H Ellis

DOUBLE DECK TRAINS

THE CONVENTIONAL stage coach of the eighteenth and early nineteenth centuries was basically a double-deck vehicle, with inside passengers travelling in some comfort and the more-numerous class riding outside in a rather unhappy state in inclement weather. The bus industry did not at first imitate this arrangement, but apparently the double-deck road vehicle was evolved in London in the busy days of the Great Exhibition traffic in 1851. A quite complicated horse-drawn double-decker appeared on the Swansea & Mumbles Railway (also known as the Oystermouth Railway) in the eighteen-sixties, inclined ladders giving access to the roof seats. Incidentally, the Oystermouth Railway, which could claim the proud title of being the world's first passenger railway, on which horse-drawn vehicles for passengers were running in

1807, ended its days with a fleet of vehicles which were virtually double-deck electric tramcars, running in the peaks as two-car trains and providing a total of 212 seats. The vehicles were built in 1929 by Brush Electrical Engineering, and lasted just over thirty years until the line closed in January 1960.

Choice of double-deck vehicles was probably due to the need to provide a high passenger capacity in trains as short as possible because of the length of terminal roads and passing loops. Moreover, double-deck carriages had been used traditionally on the line both for horse and steam traction, and control was in the hands of the British Electric Traction group, familiar with double-deck vehicles both for bus and tram services.

It is not quite so easy to explain the European passion for double-deck railway vehicles which resulted in a number being built in the closing years of the nineteenth century; if the Western Railway of France, believed to be the pioneer, is taken as an example, it was for the reason that suburban traffic was growing steadily and that double-deckers were seen to be a simple way of increasing train capacity in the peak hours without spending capital on lengthening station platforms. The first experiments were made in 1879 and a number of coaches were built as a result in the following year. They were about 27ft 6in long, had a tare weight of nearly nine tons and seated 40 downstairs (second class) and 36 up (third class), and had only the skimpiest of canopies over the top deck. The stairs at each end were only 2ft 9in wide and they were placed transversely, so that they rose about 6ft in less than half the width of the coach; there was a narrow centre gangway on the upper deck which extended to the stairhead. Despite protests from passengers who had been kippered by the fumes from a compound tank engine in Batignolles tunnel on the exposed upper deck, other railways followed suit and double-deck carriages appeared in Berlin, Frankfurt and on the Bavarian State Railways among other systems.

The Western of France built a new generation of double-deckers in 1899 and this time glazed the upper deck and added nearly 2ft to the length. There was a little more room for everybody and more space on the staircases, and four more seats were provided upstairs to give a total of 80 passengers. The glazing added about 50 per cent to the tare weight. Some of the later vehicles lasted a quarter of a century. Although they were still somewhat crude, they represented a long step forward from the stage-coach adaptations which operated on the Whitby & Pickering Railway in Britain in the 1830s or the little double-deckers of the pioneer St Etienne & Andrezieux line in France, of which a fanciful picture showed a line of coaches being hauled by horses in tandem.

They were also more civilised than the staggered-gangway double-deckers of the 1860s on the Bombay, Baroda & Central Railway, which were designed unashamedly to accommodate the maximum number of passengers of inferior class. They carried the passengers on four parallel longitudinal benches, with a dovetailing of the decks that left two rows virtually squatting on their haunches. Designed with similar purpose in 1926, but at least giving all 128 third-class passengers a reasonable seat, were double-deck coaches for Cape Town suburban services on the 3ft 6in-gauge South African Railways. The earlier double-deckers had all been smallish four-wheelers, but the South African were mounted on bogies and were nearly 13ft high and over 63ft long. The underframe was shaped to provide a well 31ft long between the bogies, in which 48 passengers were seated longitudinally facing inwards; on top of them 48 passengers sat facing outwards on a knife-

board down the centre. There was an easy slope to the stairs joining the two decks together on a platform over the bogies at each end; on each platform were the doors and 16 more seats. The tare weight was 30 tons. The vehicles were so cramped and claustrophobic that passengers are reputed to have shunned them and the design was dropped, despite the ingenious interlacing of the lower deck gangway with the headroom created by the rise of the upper-deck knifeboard.

Another interlaced-seating type, with transverse seats for 120 passengers on levels above and below a common gangway, was introduced in 1932 for suburban operation on the Long Island Railroad in the United States and lasted forty years in service. Trials of a prototype were sufficiently attractive to justify a production batch; there were apparently some hitches in getting production going at the Altoona shops of the Pennsylvania Railroad, but by the late 1940s about 60 of the double-deckers were in commission.

The present owners of the Long Island, the Metropolitan Transportation Authority of New York, do not apparently like the double-deck fleet as they describe it as 'frequently breaking down, requiring a high level of maintenance which proves excessively costly, difficult to keep clean and with a sub-standard air-conditioning system.' Anyway, it has been swept away and replaced by 770 Metropolitans—the Metropolitan Transportation Authority's own specific for all commuting problems; each pair of Metropolitans provides 240 seats in twice 85ft of length, whereas a pair of the later double-deckers stowed 264 seats in roundly twice 80ft. The single-deck Metropolitans are arranged to seat two one side of the gangway and three the other and although they are 10ft across the floor, like the vanished double-deck stock, the Metropolitans curve out to a width of 10ft 6in at seat level.

The most-sophisticated double-deckers until that time appeared in 1933 on the Western State Railway in France; they were transverse-seated push-and-pull sets, originally intended for operation from St Lazare to Sartrouville, but later known as Rambouillet sets and operated into the 'stockbroker belt' of outer Paris. Designed to operate in eight-car sets, the well-frame design was adopted, carried on Pennsylvania bogies with 3ft wheels, running in Skefko roller bearings. There was no room on the bogies for lighting dynamos, so these were transferred to the locomotives allocated to the service. The length of each coach was 75ft 6in and each deck was 6ft 2¾in high in the centre gangway in an overall height of 14ft 3in.

The handsome coaches were built by Usines des Entreprises Industrielles Charentaises and the trains were made up of two third-class vehicles with end driving compartments, four third-class cars and two first/second-class composites. Each eight-car train provided a total of 918 seats (48 first class); in addition, standing capacity based on a Government

formula brought the total lift to 2,040 persons. The previous nine-car trains had a total passenger capacity of 1,524. The doors of the double-deckers were mounted over the bogies at each end and at the point of the cranking of the frame a broad flight of five shallow steps led to the upper deck and two narrower flights of six led to the lower saloon. The end platforms offered supplementary seating, except in the control compartments. The tare of each coach was 46tons 5cwt or roundly 875lb a seat—2½ times the weight of the 1899 four-wheeler for each seat.

A private railway in Germany, the Lubeck-Buchen, was next to feel the double-deck urge and this was the more mysterious because they ran in two-coach articulated units, hauled by special streamlined tank engines. Each pair of coaches was about 151ft 4in long overall and 14ft 2in high. Headroom on the upper deck was over 6ft 4in and on the lower 6ft 2in. The frame was carried only 8in above the railhead along the well of the coach. The tare of 64 tons was spread over 300 seats, plus 18 occasional seats. The train was powered by a Henschel 2-4-2 tank engine and was put on trial for economy and capacity alongside a Henschel steam railcar with two Doble boilers. The top speed of the railcar was nominally 68mph and the best non-stop time in 1934 for Hamburg to Lubeck, 39 miles, was 49 minutes, or 47.7mph.

From the early tests and loading and unloading experiments the Germans, and particularly the East Germans in postwar years, appear to have established considerable faith in the double-deck coach and have developed it since 1950. Suburban sets have been supplied to the East German, Czechoslovakian, Polish and Roumanian railways, the latest being five-section articulated sets, with four-wheeled bogies at the ends and six-wheeled bogies under each pair of intermediate coach ends.

Top: Bound for Galati, Pacific No 231.074 leaves Bucharest Nord in September 1966 with a double-deck train. *L King*

Left: Wooden two-tiered train with locomotive No 230 2088 arriving at Valencia terminus, Spain, in September 1961. *L King*

Above: Rare model of a Doppelstöcktriebwagen circa 1882 of the Royal Bavarian Railway.

Below: Streamlined modern double-decker of Canadian Pacific Railways pictured at Windsor station, Montreal. *V Goldberg*

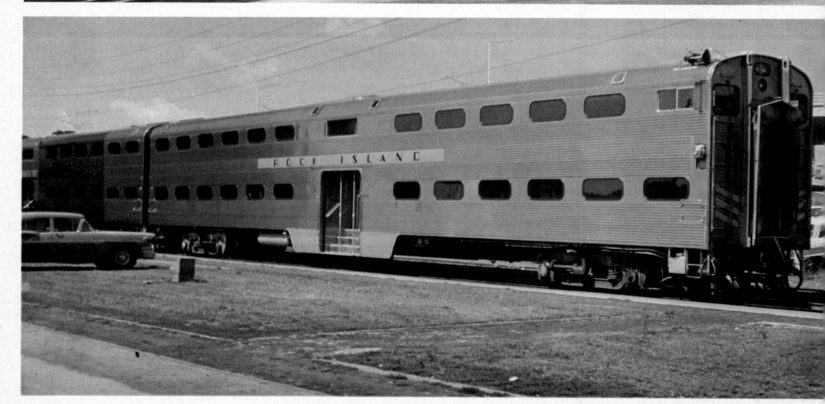

Above left: Another form of double-decker, a full-length dome lounge car as used in North America providing refreshment bar below and observation accommodation above.
J K Hayward

Left: General arrangement of the interlaced upper and lower decks of BR Southern Region experimental train. *British Railways SR*

Left below: The Budd stainless-steel double-deck coach providing 160 seats in the service of Rock Island RR. *J K Hayward*

Above: Interior of double-deck gallery car, one of over 200 used on the Chicago suburban services of the Chicago & North Western Railway. *V Goldberg*

A typical four-car suburban unit measures 241ft overall and is 9ft 4½in wide. End compartments can be arranged for driving, guard or toilet use, Vehicles can be laid out for various configurations with two-and-two or three-and-two seating, but with compensatory decreases in standing space, for example. Thus in the 63ft 4in end vehicles, 88 seats (40 down and 48 up) allow 141 standees (type A), whereas with 48 seats on the lower deck and 58 above. the number of standing spaces is reduced to 133 (type D). The 55ft intermediate coaches can provide seats for 40 and 48, plus 121 standing in type B, and for 39 and 58, plus 118 standing, in type C, which has seats for two on one side of the gangway and three on the other. Luggage vans of matching dimensions can be supplied for use with the sets on seaside and other excursions and there are also independent eight-wheeled double-deck vehicles that can be coupled in to enhance capacities of selected trains. But the well is now kept 1ft 2in above rail

level and the overall height is a towering 15ft 1in, which requires a generous loading gauge. Apart from cramming standees in during the peak periods, the advantage in terms of seated passengers is hard to take in, as the number of seats per foot run of coach comes to roundly 1.6 or 1.7 according to layout, and that sort of figure is not difficult to achieve with a single-decker. The loss of space is incurred through the need to provide stairs that are reasonably easy to negotiate to the upper and lower saloons.

If it is a question of a superior vantage point to give passengers a better view of the countryside traversed, the designer can be on a better wicket and achieve something that produces commendation from the customers, especially where steam traction has been abandoned and upper windows are no longer wreathed in smoke. Here the 1½-deck or double-deck vista dome car can well come into its own as an observation car not confined to a rear view, but one giving views in all directions. The lower deck can be used for all sorts of purposes from passenger space to kitchens and luggage storage. The Wagons-Lits company cottoned on to the idea and designed sleeping cars with dovetailed upper and lower decks.

Nevertheless, the use of double-decking seems to be developing mainly in hard-pressed suburban areas, where city terminals offer no hope of longer trains and headways are as close as signalling will allow. These considerations actuated the Australian New South Wales Government Railway in ordering double-deck trailer coaches for Sydney suburban services. In 1965 120 were planned to be built by Tulloch and to provide 132 seats each instead of 70 in the cars they superseded. Inserted between single-deck motor coaches they presented an extremely hideous appearance, but since 1968 this has been mitigated to some extent by delivery of matching motor coaches to seat 112. Aluminium-alloy bodywork is used to keep weight down. A train of eight cars, each 63ft 10in long, 14ft 4½in high and 10ft wide, can carry 976 seated passengers (89 per cent increase over the former total of 516) and an estimated peak load with standing passengers of 2,906 people.

Amusingly, a further. wave of double-decking has spread over the United States with the realisation of the valuable part the railway can play in commuter movement; at the very time when the Long Island Railroad was telling its public how beneficial the. shedding of the double-deck fleet would be, other railways were advertising the advantages of living on a railway where commuter trains would be double-decked. The Long Island saw the last of its two-storey cars in February 1972; the Illinois Central, the first of its Highliners for the Chicago suburbs in May 1971. Two cars came from the St Louis manufacturers to inaugurate the service; 130 were on order, but the management was anxious to impress users with the 156-seat vehicles. Also in Chicago, the Chicago, Burlington

& Quincy has embraced the double-deck rail coach and in the suburbs of Milwaukee 160-seat Budd cars daily demonstrate their capacity for moving commuters, as is also being done in Montreal and on many ·other North American suburban routes.

Despite the brisk interest now being taken in the double-decker round the world, its progress is uncertain. It is difficult to incorporate easy stairs for crowds without using so much space that its first-glance advantages have evaporated; usually they are so tight to gauge that special routeing is essential. Then the concentration of passengers at the end doors causes delay at stations. Delay was reputedly the British Southern's experience with the Bulleid double-deck units, put into traffic in November 1949, and withdrawn in 1971. These had interlaced compartments in pairs, each lower compartment giving access to an upper one, each pair providing 22 seats. There were 508 normal seats in each four-car set, plus 44 occasional seats, or a total of 1,104 passengers on an eight-car train. The ingenuity of design was noticeable in the tare weight of each four-car unit, which was the same as a single-deck unit at 134 tons, giving a tare of about 470lb a seat. With a flat underframe the height to floor level was 3ft 8⅛in and the overall height 12ft 10½in. The trains were passed only for the Dartford routes from Charing Cross and Cannon Street and latterly worked mainly on Bexleyheath line services. After experimental running it was decided to embark instead on the costly 10-car scheme, involving lengthening of platforms and track rearrangements at many stations and also involving new connections at Metropolitan Junction. A very small addition to the dimensions would have greatly increased the comfort of the stock, but increased vertical height under bridges and tunnels might have been very costly.

The Southern venture has not been the end of double-deck talk in Britain; in *Modern Railways* of June 1969, a design put forward by the British Airports Authority for a Heathrow-Victoria connecting train was illustrated. Very much based on the French well-frame design of 1933, it provided for 101 luxury seats in a shell 60ft 6in long, by 9ft 1in wide, by 13ft 1in high. A well design based on the Cartic 4 car-carrying wagon was suggested in 1965 inside the dimensions of 46ft between the bogie centres of an articulated set by 9ft wide by 13ft 1in high. Each 46ft section would contain 92 seats, 48 up and 44 down, with at least 6ft headroom on each deck. A train of 14 units to occupy a 10-car platform was said to have a probable capacity of 1,288 seats, or 1,750 with a modest complement of standing passengers. Further research into the double-deck suburban train might be necessary here if the prophesied population increase towards the end of the century causes heavy concentrations of peak-hour business, which might also be produced by shorter hours or the four-day week.

Travelling Post Offices

IN THE eighteenth century the British Post Office was bitterly opposed to Palmer's suggestion of the use of stage coaches to speed the mails, but half a century later its controllers were more broadminded and within two months of the opening of the Liverpool & Manchester Railway on September 15, 1830, letters were being carried by the trains. This was even before freight traffic began. By the time the Grand Junction Railway opened between Birmingham & Newton on July 4, 1837, the Post Office was able to offer a 16½-hour transit from London by stage coach to Birmingham and thence by rail to either Liverpool or Manchester. A sorting carriage (a converted horse-box) ran from Birmingham to Liverpool from January 6, 1838, on the suggestion of Frederick Karstadt.

It was decided to provide a specially built vehicle for the service and John Ramsey (appointed Inspector General of the Post Office for his idea) devised the apparatus for exchanging bags of mail at stations without stopping the train. The apparatus was incorporated in the new vehicle and used in conjunction with lineside catching nets and standards on which the bags to be collected could be hung.

Sir Rowland Hill, instigator of Post Office reform (including also the universal penny post) was a member of the board of directors of the London, Brighton & South Coast Railway on its formation in 1846 and

Top: Jubilee No 5659 heads the down West Coast Postal at the Harrow pick-up point in June 1947. *Ian Allan library*

Above: Late-fee posting box on 1885 postal sorting van of West Coast Joint stock. *British Transport Museum (B Sharpe)*

Right above: Preserved 1838 postal coach of the Grand Junction Railway. *British Transport Museum (B Sharpe)*

Right: Catching net rigged on the side of the postal sorting van. *John Topham Ltd*

throughout his service with the Post Office (1846-1864) powerfully advocated maximum use of railway facilities for mail services. As a result travelling post offices became used to a larger extent on railways in Britain than anywhere else in the world. Not only is time saved by being able to sort letters in transit, but 'late fee' letters can be posted actually on the trains.

The parcels post was inaugurated in 1883 and two years later special Post Office parcels sorting vans were in service on the railways. At one time the requirements of HM Postmaster - General were said to dominate the compilation of the railway timetable, with meticulously observed exchange points, such as Tamworth, between the West Coast route and the Midland's South-West to North-East links. Although the Great Western, with the rather pompous phrase about 'compliance with directions received from Her Majesty's PMG', was first with exclusive night mail trains in 1840, the most famous night mail was the West Coast Postal Limited, which became all-mail in 1885, had some very high-speed running between stops, and was the subject of the famous documentary film which had the theme poem:

'This is the Night Mail crossing the Border
Bringing the cheque and the postal order.'

At the maximum there were nearly 200 TPO services and 132 apparatus stations on railways in Britain. The special services have been much reduced, owing to the development of the Inter-City regular-headway passenger network, road connections and air services. During 1971 the apparatus stations, which had been eliminated of recent years on many routes, vanished entirely, their ingenious techniques having outlived their usefulness.

Top: Sorting mail inside the travelling post office. *John Topham Ltd*

Left: Trackside rig for mailbag exchange manned by Post Office staff, with bag ready for pick-up. *Ian Allan library*

Above: Vanside rig ready to drop a bag into the trackside net and snatch one into its own net. *Ian Allan library*

Overleaf: Last of steam operation at Nassington Ironstone quarry near Oundle in December 1970. *D Huntriss*

Below: A LNWR radial coach built in the 1880s for the West Coast Joint stock and fitted with TPO equipment.

6
Changing Patterns in Freight Operations

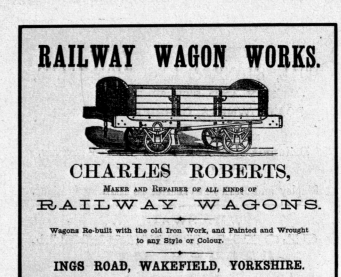

DEVELOPMENT OF FREIGHT SERVICES TO 1900

Above: Wagon builder's advertisement of 1866. *Charles Roberts & Co Ltd*

Above right: Early example of the use of iron for a wagon, on a German railway in 1860. *DB Film Archiv*

Below: Mixed passenger/goods train at Potsdam station on the Berlin-Potsdam Railway. *DB Film Archiv*

ALTHOUGH THE railway originated with the mineral business, the commercial railways which spread so quickly after the Liverpool & Manchester success of 1830 were not very eager for freight business; several, such as the London & Birmingham, put it in the hands of an agent, former stage-coach proprietor Horne. However, it was soon seen to be a highly remunerative branch of business and by the end of the nineteenth century there was a complex series of sundries services throughout the country, with 'road vans' doing station-to-station business, numerous direct services on the heavy traffic flows and tranship depots for making fast transits over less popular routes.

With the coming of the Great Northern Railway to London, there was a determined effort to sell coal by rail and the GNR did its own marketing. Coal had hitherto come to the Metropolis by sea and the North London Railway was used by the Northumberland & Durham Coal Company, which had its own engines and wagons, to deliver coal from West India Docks into London suburbs, until it bought out the cuckoo in its nest in 1859. In the eighteen-seventies the Midland became so enthusiastic for the coal business that it helped the District Railway to build a connection from Hammersmith to Ravenscourt Park to get depots on the District at West Kensington and High Street. In 1882 it went further and built a coal depot at Maidstone, 40 miles from its system, on the London, Chatham & Dover line.

Towards the end of the century, with horse-and-cart delivery from stations, small towns vied to be within five miles of the railway and places over 10 miles from the line were thought to be in the wilds; but they were rare—around Hartland Point in Devon and west of the Cheviots in Northumberland in England.

As steam shipping made the import of iron ore cheap the railways had a freight bonanza, with coal for shipment going down to the South Wales ports and ore going back up to the steelworks of Ebbw Vale and Dowlais. Consett began to rely on Swedish ore imported through the Tyne; from the west coast of Cumberland haematite ore went over Stainmore to Durham steelworks and Durham coke passed it on the 1,300ft climb going to the furnaces of Workington.

Despite many unbraked and dumb-buffered wagons in mineral service, the hand-braked 6-ton and 10-ton wagons in Britain offered speedy services, compared with the 10mph or so of the Continent, in the latter part of the 19th century. Trains of 200 tons or so ran at 30mph from London to Exeter on the GWR and the LNWR had some runs nearly as good between London Camden and Stockport. Midland Railway London to Manchester services and Great Eastern Doncaster to London Spitalfields timings came out at 23mph and the Great Northern got the goods from Kings Cross to Liverpool between nine o'clock at night and half-past seven next morning, with 28mph running on the main line to Retford, including stops. For many years the fish and cattle came from Aberdeen to London faster than the passengers!

With British business largely in the brown-paper-parcel category, there were not the opportunities that existed in America for the big bogie wagon and 1,000-ton or more loads, hauled over long distances; such services depended on bigger locomotives, developed with a more-generous loading gauge and the universal use of the air brake, where British railways made a grudging application of the vacuum brake to a few thousand of their 1,200,000 wagons used on express freight trains. The British burden of 600,000 private owners wagons had much to do with this.

This page far left: A L&NW Class G 0-8-0, originally introduced in 1893 and rebuilt in 1906, piloting a small-wheel goods 4-6-0 near Harrow.

Left: Horses used in the railway goods yard at Whitstable in the early nineteen-hundreds. *Ian Allan Library*

Below: Typical nineteenth-century goods engine with small-diameter coupled wheels, of the Prussian State Railway in 1892. *DB Film Archiv*

Overleaf: A goods train of the London & South Western Railway, hauled by 'Colossus', a Beyer Peacock 0-6-0 of 1866. *C Hamilton Ellis*

Bottom: Where the GWR 7ft gauge interchanged with the standard gauge at Gloucester, freight had to be transhipped, causing delay and inconvenience. *Illustrated London News*

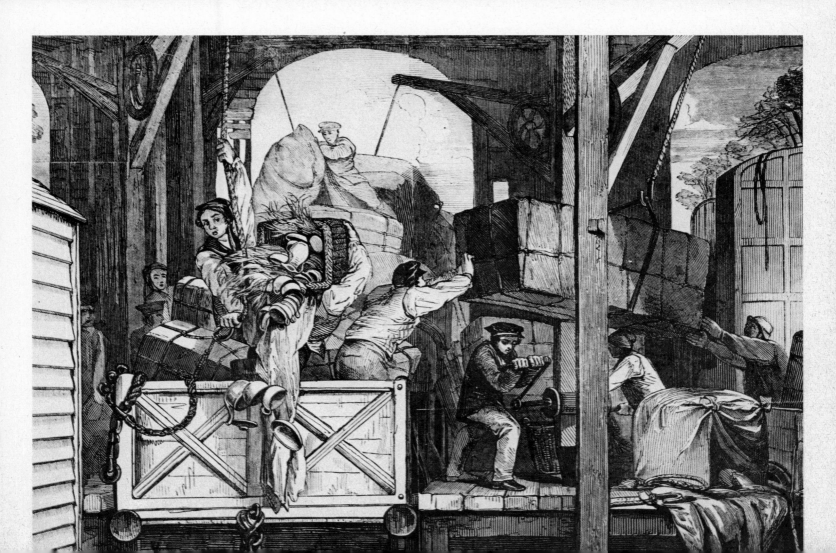

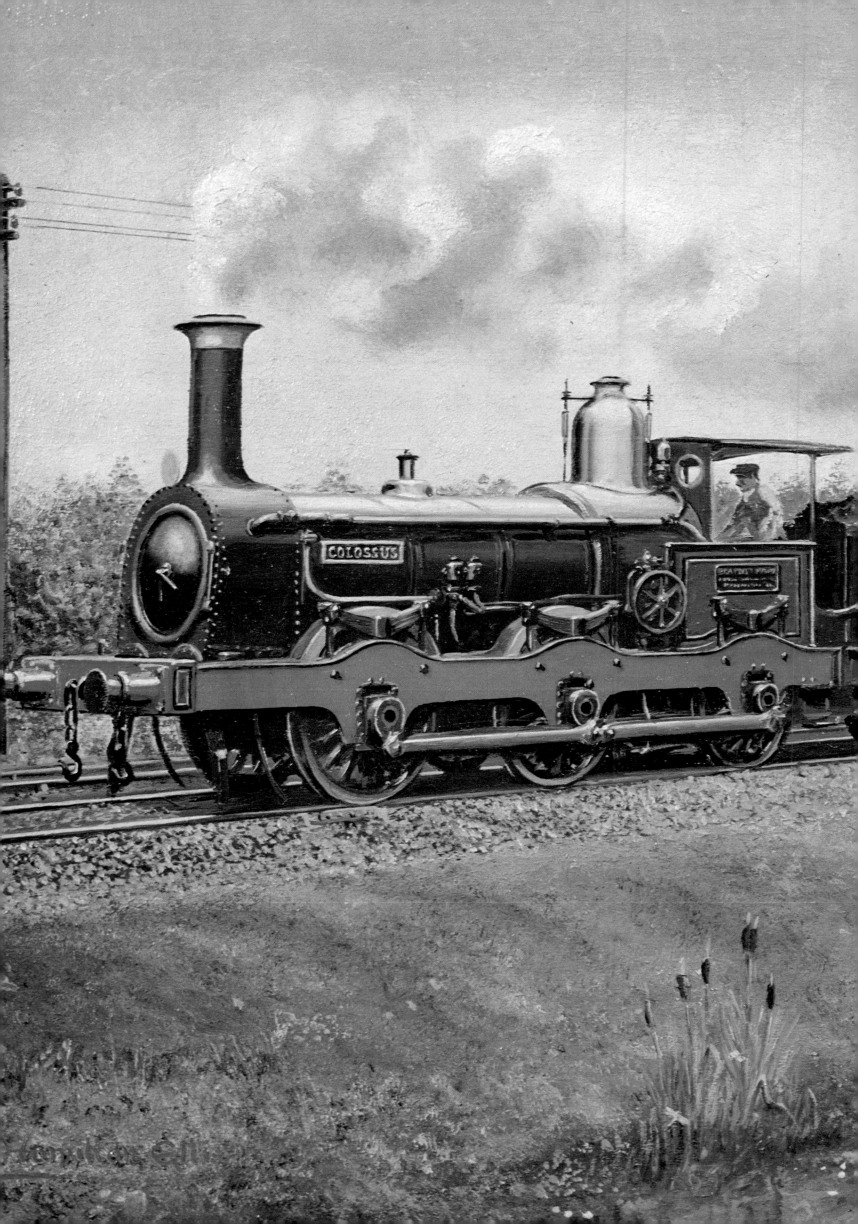

Twentieth Century Freight Services

BY THE BEGINNING of the twentieth century the depots for handling goods had grown from the 'wharf' of the early railways to a multiplicity of small goods yards set up at frequent intervals over the entire railway system, very often with domestic coal in mind as the principal traffic and with their spacing largely governed by the convenient delivery radius within the compass of a horse and cart. There was a leaven of larger depots between which regular services of sundries traffic were provided, sometimes with the aid of transhipment sheds en route.

Various degrees of sophistication were discernible, coal yards ranged from those without any mechanical aids, beyond a sack-weighing scales to comply with coal delivery regulations, to those where traffic had to be conveyed in hopper-bottom wagons to be dropped into the appropriate merchants' bins. The Midland Railway had a number where the wagons were positioned by electric traversers taking power from overhead wires, an improvement over rope and capstan methods and a considerable step from movement by pinch bar and muscle. Horses were used to move wagons in many depots and to save space in layouts. Turntables were made use of to a considerable degree; as they were usually designed round the dimensions of a 10-ton four-wheeled wagon, they helped to limit wagon sizes and explain the lack of interest in bogie freight stock.

There was discernible about 1920 a period

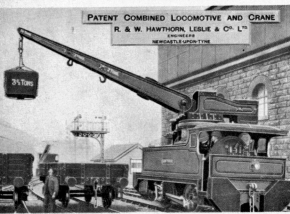

Top: Goods station at Hereford served entirely by horse transport shortly after the turn of the century. *A Wood*

Above centre: One of the early pieces of railway goods yard mechanisation, the loco crane. *A Wood*

Above: LNWR horse and cart of early 1900s with a load of empty fish boxes. *A Wood*

Right: Modern metamorphosis of the railway yard at Sotteville on the SNCF now being equipped with automatic control by the French Westinghouse company. *WABCO/Europe*

of over-mechanisation, when too many cranes were installed in some depots; the work accomplished did not match the capital expenditure. On the other hand, hand-barrowing, wasteful of manpower and time, was still the rule in many. Scientific investigation of needs, and equipment to provide logically for those needs, was initiated by the LMS in the 1930s. Wagons were placed in depots by wagon-hauling mules and power capstans instead of shunting engines; they were loaded for outward journeys by the collection vehicle circulating in the depot; inwards consignments came on to a narrow platform and were conveyed away to the delivery round vehicles by slat conveyors. Derby St Marys

and Birmingham Lawley Street were made showpieces and many others were used for various experiments, but they were brought to an end by the war of 1939. Classic depots of the period were those rebuilt by the Great Western at such points as Bristol Temple Meads, Wolverhampton and Paddington.

While wagon-load traffic and the return of empty private owners' coal wagons remained a supreme traffic consideration, marshalling yards for wagon sorting, usually mechanised for operation of points leading to the balloons of sorting sidings and with primary and secondary retarders to reduce the speed of wagons running by gravity off the hump, were vital to operation. The block

train concept and the development of the container into the Freightliner (see lengthy description pages 253-7) has reduced the use of marshalling yards and many built by British Railways in the first flush of modernisation after 1955 have already been abandoned. Slat conveyors or adaptations from moving walkways and gantry cranes for shifting containers sideways to ships and road vehicles seem to be essentials of the late twentieth-century goods depot. One can be sure also that the depots themselves, more productive through mechanisation, will be spaced very much more widely to take advantage of the mobility of motor delivery vehicles.

Left: Completely covered goods shed of the GWR at Bristol, from an 1842 lithograph by J C Bourne. *British Transport Museum (B Sharpe)*

Above: Early railway mechanical transport, a steam wagon of the LNWR in North Wales. *A Wood*

Below: A Class 8F 2-8-0 with a freight train crossing the West Coast main line at Wigan in December 1966. *M J Esau*

Overleaf: Class 8F 2-8-0 No 48448 at Cliviger, climbing towards Copy Pit with coal empties for Healey Mills yard in February 1968. *M A Collins*

COAL BY RAIL

A BR 8F locomotive hauling standard 16-ton steel wagons between Todmorden and Burnley in March 1965. *D Huntriss*

Bottom: New Santa Fe block train of coal for a steelworks pictured near Flagstaff, Arizona. *Santa Fe Railroad*

COAL IS THE traffic round which the earliest railways were built; they were the most practical way of moving heavy loads in the mines and the track spread the load instead of sinking into the ground as the wheels of common carts did when loaded. But long-distance conveyance of coal from colliery to market took some time to become commonplace—for some years it was a short downhill transit from mine to staith and then shipment by coaster the traditional way to reach London; Midlands works received their coal supplies largely by water also, but in that case by canal barge or narrow boat.

The London & North Western Railway had a snobbish inhibition against carrying coal, ranking it with manure as something to be kept out of the sight of first-class passengers—hence the screens between platforms and goods lines at their typical large stations. A decade passed after the railway reached London before a modest coal depot was built at Camden. The Great Northern on the other hand, when it reached Kings Cross, brash and out to do business wherever it could, opened a depot for the sale of Yorkshire coal in 1851. The general manager's brother, moreover, was the monopolist merchant.

Competition soon brought an end to that and the Midland began to bring Leicestershire coal to London at prices competitive not only with seaborne coal but with the Great Northern's commodity brought from half as far again. With the growth of steam shipping and appreciation all over the world of the virtues of coal as a heating agent, for gas production or the basis of steam power, enormous quantities of coal were moving from mine to factory, to every home and to ports for shipment by the end of the century. It was so cheap and labour so plentiful that no great sophistication developed in its transport. Coal was moved in 6-ton, 8-ton and 10-ton wagons which were mainly supplied by collieries and coal merchants; there were about 600,000 private owners' wagons on railways in Britain, mainly in the coal trade, and they

roundly equalled the numbers supplied by the railway companies. These small units had to be marshalled to return empty to the right collieries and outward to the correct consignees and despite several attempts to suppress the private wagons, traders clung to their rights, established from the pre-steam railway days when the railway was looked upon as a special sort of toll road.

Wagons were cheap to build and their use as warehouses either by coal merchants or by exporters was tolerated undeterred by theories about demurrage charges. Nearly every great port was distinguished by miles of sidings filled with coal wagons awaiting shipment and the railways accepted this as a penalty for handling such vast tonnages; for many years the total carried came to more than 200 million tons, although this figure counts a good deal of tonnage twice as it exchanged from one company to another—crossing London by the Widened Lines of the Metropolitan and Blackfriars Bridge, en route from the northern companies to the London, Chatham & Dover company's depots, for example. In South Wales alone nearly 60 million tons of coal were raised in the peak years; in 1913 37 million tons were exported and 11 million tons went through the loading plants at Barry Docks—a

record figure for Great Britain—for export.

The horse-and-cart era of delivery from goods and mineral stations set a pattern of small lots, no more than two tons at a time, to domestic and industrial premises and brought about a proliferation of railway depots at frequent intervals along the routes, since the ideal horse haulage radius was thought to be about three miles, with a resultant inefficiency in goods train working. There were 74 goods depots in the London area alone and each of the northern companies, with the exception of the late-arriving Great Central, secured coal depots south of the river to which they sent their own trains by means of complicated running powers. One Midland establishment was at Maidstone, to which its trains toiled, for a short period, over 42 miles of alien tracks from St Pancras by way of the Metropolitan and London, Chatham & Dover Railways.

The coal wagon gradually increased in size until the 10-ton wagon was commonplace and some owners went nap on 12-tonners; high-sided wagons came into operation in the coke trade, but the biggest types could not get under the colliery screens and coal owners seemed unwilling to invest in improved railway loading arrangements. So although early in the twentieth century several railways

were experimenting with 30-ton wagons for general goods, mineral wagons remained of modest size. When after 1920 the Great Western Railway tried to improve coal shipment traffic in South Wales by building 20-ton wagons it became apparent that what they had succeeded in most was arousing the enmity of their customers. Although between 1919 and 1939 much lip-service was paid to the virtues of all wagons in the coal trade being owned by the railway companies, it was not until the 1947 Transport Act that anything positive was done about it, although during both wars steps had been taken by pooling their use to ensure that unnecessary sorting of wagons was curtailed.

Under the 1947 Act the railway companies were nationalised and 585,000 po wagons, mostly for coal, were taken over; as a result the stock issued in compensation was dubbed 'wagon stock' at the Stock Exchange. In the meantime Mr Duncan Bailey of Charles Roberts & Co Ltd, a well-known railway wagon builder, had designed a 16-ton all-steel wagon which would fit into any colliery loading bay and British Railways set about improving on it with 21-ton and 24½-ton wagons, designed to suit more liberally designed colliery screens. A 32-ton hopper was also designed, but as it stood nearly 12 feet above rail level a cut-down version of lower height and only 26 tons capacity was quickly made available, to suit the National Coal Board.

It was in that period that it became increasingly realised that the most satisfactory and economical operation of a railway was obtained by running block trains from colliery sidings to one destination only, without going through a marshalling yard. As far as possible, consistent with the qualities of coal required by the consumer, that is now the pattern of BR coal transport. House coal concentration involves co-operation between National Coal Board, British Railways Board and local coal merchants to provide mechanised plant for dealing with many thousands of tons of fuel a year.

There have been many difficulties. Among them are the independence of small coal merchants; the cost of the necessary plant; the shortness of the haul, which allows little in the way of the charge for the traffic to be allocated to paying for the investment; and in some areas, the small demand for coal, which by the nineteen-fifties was meeting active competition from oil fuel and the threatened competition of North Sea gas. Nevertheless it was in 1957 that a start was made by a Sheffield firm, Burnett & Hallamshire Fuel, which made a decision to concentrate all its solid fuel business in the city on a pioneer mechanised handling plant in the Eastern Region Nunnery depot. It was a private venture, as was one the next year put in by Charringtons at Palace Gates in North London as a pilot scheme, which was closely watched by the trade.

Further action was slow to come, but things began moving in 1962, when the Eastern Region persuaded merchants from a large number of stations to take their coal from plant it erected at Enfield Chase. Bulk tipping lorries were provided for delivery to the merchants' own premises, which are run for the railway today by National Carriers Ltd, the company that took over railway collection and delivery fleets under the 1968 Transport Act. This arrangement enabled small wayside coal depots on the main line, such as New Southgate, to be closed, and what is more important, from its benefit in shutting down a costly freight train operation, the night service to be given to the yards on the High Barnet branch, where the passenger service is provided by London Transport electric tube trains. Enfield line depots between Wood Green and Bayford were also closed, with consequent saving in freight train mileage.

Another event in 1962 was the coming together, after much negotiation, of the National Coal Board, the British Railways Board, and the Coal Merchants Federation of Great Britain, in a tripartite agreement which, based on the experience so far obtained, settled the general lines of concentration for the future, but left local details to be cleared up by regional and local committees. As a result coal movement has been rationalised almost everywhere, although not all of it moves in lengthy block trains and not so many mechanised depots have been erected as was at one time hoped.

Mechanical plant is very costly and consequently it requires a reasonably long haul from the coalfield to keep the traffic

profitable to British Railways and at the same time to permit some contribution towards the interest on the expenditure, so a big annual throughput is also essential. A typical plant was one of the first to open under the tripartite agreement at West Drayton on the Western Region, where it was bounded by the Frays River and the curve of the West Drayton to Staines branch. It was designed for an annual distribution of 200,000 tons of fuel and the 40,000-ton stock provides 23 varieties. The designed daily peak movement is 1,200 tons, or on a weekly basis, 6,500 tons. Trains come from the South Wales or the East Midlands coalfields and are composed of 21-ton hopper wagons. The siding layout is simple; the train engine backs the train in to discharge its load into a chamber below the track and the train of empty wagons then proceeds towards London to turn back at a convenient point. A conveyor takes the fuel at 120 tons an hour from the receiving hopper to the selected one of 12 60-ton delivery hoppers or 10 10-ton hoppers. The hoppers feed 46 bagging points where lorries are loaded for the western suburbs of London. A transfer point on the conveyor feeds an automatic boom stacker which takes fuel to the desired part of the 40,000-ton stacking ground. As required

the stacker can retrieve the fuel and dispatch it to the delivery hoppers.

At Taunton in 1964 the Western Region opened an interesting combined freight and coal concentration depot, designed to serve by road destinations in the 30-mile radius. The local coal merchants joined in the £300,000 combined investment through Taunton Coal Concentration Ltd. It was intended, on the solid fuel side, to handle up to 500 tons a day, but in the seasonal nature of the coal trade this means about 80,000 tons a year.

To avoid heavy investment in conveyor belts and large hopper structures, some non-mechanised concentration depots have been set up. They are necessary in the green fields areas where block trains are unjustified but the haul from the nearest mechanised depot would be too costly by road. The equipment varies from portable conveyors and digger shovels to plain old-fashioned shovel and muscle power. But there are also manually operated concentration depots in highly urbanised areas where the run from the coalfields brings only small remuneration to the railway and it has been agreed with the coal merchants that while block trains are desirable, heavy investment in plant is not. In the West Midlands it was intended to concentrate the work of 168 depots in the

then Birmingham Division into eight new establishments, but apart from the investment aspect there were environmental reasons for not adopting a size of depot that would have involved annual throughputs of 350,000 tons a year in the heart of the conurbation, with the concomitant congestion of coal delivery lorries in central area streets. A plan was therefore hammered out for use of two dozen smaller depots, designed to pass 40,000 or 50,000 tons of fuel a year as a minimum, or at least two trainloads a week.

Three depots in Birmingham, at Aston, Monument Lane and Lawley Street, opened on November 4, 1963, and Stratford-on-Avon and Leamington Spa followed a week later. The first block coal train to a non-mechanised depot ran on December 2 to Aston, and the entire programme was on its way to completion in about a year. The distance from the pithead to many of these depots is only 15 or 20 miles, making for a low rate out of which to recoup extra investment costs. The depots are under mixed management, but there are also some private depots, such as the one on the Pensnett Industrial Estate (connected with the ancient Pensnett private railway which served the Earl of Dudley's steelworks and collieries) where conveyors take the fuel from under-

track drops to overhead bins from which the lorries are fed. The Pensnett depot also has a railhead for pig-iron to serve Black Country industry from the steelworks at the Ford Motor Company's Dagenham plant.

Coal concentration has enabled wagons to go into intensive circuit working and the regular runs have improved locomotive utilisation. This is exemplified still better in the principal industrial use of coal—in the generating stations of the Central Electricity Generating Board, where, despite the rivalry of oil fuel and nuclear power, aided in a small way by paraffin-powered gas turbine plant, the demand for electrical energy is so great that use of coal has increased from 34 million tons in 1962 to 66 million tons in 1971, thus compensating to a large degree for the reduction in domestic demand. A 2,000-megawatt power station, of which six were completed during the last part of the 1960s, will absorb 20,000 tons of coal a day and some are able to accept the output of several collieries. A little of it is waterborne, but a considerable proportion of the coal required comes by rail.

Where possible coal is handled by modern 'no hands' methods, the train running over the generating station hoppers at slow speed and the bottom doors of the hopper wagons being opened automatically by mechanical tripping gear. The unloading equipment is provided by the Generating Board under an agreement signed with British Railways in a glare of publicity at the beginning of 1964. The counterpart of automatic loading into a moving train at the colliery end has been implemented much more slowly by the National Coal Board, which has no doubt taken note of the CEGB endeavours (so far frustrated by teething troubles) to rely to an increasing extent on the commercialisation of nuclear fission. However, the ideal merry-go-round system, with the train not stopping at either end for loading or unloading, is quite practicable, and ensures that maximum utilisation of

the wagons is obtained.

First English merry-go-round at a power station to get off the ground was West Burton, in Nottinghamshire, then the largest coal-fired power station in Europe, with a consumption of about five million tons a year. Trains of up to 50 permanently coupled 46-ton-gross (32 tons of coal) wagons are chute loaded at 14 pits, including for a start the super-modern Bevercotes, and hauled by diesel-electric locomotives to West Burton where, controlled by the signalman in a modern power box, the train enters the merry-go-round loop and the six whole-width bottom doors are automatically opened while the train moves at a steady half-a-mile an hour, despite the diminishing load, under the control of a very precise locomotive speed control. Discharge takes place at a rate of 2,500 tons an hour; although the hopper capacity below the track is only 1,200 tons, the conveyor belts discharge coal into the power station at 3,000 tons an hour. In all, about 50 collieries are involved in 15 merry-go-round schemes, which beside power stations include working to the vast Northfleet cement works in Kent and the Immingham jetty for export coal.

In Scotland the South of Scotland Electricity Board station at Cockenzie was the first to have circuit working, from Monktonhall colliery over part of the Tranent-Cockenzie wagonway, which is so old as to have figured in the official account of the Battle of Prestonpans. There 84 wagons, running in 28-wagon trains, do the work that by the old rule-of-thumb methods would have needed more than 1,500 wagons and at Monktonhall four acres of sidings replace the 250 acres that would have been needed formerly. The wagons on this circuit generate three million ton-miles a year instead of the 22,000 ton-miles of the conventional coal wagon in old-time wagon-load working.

Another interesting railway task is to take import coal of certain specialised grades from port to steelworks; for the

block trains to carry it wagons of 50 tons gross weight have been designed, with 25-ton axle-loads—about the maximum that can be sustained in Britain. A new form of friction-damped pedestal suspension has been developed for working the new wagons at 60mph or more. So although the tonnage of coal moved by British Railways was only 107,318,000 in 1971, the prospects of profitability, owing to rationalisation, are bright. There are several factors that help: closing of wayside depots to the tune of over 200 in Greater London alone in 15 years to 1970; consequent movement of block trains to the remaining larger depots; circuit working and merry-go-rounds from colliery to consumer; and maximisation of wagon size with aids to quick discharge. Far from declining, railways show in their handling of coal traffic technological advance and managerial and marketing skills.

PIGGYBACK OPERATIONS OF NORTH AMERICA

CLAIMED TO BE the world's fastest freight train, the Super C scorches along the Atchison, Topeka & Santa Fe Railway's main line at better than 75 miles an hour! Clad in blue, silver and yellow, as many as three throbbing diesel locomotive units totalling more than 10,000 horsepower head a train made up of piggyback shipments riding on 89ft-long flat cars on roller bearing-equipped wheels. The load adds up to 2,000 gross tons of steel wagons, road semi-trailer vans, wheelless container vans and cargo all dynamically balanced and suspended precisely above the two thin-ribboned steel rails as it plummets along at quite remarkable speed.

Santa Fe created Super C in 1967 as a premium-rated train to piggyback trailers and containers at passenger train speeds. Running seven days a week as train No 198 westbound and No 891 eastbound, Super C slashes 17 hours from the next-best through freight schedule over the 2,220-mile route between Chicago, Kansas City and Los Angeles. The train is due out of Chicago at nine o'clock each morning, booked on a 40-hour schedule, but capable enginemen along the way frequently manage to put 'The C' into LA several hours ahead of time. Such speed compares with the timing of the famous passenger streamliner Super Chief, which boasts a best schedule of $39\frac{1}{2}$ hours over the same route. For the premium-speed freight rate of $1,484, a shipper can waybill a $17\frac{1}{2}$-ton trailerload via Super C whereby it will move faster than by road and cheaper than by air. Train speed must remain consistently near, and often above, the mile-a-minute mark. But the zenith in speed probably occurs in the great Southwestern desert country between Winslow, Arizona and Gallup, New Mexico. Along that 127.2-mile stretch of track, train 891 is scheduled to maintain a minimum overall running speed of 72.7mph.

Super C aptly demonstrates that speed and priority handling are the names of the piggyback game, where the 90ft super

flat-tops average $3\frac{1}{2}$ times the daily mileage of other freight wagons. Thundering over 46 American and the two principal Canadian railroads, hundreds of daily fast-scheduled freight trains move nearly two million piggyback wagonloads annually—a truly phenomenal traffic growth for a transport service that has existed for less than two decades. Numerous trains emulate Super C by catering only for trailer and container van payloads, while many other trains sandwich piggyback wagons among the conventional mixture of boxcars, gondolas, tanks and refrigerators. Probably for lack of a better word, the highly descriptive nickname 'piggyback' has enjoyed a popular persistence through the years to denote what is officially termed TOFC (Trailers On Flat Cars) and COFC (Containers On Flat Cars).

But whatever the name, it all amounts to a very convenient and economical way to pre-package, or containerise, freight. The slow and costly chore of intermediate manual transfer of less-than-wagonload (lcl) shipments between lorries and boxcars is avoided and indeed, this deficit operation caused the phasing out of most lcl freight stations during the 1950s. In their place, a railroad or its affiliated road haulage line can offer much the same service in its own trailers as TOFC traffic. Furthermore, the same TOFC marketing is applied to solicit trailers of all common carrier hauliers where the piggyback rate on hauls of 500 miles or more is ten cents or more per ton-mile cheaper than throughout road haulage.

The idea of transporting wheeled vehicles on railroad flat cars is not a new one. Way back in 1858, the Nova Scotia Railway (now part of the Canadian Pacific's Dominion Atlantic) offered the service for farmer's wagons. Numerous crude forms of piggyback appeared through the years, mostly experimental in nature, but perhaps the longest-lasting and best-remembered is the circus train with its ornately

decorated wagons. The highly refined high-speed concept of TOFC of today began in 1953, when Pullman-Standard introduced the first specially designed big flat to carry trailers. The 75ft wagon apparently appealed to Southern Pacific, which later that year established the first regular TOFC run carrying semi-trailers of its affiliated lorry line, Pacific Motor Freight, between Los Angeles and San Francisco, a distance of 470 miles.

How it all works and what makes it go is completely unlike anything ever seen in railroading, from the concepts of rate-making to the homogeneous mating of normally opposite transport forms and the physical mechanics of rail-haul accomplishment. First must come the Plan, the foundation of agreement and paperwork to make it all possible. Under five possible plans, rates are determined by who performs what service(s) and whose equipment is used, as follows:

Plan I — Railroad flat cars, trucker's (road haulier's) trailers. Trucker performs pick-up and delivery.

Plan II — Railroad flat cars, railroad trailers. Railroad performs pick-up and delivery, but variations can have it done by truckers.

Plan III — Railroad flat cars, private shipper's trailers. Shipper performs pick-up and delivery.

Plan IV — Private shipper's flat cars, private shipper's trailers. Private shipper performs pick-up and delivery.

Plan V — Railroad flat cars, railroad or trucker's trailers. Either party performs a road haul at one or both ends of the rail haul.

After the plan comes the hardware, that special type of wagon equipment designed to carry vehicles that, in the purist concept, were never intended to ride the rails. Today's piggybacking wagon or flat car is longer than a Pullman and must ride like one at high speed to protect the valuable cargo. Its loading deck measures 89 feet 4 inches long and 9 feet wide, coupled length is 92 feet $8\frac{1}{2}$ inches and weight is 32 tons. Running gear is two four-wheeled high-speed bogies. While earlier versions were built in 75-foot and 85-foot lengths, today's standard car just described will accommodate one 45-foot and one 40-foot trailer, or two 40-foot trailers, or three 27-foot trailers. The maximum payload capacity of most of them is 65 tons and the total combined weight of a wagon, trailers and cargo can run to 101 tons. The overhead clearance height of a loaded super flat can be over 17 feet.

The traditional method of loading/unloading trailers utilises a sloping ramp placed at the end of a stub track. Diesel tractors are used to push or pull the cumbersome trailers over the incline bridging the 42 inches between ground level and wagon deck. A string of coupled wagons is usually dealt with at one time, movable steel bridge plates affording an unbroken running surface from car to car

To secure trailers firmly in place on flat cars, special hitch assemblies are raised from the car deck to engage the trailer kingpins and chains are attached to the tandem axles.

The spectacular growth of piggyback has rendered the simple ramp method too slow. In the larger terminals it is replaced by huge power lifts on pneumatic tyres that move alongside the rake of wagons lifting the trailers on and off as required. One type straddles the wagons with steel legs and wheels on each side and works like an overhead crane; another type works from one side only. The cranes can load or unload 30-ton trailers at the rate of one every two minutes, permitting final reporting time only an hour in advance of train departure time.

The story of piggyback must necessarily include the story of Trailer Train Company, Chicago, which owns most of the wagons and leases them to all railroads, to move freely from line to line as needed and to Canada and Mexico. Pennsylvania Railroad and Norfolk & Western organised TT in 1956 and the company is today owned by 33 railroads and one freight forwarding company. Representing a total investment of $900 million, its vast fleet of 60,000 cars includes COFC/TOFC flats, two- and three-level motorcar carriers which have steel racks applied to the standard TOFC car, and other special types.

The largest part of the TT fleet is the TTX piggyback flat, of which there are 30,665. Designed principally to PRR specifications by Max Seel, Trailer Train's now-retired Manager of Engineering, today's TOFC flat costs nearly $18,000 and is built for TT by Pullman-Standard Company, Bethlehem Steel Company or ACF Industries. TTX cars are repaired and maintained at 23 contract shops located strategically on the various owner railroads. In 1970, the car fleet posted an amazing 97.8-per cent utilisation factor which was achieved with high maintenance standards, an average age of only seven years and high-demand service.

American railroads, in contrast to TT Company, have but 7,854 of their own piggyback cars, but they are also employed in through interline service to other railroads. Santa Fe and Southern Pacific/Cotton Belt are among the biggest fleet owners, with over 1,000 wagons each.

Across the border in Canada, TOFC is likewise a booming business, especially because great distances between cities, rugged terrain and severe winter weather make road haulage costly, time-consuming and downright hazardous. TOFC has given the trucker an inexpensive way out and one who might have hesitated to extend his routes westward across the Rockies can now do so with ease. But the Canadian approach to flat car equipment owned by railroads is conservative. The longest wagons are 63 feet, permitting the loading of one large trailer or two of the smaller 27-foot variety. It means more wagons or fewer trailers per train, but

provides better flexibility in switching and routeing. Canadian National owns 1,060 flat cars and CP Rail (Canadian Pacific) has 1,600; they are not permitted off the home line.

With modest piggyback forms extant for many years, the fundamental reason for its sudden boom in the 1950s seems to be that the economic climate was ripe for such a technique. Rising wages and other operating costs, due largely to inflationary pressures, seemed almost automatically to send the big highway trailers scurrying to the TOFC ramps, where they could enjoy both lower ton-mile rates and faster delivery speed. The following figures compiled by the Association of American Railroads emphasise the phenomenal growth of the traffic:

Year	Wagonloads
1955	168,150
1960	554,115
1965	1,034,377
1971	1,196,519*

*Total number of trailers and containers handled 1,962,729.

Looking now at TOFC operations of several representative railroads, the pioneering Southern Pacific/Cotton Belt system in its inaugural piggybacking year of 1953 carried just 2,634 trailers and containers. By 1969 the total had soared to 270,079 units handled through 73 terminals—approximately half of all such traffic carried in the Western District of the United States. SP operates no all-TOFC trains but its busiest through routes, handling great quantities of flat-car trade in regular fast-scheduled service, run out of the largest terminal, Los Angeles, to San Francisco (470 miles), to Portland, Oregon (1,188 miles) and to St Louis, Missouri (2,446 miles). Blue Streak Merchandise is the train making the longest and fastest run—over the LA-St Louis route in 50½ hours, running via North Fort Worth, Texas and the Cotton Belt east of that point.

In the East, the Pennsylvania Railroad (now merged into Penn Central) was an early TOFC advocate with its fast-flying TrucTrains TT1/TT2 separating New York and Chicago by only 26 hours, which was but 10 hours more than it took the crack Broadway Limited to make the run. Serving the highly industrialised New England, Northeast and Middle West areas of America, Penn Central is the undisputed king of piggybacking, as its 34 terminals include the world's largest at Kearny, New Jersey, its daily fleet of 42 all-TOFC trains is by far the most on any road, and its total of 421,000 trailers and 80,000 Flexi-Van containers of mail represented more than 26 per cent of all piggyback business handled in America during 1971.

Now named TrailVan service, Penn Central's extensive operations employ a daily average of 2,700 Trailer Train wagons, plus its own Flexi-Van container flats for the long-distance bulk mail trains. While containers are universally transferable between ships, wheeled

Top: One method of loading/unloading piggyback trains is the FWD-Wagner Piggy Packer, here seen at work for SP at Los Angeles. *Southern Pacific Railroad*

Above: In Australia the complete articulated lorries go piggyback on the Trans-Australian Railway. *Commonwealth Railways*

Right centre: A Southern Pacific piggyback train with the Rockies in the background. *Southern Pacific RR*

Right: Lorries and trailers on the Swiss low-level piggyback train for rail tunnel transits. *W H R Godwin*

chassis and railway flat cars, the overwhelming emphasis in domestic service is to take the wheels along, for it has been found more convenient to use standard tandem-axle highway semi-trailers and therefore have the wheels right there at all times. Viewing TrailVan service with an optimistic nature, PC has recently invaded the short-haul market with a $6\frac{1}{2}$-hour overnight run between Chicago and Detroit, Michigan, 272 miles.

By putting together PC's TrailVan train TV3 (New York to Rose Lake Yard in East St Louis, Illinois) and the Blue Streak Merchandise, we come up with a transcontinental running time of $79\frac{1}{2}$ hours for the 3,496 miles between East and West coasts. But the 29-hour TV3 is not a through connection so additional time is required for the necessary transfer. PC traffic managers have found that Avon Yard in Indianapolis, Indiana, is the best gathering point for western connecting cars and trains MCB1/MCB1A run from that point right on through St Louis to the Cotton Belt and onward to Pine Bluff, Arkansas, 401 miles deep in Cotton Belt territory. Even the locomotives go through and in this respect, PC engines have occasionally been seen as far away as Los Angeles. Conversely, SP and CB engines often get as far east as Harrisburg, Pennsylvania, 856 miles from their home rails.

Overall speed in long-distance TOFC service relies on elimination of the delays of interchanging wagons from one railroad to another. Such a service is exemplified by the Transcontinental Highball, a unique run-through collaboration of three railroads to forward piggyback and other priority freight between the Richmond, Virginia, area and California points. The train leaves Richmond each morning at 08.30 via Seaboard Coast Line; the second day finds it at Memphis, Tennessee, on the Frisco Lines; by a minute before midnight of the fourth day, it has arrived in Los Angeles as Santa Fe train 668.

Norfolk & Western's share of piggyback traffic in 1971 came to 186,778 trailers loaded at 52 on-line ramps. While this predominantly Midwestern railroad reaches the Eastern seaboard only in the Norfolk, Virginia, area, by means of advantageous connections with other roads, N&W can compete effectively with Baltimore & Ohio and Penn Central which serve directly the manufacturing and seaport centres of New York, Philadelphia and Baltimore.

Looking at the Canadian traffic scene, total TOFC wagonloadings for 1971, not including containers, were 185,560 in a service that is growing at the rate of about ten per cent a year, although it is quite modest in volume compared to American figures. CP Rail can get a piggyback flat car across Canada from Saint John or Frederickton, (New Brunswick) to Vancouver, (British Columbia) in $5\frac{1}{2}$ days. The longest possible run is 3,754 rail miles via Canadian National from Halifax (Nova

Trailer Train
Container Car

TTCX SERIES

BRIEF SPECIFICATIONS

- 16 pedestals
- 85'-0" overall container loading length
- 8'-0⅜" interior width between pedestals
- 6" clearance between container and deck
- 3'-5½" deck height
- 89'-4" x 9'-0" platform
- steel deck
- 15" travel hydraulic cushioning

POSSIBLE LOADING COMBINATIONS

4-20'	1-20', 1-24', 1-27'	3-27'
3-20'	1-20', 1-24', 1-30'	2-40'
2-20', 1-24'	1-20', 1-24', 1-35'	2-35'
2-20', 1-27'	3-24'	1-35', 1-40'
2-20', 1-30'	2-24', 1-30'	2-30'
2-20', 1-35'	2-24', 1-27'	1-40', 1-27'
2-20', 1-40'	1-24', 1-27', 1-30'	1-40', 1-30'
1-20', 2-24'	1-20', 1-27', 1-30'	1-40', 1-24'
1-20', 2-27'	1-20', 1-27', 1-35'	1-35', 1-30'
	2-27', 1-24'	1-35', 1-24'

CONTAINER LOCK
opens and closes **automatically** when container is loaded or unloaded

NUMBERING SYSTEM
aids in placing pedestals in proper locations when loading containers of different lengths

PEDESTAL LOCK
lugs on bottom of pedestal key into indexing holes in deck

OPERATION
will accommodate the USASI-ISO corner fitting and those of all other container fleets of relatively large size now in operation

STOWING OR ADJUSTING PEDESTALS
easily operated by one man; rotates into or out of storage position; slides along deck slot for adjustment

STOWED POSITION
pedestal back extends only ¾" above deck

Right: US Trailer Train company's flat wagon designed for carrying containers and road semi-trailers. *B Pennypacker*

Right below: Special low-level wagons of German Federal Railway for carrying lorries and trailers through tunnels. *DB Film Archiv*

Bottom: Piggyback loading/unloading area of the Burlington Northern Kansas City yard. *Burlington Northern Inc*

Scotia) to Vancouver, but such a haul, of containers from ships, would probably be a so-called 'land bridge' operation to another ship at Vancouver, thus avoiding the time of an all-water journey through the Panama Canal. Fast overnight service is run between major cities of the busy Eastern manufacturing provinces of Ontario and Quebec, with the largest piggyback terminals located in Montreal.

Canadian National has handled American TOFC traffic to Whittier (Alaska) and the Alaska Railroad, via Prince Rupert (British Columbia) and CNR's Aquatrain ships. In September 1971, CNR opened a new ship-to-rail container terminal at Halifax, thereby offering faster and cheaper general freight service to inland cities than could be offered if the ships continued onward via the St Lawrence Seaway, which since its opening in 1959 has been strangling the life out of Halifax as a seaport. But the strange paradox of it all is that this relatively new CNR COFC service is an example of the government competing against itself, for both railway and seaway have been built, owned and operated at the cost of hundreds of millions of dollars of public funds.

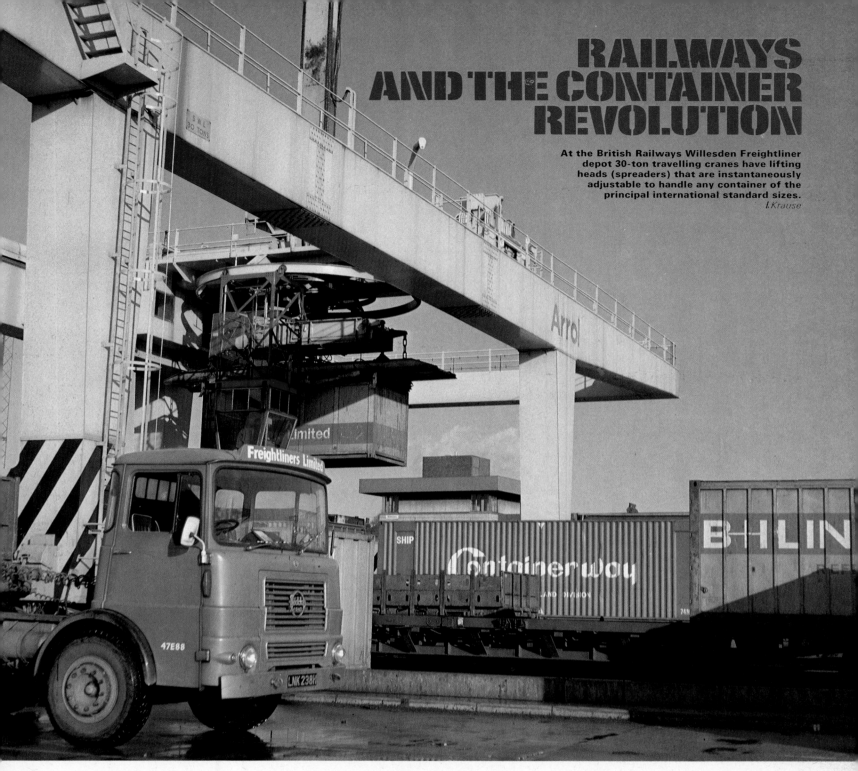

RAILWAYS AND THE CONTAINER REVOLUTION

At the British Railways Willesden Freightliner depot 30-ton travelling cranes have lifting heads (spreaders) that are instantaneously adjustable to handle any container of the principal international standard sizes.
I. Krause

WHAT HAS BEEN described popularly as the 'container revolution' is confidently expected to change the nature of four-fifths of the world's general cargo shipping before the end of the century. It is, nevertheless, not an innovation from the shipping world, but essentially a railway-evolved device which can be traced back to the earliest days of the industrial revolution in Great Britain.

There are many types of container in service, so what are the common features that make them so useful to the transport industry? A container is a strong weather-proof case, in which smaller and, if necessary, assorted goods can be securely packed, suitable for journeys to and fro between more than one transport medium —road, rail, sea or air. It should have a minimum size of one cubic metre and it should be fitted with the necessary equipment for handling at the interfaces between the different forms of transport. For international movement it goes without saying that it must comply with customs requirements and especially it must be capable of being sealed for transit without examination when it passes across intermediate countries.

There is a close resemblance between the work done by containers with lift-on and lift-off movement from one vehicle to another, and vehicles with roll-on—roll-off transfer arrangements. The latter is, as far as can be judged, the older system, having originated in the eighteenth century with cauldrons of coal which were run on to canal barges for the trunk part of their journey. In 1835 there were a number of wagon-boats on the Forth & Clyde Canal which each carried 14 wagons from the Monkland & Kirkintilloch Railway with a total load of 40 tons of coal. At the Dinorwic quarries in North Wales from 1848 until the closing down in recent years, 2ft-gauge wagons carrying slate were loaded four at a time on 4ft-gauge wagons for the transit from quarry to port, over the Padarn Railway.

The Liverpool & Manchester Railway from 1830, and a number of other early railways, carried horses and carriages on flat wagons and Pickfords sent wagon-loads of freight by train without breaking bulk. Because of the desirability of leaving household furniture undisturbed after loading, it was customary throughout the horse haulage era to send pantechnicon loads of household removals by rail in well-wagons. This has its counterpart today in the dispatch by well-wagon of semi-articulated lorry trailers on the Continent and in America to cover the trunk portions of journeys by rail at high speed. Loading-gauge restrictions prevent the kangaroo or piggy-back practice on railways in Britain, except for specially designed trailers.

Very slowly an approach was made to the true container concept. For Continental passengers via Folkestone the South Eastern Railway sent luggage in covered containers, then called boxes, which were lifted bodily on to the ship and carried across the Channel as deck cargo. Alas, the Northern Railway of France would not play ball, and without a crane at Boulogne big enough to lift the box, it had, according

Top: Santa Fe Railway in America uses a rubber-tyred travelling crane at its Corwith yard for road-rail transfer of both containers and 'piggyback' lorry trailers.
Santa Fe Railway   O Brent

Above: A rake of four-wheel wagons with containers mounted, as used on German Federal internal container services.
DB Film Archiv

Below: Half-height containers of china clay being transferred by ordinary mobile crane from road to BR Freightliner wagons for the trunk haul by rail from Par in Cornwall to the London area.   *T E Corin*

Facing page: Typical scene at a Freightliner depot with two cranes busy on road-rail container transfer, although rubber-tyred cranes have now largely been replaced in BR service by high-capacity rail-mounted machines.

to Acworth's complaint in 1889, to unload trunks and suitcases individually from ship to train for the onward journey.

In the early years of the twentieth century the container movement was for the first time named and identified, not by a transport man, but by a banker. He based studies of the sorting and expeditious delivery of goods and parcels upon the work of the Bankers' Clearing House; he proposed to reduce drastically the number of goods depots in each city — he suggested that 74 in London could be replaced by a central goods station in Clerkenwell—and that collection and delivery be brought up-to-date by using three-ton motor vehicles over a 10- or 12-mile radius instead of horse-hauled vans in a three-mile radius. All goods should be handled in containers so that items should not require individual handling; for his purpose wire round a bundle of pipes would make a container so long as the item was easily handled. Tanks, bales of goods, sawn timber in bundles would all have been acceptable to his purpose. As motor lorries developed he expanded his ideas towards five-ton units. An integral part of the Gattie plan was machinery for automatic sorting of parcels and sundries traffic at each town depot; this would have done electro-mechanically what might be attempted with the aid of computers and solid-state switching today.

A Warwick Gattie was not only concerned with transfer of traffic from road to rail and vice versa, and with the much more efficient use of the railway wagon fleet, but with the more efficient loading of ships and their quicker turn-round. A diagram he produced of an adaptation of

one of the London docks looks remarkably like a container berth of today, allowing for the fact that it is intended for smaller units. It was attacked by port and shipping pundits on the grounds that the capital cost could never be afforded. Railway officers showed no greater enthusiasm for containers as part of the daily job. But Warwick Gattie was a vociferous political animal; he ensured that there were Board of Trade inquiries and his friends wrote vitriolic literature about the intelligence of railwaymen, full of coarse statistics to the detriment of the railways and by the time Sir Eric Geddes came on the scene as the first Minister of Transport in 1919 not only had transport people heard about containers, but Geddes had even offered a North Eastern goods shed for experiments.

For some years little was heard. Nevertheless developments continued, although at first they were mostly in the direction of greater use of Lancashire flats (demountable open cart or lorry bodies) in the cotton trade and for meat traffic on the London & South Western Railway, where demountable flats enabled a quick transfer from ship at Southampton to train, and then from Nine Elms in London to Smithfield Market. During 1926 experiments were made with two sizes of open and closed containers for 2½-ton and 4-ton loads and soon the advantages of door-to-door delivery without break of bulk and with less risk of damage or pilferage were being extolled. Traffic grew and by 1935, while there was still little interest, let alone activity, elsewhere, the four great British railway companies had 10,000 containers in service.

When British Railways was formed it

found itself in possession of 15 main types and sizes of container for dry goods and a further range of demountable flats and tanks, mainly glass-lined for milk traffic, built on road vehicle trailers and designed to carry out trunk hauls by rail. There were special containers for furniture, cycles, cement and to carry glass in cradles; open boxes for bricks and tiles; ventilated types for fresh-killed meat; and insulated and highly insulated units for frozen meat and fish and for quick-frozen foods and fruit. When the International Container Bureau took a census in 1950 it was gratifying to find that British Railways was the leader in Western Europe in containerisation—and as far as could be seen, in the whole world—with 35,000 or so large containers.

With Gallic verve the French Railways had developed welded steel containers for wine traffic from Algeria and had overcome the road-to-rail transfer problem by introducing sophisticated means of securing road vehicles for long-distance transits on railway wagons. They and the Germans, and other European railways where the road authorities permitted such massive loads, delivered loaded railway wagons to factories on road vehicles—indeed, there are a number of works with railway sidings and shunting engines to which all the railway wagons are delivered by road.

During the war, for the invasion of France and other campaigns, there was developed the technique of carrying tanks, lorries and railway vehicles on ships which started from a hard rather than a crane-festooned quay and landed on a beach rather than any formal port. Although neither train ferries nor road-vehicle ferries were new concepts, this gave an immense fillip to roll-on—roll-off shipping. In a pioneering venture the Atlantic Steam Navigation Company, formed to provide a rival service to the *Queen Mary* before the war, diverted its activities to carrying commercial vehicles between England and Europe and England and Northern Ireland. The theme has progressed so that transatlantic vehicle transits on wheels are now commonplace and loads of machinery make journeys such as from a Belgian factory via England, Scotland and Skye to a destination in Lewis without the lorry being unpacked.

It became obvious to those interested in the container that it was not making the headway that might have been expected from its proved advantages, one of which is the much better use of shipping space made by packing boxes in a hold than when the hold is used as a garage to contain wheeled vehicles, a comparatively small load and a great deal of air. The container had also shown itself to be less open to loss through pilferage or damage; for example, between Europe and African Atlantic ports the loss of cement went down from 25 per cent to 0.05 per cent; for wine by rail, short measure in containers was 80 per cent of what had been experienced in barrels.

Not only that, handling required fewer men and was so much quicker that a shipping company making the circuit of the Danish islands was able to scrap four conventional ships, loaded with separate items by slings, and do the work with two specially designed container ships. The rates on insurance were reduced. The shipping line made a rigid rule that if goods could not be containerised they must at least be palletised—that is, stand on a platform, up to 40in by 48in in size, underneath which there would be slots for the insertion of the forks of a fork-lift truck so that the unit of load could be handled on the quay, in the ship's hold or in the warehouses without excessive use of manpower.

So even 20 years ago the container had many friends, but railways still moved them in rather unorganised wagon-load lots; shipping and port authorities had yet to be persuaded that there was money in it and thought the investment would have to be unreasonably high; and in Great Britain the haulier, owing to repressive Ministry of Transport Construction and Use Regulations, could not handle a container of much more than 10 tons. At American ports customs and dockers, in unholy combination, insisted on containers being unloaded on the quayside, destroying the door-to-door concept.

A major difficulty was the transfer of containers from one means of transport to another. Hundreds of ingenious devices were patented, most of which involved locking capital up in lifting gear carried on a lorry and used perhaps twice a day. British Railways used petrol-electric mobile cranes which could be sent to stations as required to handle a container. The means now generally used, the gantry crane, involves channelling container traffic to a few suitably equipped stations, but this is immaterial since the block train is now recognised as a more economic railway unit than the wagon.

A remarkable breakthrough eventually took place. On British Railways the combination of the through train, which would run the maximum distance without shunting or division, with specialised depots for road-to-rail and the other way about movement of containers led to the Freightliner concept, beginning, after trade union objections as to road haulage men bringing traffic to railway depots had been overcome, with transits at up to 75mph between London and Glasgow. American attitudes to the container eventually were softened by trucking organisations using ships on coastal links to carry out trunking operations. Once internal traffic was handled the logical extension was to take consignments for overseas, and to build special ships for the stacking of containers to best advantage in their holds. A further and necessary part was played by the International Standards Organisation which settled standard sizes for containers engaged in international transits—8ft by 8ft by 20ft, 30ft or 40ft in length. The dimension which has been allowed to vary is the height, which has been widely increased by US firms to 8ft 6in. So many containers of this height now enter Britain that most British Railways routes have been cleared for the additional 6in and it causes little difficulty in Continental Europe.

In Britain the railways for a time produced 20ft and 27ft containers, as Construction & Use Regulations would not permit 30ft containers to be handled on road vehicles. Now that an articulated lorry can be over 49ft in length even 40ft containers can be delivered by road in Britain, but the 32-ton all-up weight limit still limits the load in such a container to about 22 tons on streets in Great Britain and there have been cases of containers having to be unloaded—'unstuffed' is the trade term—before they can leave the docks. Hence comes the plea from those responsible for their delivery for authorisation of 44-ton gross weight for lorries.

The upsurge in container traffic over the past two years has stemmed from two sources—the efficient internal network of Freightliner trains between principal industrial centres operated by BR on behalf of Freightliners Ltd, a company owned 49 per cent by BR and 51 per cent by the National Freight Corporation—another state-owned body—and the growing interest of shipowners in containerising their major liner trades through consortia of the principal firms engaged in each trade. A considerable proportion of these movements involve journeys by three media— a lorry of Freightliners Ltd collects the container from a consignor and takes it to the appropriate railway depot, where a mammoth gantry crane, costing perhaps £250,000, transfers it from the road vehicle to a railway wagon. The trainload complete, it runs on a fast passenger schedule (the 70-ton wagons are designed for running at 75mph) to the port, where another crane transfers the container to a lorry and trailer engaged solely in the port shunting work; then follows positioning under a crane costing perhaps £350,000 because of its reach over the quays and across the ship's hold and in three minutes the 20ft container has been aligned with the spreaders of the crane, picked up, traversed, lowered, and deposited between the guides in the ship, gently on top of its immediate predecessor.

With considerable boldness British Railways set a pattern for their Freightliner trains that is now being emulated on the Continent. The trains are made up of disc-braked low-loading bogie vehicles in sets of five close-coupled units. The containers are located on the wagons (and on road vehicles) by cones and twist locks. Three 20ft containers can be carried on the standard 62½ft underframe. Ideas on lifting containers are diverse and as a result many have equipment for both top and bottom lift and crane spreaders are designed for either system. In addition some container owners insert boxes in the base to take the prongs of the giant fork trucks favoured by a few for transfer work. If possible the entire train of 15 or 20 wagons is worked from end to end of the route, but to cope with some traffic flows trains are split.

Some cities justify more than one container depot. The large industrial centres and the principal ports with container facilities are served; there are numerous

regular facilities to the Continent and to both Northern Ireland and the Republic. The trains operate to fast schedules with great reliability, whether there are loads or not; the user virtually buys space in a train for his container. The service is so good that some firms have been able to substitute container deliveries for warehouse facilities, making considerable savings.

The first cellular container ships built in Britain were for the British Railways Harwich-Zeebrugge service; each 4,000-ton ship carries 148 ISO 30ft long 8ft by 8ft containers—110 three-high in eight cellular compartments in the hold and 38 on top of the MacGregor hatch covers. The cellular construction can be adapted to take 20ft or 40ft containers, but odd American sizes, such as 24ft and 35ft containers, have to go as deck cargo. Trim of the ship is adjustable by water ballast. The base load for the ships was supplied by 22 containers a day from the Ford Halewood plant and 38 from Dagenham, taken by rail to Harwich and then carried from Zeebrugge to Ford factories in Belgium and Germany, with corresponding return trips for loads of parts made in Europe to be used in England.

The development of overseas container traffic has been greatly aided by the arrangement of customs examination at inland container depots in strategic parts of the country; the depots are owned by consortia of port authorities, carriers and

in some cases, forwarding agents. The importance of forwarding agents to the container trade is the provision of facilities by container to senders who cannot fill a whole container unaided and to whom 'groupage' or merging of consignments becomes vital to economical charges.

Southampton is a typical port where container facilities are in course of expansion. The Millbrook depot serves manufacturers and traders in the area and also picks up traffic from the first of the new container berths built by the British Transport Docks Board. Belgian Line began a service to the United States in October 1968; then it formed a consortium with Bristol City Line and Clarke Traffic Services as Dart Containerline, operating to the USA and Canada. Atlantic Container Line came in December 1969 with a combined container and roll-on—roll-off ship. Seatrain also began North Atlantic services and during 1971 opened a connection to the Pacific coast of America. These lines are served by two Paceco-Vickers 30-ton Portainer cranes, running on 50ft-gauge track, with outreach over a ship of 115ft and backreach of 30ft. The underside of the spreader can rise to 80ft above the quay. Hoisting is at 100ft a minute and cross-travel at 410ft a minute, giving a handling rate of 30 containers an hour. Containers are moved on the quay by straddle carriers and a fleet of fork-lift trucks and side-loaders.

Container trains are worked away from Millbrook at 18.10 to London Barking; 22.30 five wagons for Liverpool Garston and 10 to Manchester Trafford Park and 02.50 to Birmingham Landor Street.

A consortium of shipping lines serving the Far East will use 3,900ft of new quay and 100 acres of land in 1972 for container marshalling; 17 container ships, carrying 2,000 containers at 26 knots, will replace 40 conventional cargo ships and two ships will be turned round each week by 1973. For this vast increase in traffic there has been provided a new Maritime container terminal at Redbridge with four rail tracks and two roadways under the cranes. The Far East containers will be handled by special company trains to Birmingham, Glasgow, Liverpool, Leeds, London and Manchester, each of 15 to 20 wagons and there might be up to 25 trains daily as the service develops.

The opponents of the container system of half a century ago proved to have been quite right when they said that heavy investments were needed in containers and transfer equipment; Gattie has equally turned out to be right when he said the productivity of railway wagons would be immensely improved. Millions of pounds have been spent, but container wagons on BR generate 700 times as many ton-miles as wagons on wagon-load traffics on the old pattern. Traffic is going up—Freightliners Ltd carried 397,000 containers in 1969 and 480,000 in 1970; gross receipts were up £10.7 million to £14.6 million in the twelve months. After six years of development a profit was in sight on the investment. Both on land and sea the container has justified itself; its next conquest, with bigger aircraft, is in the air.

Facing page top left: A rail-mounted German Federal container crane with fully adaptable lifting head at Dusseldorf depot. *DB Film Archiv*

Facing page lower left: A transfer crane in use in France in 1971 using arms to lift at the bottom of the container. *W H R Godwin*

Top: Shunting a Freightliner train at Heysham in connection with Irish Sea container traffic in 1968. *D Cross*

Above left: Night scene at Canadian Pacific Quebec container terminal for land-sea transfer. *CP Ships*

Above: Scene at British Railways Parkeston Quay, Harwich, land-sea container terminal. *British Transport Films*

Overleaf: The Andrew Barclay 0-6-0 'Illtyd' at work at Talywain Colliery, South Wales, in March 1969. *D Huntriss*

AUTOMATIC WAGON IDENTIFICATION

Above and below: Two pictures of a huge new hump marshalling yard at North Platte, Nebraska, USA; yards of such a size make some system of ACI virtually essential.
Union Pacific Railroad Company

KEEPING RECORDS of the day-to-day movements and whereabouts of more than two million freight wagons or cars rolling constantly over 255,000 miles of North American railroad tracks is probably the industry's biggest single chore in paper-work. As every train enters or leaves each classification yard or passes through interchanges or junctions between connecting railroads, its wagons must be observed and the owner's reporting mark initials and serial numbers accurately listed. The job has always been a pencil-and-paper manual task performed by a yard clerk, car checker or 'mudhop' as he has been nicknamed. In order to secure completely accurate data, train speed past the observation points must not exceed 15mph. Occasionally, a mudhop who was endowed with a photographic memory came along; he could observe a 100-car train without writing anything, then go into the yard office and re-run the entire consist through his mind from memory, but this highly unusual breed of man was few and far between.

Once recorded and inside the yard office, car movement data through the years has undergone vast speed-ups and improved handling methods. Telegraph messages eventually gave way to telephone and teletype systems and even micro-wave transmission conducted by computer memory banks. But the only forward step in the basic old-fashioned manual gathering of wagon data has been the introduction of closed-circuit television monitors which permit the clerk at his desk, and at any distant point in the yard, to see and transmit the information to message lines or computers.

Now, through the wonders of electronics, every piece of rolling equipment from locomotives to cars to cabooses (and even piggyback road vehicles and containers) can be identified and recorded automatically as they pass a trackside equipment installation at any speed up to 80mph. Known as Automatic Car Identification (ACI), the unique system was developed in 1967-68 by the Sylvania Division of General Telephone & Electronics Corporation, Bedford, Massachusetts, who worked in collaboration with the Association of American Railroads Research Center located at the Illinois Institute of Technology in Chicago. ACI in thorough tests has proved workable and highly accurate and is today fully operational and available to all railroads.

The basic Sylvania ACI system, named KarTrak 800 Series, consists of three major assemblies: the label, the scanner and the decoder. The colour-coded label, which obviously must appear on the sides of each wagon and piggyback vehicle, consists of 13 small stripes or modules in single colours, or combinations of black, blue, red and white, arranged in proper sequence to identify the vehicle. The scanner reads the identifying label information from the moving vehicle. The scanner, an electro-optical device, installed at the trackside, converts the colour-coded data on the label into electrical analogue signals which are sent to the decoder. The decoder analyses and interprets the analogue signals and converts them into digital outputs for use in railroad communication, data processing and control systems.

The decoder in the basic system can be designed to work directly through various standard communications systems. However, as most of the communications systems transmit data at speeds of only between 60 and 150 words per minute, a message-storing buffer is necessary sometimes to balance a fast generation of ACI data against the slower transmission rate.

The basic ACI scanner/decoder installation can be made to perform other useful functions with the addition of various optional devices. Since all scanner readings obtained from labels are expressed in numbers, the optional Carrier Index converts each wagon owner's code number into the reporting mark initials; code number 022, for example, would automatically come out ATSF for Atchison, Topeka & Santa Fe Railway. There are several optional choices of data storing equipment which permit later delivery upon command, such as a controlling computer in the Santa Fe's Argentine (Kansas) yard which periodically polls 10 scanner/decoder sites for train movement data. There are also optional Message and Calendar devices which provide a topical heading for each train scan. Details included here are direction of train travel, scanning location, date and time. And finally, the optional Piggy-

back Format will scan each flat wagon and the labelled trailers or containers as well.

The success of the ACI project depends upon four million labels affixed to two million freight cars. To achieve desired results, the labels must be almost as carefully engineered as the delicate equipment that monitors them. In completed form with black borders, there are two sizes of label with colour-coded modules affixed thereon with adhesives. Modules, developed by the 3M Company of Minneapolis, Minnesota, are made from adhesive-backed retro-reflective sheeting similar to that used in road signs. Light striking the material is reflected back to its source along the path it followed when transmitted. In ordinary mirror reflection light is reflected at an angle opposite to that from which it came, or away from its source, except when mirror and light source are perpendicularly opposed. However, a retro-reflective surface reflects light back to its source regardless of the light's incoming angle. The module surface is coated with tiny glass beads, 90,000 of them per square inch, each of which is its own optical system. En masse, they reflect back to the wayside scanner light claimed to be 200 times more intense than normal reflected light from any painted or coloured object.

There are 12 different colour-coded module forms, each divided into two parts and each denoting a single number value from zero to nine, plus one for Start and one for Stop/10. The colour code is as follows and a typical label is shown in an accompanying illustration.

0—Blue/White	6—White/Blue
1—White/White	7—Red/White
2—White/Red	8—White/Black
3—Red/Black	9—Blue/Blue
4—Red/Red	10/Stop—Blue/Red
5—Blue/Black	Start—Red/Blue

For easy identification when attaching the modules to vehicles, man-readable

numbers appear on them. Each completed label must be a custom-assembled group of 13 modules to show the individual identity of each vehicle, the modules being arranged in ladder style, one above the other, to be read from bottom to top. A complete label may be assembled directly on the surface of a steel vehicle after properly preparing the area, or applied to a backing plate of steel, anodised aluminium or vinyl film for attaching to vehicles of aluminium, stainless steel or wood construction. Properly applied modules are said to perform satisfactorily in all weather conditions between temperatures ranging from minus 60 degrees F to plus 125 degrees F.

Reading from bottom to top, the general label format of 13 modules comprises: Start (1 module), equipment code number (1 module), owner code number (3 modules), vehicle serial number (6 modules), stop (1 module) and validity check (1 module). Where the owner code number is less than three digits and where the serial number is less than six digits, zero modules are inserted preceding the number in each case to bring it up to the required label spaces. Equipment code number identifies the type of rolling stock numbers running 0 for railroad and 1 for privately owned wagons, 2 to 5 for trailers and containers, 6 for works equipment, 7 for passenger coaches, 8 for cabooses and 9 for locomotives. The validity check digit is the only module that can possess a value of 10 and is arrived at through a complex multiplication, addition and division of all ten module numbers; to make it simpler for applying correct labels in the field there is a quick-calculation chart. For locomotive labelling, the first two of the six serial numbers can be used as an optional code system to identify the type of locomotive and the remaining four spaces for the locomotive number.

Proper placement and location of labels

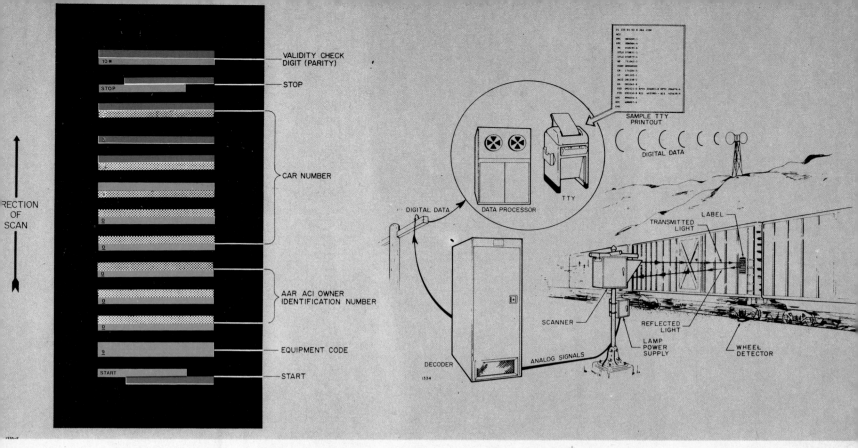

VALIDITY CHECK
DIGIT (PARITY)

STOP

CAR NUMBER

AAR ACI OWNER
IDENTIFICATION NUMBER

EQUIPMENT CODE

START

DIRECTION
OF
SCAN

SAMPLE TTY
PRINTOUT

DIGITAL DATA

DIGITAL DATA

DATA PROCESSOR

TTY

TRANSMITTED
LIGHT

LABEL

SCANNER

REFLECTED
LIGHT

DECODER

ANALOG SIGNALS

LAMP
POWER
SUPPLY

WHEEL
DETECTOR

on equipment is of importance to obtain an unobstructed scanning range. Flat areas unhindered by doors, channels, railings, rivet heads or seams should be used; on the curved sides of tankers and hoppers—special separate mounting brackets are the best solution. Tops of labels must not be more than 9ft 6in above the top of rail and there is a recommended minimum height of 6ft for normal vehicles and 16 inches for flat wagons. A label is required on each side normally and on vehicles with more than six axles there should be two labels per side.

Sylvania markets its ACI optical/electronic equipment under the registered name KarTrak. The scanner is enclosed in a sealed steel cabinet measuring 39 inches wide, 28 inches high and 16 inches deep; it weighs 160 pounds. It is mounted on a mast located about 12 feet from the track to be scanned and 7 feet above rail level of that track, permitting a vertical scanning height range from 16 inches to $9\frac{1}{2}$ feet from top of rail. The scanner is designed to withstand all weather conditions between temperatures of minus 50 degrees and plus 150 degrees F and 100 per cent humidity. A scanner cabinet contains the illuminating source, scanning optics, photo detectors, cable drivers, control electronics and electric power supply. It is connected to the decoder by a cable which can have an extreme length of 1,000 feet to reach the decoder, which must be housed in an environmentally protected building.

The scanning equipment is designed to read each passing label up to four times. The equipment starts with a 9,000-watt xenon lamp, the light from which is first routed through a series of mirrors to a multi-faceted scanning wheel, each facet of which is also a mirror. Spinning at high speed, the wheel causes the light beam to move from the bottom of the scan to the top at the same light rate. The light is projected at the label and follows the same

path back to a partially silvered mirror where the returned light is focused through a lens to create an image of the label. The light in the image is optically filtered at the mirror into two broad spectra defined as red and blue. Photo-multipliers change the optical signals into electrical pulses for input to the decoder.

The heart and brains of the ACI system lie in the computer-type circuitry of the decoder unit, which is contained in a steel cabinet measuring $24\frac{1}{2}$ inches wide by 73 inches high by 29 inches deep. The delicate equipment must be kept inside a building where heating and air conditioning ensure a temperature of 45 to 95 degrees F and humidity in the 20-80 per cent range. The circuitry of the decoder changes electrical input signals from the scanner into meaningful digital values for transmission as data. It also is designed to analyse incoming signals and decide whether a proper label has been scanned and accuracy requirements have been met.

As a train approaches a scanning site, a track circuit is activated, turning on the ACI equipment. (If the decoder has an optional message/calendar device, a heading is prepared for the train report to follow.) Incoming information from each scanned label is stored momentarily in a label data register. Positive and negative checks indicate whether information received in the label data register is correct or incorrect. A positive comparison sends information to the output circuitry. If a negative comparison occurs, the information in the label data register is held while additional scans are made; another negative check causes the output circuit to send a question-mark designation.

Another decoder component, an unlabelled car detector, works in conjunction with electronic wheel sensors fitted in the railway track. The sensors count the vehicles as they pass and relay a signal for each vehicle to the detector. If the

Facing page: A section of Santa Fe's electronic classification yard at Kansas City, which was a pioneer user of KarTrak ACI. *Santa Fe Railway*

Above left: Detail of the KarTrak label affixed to wagon sides.
General Telephone & Electronics Corpn.

Above : Pictorial representation of how the elements of ACI are arranged.
General Telephone & Electronics Corpn

Below: KarTrak scanning equipment for mounting at the trackside. *B Pennypacker*

signal is not cancelled by positive check signals from the other information processing circuits, the unlabelled car detector generates a series of zeros which go to the output circuits to indicate that an unidentified vehicle has passed. Such is the speed of today's computer electronics that the entire process of reading, verifying and the rest is completed in a tiny fraction of a second and that each and every label on every passing vehicle in a train, including piggyback containers and semi-trailers, is processed separately at train speeds of up to 80mph.

With the development of a workable ACI system, the Association of American Railroads adopted strict regulations governing the proper labelling of all equipment and set a target date in 1970 for completion of the job. The monumental task has taken much longer than anticipated and the twice-postponed date is now this year. However, extensive field tests on many railroads began in 1969 and between

October 20 and November 28 of that year, tests on the Canadian National Railways produced some enlightening results. Alongside a westbound track leading to a receiving yard near Toronto, Ontario, two Sylvania KarTrak scanner decoder units were set up to monitor simultaneously the same trains, to provide a cross-check for label reading and reporting accuracy. The results went to a teletype output in the yard office, from which the printed car lists were taken and checked manually, car by car, after each train had stopped in the yard.

One portion of the detailed test report shows that of 1,086 complete train reports, consisting of 54,165 cars, 47,650 cars had labels and 45,365 were read correctly; 2,295 were not and were termed problem labels. There were 184 labels incorrectly read, but the biggest problem was that 1,671 were dirty and/or defective. This clearly indicated the need for strict label maintenance, the repair of damaged labels and replacement of dirty ones. Sylvania also recognised the need to try and make its equipment reject fewer marginal labels. Even so, the tests suitably impressed CNR to the point of placing an initial order for ten sets of KarTrak equipment.

ACI's potential benefits to railroading lie principally in the immediate future. At the present time only a few railroads have scanning equipment, and it is being used more or less experimentally to evaluate accuracy and ways of programming system computer networks to make the best use of ACI-generated data. But with completion of the huge labelling job this year, many carriers are expected to initiate ACI programmes, just as the pioneering Santa Fe did in early 1971 with installation of ten scanner/decoder units at Argentine yard near Kansas City, Missouri. Each decoder can store 1,000 labels and is polled regularly and automatically for this information by an IBM 360-40 computer in the bill office. The bill office is expected ultimately to be interconnected to the system message-switching complex in Topeka, Kansas, from which information is immediately available to any department dialling for it.

The *Santa Fe Magazine* for July 1971 reports that ACI accuracy is perhaps the biggest problem, but there is also the reconciliation of data when manually recorded and ACI-generated lists differ. It is this writer's opinion that clean and easily readable labels will be the key to the success of ACI and from purely casual observations of numerous dirty labels already to be seen on cars that were labelled a year or more ago, this is bound to be ACI's biggest trouble spot. Referring again to the *Santa Fe Magazine,* other benefits of ACI are mentioned. For example, the calendar/time device records can be used by a computer to determine the arrival and leaving times of every car in a yard; thus slow movers, stragglers and overlooked cars might be pinpointed if they have not left the yard within a specified time.

The giant Penn Central system to date has installed only two ACI scanners, which are located on-line (not in yards) in remote areas for the specific purpose of monitoring eastbound unit coal trains as they pass over electronic weigh-in-motion scales. The combined car label and weight data goes direct to a billing computer in the Philadelphia accounting offices. One of the scan/weigh locations is on the main line at Denholm, near Lewistown, Pennsylvania, and the other is upstate in the Susquehanna River valley at McElhattan, near Lock Haven; each location is positioned to process coal movements coming from each of the two principal bituminous-producing areas of the state. All this amounts to the centralised and automated processing of most coal traffic, eliminating numerous individual freight stations, manual waybilling by clerks and even waybill rate figuring. It also eliminates many weigh scales and the time required for train crews and weigh clerks to weigh each wagon individually.

Seaboard Coast Line currently has three ACI scanners in use at Hamlet, North Carolina, site of the road's largest car distribution and classification yards. The scanners generate and feed car data to an IBM 1800 computer for system-wide use. Another scanner located at Rockport, Florida, monitors perishables trains moving out of Florida and relays the data northward by teletypewriter. SCL reports that, at the beginning of 1972, it had placed ACI labels upon 92.6 per cent of its 63,214 freight cars. Since some cars stay off-line for many months, running down that final 7.4 per cent is probably the hardest part of the whole labelling job and explains why it is taking so long to get them all tagged up.

Finally, the ACI principle has almost limitless uses both inside and outside railway operation. For example, the Seaboard Coast Line has tested experimentally what is termed a Flagger locomotive malfunction indicator with movable coloured modules. Thus, a distant terminal might be warned hours in advance of mechanical trouble in a locomotive moving toward the terminal and make preparation to attend to it. Car rental companies have also expressed an interest in ACI as a means of keeping track of what vehicles arrive at garages and rental parks so they can be immediately made available to new customers. Although developed for railroad use, ACI appears to have valuable applications throughout industry.

7
Running a Railway

Overleaf:
A British Railways Class 8F 2-8-0 locomotive
No 48327—the LMS taper-boiler design—
approaching Chinley with a Manchester-
Buxton freight in February 1968. *D Huntriss*

RAILWAYS AT WAR

Start of work on the railway at Balaclava as depicted in the 'Illustrated London News' of March 10, 1855. *Illustrated London News*

THE PRESENCE of the Duke of Wellington at the opening of the Liverpool & Manchester Railway in 1830 might well mislead one into thinking that the British, the first to make railways a practicable proposition, were also swift to see their military potential, for the speed and reliability which railways could offer obviously revolutionised man's mastery of time and space, the fundamental dimensions of strategic thinking. In fact the 'Iron Duke' was present in his civilian capacity as Prime Minister. Nevertheless in 1834 the promoters of the projected London & Southampton Railway did think it worthwhile to bring before Parliament as witnesses to support their cause Admiral Sir Thomas Hardy, General Sir Willoughby Gordon and five captains of the Royal Navy, to testify to the military value of a railway link between the capital and its major Channel ports.

The authorities were also quick to see the value of railways as a means of transporting police and troops to put down demonstrations and riots in various parts of the country. At the height of the Chartist agitation in 1842 a Railway Regulation Act was passed by Parliament requiring railway companies to carry troops, but only 'at the usual hours of starting'. This was later amended to include the possibility of running 'specials', but, whatever the arrangements, all military passengers were to be scrupulously paid for at the full rate. Apart from using railways as an aid to maintaining law and order or as a link in the chain of transport to overseas stations, the military establishment remained indifferent to their strategic potential for more than two decades after their inception. The Admiralty merely concerned itself with ensuring that structures such as the Saltash Bridge over the Tamar or the Britannia Bridge over the Menai Strait should not obstruct shipping.

The real vindication of the railway came during the Crimean War of 1854-6, and then chiefly on the initiative of private enterprise. In the harsh winter of 1854-5 Russell's despatches to 'The Times' from the battlefront revealed to a shocked public the total failure of the supply system which had reduced the army to the edge of destitution. Charles Gordon, then a lieutenant of Engineers (later the hero of Khartoum) wrote to his parents of 'officers in every conceivable costume foraging for eatables' and of 'roads bad beyond description.' Therein lay the nub of the matter. The distance from the harbour at Balaclava to the firing-line before the fortress of Sebastopol was a mere seven miles, but it might as well have been 700. Supplies which had come 1,500 miles by sea from England piled up at the supply base, while less than ten miles away the largest expeditionary force to leave England for 40 years was steadily decimated by starvation and frostbite and military operations came to a total standstill.

The answer was, of course, a railway and it was sent out from England by that titan among engineers, Thomas Brassey, at his own expense. It arrived complete with wagons and a small army of navvies and was in operation by March 1855, despite the fact that most of the rolling stock had to be rebuilt before it could be

Above: Austrian soldiers mustering at a Vienna station for transport to the front in 1866 *Illustrated London News*

Left: A railborne gun battery built for the American Federal Government in 1861 by the Baldwin company: it was proposed to carry 50 riflemen and a rifled cannon capable of bearing through the end or side ports. *Illustrated London News*

Right: An 'Illustrated London News' artist's impression of a train with American Civil war reinforcements running off the track in 1863. *Illustrated London News*

used. At first the trains were horse drawn, with a stationary engine to help the horses manage one steep gradient, but later small locomotives were sent out. Another distinguished engineer, I K Brunel, also lent his talents to the war effort, designing a prefabricated hospital which has remained the basic model for all such field medical units in subsequent wars.

By bringing supplies up to the front line and evacuating the wounded on the return trip, the Balaclava railway made possible the final assault on Sebastopol which brought the futile war to a close. The experience had taught some useful lessons —that it was not possible to leave military railways in the hands of civilians who were exempt from military discipline; that military lines must be under the direct orders of the commander in chief and insulated from disruption by local and subordinate commanders, and that, above all, loading and unloading must be organised with maximum efficiency to avoid choking the line.

Unfortunately it seems to have been necessary to re-learn the lessons in every succeeding war. And the War Office seems never to have been able to resist the attractions of doing a job on the

cheap. When a British force had to build a railway from the Red Sea port of Zula 300 miles into the interior of Ethiopia in 1867-8, they were supplied with five different types of rail and six ancient locomotives, all bought second-hand from Indian railways. Two of the engines were quite useless and two broke down in a fortnight. All spare parts had, of course, been left on the dockside in Bombay together with the augers for boring spike-holes in sleepers.

The Mutiny of 1857, which revealed the precariousness of Britain's hold over India, led to the construction of strategic railway lines throughout the sub-continent. Realising that the white garrison could never be substantially increased in size, the authorities determined to make it a mobile striking force which could be brought to bear at any threatening point. This was really an application on a massive scale of the principles already worked out in Britain for controlling domestic disorders. And investors were encouraged by a guaranteed five-per cent return, subsidised out of taxes.

In Europe, meanwhile, the French were giving the first convincing display of the strategic, rather than the merely tactical,

use of railways. Having provoked Austria into declaring war in 1859, France sent to the aid of her ally, Piedmont, 76,000 men and 4,450 horses, who made the journey from Paris to northern Italy in 10 days. The supply arrangements, however, failed to match the efficiency achieved in the initial deployment and, after the bloody battles of Magenta and Solferino, the French were unable to pursue the beaten Austrians beyond the Mincio for lack of food, despite the fact that they had a fully operational railway network at their rear. This was more than could be said of the Austrians whose incomplete system of single-track lines had been all but paralysed throughout the conflict by the patriotic desertion of its largely French personnel.

Despite the shortcomings on both sides, the spectacle of French military success revived old fears of Napoleonic ambitions in Britain. Volunteer rifle companies were formed in large numbers in 1859 and 1860 and there was talk of constructing a circular railway around London to carry armoured trains. In 1862 tension was still sufficiently high for the War Office to veto a proposed broad-gauge line from Tavistock to Launceston on the grounds

that a standard-gauge link from Exeter to Plymouth was a military necessity.

The real lessons of railway warfare were, however, to be learned, not from Europe, but in North America. On the eve of the American Civil War, Colonel R Delafield had presented to Congress a report on the state of the art of war in Europe, a report in which he had placed particular emphasis on the military potential of the railway. Despite that, both the Federal and the Confederate armies were slow to organise the railway systems at their disposal, although the field of conflict they were to contest was as large as the whole continent of Europe. Indeed, the Confederates delayed until February 1865, the last year of the war, before imposing state control in a futile effort to undo the damage inflicted by suicidal competition between the various southern railway companies. The victory of the North was largely determined by the efforts of two men—David C McCallum, a Scottish railway administrator (who was also a poet and church architect), and Herman C Haupt, a West Point-trained engineer whose speciality was bridge-building. President Lincoln spoke admiringly of Haupt's bridge over the Potomac

—'over which loaded trains are running every hour, and, upon my word there is nothing in it but beanpoles and cornstalks.'

Thanks to McCallum and Haupt a rapid programme of railway building was pushed ahead and such novelties as railway corps, armoured trains and hospital trains introduced. Prodigious feats of transportation became almost commonplace. In September 1863 23,000 men with their artillery and horses were moved 1,200 miles in seven days to save Rosecrans after his mauling at Chickamauga, a deployment which, without the railway, would have taken about three months. Sherman's decisive campaign through the South, starting from the vital junction at Chattanooga and ending with the destruction of the railway town of Atlanta and the terrible march through Georgia, was made possible by a single line of track which the Confederates never managed to cut for more than a few days at a time. The effect of this manoeuvre was to sever the railway connections between Robert E Lee's army in Virginia and his supply base in the South and thus oblige him to surrender.

The American Civil War also produced

an epic of individual endeavour which has never been paralleled in the history of railways. On April 12,1862, a band of 21 Federal soldiers, led by Captain James J Andrews and disguised as civilians, stole the locomotive *General* and a number of carriages of a north-bound passenger train which had stopped for a breakfast halt at Big Shanty, Georgia. Their aim was simple, to drive northwards to Chattanooga, destroying bridges and tunnels behind them. Wet weather foiled their attempts at arson, however, and numerous meetings with other trains involved them in long delays while their leaders explained away their unscheduled progress along the line. The delays gave dearly needed time to the intrepid conductor of the stolen train, W A Fuller. Like a determined bloodhound he pursued the train for more than a hundred miles, sometimes on foot and sometimes in the locomotive *Texas*. His relentless pursuit constantly interrupted the Federals' attempts at sabotage and made it so impossible for them to refuel adequately, that they were finally forced to abandon the *General* at the Tennessee state line and seek refuge in the woods. This entire story was, of course, immortalised in Buster Keaton's silent comedy classic *The General*.

It is tempting to speculate on whether or not the railways made the Northern victory inevitable and thus secured the preservation of the Federal Union. Had it not been possible to reach a temporary compromise over the slavery issue in 1850 and had the South seceded in that year it is doubtful whether the North, with its few disconnected lines, could ever have mounted the massive probing counter-attacks which eventually proved decisive in breaking stubborn Confederate resistance.

The 'War Between the States' naturally attracted its share of European military observers; among them Moltke, the Prussian genius, dismissed the mighty struggle contemptuously as that of 'two armed mobs chasing each other around the country, from which nothing could be learned'. The evidence suggests, however, that Moltke learned a great deal. As a young man in the early 1840s he had risked his savings in the new Hamburg-Berlin railway, of which he later became a director. In 1864 the Prussian General Staff set up its own railway sub-section, elevated to the status of a full department in 1866. At the end of the American Civil War it was responsible for translating and publishing an edition of McCallum's official report on US military railways.

In fact the Prussians were building on a long-established tradition. As early as 1833 Friedrick Harkort had urged the building of a railway from Minden to Cologne on the grounds of its defensive value in the event of a French invasion. In 1842 C E Pönitz had pointed out the value of railways to Germany should France and Russia choose to attack Germany simultaneously. But it was Friedrich List, the economist and a passionate supporter of railways as a result of a visit to the USA, who was the first to realise that they would enable Germany to transform her greatest source of military weakness, her central geographical location, into a source of strength. A Germany united by railways would be like a single vast fortress, its army a domestic garrison which could be shifted along interior lines of communication to any threatened section of frontier. 'While the French Chambers are still engaged in discussing the matter,' List wrote gleefully to his brother, 'we have laid down 300 miles of railway and are working at 200 more.' List idealistically imagined that Germany's new strength would act as a deterrent to all attackers and thus ensure the peace of Europe. It never occurred to him that Germany might herself be the aggressor, but in the year of his death, 1846, a Prussian army corps of 12,000 was despatched by rail to snuff out the tiny Polish republic of Cracow. It was a portent of greater and more-sophisticated acts of aggression.

In 1847 a German military writer asserted that transport of artillery and cavalry by train was impossible and denied that any railway could carry 10,000 men over 60 miles within 24 hours. The Austrian mobilisation along the Silesian frontier in 1850 seemed to prove his point, as 75,000 men and 8,000 horses took 26 days to travel the 150 miles from Vienna. As opponents of the railway were swift to point out, they could have done it faster on foot. Nevertheless the Prussian General Staff had already gained enough faith in the new mode of transport to begin compiling a comparative survey of railways from the military point of view and the Austrians, having digested the lessons of the debacle of 1850—the need for adequate supplies of rolling stock and numerous detraining platforms—succeeded in 1851 in moving 145,000 men, 2,000 horses, 50 guns and 500 vehicles a distance of nearly 200 miles in two days. To march would have taken 15.

When Prussia and Austria finally clashed in 1866 it was the railway which proved decisive. Using five lines to Austria's one, Prussia was able to compensate for her late mobilisation and deploy a screen of 250,000 troops over a front of about 270 miles, enabling her generals to bring the Austrians to a quick defeat at Sadowa. This 'Six Weeks War' was, indeed, so rapid that its lessons were largely lost on contemporaries. In retrospect, however, it is possible to see how the railways meshed in with other technical developments of the period. Without them it would have been impossible to keep the front line supplied with the quantities of ammunition required for the quick-firing needle-gun or breech-loading artillery. Without contemporary progress in medical science, on the other hand, it would have been impossible to concentrate and transport large numbers of men without their falling victim to typhus.

The Franco-Prussian war of 1870-71 once again demonstrated the new strategic significance of railways and this time the lessons were nowhere ignored. Despite the fact that Prussian preparations for war were incomplete, they moved 384,000 men with their horses and artillery to the assembly areas within a fortnight. Uncontrolled loading, however, created a great supply blockage between Frankfurt and Cologne, which was to create a shortage of food at the front. The importance which was attached to the railways can be assessed from the fact that 100,000 men were kept behind the lines to protect them. French mobilisation was, by contrast, extremely slipshod and totally hamstrung by quarrels between the civilian railwaymen and the military authorities. Despite great confusion, however, the French Est Company struggled on valiantly and rushed troops towards the frontier throughout the late summer of 1870.

Again it is difficult to resist the speculation that if the confusion had been that little bit worse, if the Est Company had disintegrated into total chaos, then the French army would not have been thrown into action so rashly and could have taken advantage of Prussian supply shortages to attack the invaders as they began to lose momentum. Thus might the Second Empire have been saved instead of lost. As it was the French were defeated on the frontiers and the Prussians were able to use the railways to bring up enough food and ammunition to besiege Paris and bombard it into submission, to the astonishment of all Europe. As a result of the Franco-Prussian conflict the British government gave itself the power to take possession of the railways in time of war and governments throughout Europe began to grasp the basic implication of railway transport—that it made possible the mobilisation and deployment of armies of unprecedented size. Mass conscription and a general increase in international tension was the result.

Another result was strategic railway-building at a pace that might almost be described as frantic. France greatly extended her network along the eastern frontier, neglecting the west; Germany intensified her system to the west, neglecting that of the east; Russia began to build on a massive scale. With French financial assistance, the fantastic Trans-Siberian Railway was started in 1891, stretching 4,627 miles from Chelyabinsk in the Urals to Vladivostok on the Pacific. The condition of French aid in the project was the simultaneous construction of a rather useless line to Tashkent. The French hoped to use it to stimulate British fears of a Russian invasion of India.

A similar idea lay behind the scheme for a Berlin-Baghdad railway, which gave the Foreign Office nightmares in the first decade of the present century. In the 1830s List had envisaged a joint British-German railway along the Berlin-Baghdad route which would enable Germany to colonise the Balkans and Britain to create an overland link with her Asian Empire. What in fact appeared to be materialising was a German-controlled route from the Bosphorous to Basra. This was too near the sensitive Persian Gulf for Britian's liking and diplomatic tension was only finally eased by an agreement that the section from Baghdad to Basra should remain in British hands. Ironically, the agreement was signed in June 1914, just two months before the outbreak of the first world war.

The roots of the 1914-18 war lie deep in the colonial and economic rivalries of the great powers of Europe. Many factors played their part in making general war unavoidable—the interlocking systems of military alliances, the existence of vast conscripted armies, the problem of strategic areas, like the Balkans and the Middle East which had their own explosive domestic problems; but one particularly important factor was the railway. Throughout Europe, General Staffs placed the utmost significance on the rapid initial deployment of their forces by rail. All imagined a short and bloody war whose outcome would be determined by a single decisive battle on the frontiers. All had drawn up elaborate timetables for mobilisation and none more so than the German General Staff. Every station, every siding, every wagon had its appointed role in the great Schlieffen Plan, which would rush German forces to the west, knock out France in six weeks and then turn them around by rail to throw them east against the ponderous Russians.

But once mobilisation had begun the railway timetable took over. Nothing could be altered for the first five days without causing the whole system to collapse into complete anarchy. Thus the feverish last-minute attempts of the diplomats to keep France or Belgium, England or Germany out of what was essentially a local squabble in the Balkans, were thwarted by the simple logic of the railway timetable, a logic which ironically failed to reproduce the decisive conflict of 1870, but instead led to a re-staging of the four-year carnage of 1861-65.

Above: German prisoners of the British entraining at Salonika in 1916. *Illustrated London News*

Right: Poster intended to soften complaints about driving conditions with masked lights in the 1939-45 war. *Imperial War Museum*

Below: Scene of troops entraining at London Victoria station during the 1914-18 war, from a painting by Richard Jack RA. *British Transport Museum (B Sharpe)*

The Great War of 1914-18 marked a turning - point in the history of Britain's railways, as in so many of her institutions. The pride and self-assurance of the Edwardian era were never to be recaptured. In 1914 the Regulation of Forces Act, passed in 1871 in the shadow of Prussia's railway - borne victory over the French forces, put the railways of Britain under state control for the first time in their history. Henceforth they were to be operated as a single unified system under the direction of a Railway Executive Committee presided over by the President of the Board of Trade. But it was still far from nationalisation. The membership of the Railway Executive Committee was entirely composed of the general managers of the eleven largest railway companies and the companies were guaranteed the same profits as they had made in 1913, a year which, incidentally, had been rather prosperous. Thus the system of state control which was adopted was one in which railways were run *for* the government but not *by* the government.

The wartime tasks imposed on the British railway system were immense. The flow of traffic was greatly intensified at the very time that 30 per cent of the railway labour force was recruited into the army and the diversion of railway manufacturing capacity to munitions production made it almost impossible to obtain new rolling-stock. Maintenance and investment were seriously neglected, with significant consequences in the post-war period. In retrospect this seems an incredibly short-sighted policy; but, given the task to hand, it was probably inevitable.

To grasp the overall picture is difficult and a more accurate impression may be gained by looking at the work of one or two vital lines. Consider, for example, the strains imposed on the London & South Western Railway, the main supply-route for British forces on the Continent, or on the Highland Railway, which performed the same function for Scapa Flow and Cromarty Firth, two of the Grand Fleet's most important bases. Admittedly the London & South Western, which served Aldershot and Salisbury plain, had long military experience to fall back on, but it had never before faced the problem of funnelling literally millions of men, converging along five main routes, into the single port of Southampton, which was the main point of embarkation for the Western Front. More than 20,000,000 soldiers were transported by the London & South Western in the course of the war, an average of 13,000 every day.

No less remarkable was the achievement of the Highland Railway, for it was peculiarly ill - adapted to the needs of war. Before 1914 heavy traffic on the line had been confined to a three-month summer tourist season; three - quarters of its length was only single track and there were few sidings or loops. Within a year a third of its locomotives were to be out of service and another third badly in need of repair; but still the line somehow kept the traffic flowing and remained a vital, if tenuous, link in a chain of communication which maintained the naval shield on which Britain's national security depended.

IN WAR AND PEACE
WE SERVE

GWR · LMS LNER · SR

"PERHAPS THIS'LL TEACH YOU
STAY AT 'OME NEXT 'OLID

In the autumn of 1914 the generals, and the public, had anticipated a 'war of movement' which would be 'over by Christmas'. It was expected that the pattern of the Franco - Prussian war would be repeated — a massive deployment of troops by railway followed by a single, bloody and decisive battle on the frontiers. The stabilisation of more than a hundred miles of trench fortifications created a novel situation in which railways were to play a new role as the need to supply forward positions and, later, to stockpile ammunition and stores for major offensives, led to the extemporisation of a tactical railway network behind the lines. Communications problems, revealed starkly during the Somme offensive of 1916, led to an official decision to set up an organised system of light railways, which was rapidly extended in 1917 and 1918; from the main system trench tramways, utilising men and horses for motive power, proliferated as feeder lines. By the end of hostilities the army's Railway Operating Division had a total strength of 18,400 men organised in 67 companies. In all 76,000 troops and 48,000 men in labour service units were employed in running and safeguarding this largely new network of 800-odd miles, a network which necessarily came to bulk large in Allied strategic thinking.

According to the official war history the decision of Marshal Foch, the supreme co-ordinator of the Allied counter-offensive of 1918, to grant the Germans an armistice, was largely determined by the realisation that the Allied advance was about to run out of reach of its railheads. If it had not been so, of course, Hitler and his followers would never have been able to argue so powerfully that the German army had never been defeated nor the homeland invaded. In view of the strategic and tactical importance of railways in that war, it was perhaps rather appropriate that the armistice which brought it to a close should have been signed in a railway carriage — which Hitler was to insist on using again to accept the surrender of France in 1940.

Railways were, of course, important in other theatres of war, and especially in the Middle East, where Colonel T E Lawrence's train - wrecking activities played a large part in disrupting the defence of the Ottoman Empire. In Salonika and East Africa, railway units also played their part in ensuring Allied victory, while, on the other side, German railwaymen struggled to maintain a vast network, stretching from the Baltic to the Bosphorous. In Russia the total collapse of the railway system, resulting in the cessation of supplies to the front or of food to the towns, was a major factor in precipitating the outbreak of revolution. In Britain the situation was by no means so dramatic, but it was acute enough for the Liberal-Conservative government of the day to entertain a solution which in many circles would be branded as revolutionary, and even Bolshevik, in its inspiration — nationalisation.

State control of Britain's railways, which had been debated and dismissed as far back as the 1840s, had now been vindicated by the test of war. It had not only enabled the railways to meet the extraordinary demands made upon them, it had also enabled them to achieve a number of striking economies in operation through such schemes as the pooling of wagons or arrangements to eliminate unnecessary haulage of coal. The coal distribution rationalisation alone saved 700 million ton-miles a year after its introduction in 1917. As early as 1915 the Trades Union Council had passed a resolution calling upon the Government 'before relinquishing its present control to introduce legislation having for its object the effecting of complete national ownership of the railways.'

Sir Herbert Walker, general manager of the London and South Western and de facto head of the Railway Executive stated publicly that he did not 'think that our railways will ever again revert to the independent and foolish competitive system' of the pre-war period. Lloyd George himself intimated that nationalisation was seriously being considered by the government and, in December 1918, Churchill actually asserted that that was in fact the government's policy.

In 1919 a Bill was introduced to establish a Ministry of Ways and Communications with powers of compulsory purchase which would enable the state to acquire railways, docks and canals by Order in Council. But the times were not propitious for such a momentous step, despite the success of the wartime experiment. The spectre of Bolshevism was abroad; there was a general resentment against the continuation in time of peace of war controls and a desire to 'get back to normal' which swept away the whole apparatus of state control of industry, agriculture, finance and transport which had been constructed piecemeal in the course of the war. By the time the Bill emerged from Parliament the purchase clauses had been cut away and the proposed all-embracing Ministry of Ways and Communications reduced to a mere Ministry of Transport. Nationalisation was finally rejected in the summer of 1920 in favour of a compromise measure of rationalisation which was embodied in the Railways Act of 1921.

The 1921 Act was to play a major part in determining the future development of the railways. The 120 companies of the pre-war era were reduced to four main groups — the London & North Eastern, the London, Midland & Scottish, the Great Western and the Southern. The reorganisation would, it was hoped, enable the railways to achieve new economies of scale in operation. The public interest would be protected by a Railway Rates Tribunal and an elaborate system of conciliation procedures designed to prevent stoppages like the national railway strike of 1919. Some competition would remain along the 'frontiers', and cities like Exeter, Leeds, Sheffield and Glasgow would be served by more than one group but, on the other hand, major industrial areas like South Wales and Lancashire would thenceforth depend entirely on the services of a single railway organisation.

Unfortunately the amalgamation scheme, though it looked like a step towards greater efficiency, had been determined largely by political pressures and according to political principles. The economic aspects of the problem had been pretty well ignored or were assumed to require no detailed examination. There was, therefore, no study made of the optimum or viable size for a railway unit and the maintenance of the shibboleth of private ownership, which blocked the dismantling of former companies, led to the creation of four groups which were extremely unequal in their size and capacities. The London & North Eastern, for instance, struggled with an unhappy legacy of uneconomic country branch lines and was to find itself dependent for most of its custom on a Tyneside plunged in the depths of industrial depression. The Southern, which had borne the brunt of the strain imposed by war, found itself faced with the need to accommodate a massive and expanding commuter belt around London. Thanks to the energy and vision of the indefatigable Sir Herbert Walker it found its salvation in a programme of electrification which brought Portsmouth, Brighton and Chatham virtually into London's backyard.

The 1921 Railways Act imposed on the railway companies a new outlook which required great organisational and psychological readjustments, while regrettably maintaining a tradition of Parliamentary regulation that hamstrung the railways when they attempted to meet the challenge of motor transport, which had developed rapidly as a result of the war. Large-scale production of military vehicles, plus the protectionist McKenna duties, imposed in 1915 to economise on shipping space by limiting the importation of luxury goods like French and American cars, had created the facility in Britain to turn out large

quantities of buses, lorries and cars. With their permanent way maintained at the expense of the taxpayer and with no statutory obligation to provide 'reasonable services' or to publish their freight rates, the road hauliers and bus companies were all set to cream off the profits of the best routes, leaving the railways to make what they could from such stricken customers as the coal and steel industries. Little wonder that by 1938 the railways were clamouring for a 'square deal'.

The outbreak of war in 1939 precluded any possibility of salvaging the lost fortunes of the railways and once again imposed upon them the massive strains of total war. In an age of air and motor transport and after nearly a quarter century of under-investment, the railways were still called upon to shoulder the major part of the burden. Not only did they have to cope with a vastly expanded volume of regular traffic, they also had to hold themselves ready to adapt the whole system to meet a national emergency at a moment's notice. The most spectacular exercise of the emergency machinery was, of course, Operation Dynamo, which was set in motion on May 26, 1940, to assist the evacuation of the troops from Dunkirk. The main problem was to get the men away from the South Coast ports to reception centres far inland as quickly as possible. Two thousand railway coaches were immediately pooled for the purpose and Redhill junction closed to act as a clearinghouse. There was no time to organise a timetable and all train movement orders were therefore issued minute by minute over the telephone. Thanks to the skill of the railwaymen and the enthusiasm of thousands of volunteers, all of whom put in incredibly long hours, about 320,000 men aboard 620 trains were ferried away from the danger areas in a single hectic week.

Bombing was, of course, a new hazard to be overcome. It was particularly severe in the summer and autumn of 1940, when more than half of all the stoppages and delays caused by aerial action occurred, and again during the V2 attacks of 1944.

The most concentrated damage was inflicted by saturation raids on dock areas, but direct hits on bridges also caused long delays and throughout the war unprotected trains seem to have been a temptation which few lone raiders could resist.

Stations suffered mixed fortunes. Dover naturally received considerable punishment while, far away, Middlesbrough was smashed by a stick of bombs. In London, St Pancras was badly damaged and nearby Kings Cross had part of Cubitts famous roof blown away. Locomotives seem to have been remarkably tough; of the 484 which were hit only eight were a total write-off. Three thousand or so wagons and carriages were destroyed. Doubtless many more were casualties of marshalling in blackout conditions. Total damage has been estimated at £30,000,000, a figure which pales into insignifance beside the estimated £200,000,000-worth of arrears of maintenance.

Total war meant a total mobilisation of national resources and the mobilisation of the whole population. It meant diverting more than 100 locomotives, converted at Swindon from steam to diesel, to distant Persia to serve the Allied lifeline to Russia. It meant an LNER driver and fireman earning a George Cross apiece for driving an exploding ammunition train out of Soham station into open country. It meant shuttling 100,000 men through Southampton in the six days after D-day. Total war involving such extraordinary disruptions left Britain's railways in a disastrous state. Nationalisation became, therefore, not so much a political objective to be achieved as a vital prerequisite for post-war economic recovery.

Twice in the present century Britain's railways have been called upon to make heroic efforts and great sacrifices in the nation's defence. Many of their problems have been the direct result of the loyalty and devotion with which the call of duty was answered. An honoured place in Britain's transport system is the only fitting epitaph for such a record.

Top: To war by train, Italian style.
Italian State Railways

Left: Middlesbrough station after an air raid in 1942. *British Railways ER*

RAILWAY SIGNALLING
The early days

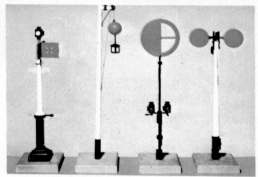

Far left: Policeman or 'Bobby' who worked at the lineside and regulated the passage of trains on a time-interval basis. *British Transport Museum*

Above left: Old crows-nest signal box at Waterloo station on the London and South Western Railway. *British Transport Museum*

Above: Hole-in-the-wall signal box at Victoria on the London Chatham & Dover Railway. *British Transport Museum*

Left: Early signals, left to right: Wood's crossbar c1840; GWR ball 1837; LSWR rotating disc c1840; horizontal axis double disc 1846. *Science Museum London*

TWO OF THE pictures in these chapters sum up the great change that has taken place in the work of the railway signalman. Today, he is seated in front of a few rows of buttons or switches and able to see from track diagrams in front of him the position and identification of every train under his control. Signal boxes are no longer concerned just with a few miles of track and their signals. Now they are control rooms often covering many miles with as many signals and points all under the eyes and control of only a few signalmen who now do the work of many individual signalmen in separate boxes.

A modern train control centre (signalbox is no longer an appropriate title) can cover train movements over greater distances than was possible with the old cabins with levers connected to the signals by wires, whose length for practical purposes was usually not much longer than half a mile. Until the widespread introduction of power - operated signals, the railways of Britain were guarded by signal cabins spaced at least every five miles and on lines with heavy traffic, particularly in the vicinity of large stations and junctions, the cabins were sometimes within a few hundred yards of each other. Pulling and pushing the heavy signal and point levers for 12 hours or more at a stretch, the old-time signalman's lot was arduous.

Signals in the very early days of the railway generally were given by flags, lanterns and hand and arm signals. 'Policemen' stationed at intervals alongside the track were responsible for the safety of trains by signalling the time which had elapsed since the preceding train had passed his position. For many years in Britain signalmen were called 'Bobbies'

because their original duty was to police the line. However, the first passenger steam railway, the Liverpool and Manchester, installed rotating 'disc' signals within four years of its opening in 1830 and on the LSWR disc signals were introduced in 1840.

As train speeds increased it was found that a man with a flag or lantern standing at track level could not be seen in time by the driver of an approaching train and means were sought to improve signalling by erecting rotatable masts with shaped boards. Although the boards were not all disc-shaped (actual shape varied according to the railway company) 'disc' is a convenient group description of this type of signal to distinguish them from the semaphores which came later.

One alternative tried in 1840, but not perpetuated in Britain, was a ball hoisted to the top of a mast to indicate when the line was clear. In North America this type of signal was used for many years and from its use came the expression 'highball' to indicate proceed.

Brunel's Great Western disc-and-crossbar signals, first used in 1838, were of exceptional size, sometimes sixty feet above the ground with the crossbar eight feet or more long; some remained in use until the 1890s. In the stop position the crossbar was presented. If the line was clear the disc was displayed by turning the post through ninety degrees. For many years these signals, and similar types on other lines, were operated by the policemen moving a lever at the base of the pole. Control by a lever at a distance through wires did not come into use for some years. It is said that a policeman at Watford on the LNWR in 1846 devised the first

system of operating a signal at a distance. He used a weight on the signal and a wire running to his hut.

The discs on rotatable posts were gradually superseded by the semaphore signals which were to become a distinctive feature of the British railway. The first semaphore signal, supposedly derived from the signal arms used by ships of the Royal Navy (but more likely derived from the Chappé land relay chain) was installed by C H Gregory on the London and Croydon railway in 1841. At first the semaphore arms could be set to three different positions: the arm horizontal to indicate 'stop'; at 45 degrees to show 'caution' and vertical, concealed in the slotted post, 'all clear'. Although in general these indications, or aspects, replicated the displaced policemen's arm signals, there was little standardisation between individual railways, nor indeed any need for it in early years, of signal aspects and their interpretation.

An essential part of a signalling system is communication between signal cabins. Despatching trains on the time-interval system had to be abandoned gradually as traffic and speeds increased above certain low levels, and the electric telegraph was introduced into railway operation to provide the answer. However, the single-needle telegraph, in which letters were represented by the deflection of the needle, could not be adopted extensively for railway use in the 1840s because the greater number of station masters and signalmen could neither read nor write. This situation was emphasised when I K Brunel gave evidence on railway safety before a Parliamentary Select Committee in 1841. The NER adopted the 'speaking'

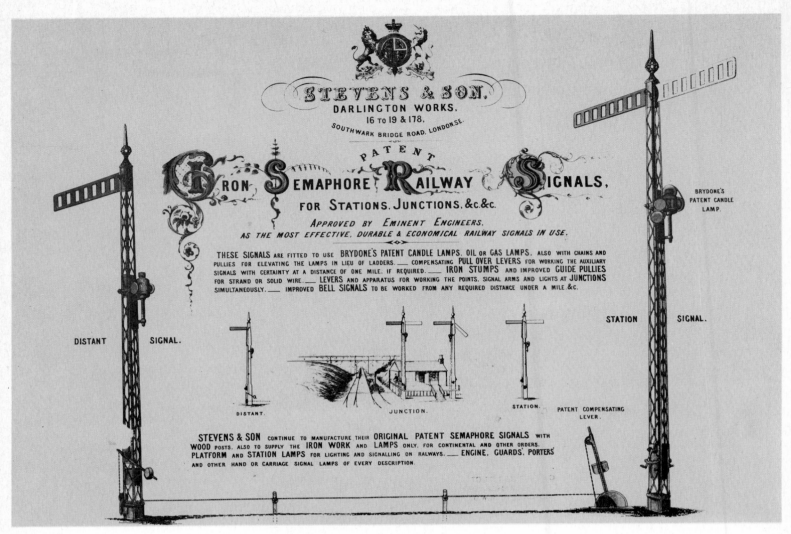

STEVENS & SON.
DARLINGTON WORKS.
16 TO 19 & 178.
SOUTHWARK BRIDGE ROAD. LONDON S.E.

PATENT
IRON SEMAPHORE RAILWAY SIGNALS,
FOR STATIONS. JUNCTIONS. &c.&c.
APPROVED BY EMINENT ENGINEERS.
AS THE MOST EFFECTIVE, DURABLE & ECONOMICAL RAILWAY SIGNALS IN USE.

THESE SIGNALS ARE FITTED TO USE BRYDONE'S PATENT CANDLE LAMPS. OIL OR GAS LAMPS. ALSO WITH CHAINS AND
PULLIES FOR ELEVATING THE LAMPS IN LIEU OF LADDERS. — COMPENSATING PULL OVER LEVERS FOR WORKING THE AUXILIARY
SIGNALS WITH CERTAINTY AT A DISTANCE OF ONE MILE. IF REQUIRED. — IRON STUMPS AND IMPROVED GUIDE PULLIES
FOR STRAND OR SOLID WIRE. — LEVERS AND APPARATUS FOR WORKING THE POINTS. SIGNAL ARMS AND LIGHTS AT JUNCTIONS
SIMULTANEOUSLY. — IMPROVED BELL SIGNALS TO BE WORKED FROM ANY REQUIRED DISTANCE UNDER A MILE. &c.

BRYDONE'S
PATENT CANDLE
LAMP.

DISTANT   SIGNAL.

STATION   SIGNAL.

DISTANT.

JUNCTION.

STATION.

PATENT COMPENSATING
LEVER.

STEVENS & SON CONTINUE TO MANUFACTURE THEIR ORIGINAL PATENT SEMAPHORE SIGNALS WITH
WOOD POSTS. ALSO TO SUPPLY THE IRON WORK AND LAMPS ONLY. FOR CONTINENTAL AND OTHER ORDERS.
PLATFORM AND STATION LAMPS FOR LIGHTING AND SIGNALLING ON RAILWAYS. — ENGINE. GUARDS. PORTERS
AND OTHER HAND OR CARRIAGE SIGNAL LAMPS OF EVERY DESCRIPTION.

telegraph in 1846, although even until as late as 1851 illiteracy among staff restricted its usefulness as a means of communication between stations and signalmen. However, in that year C V Walker, of the SER, introduced the single-stroke bell telegraph system using a simple code of bell strokes which could be learnt easily by the signalmen. For example: one stroke —'attention'; two —'train entering section' and so on.

Around 1850 there was significant progress in block telegraph systems, notably by Edward Tyer who simplified the equipment and reduced the number of wires and batteries required to operate it. He also anticipated the modern track-circuit by developing a treadle rail with electrical contacts for announcing the position of trains.

In 1861 he invented the step-by-step 'alphabetical' telegraph for communicating between signal boxes. This was the precursor of the train describers with which signalmen could supplement the single/block bell code by 'describing' each train forward to the next box. For example, in addition to 'offering' and getting 'accepted' from the next signal box and advising 'train entering section', the describer could be used to pass details of a train, eg, 'Up fast parcels train for branch line'.

The single-needle telegraph came into use alongside the block-bell telegraph as a method for passing traffic information and public messages. It survived into the era of the all-electric area-control signal box as it was an ideal system for broadcasting information without unduly distracting the signalman. Signalmen could 'listen with

one ear' to the clicking telegraph needle at the same time concentrating on the track diagrams, the signal indicator lamps and the signal levers.

During the 1870s more and more signal and point levers were being concentrated in frames at one point so that they could be interlocked with each other to prevent the signalmen displaying signals which conflicted with the position of the points. Instead of signalmen who operated the signal levers and pointsmen who stood at the point levers beside the track, all were brought under the control of one man in a signal cabin. This became the standard British arrangement and one which was encouraged by legislation administered by the Board of Trade.

It was not, however, adopted in other parts of the world even when there were traffic conditions sometimes as complicated as those of this country. To this day in some countries, the control of the block sections between stations is the responsibility of the station master while the points and signals in the station are under the control of an official in another office. In general, though, outside Britain the same intensive operating conditions did not exist and simpler forms of signalling could be used with safety.

In the 1890s the three-position semaphore went out of favour because, for one reason, it was not easy to arrange the mechanism so that the arm was accurately set. Sometimes the arm took up a position between stop and caution. It was replaced by the two-position signal with the arm falling vertically into the slot in the post, as before, to indicate 'clear'. However, the

semaphore arm moving into a slotted post had the serious drawback of occasionally becoming frozen in the 'off' position by ice or snow. Such a 'failure to danger' could hardly be considered satisfactory although in the signalling systems accepted in some countries to this day fail-safe practices have yet to be enforced.

In the UK the lesson was learned early enough. At Abbots Ripton in 1876 the signalman acted correctly and set the signals for the trains passing through his section. In driving snow and freezing air temperature, the southbound Flying Scotsman was rapidly overhauling a slow freight train on the same line. Blinded by snow, the driver of the freight overran the stop signals at Holme, where the signalman intended to shunt the freight into a siding out of the way of the Scotsman, which was only 16 minutes away. It was not until the freight train had run past two more signal cabins, which were not on the telegraph line and therefore were unaware of the developing situation, that the signalman at Abbots Ripton, advised by the telegraph, stopped the train and instructed its driver to back into the siding.

The signalman to the north of Abbots Ripton had correctly set his signals to danger behind the departing freight train and would keep them 'on' until he received the bell code, 'train out of section' from Abbots Ripton. Within a few minutes the block bell told him that the Scotsman was approaching his signals. To his surprise it did not slacken speed but swept past and disappeared to the south, lost in the swirling snow. At Abbots Ripton it crashed into the side of the freight train

Above: Inside the London & North Western box at Willesden around the turn of the century, showing block telegraph instruments on the right. *Ian Allan Library*

Facing page: Early semaphore signals used on the Great Western Railway. *British Transport Museum (B Sharpe)*

Right: Manual lever-operated boxes have continued in use until the last quarter of the century. This view shows a box in the Lincoln area. *I Krause*

which had not completely cleared the main line. The driver of the express had seemingly ignored the distant signal for Abbots Ripton; the lever for which and that for the home signal were both in the 'on' position. The disaster was worsened because of poor communications and the appalling weather conditions, which prevented a northbound express from being stopped before it crashed into the wreckage.

The driver of the Flying Scotsman had been lured into danger by signals giving a false indication that the line was clear. The signalmen concerned had acted correctly but the signal arms were frozen in the clear position by snow packed in the slots in which the arms moved. The balance weights designed to pull the arm to the stop position in the event of a broken wire could not overcome the resistance of the frozen arm and the pull of wires weighed down by frozen snow.

Abbots Ripton highlighted inadequacies in the signals and their equipment of the 1870s and the difficulties of drivers and signalmen working in adverse conditions. However, as has happened before and since, the report of the Board of Trade Inspector on the accident contained recommendations intended not only to avoid a recurrence but to improve the safety of the railways generally. Among them was the abandonment of the type of semaphore signal which fell to 'clear' into a slot in the signal post.

Even more important however was the abandonment of the principle of keeping signals normally in the 'off' position and putting them to danger after a train had passed. (In France and some other countries this method of working signals remains in use even now.) Instead, in British railway practice, the signals were to remain normally in the 'on' position and were to be cleared only after the necessary bell signals had been exchanged and the line proved clear.

Had that been the practice at Abbots Ripton then the signal arms might have frozen in the danger position which, while inconveniencing operations, would have been a 'fail-safe' method. Another outcome of that historic accident was the adoption by the Great Northern and by some other lines, of the balanced or somersault signal designed to be unaffected by such things as the weight of snow.

Safety of train movements had been the subject of a number of Governmental regulations which were introduced successively from 1839 onward. The Board of Trade and its inspectors were empowered to investigate operating practices and the provision of satisfactory methods and equipment for the safety of railway passengers. However, it was in the Railway Regulations Act of 1889 that the Board of Trade finally consolidated and codified regulations and orders applying to all British railways. The regulation covered the adoption of the absolute block system of working for all passenger lines, ie one

train only in a section at a time; the interlocking of all points and signals on passenger lines; and the adoption of continuous brakes, operated by air or vacuum, on all passenger rolling stock.

Signals proliferated as railway companies complied with the Board of Trade requirements that all passenger train movements had to be under the control and protection of signals interlocked with the points and with other signals which might conflict. Even every exit from little-used sidings had to have the appropriate shunting signals to govern movements. There were of course variations in the way each company arranged and operated its signals. On some lines there was a separate signal for all possible moves; on others only the minimum to satisfy Board of Trade regulations.

In this chapter we have seen a little of the signalman's job in the days of the lever-and-wire-operated semaphore signals. He was then primarily concerned with operating in accordance with sets of rules, or communicating in accordance with codes designed to obviate mistakes or misunderstandings, with responsibility for train movements only within the boundaries of his own block sections. Next, we will deal with the transitional period up to about the 1940s, and finally the modern signalman assisted by electronic systems which have taken out of his hands much of the routine operation of the signals and points so that he can concentrate more on traffic control. Now he has a working environment not unlike that of the air traffic controller; both are provided with electronic displays of the position of the traffic moving within their area.

Above: The massive array of semaphore signals needed to control the approaches to Waterloo station as it was between about 1892 and 1900. *British Transport Museum*

Left: Self-balancing somersault signals needing lower operating power in use on the Great Northern line in 1952. The one on the right is just returning to danger. *Ian Allan library*

SIGNALLING 1890~1940

THE DEVELOPMENT of the electric telegraph in early Victorian times and its adoption by the railways laid the foundation of modern railway signalling, yet it took 60 years of haphazard railway operation and many accidents before it was made compulsory. Some railways adopted a primitive form of telegraph for sending messages about trains running over dangerous sections of line, tunnels, for example, as early as the late 1840s. But the equipment was cumbersome and messages were spelt out letter by letter. Soon the railways adapted telegraph instruments into a simpler form to show the state of the line between two stations merely by the position of the telegraph needle supplemented by bell code signals so that signalmen could advise each other of the movement of trains.

Some of the most progressive railways quickly realised the advantages of the telegraph system for it meant that signalmen had a positive indication of whether the section of line they controlled was occupied by a train or not, a far better state of affairs than the old time-interval system in which signalmen had no means of communication between one station and the next. The sections of line, which generally ran from one signalbox to the next, were known as block sections, and the method of controlling trains by the electric telegraph became known as the block system. The principal rule was that there should not be more than one train in a block section on one line at one time and signalmen were able to advise each other as trains passed into and out of each block section by the electric telegraph and bells.

A system was evolved whereby a signalman, before he could clear his signals for a train, 'offered' it by bell code to the next signalbox ahead and if the block section was clear the train was 'accepted' by repetition of the bell code back to the offering signalbox. As the train passed the first box the signalman sent the 'train entering section' bell signal to the box ahead, and when it arrived or passed the signalman there sent back the 'train out of section' bell signal. The block indicator needle, worked by the signalman at the exit end of the block section and electric-

ally repeated at the entry end box, was used to show the state of the line and whether a train had been accepted or was actually in the section. This system remains in use today on lines still controlled by old-style mechanical signalboxes.

Some railways were slow to adopt the block system but it was finally ordained by Parliament in the Regulation of Railways Act 1889 that it should be installed compulsorily. This Act also required that all signals and points controlled from one signalbox should be interlocked with each other at the lever frame so that conflicting indications could not be given. This meant that a signal could not be cleared unless the points were correctly set, and at junctions two signals from different lines leading to a conflicting route could not be cleared at the same time.

Facing points, that is points giving a direct running move from one track to another, were avoided wherever possible except, of course, at route junctions or large stations; at small country stations facing crossovers from a line in one direction on to the line in the opposite

Top left: Three-position upper-quadrant semaphore signals at London Victoria station in the 1920s. *Ian Allan library*

Top right: Standard 1930s form of station layout diagram and telegraph instruments in Dunbar West manual signalbox on the East Coast main line. *G Ogilvie*

Above centre: Extract from signalman's bell code book as posted in signalboxes as a constant reminder. *British Transport Museum (B Sharpe)*

Above: Old semaphore and new four-aspect colour-light signals side by side between Holborn and Elephant & Castle, SR, in preparation for the changeover in 1925. *Topical Press Agency*

G.O. 246. **MIDLAND & GREAT NORTHERN JOINT RAILWAY.**

BELL OR GONG SIGNALS

(As provided in the Block Telegraph or Electric Train Tablet Regulations).

EMERGENCY BELL OR GONG CODE.

		Beats on bell or Gong	How to be given. a stroke thus - represents a pause.
12	OBSTRUCTION—DANGER	6	6 consecutively.
17	STOP AND EXAMINE TRAIN	7	7 consecutively.
19	TRAIN PASSED WITHOUT TAIL LAMP	9	9 consecutively to box in advance. 4-5 to box in rear.
20	TRAIN DIVIDED	10	5-5
22	VEHICLES RUNNING AWAY ON WRONG LINE	12	2-5-5
22	VEHICLES RUNNING AWAY (SINGLE LINES ONLY)	12	2-5-5
23	VEHICLES RUNNING AWAY ON RIGHT LINE	14	4-5-5

Traffic Manager's Office, King's Lynn. January, 1905.

JNO. J. PETRIE, Traffic Manager.

direction were almost unknown. Indeed, this sort of crossover was nearly always provided as a trailing connection so that if a train had to cross to the opposite line it had to run beyond the points, stop, then reverse back through the crossover. By this means the risk of head-on collision by trains being accidentally diverted on to the opposite line was virtually eliminated.

Signals themselves by that time were almost entirely of the two-position semaphore pattern which denoted stop with the arm horizontal and clear with the arm lowered at 45 degrees. In the danger position at night they showed a red light and in the clear position a white light. Arms were generally painted red with a white vertical stripe near the left hand end; distant signals, that is the advance warning signals which repeated the indication of the next stop signals ahead, had a vee notch cut out of the left hand end. Signal arms on most lines were by then pivoting outside the post instead of within a slotted post, but some railways adopted the somersault arm which was formed of a centrally balanced arm coupled to a separate glass spectacle casting designed to defeat the unbalancing action of a snow build-up. A number of accidents had been caused because snow had affected the working of normal semaphore arms and caused them to show a false clear indication.

Other safety devices included facing point locks in which a bolt positively locked the point blades fully home in their normal and reverse positions so that there was no danger of a point blade standing away from a rail and causing a derailment. The point lock bolt was connected to a steel bar longer than the space between any two pairs of wheels on locomotives and coaches laid against the inside edge of the rail approaching and through the points. Before the points could be moved they had to be unbolted by a point lock lever in the signalbox, during which operation the bar, called the fouling bar, rose up to rail level. If a train was standing or passing over the fouling bar the wheel flanges prevented the bar from being lifted and in turn the points from being unlocked and moved.

On single lines it was thought necessary to have something more than the block system to prevent head-on collisions and the staff system was used. At first this consisted of a large wooden staff, one for each block section, and the driver of every train passing through the block section had to carry the staff as his authority to be on the single line. As there was only one staff for each section it followed that if everyone obeyed the rules there could be no collison. The basic system proved inflexible because it meant that ideally trains ran alternately in each direction and this did not always happen in practice.

From it was developed the staff and ticket system in which if several trains had to follow each other in the same direction over the single line the drivers of all but the last train were shown the staff but given a written ticket to proceed, while the last train of the group carried the staff. The tickets were kept in locked boxes opened by a key on the staff. Even this system was cumbersome,

although it survived on one or two lines until recent times; its place was taken on many single lines by the electric staff instrument or its similar but smaller related systems—the tablet and key token. The signalboxes at each end of a single line section were equipped with electrically interlocked staff instruments with several staffs in the system. Electric locks were fitted to the two instruments so that only one staff could be taken out of either instrument at one time, thus again ensuring the security of the single line.

With the virtual standardisation of the two-position semaphore signal and the abandonment of the old three-position type which, at night, showed red for danger, green for caution and white for clear, the green light was gradually adopted for the clear indication instead of white, which could be confused with ordinary lineside lighting, and particularly gas lights, then being adopted more widely in towns and on stations.

By 1900 the wonders and use of electricity were becoming known. The early years of the present century saw the introduction of track circuits, in which a weak electric current was passed through an insulated section of the running rails and when short-circuited by the wheels of a train occupying the line could be made to operate electro-magnetic relays, which in turn were employed to illuminate lights of signalbox track diagrams or to operate locks on signal levers.

Electricity was also used to power electric motors connected to points or signals which could be controlled a greater distance away from a signalbox than by mechanical means. Indeed there was (and is) an absolute limit of 350yd on the mechanical operation of points by rodding from a signalbox and the practical limit for a wire-worked signal was about three-quarters of a mile.

The earliest application of automatic signalling in Great Britain was on the Liverpool Overhead Railway in 1893 where electrically worked semaphore signals were placed to danger by an arm on the back of a passing train striking a lever on a contact box fixed on the lineside. As the train progressed the operation of the striker arms altered the electrical connections to place the signals immediately protecting the train to danger and cleared the signals at the previous station to allow another train to proceed.

During the next 20 years, which saw the construction of most of the deep-level underground lines in London, improvements in signals and signalling systems were evolved gradually. At first some of the tube lines used the normal block system with signal cabins at each station controlling miniature semaphore signals illuminated by oil or gas lighting. Later, electricity was used for signal lights, still retaining a moving arm or vane containing coloured glass, but eventually the colour-light signal, which employed separate bulbs for each colour indication and had no moving parts, was adopted. Track circuits were gradually introduced to allow automatic operation of signals, which permitted the closure of many signalboxes at intermediate stations where no points existed.

Main-line railways also took advantage of power operation in some new signalling installations; in 1898 the London & North Western introduced electric working of signals and points in the Crewe area. The lever frames no longer needed to be fitted with the long levers necessary for mechanical operation to obtain adequate movement of wire or rodding, and instead short levers, still with mechanical interlocking, were used to operate electrical contacts which transmitted the current to the signal and point-operating equipment. In 1902 the London & South Western Railway introduced automatic signalling

Above left: A fairly modern key token instrument used for security of single-track lines. *British Railways SR*

Top: Early power frame, train describer telegraphs and indicator lights at London Bridge station. *Ian Allan library*

Left: Reconstruction of a signalbox of the Great Eastern Railway showing a power frame in the foreground and 1884 single-line tablet instrument. *Science Museum London*

Above: Early electric train-describer instrument of the middle-1920s. *Ian Allan library*

controlled by track circuits, with semaphore arms powered by low-pressure compressed air through electro-pneumatic valves, on its main line between Woking and Basingstoke.

The track circuit was also gradually adopted to provide better protection in mechanically signalled areas controlled by normal block working, for it could be used to prevent a signalman clearing a signal leading to a section of line already occupied by a train.

Other allied safety devices similar in effect, if not in principle, were also used, including the lock and block system. This pre-dated the track circuit and was used extensively on some lines in Southern England and in North East London. It employed treadles situated along the rail edge which were depressed by the wheel flanges of a passing train and used to actuate or release locks in signalbox equipment. Generally the system provided complete locking between the block instruments and the signals in such a way that a train had to pass the signals at one signalbox and the signals had to be restored to danger behind it before the block instrument for the section the train had just left could be released and cleared for a second train. In turn, the signals at the previous station could not be cleared for a second train until the block instrument for that particular section was put in the clear position. In this period also the telephone had been perfected and was installed widely for giving information on train running to supplement the block system and the needle telegraph still employed in its original form for sending general train messages.

In the years before and after the first world war more changes became apparent in signals, particularly distant signals. One or two railways had begun to install three-position signals again but this time the arms worked in the upper quadrant, that is to say, from the horizontal danger position they were raised to 45 degrees for caution and upwards vertically for clear. In the caution position at night they showed a yellow light which conflicted with the normal caution indication of two-position distant signals which on most railways still showed red; gradually, however, some companies adopted yellow for the night-time indication of a distant at caution and at the same time painted the arm yellow with a black vee stripe.

Indeed, because of the possible confusion between the two types of signal, the growing introduction of colour-light signals and automatic signalling, and the possible need for additional signal indications, a signal engineers' committee was set up in 1922 to examine signalling needs for the future. It advised against the adoption of the three-position semaphore and found that the normal two-position semaphore would be adequate for ordinary working. However, in closely signalled areas with a frequent service the committee recommended the adoption of the four-aspect colour-light system using red for danger, one yellow for caution, double-yellow for preliminary caution, and green for clear.

The Great Central Railway was the first to adopt automatic colour-light signalling out of doors (as distinct from the under-

ground lines in tunnel) in 1923, and two years later the first re-signalling schemes on the Southern Railway's South East London approaches embodying the four-aspect colour-light system were introduced. The final abandonment of the three-position semaphore left the way open for the adoption of the upper-quadrant two-position semaphore which was raised to 45 degrees for the clear position. The upper-quadrant type of signal was of lighter construction than the lower quadrant, since it returned by gravity to danger instead of being weighted to ensure that the arm returned to the horizontal position, both when the lever was put back to normal in the lever frame or in the event of a broken wire. As a point of later railway history the upper-quadrant signal did not completely oust the lower-quadrant type, for the Great Western Railway continued to use the lower-quadrant semaphore, and indeed its successor, the Western Region of British Railways, still does where it retains mechanical signalling, and even on other lines isolated lower-quadrant signals survive in one or two places. The recommendations of the committee were so

far reaching that there has been no radical change in signalling indications in Britain from then until the present time, nor is there likely to be while lineside signals exist.

The 1920s and 1930s saw the gradual extension of colour-light signalling but still largely worked by signalboxes controlling limited areas. While the old mechanical limits no longer applied, the power signalbox of that period still controlled signals and points by individual miniature levers—one lever per function—and control areas were generally not much more than a mile or so from the signalbox. Sometimes lengths of automatic signalling intervened between adjacent signalboxes. In 1927 the Great Western took signalling control a stage further by the adoption of route levers at Newport (Monmouthshire). In this system the levers controlling the signals (which were electrically operated semaphores) also set the points to which the signal applied in the one operation. The movement of the miniature lever by the signalman was in stages, first to a check-lock position as the equipment

proved that the line was free to be used and that no other conflicting move had been set (this was achieved by track circuits and normal interlocking), then to a position which operated the points, and, finally, when they had been proved in the correct position, the lever movement was completed which cleared the signal.

During the 1930s the LNER introduced the first all-electric signalbox control panels which laid the foundations for present-day power signalling. Instead of being controlled by levers, signal and point movements were initiated by thumb switches. The turning of a switch on the signalman's control desk, like the Great Western's system at Newport, proved the section of line free for use, operated the points and cleared the signal, from one signal to the next; in this case, however, the signals were colour-lights. By now the locking between the signalman's control switches was achieved electrically by relays instead of mechanical locks. This system, known as the OCS (one control switch) pattern was adopted more extensively in British signalling during the next 20 years. It is covered in the next chapter.

THE BIG POWER BOX

WE HAVE seen in the previous chapters that the first, and undoubtedly irregular, signal to be given by lights to show whether the line was clear was recorded in the 1840s. It is said to have been given by a lighted candle placed in a window of a house beside the line if the way was clear, and if the light was not there the line was blocked.

The first true signals to be given solely by lights were on the pioneer London Underground railways, built just before and after the turn of the century. At first a single light source gave the indications by a moving arm containing coloured glass spectacles which passed in front of it; later the true colour-light, with a separate bulb for each indication illuminated coloured glass lenses which magnified the light. Indeed the lenses were designed to concentrate the light into a beam directed towards the driver of an approaching train. It was this feature which later made colour-light signals out of doors so useful in fog, for the diffused lights can usually be seen from a distance in front of the signal during fog, even though the signal post itself is invisible.

The first automatic signalling system was installed on the Liverpool Overhead Railway in the 1890s and by the turn of the century electrically operated semaphore signals and points had been introduced by one or two main-line railways, for example the LNWR at Crewe on the main line from Euston to the North. Track circuits were evolved during the first 20 years of this century, and most of the ingredients were thus present for the introduction of power signalling on a more widespread scale after the first world war. The Southern Railway was the foremost exponent of power signalling during the 1920s and 30s with new installations at all of its London terminus stations.

In these early power signalling schemes points and signals were controlled from lever frames having small levers no more than about 6-9in high; interlocking between levers to ensure that signals could not be cleared unless points were correctly set or that conflicting signals could not be given, was at first achieved mechanically in exactly the same way as the levers in a normal mechanical signal-box. Later miniature lever frames used by the Southern Railway employed electric locks between levers but the principle was the same and the lever could not be operated unless it was free to be used.

The signalling at Newport, Monmouthshire, was modernised in 1927, but there the electrically operated semaphore signals were controlled from levers which served more than one function; as they were pulled the lever was checked in two intermediate positions while the equipment first proved that the line on which the train was to be signalled was clear and that no other signal leading to the same route was already clear, and second, that the points were switched to the correct position. Finally, the signalman pulled the lever to the fully over position which cleared the signal.

This equipment was known as route lever operation since the movement of a single lever set up a complete route from one signal to the next. At that time, however, no overall advantage could be seen in its more widespread adoption and during the following decade nearly all new power signalling schemes on the Great Western and Southern Railways used miniature levers having only one function per lever. A feature of most of the SR lever frames was the repeater lights behind the levers which showed the position of points by the letter N (normal) or R (reverse). Signals were indicated by the lights repeating the aspect shown on the signal itself.

The signalbox track diagrams had also come to life by this time. In mechanical boxes without any track circuiting the signalman had a display of the lines he controlled, with points and signals shown in their geographical positions and bearing a number alongside corresponding to the lever numbers which operated them. When track circuits were installed the presence of a train on the section of line concerned was indicated either by red lights being illuminated on the track diagram on the section concerned or by other forms of indicator such as a needle pointer which swung towards a label 'line clear' or 'line blocked' depending on whether there was a train there.

Sometimes track circuits were used only for indication purposes but usually they

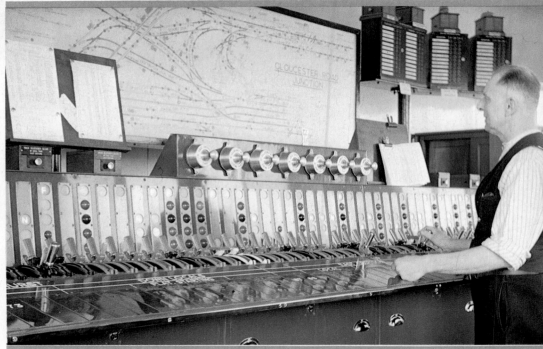

Above: At Newport West box, the first route lever installation in Britain in 1927. *British Railways WR*

Right above: Typical intermediate-period installation, at Gloucester Road, SR, with one lever per function, electro-mechanical interlocking and signal indications behind levers. *Westinghouse Brake and Signal Company*

Right below: Typical control panel in a modern big power box, at Derby, LMR. *Westinghouse Brake and Signal Company*

Far right: Another modern LMR control panel, at Wolverhampton. *British Railways LMR*

also operated locks on other signal levers leading to that section of line. In power signalling areas, however, all lines were usually track-circuited and the track circuits were not only indicated on the signalman's track diagram but were used to place signals to danger automatically as trains passed them. This was an added safety feature which made sure that there was a red signal behind a train even if the signalman forgot about it. The signal would clear for a second time only when the first train passed beyond the next signal ahead so that the track circuit became free, and also after the signalman had put the lever back to the 'danger' position and pulled it clear again.

On some sections of line the signals worked automatically and were not controlled by signal levers. This was achieved solely by track circuits; some small signalboxes at local stations, which only needed to work points perhaps once or twice a day, for example to let a goods train in or out of a yard, could be closed at other times and a special lever operated before the signalman went home which set the signals to work automatically. When the signalbox was open, however, the signals would be controlled by the levers.

There was usually none of the offering and accepting routine described previously for mechanical signalboxes between power signalboxes, and signalmen were normally warned of the approach of a train by the track circuit lights as the train entered the control area. However, the signalman

needed to know the identity of the train and this was advised to him by a train describer. The early train describers were in the form of a clock face with a single hand which pointed at different descriptions on labels around the face. The describers were worked by electric impulses from signalbox to signalbox. As signalbox control areas became more complex, it was sometimes possible for a signalbox to supervise an area long enough for the signalman to have two or even three trains approaching him on the same line at a safe distance, and train describers in use by the end of the 1930s were able to display first, second or third train approaching by means of lights illuminated against a written description.

In 1935 the LNER introduced a new signalling scheme at Thirsk on the East Coast main line in which the colour-light signals were controlled from thumb switches on the signalman's track diagram. It was not a very large installation and the signalman could sit at a desk with the control console in front of him. Each switch set up the route to a particular line, checking that the line concerned was free, changing the points if necessary, and clearing the signal.

Interlocking between switches was achieved electrically by relays rather than by electric or mechanical locks. Briefly, a relay is a piece of equipment containing an electro-magnet. If the magnet has an electric current passing through it is energised and attracts a metal arm towards it.

The arm is linked to a series of other electrical contacts which by the movement of the arm can be opened or closed, thus making or breaking other electrical circuits. When the relay is de-energised, that is with no electric current passing through the magnet, the arm drops away changing the position of the connected contacts. A series of these relays linked together between track circuits and signal operating switches can thus be used to pass electric current to signals and points, or to prevent the passage of electric current if the conditions are not right. The system is called relay interlocking and forms the basis of today's railway signalling.

The LNER pioneered the thumb switch type of signalling control panel known as the OCS (one control switch) system. Just before the second world war this company introduced a small signalling panel in a rather out-of-the-way place in the Liverpool Dock area at Brunswick, which might have seemed insignificant at the time, for it controlled only a very short section of line, but it proved to be the pioneer of the standard method of signalling today. Instead of using a thumb switch for each route controlled by a signal as in the OCS system (for example, if the signal concerned led to four different lines then four separate switches were provided) the new panel employed one switch only, called the entrance switch, situated on the diagram alongside the signal to which it applied, and a second switch, known as the exit, placed further along each of the lines which

could be reached from that signal. The operation of the two switches set up the route between them culminating with the clearance of the signal.

Signalling development made little progress during and after the second world war and the first of the post-war resignalling schemes on the LMS and Southern Railways and their successors, the London Midland and Southern Regions of British Railways, followed established methods using miniature lever frames. At York, however, the LNER was much bolder and introduced what at that time was the world's largest signalling scheme controlled by an OCS route-relay-interlocking system. Indeed, the LNER never looked back and used this type of control for a number of its resignalling schemes of the 1950s. At the same time the entrance/exit type of panel was also being developed and was used for one or two installations in the early 1950s. By that time, too, the signalman was being assisted on the more complex layouts by rows of white lights along the track diagram in front of him showing which routes had been set and signals cleared, a feature first seen at Northallerton in 1939. The white lights turned to red as the track concerned was occupied by a train.

The areas supervised by power signalboxes were gradually becoming larger but were still limited to the immediate station area and perhaps a mile or so on each side. During the mid-1950s two developments were perfected which

changed the whole course of British signalling. First, the design of much smaller relays which allowed more equipment to be housed together in a signalbox of moderate size, and second, and most important, an electronic development whereby a number of electrical circuits could be converted into electronic impulse signals and sent over the same pair of wires to be decoded at the far end into individual circuits again for the operation of specific signalling equipment.

The developments opened the way for the remote control of signalling several miles away from a signalbox and it was thus possible to think in terms of a signalling control area 30 or 40 miles long instead of 3 or 4 miles. This would not have been possible because of the cost if each electric circuit to individual signals and points had to be carried over separate pairs of wires. Moreover, it meant that many intermediate signalboxes could be closed and their function taken over by one central signalbox. Many of the signals could be arranged to work automatically from track circuits, although their indications were shown on the track diagram of the supervising signalbox so that the signalman had a continuous picture of train working throughout the area.

The new principles of larger control areas were introduced on a moderate scale with the LMR electrification in 1959 between Manchester and Crewe and during the following few years new signalboxes with more extensive control areas

were brought in by the dozen, mostly for electrification extensions: Barking, Tilbury, Pitsea and Southend on the Fenchurch Street-Shoeburyness line: Hither Green, Orpington, Sevenoaks, Tonbridge, Ashford and Folkestone on the London-Dover main line; and the extensive Euston, Willesden, Watford, Bletchley, Rugby, Birmingham and Wolverhampton boxes on the LM electric lines.

Each new signalbox seemed to set more records for the number of signals and points that it controlled and the number of miles of track it supervised. The Western Region also put in hand similar schemes so that today the vital routes between London, Swindon, Bristol and Taunton, also to South Wales, and the important cross-country route via Gloucester to Birmingham and onwards through the London Midland Region to Derby and Nottingham, are controlled by no more than about a dozen signalboxes. The latest, completed early in 1972, is that at Bristol which looks after 117 route miles of line.

All these boxes employ the entrance/exit type of control, some retaining an entrance switch and an exit button, but others employing solely push buttons, most of which serve as the exit button from one section and the entrance button to the next section ahead and thus have to be pushed twice, once for each function. It is fascinating to watch the signalman setting the route through a complex area merely by pushing buttons. White lights on the diagram trace the route which has been set,

signal lights on the diagram change from red to green and then as the train passes a series of red lights is seen weaving itself along the route that has been set. The train itself may be many miles from the signalbox and indeed the signalmen in these modern power boxes rarely see the trains they are signalling.

New forms of train describer have been developed because obviously much more information is wanted than the old first, second, third train approaching describers could give. There may be as many as 20 or 30 trains on the diagram at one time and a new system was adopted in which code figures and letters denote the class of train, its destination and train number or route. This is the code that is carried on the front of nearly all BR trains and is generally displayed as a figure, letter and two figures.

The train code is displayed on the signalman's track diagram, for in each signal section there is space on the line diagram for the code to be shown. It is reproduced either on a miniature cathode ray (television) tube no more than an inch or so in diameter or by electro-mechanical counters, and sometimes by other means. As the train runs through the layout its presence on the signalbox diagram is shown not only by the moving row of red lights but also by the code number, which steps from one signal display to the next, and so on through the layout, keeping pace with the red lights. The codes are set up by the signalman at the starting station either operating push buttons or dialling on a telephone-type dial, after which the electronic equipment makes sure that the code is passed from one display to the next. When it leaves the control area of one signalbox it is automatically transferred to the incoming display of the next signalbox ahead.

While railway discipline was essential in the safe working of trains, and numerous safety devices were adopted to try and prevent signalmen's errors, from the earliest days accidents could be caused by a driver running past a signal at danger into collision with another train. Almost from the start of the London Underground system this was recognised as a considerable danger in the confined tunnels and mechanical train stops were provided at stop signals. The automatic stopping device (automatic train stop or ats) consisted of small arms close to rail level which when the signal was at danger were raised into such a position as to engage with an arm suspended from the train. If a train passed a signal at danger the trip arm on the train was knocked back and opened a valve which applied the brakes automatically.

On main-line railways this system was not satisfactory because of the different speeds and weights of train. A few railways experimented with automatic warning systems (aws) and automatic stop systems but the only one that came to fruition to any extent in the 1930s and '40s was that of the Great Western Railway. This system employed a sloping ramp about 40ft long between the rails; it engaged a shoe under the locomotive which was lifted as it passed over the ramp. Ramps were placed near distant signals; if the signal was clear an electric current was passed into the ramp and through the shoe to equipment on the locomotive which rang a bell in the driver's cab. If the signal was at caution there was no electric current and the raising of the shoe by the dead ramp caused a horn to sound in the driver's cab which the driver had to acknowledge by pressing a plunger. If he did not do that the brakes were applied automatically. Despite recommendations that some such form of protection should be used on all railways, it remained virtually unique to the Great Western until the end of the 1930s. It also provided the Great Western with a remarkable safety record.

On the Fenchurch Street-Shoeburyness line the LMS experimented with a form of automatic warning system but unlike the Great Western pattern it involved no physical contact between the locomotive and track equipment. Instead it employed magnets, a permanent magnet to initiate an indication at a distant signal, followed by an electro-magnet which was energised if the signal was clear and opposed the warning which would be given by the permanent magnet. If the signal was at caution the electro-magnet was not energised and the permanent magnet acted on the locomotive equipment which caused

Far left: Four-aspect colour-light signals, approaching Old Oak Common, with light indications covering three routes diverging to the right. *British Transport Films*

Left centre: Section of the control panel at Wilmslow, of the one-control-switch (OCS) type. *Westinghouse Brake and Signal Company*

Left: Three-aspect colour-light main signals, with call-on and shunting signals, installed at Glasgow St Enoch in 1933. *Ian Allan library*

Above: Panel for entrance/exit type of control, at Portsmouth SR, in which the control buttons are on the route diagram itself. *British Railways SR*

Overleaf: British Railways class 8F No 48744 heading a freight train up Doveholes cutting in November 1967. *D Huntriss*

a horn to sound a long blast in the driver's cab; if it was not acknowledged by the driver pressing a button, the brakes were applied automatically.

During the 1950s British Railways developed a form of aws which combined the best features of both the GW and LMS types, using magnets to operate the system and the GW horn and bell indications in the cab. They were supplemented by a visual indicator to show a driver whether he had passed a clear signal or whether he had cancelled a warning indication. This system has gradually been installed during the last 20 years and is now standard on practically all BR main lines. It is also used on lines with multiple-aspect signals but cannot distinguish between double yellow, yellow or red, all of which will give a caution indication in the cab. Because of that and the need for faster trains to have a more positive indication, a new form of aws is being developed based on the existing system but with added refinements which will show the indication of the last signal passed.

More comprehensive, however, are the experiments now being conducted with full cab signalling, even possibly embodying some form of automatic control of train speed, in readiness for the 150mph trains of the future. It employs either conductor wires laid between the track or uses the running rails to carry coded impulse signals which are detected by equipment on the train. All sorts of information can be fed into the train equipment by the codes as well as signal aspects, including line conditions, for example gradients, permanent speed restrictions or similar physical features which might affect speed; the data can be assessed by train-borne equipment to show the driver continuously the maximum permissible speed at which the train may run and, if it is exceeded, apply the brakes automatically.

The driverless train might sound remote but already automatic trains are running on the London Underground and a few other of the world's railways. The Victoria Line tube trains have a man in the front cab but once he has opened and shut the doors at stations and pressed a start button the train accelerates and runs automatically; its speed is regulated and the train is stopped at stations by equipment picking up coded signals from the track. If it closes up towards a train ahead the equipment will automatically slow it down and if necessary stop it. When the line is again free it will restart automatically.

Points and signals at junctions on the Victoria Line, including the coded impulses to the train equipment, are controlled automatically by programme machines. These consist of rolls of paper with punched holes rather like a pianola roll. The punched holes contain details of each train on the line, the route which it is to take and the time at which it is due to pass. Feeler arms make contact through the punched holes to initiate the operation of signals and points. As each train passes so the roll steps forward for the next train and the next programmed route is prepared automatically. If a train is late the equipment is able to store the details and when the train eventually arrives its route will be set for it.

The whole of the Victoria Line and other London Transport railway routes are controlled in this fashion with the programme machines supervised from a control centre where the traffic controller and the signalman look after the entire line. Normally the signalman does not intervene except in an emergency or if equipment fails. When an item fails in all British signalling it does not mean that trains are allowed to proceed uncontrolled; if any component does not carry out its proper function the signals will always show or go to red and trains will come to a normal stop. Throughout most of the history of British signalling the equipment has been designed on fail-safe principles.

In the 80 or so years since the Regulation of Railways Act was passed in 1889, signal engineers in particular and railways generally have been working towards making railways the safest form of travelling. It might seem sometimes that new developments have been adopted rather slowly, but in an area where the loads of meeting or passing vehicles might be 1,000 passengers or more the functions of new equipment have to be proved safe beyond all doubt.

ONE OF THE MOST fascinating aspects of railway working is the complex task of preparing and publishing the timetable. In any large industrial undertaking production planning is an essential part of the business process and this is particularly so in the railway industry. Here the commodity produced—rail transport—is not normally a single standard unit, but a wide range of individual items embracing high-speed inter-city expresses, heavily loaded commuter trains and various types of freight working. The job of a train planning organisation is to co-ordinate the use of various resources—the track, signalling, stations, yards, locomotives, passenger stock, crews, wagons—so as to produce a passenger and freight timetable plan to meet the requirements of the railway's customers. They are also responsible for the production of both the public and internal railway working timetables and supporting publications, such as locomotive and coaching stock programmes, which are the means of communicating to the railway staff concerned the detailed information necessary to keep the trains on the move.

Since the business of a railway is to convey passengers and to move freight, the first stage of timetable planning is the basic commercial decision regarding the level of service to be provided. While the probable requirements of passengers can be fairly easily established, because of the nature of much of today's rail freight movement—bulk trains of cement, oil, steel, coal and high-speed Freightliner container services—finalisation of freight train schedules involves close consultation with the individual companies concerned.

Preliminary planning of passenger train services usually starts with analyses of ticket sales and train loadings, which are considered against estimates of the future level of business from certain passenger stations and on the trains in the service. From this data the commercial department defines the outline of the type of service to be offered. The outline would include: frequency of service on weekdays, Saturdays and Sundays; the time of first and last trains; selection of intermediate stops; average speed and journey time; train formation; proportion of first- and second-class accommodation; and type of catering. With the basic commercial requirements agreed, work can start in the train planning department on the first draft of the timetable.

There are many factors which affect the running of a train—the power of the locomotive and weight of the train, the maximum permitted speed on each section of route, the type of signalling governing the headways between successive trains and so on—so the train planning staff first settle the basic timetable data for each service. This would usually include: train timing based on power/weight ratio; additional recovery allowances to be added to schedules to offset the effect of temporary engineering work on the route;

The signalling characteristics of each route, which sets the headways necessary between trains, are also known to the planning staff. From the foregoing commercial and operating considerations train planning can then proceed.

Before describing the techniques of train planning and timetable production it would be helpful briefly to outline the scope and function of this part of a railway organisation. Past experience has shown that train planning activity is best organised on a centralised basis. The consultation necessary if the timing of trains is divided between different offices slows down the administrative process; also, as rolling stock is programmed to run not only throughout a railway region but, if circumstances dictate, anywhere in the country, centralised planning is an advantage. On British Railways today each of the five railway regions has its own centralised train planning organisation forming part of the chief movements manager's organisation. The largest of BR's five train planning offices is that for the London Midland Region located at Crewe. Over

Planning the Timetable

signalling; station allowances; focal point on which service is to be planned and principal connections. In addition the type of traction power, availability of crews and provision of rolling stock has also to be settled.

All the basic data required for train planning is of course established. The motive power department has on record point-to-point running times for each type of locomotive hauling varying train loads covering the entire system. Compared with steam power, where the performance of the locomotive depended on the quality of the coal and the physical efforts of the fireman, running times for electric or diesel locomotives can be calculated with much greater precision.

200 people work on the planning and production of the London Midland Region timetable. Broadly, the work covers the preparation of all train service details, programming of rolling stock and crews and the forward planning of new projects. Organisational arrangements vary on European railways, but most also seem to favour a centralised approach.

Despite the development of computer techniques and sundry trials and demonstrations, it has not yet been found practicable or advantageous to utilise computers for train timing on BR and the traditional method of timing on a large graph is still used. A train graph consists of a time scale along the top from left to right and a distance scale, representing a specific section of line, along the side. In addition to the distance scale a plan of the track layouts, junctions, loops and stations is also set out on the left-hand side of the graph. Lines representing the position and progress of individual trains are plotted on the graph in accordance with the point-to-point running times. The lines drawn on the graph vary for different types of train, and different colours are sometimes used to identify trains running on fast or relief tracks.

Simple graphical presentation has many advantages. The capacity of any section of route can be seen at a glance and the situation at junctions or stations, where trains have to cross other tracks and possibly conflict with the passage of other movements, can be quickly assessed. The position at large passenger stations and freight yards is a particularly important part of the timetable plan, since no purpose would be achieved if a path for a train was established from say Crewe to Euston if no platform was available to receive the train at the proposed arrival time. The availability and occupation of platforms at large stations is sometimes worked out on a bar chart graph in association with the main train graph.

Although the feasibility of a proposed timetable plan is verified by plotting the paths for the trains on the graph, certain preparatory work is of course possible in advance. For example, the departure times of the principal inter-city services from large centres such as London, Manchester, Liverpool, Edinburgh, Bristol and so on can be settled at an early stage of the basic planning. As is the case on almost all main routes on BR, departure times from starting stations are standardised for particular destinations—on the hour from Euston to Manchester or Liverpool, 10 and 40 minutes past for Birmingham, five minutes past for the North West and Scotland, for example—and as the paths for fastest trains have obviously to be allocated first, the skeleton outline of the most important train times is decided prior to the graphing stage. The importance and value of the train graph occurs at the second stage, when track space has to be found for the many less important passenger and freight trains.

Preparation of a train graph thus starts with the plotting of the paths of the principal inter-city trains. Then follow stopping passenger trains, particularly those that have to be timed to connect with express services at certain stations. But although express services are usually given priority, it is not always the case; for example, city terminals often have to cope with the simultaneous requirements of homegoing commuters and the early-evening inter-city trains for businessmen returning to the provinces. London's Kings Cross station illustrates the problem. There trains are timed to run in groups to maximise the number of trains which can leave the station in the peak hours. Three inter-city trains leave in close succession at 17.00, 17.05 and 17.10, when three

commuter trains are despatched on the down main line before the next inter-city departure at 17.30; from 17.30 to 18.00 the line is again available for a group of four more commuter trains.

A simple principle of timetabling is that a greater number of trains can be run over a section of line if they all travel at equal or near equal speed—a classic example is the London Transport underground where as many as 40 trains an hour can be worked at 1½-minute intervals on a given section, but only because they all stop at reasonably equally spaced stations and run at similar speed. Conversely, if the trains out of Kings Cross just mentioned were timed to depart in any order, without regard to the speed or sequence of stops, an absurd situation would ensue with fast trains forced to dawdle behind slow trains and wasting valuable line capacity. Hence, the grouping of trains in flights—railway operators call it the correct speed mix—is a widely used timetabling tactic.

As the timing and scheduling of each group of express trains is finalised, the train graphs for the sections of route are built up, showing the planner at a glance whether track capacity is being allocated efficiently and train timings are feasible. As an example, does the timing of the 10.00 Flying Scotsman affect the path of any up trains from Leeds to Kings Cross as the train passes Doncaster at 12.08; if so, is it possible to start the Leeds train earlier or later, or is it preferable to add three minutes to its timing to obviate the problem?

With the important stage of planning of passenger trains completed, work will start on timing the slower—but no less vital—freight services. Compared with the situation 15 or even 10 years ago, the basic tempo of freight train operation on BR, and on many other railways, has drastically changed. Today a substantial volume of freight is moved in block trains running at speeds up to a maximum of 75mph. There is less of a problem running the fast freight services at night but slower freight trains continue to create timing problems at all times of day.

There is an interesting train timing situation on the West Coast main line between Crewe and Carlisle in the night hours. Between 23.30 and 04.30 no fewer than 18 trains—overnight sleeping car services; newspaper, postal and parcels trains; company freight trains and Freightliner services—have to be accommodated over the long two-track section of route on the climb up to Shap summit. Sleeper trains must not reach their destinations unduly early—passengers would not wish to be turned out of their berths at say 04.00—and it is possible to run them on timings similar to the express freights. But the 45mph freight trains are difficult to work into the train graph paths. They are obviously allocated paths on relief lines wherever possible, but on two-track sections it is often necessary for slow freights to stand in loops or sidings and wait for a

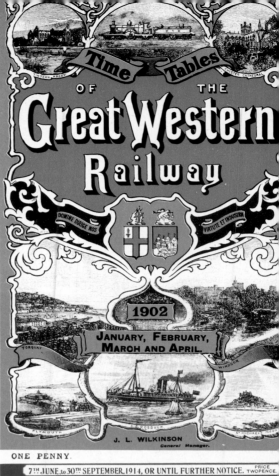

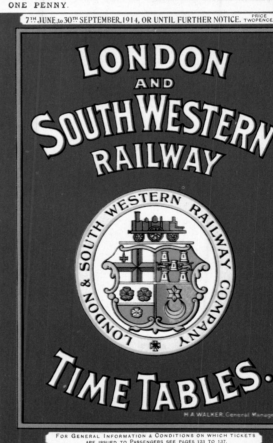

Top and above: Decorative covers of earlier years of the Great Western Railway and the London & South Western Railway *Ian Allan Ltd*

Facing page: Part of a BR Western Region timetable planning graph; it covers Saturday trains over about a two-hour mid-day period for the Paddington-Reading section of the London Division. *British Railways WR*

path to the next loop behind a group of faster trains.

Train timing is a continuing process and work on the next, or even the next but one, timetable is in progress before the current timetable year is brought into effect. To reduce the very high costs of timetable production BR opted several years back for an annual timetable to run from May each year, instead of separate books for the summer and winter periods.

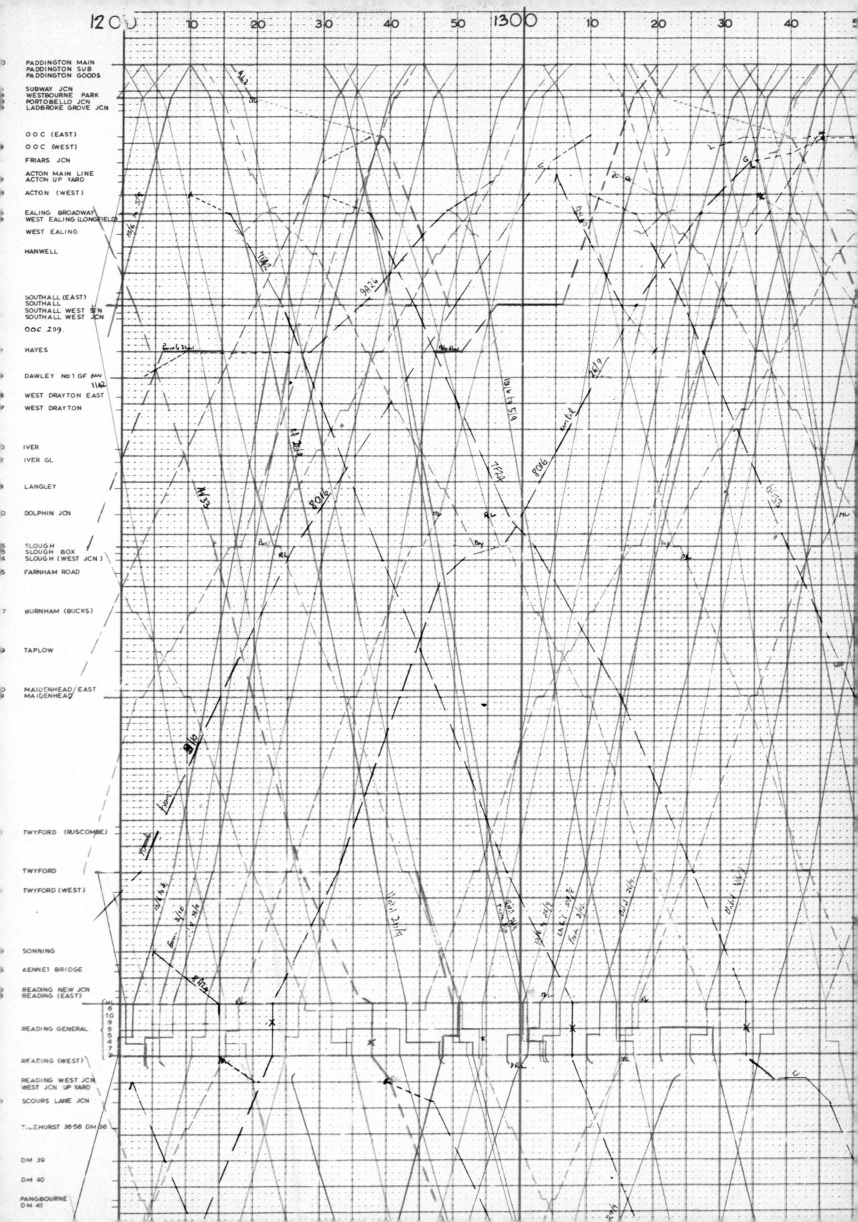

GREAT NORTHERN RAILWAY.

The PUBLIC is respectfully informed that in consequence of the Trains of the GREAT NORTHERN RAILWAY COMPANY having been prevented from proceeding to LEEDS by the METHLEY JUNCTION, they will run between DONCASTER, WAKEFIELD, NORMANTON, and LEEDS, by the LANCASHIRE AND YORKSHIRE RAILWAY as follows, until further Notice; and that in all other respects the Trains will correspond with the published Time Bills.

Superintendent's Office, Lincoln, 4th September, 1849.

BY ORDER, JOHN DENNISTON.

ROBERT HARTLEY, PRINTER, HIGH-STREET, DONCASTER.

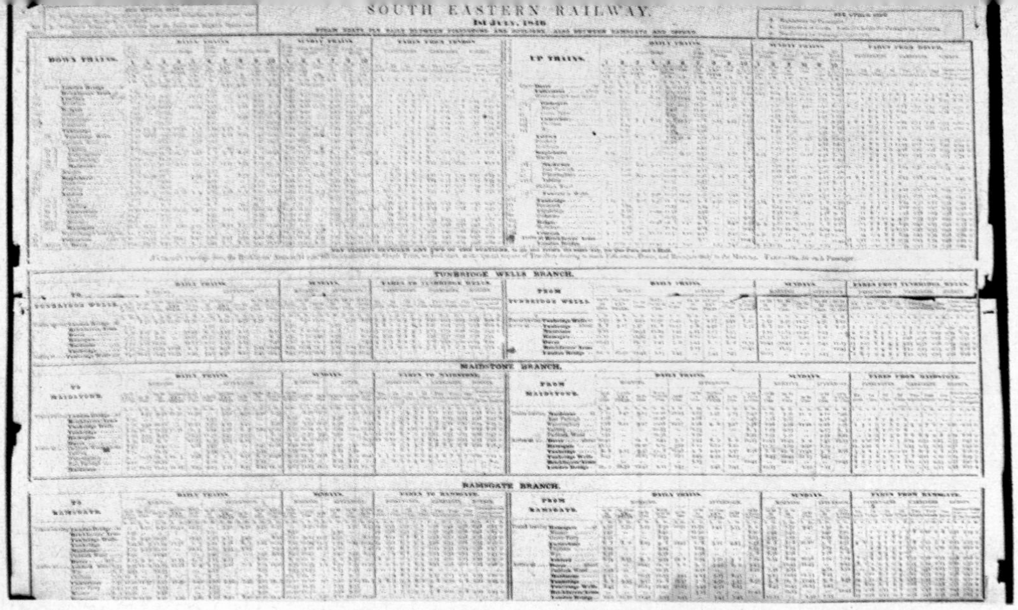

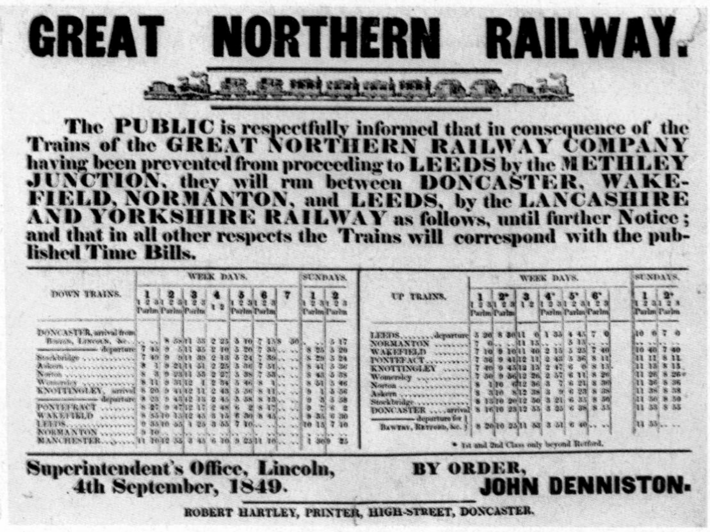

Top: Poster timetable of the South Eastern Railway for 1846.
British Transport Museum (B Sharpe)

Above: Great Northern Railway 1849 poster notifying changes to its published timetable, probably caused by an inter-company squabble.
British Transport Museum (B Sharpe)

A year-round timetable only became possible after a majority of inter-city routes were put on to fixed-interval timings and the one-time steep peak of July and August holiday train demand was blunted by the rise in air and road travel.

To ensure that the timetable is completed in time for implementation, the production of the timetable is itself strictly phased and controlled by a production schedule plan. Plans for the May 1973 timetable were already being considered before the May 1972 service had started. The 1972-73 year was an unusually complex one for BR timetable planning as the completion date for the extension of electrification over the West Coast route from Weaver Juntion to Glasgow approached. To avoid consequential extensive changes, the train services on the London Midland Region, and those on the inter-regional NE-SW route from Bristol and Cardiff through Birmingham to Lancashire, the West Riding and the North East, were then altered to fit in with the now completed Glasgow electric main-line service.

Timetable planning is not concerned only with use of the track. Among other equally important resources of the railway to be considered is, of course, the provision of rolling stock, locomotives and train crews. Simply stated, every train planned needs a set of carriages or wagons, a locomotive and a crew, and these requirements must be given due weight as part of the timetable production process. No separate part of the basic planning can be undertaken in isolation and the first ideas for even small changes to a service have to take account of the availability of passenger stock and locomotives. In practice the availability is established at the outset although not necessarily in finalised detailed form.

A simple case in point is the passenger stock situation on the LMR Euston-Manchester-Liverpool electrified service. On this route the utilisation of stock has reached a level of efficiency unheard of in steam days—many sets of stock run four single journeys each day and cover regular daily distances of nearly 800 miles. Other train sets only complete three or two trips. So when it was recently agreed to meet a public need for early-morning trains to get businessmen to their destination by 09.30, involving departures around 07.00, there was no stock problem as the additional early journeys could be programmed by bringing trains into service earlier than previously.

In contrast, an additional train in the middle of the day when all of the train sets are fully employed could mean the provision of an additional set of stock, which might or might not be economic. The situation is also true of locomotives. A planning factor for the 1970 Anglo-Scottish acceleration over the West Coast route, by double heading trains on fast timings with pairs of Class 50 diesel locomotives, was the availability of additional locomotives. As the peak employment period for Class 50s was at night, additional utilisation could be programmed during the daytime hours.

The magnitude of the programming side of train planning can be seen from the workload of the sections dealing with rolling stock allocation in the regional office at Crewe. There the detailed daily plan of work for around 1,000 diesel locomotives, 250 electric locomotives, over 2,000 diesel and electric multiple-unit vehicles and around 5,300 passenger coaches is produced. Systems for working out the daily programmes vary but are less formalised than the techniques of graphing train movements. In certain cases, where a fleet of special trains or locomotives is used exclusively for a special train service, it is often helpful to plan the use of the fleet on a bar chart graph, so that the actual hours in traffic of each separate unit can be seen at a glance and opportunities for further utilisation can be readily identified.

As an example, the programme of work for the 22 Deltic diesel locomotives working on the East Coast route is planned on that method; since the speed and performance of the Deltics are higher than the rest of the Eastern Region traction fleet, the programming of Deltics is settled at the outset when changes to the service are contemplated. There is a similar situation with the 10 Turbotrain sets on the Paris-Caen-Cherbourg route of French National Railways.

Locomotive programme and train crew work rosters are finalised and circulated to the various depots throughout the railway. Generally speaking—as can be seen from the accompanying illustrations—the detailed information is set out in tabular form. Various factors in preparing locomotive programmes have to be considered including suitability of the locomotive for the train load, suitability of locomotive for the route, availability of crews authorised to drive that type of locomotive on that route, and the requirements for fuelling and maintenance.

Programming of locomotives and rolling stock is one of the most rewarding parts of the timetable production exercise and calls for a high degree of expertise. Staff involved in the work can see the results of their efforts where, by a judicious reshuffle of work programmes, they can provide for a number of additional trains by better use of the existing fleet. In order to make the best use of a fleet of locomotives or passenger train sets it is often necessary to arrange complicated cycles of work covering a wide geographical area for several consecutive days.

A MAJOR ECONOMY resulting from the replacement of steam by diesel traction is that it permits a drastic reduction in motive power maintenance and servicing facilities. This is because, with its greater fuel capacity and less frequent servicing requirements, the diesel locomotive can be operated more continuously than a steam engine, and can therefore be diagrammed to work much higher mileages between depot visits. As fewer units are required in traffic to perform an equivalent amount of work, and since operating can be extended over greater distances, minor depots and sub-sheds can be dispensed with, and all servicing and maintenance concentrated at a few strategically sited major depots which may be anything from 50 to 100 miles apart.

As an example, the Western Region of British Railways, which relies entirely on diesel power, has replaced a total of over 60 steam depots (excluding sub-sheds) with only six main depots with maintenance and servicing facilities and nine servicing points. The servicing points are depots without the facilities to carry out extensive repairs.

During the first phase of diesel working, when all maintenance and servicing had to be carried out in existing steam depots, it soon became evident that such conditions were quite inadequate and that to achieve anything like optimum efficiency a new type of motive power depot designed to meet the specific requirements of diesel traction was imperative.

Fortunately it was possible to draw generally on the extensive diesel experience of American railroads and, in particular, on the first example of a modern diesel depot in this country, which had been installed by the Steel Company of Wales at its Abbey Works, Port Talbot in 1955. Although designed for the maintenance and servicing of shunting locomotives, this depot had been lavishly equipped and planned in a manner that was equally well adapted for line service locomotives. It proved an excellent prototype and many of its main features were subsequently adopted as standard practice by British Rail.

The most notable difference between the type of diesel depot evolved by BR and the old steam shed is the emphasis on preventive maintenance, which is now carried out in specially designed workshops in accordance with predetermined schedules—whereas in steam days it was done very much on an ad hoc basis—as and when required, and then often in some available corner of the running shed. Today the maintenance block is the principal feature of a diesel depot; it consists of a main shed which houses the locomotives and a number of subsidiary workshops, stores and premises for staff amenities. As a rule the main building contains from three to five tracks, with pits beneath, set about 15ft apart and providing examination and repair berths for up to about a dozen main-line locomotives.

The principal feature of the general

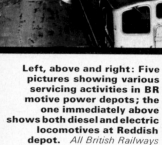

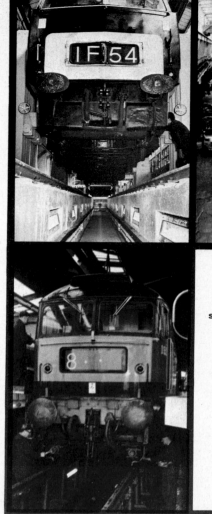

Left, above and right: Five pictures showing various servicing activities in BR motive power depots; the one immediately above shows both diesel and electric locomotives at Reddish depot. *All British Railways*

Below: BR Warship and Hymek diesel-hydraulic locomotives (both types are now withdrawn from service) at Bristol Bath Road depot. *G R Hounsell*

Inside a Diesel Locomotive Depot

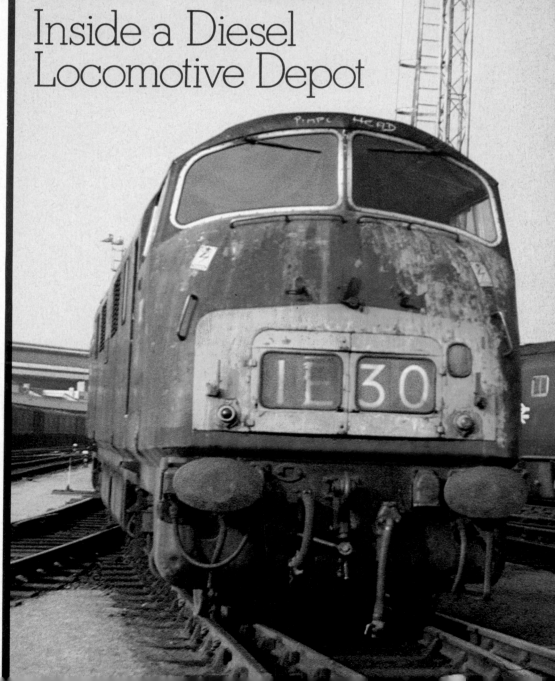

design is the provision of three working levels, arranged to permit the maximum degree of access to all parts of the locomotive. The lowest working level is in the pits between the rails, which allows work to be carried out on the traction motors, brakes and other underside equipment. The concrete floor is usually rather more than four feet below rail level in order to provide sufficient headroom, and for general cleanliness the sides are faced with glazed tiles. Lighting is provided by flourescent panels flush-mounted at suitable intervals in the side walls, and access is by a short flight of steps at each end.

The middle working level is provided in the space between the tracks which forms the main shop floor. The tracks themselves are raised about 2ft 6in above the general floor level to give a convenient height for working on the springs, bogies, brake gear and other equipment mounted externally below the footplating. Access to this level is usually by means of a short ramp to facilitate the movement of mobile equipment.

The top level takes the form of a continuous concrete platform or decking on a level with the footplating of the locomotives, supported from the floor by concrete posts. The platforms give access to the diesel engine, generators, batteries, cab and all other equipment above the running plate. It is in effect the principal working area and is at the same level as the various ancillary workshops for battery attention, coach repairs, riggers, welding, electrical testing, general fitting and general stores, to give direct access to this level and avoid the effort of running up and down stairs.

All the maintenance bays engaged on major overhaul and repair work are spanned by overhead gantry cranes—usually one at each end of the shop—to carry out the replacement of heavy parts, such as engines and generators. Where the platforms are continuous this requires the provision of removable metal grilles in the decks so that the parts can be raised and lowered through them to the ground floor level.

Another essential requirement is to equip one track with a set of synchronised lifting jacks capable of raising locomotives so that the bogies and springs can be removed for changing or cleaning. In addition this track is usually fitted with locomotive weighing equipment. Outside the shop is a heavy-duty hoist to lift the bogies on and off rail wagons used to transport them to and from the bogie shop.

A number of electric power and compressed-air points for operating various tools and equipment are dispersed throughout the shop. There are also conveniently placed dispensing points for fresh lubricating oils, steam and water, and similar points to which pipes are coupled for the drainage of dirty oil from the engines to a collecting tank outside the shed, and for the dispersal of steam from the train heating boilers to the atmosphere.

Where the maintenance shop layout consists of bays at each end, as illustrated in the drawing the central area is used as a working or storage space, with direct access to an adjacent section housing offices, stores, canteen, mess rooms, staff amenities and ancillary workshops. Many types of engineering are catered for in the ancillary workshops, including a general shop for the cleaning and adjustment of engine parts, equipped with drills, sanders, saws, wire brushing machines and valve grinders; there are also fuel pump- and injector-testing and air equipment rooms, a battery-charging room where batteries are periodically serviced, and if suspect, stripped and rebuilt, an electrical shop where control gear, contactors, relays, automatic voltage regulators, dynamos and alternators are dealt with, and welders and coachbuilders shops. There is also a large stores department holding supplies of special-purpose tools and stocks of several thousand electrical and mechanical spare parts.

Fume extraction equipment consists of electrically driven fans supplemented by pneumatically controlled air inlet louvres built into the walls to maintain a through flow of fresh air. Depot interior lighting is mainly flourescent strip, and there is also a 110 volt supply to feed the electric circuits of the locomotives. Electric power socket outlets are provided at the locomotive berths for the connection of welding plant, battery chargers, tools etc. Space heating is usually by means of an automatic high-pressure hot-water system burning waste engine oil in a central boiler.

To save expense many diesel maintenance shops have been adapted from existing buildings, but where they are of new construction the main structure is of steel and concrete with extensive glazing in both the walls and roof to provide maximum natural lighting. In sharp contrast to the dark and cramped conditions that characterised so many of the old steam workshops, their bright well-designed modern interiors rank them among the best examples of industrial architecture in Britain today.

Perhaps the greatest difference between past and present practice is that nowadays the Depot Master of a maintenance shed is not concerned with the employment of his locomotives nor the engine crews that man them. His responsibility is simply to supply the Movements Officer with reliable locomotives. The day-to-day allocation of locomotives to work diagrams is the responsibility of the Diesel Locomotive Controller, with the proviso that the depot is supplied with accurate information concerning the mileage and engine hours needed to determine a unit's maintenance requirements. At the end of each week the data thus obtained is entered on each locomotive's individual record card so that its next scheduled maintenance period can be readily ascertained and provided for. On some railways the running information is fed to a central computer which does the

calculations and issues notice when a schedule examination is approaching. British Railways is at present installing such a computer system.

The whole system of diesel maintenance is based on predetermined hourly periods in service—the specified work being carried out at scheduled intervals in accordance with the requirements of the type of locomotives concerned. For example, on the Western Region of BR a general examination check-up is carried out every 125 engine running hours, and these routine inspections coincide with more important maintenance carried out at intervals of 750, 1,500, 3,000, 6,000 and 12,000 engine hours.

High-speed diesel engines need a complete overhaul every 6,000 hours, which entails the removal of the engine for dispatch to the main locomotive works for attention. In the meantime the locomotive is fitted with a replacement engine fresh from overhaul. This system of unit replacement is especially useful for dealing with major components as it cuts to a minimum the time that the locomotive is out of traffic.

Repairs to major locomotive components come under four categories, namely, unscheduled, light attention, intermediate and general. Light attention covers such items as fitting a new engine turbocharger, or tyre-turning on a ground lathe without removing the bogies. Intermediate repairs apply primarily to bodies, bogies, engines and transmissions. A general overhaul (every 12,000 hours in the case of line-service locomotives with medium-speed diesel engines) is given approximately every five years and entails a visit to the main works, where in addition to a rebuilt engine it will probably have a body overhaul at the same time.

Unscheduled repairs occur as a result of accidents and locomotive failures, and part of a depot's capacity must always be held in reserve for such occurrences to avoid interfering with scheduled maintenance. Other suspected faults such as axle flaws and fractured castings might require a whole class of locomotives to be called in for examination at short notice, so that even with carefully controlled planning disruptions are not always avoidable.

Although diesel maintenance depots differ in layout, they are all basically alike in having the same components, and Fig 2 illustrates a typical arrangement at the Canton depot of the Western Region at Cardiff. The key position and size of the maintenance shop clearly indicates its importance, while immediately to the north is the servicing shed, which provides facilities for the daily inspection, servicing and fuelling of locomotives in traffic as distinct from those undergoing maintenance. Servicing sheds deal with any locomotive regardless of its allocation and their accommodation consists of a simple shed with sufficient berths to stand the maximum number of locomotives requiring simultaneous attention.

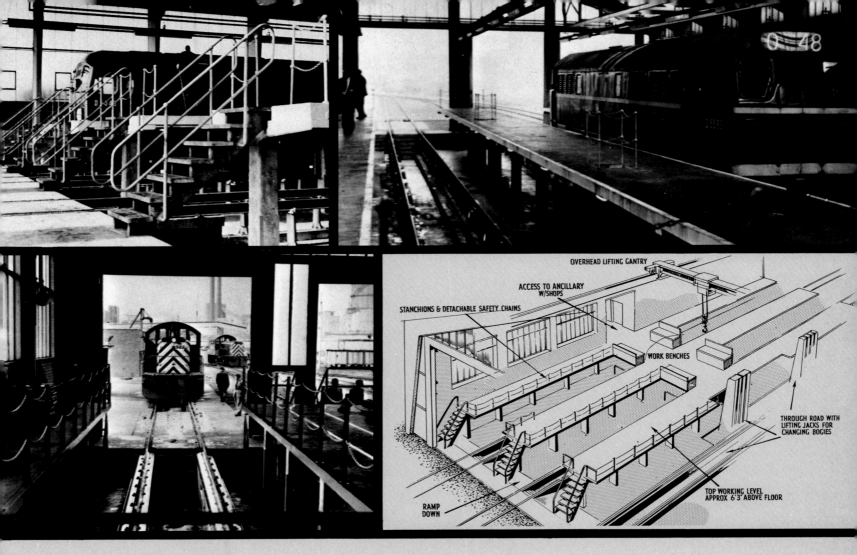

OVERHEAD LIFTING GANTRY

ACCESS TO ANCILLARY W/SHOPS

STANCHIONS & DETACHABLE SAFETY CHAINS

WORK BENCHES

THROUGH ROAD WITH LIFTING JACKS FOR CHANGING BOGIES

RAMP DOWN

TOP WORKING LEVEL APPROX 6'3" ABOVE FLOOR

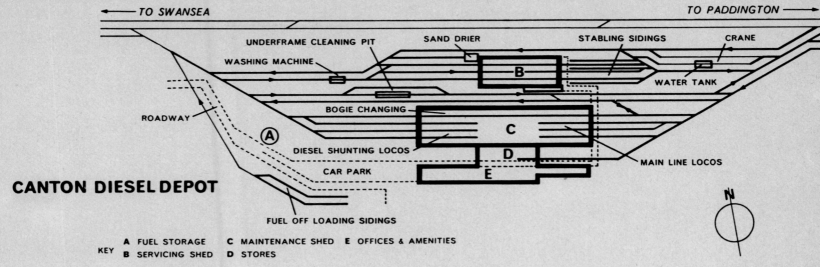

← TO SWANSEA

TO PADDINGTON →

UNDERFRAME CLEANING PIT

SAND DRIER

STABLING SIDINGS

CRANE

WASHING MACHINE

B

WATER TANK

ROADWAY

BOGIE CHANGING

C

D

DIESEL SHUNTING LOCOS

MAIN LINE LOCOS

E

CAR PARK

CANTON DIESEL DEPOT

N

FUEL OFF LOADING SIDINGS

KEY
A FUEL STORAGE **C** MAINTENANCE SHED **E** OFFICES & AMENITIES
B SERVICING SHED **D** STORES

The top four illustrations show various aspects of the three working levels in a modern diesel maintenance depot; the photo above centre left is of the Steel Company of Wales prototype layout at Port Talbot. *All P F Winding*

Above: General layout of the BR Western Region Canton depot at Cardiff. *P F Winding*

Right: A BR Class 35 Hymek diesel-hydraulic locomotive at Gloucester depot in February 1970. *E Preedy*

Like many other servicing sheds, the one at Canton has been adapted from the original steam shed, the main alteration being that the number of engine roads is reduced so that the available width between them is sufficiently increased to allow for the installation of fuelling points and other servicing equipment. This reduces the number of locomotive berths to about a dozen, but even for a depot with an allocation of over a hundred engines this is more than adequate because, unlike the steam engine, which once the fires are dropped requires a lengthy period of servicing, diesel locomotives can be dealt with almost as rapidly as road vehicles.

Apart from fuel and water points a servicing shed also requires a compressed-air system for power greasing and the topping up of lubricating oils and engine coolant at each berth. Exhaust steam pipes are also provided at convenient points to allow steam generated during the routine testing of train heating boilers to be discharged through the roof. There are inspection pits to each road with fluorescent lighting to facilitate inspection, and some sheds also have lowered sidewalks and platforms at footplate level. With diesel locomotives a thorough daily routine examination is essential, since even a minor fault if undetected, can easily result in a total failure of the locomotive in traffic.

The routine examinations consist of a general visual inspection to detect loose, leaking or defective parts, and with the engine running or the locomotive moving, checks are made on brakes and deadman's apparatus, windscreen wipers, sanding gear, auxiliary generator voltage and battery charging. A sample of the engine sump oil is taken with the engine running to establish the approximate percentage of fuel dilution, content of water, and content of insoluble solids in the sample. Should any tests show that the allowable amount of contamination has been reached, the lubricating oil is partially or completely changed.

Other depot equipment includes a sand drier with oil-fired heating in the immediate vicinity of the servicing shed or, where metallic grit is used, a gravity feed to the locomotives from overhead hoppers. Also in the yard and usually sited on an approach road to the servicing shed there is usually a two-stage automatic washing machine, in which the first stage is a detergent-solution application and the second a water wash. The machinery is brought into operation when a locomotive approaching the wash intercepts the beam of a photo-electric cell; the duration of each application is governed by a time-switch. In addition to body cleansing plant many depots have an underframe cleaning plant employing either steam or hot water jets.

With the changeover from coal to oil, depot fuelling arrangements have also undergone a complete transformation. Open coal trucks have given place to tank wagons which discharge directly into big diesel oil storage tanks, from where it is distributed through pipes to the locomotive fuelling points in the servicing area. Fuel oil has also eliminated the problem of ash disposal, and such waste as there is from sump oil can now be usefully employed for fuelling the oil-fired boilers of the depot heating system.

The overall picture that emerges by comparison with steam traction is one of much higher productivity, cleaner methods and a big saving in labour requirements.

Above left: BR Class 31/2 Brush diesel-electric locomotive with body lifted clear of bogies and engine being removed at Stratford diesel shop. *British Railways ER*

Above: BR Class 47 diesel-electric locomotive No 1606 at Western Region's Landore diesel depot in May 1970. *G R Hounsell*

Left: Class 45 and 47 diesel-electrics outside the running shed at Bristol Bath Road diesel depot. *G R Hounsell*

RAILWAY WORKSHOPS

BEHIND EVERY MAN, it was once said, stands a woman organising, influencing, backing him up and generally steering his public image into the spotlight of public attention. The reality of this *eminence grise* is, of course, debatable, and such a description is actually far more apt in the context of the great organisations that dominate the industrial life of Britain.

It is particularly so in the case of railways. For behind the scenes, modestly located, often on outwardly dingy sites full of the dust and muck, grit and grime of technology at its most venerable, there exists the vast range of skills, expertise, inventiveness and energy that maintains the services, safety and standards of British Rail. All over the country, from Eastleigh in the south to Glasgow in the north-west, BR's railway workshops between them build and repair locomotives, carriages, wagons and containers and develop new equipment for the rail travel of the future.

In 1971, about £57.7 million were spent on repairs to locomotives, carriages, wagons and containers, and the output in that year totalled 2,196 locomotives, 13,050 carriages, 108,119 wagons and 7,714 containers. In this vast undertaking, around 34,000 people are employed over the whole spectrum of technical and mechanical skills, in metal forming, forge and foundry work, plate preparation and fabrication, machining, testing, pattern-making and such ancillaries as tarpaulin, PVC and nylon sheet, chain, shackle and wire-sling manufacture. The organisation which controls it all, as well as nine works training schools, is British Rail Engineering Ltd, a wholly owned subsidiary company of BR formed in January 1970.

BRE's inheritance was handed down to it by British Railways Workshops, the division formed in 1962 to unify and modernise the network of regional workshops then operating as separately controlled entities. A five-year plan of rationalisation entailed the closure of fifteen out of thirty-one works, a reduction in shop staff from 60,000 to 35,500, modernisation expenditure which to date has reached £20 million and, inevitably, a good deal of heated public debate.

Public opinion today, unlike its nineteenth century counterpart, can countenance wholesale public spending rather more easily than it can accept wholesale social disruption. However, concern over redundancies was mollified by the findings of two university investigations which emphasised the humanity as well as the thoroughness of the five-year Workshop Plan. Similarly, traditionalist sensitivities were soothed by the survival under the plan of several of the more historic workshop sites.

One was at Doncaster, where Stirling's

Diesel-electric power car of BR's new 125mph train (HST) under construction in BRE works. *British Rail Engineering*

eight-foot Singles, the Ivatt Atlantics and the Gresley, Thompson and Peppercorn Pacifics—all renowned locomotives— were built after 1866. Another was at Swindon, where the original workshops built between 1841 and 1843 used stone from the boring of Brunel's Box tunnel. A third was at Crewe, where the stone sleepers once used on the old Grand Junction Railway decorate the wall of the main administrative building. This building in fact, curves with the line of the former London & North Western main tracks to Holyhead.

Possibly the most notable survivor of the inevitable axe that fell in 1962 was Shildon Railway Works, near Tees-side. It was near the site, where today wagons are built and repaired, that in 1825 the first passenger train in the world to be drawn by a steam locomotive started on its journey to Stockton. The original shops at Shildon were, in fact, built eight years

later by the Stockton and Darlington Railway Company.

These were the sites on which workshop activity was concentrated, together with shops at Ashford, Eastleigh, Glasgow, Horwich, Temple Mills, Townhill, Wolverton, York, Barassie, Inverurie, Derby (Litchurch Lane) and Derby Locomotive Works. Since 1962, further shrinkage of the railways has pruned away the workshops at Inverurie, with Barassie closing at the end of 1972, and Townhill has been transferred to the Scottish Region.

Its location almost at the centre of England made Derby a natural choice in 1963 for the headquarters of BR Workshops and, later, of British Rail Engineering. It is not, however, on geographical grounds alone that Derby is notable in railway lore. The town was the principal centre of the Midland Railway, formed in 1844, and at its locomotive works, nearly three thousand steam locomotives were built between 1851 and 1957. At the Derby works, where today diesel main-line and shunting locomotives are repaired and overhauled and diesel multiple-unit engines and transmission equipment are reconditioned, the first experimental diesel was produced in 1932, and the first two main-line diesel-electric locomotives to operate in Britain were built in 1947 and 1948.

Derby's other railway works, at Litchurch Lane, possesses similar historic lustre, for since it was opened in 1876, it has been the scene of many innovations. They have included the Standard wagon of 1882, flow-line wagon production (1921) and the all-steel passenger carriage adopted on the eve of nationalisation in 1948. Today, after the modernisation of 1963/7 was carried out at a cost of £1.25 million, Litchurch Lane builds freight containers and overhauls and repairs carriages, wagons and diesel multiple-units.

The main activity, however, is the building of fully air-conditioned passenger carriages for British Rail's Intercity services and for export. Each week, a basic eight coaches of the Mark II type emerge from Litchurch Lane. To the casual visitor, the completed carriage, handsomely painted dark pearl grey and blue over its grey-green primer and light blue undercoat, bears little resemblance to the dismembered units that go into it. In one shop, the bogies stand looking curiously bereft, with their carriages lying in several separate parts in several separate shops. Carriage roofs and sides lie upside down, almost unrecognisable as such, while row upon row of seats stand on the shop floor as if patiently waiting for admission. Inside carriages which outwardly look complete, men are working on what is actually an empty shell, fitting windows, doors, panelling and electrical and heating systems.

Litchurch Lane's innovating tradition lives on today in the prototypes of carriages of the immediate future which were built there in the first half of 1972. They are the 75-foot Mark III coaches with resin-glass fibre wrap-around doors, gangway ends covered in pliable foam and inside framework sprayed with plastic material designed to provide insulation, sound-proofing and vibration reduction. After the testing had taken place during 1972, the new coaches were put into service on Britain's railways at 125mph hauled between the new HST power cars, of which prototypes were built at the locomotive works at Crewe. Power cars of the high-speed train—precursor of the 150mph Advanced Passenger Train— are packed with electronic devices, fitted with a small but extremely tough driver's window and match the elegance of the high-speed carriages with sleek, aerodynamic looks.

The Crewe Works, covering 98 acres, is the scene of British Rail Engineering's most extensive locomotive-building operations, and has included on its order book 34 110mph 5,000hp electric locomotives designed to be capable of cutting the journey time of London-Glasgow expresses down to a mere five hours, after the Glasgow extension of electrification was completed in 1974. At Crewe, between 1845 and 1958, more than seven thousand locomotives were constructed for the LNWR, LMSR and British Railways. Construction of diesel locomotives began in 1957 with a series of diesel-electric shunters and two years later, the first main-line diesel-electric 1,160hp Type 2 locomotive was built there.

Naturally, the details of Crewe activities have changed over the years, even if the essentials have not. Within the Crewe works, oil has replaced the soot of steam days, and life is relatively quieter now that there is more welding than riveting. Today, cranes no longer lower massive boilers on to open steel frames. Instead, overhead cranes, two of which are capable of lifting a complete 90-ton locomotive, handle delicate and expensive pieces of electronic equipment, as well as huge diesel engines and generators, dangling them with apparent carelessness in mid-air. The casual impression is, however, completely deceptive, for with their keen eyes and practised hands, crane operators lower them exactly into position within the locomotive body with inches to spare.

Elsewhere at Crewe, computerised machines making trunnion pins, bars for couplings and other components clatter, grind or whirr away virtually untouched by human hand. A multi-head cutter, with a row of blue flames streaming down onto a steel plate and burgeoning out in a shower of orange sparks takes its instructions from a photo-electric cell.

Outside, in areas crisscrossed by rail tracks, locomotives travel by traverser from one shop to the next, looking strangely pathetic when moved by a power other than their own. And screened from local ears by a sound-proof barrier, diesel engines are run and brakes and controls are tested for a period of five days. The complete overhaul and testing of diesel-electric locomotives, which is carried out every three years (or 240,000 miles), takes on average 21 days.

Crewe also houses BRE's steel foundry, a seemingly desolate indoor wasteland where grey, brown and sand yellow materials lie heaped on the floor, and vivid light leaps and glows behind the doors of two four-ton electric arc furnaces. The foundry has the capacity to produce steel castings sufficient for all BR's locomotives, carriages and wagons, as well as general items for all BRE works and private contracts.

The Crewe foundry is one of three owned by British Rail Engineering. Another, an iron foundry, is at Horwich, where the main work consists of repairs to carriages, wagons and containers and the manufacture of sheets and tarpaulins. The third, at Swindon, is an aluminium/brass foundry

Above: Underfloor air-conditioning equipment being fitted to Mk IID coach body shell raised on jacks at Derby Litchurch Lane. *British Transport Films*

Above right: Welding work on a coach underframe/floor unit being assembled in a turnover fixture. *British Transport Films*

Right: Laying up a plastics roof panel at Derby by machine which sprays glass-fibre and resin simultaneously into the mould for curing. *British Transport Films*

BR Class 33 locomotive body being lowered on to its bogies after heavy repairs at Eastleigh works. *British Transport Films*

Below: BRE locomotive works at Swindon, with diesel engine testing house in foreground. *R C H Nash*

Below right: Container-crane grappler beams with pressbutton adjustment for handling different types and sizes of container under construction at Doncaster. *British Transport Films*

Manufacture of seat cushions and squabs in a BRE carriage fitting-out shop at Eastleigh.
British Transport Films

Below: Pouring molten metal into moulds at the steel foundry at Crewe.
British Transport Films

Below right: Interior fitting-out of a new BR Mk IID coach at Litchurch Lane works.
British Transport Films

producing non-ferrous castings for the whole of British Rail.

Swindon, like many other workshop sites, has a very strong claim to prominence in railway history. Railways, and more particularly the seven-foot-gauge Great Western Railway completed by Brunel in 1841, converted it from an ancient and somewhat sleepy market town into a vibrant centre of activity. Almost immediately after the GWR London to Bristol line was completed, Swindon was selected as the site of a new locomotive building and repair depot, and by January 1843 was in full operation. Later, carriage and wagon works were set up there. Two notable locomotives were built at Swindon in recent years—the first diesel-hydraulic main-line locomotive in 1958 and BR's last steam engine, No 92220 *Evening Star,* in 1960.

After the £2.3-million modernisation was completed in 1967, Swindon's main task became the repairing and overhauling of diesel main-line and shunting locomotives, as well as diesel multiple-unit and service vehicles, wagons and containers, but the reduction in BR's locomotive fleet will inevitably mean a gradual fall in locomotive repair work. The diesel testing station situated on the eastern edge of the 104-acre Swindon site is among the most modern in Britain and can test all types of engine and transmission up to 1,700hp.

The decibels register even higher at Doncaster, where two locomotives of up to 2,000hp can be tested together or, alternatively, one of 4,000hp on its own. The Doncaster and Swindon workshops have other similarities. Like Swindon, Doncaster also concentrates on repair, in this case repair to locomotives, diesel multiple-units, wagons, rail and mobile cranes, fork-lift trucks and the wide range of lifting tackle used by British Rail.

Doncaster's building tradition is an illustrious one for in pre-nationalisation days, it was the major LNER centre for the building of special vehicles. The more-famous sets of coaching stock to emerge from Doncaster in the late 1930s included the Silver Jubilee, Coronation and West Riding Limited high-speed trains, and ten years or so later, the special named trains inaugurated for the 1951 Festival of Britain.

The building history of BRE's other Yorkshire workshop, about thirty-two miles from Doncaster, in York, is perhaps more mundane but hardly less notable. On the original York site, where the carriage works was established in 1884 by the North Eastern Railway Company, timber in the form of logs would arrive at one end and emerge from the other as completed coaching stock. In the intervening years, however, steel has gradually infiltrated into York's carriage manufacture, starting as a composite material with timber in underframes, then forming complete underframes for timber bodies, subsequently spreading as a composite with timber in the bodies and finally taking over completely in the all-steel coach.

Today, in the building shop on a 45-acre site which cost £1 million to reorganise in 1965/7, steel carriages with body and roof frames, built up from pressed steel electrically welded and then skinned with steel sheet, progress in flow-line fashion towards the adjacent paint shop, reaching there complete with doors, window frames, partitions and interior detail. In the paint shop, the newly built carriages, as well as those which have undergone major repair, acquire fresh new colours through quick and economic airless spray techniques.

This sort of work—the building, repair, renovation, overhaul and general maintenance of British Rail locomotives, coaching stock, wagons and other assets—forms the major part, at least 80 per cent, of BRE workshop activity. The other 20 per cent represents work done for outside customers, and has on occasion included a fair range of non-railway work—the production, for example, of anchors for ships, wicked-looking long-toothed anchors for oil rigs and magnet frames for the heavy electrical industry. More traditionally, it is often on outside work that the skills derived from more than a century of experience with steam come into action. These skills have, for instance, been used at Swindon, where steam engines have been repaired for privately owned lines such as the Dart Valley Railway. At Crewe, too, a steam locomotive boiler was recently built for the Bluebell Railway and cylinders have been made for the Festiniog narrow-gauge railway.

Export outside Britain figures healthily in BRE's outside work; in 1971, its value topped the £2.5 million mark. The first export order, a £6.25 million five-year contract won by BRE within four weeks of its inception, involved the building of containers at Derby (Litchurch Lane) and Horwich for Mafi-Fahrzeugwerk of Stuttgart, Germany. Rather farther afield, BRE has built, at Shildon, 150 bogie covered vans fitted with air brakes for carrying palletised traffic on Malayan Railways.

Derby Litchurch Lane has provided four BR Mark II carriages with anti-termite protection, a pressure-ventilating system and brakework and bogies modified to suit conditions at their destination—the bauxite mines in Guinea. And in neighbouring Liberia, four diesel railcars converted at Glasgow works serve the 165-mile mining railway that runs between Lower Buchanan and Nimba, and do so grandly emblazoned with the name "Lamco Intercity" and painted in British Rail's Intercity grey and blue. In the absence of a public railway system in Liberia, about 18,000 passengers a year are carried on this private company's route.

In Britain, about 110 million passengers a year use Intercity services on less-exotic but more-familiar routes. For them, as much as for their Liberian counterparts, the vast and varied enterprise carried out behind the scenes by the railway workshops proves that there is very much more than meets the eye to the train now standing on platform three.

Above: One of the diesel railcars converted by BRE'S Glasgow works for Lamco in Liberia. *British Transport Films*

Right: Main carriage assembly lines at BRE's York works. *British Transport Films*

A CHAPTER OF ACCIDENTS

Below: Scene at the Harrow &
Wealdstone crash in October 1952.
Conway picture library

Below centre left and right: Three
pictures of the Liverpool-London
express crash at Weedon in
September 1951.
All Conway Picture Library

Bottom left: Railway crane starting
to clear pile-up of locomotives and
wagons at Linton Junction,
Nottingham in December 1971. *J Hooke*

Facing page: Three more scenes from the
1952 Harrow & Wealdstone station
three train crash. *All Conway Picture Library*

ACCIDENTS will happen, so the proverb
runs, even in the best regulated families.
To this rule railways, despite all their costly
and elaborate safety precautions, are no
exception. And when there is a casualty
like a derailment or a collision, such is the
energy stored up in the mass of a weighty
train travelling at speed that the consequences can be disastrous, not only in
damage to or destruction of rolling stock,
but also in terms of human life and injury.
Some of the most terrible railway accidents
in British history have been due to relatively simple causes, and of them the
Quintinshill collision of May 22, 1915,
was the most fearful in its consequences
in British history.

Quintinshill signalbox is 1½ miles north
of Gretna Junction, on the former Caledonian main line from Carlisle to Glasgow;
it had no special features other than down
and up loops into which trains could be
diverted if it was desired to clear the main
line. Every morning an 'all stations' slow
left Carlisle at 06.10 for Beattock, the
timekeeping of which was important, as it
connected at Beattock with the Tinto, an
express carrying commuters from Moffat
and the Clyde valley to Glasgow. Normally
this should have followed from Carlisle the
23.45 and 24.00 sleeping car expresses
from Euston, but if they were running late,
as frequently happened, the practice was
to start the 06.10 from Carlisle on time,
and to shunt it where necessary to let one
of the sleepers by. On this particular
morning the 23.45 was half-an-hour behind time, so the 06.10 was started on
time, and was to be held at Quintinshill.
It so happened that both the reception
lines there were occupied by freight trains,
and the only track on to which the slow
train could be shunted was the up main
line.

Now the signalman at Quintinshill was
due to be relieved at 6 o'clock in the
morning, but the practice had arisen,
completely unauthorised, that if the 06.10
was to be shunted at Quintinshill the
relieving signalman would travel on it
from Gretna to Quintinshill and so be
saved a 1½-mile walk. So that his late
arrival might not be noticed by the
authorities, what should have been entries
in the signalbox register from 06.00 onwards were made by the night signalman
on scraps of paper, and copied into the
book by the relieving man after his
arrival.

While he was catching up on the entries
on the morning in question, and the night
signalman was reading the newspapers
that the relieving man had brought with
him, the signalman at the next box to the
north (who had not received from Quintinshill a 'blocking back' bell signal, as he
should have done, to advise that the up
main line at Quintinshill was occupied)
offered to Quintinshill an up troop train,
which was approaching at speed. Dis-
tracted by chatter in the box and by his
work with the register, and evidently
without looking out of the signalbox
window at the train standing on the up

line, the relieving signalman accepted the troop special, and pulled off all his up line signals. He had meantime pulled off all his down line signals for the sleeper from Euston.

The troop train driver had no chance. An overbridge concealed from his sight the standing train until, at 70 miles an hour, he was almost on to it. The effect of the impact was such that the 213-yard length of his 21-vehicle train was reduced to a heap of matchwood only 67 yards long. And into this wreckage a few moments later there ploughed the double-headed 13-coach down sleeping car express, also travelling at a mile-a-minute. Most of the coaches were of wooden construction, there was gas escaping from the coach storage cylinders, and with live coals from the fireboxes of four engines, fire was inevitable; it raged for a whole day and burned out a total of 25 vehicles.

In this holocaust there perished no fewer than 227 persons, mostly officers and men of the Royal Scots. Both signalmen were subsequently tried and convicted for manslaughter, and sentenced to lengthy terms of imprisonment, but this could in no way atone for the dreadful havoc caused by their gross dereliction of duty. With modern signalling, interlocking, AWS (automatic warning system) and track-circuiting, such a catastrophe is, of course, virtually impossible.

About 37 years later, on October 8, 1952, another disastrous accident involving three trains took place, at Harrow Wealdstone; in this case the real reason for what happened was never fully established. An up outer suburban train was standing in the station at the up fast line platform picking up passengers, and fully protected in the rear by home and outer home semaphore signals and by a colour-light distant signal a mile away at Headstone Lane. The morning was misty, but could not be described as foggy. Suddenly there appeared through the mist a night sleeping car express from Perth, headed by the Pacific locomotive *City of Glasgow*, running one and a half hours behind time, which crashed at full speed into the standing local. At that very moment the heavy 07.55 express from Euston to Liverpool and Manchester, double-headed by the Jubilee class 4-6-0 *Windward Islands* and the Pacific *Princess Anne*, was approaching Harrow at 60mph without the remotest chance of being stopped, and crashed into the already considerable wreckage.

Since Quintinshill no such frightful a pile of wrecked locomotives and coaches has ever been seen to equal that which was spread all over Wealdstone station on that tragic morning. The disaster cost 112 lives. As the driver of the Perth express was killed, the reason why he failed to stop or even to reduce speed was never established; the only possible explanation was that he might have been dozing or even asleep. If that was so, the AWS horn might have awakened him in time, but at that date there was no AWS on the LMS main line.

The third most serious disaster in British railway history, measured by the number of casualties, was on December 4, 1957, at Lewisham, on the Southern Region, and was due primarily to a driver overrunning signals at danger. It was a foggy evening, and the 16.56 express from Cannon Street to Ramsgate was following a suburban train to Hayes on the fast line from New Cross. The engine of the express was *Spitfire*, one of the original Bulleid light Pacifics, which never had a good reputation for lookout from the footplate, especially with drifting exhaust in thick weather. Anyway, just beyond St Johns the driver passed a double-yellow and then a single-yellow signal, both colour-lights, without any reduction of speed, and only when the train was passing the next signal at red did he take action.

But it was too late; a few moments later he ran into the back of the stationary suburban train. And as fate would have it, the collision took place under the Nunhead flyover, carrying away the columns supporting the overhead girders, which came crashing down on to the wreckage. It was a most unfortunate location and undoubtedly contributed to the heavy death roll of 90 persons. Here again AWS would probably have prevented the collision, and shortly after the accident Southern Region started to instal this most valuable safeguard against the overrunning of signals.

While many railway accidents have been due to drivers passing signals at danger, or to derailments resulting from excessive speeds on curves, there have been others resulting from happenings of a completely unprecedented kind. Two such occurred within a mile of one another near Weedon, on the main line out of Euston, though separated in time by 36 years. The first was on August 14, 1915, in London & North Western days, and the second on September 21, 1951, on what had then become the London Midland Region of British Railways. The trouble which resulted in the 1915 accident began with the George V-class 4-4-0 *Wolfhound,* at the head of the 08.45 from Birmingham to Euston. The driver was looking round his engine at the Rugby stop when he noticed that a split pin was missing from the washer which secured the right-hand coupling-rod to the crank-pin of the driving axle.

A fitter was on the platform, and so that the train might not be delayed he extracted the corresponding pin from a neighbouring engine which was shunting, and transferred it to *Wolfhound;* he maintained that he opened the two ends of the pin out properly, but evidently he failed to do so. For as *Wolfhound* was approaching Weedon at 70mph, the fireman saw something strike the ballast on the right side of the engine, throwing a mass of stones up into the air. The engine then began lurching violently from side to side, but the driver managed to bring the train to a stand, with the engine just inside Stowe Hill tunnel.

What had happened was that the pin had worked out of its hole and five miles later the washer had become unscrewed and dropped off (both were found later where they had fallen on to the track). Then the coupling-rod itself had broken loose at one end, with its 10ft of length flailing round. The first impact with the ballast bent the rod considerably and after

that, at about seven-yard intervals, with every impact the sleepers of the down main line were disturbed, pushing the rails of the down track as much as seven inches out of line. Once again, by sheer misfortune, the second portion of the down Irish Mail was just approaching at full speed, and both its locomotives, with their 15 coaches, were derailed, ten passengers being killed. The remarkable feature of this accident was that the defective engine and its train escaped unscathed, while another express left the track.

In the 1951 accident the train involved was the 08.20 from Liverpool to Euston, with Pacific No 46207 *Princess Arthur of Connaught* hauling a formation of 15 coaches. At precisely the same point as that at which *Wolfhound's* coupling-rod came off its pin, the Pacific's leading bogie came off the rails, derailing to the right. Because of tyre wear, the two bogie axles had earlier been transposed, but the fitter who did the work had not left the axleboxes properly free to move up and down in the horns. The leading pair of wheels had therefore been relieved of their share of the engine's weight, and had lifted off the track as the engine was rounding a left-hand curve.

The extraordinary thing is that the locomotive travelled on for a full mile without the crew suspecting that anything was wrong, mainly because this section of the line had been relaid a short time previously with heavy flat-bottom rails

without chairs, so that the derailed wheels encountered no obstructions. With the bogie off the rails, the train went through Stowe Hill tunnel, in which the walls tended to set up a resistance to movement of the ballast. But once out of the tunnel and on to bull-head track, the derailed wheels started hitting the rail chairs, which soon caused distortion of the track; once the driver realised that something was wrong he evidently applied the brakes, but it was too late. The locomotive derailed and went down the embankment, followed by eleven of the fourteen coaches, 15 people losing their lives.

It might be imagined that a serious accident could hardly be caused by anything as innocent as a platform barrow, but on two occasions barrows have caused disastrous derailments. One such was on August 2, 1898, at Wellingborough, on the Midland main line. Some boys were playing about on the down platform with a postman's barrow when it ran away, down the slight slope of the platform, and fell on the track just as the 18.30 Manchester express from St Pancras, composed of some of the latest vestibuled stock, was approaching at full speed. The leading bogie wheels of 4-4-0 locomotive No 1743 picked up the barrow and carried it as far as the points at the north end of the station, where derailment occurred, with the loss of six lives.

A much bigger barrow was involved in the derailment of an up Liverpool express

at Wembley on October 12, 1940. The heavy barrow, loaded with parcels, was being taken across the line from the up slow to the up fast platform by three men, and had nearly reached the top of the fast platform ramp when one of them slipped; the weight of the barrow then overpowered the other two, neither of whom was very strong, and ran back down the ramp. The men did all they could to stop it, but unsuccessfully, and finally it skewed round and stopped with one corner fouling the up main line, just as the Liverpool train was approaching at speed. The bogie of the Patriot-class 4-6-0 *Stephenson* caught the barrow, and at the crossover roads immediately beyond the engine derailed and turned over, most of the coaches following it. Eleven lives were lost, and the tragedy in this case was that the train was running very late; had it been on time there would have been no accident.

Fouling of another kind was responsible for a serious accident on February 11, 1942, at Beighton, on the Great Central main line just south of Sheffield. Three days earlier seven steel plates, each 9ft 6in long and 8ft 7in wide, had been loaded at Frodingham steelworks on to a 20-ton LNER plate wagon, itself 8ft 4½in wide inside. Had the plates been 8ft 9in wide or more, they would have been loaded on edge in wagons fitted with trestles, and secured by binding chains, but at this intermediate width it was regarded as safe to load them with one edge on the floor of the wagon, and the other supported on packing-pieces to come just above the wagon side, over which they slightly projected. Shortly before eight o'clock in the evening of the day of the accident the wagon reached Holbrook sidings, and in some marshalling operations a more than usually hard impact caused the load to shift, so that the top plate, though unnoticed in the blackout, projected nearly three feet over the wagon side. As ill-luck would have it, the wagon was standing in a siding which had a clearance of only just over seven feet from the adjacent main line, instead of the standard nine feet.

The next train that passed on the main line was a freight, which was not fouled, but after that came a troop special of 13 coaches and two vans, carrying 400 soldiers and sailors. The 4-6-0 engine got by, and then three coaches with no more damage than the loss of door handles. But the fourth coach caught the plate and swung it round so that it cut to a depth of 6ft into the side of the sixth and succeeding coaches. But for the fact that the sixth and seventh coaches had their corridors on the near side, the casualties might have been greater, but as it was 14 of the men in the special lost their lives. Subsequent experiments showed how easily plates loaded in that manner could be shifted on impact, and the practice was stopped.

Such have been some of the totally unexpected happenings that can cause a railway disaster; fortunately, viewed in the context of the millions of passenger-miles run, they can be classed as very rare.

Above: Workers shoring up collapsed flyover in the St Johns, Lewisham, accident in December 1957. *Conway Picture Library*

Left: Recovering derailed locomotive after the accident at Hither Green in February 1960. *D Cobbe*

8
The Railways of Britain and Ireland

The LMS

THE LONDON MIDLAND and Scottish Railway was the largest of the four Main Line companies to come out of the grouping of railways in Britain in 1923. Its main constituents were the London & North Western Railway and Caledonian Railway, forming the West Coast route to Scotland, and the Midland Railway, which, as well as having an excellent cross-country service from Leeds to Bristol, also provided a rival trunk route to Scotland in association with the Glasgow & South Western Railway. Other medium-sized lines thrown into the pot included the Highland Railway, running from Perth to Inverness and then farther north, and the North Stafford Railway in the bustling smoky Potteries and North Midlands. Technically, the Lancashire & Yorkshire Railway based on Manchester did not come into the 1923 amalgamation, as it had already joined forces with the London & North Western in 1922. Oddly, the LMS acquired (through the Midland) the London, Tilbury & Southend Railway which, by logic, ought really to have gone to the easterly-based London & North Eastern Railway. The LMS also shared the ownership of two joint lines—the Midland and Great Northern (with the London & North Eastern Railway) and the Somerset & Dorset (with the Southern Railway). In addition it took over railways in Ireland, including the extensive Northern Counties Committee system and the Dundalk, Newry & Greenore Railway. All in all it formed a very impressive organisation.

To go back a little farther in history, the LMS can perhaps claim descent from one of the earliest of railways, the Kilmarnock & Troon Railway, which opened in 1810 and had steam locomotive trials as early as 1817. The Kilmarnock & Troon came into the consortium as part of the route of the Glasgow & South Western (opened 1840 to Ayr). The G&SW was one of three Scottish railways of the LMS which together totalled 2,200 miles at grouping. Of the other two, the 896-mile Caledonian started operation in 1845, and the Highland was formed of several smaller constituents in 1865, including the Inverness & Nairn which opened in 1855. The Highland brought in the line over Drumochter pass, with a summit of 1,484ft the highest main line in Britain.

Of the English constituents, the Liverpool & Manchester was perhaps the most important; it opened in September 1830 as the world's first railway with all steam locomotive operation. The L&M joined with the Grand Junction Railway (1838) in 1845, and the pair linked with the

Manchester & Birmingham and London & Birmingham in 1846 to form the London & North Western Railway. The LNWR absorbed the Chester & Holyhead in 1858 (inheriting the Conway and Britannia tubular wrought-iron bridges) and several other smaller lines during the next 10 years.

The Midland Railway was formed in 1844 by the amalgamation of the joint York & North Midland (1839) and the Midland Counties (1839) with the Birmingham & Derby Railway (1839). It took in the Leicester & Swannington (1832), the Bristol & Gloucester in 1846, and other smaller lines, and opened to London St Pancras in 1868, though some Midland trains already operated to London over Great Northern Lines.

The other LMS major constituent, the Lancashire & Yorkshire Railway, started in 1846 with the amalgamation of the Manchester & Leeds (1841) and the Manchester & Bolton (1838) and matured a year later by merging with five other railways. Other constituents included the Furness Railway, the North Staffordshire Railway and the North London Railway.

On formation at the beginning of 1923, the London Midland & Scottish Railway was indeed an impressive organisation. It had a total single-track length, including sidings, of almost 19,000 miles and a main line 729 miles long from London to Wick (and the most northerly British station at Thurso). It operated in 32 of the 40 English counties and until 1939 had a staff bigger than the British Army. At one time the LMS in fact was the largest joint stock corporation in the world. Not an unmixed blessing was its inheritance of 10,316 steam locomotives, of nearly 400 different designs!

Somewhat naturally the early years of the LMS were a period of rather slow consolidation, for it was no easy task to forge erstwhile rival lines and strong personalities into one strong unit. Certainly at the beginning, the railway tended to operate in Divisions based roughly on the territories of its principal constituents, and it is doubtful whether the general public really noticed much difference for some considerable time. It even took around six or seven years for some of the old distinctive liveries to disappear.

The main line of the LMS was the North Western route to Scotland, running from London Euston via Rugby, Crewe, Preston and Carlisle (where it joined the Caledonian) to Glasgow and Edinburgh. Branching off the trunk line were heavily trafficked routes to Manchester, Liverpool,

North Wales (for Holyhead and Dublin) and a great loop from Rugby to Stafford, taking in Coventry, Birmingham and the industrial Black Country. Trains over these sections had always been among the elite of the old L&NWR company and continued to be so of the new; many of them became the famous named expresses of the inter-war years. They included the Royal Scot (London to Glasgow) the Comet (London to Liverpool) the Mancunian, the Mid-day Scot, the Welshman, and later the Coronation Scot.

The Midland Division, not to be outdone, produced the Thames Clyde Express from London to Glasgow via Leeds and the Settle-Carlisle line, and the Devonian running across country from Leeds to Birmingham, Bristol, and on to South Devon via the Great Western. Scottish services were good on the old Caledonian line between Glasgow and Edinburgh, and up to Perth, but on the Highland and Glasgow & South Western section, where

most of the track was single, it was the service provided and not the speed, which mattered. High speed in any case, did not become the hallmark of even star expresses until the late 1930s.

In a way the progress of the LMS in the early years after formation was very much like that of any modern company take-over or merger. Of economic necessity, it became a slimming down, a centralising and standardising operation. By 1930, limbs in the shape of unremunerative branch lines began to be lopped, and the shape of things to come, mirrored in the motor car, bus, and lorry, became slowly apparent, over thirty branches closing to passengers in that year alone.

On the mechanical side matters were also somewhat complicated, with the huge collection of locomotives of varying age and efficiency, not to mention the differences of mechanical engineering and running policies. The London & North Western, for example, thought nothing of hanging 450 tons behind one of the George V-class 4-4-0s, whereas the Midland would have provided two engines of similar classification for such a load. It was the Midland which dominated the LMS and nowhere more than in the mechanical and running departments. Gradually the weak and the non-standard went to the scrapheap (usually the smaller company's engines) and a stop-gap policy of continuing to build what was considered the best of the old companies' engines lasted for a while, though in the main it meant Midland designs.

It became obvious that steps would need to be taken to obtain an LMS-built express engine suitable for the heavier trains and as the star of the Great Western was rising high in the locomotive world, the company borrowed a Castle-class locomotive in 1926 and ran it over the LNWR route where it easily mastered the heaviest loads set for it to haul. The experiment confirmed the LMS running department's prognosis that a good 4-6-0 would fill the bill. So, to get over the immediate problem quickly, the company borrowed a set of

S. HIBERNIA LEAVING DUBLIN (NORTH WALL) FOR HOLYHEAD.

Facing page top to bottom:
A North Staffordshire Railway 2-4-0 passenger engine on the turntable. *Ian Allan library*
London, Tilbury & Southend Railway 4-4-2T 'Thundersley' of 1909, not quite in original condition but restored to original livery, preserved at Bressingham Hall, Norfolk. *F V Archer*
Midland Railway Kirtley 2-4-0 of 1866 which continued in service until 1947 and is now preserved at Leicester museum. *J Adams*
Midland Johnson three-cylinder compound 4-4-0 of 1902, rebuilt by Fowler in 1914 near Mill Hill. *F Moore*

Top: No 5593 'Kolhapur', one of Stanier's three-cylinder 'Jubilees' of 1934, now preserved at Tyseley. *J Adams*

Above: London & North Western Railway ferry 'Hibernia' leaving Dublin North Wall for Holyhead. *A Wood*

Below: LNWR mishap on the Manchester side of Standedge tunnel in 1904; the engine was running chimney first and swung completely about after derailing. *A Wood*

Lord Nelson drawings from the Southern Railway for overall guidance, and arranged for the North British Locomotive Company to build fifty of the three-cylinder Royal Scot class.

The first of the new engines emerged in 1927 and the class proved to be a reasonable stop-gap until the next step in the process of consolidation and rationalisation began. That was the importation from the Great Western Railway of the second-in-command at Swindon Works, Mr William Stanier (later Sir William) to be the LMS Chief Mechanical Engineer. Stanier immediately began a programme of standardisation of locomotives and rolling stock, introducing his own efficient designs and quickly reducing the numbers of the pre-grouping locomotives. Among his famous classes were the Princess Royal and Coronation classes of Pacific wheel formation, the latter being some of the finest express engines to be designed and operated in Britain. Stanier also introduced a three-cylinder mixed-traffic 4-6-0 in the Jubilee class, and hundreds of the ubiquitous two-cylinder mixed-traffic 4-6-0s and their tank engine counterparts.

Freight was worked generally by a large class of ex-LNWR 0-8-0s and Midland 0-6-0s of varying power definitions. Later Stanier brought in his well-known 8F class 2-8-0 for freight work. In all, over 600 of the 8Fs were built, as they were ordered by the Ministry of Supply for wartime service; some ended their days in Palestine, Egypt, Iraq and Persia, but most were eventually brought home. One was seen still working in Istanbul in 1966. They were built in far-flung works, including

Brighton on the Southern, Darlington and Doncaster on the North Eastern, and even at Swindon, their designer's Alma Mater.

The LMS operated an excellent service of suburban trains based on the larger towns, and the pattern with those followed that of the main line in that gradually standardised 2-6-2 and 2-6-4 tank engines replaced the heterogeneous collection of small tank engines from the pre-grouping lines. To the end however, some of the small engines were kept to work certain branch and push-pull shuttle services, which lasted well into nationalisation. The Stanier 2-6-4 tanks could be found anywhere from Tilbury to Bangor or Birmingham to Glasgow.

Cross-country routes were slower in modernising, but as motive power was improved so were the services, and by 1935 such lines as the Somerset & Dorset, and the single-track main lines of the Glasgow & South Western, and the Highland, began to hear the sound of Stanier's deep-toned hooter instead of the shrill whistle of the older engines.

Rationalisation was also carried out with force in LMS workshop practice. Small works, such as that at Lochgorm (Inverness) on the Highland, and at St Rollox (Glasgow) on the Caledonian, were downgraded for repairs only, and locomotive building was carried on solely at Crewe and Derby—with outside help from the private locomotive builders when necessary. The North Western carriage works at Wolverton and the Midland works at Derby produced the new coaches. A start was also made on the vacuum fitting of wagons for higher-speed

freight services, and large concentration and hump yards, such as that at Toton, were built and put into operation.

The first ten years to 1933 were those of formation, and the following period to 1939, and the war, saw the emergence of a new pattern for the future. There were two important factors; the first was the general overall financial position, which demanded efficiency and economy, and second was road competition, which was an enemy stronger than had been thought possible by those used to thinking in terms of the railway as a transport monopoly. Diesels for shunting were introduced in 1934 and orders were placed for more the next year; mechanisation in the form of coaling and ash-lifting plants were installed in running sheds; the 'mechanical horse' with its trailer was brought into use for railway road services; and over in Ireland petrol railcars were introduced on the jointly owned County Donegal Railway.

Freight revenue, especially from coal traffic, was still good—it was the passenger traffic which had to be kept and improved if possible. By 1935 the East Coast rivals, the LNER, had inaugurated the Silver Jubilee, a very fast service between London and the Tyneside, running at 100mph using streamlined locomotives, and speed became a publicity feature of some importance. The year 1936 found the LMS making experimental runs with its Pacific No 6201 *Princess Elizabeth* from Euston to Glasgow and back, and by 1937 the Coronation Scot had been introduced complete with streamlined locomotive; it was in truth the Mid-Day Scot on a faster schedule. What is now known as Inter-City traffic was also speeded up and well publicised with improvements to schedules, particularly between London and Liverpool, and London and Manchester.

The London to Birmingham services, though loading to heavier trains, remained on the two-hour timing originated by the old North Western. It was only ever improved by a few minutes until electrification of the route in 1967. Although for publicity purposes the crack trains were the

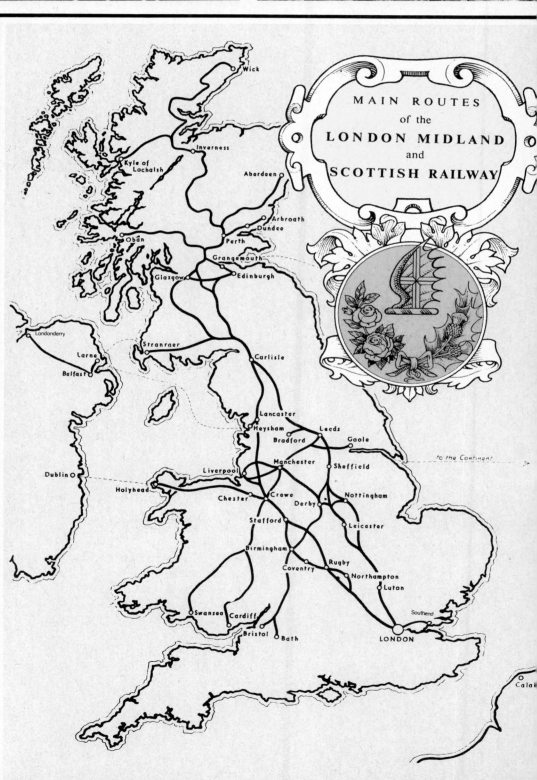

MAIN ROUTES
of the
LONDON MIDLAND
and
SCOTTISH RAILWAY

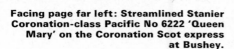

Scottish expresses, the Midland division did well enough for the businessman, and the London to Nottingham, Derby and Leeds trains were well filled, as were the Bristol to Birmingham and the Birmingham to Leeds expresses. Average speeds were not high, being generally under 50mph start to stop. Holiday resorts in Lancashire (such as Blackpool) were extremely well served, as were the principal holiday resorts in North Wales, particularly Llandudno.

The LMS was well to the fore in its signalling programme, replacing the familiar lower-quadrant arms of the old companies with the American-looking fail-safe upper-quadrant arms. Multi-aspect colour-light signalling was also introduced, and the company was the first in Britain to concentrate on that side of safety in high speed running.

Like its three competitors, the LMS invested in other means of transport, taking a considerable interest for example, in the large Midland Red bus company among others, and operating shipping services mainly inherited from the London & North Western and Midland companies, sailing from Wales and Western Scotland to Ireland. They included the Holyhead-Dublin, Heysham-Belfast, and Stranraer-Larne boats and there was also a service (later only freight) to Greenore just south of the Irish border. The Greenore route was the remnant of an attempt by the LNWR to obtain its own private foothold in

Ireland, where it owned the short Dundalk, Newry & Greenore Railway, connecting with the Great Northern Railway of Ireland. It operated 5ft 3in-gauge replicas of ancient North Western 0-6-0 saddle tanks and six-wheeled coaches, painted in 'plum-and-spilt-milk' livery.

In Ireland the LMS took over the Midland's Belfast & Northern Counties Railway, changing its name to the Northern Counties Committee. This organisation, based on Belfast, was built to the standard Irish gauge of 5ft 3in and served principal towns in the Six Counties with a good express service between Belfast and Londonderry. In LMS days its locomotives and stock were built at Derby and patterned very much on Derby designs. There were some 3ft-gauge lines merged into the NCC, including the Larne to Ballymena section which actually operated boat trains for a while. The company also owned a narrow-gauge line from Londonderry to Strabane which connected with the extensive County Donegal system, jointly owned with the GNR(I).

In the days of expansion the larger railway companies built themselves hotels and the constituents of the LMS were no exception to the rule. Most of the London main-line termini had hotels, as did the principal cities and towns, and without doubt they were of a very high standard for the period; today some of them, such as the Queen's in Birmingham, are sorely missed. The Queen's was a North Western hotel, and that company regarded itself regally, even using the word BESTOTEL as its telegraphic code, but the Midland had no such pretensions—its hotels, of equal standard, were named after the company. The Caledonian in Scotland pursued a similar policy. The smaller companies were also hotel owners, and one of the most memorable of them is the Station Hotel at Inverness, where surely some of the excellent plumbing and the huge comfortable baths were made in the works at Lochgorm! The Irish lines also had their establishments, including that at Greenore where one's bedroom looked

over the Mountains of Mourne and the bathroom window opened on to the platforms and the sound of an old LNWR tank engine.

By the coming of the 1939-45 war, the LMS had established a pattern, but its last eight years, mainly in times of austerity, exceedingly heavy traffic and minimum maintenance, left their mark, though there is little doubt that Stanier's policy of standardisation must have paid off many times. In fairness it must be stated that it was during the war period (1943) that the first of the Royal Scots was rebuilt, turning a reasonable engine into probably one of the most successful and efficient 4-6-0s to have run on any railway in Britain. The LMS performed its duty to the nation and emerged with plans for the future, which were carried on into nationalisation, one of them being the changeover to diesel motive power. It also provided the men who were certainly to influence steam's remaining years in Britain, and a large part of the thinking behind the modern systems of signalling.

To conclude, the LMS of all the four Main Lines was probably the greatest pointer to the way the railway system of Britain would go in the future. It pulled a conglomeration of smaller organisations, all with their personalities and idiosyncrasies, into a homogeneous whole, more efficient but less personal, and it provided a transport system which, though far from perfect, was an example to many others in Europe and overseas. Sadly it was never a maker of money for its shareholders, for it passed its ordinary dividends altogether after only five years, and certain preference dividends in three. Even so, it was not by any means the worst of the four—that doubtful honour goes to the LNER.

To try to compress the story of the London Midland & Scottish Railway into a few words, or even a book, would be impossible—suffice it to say that it played a leading part in the gradual integration of Britain's railways, where its influence is still felt.

"THE SILVER JUBILEE"
SILVER LINK
2509 L N E R
BRITAIN'S FIRST STREAMLINE TRAIN
FRANK NEWBOULD
NEWCASTLE AND LONDON IN 4 HOURS
AVERAGE THROUGHOUT SPEED 67.08 M.P.H.
Weekdays (Saturdays excepted) from 30th. September 1935
NEWCASTLE dep a.m. 10. 0
DARLINGTON " 10.42
KING'S CROSS arr. p.m. 2. 0
KING'S CROSS dep. p.m. 5. 30
DARLINGTON arr. 8. 48
NEWCASTLE " 9. 30
Connecting trains serve Tyneside and Tees-side
SUPPLEMENTARY FARES: (FOR EACH SINGLE JOURNEY) First Class 5/- Third Class 3/-
LONDON & NORTH EASTERN RAILWAY
LONDON & NORTH EASTERN RAILWAY

LNER

IT CAN BE SAID with some truth that the London & North Eastern Railway had its roots with George Stephenson and the world's first public railway. Certainly its largest, wealthiest, and most influential constituent company—the North Eastern—evolved from the Stockton & Darlington, which opened in 1825. The North Eastern had a virtual monopoly in the North and East Ridings of Yorkshire, the counties of Durham and Northumberland, and running powers right through North British territory to Edinburgh, with tentacles as far west as Cumberland and Westmorland. In 1922 it gobbled up its rival, the Hull & Barnsley, and finished up with a track mileage of 5,407.

The next largest company was the Great

Northern abutting and south of the North Eastern; the two lines, with the help of the North British over the border, formed the East Coast route to Scotland. The Great Northern did not come into being until 1846 and from the start set Yorkshire as its target. Kings Cross was its London terminus from 1852, and at amalgamation its mileage was 3,124.

The other two English constituent 'greats' were the Great Central (2,698 miles) and the Great Eastern (2,637 miles). The former was a descendant of the Manchester, Sheffield and Lincolnshire, which was part of the Watkin 'empire'—Watkin was also chairman of the Metropolitan and the South Eastern Railways. This was the final fling in Sir

Edward's determination to have a line of railway from Manchester to the Channel coast. The line's name was changed to the Great Central once the MS&L extension southwards to its new London terminus at Marylebone was completed in 1899. The Great Eastern began life as the Eastern Counties Railway in 1836 and merged with four others to form the new railway in 1862. It shared with the Midland Railway the distinction of being the first to admit third-class passengers to all its trains and had the honour also of being a Royal line, serving Sandringham, which was reached from London via the terminus at Liverpool Street. Neither of these two 'greats' was ever wealthy.

In Scotland the LNER absorbed the

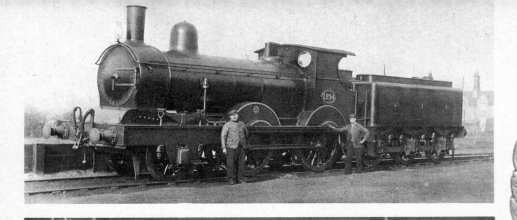

Nº 4468

CLASS A-4

LNER

ON 3ʀᴰ JULY 1938 THIS LOCOMOTIVE ATTAINED A WORLD SPEED RECORD FOR STEAM TRACTION OF 126 MILES PER HOUR

MALLARD

Top left: A Holden GER 2-4-0 for mixed traffic, 100 of which were built 1891-1902.

Left, top right and above: Details of the steam speed record holder, Gresley streamlined A4 Pacific 'Mallard' as preserved in the British Transport Museum Clapham
All J Benton Harris

Below: Gresley A4 No 60034 'Lord Faringdon' with an Aberdeen-Glasgow train at Stonehaven in September 1965. *R Bastin*

North British, (2,675 miles) the Caledonian's deadly rival, plus the last 'great' the Great North of Scotland, a once terrible railway (526 miles). The North British was the largest railway in Scotland and ran its trains over two of Britain's more famous bridges, those of the Forth and Tay. It started off as the Edinburgh & Dalkeith Railway, a horse-worked line of 1826, originally built to 4ft 6in gauge but widened to the standard 4ft 8½in in 1846. The board of the NBR held its first meeting in 1844 and construction of the railway proper began in that year. It was based on Edinburgh, and its Waverley station in that city has always been one of Scotland's finest. During its later days the Great North of Scotland (which dated from 1852) was a prim little railway based on Aberdeen, whose General station it shared with the Caledonian. The Great North, like the Great Eastern was a 'royal' line in that its branch from Aberdeen to Ballater served Balmoral.

The LNER participated in Joint lines, the two largest of which were the Cheshire Lines Committee (partly in Lancashire) and the Midland and Great Northern. Both were joint with the LMS. The former possessed its own passenger stock but the motive power was LNER (Great Central) while the permanent way came under the LMS. The M&GN was a self-contained railway which owned its own locomotives, coaches and wagons, based on Melton Constable. The locomotives were for many years painted a distinctive yellow ochre and had a marked Derby parentage.

In some ways the final evolution of the LNER confirmed a long-standing arrangement of alliances which had become known as the East Coast route, rivalling the equally well-known West Coast route activated by the London & North Western and Caledonian Railways. The East Coast companies, the Great Northern, North Eastern and North British, although not always the happiest of bedfellows, provided a fast service from London to Edinburgh. The addition of the Great Central, Great Eastern and Great North of Scotland companies, all of them poorer relations, was complementary. Fortunately there was no unpleasantness in the merging of the LNER's constituents, though the North Eastern was almost certainly the most wealthy and consequently the strongest.

So, LNER expresses ran from London Kings Cross to York, Newcastle and Edinburgh, London Liverpool Street to Norwich and the East Coast, and London Marylebone to Manchester via Rugby and Leicester. In Scotland the North British section provided an excellent service between Glasgow and Edinburgh and Edinburgh to Aberdeen. Other lines of some importance included those between Manchester, Sheffield and Lincoln, Doncaster and Leeds, Newcastle and Carlisle, Aberdeen, Keith and Elgin, and that magnificently scenic route the West Highland to Fort William, extending to Mallaig for Skye.

In 1925 the new company was the host for the Railway Centenary celebrations, when exhibits ranging from the ancient Hetton Colliery locomotive built in 1822 to an ex-Gresley Pacific, a Southern King Arthur and, above all, a Great Western Castle ran over the Stockton & Darlington route in the presence of Royalty. The same year also saw the famous locomotive exchanges between the LNER and the Great Western, when Gresley's Pacifics were tried against Collett's Castles.

Over the years, most of the fast running on the LNER was over the East Coast route, mainly on the old Great Northern section, and many of the trains were of special interest in that they were made up of Pullman stock. There were the Harrogate Pullman, the West Riding Pullman, the Yorkshire Pullman and above all the famous Queen of Scots Pullman. All were luxury trains subject to supplementary fares, but they were very popular.

Competition between the West and East Coast routes began to intensify by 1928 when the LMS, with its new Royal Scot-class locomotives began to run non-stop between London and Carlisle. In retaliation the LNER brought in the new Flying Scotsman, inaugurating the longest non-stop run in the world, 393 miles, between London and Edinburgh.

It was made possible by the use of Gresley's now well-known corridor tender which enabled locomotive crews to change over en route. By 1935 streamlining had come into vogue with the Silver Jubilee train which brought Newcastle within a four—hour journey of London. So successful was this train that a further flyer, the Coronation, began to run in 1937. The Coronation was able to wrest the then speed record from the Great Western's Cheltenham Flyer by being booked to run between Kings Cross and York at an average speed of 71.9 miles per hour—Edinburgh, the next stop, was reached in six hours from London. By the following year a third streamlined train was in operation—the West Riding Limited running from Kings Cross to Bradford with a timing not equalled until 1966 with modern 3,300hp Deltic diesels.

Other main line services were also of a high standard and included such names as the Scarborough Flyer and the East Anglian. Expresses were speeded up between London and Manchester on the Great Central section and to Cambridge on the Great Northern and Great Eastern lines. One of the more important improvements was that between Edinburgh and Aberdeen, where fast trains connected with the down Flying Scotsman and up Coronation expresses.

As on all other railways, LNER services suffered a severe downward trend during the 1939-45 war. Trains such as the Flying Scotsman still ran but only in name—it took almost nine hours to reach Edinburgh. Trains were slower and heavier—loads of 25 coaches being not uncommon. It was very much a case of 'Is your journey really necessary?' and es-

pecially at night time, travel was no joke. The war probably saved a large number of LNER branch lines from the axe, for, with petrol rationing, the road competition which had grown increasingly heavy since 1930 became almost non-existent, but it was only a temporary respite. The LNER had itself invested in certain road undertakings by the early 1930s.

From the motive power point of view the LNER was particularly fortunate in having the services of Mr (later Sir) Nigel Gresley, whose locomotives became world famous. Gresley's policy was to use the best of the old, supplemented by his own designs, and there is little doubt that it paid dividends. Of all British express engines in the early days of the Grouping (many would say for all time) his A3-class Pacifics named after racehorses and of course the evergreen A1 *Flying Scotsman* were not only the most handsome, but also the epitome of what was best in express steam locomotives. The Great Western Castles beat them on their own ground in 1925, but even that lesson was absorbed and acted upon.

In 1925 the LNER obtained a 2-8—8-2 Garratt articulated engine, built to Gresley's design by Beyer Peacock & Co. It was the most powerful steam engine ever to be built for use in Britain and was constructed for work on the formidable seven-mile Worsborough incline on the old Great Central route from Wath to Lancashire via the Woodhead tunnel.

Gresley was a firm advocate of three-cylinder propulsion and his engines of this type ranged from the K3 class 2-6-0 through the large O2 class freight 2-8-0s to the A1, A3 and later the A4 streamlined Pacifics. By 1935, test runs had been carried out with the A3s to investigate the possibilities of steam in comparison with the German streamlined diesel, the Flying Hamburger. Somewhat naturally the Germans had publicised the Hamburger well and questions had been asked. Gresley claimed that he could do better with steam, using British coal rather than imported fuel oil. Encouraged by the LNER Chief General Manager and the board, Gresley went ahead with the design of the A4 Pacific, which many consider to be his masterpiece; the first engine was named *Silver Link* in honour of King George V's Silver Jubilee in 1935. On trial runs the new engine twice reached the record speed of 112½mph. By 1938, 35 A4s had been built and were in regular service; of them No 4468 *Mallard* on a further test run attained the world speed record for steam of 126mph.

But it was not only for his Pacifics that Gresley has been recognised by historians. He also designed numerous locomotives capable of the whole range of duties required by his company, of which probably the star was the V2 2-6-2, named Green Arrows after the first of the class. The company adopted a big engine policy which certainly paid dividends, particularly during the war years when loads were prodigious. Other notable

Top: A W Worsdell 0-6-0T, a NER shunter design standardised by British Railways for the North Eastern Region, at work as a Newcastle pilot. *J Adams*

Above: A pair of the renowned Ivatt GNR Atlantics heading a special train out of London Kings Cross. *P B Whitehouse*

Facing page top: Modern keeper of the tradition of fast passenger services on the East Coast route, a BR 3,300hp Deltic diesel-electric locomotive at Kings Cross. *G P Cooper*

Facing page bottom: Map showing principal lines of the LNER at grouping.

classes included the B17 4-6-0 for use on the Great Central and East Anglian routes and an excellent range of 2-6-4 tanks. The largest passenger engine class was the P2 of which the first engine, No 2001 *Cock o' the North*, incorporated certain features of the Chapelon designs and was tested in France on the plant at Vitry.

Nor were the older classes forgotten. The ex-Great Eastern B12 class 4-6-0s, once the star turns of the Liverpool Street to Norwich expresses, were sent to Keith and Elgin to work the Great North of Scotland expresses, which they did until well after nationalisation of the railways. New Director-class 4-4-0s were built and also sent to Scotland, while the older engines of their class performed well on the Great Central main line until ousted by the B17s in the later 1930s. Pre-grouping classes were retained for many secondary branch-line duties, including wheel arrangements such as the 2-4-0 which disappeared on the other main lines much earlier—several of these engines were running in East Anglia well into the 1950s.

After Gresley's death in 1942, first Thompson and then Peppercorn took over the reins, the former rebuilding and modifying several of his old CME's designs. Two cylinders were now to be the rule. Notable among the conversions was the

K4-class 2-6-0 built for the West Highland line, from which came the very capable two-cylinder K1. A most successful class introduced as early as 1942 was the B1 4-6-0, a general-purpose locomotive comparable to the LMS Class 5 and the Great Western Hall. Most LNER engines were either built at the old Great Northern works at Doncaster or the North Eastern shops at Darlington.

Although the LNER had not been diesel-minded, it had turned its thoughts towards electrification. It inherited the Tyneside electric trains from the North Eastern and joined with the LMS in the electrification of the joint Manchester South Junction and Altrincham line. In London the company worked with the London Passenger Transport Board in the electrification of some of its suburban routes. The most comprehensive plan, however, was the proposed Manchester to Sheffield electrification, but it could not be completed until the long Woodhead tunnel was rebuilt, and the project was not finished until after nationalisation.

Like its competitors, the LNER had maritime interests, in fact not only did it own a considerable shipping fleet, but also the largest number of docks and harbours of any of the railway companies. Most were on the Tyne, Tees and Humber, though to travellers Harwich was no doubt the best known. There were also extensive installations in Scotland at Methil in Fife, with smaller docks at Burntisland and Bo'ness. Passenger steamships to the Continent left Grimsby for Hamburg, Harwich for Holland, and Hull for Germany, France and Belgium. Parkeston Quay at Harwich also served the Belgian port of Zeebrugge with a train ferry service inaugurated in 1924, and was the port for a regular nightly ferry service to the Hook of Holland. In Scotland the company also operated a delightful fleet of ex-North British Railway paddle steamers, named after Walter Scott's novels.

Hotels were profitable investments and the LNER inherited a large number from the constituent companies. Among the most notable were those at Liverpool Street (the Great Eastern) and at Edinburgh (the North British). The Great Central built a huge edifice at Marylebone (now the headquarters of British Railways Board), the Great Northern appeared at Kings Cross, and most provincial towns of size had their railway hostelry if served by the LNER and the Great Northern in particular.

The LNER (though it was not alone) realised a little late that other forms of transport, particularly the road, were thorns in the side which could only fester and needed drastic treatment. With the other three companies it put a great deal of effort into the 'Square Deal' campaign in the nineteen-thirties when it was argued, with some justice, that legal restrictions put on the railways in the days of their monopoly were unfair. The complaint applied particularly to the old basis of freight charging, which was roughly to equate the charge with the service rendered and that in turn depended on the value of the article moved. So road transport often got a high-rated job of carrying full cases by slightly undercutting the published rail rate. Nothing however, was to happen until the Transport Act of 1953, by which time it was too late.

In the end, times and the war made it necessary that either the railways were given a massive subsidy in one form or another or they should be nationalised outright. The latter course was chosen and the LNER disappeared, except in nostalgia and history, on December 31, 1947. Unfortunately, from its shareholders point of view it had not been a great success—in fact the LNER had the worst record of the Big Four companies. Not one of its several series of dated or first or second preference shares was regularly paid, or in full, and its ordinary preference shareholders had nothing after 1930. Money was always tight and it is to the company's credit that it was able to perform so well under the circumstances. It had a first-class line of railway officers, and one of its memorials must be that many of them reached high, and indeed the highest, ranks in the new British Railways organisation.

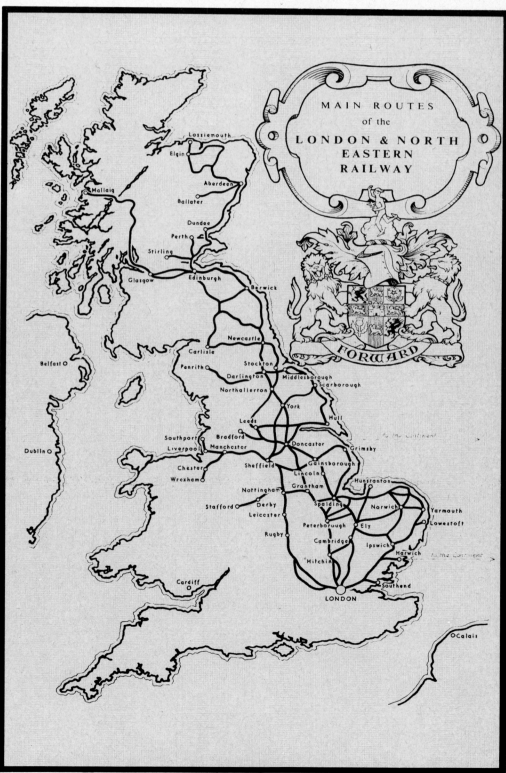

THE HISTORY of the Southern is bound up with the stories of the first 'public' railway in the world—the Surrey Iron Railway of 1803; the first railway to carry passengers by means of a locomotive—the Canterbury & Whitstable Railway of 1830; and the first railway into London—the London & Greenwich of 1836. It is true that the Stockton & Darlington line was opened as early as 1825 but all that company's passenger coaches were horse-drawn until 1833, and although the Liverpool & Manchester is sometimes thought of as being the first major public railway to use steam haulage, the *Invicta* of the Canterbury & Whitstable started running about five months earlier.

The main constituents to form the Southern in 1923 were the London & South Western, the London, Brighton & South Coast, the South Eastern, and the London, Chatham & Dover Railways—the two last-named coming under the banner of the South Eastern & Chatham Railway Companies Managing Committee. Other lines to be drawn into the new organisation included those in the Isle of Wight (the Freshwater, Yarmouth & Newport, the Isle of Wight and Isle of Wight Central Railways). The Southern also shared the Somerset & Dorset Joint Railway with the London Midland & Scottish Railway. In addition there was a unique and delightful narrow gauge line, the Lynton & Barnstaple, which came in under special parliamentary powers.

These railway companies covered virtually all Southern England and spread well into the South West. The London & South Western was the largest, with a total route running line of 1,019 miles, of which 324 miles was single track. It sprang from the London & Southampton Railway of 1837 whose contractor was the famous Thomas Brassey. The next in size was the South Eastern & Chatham Committee's line comprising the South Eastern and London, Chatham & Dover Railways. It had a total route running line of 638 miles and its ancestry is traceable back to the Canterbury & Whitstable. The London Brighton & South Coast was the smallest of the 'Big Three' having a route running line of 457 miles, its beginnings going back to the London & Croydon Railway opened in 1839. The Southern Railway's historian Dendy Marshall tells us that the company inherited in total 2,178 miles of first running track, 4,175 miles of total track (running line) and 1,205 miles of siding. There were 2,281 locomotives, 7,500 coaches and 36,749 wagons, as well as 41 steamboats and 11 hotels.

The Southern was very much a passenger line; it dealt with vast numbers of commuters in the London area as well as holidaymakers, cross-Channel and ocean-going travellers. It spread its commuter belt wider and wider, encouraging suburban growth down to Margate, Ramsgate, Brighton and Sevenoaks. It advertised and encouraged its seaside resorts from Kent to North Cornwall. Its cross-Channel

Left: A London & South Western Railway 1d platform ticket machine seconded for duty at Clapham Transport Museum.
British Transport Museum (B Sharpe)

Below: Southern Railway West Country Pacific No 34023 'Blackmore Vale' seen here on the Longmoor military railway; the locomotive is owned by the Bulleid Preservation Society and is now housed on the Bluebell Railway. *M Pope*

Bottom: An F Moore painting, showing an LBSCR Class H1 4-4-2 at Victoria.
Ian Allan Library

Facing page: Nameplate and crest shield of Bulleid SR West Country class Pacific No 34013 'Okehampton'. *M Pope*

Far left: Part of the motion of a Bulleid Pacific locomotive. *M J Esau*

Left: Last active original West Country Pacific, No 34102 'Lapford' on a Salisbury-Waterloo train in July 1967, just before the end of steam on the Southern. *A H Ellis*

Above: Bulleid Austerity Q1 No 33035 on a Dover train at Folkestone Warren in 1961. *M Pope*

Below: A Q1 0-6-0 being cleaned out at Guildford shed. *I Krause*

Below: Bulleid's shock-absorbing wagon of 1940 with body mounted to frame on sliding blocks on shafts with fore-and-aft springing. *British Railways SR*

Right: Adams LSWR 02-class 0-4-4T No W26 'Whitwell', on the drawbridge at Newport IoW. *M J Esau*

Facing page: Maunsell SR Schools-class 4-4-0 No 926 Repton, at Eastleigh in February 1967, just before shipment to the United States, where it is preserved *Colourviews Ltd*

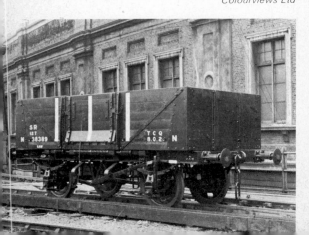

steamers plied from Dover or Folkestone to Calais or Boulogne, Newhaven to Dieppe, and Southampton to Cherbourg, Le Havre and St Malo. There was also a Channel Islands service. Train ferries crossed over from Dover to Dunkerque, and Southampton docks was built up into the vast Ocean terminal, rivalling and then eclipsing Liverpool for the Atlantic passenger trade.

The Southern Railway's expresses, apart from those serving Devon and Cornwall, were comparatively short-distance ones. The South Eastern & Chatham's termini at Charing Cross and Cannon Street were the starting points for the Kent Coast trains running via Chatham or Ashford, and the South Eastern's westerly route, into Hastings via Tonbridge. Victoria served the lines to Brighton, Newhaven, Hastings, Bexhill and Eastbourne, and trains from Waterloo ran to Southampton, Bournemouth, Salisbury, Exeter, North Devon and North Cornwall. Portsmouth and the Isle of Wight trains ran over both the old LBSC and LSW sections from Victoria and Waterloo. Pullman cars ran regularly on the Golden Arrow (Victoria to Dover) the Southern Belle (also from Victoria) and the Bournemouth Belle. The latter was the Southern's longest express journey and the train carried portions which were shed beyond Exeter for Plymouth, Bude, Padstow, Barnstaple, Ilfracombe and Torrington. Through trains ran regularly to its connecting northerly neighbours, the old

LBSCR's Sunny South express route to the LMS, and trains from Bournemouth or Margate to Birkenhead via Reading and Birmingham on the Great Western. Bath and the Midlands were reached from Bournemouth via Templecombe and the Somerset & Dorset line.

Barnstaple was the junction for the 1ft 11½in-gauge railway to Lynton, which was closed by the Southern in September 1935. It was one of the most delightful journeys that could be made, and had it survived the 1939-45 war there is little doubt that it could have become one of Britain's finest tourist railways. The locomotives were, in the main, Manning Wardle 2-6-2 tanks with lovely river names like *Exe, Taw* and *Yeo,* all of 1897 vintage, assisted by an American Baldwin-built 2-4-2 tank *Lyn,* also of 1897. The Southern obtained a third 2-6-2 tank *Lew* and it

was the only engine to survive the line's demise, having been, it is said, sold out of service to Brazil. It has never yet been traced and remains one of the interesting speculations of narrow-gauge railway lore.

The Isle of Wight lines were retained by the Southern and although Ryde and Portsmouth were the principal pierheads, ferries also ran to Yarmouth (from Lymington) and Cowes (from Southampton). The train service from Ryde to Shanklin and Ventnor was as busy in the summer as the single line could take. By the early 1930s, most of the old Isle of Wight companies' engines had gone and the traffic was worked by imported tank engines from the mainland. There were ex-LSWR 02-class 0-4-4 tanks, with enlarged bunkers (which worked most of the trains), ex-LBSCR 0-6-0 Terrier tanks (mostly on the 'branch' trains) and two ex-LBSCR E1-class 0-6-0 tanks for freight. All carried names of towns or villages on the island.

Electrification of the Southern suburban lines made considerable headway immediately after the Grouping. They ran out to Rochester, Chatham and Gillingham on the South Eastern section, spread during the decade over much of the LBSCR (Central section) and took in the South Western's remaining steam suburban services out of Waterloo, as well as the Portsmouth line. The London & South Western had already carried out an electrification project in 1915, trains running out of Waterloo to East Putney, Shepperton and Hampton Court. This followed the lead set by the London Brighton & South Coast, which had put in an overhead system as early as 1905, having in all about 62 miles of electrified track out to Crystal Palace and West Norwood. The Southern followed the South Western's principle of third-rail direct current whereas the LBSC favoured overhead-line and alternating current.

The Southern's first chief mechanical engineer was R E L Maunsell, who came from the SE&CR; he inherited a collection of somewhat ancient engines from each of the constituent companies. They were augmented by further 2-6-0 engines of the SE&CR N class, the ill-fated River class 2-6-4 tanks, some L1 4-4-0s based on the SE&C's L class, and more 2-6-0s of U, U1 and N1 classes. In 1925 the famous

King Arthur class was born at Eastleigh works; they were based on the LSWR Urie H15 4-6-0 and were an immediate success. This was perhaps the most famous Southern Railway class and until final withdrawal almost forty years later the King Arthurs were used on express work. During their heyday they hauled virtually every important fast train, including the Continental services, the Atlantic Coast Express and the Southern Belle (the predecessor of the electric Brighton Belle).

Between 1926 and 1929 an even more powerful 4-6-0 class was tried out—the Lord Nelson, a four-cylinder design whose eight beats per revolution of the wheels sounded rather odd to the uninitiated. When originally built, the Lord Nelson was the most powerful locomotive in the country and drawings of it were borrowed by the LMS when contemplating its Royal Scot class. In 1930 Maunsell produced the most powerful 4-4-0 in Europe—the Schools class; the new engines were put to work on the South Eastern main lines, including that to Hastings which had been worked until then mainly by the old L-class 4-4-0s.

Maunsell retired in 1937 and was succeeded by O V Bulleid, whose designs were revolutionary to a degree. His first class (Merchant Navy) came out in 1941 at a period when wartime restrictions on the building of express engines were in force; the restriction was avoided by terming the engine a mixed-traffic type—because the driving wheels were only 6ft 2in in diameter! The Merchant Navys were the Southern's first Pacifics and they boasted a form of streamlined casing, chain-driven radial valve gear (peculiar to their designer), disc wheels and electric lighting. They were followed by two classes of a lightweight version, the West Country and Battle of Britain classes. After nationalisation of the railways all the Merchant Navy engines and a large number of the light Pacifics were rebuilt with orthodox valve gear and had their streamlined casings removed. They ran over the Bournemouth line until the end of steam in 1967. Probably the most controversial of all Bulleid's designs was the Leader class running on two six-wheel power bogies. Although ten were ordered, only one engine was ever completed. Southern engines were built at Ashford (SE&CR) Brighton (LB&SCR) and Eastleigh (LSWR) works.

Partly because of the Southern's determination to electrify and partly because existing locomotives were still able to perform their duties on secondary and shunting services, a largish number of pre-grouping engines lasted well into nationalisation—some almost to the end. Of them, the SE&CR's efficient 4-4-0 D1 and E1 rebuilds remained hard at work on the Eastern section—especially to Margate and Ramsgate—until electrification at the end of the 1950s, and Drummond's T9-class 4-4-0s took the subdivided Atlantic Coast Express to Plymouth, Bude and Padstow.

Drummond's 0-4-4 tanks of Class M7 lasted as long as most of the push-and-pull services in Devon or the shunters at Waterloo were required. Two ancient London & South Western classes had particularly long lives—the old Beattie 2-4-0 well tanks which worked the Wenford Bridge line out of Wadebridge, and the Adams 4-4-2 tanks which ran from Axminster to Lyme Regis over a hilly and twisting road where they needed to double-head on a load of three coaches. Other classes working almost to the end of steam included the N15 class 4-6-0s, the 02 0-4-4 tanks on the Isle of Wight, and the Maunsell Moguls.

Like its competitors, the Southern was a ship- and dock-owning company. The ships were cross-Channel steamers (some owned jointly with French Railways) and were generally in service on the short sea route to France. Two larger vessels, the *Dinard* and the *St Briac,* were put to work on the overnight Southampton - St Malo run. Other steamers ran from Weymouth and Southampton to the Channel Islands, Dover to Ostend, and Gravesend to Rotterdam; there was also a ferry service to the Isle of Wight. Passengers from London could travel to Paris via the Night Ferry from Dover, and in 1939 the Southern introduced a new ship, the *Invicta,* for the luxury Golden Arrow service from London to Paris. No fewer than twelve of the Southern's ships became casualties during the 1939-45 war.

Of all its docks, Southampton was the most valuable and certainly the most famous—it has a remarkable double high tide—the second high water occurring only two hours after the first, with only a slight fall in between. The docks were inaugurated by the London & South Western Railway and were developed by the Southern into the country's premier Atlantic terminal. Other docks owned by the company included Dover, Folkestone and Newhaven for the Channel crossings, and Ryde in the Isle of Wight.

The Southern system, in general, was badly hit by the war, as a large proportion of its Channel holiday resorts were prohibited areas. It made tremendous efforts during the retreat from Dunkerque, and in the events prior to the D-day landings; it was not only a target for marauding aircraft, buzz-bombs and rockets, but the Dover district also suffered constant shelling.

The two years between 1945 and the end in 1947 were ones of austerity, but in 1945-6 some cross-Channel services were restored; the same year saw the luxurious Golden Arrow/Invicta service re-opened and Pullman restaurant cars back on some trains. In 1947, a hundred engines were converted to oil burning and the all-Pullman Devon Belle came into operation, bringing an appearance of normality again. Once more the Southern turned its attention towards leisure and holidays instead of just troops and commuters. New plans were brought forward and old ones taken

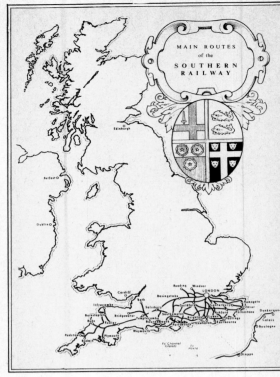

from cupboards and dusted, mostly for further electrification, and when the new Railway Executive was formed to administer Britain's newly nationalised railways, it was the Southern's general manager, Sir Eustace Missenden, who became its chairman.

The Southern came second to the Great Western in its returns to its shareholders, having always paid a preference dividend—though not necessarily at the promised rate. It had the best record of all the four group companies for forward-looking improvements, especially in the ambitious electrification schemes, and the docks at Southampton which have long proved a great asset to the nation. Because it was very much a passenger line and served most of south London's long-suffering suburbanites, who were (and still are) crammed like sardines in peak-hour trains, the Southern never had the popular image of the Great Western. It helped to push and develop suburbia in its crowded electric services and consequently had its share of public stone-throwing, but like

the tubes it became an essential part of the pattern of London and outer-London life.

But as well as suburban and commuter electrics, it had the more-leisurely hop-pickers' train, ramblers' trains, race-goers' trains, boat trains, and even opera trains; it used Pullmans to give comfort to the well-off and the overseas visitor and can be said to have served every facet of life from Royalty en route to Ascot to the day tripper on Margate excursions. However, the pattern changed very quickly and apart from its holiday trains and Continental traffic (which tended to be seasonal anyway) the Southern became more and more a railway whose future lay in the none-too-profitable job of taking the willing but un-grateful public from home to work and back, five days a week. Had it not been for the excellent planning of its management in bringing forward the electrification works, then road traffic congestion in and out of London would have become so bad that the thought is hardly bearable. It is worth remembering.

Left: One of the famous William Dean Singles, 4-2-2 'Achilles', a basic design which bridged the changeover from broad to standard gauge. *British Railways Board*

Above: Twin shields of the Great Western Railway Coat of Arms. *J R Batts*

The Great Western Railway

OF THE FOUR British railway companies to emerge from the Grouping of 1923, the Great Western was unique. It was the only line to absorb others, to keep its own territories and networks inviolate, and to retain its original identity. These facts are probably the main reason for the adulation which the GWR has received for the past fifty years. It absorbed thirty-two smaller railway companies embracing practically all the Welsh railways and the whole of the railway-owned docks in South Wales. At the Grouping it had 8,000 miles of track, 1,500 stations and halts, over 3,900 locomotives and over 10,000 coaches, and during the last years before Grouping the total number of engine miles run was 86,309,020. A great deal has been said and written about the 'Great Western Tradition', the saying and writing depending to some degree on whether one considered the concern to be 'God's Wonderful Railway' or the 'Great Way Round'. But, there is no doubt at all

that there *was* a tradition and it *was* a magnificent railway — stubborn to the end in that even during the early days after nationalisation it could still be thought that there were five Regions of British Railways, and the Great Western Railway.

So, the Great Western was different; indeed, it was different from the very beginning in that it was built to the unusual gauge of 7ft. This was due to the imaginative thinking of its first great engineer, Isambard Kingdom Brunel (Mr Brunel Junior, as the Annals of Bristol describe him). The selection of that young man and its momentous consequences was made by Bristol men in the year 1832, the year of the Great Western's birth, and by 1835 the decision was made to construct the line to the 7ft gauge. Those were early days, and although George Stephenson was advocating one gauge for all railways laid down in Britain, Brunel so convinced his board of the superiority of his proposals that he won the day.

Below: Great Western 2-6-2T No 4555, built at Swindon in 1924, and now owned by Dart Valley Railway, at Alverley Colliery, Severn Valley, in September 1965. *P B Whitehouse*

Bristol later had some cause to regret the decision, for much of the city's trade was with the Midlands, and the use of the broad gauge meant railway frontier points with other companies at places such as Worcester, Warwick and, in particular, Gloucester. In fact, so bad did matters become that the delays in transhipment forced merchants to send their wares for foreign lands via London or Liverpool, where no such problem arose.

By 1846 the Government had put the Gauge Act through parliament forbidding anything but the standard 4ft 8½in for use on any new railways. The Great Western then had 270 miles of broad-gauge line; it reached from London to Bristol and on to Exeter. Further extensions took it to Penzance, Haverfordwest, Shrewsbury, Hereford, and Salisbury. Mixed - gauge tracks were laid from Oxford through Birmingham to Wolverhampton. By 1859 the maximum mileage of the broad gauge had been reached, and slowly the standard gauge took over. Brunel himself died the same year at the early age of fifty-three, only months after the Prince Consort had opened his magnificent bridge over the Tamar at Saltash.

In the early days of railways there were great opportunities, and in 1837 Brunel had taken on a young man of 21 as his Locomotive Engineer — Daniel Gooch, who was to serve the company for fifty-two years, ending up as Sir Daniel and its Chairman. By 1846 Gooch had designed and built at the new works at Swindon the magnificent express engine aptly named *Great Western,* which was to be the prototype of the class which served the company during the whole of the broad-gauge era.

It was Gooch who steered the company through the years of change—he, more than any other man helped to bring Brunel's dream of the broad gauge to fruition and almost completion. For speed and comfort as well as power no standard-gauge engine of 1850 could approach those of the Great Western, but Gooch realised that the ultimate success and perhaps salvation of the company depended on co-operation with standard - gauge concerns, such as the Midland and the London & North Western, which connected with his own railway. He remained convinced that the broad gauge was the better system, but common sense prevailed. Gooch died in 1889 when his own eight-foot - single - driver locomotives were still taking the expresses out of London. Three years after his death the very last broad-gauge train left Paddington for Penzance and an era was over.

The Edwardian years were those of development and consolidation. The Great Western was primarily a railway of the West of England, the Midlands and South Wales, and its mileage in the London area was small compared with the others. It was a line which served the less-developed parts of the country, where it was the main employer, albeit a disciplined but benevolent one. Among its staff the soft burr

of Devonshire, Wiltshire and Gloucestershire mixed with the broader Black Country dialect and the Welsh lilt. It built up a loyalty which politics could not break—it was the Great Way to the West and to Wales—so its publicity organisation told the world as far back as 1905.

By 1910 the wind of change had begun to blow strongly and the railway began to implement a huge modernisation plan, organised as a two-fold operation. The first was the new lines which were planned and built to straighten out the old Great Way Round and effectively to compete with the Midland from Bristol to Birmingham and later the London & North Western from London to Birmingham. The long-awaited straightening of the line to South Wales via Badminton was also completed. The second was in the locomotive department, and was perhaps the more radical. It certainly affected Great Western locomotive designs and classes for the rest of its existence; it also influenced considerably locomotive design and practice in Britain for at least thirty years.

During the later years of the nineteenth century, the whole of the locomotive design, construction, maintenance and running had been under the charge of William Dean, with senior assistant George Jackson Churchward as second in command. Dean's health had not been good and during his last years Churchward had virtually assumed control, with the full authority of the GWR locomotive committee of the board of directors. During that period Churchward laid down the foundations of the locomotive policy to be followed, and which *was* followed for a quarter of a century and more. It was a radical departure from precedent, but it worked. Some of the basic thinking was American.

The new policy was to produce a boiler design which was extremely sound and capable of being reproduced in a considerable range of standard capacities, and thus to lead to a general standardisation of locomotive stock. Once the new boiler (which was coned) was settled, Churchward turned his thoughts to the re-design of the front end, developing principally an internal streamlining designed to pass the necessary large volumes of steam freely through the valves and cylinders. It involved a new arrangement of valve motion which proved most effective and by 1902 the first of the big 4-6-0 express passenger engines had been built at Swindon and put to work.

Churchward next began a scheme for replacing the many and varied classes of older engines by modern locomotives of as few different types as possible. Between 1903 and 1911 the programme was completed and nine new standard classes were constructed and put into use. They included a two - cylinder 4-6-0 (Saint class), a 4-4-0 (County class), a 2-6-0 (43XX class), a 2-8-0 (28XX class), a 4-4-2 tank (22XX class), two classes of 2-6-2 tank (31XX and the small-wheeled 45XX), a 2-8-0 tank (42XX class) and a four-

cylinder 4-6-0 (Star class), which formed the basis of all Great Western motive power for the future.

The Grouping had little effect on the Great Western locomotive scene, apart from the absorption of engines from the various Welsh lines. The older and smaller classes of Welsh engines were rapidly withdrawn; the more-modern and efficient locomotives were equipped with standard GWR boilers and boiler fittings. The Midland & South Western Junction Railway, also absorbed by the GWR, had its locomotives treated similarly.

Shortly before the Grouping, G J Churchward retired, having left his mark on Swindon for all time. He was succeeded by C B Collett, who continued in his footsteps, providing the famous Castles (which were really modernised and modified Stars) Halls (which were smaller-wheeled Saints) and hundreds of little 0-6-0 pannier tanks which were developments of Dean's old 0-6-0s of the 23XX class. Other new classes and improvements on the old included the 51XX 2-6-2 tanks, the taper - boilered 0-6-0s of the 22XX class and the South Wales 0-6-2 tanks of the 56XX class.

So successful were the Castles that both the LMS and the LNER borrowed examples for test running in the 1920s, the results going a long way towards changing the course of locomotive development on both railways. The Castle had appeared in 1923 and in 1927 the first King was completed at Swindon. Not that any deficiency had been found in the Castle class, but an extra-powerful machine was required to deal with the heaviest West of England and Birmingham trains. At the time of building, the King was the most-powerful locomotive in Britain. Both Castles and Kings were finished in the ornate livery of green and polished brass so beloved of the Great Western over the years.

By 1941 Collett had been succeeded by F W Hawksworth, who introduced the two - cylinder County class 4-6-0s, with boiler pressure of 280lb per square inch, which carried the Great Western banner high into the post-war era. Conditions had deteriorated considerably during the war, and the Counties were unable to show their prowess as well as might have been hoped. Other innovations made after the war included the conversion of some Halls and other classes to oil burning, but because of difficulties with the then almighty dollar and the need to use home-produced fuel, this was not continued. Another was the experimentation with gas turbine locomotives, described in a previous chapter. Two engines, roughly of the power classification of the Castles, were built and passed into the era of nationalisation; the experiment was not conclusive.

The Great Western was one of the first of Britain's railways to introduce a system of automatic train control (the North Eastern also had an automatic warning alarm). The system introduced by the

GWR as early as 1905 was simple, enterprising and safe. It was the precursor of the automatic warning device at present used on British Railways and it went a long way towards ensuring that the Great Western was one of the safest lines in the country. The primary object of the system was to give audible warning to a driver when his train was approaching a distant signal in the on position, and in the event of it being disregarded, automatically to apply the brakes to ensure that the train pulled up before the home signal was reached. Another distinctive audible indication was given in the cab when the distant signal was off.

The Great Western was always noted for fast running and as early as 1848 broad-gauge trains were booked over certain sections at an average speed of nearly 57 miles per hour. Some of the well-known named trains included the Flying Dutchman, at 11.45 from Paddington to the South West, and the Zulu, at 15.00 from Paddington to reach Exeter in $4\frac{1}{4}$ hours. By 1904 Plymouth was reached non-stop from Paddington with long stretches booked at over 60mph. The year 1906 saw the opening of the shortened route via Castle Cary, and slip coaches for Taunton and Exeter were put on the down trains. Over the years, slip coaches were a regular feature of Great Western express running and they did not finally pass out of use until the end of the 1950s. The run from Swindon to Paddington was for a long time the fastest booked start-to-stop run in the British Isles.

There is one special run which must be mentioned — the record - breaking journey made by the Ocean Mail train from Plymouth to London in May 1904. The train from Plymouth to Bristol was

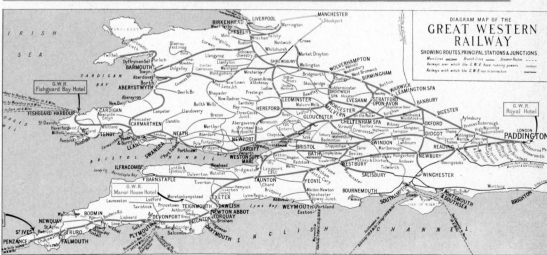

Facing page: Roll of Honour of GWR casualties in the 1914-18 war. *J R Batts*

Above left: One of the famous Castle class of the 1920s: No 4079 'Pendennis Castle' on the Birkenhead Flyer in March 1967. *J A Bingham*

Top: Imposing front end of 'Pendennis Castle', at Southall in August 1965. *M Pope*

Above: Principal routes and stations of the Great Western Railway. *P B Whitehouse*

made up of five eight-wheeled vans headed by locomotive No 3440 *City of Truro* and timed by that doyen recorder of the day, Mr Charles Rous-Marten (though some students of locomotive performance doubt the accuracy of his recording on that occasion). During the descent of Whiteball bank the maximum speed reached, according to Rous-Marten, was 102.3mph, the highest recorded until the 112mph by the LNER A4 *Silver Link* in 1935.

Of all the Great Western expresses two stand out—the Cornish Riviera Limited and the Cheltenham Flyer. The former left Paddington at 10.30 each day until May 1, 1972, when it was retimed at 11.30. The Ten-Thirty Limited, as it was known on the railway, was one of Britain's most famous trains. South Wales to Newport, Cardiff and Swansea, and northwards to Banbury, Birmingham and Wolverhampton were all well served by fast and comfortable Great Western trains. Beyond Swansea to the west and Wolverhampton to the north, the expresses usually became semi-fast trains, as they did beyond Plymouth into Cornwall. Once the Bicester cut-off had been built, two-hour expresses vied with the North Western to Birmingham over a generally harder route, but it was the only really competitive main line the Great Western had. The line from Shrewsbury to Hereford was joint with the LNWR and some of its trains were also smartly timed.

Top: Up Cambrian Coast express behind No 6016 'King Edward V' in Saunderton cutting. *M Pope*

Above centre: Memorial tablet to I K Brunel on his Royal Albert Bridge at Saltash. *R C H Nash*

Above: The preserved Dean Goods 0-6-0 No 2516, representative of a numerous and successful GWR class, in GWR Museum, Swindon. *R C H Nash*

Of the absorbed companies, trains of the Midland & South Western Junction from Cheltenham to Andover, those of the Cambrian from Machynlleth to Pwlhelli and Aberystwyth, and the little Wantage tram from Wantage Road to Wantage, all ambled. In South Wales the business was mainly freight, and coal at that, train after train running loaded down the valleys behind varieties of 0-6-2 tanks. There were Barry engines, Port Talbot engines, Rhymney engines and Cardiff engines, and out of the smoke and into the hills

there were the Brecon and Merthyr engines. It was quite a collection.

The Great Western's hub for mechanical matters was Swindon, but even before the "Absorption" it had smaller out-stations, the principal ones in later years being at Wolverhampton, which dealt with the Northern division, and Caerphilly which looked after South Wales. The Cambrian's works were at Oswestry, which to the end dealt with most of the engines on that section.

From the point of view of way and works, the Great Western had a number of unique and interesting items. The Severn tunnel, with its huge beam pumping engines, was the longest underwater tunnel in the world, while Brunel's timber viaducts in Devon and Cornwall were, to say the least, extremely handsome, as was, and is, the Saltash bridge across the Tamar, and a similar though smaller structure over the Wye at Chepstowe. The Cambrian brought in that long timber viaduct over the Mawddach at Barmouth, ending with a steel swing structure hardly ever used, though it *was* swung for the making of a film *The Ghost Train* in the early 1930s.

Compared with the LMS and the LNER, the Great Western owned few hotels and even fewer ships. Paddington, of course, had the Great Western Royal Hotel and Weymouth served the Channel Islands by Great Western ships. But like the LNER the company considered itself to be a 'royal' line, carrying the Crown — Royal funeral specials tended to start at Sandringham and end up at Windsor; special plaques and headlamps were kept for such sad occasions.

To conclude, there was one further thing that the Great Western did superbly well— it sold itself not only to the travelling public, but to the public at large. Its staff were smartly dressed, and one always *felt* that they were efficient, and the public relations department carefully fostered that image. This was especially so during the period between the wars when it seemed almost a crime to go to 'Glorious Devon' in any other way than by Great Western train — and if you were lucky enough to travel on the Cornish Riviera Limited, the Torbay Express or the Cornishman, then that really *was* something.

The Great Western produced books of engine classes, names and numbers, books on its glories such as the Ten-Thirty Limited, the Cheltenham Flyer and Locos of the Royal Road—all for a shilling, and really superb jig-saw puzzles of its trains, engines and the places of tourist interest it served—150 pieces of plywood for two shillings and sixpence. Above all it produced the great thick handbooks on the areas it served, full to the brim with information and advertisements, called *Holiday Haunts*. Without doubt it was an enterprising railway and of the big four it was the Great Western which produced results for its shareholders—not as much as one might have liked, but it produced them, to the end.

Railways of Scotland

Above: Wemyss Private Railway 0-6-0ST
No 16 at Methil, Fife, hauling coal to
Wellesley Colliery for washing in March
1970. *R Lush*
Below: Ballochmyle viaduct, the
biggest stone arch in the world when built,
and probably still. *D Cross*

LET ME GIVE YOU four names: Locke, Mitchell, Foreman and Grainger; engineers all, but even the intelligent student of railways could be forgiven for asking who was Grainger? These four men shaped the railway map of Scotland. Joseph Locke had much practice in such things with the Grand Junction and Lancaster and Carlisle line under his belt, he was already well known as the sun rose on the Scottish railway scene 130 odd years ago. Joseph Mitchell's hour was to come later when his burning vision and 'eye' for the country blazed the most romantic of all Scottish railways across the great hills from Inverness to Perth, the line known as the Highland, a great name for a very great railway. Charles Foreman was the calculator to the romanticism of Mitchell and his West Highland, though a great conception superbly engineered, somehow lacked the all-out challenge to nature that Mitchell tackled on his line through the Grampians. But who was Grainger? In a purely Scottish context the answer is the greatest of the four. Much of the Edinburgh & Glasgow was his, the Edinburgh & Berwick was all his. . . . Fife knew of his ways and Galloway felt the sure touch of his son, but his greatest and most lasting monument is the Nith Valley line of the old Glasgow & South Western, with its wonderful use of the landforms—a trait shared by Locke—and its great viaducts.

Most of the early railway civil engineers had their traits; Locke loathed tunnels and come to that Mitchell did not much like them either. Stephenson and Brunel were rather worried by grades but Grainger loved viaducts, he must have done for he could have avoided many of them. The sun shone through the Box tunnel on Brunel's birthday—or so they say. I have never heard even the most dedicated G&SW man suggest that the sun shone across Ballochmyle Viaduct on Grainger's. But the great stone viaducts of the G&SW, and Bathgate and Linlithgow on the Edinburgh & Glasgow, were Grainger's 'masons mark'. His lines were superbly laid out, taking advantage of every twist and turn of the countryside; his great bridges were superbly built, for 120 years after their construction they were carrying engines as heavy as the whole trains they were designed to take. Yet for all his work on Scottish railways he is nearly completely unknown. Could it be because his works grew naturally from the land they crossed and in the fullness of time have become very much a part of that landscape? We tend to remember the despoilers of our environment and not the improvers.

However, for an understanding of the railways of Scotland we must go back before those four great engineers . . . back to the Duke of Portland who used his money to build a railway from Kilmarnock to the port of Troon on the Ayrshire coast in 1808; it was a well-laid-out railway and much of it is still the present Brassie Junction to Kilmarnock line. The Duke of Portland's Railway, as it is known to the present day, was built to link a few small and rather scattered coal mines around the western edge of Kilmarnock with the port of Troon. It was originally of 4ft gauge with a branch of 3ft 4in gauge joining it about halfway to the coast at Drybridge (the history of the branch is lost in antiquity, but it must have been a unique gauge anywhere). The railway opened with horse traction on plate rails, but about the year 1817 a steam locomotive, thought to have been of George Stephenson's design, was tried, with disastrous results on the track.

Although built as a coal-carrying line, passengers were conveyed from the start, so long as nobody in authority was looking. In 1837 an Act enabled it to be worked by locomotives and carry passengers, from which one can assume that the track had been considerably improved and probably converted to standard gauge. Nine years later it was leased to the infant Glasgow, Paisley, Kilmarnock & Ayr Railway and thus became a founder unit of the Glasgow & South Western. For a number of years the Duke of Portland's line was the prototype of infant railways in Scotland—built locally to serve local needs. Until recently the original station house at Troon harbour stood to the east of the present lines, but it has now been demolished, for no very good reason other than a hatred of a past more efficient and tasteful than the architecture of today.

Chronologically the next railway in Scotland was the Monkland & Kirkintilloch, again a local line and again built to carry coal from pits near Monkland to a basin on the Forth and Clyde at Kirkintilloch. This 11-mile-long standard-gauge line was started in 1824 and worked by locomotives from the outset. Despite being absorbed by the North British latterly, a mile of the original formation is to this day part of the main line from Carlisle to Perth.

Two years later came the inception of no less than three railways in Scotland. The most notable was the Garnkirk & Glasgow, a standard-gauge line linking the Monkland & Kirkintilloch with St Rollox (Glasgow). Again easy conveyance of coal from the Monkland pits to Glasgow was the stimulus for the line, but passengers were carried from the start and so many people think it was Scotland's first railway.

The other two lines authorised in 1826 were on the east side of the country. The Edinburgh & Dalkeith was mostly a horse-worked line built to bring coal to Edinburgh from Dalkeith. The Edinburgh end had a rope-worked incline powered by a stationary steam engine. Part of the line was to survive to become part of the famous Waverley Route of the North British and later of the LNER. The third line, the 4ft-gauge Dundee and Newtyle, was the strangest of them all. It was a freak from the word go; there was no coal at stake and there was not very much else for that matter. The line was made up of several inclined planes worked by stationary steam engines built locally, plus some short level stretches worked by horses. Ultimately it became part of the Caledonian, not I suspect as they wanted it but simply to keep the North British from getting it, for that is what Scottish railway politics were all about. Strange to say this Cinderella among railways lasted into British Railways days, albeit rather altered in route, but it has gone now. The year 1827 might be considered the last year in which the strictly local railway was suggested; after that railways tended to have a wider concept, and the age of the great trunk line was at hand. The only Scottish line started in 1827 was the Ardrossan & Johnstone, with the

aim of linking the port of Ardrossan on the Ayrshire coast with the Paisley canal at Johnstone. It got no farther than six miles, to Kilwinning, where it was able to tap the northern fringe of the Ayrshire coalfield; thereafter the proprietors found that they could make money by carrying coal to the coast with horse transport and rather lost interest in going any farther. When the Glasgow, Paisley, Kilmarnock & Ayr was opened in 1840 the stunted spur of the Ardrossan line was linked with it and steam locomotive traction began.

In the 1830s, the decade which produced the skeleton of the English railways (the Newcastle & Carlisle, the London & Southampton, the London & Birmingham and the Great Western, for example) there was a strange pause in Scottish railway development. A few minor branches were constructed to feed into lines built a decade earlier, many of them in the Dundee area and built to varying gauges. The one line whose coming cast important shadows before it was the Edinburgh, Leith & Newhaven, formed in 1836. But if there was a hiatus in railway development during the 1830s, it does not mean that nothing was being done. The Scots were fighting among themselves, not only over what was to be done but about how to do it. There was Nithsdale versus Annandale for the main line from Carlisle to Glasgow, surely the classic case of all railway rows, especially as in the end both were built.

By 1840 Scotland was trembling on the brink of the great trunk lines to link Glasgow or Edinburgh with the South; stimulus was given by the inception in 1838 of the Edinburgh & Glasgow line, which can fairly lay claim to the title of Scotland's first 'main' line and was destined to become a founder part of the North British. It was the Edinburgh & Berwick part of this consortium that was the first railway across the border in 1844; though only on a technicality, as the border was not the natural barrier of the River Tweed but a point two miles north of the town of Berwick-on-Tweed, owing its existence to the antics of sundry border wars.

To the south of the Tweed there was a power that did stop the territorial ambitions of the North British and initiate a running sore for many years. George Hudson, flushed with success in various lines in the Midlands, cast eyes across the border, looking on the infant North British as a ripe plum ready to drop into his lap. He miscalculated, as the hard-headed North British directors were unwilling to part with their bawbees for pieces of embossed paper—how right they were! In later years the NB was to spend much time and substance trying to get its fingers into England; it managed it at Carlisle and at Silloth—that ephemeral Southampton on Solway, and even waved a digit at Hexham. It would have been far more profitable had it stayed at home. But at least the North Eastern, tainted by the goings-on of the notorious Hudson, never got to Scotland and after all, to a Scot, what better reason

was there for building a railway than to stop someone else doing so?

Nothing like the financial bickerings that clouded the early days of the North British tarnished the rise of its great rival to the west, the Caledonian. This was an aristocrat among railways; not for nothing did it appropriate the Royal Arms of Scotland for its crest. Certainly it had the statutory smattering of squabbling politicians at the outset, but it overcame them as it overcame Beattock. To this day it is a disputable point whether the line over Beattock should ever have been built; there was a lot to be said in favour of the Nithsdale route. A link with Edinburgh was the clinching argument for Annandale and I wonder how many people realise that the summit of the line from Carstairs and the Scottish capital, near Cobbinshaw, rises to within 100ft of Beattock. Locke was the engineer of the 'Caley' line and a splendid job he made of it, even if in some ways Grainger's Nith Valley line was the finer aesthetically. But Grainger had already had a lot of practice in Scotland with the Edinburgh & Glasgow and the Edinburgh & Berwick lines. The Caledonian line from Glasgow to Carlisle was opened throughout in 1848.

Two years later the Nithsdale line of the Glasgow & South Western was opened from Glasgow to Gretna Junction, with running powers over the 'Caley' from there to Carlisle. The Duke of Portland's railway had certainly grown, for the Nithsdale

route was the outcome of that line, plus the Glasgow, Paisley, Kilmarnock & Ayr blending into the Glasgow & South Western. It was this infant company that for years had fought against the Caledonian Annandale route. It is very much in the Lowland Scots character when the decision goes against you to build your line none the less; British Rail must appreciate the fact today, for while the Caledonian line is electrified, much of the traffic from Glasgow to the south goes down the Nith Valley. Thus by 1850 the main lines from Scotland to the south were in existence. Then, 12 years later the North British Railway's long, lonely and lovely Waverley route was completed from Edinburgh to Carlisle, but it could never seriously be considered an Anglo-Scottish main line, and significantly has been the first to be closed and lifted in 1971/72.

North of the Lowland valley railway development was slower, lacking the stimulus of communication with England. Even so two companies, the Scottish Central and the Scottish North Eastern,

had formed a line between Glasgow and Aberdeen in 1848. Our old friend the Dundee & Newtyle found itself at the centre of a burst of railway development round Dundee and along the Angus coast, initially all at differing gauges bearing no relationship to any other railways of that time. Ultimately the trouble was sorted out, with little credit to the Dundee & Newtyle which by that time was getting rather out of its depth. Railways in Fife were like the mythical Topsy and 'just growed'. The trouble with Fife was that it was surrounded on three sides by water and on the fourth by the Scottish Central/Caledonian; there could have been more sympathetic surroundings. With one exception before the construction of the great bridges across the Tay and Forth estuaries, the railways of Fife were localised and based on coal, with no more than a rather tenuous idea of a north-south trunk route.

They all ultimately fell into the North British camp and the reason for that is interesting. Among the lines started in 1836 was the Edinburgh, Leith & Newhaven;

now it was a very strange line, starting at right angles from the present Waverley Station and dropping on a cable-worked incline through the notorious Scotland Street tunnel to Leith and then by locomotives along the coast to Granton and ultimately Newhaven. From there contact was made with Fife by a ferry to Burntisland. In 1850 this line attained immortality by innovating the first train ferry in the world between Newhaven and Burntisland with the steam ship *Leviathan*. This vessel carried only goods wagons and the passengers had to detrain and travel in some degree of discomfort, as before. Their ordeal might have been mitigated had they known that the ship was designed by Sir Thomas Bouch, whose subsequent efforts in estuary bridging were rather less than successful. The great bridges were bound to come and when they did the whole pattern of Scottish railway building fell into place.

So in the year 1850 the basic railway pattern in southern Scotland was more or less established; certainly many branches remained to be built and much bickering

Far left: An Aberdeen-Edinburgh train behind a Class 40 diesel passing Princes Street gardens approaching Waverley station in May 1965. The red ballast came from a Carstairs quarry. *D Cross*
Above: Bridge of the Clyde Valley line near Crawford with BR standard Class 5-hauled northbound goods train in March 1964. *D Cross*
Left: Glenfinnan viaduct at the head of Loch Sheil on the Mallaig extension; it was the first major concrete viaduct in Britain. *J R Batts*
Right: No 46254 'City of Stoke on Trent' climbing Beattock bank with a Birmingham-Glasgow express in 1962. *D Cross*

was to come on the Clyde coast or Galloway. North of a line from Glasgow to Aberdeen there was nothing other than the Scottish North Eastern making ineffectual eyes at Dunkeld. Two of my four great Scottish railway engineers were still waiting in the wings, and sadly the other two, Locke and Grainger, were dead. The key to the great romantic lines to the far north and west of Scotland lay in the tightly knit County of Aberdeen and the Great North of Scotland railway. For the last five years of the 1840s rumblings were made to form a railway to serve the north-eastern parts of Aberdeenshire, but those concerned fell a' feuding and a' fussing more than most of the Scottish railway founders and it was not till 1852 that start was made on this railway.

Its tempestuous birthpangs carried on into its working life, for it ever there was a thoroughly cantankerous railway it was the Great North of Scotland. It fought with its neighbours, it fought with its shareholders, it was lampooned by many early railway writers—and then it turned about and put on its finest raiment for taking the Queen to Balmoral. Above all it fought with certain gentlemen in Inverness, which was a mistake, for initially those gentlemen simply wanted to get from Inverness to London in a reasonable degree of comfort . . . possibly even spending the odd sovereign in Aberdeen on their way. But that the Great North would not allow and from such an attitude the Highland Railway was born.

To those of us who know the Scottish railways mile by mile and sleeper by sleeper, the Highland is the most Scottish of them all. It was born in trouble, it challenged the toughest that nature could throw against it, it lived and worked on a shoestring but produced two of the most remarkable classes of locomotive ever built in Britain; even more surprisingly it never produced a dud—a proud boast that could not be upheld by any other company. Above all else it produced the man for the job of driving that great main line through the Grampians, Joseph Mitchell. In stating that the Highland was born out of the cantankerousness of the Great North, I must sound like Schiller's 'The Star that gave us Birth has had elsewhere its setting'. In many ways this was true, but after one or two severe doses of purgative the GNSR served its part of Aberdeenshire well; it also weaned two notable locomotive engineers, Manson and Pickersgill.

The Highland was a unique line for Britain as it was built to open up the countryside and the only main centres of population it had to link were Inverness and Perth. It grew from the Inverness & Nairn, a line built in protest against the acrimonious antics of the Great North, but which got as far as Keith due to the inefficiency and bickering of the latter. The ground along the Moray coast was flat, but between there and Perth there was the great barrier of the Grampians. Mitchell had only one option and that was up and over, which, making use of every river valley

and every pass he could find, he did superlatively well. The Highland, unlike many lines in the Scottish mountains, was laid out to main-line standards. Its limiting factor was long fierce grades and not the curves or skimped construction of so many mountain lines. Moreover it was built in a remarkably short time considering the terrain.

Once Inverness was linked with the south the opening up of the country could begin. Came the Inverness-Wick, a long meandering line but tapping every established centre of population; the Dingwall & Skye to open up the islands and the far north-west; and many shorter branches—to Dornoch, to the Black Isle and smaller places like Burghead. The Highland Railway was the antedote to the Highland Clearances of a century before and strange to say for much of its life showed a profit.

In the years following the consolidation of the main lines to the south and the inception of the Highland, other attempts were made to open up the Highlands of

Scotland. The Callander & Oban line, in a rather scratchy way under the wing of the Caledonian from the outset, linked Oban with the south. After much bickering Stranraer came into the pattern of Scottish railways involving both the Midland and the LNW on the road from Dumfries—an unholy alliance formed only because they had heard that the Great Northern was interested. In face of such an insult even the 'Caley' and the G&SW buried the hatchet for a short while, though once dug up again the hatchet was all the sharper for its interment. The 'Caley' and the 'Sou West' went in for some very competitive railway buildings round Muirkirk; at one stage even the remote hamlet of Leadhills was considered worthy of a G&SW branch over the Mennock pass. Luckily sanity stopped that one; although it would have been a most photogenic line, its profitability would have been more open to question.

There was yet one area on the Scottish map untrammelled by railways, and that was Fort William. Here I must introduce my fourth engineer, Charles Foreman. Ironically we first hear of him in the field of railway construction in connection with an underground railway in Glasgow for the Caledonian. Yet his greatest work was to be on the West Highland, a line whose sole purpose was to keep the Caledonian out of Lochaber. No! that is unfair. The 'Caley's' protege—the Callander & Oban—was going to build a branch from Oban to Fort William; its builders got to Balla-

chulish, took one look at the water and got cold feet. In that they were not alone, for only now are road builders tackling the task.

As far back as 1880 noises had been made about a Glasgow & North Western railway linking Glasgow not with Fort William as its main objective, but with Inverness. The Highland did not like that idea one little bit and the usual round of Parliamentary battles was fought, with no benefit to anyone apart from the lawyers. However, in 1889 an Act was passed authorising the building of a line from Craigendoran, north of Dumbarton, to Fort William and work started in October of that year. While the project was still officially known as the Glasgow & North Western, the more familiar name West Highland was used from the outset. It was to become a splendid line, built rather on the lines of the Dingwall & Skye with no pretensions to being a fast main line, as was the Highland between Perth and Inverness. This was rather surprising as the North British, which was the power behind the West Highland, had not forgotten about Inverness and there was to be more bickering later. But despite that it never got nearer than an abortive branch to Fort Augustus and the only extension of the West Highland was to the port of Mallaig, opened in 1901. With the opening of that extension the railway map of Scotland was complete; alas! the twentieth century has seen nothing but reductions.

Facing page: LNER Gresley Class V2 2-6-2 mixed-traffic locomotive on a Carlisle-Edinburgh goods train at Riccarton in December 1965. *R Bastin*

Above: Part of the industrial railway scene in Scotland. Two of the NCB's Barclay 0-4-0STs shunting spoil trains in an Ayrshire coalfield in March 1972. *D Cross*

The evolution of motive power on the Scottish railways is so closely bound up with lines south of the Border that it is necessary only to touch on the highlights. Initially, as in many cases elsewhere, single-drive and four-coupled locomotives of typical early Allan and Bury derivation were used, but soon the high curvature of many of the lines brought the bogie engine into prominence. Indeed, as early as 1871 the first typical British 4-4-0 with inside cylinders was produced by Thomas Wheatley for the North British; two of the engines were built, one of which—No 224 —achieved immortality of a kind by going down with the wreck of the first Tay Bridge, lying on the bottom of the river for a few months before being fished out, repaired and run for another 40-odd years.

One could say that the advent of the bogie 4-4-0 locomotive in Scotland came by accident; it was the need for better riding that gave it birth rather than the possibilities of a larger engine and greater power. That possibility was realised by the remarkable David Jones, engineer of the Highland Railway, and came about in an interesting manner. The Dingwall and Skye line has always been a brute to work

owing to its short sharp grades and continuous curvature and in 1873 Jones rebuilt a typical Allan 2-4-0 with a front bogie to try and improve the riding on the line to Strome Ferry. It was a great success and after rebuilding another of Allan's 2-4-0s he produced the very celebrated F-class 4-4-0s. The F-class engine was unusual for the day in having outside cylinders, as did most of the Highland engines throughout the company's career. But the Highland 4-4-0s also used the greater flexibility of the bogie engine and its longer frames to take a bigger boiler; when they took the road they were the largest passenger engines in Britain and they were also the most efficient.

The success of the Fs on the Highland started the fad for big-boilered 4-4-0s in Scotland, to be taken up by Drummond on the North British and the 'Caley', and Smellie on the Glasgow & South Western, though all the engines of the Lowland companies had inside cylinders—a style that culminated with the immortal Dunalastairs on the Caledonian. One of the ironies of the 1923 grouping, and the disastrous 1947 nationalisation, was that

the last series of Dunalastairs were to come back north to be the last 4-4-0s to work on Highland metals.

Because the Highland Railway was the northernmost and the most-isolated part of the British railway system, it is doubtful whether the Jones F class made any directly traceable impact on the rest of British practice; its importance was taken up by osmosis rather than deliberate policy. David Jones's next innovation hit the railway scene with all the shattering impact of a Pop group giving a brilliant performance of the Messiah, for in 1894 the Highland, so long taken by the Moons and Webbs of the country to be the Cinderella of companies, appeared with the first British 4-6-0, the famous Jones Goods. Nor was Jones content to produce one example to see if it would work; between September and November of 1894 the Highland took delivery of no fewer than fifteen of the engines, ordered from Sharp Stewart straight off the drawing board. For what in British locomotive circles was not merely a new class, but a wholly new concept, it was a staggering display of confidence—or an equally staggering gamble. Large, simple, rugged, with outside cylinders, these locos were a success from the word go, and while classed as his Big Goods there is no doubt that Jones thought of them as mixed-traffic engines, and as such they were used. The last and greatest offspring of the Jones Goods was the Stanier 5 which came to dominate the Highland line in its last years of steam; it was a fitting chicken to come home to roost!

A slight mystery about the Big Goods concerns its parentage. The designer was certainly Jones but in those days loco-motive engineers were tacitly allowed to do work 'out of hours' for various inde-pendent locomotive manufacturers and there is evidence that Jones had designed a 4-6-0 some years earlier for an Indian railway. The author's own opinion is that he also had a hand in a very early series of 4-6-0s for the New South Wales Govern-ment Railways; certainly many of that system's older 4-6-0s and 2-8-0s had a remarkably Highland look about them. Significantly both the Indian and Aus-tralian classes were built by Sharp Stewart and it does seem rather odd that fifteen engines of a revolutionary design for this country were turned out in a space of six months by that firm for the Highland, and what is more worked brilliantly with no modifications.

By a stroke of genius, the LMS pre-served one of the Jones Goods engines—No 103—and thanks to the efforts of Mr James Ness, sometime manager of British Railways Scottish Region, it was restored to Highland livery (probably the wrong one but a good try) and from 1955 ran excursions for about ten years. No 103 now rests uneasily in Glasgow Transport Museum; a museum is no place for such a treasure of industrial archeology and if ever the BR ban on steam excursions is lifted this is an engine that MUST run again. With his F and his Big Goods, Jones had scored the proverbial right and left in British locomotive engineering; it was a notable feat but as I said earlier men who live girt about with hills have to have vision. Whether he could have seen his vision of the F culminate in Maunsell's Schools class or his 4-6-0 in Stanier's Black 5 I know not—but he was the type of man who might have.

Compared with the revolutionary inno-vation on the Highland under Jones much of the rest of Scottish locomotive practice down to the 1923 grouping can be best described as sound. Value for money might have been the watchword, for the engines of the Scottish companies tended to be simple, capable of hard work and endless abuse and to have large capacity boilers wherever possible. Such was the secret of the success of the Drummond and McIntosh 4-4-0s on the Caledonian and of Manson's for the 'Sou-West'. The GNSR was a line differing in both terrain and type of traffic from the other four and so tended to stick with smaller-boilered 4-4-0s throughout its career, designed by two men covering a great span of years—Manson who went to the G&SW and

flowered and Pickersgill who went to the 'Caley' and wilted. Their small and elegant engines for the Aberdeen line worked it well for all its independent career and beyond—and they worked it economically. Economy is a trait of the Aberdonian.

The North British throughout its career stuck to four-coupled engines culminating in some very handsome Atlantics, and only representatives of that wheel arrange-ment in Scotland. The Highland quite naturally developed the 4-6-0 with the Castles (nearly pure Jones), the Clan Goods and the Clans of Cummings, and the ill-fated Rivers of F G Smith which, but for civil engineering ignorance of modern work in locomotive balancing, would have been the greatest Highland locomotive of them all.

The Glasgow & South Western around the turn of the century could well have been the most interesting of them all, for James Manson was not content with taking up Jones's F principles and pro-ducing a series of large and efficient 4-4-0s. He made locomotive history in 1897 when he produced Britain's first four-cylinder simple 4-4-0, beating Webb for the honour by a very short head. Alas, Manson's four-cylinder 4-4-0 could have worked better, but then so could Webb's! It was underboilered and when in 1922 Whitelegg, then the CME of the 'Sou-west', gave it a superheated boiler and modified the cylinders it became a reasonable locomotive. Manson also gave the G&SW a class of very handsome 4-6-0s on the Jones principle with outside cylinders, which had they all been superheated would have lasted far longer than they did. Peter Drummond came from Inverness in the last years of the independent G&SW and tended to make matters rather worse, so that the 'Sou-West' at the grouping in 1923 sank without trace; it was a sad end to a fiercely individual line.

The Caledonian in its last independent years faired little better. McIntosh carried the Scots precept of bigger boilers and better brakes to its limits with the inside-cylinder Cardean 4-6-0 and her sub-sequent sisters; he produced some of the finest 4-4-0s to run in the world, but the adherence to inside cylinders for big engines was a mistake. When Pickersgill tried to alter this with his 60-class engines and the ill-fated three-cylinder derivatives, the 'Caley' tradition was swamped by waves of Derby compounding and all. Strange to say, the Scots never tried compounding in locomotives, though their marine engineers were among the first in the world to apply the principle success-fully. Even stranger it was a Scot, Walter Mackersie Smith, who in association with the Worsdells on the North Eastern and latterly and more strikingly Deeley on the Midland, was responsible for the most successful application of compounding in Britain. Ironically enough, the 'Caley' and 'Sou-West' men got far better work out of the Midland compounds when they got to Scotland than was ever wrung from them on their home system.

After the grouping locomotive design passed south of the border, but it was a kindly transfer, for the CMEs of the LNER, and even more the LMS, served Scotland well. Many of Gresley's locos did splendidly between Edinburgh and Aberdeen, even if some of the Great Central's cast-offs were heartily detested. The contentious Cock o' the Norths were welcomed on the Aberdeen road by the drivers, if not by the permanent-way men. On the other side of the country the compounds were flogged to death, for to a driver among the great hills of Clydesdale that was what a locomotive was for. Then came the 'Crabs'—they got everywhere on the old LMS system but the Highland and the G&SW men took to them like ducks to water. Within a year of all steam going from the 'Sou-West' I knew many drivers who would take a Crab in preference to a Black 5 on a hard freight turn.

Still, if ever there was an ideal steam engine for Scotland it was the Stanier Black 5—how dramatically had the Jones Goods come home to roost. They worked nearly everywhere, apart from the North British, though in the twilight hours of steam over the Waverley route an Edin-burgh driver told me that one Black 5 on a goods was worth 'twa o' they damned things'; the locos so abused were the LNER A1 Pacifics! The Black 5s were even accepted on the West Highland, despite some unfortunate experiences with the B1s making the drivers rather suspicious of 4-6-0s, through a tendency

Above: Two of the preserved locomotives of pre-grouping companies, Caledonian No 123 and Great North of Scotland No 49, at Whithorn in 1962. *D Cross*

Facing page top: Workhorse of the Ayrshire coalfields, 'Crab' 2-6-0 No 42789 working coal empties at Falkland junction in November 1966. *D Cross*

Facing page lower: F Moore painting of a Caledonian 4-6-0 climbing Beattock. *Ian Allan Library*

Right: Class 29 NBL diesel No 6107 with an Oban-Glasgow train at Crianlarich Junction on the West Highland line in April 1967. *D Cross*

to slip on the banks. Some BR standard classes got to Scotland but were considered to be no improvement on the locomotives that were already there. Strange to say, the one standard class—the 9F 2-10-0s—that would have been ideally suited for many of Scottish steeply graded lines never came north. So to diesels and the philosophy of 'if one won't pull the train use two'. An expensive way of running a railway and the Scottish railways were nothing if not cost-conscious.

Finally to turn to the civil engineering works on the Scottish railways. In view of the country traversed they were remarkably few; there were no Tring cuttings or great embankments. There were remarkably few tunnels and of them the G&SW and North British had a near monopoly. How much of this was due to Locke's influence (for that gentleman loathed tunnels) and how much to good sound engineering that used the landforms without having to abuse them, is hard to say. Only in one form of civil engineering were the railways of Scotland pre-eminent and that was the great viaducts. The Forth and Tay bridges are world-famous, but not typical as they were designed specially to cover a special purpose.

Far more typical are Grainger's great stone viaducts of the Nith Valley line and the Edinburgh & Glasgow. The Caledonian had its own style with stone piers and metal girders, a feature of the Annandale route to the south and its branches.

The original main line of the Highland had few viaducts but the cut-off from Aviemore to Inverness by Carrbridge had two of the most massive and graceful structures in Scotland, at Tomatin and Culloden; the latter used conventional stone on a vast scale and the former a mixture of lattice girders on stone piers. For the bridges on the Far North lines anything went, stone where there was stone, or metal girders on stone bases rather reminiscent of the Caledonian in other places. In many ways the Tomatin viaduct could be considered the archetype of its contemporaries on the West Highland. Between Craigendoran and Fort William, Charles Foreman's slender lattice girder viaducts on their massive stone bases are the most distinctive feature of the line.

The Mallaig extension introduced a new feature in bridge building with the use of concrete for the curving viaduct across the head of Loch Shiel at Glenfinnan. There is a macabre story about this structure; during the pouring of the concrete a horse and cart are reputed to have slipped into one of the arches and to be entombed there to this day! It is a unique structure by British standards, born of necessity, for by the 1900s stonemasons were becoming scarce, as the brick buildings of the Victorian epoch replaced the more graceful stone of the Georgian. How lucky the early railways were in having such wonderful craftsmen at their disposal; it is very true that from 1850 onwards it was the engineers who produced more lasting memorials to our cultural heritage than the architects. In many cases it was the railways that gave them the stimulus. Men of vision, skilled craftsmen and good sound engineers made the Scottish railways what they were. They challenged a difficult terrain and beat it, but they never abused it; this was their genius and this their memorial.

Above: A Caledonian Class 72 Pickersgill 4-4-0, introduced from 1920, in spick-and-span BR livery and number. *J Adams*

Below: Most famous of the Scottish locomotive developments, the preserved Highland Jones Goods No 103 at Hurlford in June 1963. *D Cross*

Ancient Holmes J36 0-6-0 working alongside Class 37 EE diesel at Seafield colliery near Kirkcaldy in March 1967, three months after steam was officially withdrawn by BR in Scotland. *D Cross*

BRITISH RAIL IN PICTURES

Top: English Electric Type 3 Co-Co diesel-electric No D6894 leaving Sunderland with empty coal wagons in August 1967. *B Stephenson*

Left: English Electric Type 1 Bo-Bo de No D8127 passing Shap village with empty hoppers from Carlisle to Shap quarry in April 1967. *B Stephenson*

Bottom: British Rail's experimental gas turbine-powered APT (advanced passenger train) at the Derby Railway Technical Centre. *British Transport Films*

Above: SR 4VEP third-rail electric mu approaching Vauxhall from Waterloo. *British Transport Films*

Left: A Brush Class 47 diesel-electric Paddington bound with a passenger train, near Bath *British Transport Films*

Below: BR experimental 4PEP sliding-door emu for high-density service, at Shepperton. *J A Bingham*

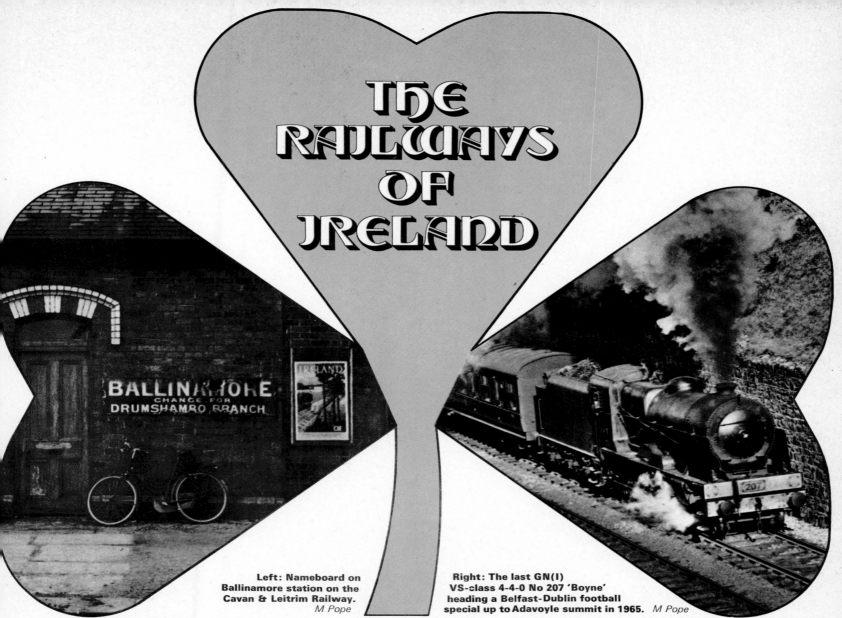

THE RAILWAYS OF IRELAND

Left: Nameboard on Ballinamore station on the Cavan & Leitrim Railway. *M Pope*

Right: The last GN(I) VS-class 4-4-0 No 207 'Boyne' heading a Belfast-Dublin football special up to Adavoyle summit in 1965. *M Pope*

IRELAND HAS ALWAYS been a great source of interest to both the railway historian and the seeker after the unusual, for its railways have, through political necessity, remained individualistic until very recent times. At the beginning, as in Britain, clusters of comparatively short sections of railway were planned and opened between centres of commerce—but, while Britain had only two gauges for its main lines, the standard Stephenson one of 4 feet 8½ inches, and Brunel's 7 feet of the Great Western, Ireland had virtually as many different gauges as it had counties. For example, the first section of the Ulster Railway out of Belfast was laid to 6 feet 2 inches gauge, the original gauge of the Dublin & Kingstown was 4 feet 8½ inches, and the Dublin & Drogheda projected a third gauge of 5 feet 2 inches.

Such a state of affairs could not be allowed to continue and consequently a Gauge Commission sat in 1845 to determine the matter, the Ulster and the Dublin & Drogheda Railways having asked for an adjudicator as the two lines had eventually to be joined. The Board of Trade put the inquiry into the hands of its Chief Inspecting Officer of Railways, who canvassed the opinions of most of the leading engineers of the day (except Brunel, who, it was considered, was too committed to be impartial). These pundits put forward 5 feet as the narrowest desirable gauge and 5 feet 6 inches as the widest. Having

obtained this information the Board of Trade, by carrying out a small arithmetical calculation, split the difference, coming up with the Irish Standard Gauge of 5 feet 3 inches, which was fixed by Act of Parliament in 1846.

Later, when it became policy to open up the poorer parts of the country by means of Light Railways, a further standard of 3 feet was introduced for the narrow-gauge lines. The origin of the 3-foot gauge as such is somewhat obscure, but it is thought that it was probably influenced by H Vignoles, the Engineer to the Isle of Man Railway in 1870. The first 3-foot gauge railway to be open to traffic was the Glenariff Iron Ore Company's line in 1873. Each narrow-gauge railway in Ireland was entirely local and even at the few places where they did meet, interchange of traffic was difficult, due to the varying levels of buffers and couplings adopted by the companies concerned. Most of the narrow-gauge lines were subsidised by the Government and many were made a charge on the county rates, which caused plenty of argument and some trouble.

As with Britain, the various main line railway companies gradually amalgamated during the eighty-odd years from the Gauge Commission to Irish Independence, which roughly corresponded in date with the British grouping into four major companies. Naturally, the two main headquarters became Dublin and Belfast,

and the railways concerned linked those two principal towns with each other, and the larger centres of population such as Cork, Limerick, Galway, Sligo and Londonderry. In what is now Eire, the main companies were the Great Southern & Western (Dublin to Cork and the South West) the Waterford, Limerick & Western, the Dublin, Wicklow & Wexford, and the Midland Great Western which ran from Dublin west to Galway and Sligo. There was also the Cork, Bandon & South Coast Railway. The Great Northern of Ireland ran between Dublin and Belfast with a junction at Portadown to Londonderry, and a long branch west to Bundoran on the Atlantic Coast, while the Belfast & Northern Counties joined with the Midland Railway of England to exploit the Belfast-Londonderry territory. There was one other standard-gauge line of importance—the Belfast & County Down Railway, which served the county of that name with efficient and intensive suburban and local trains.

As time progressed the British and Irish companies formed loose alliances, particularly where cross-channel shipping services were concerned, the Midland, London & North Western and Great Western in particular, providing their own ships. The Midland, with its interest in the Belfast & Northern Counties, docked its ships at Larne, the North Western made a two-pronged attack by operating a Holyhead-Dublin service, and penetrating into

Above: Preserved GN(I) 4-4-0 No 171 'Slieve Gullion' at Coleraine shed in 1969, with a 2-6-4T at the coaling plant. *M Pope*

Left: Old Midland Great Western sign at Edgeworthstown station on the CIE in 1959. *M Pope*

Right: The Dublin & Blessington steam tramway at Blessington in June 1932. *H C Casserley*

Far right top: First railcar in the British Isles, by County Donegal Railway, pictured at Strabane in April 1948. *H C Casserley*

Far right bottom: Bulleid novelty designed for CIE in Ireland—a peat-burning steam locomotive with mechanical stoker and additional tender-wagon with ic-engine-powered fire blower. *T K Widd*

PUBLIC WARNING
BY
THE MIDLAND GREAT WESTERN
RAILWAY OF IRELAND COMPANY
TO
PERSONS TRESPASSING UPON THEIR
RAILWAYS AND TO PERSONS
ALLOWING THEIR CATTLE OR
OTHER ANIMALS TO TRESPASS
THEREON, THAT IF EITHER
SUCH TRESPASS BE COMMITTED
AFTER THIS WARNING, THE
OFFENDERS WILL BE PROSECUTED
UNDER THE MIDLAND GREAT WESTERN
RAILWAY OF IRELAND ACT 1903.
BY ORDER
MAY. 1909.

Ireland with its own Dundalk, Newry & Greenore Railway, with a port at Greenore. The Great Western met the Great Southern & Western at Rosslare, Waterford and Cork, the GSWR having absorbed the Waterford, Limerick & Western and other smaller railways at the turn of the century. The Dundalk, Newry & Greenore Railway was pure London & North Western, built to the 5 feet 3 inches gauge, even to Webb-designed Crewe-built 0-6-0 saddle tanks and six-wheeled coaches in 'Plum and spilt milk' livery.

The main-line companies in Ireland developed their motive power requirements on similar lines to those on the other side of the water in Britain, relying very much on the 2-4-0 and later the 4-4-0 for express passenger work, the 2-4-2 tank and the 4-4-2 tank for suburban trains, and the 0-6-0 for freight. The 2-6-0 became a mixed-traffic engine in the South and an express engine in the North, while a limited number of 4-6-0s was built for the Great Southern lines. Speed was never of the essence (except on the Belfast-Dublin services of the GNR) for, apart from the Dublin-Cork, Dublin-Belfast, and Belfast-Londonderry lines, single track was the norm. Of the respective locomotive engineers, perhaps Alexander Mac Donnell of the Great Southern & Western, who carried standardisation to considerable lengths, Cusack of the Midland Great Western, and Park and Glover of the Great Northern of Ireland stand out.

Considerable changes came to the railways after the advent of the 1914-18 war, when costs rose steeply and quite out of proportion to the meagre income from all but the busiest sections. The narrow-gauge lines suffered particularly badly. Matters were not made any better by the 'Troubles' and the Civil War, when considerable damage was done.

The year 1925 saw the grouping of railways in the Irish Free State under the banner of the Great Southern Railway—all lines were included in the merger, even those rural 3-foot organisations which were a necessary evil and a perpetual drain on finances. Certain railways crossing the border, in particular the Great Northern, retained their old identity, but partition went a long way towards that magnificent railway's eventual death in the 1950s. It also hastened the end of the two large narrow-gauge enterprises, the County Donegal Railways Joint Committee and the Londonderry & Lough Swilly Railway.

The railways in Ulster remained independent, though the Belfast & Northern Counties (which also owned the Bally-mena & Larne, and the Ballycastle branches built to the 3-foot gauge, plus the London-derry to Strabane line worked by the County Donegal) changed its name to the Northern Counties Committee of the London, Midland & Scottish Railway. The last-named concern also became the proprietor of the LNWR-sired Dundalk, Newry & Greenore which was another cross-border line. Customs at the border made journeys slow, and the traffic fair game for the intruding motor car and motor lorry.

The Great Southern Railway inherited a considerable variety of locomotive types and classes, and over 2,600 miles of trackage from its constituents. They included some notorious narrow-gauge lines; the West Clare, the Tralee & Dingle, the Schull & Skibbereen, and the Cork & Muskerry Railways, plus the suburban Cork, Black Rock & Passage Railway, and the Cavan & Leitrim serving Ireland's only commercial coal mine.

Very few new locomotives were built by the GSR because of the financial position of the company and the increasing inroads made on traffic by road competition. One class stands out in particular, the Wool-wich 2-6-0s which were kits of parts of standard locomotives of South Eastern & Chatham parentage made at Woolwich Arsenal. About a dozen of them had been ordered by the Midland Great Western prior to amalgamation and the Great Southern purchased 15 more. In 1939 came three large named 4-6-0s of the 800 class, and with the exception of the GWR Kings, they were for many years the most powerful engines in Britain and Ireland. The introduction of the 800s was intended to produce a considerable acceleration of the Dublin-Cork expresses and the new schedule was kept with power to spare. These engines were painted dark green in contrast to the dark grey of the general run of GSR locomotives. Railway services reached their peak in 1939 and some sharp timings were recorded on the Dublin-Cork main line.

The Great Northern was the second largest railway system in Ireland and the main connecting line between North and South with a total track mileage of 827. It was badly hit by partition as there were ten points where it crossed the boundary and customs formalities had an obviously detrimental effect on the timekeeping and speed of trains. The principal customs stations were at Dundalk and Goraghwood on the main line between Dublin and Belfast, and also on the Irish North Western section from Dundalk to Ennis-killen, as well as between Strabane and Londonderry. In its heyday the Great Northern owned over two hundred steam engines but nothing larger than a 4-4-0 or 0-6-0. The 4-4-0s introduced by Park were rebuilt and superheated by Glover, resulting in the magnificent inside-cylinder S class carrying the names of mountains, and the huge three-cylinder compounds, and later simples, with the names of birds of prey.

These big engines were introduced in 1932 to work the Dublin-Belfast Enter-prise express, and were limited to the main line because of their axle loading. Great Northern engines were painted sky blue and lined out in scarlet, and they looked magnificent at the head of their trains of varnished teak coaches. Like its more southerly and northerly neighbours, the Great Northern also had a finger in the narrow-gauge pie, sharing with the Mid-

Above: CIE (Cavan & Leitrim) 3ft-gauge No 3T locomotive (ex-Tralee & Dingle Railway) at Ballyduff in July 1958. *C F Firminger*

Left: Horse-tram on the Fintona line, part of the Great Northern system, in County Tyrone; the line closed in 1957. *P B Whitehouse*

Below: NIR'S new Enterprise '70 train at CIE's clean and colourful Connolly station, Dublin, in October 1970. *R C Flewitt*

Right: CIE diesel-electric locomotive No B113 at Limerick junction in July 1958. *C F Firminger*

Right below: A 1ft 10in-gauge 0-4-0T locomotive specially designed by Samuel Geoghegan for the extensive Guinness works lines in Ireland; it was in service from 1882 until 1950.
Arthur Guinness Son & Co (Dublin) Ltd

Above, top to bottom: Clogher Valley No 5 'Colebrooke' built by Sharp Stewart in 1887. *B Jackson*
CIE No 100 0-6-0T at Cork in 1959. *M Pope*
Midland & Great Western 0-4-2 'Dunsandle' built in Glasgow by Neilson in 1872. *B Jackson*
CIE No 470 4-6-0T on station pilot work at Cork in June 1959. *M Pope*

the Midland, Derby began to take a serious hand in the locomotive side, though, as with all things in Ireland at that time, progress until the late 1930s was slow. Gradually however, the old classes began to disappear and 5-foot 3-inch gauge versions of Midland class 2P 4-4-0s and 0-6-0 tanks began to come on the scene, the 4-4-0s being named after Castles.

The mid-'thirties, as with the other big two, produced a new express engine in a Derby-built 2-6-0 named after Hunts, Earls, Kings and Queens; they worked the principal Belfast-Londonderry trains to the end of steam. The last class of locomotive to come out of Derby was a 6-foot driving-wheel version of the LMS 2-6-4 tank. The year 1939 was again the peak period of express services when a timing of 60mph was in operation between Ballymena and Belfast on the Derry line. The NCC ran passenger services on two of its 3-foot gauge lines—the Ballymoney to Ballycastle, and the Ballymena & Larne. From 1928 until the introduction of the Greenisland loop on the main line in 1933, the Ballymena and Larne section ran *boat trains* with newly built first- and third-class corridor coaches with lavatories and electric light—an unheard of luxury on the narrow gauge.

The 1939-45 war had its effect on Irish Railways — those in the South suffering from the comparative isolation of Eire as a neutral country, and from a wartime shortage of fuel and materials, while the companies in the North, like their sisters in Britain, became overworked and undernourished. The situation was aggravated during the winters of 1946-47 due to coal troubles in England and many services were cut back 'temporarily' never to be resumed. 1945 saw the nationalisation of railways in the South in the form of Coras Iompair Eireann or the Transport Company of Ireland, while 1948 brought the end of the NCC with British railway nationalisation and the beginning of Ulster Transport.

Strangely enough, many of the narrow-gauge lines staggered into the 1950s, for in many parts of the country roads were still inadequate for lorry traffic. Of the lines to survive for a while, the two largest were the Londonderry & Lough Swilly and the County Donegal Railways. The former continued to run freight and the occasional excursion on its sections to Letterkenny and Buncrana until 1953, though the huge 4-8-0s built for the Burtonport extension (lifted beyond Gweedore during the war) rusted away unused. Occasionally the great 4-8-4 tanks came out for the Buncrana excursions at Bank Holiday periods but the freights were usually hauled by the 2-6-2 tanks. Now the Lough Swilly is a bus and lorry company, though retaining its grand railway title.

The County Donegal languished on until the close of 1959 when the last of the steam locomotive crews, the McMenamin brothers, worked the final train into Strabane by steam, instead of the usual

railcar, because of the crowds. The Donegal had made railway history by the introduction of petrol, and later, diesel railcars for passenger service in 1931, cuttings costs considerably and thereby saving the line for about thirty years more. Freight was hauled by the geranium-red 2-6-4 and 4-6-4 tanks, all named, and a heterogeneous collection of old coaches was kept for Bank Holiday passenger trains to Ballyshannon on the West Coast. They were the last steam-hauled passenger trains on the narrow gauge in Ireland, and were very popular excursions when many of the passengers were—as the Irish say—the better for drink.

The narrow gauge in the South had begun to wither in the late 'thirties when the Cork lines went, but the Schull & Skibbereen kept going until the coal shortage of 1947 and the infamous Tralee & Dingle, with its mountainous gradients and one-day-a-month operation, kept adventurous railroading alive until 1953. Of the two sections which remained, the West Clare based on Ennis, which took a circuitous route to Kilrush and Kilkee, succumbed to dieselisation (which did not save it) and the Cavan & Leitrim still brought the coal out of Arigna. Both were gone by autumn 1960 when the West Clare put up the shutters; the Cavan & Leitrim, with engines from the Tralee & Dingle and Cork, Blackrock & Passage, as well as its own, finished on March 31, 1959. With this passing a sometimes dramatic and mostly turbulent part of the railway story of Ireland went into history.

Since the nineteen-fifties Ireland's railways have gone into decline; dieselisation began early on the CIE—before it really caught on in Britain, and everything except the principal main lines has gone with the exit of steam. You can still go on the Radio Train to Killarney, take the Sligo and Galway expresses, a trip to Cork, or ride on the boat train to Rosslare; but the variety has gone for ever, though being Irish, untold legends have been left behind. The Great Northern is no more—circumstances leading from partition to the last war and its aftermath having bankrupted it. For a while both North and South combined to run the Great Northern Railway Board, but it became impossible to work. Now there are only the CIE and Ulster Railways combining to provide a Belfast-Dublin service, while the latter runs a very truncated system in the Six Counties—including one section of the old Belfast and County Down line to Bangor. Steam hung on by a thread in the North in the form of the 2-6-4 tanks, but by 1972 they too have finished their normal working life, and another chapter of Ireland's story is done.

Steam still lives on however, in preservation, for an S-class 4-4-0 resplendent in Great Northern sky blue and scarlet, No 171 *Slieve Gullion*, a Derby-built 2-6-4 tank, and an ex-Great Southern & Western J15 class 0-6-0 are kept in working order for the occasional special train.

land (later the LMS) of England the ownership of the County Donegal Railways Joint Committee. The Great Northern also owned and operated a unique branch line from Fintona Junction to Fintona, a distance of half a mile. The motive power was one horse, and the vehicle a double-deck tram which made connections with all trains at Fintona Junction.

The Northern Counties Committee served the northern part of the Six Counties, providing a service between Belfast and Londonderry, Coleraine, Portrush and Larne with the important mail and sea route via the latter port. After the acquisition of the Belfast & Northern Counties by

Above: GS&W 0-6-0 No 186 on an excursion in June 1972, near Listowel. *C J Gammell*

Right: UTA diesel mu train on the Enterprise Belfast-Dublin service at Poyntzpass in September 1967; one coach is in the blue-and-cream livery. *R C Flewitt*

Below: One of CIE's new air-conditioned trains. The coaches were built by British Rail Engineering and finished at Inchicore.
Coras Iompair Eireann

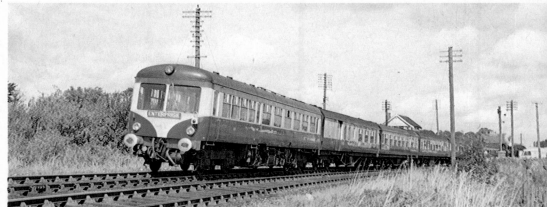

9
The Railways of Europe

FRANCE – FASTEST INTER-CITY

VITESSE, CONFORT, exactitude (speed, comfort, punctuality)—that is the French Railways (SNCF) claim for passenger services and more particularly for inter-city trains in France. In its current usage the term 'Inter-city' means fast and, usually, frequent day trains between big cities or other important centres on timings acceptable to travellers on business. Inter-city trains are often, but not always, first-class only and an extra fare is payable for travel by most of them; some are Trans-Europ Expresses (TEEs), described in a later chapter of this book. As examples, the summer-only gas turbine-driven multiple-unit trains between Paris and Trouville-Deauville (140 miles) on

the Normandy coast rank as inter-city, and so does the Paris-Marseilles-Riviera Mistral TEE that covers the 676 miles to Nice in just over nine hours.

Speed characterises inter-city trains in Great Britain, France and other Western European countries and many of them consist of or include specially comfortable vehicles. Punctuality is an aim, largely because of the competition of the private car and to a lesser extent of the airliner over inter-city distances, which can exceed 500 miles in France. Also, because the rolling stock is rostered to afford the highest possible mileages in a day, punctuality is important from the train operating aspect, for a late arrival might not allow enough time for cleaning and servicing the stock before its return journey, or cause a late start on the next rostered duty.

Many SNCF night trains are fast. The Palatino, which covers the 912 miles from Paris to Rome overnight in just over 14½ hours, takes 6 hours 40 minutes for the 432 miles from Paris to Modane, the

frontier station where Italian Railways (SF) takes charge of the train. This is an average speed of 64.8mph including one eight-minute stop and a 60-mile climb through the Alps up to Modane. The luxurious Blue Train is allowed 11 hours 19 minutes for the 676 miles from Paris to Nice—almost a mile-a-minute average— and it could easily be accelerated but for the need to allow sleeping-car passengers a good night's rest before reaching the Riviera resort of their choice.

Compared with Britain and Germany, really big towns in France are few and far between and with few exceptions the only routes which promise reasonable inter-city traffic in the specialist sense are those which radiate from Paris. During the last century the French railway companies, as they then were, made little attempt to run fast and frequent expresses between Paris and provincial cities comparable with those between London and, say, Manchester and Leeds (and in England there were services over competing routes). Before they were nationalised in 1938 the French

railways served fairly well-defined territories and there was little scope for competition, at least for inter-city traffic, except between Paris and Bordeaux, which were linked by both the Paris-Orleans (PO) and the State (Etat) Railways. There the competition resulted in some fast—for that period—services by both routes and, early in the century, led to the installation by the Etat of some of France's only locomotive water troughs to avoid wasting time at water columns.

Curiously, the only other French inter-city service before 1914 worthy of the name was on a non-competitive route— that of the Chemin de Fer du Nord (Northern Railway) between Paris and the Lille-Roubaix-Tourcoing conurbation, the biggest concentration of population in France apart from Greater Paris, and serving also Arras on the way. Also qualifying as inter-city were the Nord's day expresses between Paris and Brussels and Liège, where most of the fastest running over the Nord, the Belgian State and the Nord's Belgian subsidiary the Nord Belge, was

done by the French company. The day trains between Paris and Lyons, France's second city, were relatively infrequent and slow until after nationalisation, partly because the Paris Lyons & Mediterranean Railway (PLM) did not believe in speed and partly because the distance—318 miles—was thought more suitable for overnight business transits. The Chemin de Fer de l'Est did not provide a true inter-city service between Paris and Nancy (and Strasbourg after it was ceded in 1918) before nationalisation. The Etat, until its invigoration by an outstanding general manager, Raoul Dautry, in the 1930s, did not try to link Paris, Rouen and Havre by reasonably fast services, though eventually it ran some of France's first express diesel trains on that main line before the 1939-45 war. In steam days Toulouse, 440 miles, and Marseilles, 536 miles, from Paris, were considered too far for inter-city day journeys.

From the turn of the century there were a good many day expresses that did credit to the French steam power of the era. There were the Paris-Lille, Paris-Brussels, Paris-Liège and Paris-Bordeaux expresses; the Nord's boat expresses between Paris and Boulogne and Calais—some of the fastest trains in the world at that time, and over a difficult route; and (after 1918) the Est's Paris-Belfort-Basle expresses. Most of them competed for international traffic and indeed had done so ever since completion of most of the French trunk routes before the Franco-Prussian war of 1870. The Nord's Paris to Boulogne and Calais (for Folkestone and Dover) trains were in competition for Anglo-French traffic with those of the Etat between Paris and Dieppe (for Newhaven). The Est and the PLM offered competitive routes to large parts of Switzerland and, after the opening of the Simplon and Lötschberg tunnels in the Edwardian era, via Switzerland to Italy. The PO and PLM were rivals for the traffic to Barcelona via the Mediterranean frontier of Spain; the Chemin de fer du Midi handled both their traffics before they reached the border and competition was not acute.

None of those rivalries resulted in inter-city expresses as such. The Nord and the Est suffered badly during the 1914-18 war and they and the other French lines were slow in recovering even pre-war standards of speed. However, by the 1930s the Nord was running Paris-Lille expresses at something like a two-hour standard interval and taking 2¾ hours or slightly less for the 160 miles including two stops, to form the first real inter-city trains in France. The Paris-Bordeaux timing was cut to 6 hours 40 minutes for the 360 miles. The Flèche d'Or Pullman train was allowed 190 minutes for the 185 miles from Calais Maritime to Paris over a difficult route—like most of the Nord's routes in the allegedly flat North of France —but was not an inter-city train. The 1929-39 decade saw the introduction of many Pullman and other fast trains in France, most of them radiating from Paris and some using cross-country routes, but with few exceptions the inter-city routes remained Paris-Lille, Paris-Bordeaux and Paris-Rouen-Havre. At that time the PO and Midi were busy electrifying the Paris-Bordeaux-Irun (Spanish frontier) and Paris-Toulouse main lines, but until 1939 nearly all other French trunk lines were steam-worked, though a start had been made on the introduction of diesel traction and on one or two other main-line electrifications.

The principal railways were nationalised as the SNCF in 1938, which gave a fillip to electrification and the sharing of individual railway's technical know-how. The Midi, for instance, was a pioneer of electrification on its Pyrenean lines; and most of the constituent companies, perhaps most notably the PO, Nord and Est, had developed outstanding express passenger steam locomotive designs before the outbreak of war in 1939, and the general level of speeds had risen. Even so, despite the growing competition of road and air transport, business travellers in France were served by relatively infrequent (though comfortable and spasmodically fast) day trains and many

overnight sleeping-car services. Many long-distance services were from Paris and other large towns to seaside and mountain resorts and inland spas rather than inter-city in its modern context.

Soon after the end of the 1939-45 war electrification of SNCF main lines at the two voltages inherited from pre-nationalisation practices proceeded apace. A start was made on the 697-mile Paris-Marseilles-Riviera main line, which had previously been steam-worked apart from a few diesel multiple-unit services; the project, partly 1.5kV direct current and partly 25kV alternating current was finished in 1969. The most heavily trafficked main lines of the Northern and Eastern Regions and other important sections have been electrified in the past 20 years. Use of two voltages and evolution of the two-voltage (and three- and four-voltage electric locomotives for running over foreign railways' 3kV and 15kV electrified lines) allow through working without stops for changing locomotives.

The quarter-century since the war has also brought powerful diesel locomotives for use on non-electrified lines, such as Paris to Basle, (Paris-) Amiens to Calais, (Paris-) Le Mans to Nantes and Paris to Vichy and Clermont-Ferrand. At long last, spurred by road and air competition, service frequencies have been increased.

A new form of motive power, the gas-turbine, has been adapted for rail traction in the past four years or so; it has been in successful service in combination with hydraulic transmission in multiple-unit trains on the Paris to Caen and Cherbourg and (in summer) to Trouville-Deauville routes for over a year. A more-luxurious form of gas turbine-powered train is making its début on cross-country services radiating from Lyons and a higher-speed experimental gas-turbine-electric multiple-unit train is being built. The availability of greater motive power in various forms has caused acceleration of many day services between Paris and Lyons and Marseilles and other French

SNCF RUNS AVERAGING OVER 87mph, SUMMER 1971

From	To	Distance miles	Time hr	min	Average speed mph	Rostered load (tons)
Paris	Bordeaux	359.8	4	00	89.97	505/515
St Pierre	Poitiers	62.8	0	42	89.7	559/570
Angoulême	Poitiers	70.1	0	47	89.5	505/515
Poitiers	Paris	206.0	2	19	88.9	505/515
Arras	Longueau	41.0	0	28	87.9	410/500
Paris	Limoges	248.1	2	50	87.6	561/570
Paris	Limoges	248.1	2	50	87.6	617/625
Paris	Montbard	150.9	1	44	87.0	600/800
Limoges	Paris	248.1	2	51	87.0	617/625

Facing page: A 1959 SNCF inter-city express, headed by electric locomotive 2D2 9114 of 1950 vintage. *E S Russell*

Top: L'Aquitaine Paris-Bordeaux inter-city train of 'Grand Confort' stock headed by CC6500 locomotive. *SNCF*

Below: A BB9200 in sparkling fresh paint, probably just outshopped. *SNCF*

FASTEST TRANSITS BETWEEN PARIS AND PROVINCIAL CENTRES, SUMMER 1971

Town	Distance miles	Time hr	Time min	Average mph
Lyons	318	3	43	85.5
Marseilles	536	6	33	81.7
Lille	156	1	55	81.3
Bordeaux	360	4	00	90
Toulouse	442	5	56	74.6
Nice	675	9	02	74.7
Nantes	245	3	18	74.2
Strasbourg	312	3	48	82
Havre	142	1	47	79.3
Clermont-Ferrand	261	3	57	66
Dijon	195	2	16	86.1
Tours	145	1	49	79.8
Brest	387	5	17	70.9
Amiens	81	1	00	81
Calais	183	2	56	62.5
Cherbourg	230	2	56	78.4

cities and some foreign destinations such as Brussels, Amsterdam, Cologne, Zurich and Milan. As stated, some are TEEs.

The accompanying tables show some of the fast runs scheduled in the 1971 SNCF summer timetable. The motive power in all cases was electric, diesel or gas turbine. None of the SNCF's remaining steam locomotives is rostered for fast working. There are indications at the time of writing that this year's summer services might include more such fast runs. All the trains concerned rank as inter-city and some are the SNCF portions of international services. In summer 1971 the total number of runs at an average speed of 68mph was 936 and there were 337 at 75mph and over.

Worthy of note in the French high-speed services is that most are on electrified lines and nearly all are locomotive-hauled. The Paris-Bordeaux and Paris-Limoges (-Toulouse) main lines made the best showing, being specially signalled and otherwise equipped in sections for 124mph (200km/h) running. Loads on these lines were heavy, many 570 tons and some up to 700 tons. Loads tended to be heavy also on the Paris-Lyons main line, with many up to 800 tons.

Diesel locomotives and diesel multiple units played a relatively minor part in very high-speed working, but there were and are many diesel runs at averages between about 62 and 70mph.

Comparisons of the total SNCF inter-city network with those of other Western European countries are idle, largely for reasons of population (and therefore traffic) density, distance, railway geography and of the dominant position of Paris as the commercial and railway centre. The table of fastest transits between Paris and many provincial centres shows that the SNCF can compete with the motorway (taking comfort, availability of refreshment services and other factors into consideration) and even with the air over medium distances.

The number of runs at over 87mph might not be bettered this year. All the runs listed for 1971 were by trains hauled by electric locomotives. The fact that only one of the lines concerned is ac rather than dc is fortuitous. All nine trains are heavy and gradients range from easy to (by steam standards) moderately severe, including 1 in 100 in the foothills of the Massif Central approaching Limoges and the long ascent at 1 in 200 of the Plateau de Langres between Laroche and Montbard—but nothing of any consequence to electric locomotives geared for express passenger working.

The fastest runs naturally continue to be on routes which are laid out for high speeds in respect of signalling, permanent way and elimination of sharp curves. The SNCF is busy equipping its trunk routes for very fast running. One complication is the discomfort to passengers through lateral forces caused by running over curves at speed, which is noticeable well below the speed at which danger of derailment occurs with modern vehicles on modern track. The discomfort can be minimised by various methods. One of them is suspension of the coach body to allow it to roll or swing about its fore-and-aft axis on curves independently of the banking or superelevation of the track. Like other major railways the SNCF is conducting experiments and has built some main-line vehicles now in service to allow subsequent fitting of a body-tilting device.

Until the development of the gas turbine, the trend in high-speed inter-city services had been towards locomotive-hauled trains. The principal exceptions in service at present are the Japanese New Tokaido Line trains and the American Metroliners, both of which are electric multiple-units. The gas turbine also is being used in multiple-unit trains, such as those in the SNCF Paris-Cherbourg service and still under development in the United States. Gas-turbine multiple-unit trains are also proposed for the high-speed line planned between Paris and Lyons, while several other designers favour trains with power units dispersed along the length of the train for very high speeds. This seems to be the trend also for electric passenger trains of the future. Another proposed SNCF high-speed line seems likely to be electrified at the standard 25kV, but with modifications for 300km/h running. The projected line would run from Paris northwards to a point south of Lille, where there would be a Y-junction; one branch could connect with a Channel Tunnel and on to London and the other east to Brussels and thence to Amsterdam and to Western Germany, connecting possibly with a German high-speed line.

FRENCH RAILWAYS IN PICTURES

Inset: A breath of French narrow gauge, now virtually defunct as working systems — St Bonnet station on the PO-Correze Railway.

Above: One of the big SNCF big tank engines, Ex-PLM Class 242TA four-cylinder compound, leaving Croix-Wasquehal with a Paris-Tourcoing express in September 1968.

Below: Also representative of the earlier extensive minor French railways, a narrow-gauge Mallet at Tournon, on the preserved section of the old Vivarais system, in September 1971.

Top: Standard SNCF two-car diesel mu sets made up into a train for local service on the Nice-Marseilles electrified line. *La Vie du Rail (Broncard)*

Above: SNCF diesel locomotive BB66111 at Pont-de-Briques with a local goods train in September 1968. *B Stephenson*

Right: One of the latest SNCF electric mu trains of Z6300 series for local and suburban service on 25kV alternating-current lines, taken near Achères. *La Vie du Rail*

Above: A pair of SNCF diesel railcars forming a Laquille-Le Mont Dore train leaving La Bourboule in June 1967. *B Stephenson*

Below: SNCF Class cc 6500 high-speed electric locomotive for direct-current lines, on the Paris-Bordeaux l'Etendard express, one of the fastest trains in the world, in May 1970. *La Vie du Rail (Broncard)*

Above: SNCF two-current (ac/dc) locomotive of series BB25200 on a Nice-Paris train at Le Trayas on the Mediterranean coast. *La Vie du Rail (Broncard)*

Below: Forward-looking French railway technology is given practical expression in the TGV001 gas turbine-electric experimental train now under test. *La Vie du Rail*

MINOR FRENCH RAILWAYS

Above: Locomotive of the Vivarais system, now a Touristique railway, joining mixed-gauge track at Tournon. *R A H Casling*

Left: No 101 of the PO-Corrèze Railway on a special train at Tulle. *J R Batts*

Below: Côtes du Nord No 39 0-6-0T and train at St Brieuc. *Colourviews Ltd*

ONE ROARS ACROSS France in a streaking juggernaut of an express—a most impressive engineering achievement. It is perhaps no longer quite the *stupor mundi* it was ten or fifteen years ago, but it is not difficult to realise how much the engineering side of the railways of the country has altered over the last twenty years. The main lines have changed considerably; steam traction has dwindled in an orderly fashion, towards extinction. Electrification has spread to most of the main arteries, and diesels roar in many places, but commercially, the standard-gauge network has altered comparatively little. A number of branch lines have lost their passenger services, though not as many, pro rata, as in Britain; a high proportion of them survive to handle freight, which after all is what railways are really for. Total abandonments there have been, but even so there are few parts of rural France far from a rail connection of some kind.

The decisive change in the French railway map has been the almost total disappearance of the railway underworld. The filigree of French National Railways (SNCF) lines which survives, its texture mainly intact, owes its final development to the Freycinet Plan of 1879, which decreed that the trunk route system, then pretty well completed, should be complemented by a further 6,500 miles of new construction. This was intended to place every Sous-Préfecture, or in effect most towns of more than a couple of thousand inhabitants, on the standard gauge.

But between the veins and capillaries of standard track that came to be established, there grew a fantastic mini-network of secondary and independent lines, normally of metre gauge, but a few standard and even an occasional two-footer. Their development was mainly in the richer agricultural areas, and they were few in the mountains of the Vosges and the Massif Central. They did not often link up with each other and so a journey on them (albeit unlikely except by hardened enthusiasts) from Calais to the Pyrenees or Brest to Nice, would have been broken by a dozen or so gaps, mainly relatively short. But during the forty years before 1914 a total of over 13,000 miles of secondary railways was built. Almost the whole of the impressive total has now been closed completely.

Being a logical people, the French were always very exact about the classification of a railway, whether it was 'principal' or 'secondary'. The principal lines were those legally established as of national interest; the secondary lines were alternatively classed as of local interest only. However, clarity of the law was one thing, and actual clarity occasionally something else. All the Freycinet Plan lines were of Intérèt National, but not all principal lines were of standard gauge as some narrow-gauge ones were important enough, and soundly enough built, to be ranked in the first category. Most secondary lines were of narrow gauge. However, generally the

only rule, whatever the gauge, was that though they might form considerable systems, they must be lightly and cheaply built, often running on the roadside.

None of them was owned—at any rate, directly—by the SNCF or its predecessors, the five great main-line companies. But plenty of principal lines were independently worked. There were at one time well over a hundred public railway operating authorities in France, companies or local government bodies. In time, most of the principal independents came into the control of two or three national organisations, who were private companies in receipt of government subsidy, each one run as a separate entity, but sharing common services such as main workshops.

Construction of secondary railways was booming still in 1914, with another 4,000 route-miles still planned or actually building when the war broke out. After 1918, work was resumed, but on a slower pattern due to the impoverishment of the country. It stopped again as the development of road transport began to make an impact in country areas. The last new secondary lines were opened in 1925 and not long after that closures began. Most of the railways had been built simply to provide a public service, even though it was well known that they could never pay. When it was realised that an acceptable and cheaper alternative was provided by bus and lorry, there was no justification for continuing. Some of the newer lines in less populous districts were very short-lived; the record was held by a branch in the Côte-d'Or which lasted for only six years. During the 1930s closures continued apace; they more or less came to an end during the German occupation of the second world war, when road transport was paralysed by lack of fuel, and a number of railways which had been closed but not dismantled prior to 1940 were hastily reopened. Thus, about 7,000 miles of narrow-gauge railway survived until 1947.

two limbs of the once mighty South of France company to escape fatal war damage; the 100-mile Vivarais system in the mountains of Ardèche; and the electrified SNCF-owned line from St Gervais through Chamonix in the Savoy Alps to the Swiss frontier at Vallorcine. Many of the local systems survived the second war, at least in part. Some of them were electrified, ranging from the modern Samoëns-Sixteline in the Savoy Alps, through some very creditable suburban and interurban railways. For example, those at Toulouse and Bayonne, down to some perfectly incredible rural electric trams, such as that which sparked its way twice daily out of Ambérieu towards Nantua.

Most of the other lines used petrol or diesel railcars, since the potentialities of this type of vehicle for cutting costs and competing on more level terms with the bus were realised quickly; some remarkable vehicles were evolved very early, including Model T Ford rail buses on the Côtes-du-Nord in Brittany. During the 1930s the firm of Billard, at Tours, produced a standard range of light and economical diesel railcars, some of which are still working. The most popular of them, incidentally, was a 27-seater; that is, about half the size of the average bus, which gives some idea of the low traffic potential in most of the areas these railways were built to serve. Diesel locomotives, however, never really spread very widely, although at least four of the last-surviving lines used quite modern and powerful ones exclusively for freight. There was no great incentive to replace the steam engine since diesels would do nothing to increase non-passenger receipts and running costs were in any case met by subsidy.

So the typical post-war French narrow-gauge line had railcar-worked passenger and steam-powered freight trains right to the end. The steam locomotives ranged all the way from 53-ton 0-6-6-0T Mallets hauling 400 tons or more on the Réseau Breton, to 0-6-0Ts on such unforgettable little lines as the Tramway de la Corrèze, squeaking and graunching along the roadside round dog-leg hairpin bends and panting up 1 in 25 grades with four loaded wagons at a time. In that particular case, also suddenly diving down into a horrifying gorge to leap across it on a spider's web of a suspension bridge.

Not to be overlooked were the quite large number of lines which survived only to haul sugarbeet to the factories; several were of only 2ft gauge, and some had never handled any other traffic. They slept invisibly under the long grass for nine months of the year, then sprang into busy action from October to Christmas. Many of the two-footers used track, rolling stock and locomotives inherited from the military light railways used by both sides during the first world war, but some were more grand. The aristocrat of them all was the Pithiviers-Toury, which until it died at the end of 1964, still worked

Top: Vivarais Mallet 0-6-6-0T No 403 with a British railtour near Raucoules-Brosettes in September 1968. *C J Gammell*

Left: Ex-Vivarais Mallet 0-6-6-0T of Réseau Breton at Carhaix. *P B Whitehouse*

Above: Diesel railcar on the Nice-Digne Railway in September 1969. *F L Pugh*

They included a rich and wide variety. Most senior and respectable, of course, were the National Interest lines. The largest of them in route-mileage in 1947 was the Réseau Breton, a five-pointed star centred on Carhaix in the middle of the Breton peninsula, with 244 miles of metre gauge. But there were others more interesting and spectacular, notably the 95-mile Nice-Digne line, one of the only

300-ton trains hauled by imposingly big 0-8-0Ts built as recently as 1945. This line too, used some ex-War Department material including at least one Alco 2-6-2 tank, which was recently rescued and has now been acquired by the Festiniog Railway in North Wales.

The field was still so wide in 1945 that it would take a whole book to give a sufficient account of what was to be found in it; all one can do here is to mention some particular favourites. Few English people ever seemed to get to know the Pas-de-Calais system, which was the first to be seen after crossing the Channel; there might be a scruffy railcar sitting in the bay at Calais-Ville, or an 0-6-0T smoking it up at the head of a mixed train at Rang-du-Fliers, where another branch of the system crossed the Paris main line. But the Super-Pacific at the head of the boat train was panting to be off to more interesting parts of the country, and there would always be time later to examine something so nearly on one's doorstep. Of course, as it turned out there was not; it went out like a light in 1954.

But one saw two more narrow gauges even before getting to Paris in those years; the Réseau de la Somme at Noyelles, and the branch to Grêvecoeur at St Just-en-Chaussée, and one might even be lucky enough to see a train. The freight to Heartbreak was particularly appealing, with a splendid little 0-6-2T at the head of it. Thereafter, the narrow gauge menu depended on which direction was taken, and although the pull of the Mallets on the Réseau Breton was strong, one tended towards the mountains, where luscious, dirty little coal-burners still panted up the valleys. At Tulle, there was not only the Corrèze tram, but the PO-Corrèze, a more respectable concern which the SNCF was not ashamed to include in its main body of its timetable (an honour shared with the Réseau Breton but not many other narrow-gauge lines), which boasted four 0-4-4-0Ts for mixed trains and still a 2-4-0T for emergency use when all the railcars had broken down. Being

France, that did not happen often.

There was also the Castres-Murat-Brassac, the Nice-Digne, dieselised, but still with cavernous empty sheds and rusting water columns to show what a splendour must have been there in steam days. They also had some ex-Tunisian Pacifics there for a while. Above all, there was the Vivarais, with its reliable railcars, its magnificent gorge and mountain scenery, its formidable climb with a ruling grade of 1 in 32 from Le Cheylard up to St Agrève, and despite the diesel locomotive rebuilt from a 2-6-0T, the occasional and elusive Swiss-built Mallet 0-6-6-0T which could be found on freight work if you knew exactly where and when, and on the famous 18.53 summer Sundays-only St Agrève-Dunières.

But a massacre has taken place. Not one of the narrow-gauge secondary railways of France survives; their often imposing arched-roofed terminals are converted to bus depots, their bridges and tunnels stand pointlessly, premature archaeological remnants of the industrial age. And few of the National Interest lines remain either, the knell having been sounded for them by the abandonment of the Réseau Breton in 1967, apart from the conversion to standard gauge of one limb. The Vivarais, too, has gone in its old form, but, *mirabile dictu,* it has resurrected itself in the form of a Chemin de Fer Touristique on one of its legs—that from Lamastre to Tournon. The SNCF electrics at Chamonix and from Villefranche to La Tour-de-Carol, in the Pyrenees, still run, but despite the recent re-equipment of the former, rumours of closure are heard. The PO-Corrèze and the La Blanc-Argent lines still appear in the SNCF timetables, both now dieselised, but their survival is surprising since neither are particularly busy and both are paralleled by good roads. The same thing applies to the Réseau de la Somme. The Nice-Digne too, though well built and reasonably busy, seems to be unpopular with those who consider whether its subsidy should be renewed, and it lives from hand to mouth.

Most surprising of all was the survival until 1971 of the Ligne de la Lozère, supported by the last thin strand of a shoestring, whose six-wheeled railcars (sometimes hauling a two-wheeled trailer, for luggage only!) and occasional diesel freight still staggered up and over the Col de Jalcreste on their way from Ste Cécile-d'Andorage to Florac, in the Gorges du Tarn. There was a 2-4-4-0T stored serviceable, at Florac, but it had not been used for twenty years. Why the line survived is hard to see; possibly it was because its 2,747ft summit level was sufficiently lower than the road to make snow clearance less of a problem in winter.

These are all the survivors bar such excellent museum schemes as that set up at Pithiviers. Those which are still open to public traffic do not seem likely to survive the 1970s.

ITALIAN RAILWAYS
IN PICTURES

Top left: An Italian State Railways diesel railcar for Chivasso pictured near Crescentino, northern Italy, in May 1972. *L King*

Far left: Another railcar, this time at Villabassa heading for Fortezza in May 1972. *L King*

Top: ETR220 electric mu train forming thè Trieste-Genoa Rapido at Brescia in October 1971. *E Tonarelli*

Above: A diesel-powered TEE train, the Milan-Marseilles La Ligure, pictured at Agay on the French Riviera in September 1958. *E S Russell*

Left: Italian State Railways track maintenance men at work at Ventimiglia near the Franco-Italian frontier. *Italian State Railways*

Left: Steam and smoke billowing from Franco Crosti 2-8-0 locomotive No 743 377 on a westbound freight at Nizza Monferrato in May 1972. *L King*

Below: A Cavaller Maggiore-Alessandria train headed by 2-6-0 No 640 037 pictured near San Stefano in May 1972. *L King*

Right: Two 625-class 2-6-0 locomotives heading an evening train to Bassano out of Venice in September 1971. *D H Wilson*

Below right: Another 625 2-6-0 crossing a viaduct near Cisano-Caprino Bergamasio with an evening Lecco to Brescia train in March 1970. *L King*

Spain-Europe's last stronghold of steam

Top: RENFE 2-8-0 No 140 2066 with a freight at Baza, near Granada, in September 1963.
D Trevor Rowe

Centre: An 0-4-0 tank engine pictured at work in San Jeramino in 1963. This engine, which is now preserved in Madrid, is the one mentioned in the text whose boiler was on occasion allegedly filled with wine.
D Trevor Rowe

Above: Busy scene at Calzada in April 1962 as 750mm-gauge 'Belgica' of the now defunct Valdepeñas Puertollano Railway makes up a train. *D Trevor Rowe*

SPAIN IS well known as one of Europe's favourite playgrounds, and holiday posters are to be seen everywhere extolling her seaside attractions of sunshine and sand, and the marvels of her southern cities such as Seville and Granada. The holiday areas are well defined and neatly labelled Costa del Sol, Costa Brava, etc. The number of tourists flocking to Spain each year is impressive, but the majority travel in package tours, arrive by air, and are concentrated in very limited geographical areas.

All this is a comparatively recent phenomenon and has brought dramatic change to a way of life virtually undisturbed for centuries. Spain's political troubles hindered her development during the first half of this century and economic difficulties after World War II (in which she did not take part) further slowed advancement in many fields. Thus, while the railways of many other European countries pressed ahead with modernisation, Spain had neither the foreign aid nor resources of her own to undertake large projects, and had perforce to be content for many years with a policy of 'make do and mend', which barely managed to keep pace with the rate of deterioration evolving from the ravages of the Civil War of 1936-39 and the lack of materials available thereafter.

These factors help to explain our title, though it is no longer completely true today. Foreign aid and economic recovery have now provided the wherewithal for one of Europe's most ambitious railway modernisation plans, the RENFE ten-year plan for 1964-1973. During this period two main lines, one of international importance (Madrid-Burgos direct railway) have been completed, many important

routes electrified, track and signalling drastically overhauled, rolling stock renewed, and steam traction, previously paramount, virtually eliminated.

Railways in Spain began effectively in 1848, when British engineers built the short Barcelona-Mataro Railway. Other lines soon followed, and were built to the wide gauge of 5ft 6in (1.671m), which was six Castilian feet and had been recommended in a report prepared for the Government in 1844. This decision, which was instrumental in causing neighbouring Portugal also to adopt the broad gauge, has always made through rail connection with the rest of Europe difficult, although it has been overcome to some extent by using wagons (and recently passenger coaches) which are converted at the frontier.

Historically, the high cost of construction contributed to the authorisation of a large network of narrow-gauge railways, mostly metre, which, when they were of more than local importance, were also inconvenient for the nationwide transport of freight, fruit in particular requiring quick transits and minimum handling. By 1900 there were about 7,100 miles (11,400km) of broad-gauge and 1,450 miles (2,100km) of narrow-gauge railways, and at least many of the small broad-gauge companies were being absorbed into larger ones. In time this process resulted in two companies emerging to control a large area of the country. The two almost equally matched concerns were the Madrid, Zaragoza & Alicante Railway (MZA) and the Norte Railway. Behind them came the Andaluces Company which, however, never gained complete ascendency in the south, where small companies, some British financed, abounded until the formation of one national railway system for the broad gauge.

The single authority was formed in 1941 with the creation of the Red Nacional de los Ferrocarriles Españoles (RENFE), which took over around 8,000 miles (12,800km) of broad-gauge track and over 3,000 steam locomotives. Some of the locomotives dated back almost to the first years of railways in the country; they were of such great variety that visitors from almost every locomotive-building country in Europe (including Russia) and North America could find some of their national products in action. New locomotives were built, but few withdrawals took place as traffic grew constantly; after a few pioneer enthusiasts had visited the country in the early 1950s tales trickled back of the wonderful machines still active and other fans set out on a pilgrimage quite different from those who for centuries had travelled the road to other Spanish shrines, such as that of Santiago de Compostela.

The new saints were locomotives 100 or more years old; their shrines the steamy depots of junctions like Miranda de Ebro, on the windswept Castilian plain, and the rain-sodden industrial valleys of Asturias, where coal mines provided a selection of little railways not at all like those touristic ones in Wales as they are today, though sometimes in rather similar terrain. As the enthusiasts grew more numerous, they penetrated into remote valleys, until to add to the stocklists of the broad-gauge RENFE, came booklets on the industrial and minor railways of various areas. With the decline of steam even the RENFE, which had always been sympathetic to railfans, took to publishing lists of withdrawals and details of where certain types could be found.

Now for a few words on the objects of this article—the steam locomotives of Spain. The oldest class active when the RENFE was formed in 1941, and still going strong on shunting duties until the mid 1960s, were some 0-6-0 tender engines built by Kitson, Thompson and Hewitson at the Railway Foundry Leeds in 1857/58 and by Cail of Paris in 1858. To the end they remained almost as built, some having had rough wooden cabs added while the original 'weatherboard' or 'spectacles plate' remained in place. In Spain, unusually, it was not the fine modern express locomotives which carried names, but the shunters and tank engines, some with historic names such as *Isobel la Catolica* (I doubt if *she* would have been amused) *Alfonso VIII* and *El Cid* (stationed at Valencia, of course). Others were named after towns, rivers and one, perhaps aptly, *Terrible*.

Passing from the huge variety of 0-6-0s and 0-8-0s to the larger types, Spain always had a large proportion of eight-coupled machines, including many 4-8-0s and 4-8-2s. The Mountains class (4-8-2s) was perpetuated by the RENFE and in production up to 1952, when the standard mixed-traffic engine selected as standard successor and built in large numbers up to 1960 was a 2-8-2 of North British design. Latterly, these modern types were built for oil firing, and older types were converted from coal, which in Spain is of indifferent quality.

Tank engines have never been numerous in Spain; one little 0-4-0T now preserved in Madrid came from the FC Urbano de Jerez, the sherry wine town where legend has it that at the annual festival the boiler was filled with wine instead of water! Many tank engine classes consisted of one or two machines only, from small concerns like the Mollet-Caldas and Cinco Casas-Tomelloso railways, although a batch of 4-8-4Ts, built in Barcelona in 1923/24 was distributed to various lines under State control.

Of articulated locomotives, Spain had a great variety quite unequalled in Europe. Mallet compound tender locomotives came first, built for the Central of Aragon Railway in 1906, 1912 and 1927/28, the more recent ones still being active around Valencia in 1969. Some Kitson-Meyers went to the Great Southern of Spain in 1908 but were withdrawn in 1953. Garratts were introduced in 1930 by the Central of Aragon for express passenger working between Valencia and Calatayud. Six were built by Euskalduna at Bilbao and latterly they were used on the very heavy Seville-Barcelona through train between Valencia and Tarragona. They were the only Garratts used on passenger trains in Europe, although this is quite common practice in Africa. These passenger Garratts were of 4-6-2+2-6-4 wheel arrangement, but in 1930 the same operator had six 2-8-2+2-8-2 Garratts built by Babcock & Wilcox at Bilbao for freight traffic. Until the RENFE built some Santa Fe (2-10-2) machines for coal traffic around Leon in 1942, these last-mentioned Garratts were the most powerful steam locomotives in the Iberian peninsula. Most surprisingly, as late as 1961 the RENFE had a further six very similar Garratts built; they were the last large steam locomotives built for service in Western Europe.

It is a fact that right until the end of steam the RENFE continued developing this form of traction. Although the 1961 Garratts were the last steam locomotives built in Spain, they were essentially repeat orders of a well-tried design, but in 1956 the RENFE had put into service ten express passenger 4-8-4s of a new design and the only tender locomotives of this wheel arrangement in the country. They were built for heavy international trains between the French frontier and Madrid, and worked the non-electrified section between Alsasua and Avila. This main artery was gradually electrified under the 1964-73 plan and the fine machines were relegated to freight duties. Some continued in service into 1971, but it is doubtful if they will last much longer.

Modern developments were not neglected, and several standard 2-8-2s and a 4-8-0 were fitted with Giesl ejectors, while there was one experiment with a Franco-Crosti boiler on a 2-8-0. Under the ten-year plan, steam was expected to be extinct by 1973, but present indications are that it might not finish until 1976. Very little steam activity on a regular basis has been noted recently, although the traffic generated by fruit crops brings back into action locomotives out of store. Even the Garratts came out of retirement recently for a brief spell. The RENFE is certainly not unaware of the historic value of its locomotives, and some have been put aside for preservation, along with interesting coaching stock and other relics.

This brief look at the steam stock of the RENFE only touches on a vast subject and mention of many types has perforce been omitted. Although in the early days locomotives came from abroad, Spanish industry was building 4-8-2s in 1925 and after the Civil and World Wars local industry expanded as fast as was possible under difficult conditions. Steam locomotives were built by La Maquinista Terrestre y Maritima (MTM) of Barcelona, Babcock and Wilcox and Euskalduna, both of Bilbao and Devis (later Macosa) of Valencia. In steam days these companies built solely for the Spanish market (apart from an isolated batch of Spanish type 4-8-0s for Portugal), but today Macosa and the Bilbao firms export diesels to South American countries.

Turning to the narrow-gauge railways of Spain, these have ranged from local roadside tramway-type lines to electrified main lines operating Pullman cars. Most of the former category are now extinct, especially all those charming little lines of sub-metric gauge—60 and 75cm. Particularly interesting were the 75cm Veldepeñas-Puertollano Railway, with 0-6-0 tender engines, and the Onda-Castellon line of the same gauge which passed through the town streets and paused briefly in the main square of Castellon de la Plana before being given 'right of way' at the road junction by the policeman on traffic duty! Last of the 75cm lines to go was San Feliu-Gerona, closed only a year or two ago, and probably unnoticed by the holiday crowds at this quite well-known Costa Brava resort. Publicity could perhaps have made it a tourist attraction, but it died mourned only by a few local people, steam worked to the last by 0-6-2Ts, some of them built for the opening of the line in 1892.

On the metre gauge, closures have included many of the lesser isolated lines, but at least one, Malaga-Fuengirola, has closed not because of lack of traffic, but because it is to be converted to the broad gauge! And up along the northern coastline a long metre-gauge link has been under construction for many years; when the last section is completed it will be possible to travel from Hendaye, across the border in France, over 800km to El Ferrol, via Bilbao, Santander and Oviedo. It is along Spain's northern coastline that the

Above: JOP Huelva Railway's No 5, an
0-4-0 tank engine built by the German firm
Orenstein & Koppel.   *D Trevor Rowe*

Left: 0-4-0T 'Odiel' at Corrales on the Tharsis
Railway in the Rio Tinto copper-mining
area in southern Spain.   *D Trevor Rowe*

Below: RENFE No 282F 0405, an oil fuelled
Aragon Garratt built by Babcock & Wilcox in
1930, withdrawn in 1969.   *D Trevor Rowe*

Left: RENFE 0-8-0 No 040 2184 heading a freight train at Linares in September 1963.
D Trevor Rowe

Below: RENFE old and new types pictured side-by-side in 1963; an oil-fired 2-8-2 No 141F 2313 and 0-6-0 No 030 2472.
D Trevor Rowe

Bottom: Ex-MZA 1400-series 4-8-0 No 240 2325, one of a big RENFE class built in Spain by MTM in 1920s and 30s, pictured at Valencia. *D Trevor Rowe*

narrow gauge is strongest, with electric traction between the French frontier and Bilbao since the 1920s, and nowadays fast diesel railcar services thereafter. In the heyday of steam, less than a decade ago, the trains between Bilbao, Santander and Oviedo were hauled by steam, Engerth-type machines of the Cantabrico, and tank engines of the Economicos de Asturias, all bright green with polished brass nameplates.

On the inland Robla railway, old American Baldwin 2-8-0s rubbed shoulders with ex-Swiss Rhaetian Railway machines of the same wheel arrangement, while metre-gauge Garratts with long names hauled the heaviest coal trains. This railway worked its daily through passenger train with fine green Pacifics, sold by Tunisia for scrap in the furnaces of Bilbao but rescued and given a new lease of life by the Robla. Other ex-Tunisian types also saw service in Spain, some 2-10-0s on the Peñarroya-Puertollano line and Mallett tank engines on the

Utrillas railway serving Zaragoza. Metre-gauge Garratts were in Catalonia on the long line up into the mountains, and there was a 3ft 6in-gauge pair on the Rio Tinto mining line near Huelva, their place today being taken by Robert Stephenson-built 2-6-0s of 1953.

Tender Mallets and more Garratts saw service on the long mineral line from the Ojos Negros mine to Sagunto Steelworks near Valencia. Replaced by diesels, the whole railway is now to close and traffic will be diverted over the nearby broad-gauge RENFE, once the Central of Aragon road of the Garratts and Mallets. At the other end of the scale, many railways had little British built 4-4-0Ts from Falcon of Loughborough, and the Alcoy-Gandia railway near Valencia had a stud of Beyer Peacock 2-6-2Ts in 1890-91, which lasted until closure of the railway a few years ago. When funds were low they sold one to the Sagunto Steelworks and kept going with the rest!

Even more remarkable, the Sestao-Galdames Company, an ore line near Bilbao, has not bought a new loco since 1877, and its shed is full of the cannibalised remains of the two types still in use, Kitson 4-6-0Ts of 1873/74 and Manning Wardle 0-6-0Ts of 1873/77. Mind you, this railway has the unusual gauge of 3ft 9¼in. Unusual gauges have abounded in Spain, for instance the 4ft Tharsis railway shares its gauge only with the Glasgow underground, and since it was built by a Glasgow company perhaps that is no coincidence! The island of Mallorca is exclusively 3ft (nowhere else in Spain is) while the European standard gauge of 4ft 8½in is only to be found on metros, one Barcelona suburban line and the Langreo Railway, one of the oldest in the country.

Not so long ago, locomotives of three gauges could be seen in the same shed at the Poveda Sugar Factory and at the Cuatro Vientos air force establishment, both near Madrid, the gauges being 60cm 1m and 5ft 6in. On the metre gauge serving the Sugar Factory were tender Mallets built in Belgium and the broad-gauge shunter at the factory was a 4-4-0T of the type built by Beyer Peacock for the British Metropolitan Railway. Another of this type remained in use until it was withdrawn recently for preservation at the Basconia Steelworks, Bilbao. They came originally from the Bilbao-Tudela Railway and were sold out of service long before the formation of the RENFE.

Today, much of the metre gauge still exists, but in modernised form, with diesel or electric traction, although a few steam locomotives survive here and there, particularly in industrial use. The one railway which is still entirely steam worked, and truly European steam's last stronghold, is Ponferrada-Villablino situated on the old main line from Madrid to Galicia beyond Leon, where locomotives include the last Engerths still active, Baldwin-built 2-6-2Ts of 1919 and Spanish 2-6-0s, the most recent of which was built in 1956.

Below: Portuguese Railways (CP) metre-gauge railcar at Porto (Oporto) Trindade in May 1968. *B Stephenson*

Bottom: Electric multiple-unit trains of Bilbao Railways and Suburban Transport in June 1968. *B Stephenson*

Right: A look down on the Regua yard, with a pair of 2-4-6-0T Mallet engines of the Corgo metre-gauge line in view. *B Stephenson*

Far right: A CP broad-gauge Bo-Bo diesel-electric locomotive of English Electric origin leaving Porto Sao Bento station with a passenger train in May 1968. *B Stephenson*

The Narrow Gauge in Portugal

WITHOUT QUESTION the time to visit the narrow-gauge railways of Portugal is early autumn, for in late September and early October the precipitous valleys along which many of the railways run are busy with the vintage harvest. Up along the Douro valley and its tributaries, the grapes ripen at much the same time, and as it once was with the hops of Kent and Sussex, there is seldom enough local labour to go round. So groups of harvesters and treaders, whole families, entire villages even—often of three generations—make up teams of up to a hundred or so and go forth on their annual outings. Then the little metre-gauge trains chug along the vine-clad valley of the Corgo from Regua to Vila Real and up to Chaves, coaches packed to the roofs, with a magnificent selection of sounds coming from the accordians, guitars, mouth-organs and drums.

In other seasons the valley railways are much quieter, and the traffic is more suitable to the diesel railcar which is beginning to throb along them; but steam is still there in abundance and many of the trains are mixed, with wagon-loads of grain or fruit, or metallic ores, trundling along with the passenger stock, and the ever-present dark-red postal van. Mostly the passengers are country folk off to market or a regular country fair, and children going to and

Top: Henschel-built 0-4-4-0 Mallet tank on waiting duty turn at Porto Trindade station. *P B Whitehouse*
Above: A Mirandela-Tua freight train nears Tua at evening time in September 1971. *A G Orchard*

from school. Most trains carry first-class and third-class stock, the former with seats protected by white linen covers and very clean, the latter with hard wooden slatted seats.

There are no dining cars on the narrow-gauge lines, nor are there refreshment rooms except at the larger termini or junctions, though there is usually the odd wine counter hidden away in most of the station buildings; they are not to be

despised. Most of the passengers, be they locals, priests, returning emigrants, or members of the services, bring their own food—fish-cakes made with dried cod (bolinhos de bacalhau) or smoked ham from Chaves and delicious crusty bread, accompanied by wine in bottle, cask or leather wineskin. Most of the stations are inhabited by a water seller during the summer months, for Portugal can be a very hot country then and the valleys can be particularly grilling.

These little lines serve some historic and attractive places up in the province of Tras os Montes (Behind the Mountains), such as the great fortress churches of the Sabor valley on the line close to the Spanish border. They have romantic names too—Mogadouro, Miranda do Douro, and Freizo de Espada a Cintra (the Ash of the Girt Sword), remembering the days of the border wars and the Moorish raids; then there is Braganca, the railhead of the Tua line, another border town giving its name to the Royal House of Portugal and the Imperial House of Brazil.

There are three main groups of metre-gauge lines, all in the north of the country. The first and easiest to visit is probably that based on the Porto Trindade station. From there, all trains run out over a steeply-graded section of double track to Senhora da Hora which is the junction for

Vila do Conde and Povoa de Varzim in one direction, and Fafe in the other. This busy suburban service is worked by 0-4-4-0 Mallet tanks, 2-6-0 tanks and modern 2-8-2 tanks, with a sprinkling of diesel railcars. Moving eastwards, there are the picturesque lines (each completely separate and unconnected with any other narrow-gauge system) along the Douro Valley. Going east from Porto they are the Tamega line (Livracao to Amarante and Arco de Baulhe), using railcars for passenger services and steam only on the occasional freight; the impressive Corgo line (Regua to Vila Real and Chaves), using 2-4-6-0 Mallet tanks for all its trains, which are mixed; the Tua line (Tua to Mirandela and Braganca), using railcars and 2-6-0 tanks on mixed trains; and the Sabor line (Pocinho to Dua Igrejas, for Miranda), using -minute railcars and 2-4-6-0 tanks on mixed trains. All these narrow-gauge trains connect with those of the Portuguese State Railways on the Douro Valley line—itself worked by steam beyond Regua. Then there is the group of lines which centre on the somewhat remote junction of Sernada da Vouga. Of them, two run to the Atlantic coast towns of Espinho and Aviero, whilst the third goes east to the cathedral city of Viseu; from there a further branch runs on to Santa Comba Dao.

The motive power used on the Portuguese narrow-gauge system is delightfully various, as is the rolling stock. Certain types and classes are restricted to their own particular lines, and each system or separate line has its own workshops (usually at the main junction point) fully capable of all but the heaviest repairs; for the heavy work, engines are sent to Porto on a low-loader, rather as the Leek & Manifold sent its engines to Crewe in the good (or bad) old days.

Looking at each of the groups separately we find that they have no common locomotive class, though most lines use the small 2-6-0 tank and each has its own form of Mallet tank. At the time of writing no diesel units have reached the Sernada da Vouga system.

The Porto lines use three main classes of tank locomotive. The Henschel-built 0-4-4-0 Mallet of 1905 vintage with really magnificent copper-capped chimneys and sparkling black paintwork; varying makes and classes of 2-6-0 (including Decauville, Kessler, Orenstein, Koppel and Esslingen), most sporting stovepipe chimneys, but with the odd engine dating back to 1886 with copper-capped bellmouths; and then the large 1931-built smoke-deflectored Henschel 2-8-2 tanks. Unlike the smaller locomotives, the last-named never seem to be turned but run chimney-first into Porto. All the engines on the Porto system are maintained in the workshops at Boa Vista, between Porto and Senhora da Hora. Once, a British-built Vulcan Foundry 0-4-4-0 Fairlie tank dating back to 1875 ran over the line, ending its days banking heavily overcrowded holiday specials, with surplus passengers clinging happily on to the buffers and drawgear with the good-natured irrepressible air of those clinging to the sides of a Cairo tramcar.

The Douro Valley railways rely, in the main, on a remarkable wheel arrangement —a 2-4-6-0 Mallet compound tank engine, dating from 1911. Clearly the twisting and heavily graded lines needed something more powerful than the 0-4-4-0 Mallets on the Porto system, and the odd Henschel engines were introduced as a sensible modification of the more normal 0-6-6-0 tank. The Tamega line runs one engine only at a time, usually one of the odd pair of 0-4-4-0 Mallet tanks, slightly larger than the Porto engines and carrying stovepipe chimneys. The precipitous, heavily graded and tortuous Corgo line relies solely on the 2-4-6-0 tanks for all its services; as all its trains are mixed, loads are usually heavy even in the quiet season. There are workshops at Regua and the Corgo's copper-cap-chimneyed engines are smartly turned out and a delight to behold. There is, in addition, an old 0-4-0 tank (No E1) which had lain derelict at Regua for many years, and which was recently put through the big works at Campanha—ostensibly for preservation; however, the engine has recently returned to Regua to act as station pilot.

Next up the valley, the Tua line has 2-6-0 tanks for its few mixed trains and the engines, as well as the railcars used for most passenger turns, are serviced in the small modern shops at Mirandela. Sometimes one can also find one of the small 0-6-0 tanks working on this branch. The last and most remote of these railways, the Sabor, again uses 2-4-6-0 Mallets for its mixed trains, for it is another very steeply graded line. In recent years, one of the Tua Mallets has been the sole example of a Portuguese narrow-gauge engine using the Giesl ejector, with an ugly flat chimney which does not enhance its appearance. The Sabor line workshops are at Pocinho and traffic on this section is at a low ebb.

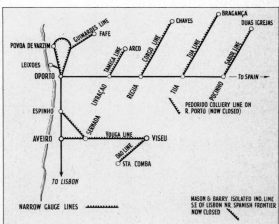

**Facing page: A narrow-gauge 2-8-2T of
Portuguese National Railways at Trindade
station in Porto.**
P B Whitehouse

**Top: CP Kessler-built 0-6-0T at Tua in
September 1970.** *C J Gammell*

**Left: Diesel railcar and trailer of the Tamega
line at Amarante station.** *P B Whitehouse*

Somehow, the Sernada da Vouga system has an individuality which is particularly appealing. Its centre at Sernada is almost nowhere, it is the personification of an old-time country junction with a wine shop-cum-cafe and a locomotive works to boot, and it also has a greater variety of motive power than either of the other two. Locomotives include the 2-6-0 and 2-4-6-0 tanks, but two other classes are unique to the line—they are another Henschel 2-8-2 tank dating from 1924, machines with a very handsome outline and steel ladders running down the sides of their smokeboxes, and a class of 4-6-0 tanks by Borsig, dating back to 1908. The latter are foreshortened in looks and remind one very much of some of the locomotives which once worked the late-lamented Irish 3ft gauge lines. Quite often engines of each class can be seen working at Sernada at once, generally at the three times during the day when trains from each of the three limbs connect and intershunt, when the station becomes a sort of Portuguese narrow-gauge Crewe of fifty years ago.

The diesel units, which often run with trailers, are painted in a smart blue, and are of two main types—to the un-technical, large and small! The former are used on the Porto suburban and the Tamega lines, while the diminutive cars that run out of Pocinho seem like bumping juveniles in comparison. Blue is also the colour for the newer steel-bodied passenger stock, though the older coaches more often found on the country systems are painted dark green. Fares are cheap, and you are recommended to travel first class if you intend to go far.

There is one other narrow-gauge system —that of the Porto Docks and Harbour Board. The system was originated back in 1884 when the artificial harbour was made at the mouth of the River Douro. Two long breakwaters were built to protect the man-made port and the metre-gauge railway was constructed to carry the granite used from the quarry of San Gens just outside Porto. Today this little railway is diesel operated. It is rumoured that there are still three spotless and shining Belgian-built steam tank engines tucked away in a shed, waiting either for a buyer or an emergency.

Taken all in all, the metre-gauge railways of Portugal are a delightful anachronism, and under a recent review of their health by the authorities, the lives of the more countrified lines are bound to be limited. The railways run in modest-living country where the general economy is limited and includes few natural resources, so that their first objective was, and must continue to be, the provision of economical transport services for the local regions which they serve. Because of the necessity for economy in their construction, like other narrow-gauge railway of the same ilk, they have a tendency to 'go round' rather than 'up and down' and follow the river valleys where possible. There are one or two examples of tunnelling and bridging, notably on the Porto line and on the Tua railway; on the latter there is one place where the line emerges from a short tunnel parallel to a precipice where it is carried on a bridge built along the rock face, before diving into a further tunnel.

Most of the country lines link the towns and villages along their various river banks and take the seeker of the genuine rural life into terrain full of history and Roman or medieval remains, as well as the more active industry of wine making. This, together with the unusual and interesting variety of tank engines (about 80 all told, divided into 20 classes of varying character), makes a visit to that lovely land a must for those who want to see a little of yesterday while it is still left—the motor car will soon bring it to an end.

Below: A 2-6-0T and passenger train of the Aviero line at Sernado da Vouga in September 1970. *C J Gammell*

Bottom: A mixed train headed by a Henschel-built 2-8-2T about to leave Sernada for Aviero. *P B Whitehouse*

Railways through the Alps

The Gotthard Line

GOTTHARD IS THE first name of a railway through the Alps to occur to most people. The St Gotthard pass, under which the railway runs in the tunnel of that name, has for centuries been one of the chief of the many Alpine passes between Italy and Central and Northern Europe. Over it there was first a footpath, then a bridlepath and then a carriage road; it is snowbound for much of the year.

The Gotthard railway is the usual term for the Swiss Federal Railways' 140 miles of line (as the crow flies only 92 miles) from Lucerne on the Rhine and North Sea side of the Alpine watershed, through the Gotthard tunnel to Chiasso on the Italian frontier near the sub-tropical lake of Como and in the basin of the Po that flows into the Adriatic. The engineering feats by which the Gotthard line crosses the Alps—the $9\frac{1}{4}$-mile Gotthard and many other

tunnels, including some of spiral form, the lofty bridges and viaducts and tortuous alignment with many loops—and the mountain and lakeside scenery are the best-known features. But what makes it the world's greatest rail traffic artery through some of the world's toughest country are its ever-growing traffic, already totalling nearly 11 million tons of freight and 7.5 million passengers a year and the modernity and efficiency of its motive power and signalling.

Like the old bridlepath that preceded the road, the line is a vital link. Today it moves a variety of traffic between a vast area, including Britain and Scandinavia, north of the Alps, and Italy—and, via Italian ports, the oil-producing countries and importers overseas of Central European industrial products. Fuel oil from Italian coastal refineries is essential to much of Germany.

Above: A 1963 view into the Rhone Valley over the BLS Railway as it crosses the Luegelkin viaduct in Switzerland.
Swiss National Tourist Office

Below: A Loetschberg express passenger train crossing a viaduct near Frutigen, Switzerland, in the late 1930s.
Swiss National Tourist Office

Italian fruit and vegetables and wines reach markets in Manchester and Stockholm—by means of train ferries. The products of the Italian motorcar works are moved to markets in Germany and beyond. German and Swiss machinery and electrical components and chemicals and—in diminishing quantities—German coal help to keep the Italian economy ticking over. As important as its heavy tourist traffic, which bears up well in the age of the private car and motorcoach and is carefully fostered by aggressive marketing, including a variety of cheap fares, are travellers on business. There are also the many thousands of Italians working in Switzerland and Western Germany, whose movements home and back at holiday times tax the railway resources of motive power and rolling stock and take up additional train 'paths' on the already congested Gotthard line. What started as a profitable sideline and has since developed into a major traffic is the conveyance through the Gotthard tunnel of accompanied road vehicles between the north and south portals at Goeschenen and Airolo—traffic that is liable to fluctuate with the weather on the pass, and is handled with great despatch at peak periods.

The Swiss Federal Railways which absorbed the Gotthard Railway on nationalisation in 1909, strives constantly to increase the capacity of the line by applying signalling techniques which enable more trains to be run. The most notable example is the division of the Gotthard tunnel into 13 block sections; this allows several trains to run simultaneously on each track, protected by automatic signalling which is controlled from Goeschenen station. New electric locomotives of greater power enable train weights to be increased and, on certain sections, the 72kmph (46mph) speed limit in force generally on the mountain sections to be raised. The maid-of-all-work on the Gotthard line has for some years been the 5,940hp Ae 6/6 class of Co-Co wheel arrangement. This type can haul 600-ton trains up the 1 in $38\frac{1}{2}$ gradients and 1,200-ton freight trains are worked with two Ae 6/6s, one marshalled in the middle of the train to minimise strain on the drawbar between the locomotive and vehicles. Some passenger trains are made up to nearly 700 tons. This involves difficulties, such as boarding and alighting where the low Continental platforms are too short, long walks along the moving train to the restaurant car at the end, and providing enough ticket inspection staff to deal with, say, 700 passengers holding various types of ticket. But almost any step is desirable which allows one train to be run instead of two on this highly trafficked route.

With vast expenditure of money and engineering resources the SFR in recent years has double-tracked the remaining single-line sections of the route. Among them are the causeway built on an underwater ridge across the south end of the lake of Lugano and along the precipitous shore of the lake of Lucerne. Even so,

The Gotthard line abounds in bridges, viaducts and tunnels. Above and right: respectively the Lower and Middle Meienreuss bridges near Wassen on the northern ramp. *Both Swiss Federal Railways.* Far right: A typical winter scene of an overline bridge near Wassen. *Swiss National Tourist Office*

European economic expansion is creeping up on Gotthard line capacity. Hence proposals for alternative north-to-south rail routes through the Swiss Alps. There is one for a level 30-mile Gotthard 'base tunnel' from Amsteg on the Gotthard line, before the steep climb southwards to the Gotthard tunnel, to Giornico in the Ticino valley, beyond the descent from Airolo. Also proposed are two alternative routes east of the Gotthard that both involve extensive tunneling works but are easier than the Gotthard. The Swiss Confederation will have to make a decision very soon, but even after the opening of whichever route is chosen, the present Gotthard line must continue to move heavy traffic even though the heaviest freight trains would be routed by a less severely graded route.

The present line may seem obvious as a link between traffic collection and distribution points north and south of the Alps—Basle, for instance, and Zurich and the freight marshaling yards and traffic centres of South Germany, and Milan, Turin, Genoa, Bologna and so on. It is certainly the obvious route between these points and areas when compared with the Alpine passes to the west (including the Simplon) and to the east. All involve difficult rail approaches, even the comparative low Brenner pass between Austria and Italy, over which the railway runs without a tunnel.

Nevertheless the Gotthard line, opened in 1882, was only the fourth trans-Alpine railway. The first was the Semmering, in Austria, completed in 1854, which was comparatively easy to build yet still afforded valuable data for use by later engineers. Next came the Brenner, opened in 1867. Both had the backing of the imperial Austrian government, which wanted to develop its modern port of Trieste and to strengthen strategic links with its possessions in Northern Italy. The third was the Mont Cenis (1871) including the eight-mile tunnel that replaced the Fell-system rack railway over the pass. The Mont Cenis was the result of concerted action by France under Napoleon III and the kingdom of Piedmont, later part of the kingdom of Italy. Democracies are accused of being slow to act. That might be why

the Gotthard Railway Company was not incorporated until 1871, with its headquarters in Lucerne in the heart of that democracy *par excellence* the Swiss Confederation. The industrial pattern of Italy, not yet unified, to which sea routes from North Sea and other European ports could not be so attractive as a direct overland route from Central Europe, had not been established in the 1850s and 1860s.

Yet the Swiss were quick to spot the potential of a Gotthard railway. Maps show how much more direct is its route to Milan, Turin, Genoa and even Florence and Rome from most of Germany and beyond compared with those of the Brenner and other trans-Alpine railways. Study of physical maps shows the difficulty of rail approaches to other passes such as the St Bernard and the Splügen. The first conference on the Gotthard railway was in 1860. It commissioned a Swiss engineer Kaspar Wetli to survey a route from the lake of Lucerne to lake Maggiore. Delays followed while Wetli's plans were toothcombed and the Swiss Confederation and cantons that would be directly affected discussed how to raise the money.

Italian and eventually German subventions were forthcoming. A treaty of 1871 between Switzerland and the newly formed German empire and kingdom of Italy provided for construction and management of the line. The absurdly small, by present standards, sum of 187 million Swiss francs (£7.5 million) was deemed sufficient. More than half was raised as private capital and the rest was in the form of subventions from the Swiss, Italian and German governments. In the event this proved too small and the project had to be pruned before an additional 40 million francs could be made to cover it.

On formation of the company a German, Robert Gerwig, was made chief engineer. In 1875 he resigned and after another German had been appointed and resigned, a Swiss, Gustav Bridel, was made responsible and saw the construction through. Building the line took 11 years. The contractor for the Gotthard tunnel was another Swiss, Louis Favre, who had had wide experience of French and other Swiss rail projects; he died suddenly in 1879 on an inspection of work in the tunnel.

The tunnel was begun in September 1872. The bores from opposite ends met in February 1880; they were out of alignment by only 2in vertically and 15in horizontally. Opening of the line was in January 1882 for freight and in the following June for passenger traffic. The tunnel and its approaches presented greater difficulties than had any other main-line railway through mountains at that date. About 2,500 workers, mostly Italians who were considered to have a special aptitude for tunnelling, worked in the tunnel at any one time. Mechanical boring was introduced in 1873 and compressed-air locomotives—one of their first applications to underground work of this kind—were used with horses and mules to haul wagons of spoil inside the tunnel. Dynamite was used

for blasting. There were rock falls and flooding from springs. Temperatures in the heart of the mountain sometimes made working conditions intolerable. Ventilation was faulty when the hydraulically worked air pumps proved ineffective. Small wonder that 177 tunnellers died by accident or disease and over 400 were injured or suffered serious illness—and that the tunnel was not finished within the eight years stipulated in the contract.

From Lucerne the Gotthard line runs near the lake of Lucerne and then turns away through Immensee, the junction with the original Gotthard line. The old line runs in from Rotkreuz to the north and carries the freight traffic which an awkward layout at Lucerne and the detour involved preclude from taking the Lucerne route. Shortly comes Arth-Goldau, separated by the Rigi peak from the lake of Lucerne and the junction for Zurich and the industrial area of north-eastern Switzerland and Germany via Schaffhausen. Later it rejoins the lake of Lucerne at Brunnen and runs along the steep rocky shore under the well-known Axenstrasse road, with its tunnels and gallery. This is one of the sections to have been double-tracked since World War II. At Flüelen, at the head of the lake, the line heads south up the flat portion of the valley of the Reuss to Erstfeld.

There starts the 18-mile climb, mostly at 1 in $38\frac{1}{2}$ and 1 in 40, to the summit at an altitude of 3,780ft in the Gotthard tunnel. The steepness of this ascent caused misgivings in the 1870s in the light of the steam motive power of that era; and certainly until electrification, speeds of both passenger and freight trains were necessarily low. Like nearly all SFR lines, the Gotthard is electrified at 15kV $16\frac{2}{3}$Hz. The SFR's first main-line electrification, up the slope from Erstfeld to Goeschenen, through the tunnel to Airolo and down the Ticino to Bellinzona in the Italian-speaking Canton Ticino, was begun just before World War I; it was completed to Airolo in 1920, to Bellinzona in 1921 and the whole route had been electrified by 1922.

The section to Goeschenen affords one of the most spectacular rail journeys in the world. The vertical rise in the 18 miles is more than 2,000ft. To gain height in the ascent of the valley the engineers resorted to the ingenious spirals and loops that figure in so many photographs—notably the spiral and two semi-spiral tunnels near Wassen. Tunnels abound. The train crosses the Reuss and its tributaries by bridges and viaducts, many of them of great size, including the Kärstelenbach viaduct, 178ft high above the floor of the abyss which it spans.

Not all trains stop at Goeschenen before plunging into the tunnel. The fastest that stop there and at Airolo are allowed 11min between the two stations adjoining the portals. From Airolo the line drops to Bellinzona, continuing to overcome differences of height by loops. Many people have seen or know of the convolutions and spiral tunnels in the 15 miles between

Rodi-Fiesso and Giornico as the line loops down the Ticino gorges, and the famous view of the three levels of line near Giornico. The start of Mediterranean vegetation can be seen near Biasca.

Bellinzona, lower down the Ticino, is only 800ft above sea level. Here diverges the original Gotthard line that runs to Lake Maggiore and along its eastern shore to the Italian frontier at Luino and is still used by some freight trains. What is now the main Gotthard line ascends from Bellinzona and runs via the tourist resort of Lugano and crosses the lake by the Melide causeway mentioned above and so to the frontier at Chiasso, a short distance from Como in Italy. In the 140 miles from Lucerne a train threads more than 80 tunnels and crosses nearly 80 bridges that are over 35ft long.

The SFR has constructed at Chiasso a marshalling yard for freight traffic in both directions and extensive customs and other installations for dealing with freight. Many consignors in Italy forward fruit and other commodities to Chiasso whence they are reconsigned via the Gotthard line after sale. Because the voltage of the Italian State Railways is 3kV, motive power must be changed at Chiasso except for the multi-voltage electric multiple-unit Trans-Europe Express trains mentioned below.

Gotthard line passenger services are many and various. The Basle and Zurich to Milan Gottardo and Ticino TEEs are four-voltage multiple-unit sets incorporating 15kV (SFR), 3kV (Italian State), and French 1.5kV and 25kV. The latter two voltages are for running over the French railways when the rostering of these sets involves working the Milan-Paris Cisalpin TEE service over the Italian lines to Domodossola, thence over the SFR through the Simplon tunnel via Brig and Lausanne to the French frontier at Vallorbe, then over the French 25kV section to Dole in Burgundy, the voltage changes to 1.5kV for the run to Paris. The southbound Gottardo train is allowed only 3hr 49min for the 183 miles from Zurich to Milan, stopping only at Lugano and Como. The voltage changeover is made at speed.

Other Gotthard passenger trains are long caravans, like the Holland-Italy Express which is made up of a variety of sleeping cars, ordinary coaches, vans and a restaurant car on the Gotthard part of the route and is consequently very heavy. Carsleeper trains on the Gotthard include a pair between Holland and Biasca, south of Airolo, where the station is near the Gotthard road, enabling motorists to start and end their holiday journeys in the scenery of Italian Switzerland.

More than 90 freight trains a day were recently working over the Gotthard. (At peak periods more than 350 trains including passenger trains have run through the Gotthard tunnel in 24hr.) Wagons of many types including tank wagons and car-carrier wagons can be seen, and high-capacity bogie wagons are gradually replacing the familiar standard four-wheelers,

Above: A Gotthard line passenger train at Bellinzona on the southern ramp. *Swiss National Tourist Office*

Above right: A stop at Erstfeld for SFR No 11409, a 6,000hp Type Ae 6/6 co-co electric locomotive. *Swiss Federal Railways*

Right: SFR four-voltage 3,300hp mu stock forming the Ticino Zurich-Milan Trans Europe Express passing Brunnen in central Switzerland. *Swiss National Tourist Office*

Below: A Gotthard freight at the Lower Wattinger bridge near Wassen. *Swiss Federal Railways*

though the patterns of traffic still tend to require the smaller vehicles. The greater part of Gotthard line freight traffic is in transit through Switzerland. Apart from its engineering and scenic distinctions, the Gotthard railway deserves fame as a generous contributor to Swiss invisible exports in the form of freight receipts.

The Loetschberg line

In contrast to the Gotthard line the Loetschberg line, the main line of the independent Berne - Loteschberg - Simp - lon (BLS) Railway (one of Europe's few railways that pays a dividend), follows no centuries - old trail. It was conceived partly as a rival to the Gotthard route and, rather more, to improve passenger and freight communications by reducing the distance between Berne—and the important Bernese Oberland holiday district — and the upper Rhone valley and Italy; it is also a more convenient link between Italy and a northern *debouche* comprising north - western Switzerland, Alsace - Lorraine and eastern and northern France, Belgium and Holland, lying west of the traditional area served by the Gotthard line.

Conveying, like the Gotthard line, a heavy transit freight traffic through Switzerland, the Loetschberg line today can be said to be largely complementary to the Gotthard (without going into the complex question of freight rates via the different Alpine routes). Because it is still largely single track its capacity is limited and it cannot therefore relieve the Gotthard to

the extent that is desirable at peak periods.

The Loetschberg at its southern end, at Brig in the upper Rhone valley, feeds traffic into and takes it over from the Simplon line. The latter is basically a link between France and French - speaking Switzerland on the one hand, and Italy, Jugoslavia and south - eastern Europe on the other. The Swiss Federal Railways work traffic through the 12-mile Simplon tunnel to Domodossola, where the Italian State Railways take over. All through BLS traffic is handled by the SFR—but often hauled by BLS electric locomotives— between Brig and the Italian frontier. Relations between the BLS and SFR are close and there is much inter - working of the two concerns' electric locomotives and train crews. But whether the BLS will be nationalised in the near future is still a moot point. Such a step would have comparatively little effect on traffic working.

The Loetschberg route through to Italy starts from Thun, south of Berne and on the lake of Thun and runs via Spiez and Kandersteg and through the nine-mile Loetschberg tunnel, named after the mountain massif which it pierces, to Brig. At Spiez branches which are comparatively little concerned with Italian traffic diverge to Interlaken, the junction for minor railways serving many Oberland resorts, and Zweisimmen, terminus of the Montreux-Oberland Bernois Railway. The Loetschberg railway stems from a branch of the Thunerseebahn (Lake of Thun Railway)

from Spiez to Frutigen, en route to Kandersteg. Construction of the international line as now conceived started in 1906 shortly after the two single-line bores of the Simplon tunnel were opened, and the concept had been formed of the combined Loetschberg and Simplon international route. Part of the capital was provided by a French consortium and part by the Swiss Confederation. The BLS Railway came into existence in July 1906.

From Thun, the route is alongside the lake as far as Spiez, where it starts to climb. After Frutigen, the line is single track to Kandersteg and gradients are severe. The route includes a spiral and many other tunnels before Kandersteg, the northern portal of the Loetschberg tunnel, which is only 424yds shorter than the Gotthard, and with a summit altitude of 4,070ft. From the southern portal at Goppenstein, the line drops down to Brig. The ruling gradient is 1 in 37 and there are avalanche galleries, and many tunnels and bridges as the line descends the north side of the Rhone valley.

The tunnel was finished in 1913. Construction was quicker than that of the Gotthard, partly because improvements in tunneling methods had been introduced in the meantime. Nevertheless it would have been faster but for an inrush of water from an unsuspected fissure in the rock that was waterlogged; the fissure was breached by a routine blast, and twenty-five men were killed. The site of the disaster was sealed off by a massive wall and the alignment of the tunnel altered, involving curves and an addition of half-a-mile to the total length.

The whole line eventually is to be double track. The passing loops on the sections between Spiez and Brig that are still single track are now being doubled; the 11 miles through the Loetschberg tunnel between Kandersteg and Goppenstein has always been double. There will be complete doubling from Goppenstein to Brig. When the line was laid out all tunnels were prepared in part for doubling, as were certain bridges. Electrification came early. After experiments on the Spiez - Frutigen section in 1910 with electrification at 15kV 15Hz, the BLS adopted 15kV 16⅔Hz, the same as for the SFR. The line was electrified through to Brig from its opening in 1913. The BLS has been prominent in both electric traction and signalling developments—but to describe them would need a book.

BLS traffic resembles that of the Gotthard in essentials. The company has always been active in seeking to develop international passenger traffic, both transit to Brig (including traffic to Zermatt by the Visp - Zermatt Railway from Brig) and Italy and including through vehicles from Paris and the Channel ports and from Germany, all via Berne, and also to its own stations serving the Oberland. The journey from Thun to Brig is through incomparable scenery; the high spots are probably on the descent into the Rhone valley after Goppenstein.

Mountain Railways of Switzerland

Above: Train on the Arth-Rigi Railway on the final mile to the summit above Staffel, with the Vitznau-Rigi track alongside. *D R Stopher*

Below: Train on the Wengernalp line from Lauterbrunnen in the valley to Kleine Scheidegg, on the 1 in 4 section above Wengen. *G M Kichenside*

IN THE YEAR 1971 a notable Centenary was celebrated in Switzerland. It commemorated the opening of the first true mountain railway in Europe, from Vitznau on the Lake of Lucerne to the summit of the Rigi. A Swiss engineer named Niklaus Riggenbach had been interesting himself in the problem of climbing railway gradients steeper than could be negotiated by ordinary adhesion methods, and in 1863 had taken out a patent for traction by rack-and-pinion gear. At first nothing came of the invention, but in 1869 news came to Riggenbach that an American inventor named Sylvester Marsh had opened what he called a cog-wheel railway up Mount Washington in New Hampshire, which Riggenbach hurried across the Atlantic to see in action. On his return he built a short line in some quarries near Berne in order to try out his theories; when that proved successful he looked round with some associates to find a mountain viewpoint popular with the public up which a permanent rack-and-pinion line might prove a profitable enterprise. Their choice fell on the Rigi.

A concession having been obtained from the Canton of Lucerne, work started without delay, and the first section of the line, up to Staffel, was opened on May 23, 1871. Then an unexpected delay occurred, because to reach the summit the line had to run from the Canton of Lucerne into the Canton of Schwyz, which at first refused to grant the necessary concession. A compromise was eventually reached whereby the Canton of Schwyz built the final mile from Staffel to the summit, for use of which the Vitznau-Rigi Railway had to pay (and still does) a rental. So the complete $4\frac{1}{4}$ miles from Vitznau to Rigikulm, conquering a difference in level of 4,300ft and with a maximum steepness of 1 in 4, came into use in 1873. It was followed in 1875 by a line up the opposite side of the mountain, from Arth-Rigi, paralleling the Vitznau-Rigi Railway up the final mile from Staffel to the summit.

Riggenbach's rack is considered to be an improvement on that used by Marsh up Mount Washington. Both are in the form of a steel ladder, but whereas Marsh used rungs of circular section, Riggenbach had rungs of tapered section, designed to ensure better locking of the locomotive's pinion-wheel teeth with the rack and to counteract any tendency of the teeth to climb out of the rack. On a rack railway where locomotives and independent coaches are used, as was originally the case on the Rigi line, each coach has a pinion to engage the rack to provide an added safeguard against any tendency for the train to run away out of control.

Additional safety is provided by the type of rack devised by Dr Roman Abt, which is widely used on lines on which the working is partly by adhesion and partly by rack-and-pinion. Abt track has two parallel rows of vertical teeth machined out of solid bar; the teeth are staggered in pitch, and the locomotive pinions have double rows of teeth to correspond.

But neither the Riggenbach nor the Abt system would have ensured safe operation of what is the steepest and probably the most remarkable rack-and-pinion railway in the world; that is the line from Alpnachstad on the Lake of Lucerne to the summit of Pilatus, which climbs 5,344ft in a distance of 2.66 miles, giving an average gradient of 1 in $2\frac{1}{2}$ and a steepest inclination of 48 per cent, or practically 1 in 2.

The engineer of the line, Edouard Locher, devised a rack of unique design, in the form of a central rail with teeth on both outer edges which are gripped by pairs of horizontal pinions under the vehicles. The system has been in use on both former locomotives and the present electric motor-coaches since 1889, when the Pilatus Railway was opened, and the Locher rack has operated without any kind of accident. At such a steepness, no form of switch could be used safely to divert vehicles from one track to another; such movements have to be carried out by electric traversers at the terminals, and at both ends of the midway crossing loop at Aemsigenalp.

The record climb by a Swiss rack-and-pinion railway today is made by the only line which is still steam-operated, that from Brienz to the summit of the Brienzer Rothorn, in the Bernese Oberland. In a distance of $4\frac{3}{4}$ miles its small locomotives, with boilers tilted on the chassis to keep the water on the level on a gradient of 1 in 4, mount a total of 5,515ft. The highest altitude reached by any Swiss rack-and-pinion line, however, is the 11,333ft terminus of the Jungfrau Railway, in tunnel at the Jungfraujoch, the ice-mantled pass between the Mönch and the Jungfrau. This $5\frac{3}{4}$-mile line uses a fourth variety of rack, the Strub, with teeth machined out of the head of a flat-bottom rail section. The total climb of the Jungfrau line is 4,571ft, but it is beaten by its nearest rival in altitude, the Gornergrat Railway, which mounts from 5,262ft at Zermatt to 10,134ft at the Gornergrat, commanding one of the most marvellous glacial panoramas in the whole of the Alps.

The Vitznau-Rigi, Arth-Rigi and Rorschach lines are all of 4ft $8\frac{1}{2}$in gauge. All other Swiss rack-and-pinion railways are of metre gauge with one exception; this is the line with the most lengthy continuous rack equipment in the country, the Wengernalp Railway in the Bernese Oberland. Starting at 2,615ft altitude at Lauterbrunne, it climbs on a gauge of 80 centimetres through Wengen to 6,762ft at the Kleine Scheidegg, where it connects with the Jungfrau Railway, and then descends to 3,097ft at Grindelwald Grund, with a final brief climb to 3,392ft into Grindelwald, a total length of just over 12 miles. Scenically the Wengernalp provides one of the most spectacular routes in the whole of the Alps, immediately under the towering summits of the Eiger, Mönch and Jungfrau.

In the realm of motive power, there is only one other exception to electricity

beside the steam-operated Brienzer Rothorn Railway; it is the line from Capolago, on the Lake of Lugano, that climbs for 4,327ft to the summit on Monte Generoso, at 5,223ft altitude.

Altogether, there are 15 Swiss mountain lines that have rack-and-pinion operation throughout their length, and a number of others on which the rack is needed only on the steepest sections. Of the rack-and-adhesion lines the most notable is the Furka-Oberalp Railway, which in its 61-mile course between Brigue and Disentis climbs over both the mountain passes named in its title. Beginning at an altitude of 2,201ft at Brigue it attains 7,088ft in the Furka tunnel, drops to 4,710ft at Andermatt, rises again to 6,670ft on the Oberalp pass and finishes at 3,706ft in Disentis. Lengthy stretches at 1 in 9 have to be negotiated by locomotive-hauled trains up to 100 tons in weight. Brigue is also served by the Brigue-Visp-Zermatt Railway, which in its 27-mile course has four rack-and-pinion sections, the steepest of 1 in 8 past Stalden. Traction over it is mainly by twin motor-coaches of 1,600hp, which can handle trains of five or six lightweight bogie coaches up and down the steep climbs.

The Swiss Federal Railways has one line only which requires rack-and-pinion traction over a mountain pass, and that is the metre-gauge line connecting Lucerne with Interlaken. Between Giswil and Meiringen it has three rack-equipped stretches over the Brünig pass, with gradients up to 1 in 8 in steepness. The Bernese Oberland Railway, part of the group which also includes the rack-operated Wengernalp and Jungfrau Railways, needs rack sections on its lines from Interlaken up to both Grindelwald and Lauterbrunnen, where it connects with the two ends of the Wengernalp Railway.

On the rack-and-adhesion railways, as points where rack drive takes over from adhesion drive are approached, speed is reduced and for the moment of engagement the train is slowed to a walking pace; as the pinions on each coach engage the rack a slight shock is plainly noticeable by passengers. No reduction of speed is needed for disengagement.

In Switzerland and other Alpine countries there are also short railways that are considerably steeper than any of those worked by rack-and-pinion. They are the funiculars, or cable-operated lines. The principle, like that of a number of cliff railways at British seaside resorts, is that of two cabins, connected by one common haulage cable passing round a winding wheel at the upper terminal, so that the weight of the descending cabin helps to balance that of the cabin making the ascent, and power thereby is economised. A single track only is needed, except that at its centre a loop is necessary to enable the cabins to pass one another.

At the two ends of the funicular passing loops movable switches are unnecessary; the cabins have the wheels on one

side double-flanged and unflanged wheels on the other side. The double flanges grip the rail-head and guide the cabin to that side of the loop, while the other cabin has its double-flanged guiding wheels on the opposite side, and so must always take the other side of the loop.

Funicular gradients in steepness up to 1 in 1½ are common. The record is held by two lines which originally were engineered up steep mountainsides in order to carry to the upper level materials to be used in hydro-electric dam construction. One is from Piotta up to Piora, just south of Airolo, and the other at Châtelard, not far from Chamonix on the Franco-Swiss border; both have steepest inclinations of 88 per cent, or 1 in 1⅛. Much more heavily used than either of them is the line from Schlattli up to Stoos, near the town of Schwyz; it makes an ascent of 2,306 feet in a length of 1,488 yards, with a steepest gradient of 78 per cent, or 1 in 1¼.

The longest Swiss funiculars have more than one section, with a change of cabin intermediately, to avoid the use of haulage ropes of excessive length. The longest is the two-section line which serves the famous winter sports resort of Montana, in the Valais; on its length of 4,601 yards (2⅝ miles) from Sierre in the Rhône valley the steepest gradient is 1 in 2. Also with a ruling gradient of 1 in 2 is the Parsenn Railway at Davos, so heavily patronised in winter by skiers that it has to run twin cabins with a capacity of 140 passengers each. This two-section line, 4,427 yards long, also has the distinction of attaining the greatest altitude of all Swiss funiculars, 8,737ft on the Weissfluhjoch. Not far from Lucerne there is the somewhat more primitive funicular up the Stanserhorn—a conical peak with an even finer all-round view than its more glamorous neighbour Pilatus—which requires two cabin changes in its three-section length of 4,280 yards and total climb of 4,593ft.

Another conical peak which provides a famous viewpoint in the Bernese Oberland, is the Niesen, which boasts the funicular with the greatest climb of any —5,390ft—and has a steepest inclination of 68 per cent. It is in two sections, with a change of cabin at Schwandegg. In the Engadine we find the line with the longest moving cable, 2,390 yards, for the line from Punt Muragl, near St Moritz, up to the 8,031ft altitude of Muottas Muragl has a single section only.

An interesting funicular is that from Lugano Paradiso up Monte San Salvatore, for although it has two sections its two balanced cabins never pass one another. As one starts from the lower terminus the other sets out from the upper terminus; they meet and stop on opposite sides of the platform at the middle station, where their passengers change from one to the other. Another interesting variation is found on the funicular from Territet, a suburb of Montreux, up to Glion, 689 yards long. It is distinguished by being operated by water-balance instead of by

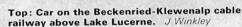

Top: Car on the Beckenried-Klewenalp cable railway above Lake Lucerne. *J Winkley*

Above, left and left below: Three views of one of two veteran steam locomotives of the Vitznau-Rigi Railway, No 17, at the lakeside station and on the climb of the Rigi. Although the line is now electrified, the steam engines are still used for special excursions. *all G M Kichenside*

EAST EUROPEAN RAILWAYS **in pictures**

Far left: Austrian-built (SGP) diesel locomotive with a passenger train on the Sofia-Pernik line in Bulgaria. *C J Gammell*

Left: USSR Class VL60 Co-Co 4,160kW 25kV electric locomotive with a passenger train at Ulan Ude, E Siberia, in November 1971. *J Holwell*

Below: Greek metre-gauge diesel railcar at Volos station on the Thessaly Light Railway in August 1961. *F L Pugh*

Facing page bottom: Unofficial double-deck commuter train of Roumanian State Railways in the Bucharest rush hour. *L King*

This page bottom: Polish State Railways Type SM42 diesel freight locomotive at Poznan in June 1967. *C K Hemphill*

Above: Czechoslovak State Railways 4-8-2 engine No 498 112 at Zdice in April 1972.
C J Gammell

This picture: East German Pacific No 01 525 on a cross-border express near Honebach, W Germany, in June 1968. *C J Gammell*

10
The Railways of Asia

The Trans-Siberian Railway

Top: Soviet Railways Trans-Siberian train No 2 The Russia. *D J Holwell*

Above: The Russia at Khabarovsk. *K Westcott Jones*

ONLY THE BRITISH call the 5,778 miles of railway stretching from Moscow to the Siberian Pacific coast the Trans-Siberian. The title came naturally to interested travellers of the Edwardian era when the long line was completed after ten years of work. For West Europeans it meant a relatively quick passage to the Far East and was of paramount importance to embassies staffing missions at Peking and in Tokyo, also to business travellers bound for Japan and Shanghai. The promise of a fortnight's overall journey compared to at least six weeks by mail steamer had an impact in the early years of this century as great as that of flying the Atlantic compared to crossing by sea did in the 1950s.

The Russians under the Tsar called it the International Railway and named the through train the International; the Americans, who began to use the line to visit Europe after crossing the Pacific to Vladivostock, called it the Great Siberian Railway.

The Tsar laid the foundation stone in 1891 and the line was virtually complete ten years later, except that passengers and goods had to cross Lake Baikal, by a British-built train ferry in summer or on sledges in winter. Building the line through the rugged terrain around the southern shores of the great lake took five more years. The original single-track line was lightly laid and not geared for express running, and most trains derailed at least once during the journey. Services were not

a great success and efficiency was low, so much so that inability to use the line to its full extent during the 1905 war against Japan contributed to the Russian defeat.

But after the Japanese war, the Holy Russian Empire pulled itself together in remarkable fashion and from 1907 to 1914, the railways at least worked well throughout the massive country. The Trans-Siberian began to fulfil the dreams of Westerners, and the International carried diplomats and their wives, businessmen, and rich tourists in its brown International Sleeping Cars. The train, which ran as a deluxe express weekly (and later twice weekly) was equipped with a bath car (a lavish porcelain bath being provided) and a reading room cum library. Cooks Continental timetable of 1912 was able to advertise schedules of 11 days from Moscow to Tokyo, or 14 days throughout from London to Shanghai, timings which were kept.

Such luxury has not been repeated, although today's frequency is much greater and the journey takes one day less. The 1914-18 war naturally disrupted services, and during the 1917 Russian revolution the Czech divisions somehow managed to take over the line, transporting their soldiers right across it and then through America to reach Europe and establish the independence of their country. Later, the civil war between Reds and Whites, with American intervention through the port of Vladivostock, caused chaos along the route. It was not until 1925 that scheduled services were restored, and by 1930 foreigners travelling under the auspices of Intourist were again allowed to use the Trans-Siberian.

Although the original line passed through Mongolia by means of the Chinese Eastern Railway, a route keeping exclusively to Russian territory by following the North bank of the Amur river via Khabarovsk was established in 1914. By 1939 the entire line from Moscow through Irkutsk and over the Amur route was doubled and although the 1939-45 war shattered most railway lines in European Russia, the Trans-Siberian behind the Urals was strengthened.

The port of Vladivostock was, and still is, banned to foreigners, but a new port on the Siberian Coast at Nakhodka, about 85 miles to the north, was developed as the packet station for regular ships of the Soviet Far East Line running to Osaka, Tokyo Bay, and Hong Kong. Foreigners must change trains at Khabarovsk and spend a day in that city sight-seeing with Intourist before boarding a special boat train for the 564-mile run to Nakhodka. The boat train follows the Trans-Siberian Vladivostock line as far as Ussurisk junction and then travels under newly erected wires for the rest of the way to the ship's side.

Coming westwards, foreigners depart at Nakhodka from the ship to a train of ultra-modern green-and-cream rolling stock hauled by a powerful electric engine. They find two-berth sleeping cars with a shower compartment set between the double sleepers, and a smart restaurant and club car for convivial pursuits. This luxury is with them for only 16 hours, the last 14 hours behind a diesel, until arrival at Khabarovsk, where the boat train stops. After the required sight-seeing they join Train No 1, named Russia (the Soviets still do not use the title Trans-Siberian), which comes in from Vladivostock in charge of a splendid P36-class steam locomotive, one of a batch of huge 4-8-4s built at Lugansk between 1949 and 1956 by the dedicated steam designer Kaganovich. He was the man who declared at an international railway meeting in Moscow, 'I am for the steam locomotive. It is simple and reliable and will never give up. Although diesels and electrics will come for the best trains, steam must go on alongside them'. He was dismissed from his post but his work lives on and will be in evidence, on the Far Eastern section of the Trans-Siberian at least, for several years. It is intended that the entire Trans-Siberian line shall be electrified by late 1975.

But the train behind the P36 tends to be rather a let-down compared to the boat special. It usually consists of ten or eleven coaches in red and cream, several of them hard class, two of them soft, plus a dining car and a baggage car with crew accommodation, and one or two day coaches for short journeys. It might now have one or more of the new SZ two-berth sleepers, but in 1969 and 1970 they had not yet made their appearance on the Russia although they are used extensively on trains running to Western Europe.

In winter the Russia runs four times a week in each direction, but in summer the service is daily. It is available to foreigners at all times between Khabarovsk and Moscow, but the boat train to Nakhodka runs only in connection with ships, which means fortnightly in winter or weekly in summer (except occasionally when it is twice weekly at peak periods). The great advantage of the Far East ports of Vladivostock and Nakhodka, of course, is that they are ice free. The Amur river, though, is frozen from early December to late April.

There are 91 stops to Moscow from Vladivostock and 78 from Khabarovsk. None of them exceed 17 minutes (only those at Irkutsk and Sverdlovsk are allowed that long) and most are between eight and 12 minutes. The traveller should make a point of studying the timetable giving the list of stops and their duration displayed in each corridor. For this purpose it is essential that any persons travelling on their own, or without a special Intourist guide, should be able to read the Cyrillic alphabet, a study of which takes not more than three days. Without such knowledge, station names mean nothing. It is not, of course, necessary to speak or read Russian (although that is a great asset) to ride the train. The restaurant-car menus are in six languages, including English and Japanese, and the train staff are well used to travelling foreigners.

People use the station stops, which at the Far Eastern end of the line tend to be longer than average and are for watering purposes or changing locomotives, to go for walks up and down the platform. With a week on the train, exercise is important. There are also interesting little 'bazaars' at all the stops, where postcards, ham delicacies, and a fierce Siberian 'brandy' are sold. Villagers often use the stops to board the train and buy ice cream or beer from the restaurant car, which is usually a better 'shop' than any they have in their home town.

The Far Eastern section is the most interesting part of the Trans-Siberian Railway, not only for the steam traction and the engine changes (each P36 runs about 200 miles) but for the dramatic scenery. The bare hills and mountains seen to the south of the line are China, or at least Chinese Manchuria. There are rushing rivers, the mighty Amur (crossed on a long bridge shortly after leaving Khabarovsk), glimpses of semi-desert, and forests of varied trees.

Shortly after leaving Chita, junction for the former Chinese Eastern Railway, the line climbs beside the Silka river away from the fringes of the Gobi desert with the Mongolian People's Republic to the south. Then a massive range of mountains, the Yablonovoi, stands in the way of the route towards the great Lake Baikal and the high

Below: One of the 38 tunnels (and 13 covered cuttings) in the 50-mile line round Lake Baikal, showing typically Russian cross-section and armed tunnel guard.
Illustrated London News, December 1904

Overleaf top: A P36 4-8-4 steam locomotive replacing the electric engine at Petrovski Zavod to take the Trans-Siberian on to Vladivostok, still 3,000km distant. *D J Holwell*

Overleaf centre: Route of the Trans-Siberian Railway from Moscow to Nakhodka. *K Westcott Jones*

Overleaf bottom: Railway coach rigged out as a travelling church for benefit of workers on the Trans-Siberian and their dependants with a service in progress in 1906. *Radio Times Hulton Picture Library*

Central Siberian plateau. The Russia stops at Yablonovaya station where another P36 4-8-4 locomotive joins the train to double-head the formation, while an Ea-class 2-10-0 banks at the rear. Many retired steam locomotives are still at Yablonovaya and a few survivors are kept for banking and double-heading purposes, intended to be kept in good order until the wires come.

Apart from the heaving of the Taurus Express up to the Anatolian plateau from southern Turkey, and lifting weighty trains up from Port Elizabeth to the High Veldt in South Africa, there are no other examples of triple steam workings on main line trains left in the world. It is a great experience to thunder up the Yablonovoi bank, twisting and turning with the thunder of the locomotives resounding through the train. The climb takes the Trans-Siberian line up through 3,512 feet and as late as May or as early as October can transform a warm and sunny scene down on the Gobi fringe to one of snow, forest and desolation at the summit. Mogzon, where the pilot and banker were detached, is nearly 6,000 feet above sea level and on the writer's April 1969 trip it

looked like a wintry scene from Tolstoy.

Spectacular scenery, some of which is missed during the hours of darkness, can be enjoyed during the journey around the southern shore of Lake Baikal. This section is already electrified, the wires reaching Selanga in 1970 and the summit station of the Yablonovoi bank in mid-1972. Apart from a change of electric engine at Irkutsk, there will be a continuous run behind one locomotive all the way to Moscow, 3,226 miles, and the longest electrified line in the world.

A stop of 17 minutes at Irkutsk enables some restocking of the restaurant car to take place, and changes of bed linen and towels for the soft-class passengers. The train crew make the entire journey, only the locomotive engineers and guard being changed at various points, but the two provodniks serving in the soft-class coaches, whose duties include stoking the coke boilers at each end, keeping the samovar of tea on the boil, and making sure passengers do not get left behind at station stops, work turn and turn about. The restaurant-car staff work continuously during the time the car is open, from nine in the morning until ten at night. About 75 per cent of the on-train staff are women; sometimes the electric engines are driven by women.

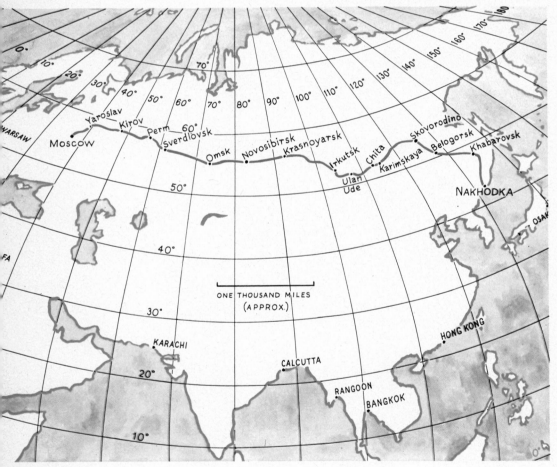

It is as well that the electrified journey to the Urals is faster, since the scenery becomes monotonous, with constant forest, usually consisting of beriozhka (silver birch trees) interspersed with a few big rivers. One can always tell if a traveller really knows the Trans-Siberian, for those who do *not* speak of stops at Tomsk and Omsk whereas Tomsk is 54 miles to the north of the main line and is reached after a change of train at Taiga junction. The most impressive city stopped at, where foreigners may alight and stay if they wish (as at Irkutsk) is Novosibirsk, close to the futuristic city of Academiegorsk, seat of scientific learning. The bridge over the Ob just outside this city is one of the major engineering achievements of the Trans-Siberian. Omsk is a 12-minute stop with a view outside the station to a broad avenue ending at a tremendous football stadium on the banks of the Irtish river.

The Urals are a bit disappointing, relatively low mountains which the line penetrates by means of tunnels and rock cuttings. There is a signboard showing Asia to one side and Europe the other. Sverdlovsk is an important stop, and later so is Perm. Finally, the train comes to rest at Yaroslavl station in Moscow, in the Square of the three Terminals (Komsomol Square), a building in the style of an ancient Russian manor house with a graceful tower designed by architect Franz Shekhtel.

Covering the 3,226 miles from Irkutsk to Moscow will have taken just under 76 hours at an average speed of about 43 miles an hour including stops. The Russia is very rarely late in either direction; if it is, then the lateness is severe, due perhaps in spring to the thaw destroying track or a

Above: A typical Siberian station of timber construction, on arrival of The Russia. *D J Holwell*

Left: A pair of Smirnov N8 electric locomotives heading a train through the Urals in 1956. *Novosti Press Agency*

Below: Nakhodka—eastern end of the journey, with a ship for Japan at the quayside. *K Westcott Jones*

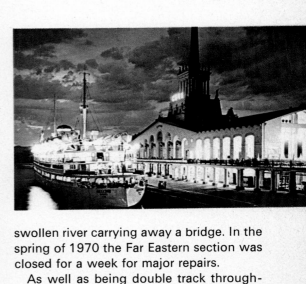

swollen river carrying away a bridge. In the spring of 1970 the Far Eastern section was closed for a week for major repairs.

As well as being double track through-out, the Trans-Siberian Railway is equipped with centralised train control (CTC) and at busy times carries a train every 20 minutes, the vast majority of them heavy freights. Most of them are diesel worked in the Far East, two locomotives being coupled together. In addition to the Russia, which goes all the way to the Pacific, two other express trains share the line as far as Krasnoyarsk, the Yenesei and the Baikal. The latter, a train of blue coaches of the latest type, is a twice-weekly holiday express which runs to Irkutsk and makes slightly better time than the fabled Trans-Siberian proper.

TURKISH RAILWAYS
IN PICTURES

A diesel mu train of Turkish State Railways (TCDD) at Bandirma, in Western Turkey, about to leave for Izmir in October 1969. *C J Gammell*

Far right: American built Vulcan 2-10-0 engine looking busy at Zonguldak in September 1969.
I Krause

Bottom: Turkish State Class DE20 1,980hp diesel-electric locomotive at Haydarpasa.
C J Gammell

Bottom right: One of the 4,000hp 25kV Bo-Bo electric locomotives recently supplied to Turkish State Railways, at Halkali.
C J Gammell

Above: Czech-built (Skoda) 2-10-0 on an express passenger train at Irmak in May 1970. *T B Owen*

Left: German-built (Henschel) 2-6-0T on the Samsun-Carsamba 750mm-gauge line, at Sansum shed in September 1969. *I Krause*

Below: German-built (Maffei) 2-6-2WT at Mersin on the Baghdad Railway in September 1969. *I Krause*

HPS-class 4-6-0 No 24262 on a local train at Futwah in November 1970. *L G Marshall*

Below: Electric locomotive for 25kV ac operation built by Chittaranjan locomotive works. *N Viswanath*

The Railways of India

THE INDIAN RAILWAYS are now 123 years old. It was on April 16, 1853, that the first train in India, and indeed in Asia, steamed out of Bombay for Thana. The train, with 14 carriages and about 400 guests, left Bori Bunder at 3.30 in the afternoon amidst the loud applause of a vast multitude and to the salute of 21 guns.

From that 33 km track to the present network of over 58,000 route-kilometres is, indeed, a far cry. But then, that is the story of Indian railways, which has been one of continuous expansion both in their extent and the volume of traffic carried by them.

Today, the Indian railways organisation is the largest nationalised undertaking. It also constitutes Asia's largest and the world's second largest rail transport system under a single management. Total investment in this lifeline is about 35,000 million rupees. Over 1.3 million persons are directly employed in their giant network, and there are many more indirectly who help to carry about six million passengers and half a million tonnes of freight every day. One in every 20 persons in India is earning his livelihood directly or indirectly from the railways.

How did the railway come to India? In the 1840s, British investors were passing through a 'railway mania', and it was the official attitude of the then Government of India generously to assist those investors which was responsible for the advent of railways in India. Particular mention must be made of Lord Dalhousie, who as Governor-General played a very important part in shaping the policy of railway construction in the country. It was he who recommended a system of trunk lines

connecting the hinterland of the Bombay, Bengal and Madras Presidencies with their principal ports and with each other.

But the Government had neither the resources nor the technical personnel to undertake the construction of railways themselves. They had to entrust construction to private companies which were guaranteed a return of five per cent on their capital investment for a period of 25 years and free land needed for construction.

In return, the companies were required to share the surplus profits half-yearly with the Government after meeting the guaranteed interest and to sell the railways to the Government after 25 years. The expected profits, however, remained unfulfilled mainly due to high costs of construction. And the guaranteed interest proved so high that it affected the Government adversely. Therefore, after the expiry of the contract period, the Government purchased many railways, though their management by the companies continued for some time longer. The Government had also to undertake construction of new lines for social and strategic purposes, particularly in the context of recurring famines of

the 1870s, and the Afghan War. Thus, by 1920, the Government owned nearly 73 per cent of the total mileage of the railways. But their management continued to rest in the private companies with boards of directors in London.

Needless to say this arrangement was extremely unsatisfactory and evoked considerable public criticism. Following the recommendations of the famous Acworth Committee, by 1922 the Government had taken over the management of the bulk of the railway system. In 1924, railway finance was separated from general finance.

Those were prosperous years for the railways and large amounts were spent on the construction of new lines, renewals and replacements. An outstanding development was the introduction of electric traction in 1925. The Harbour Branch section from Victoria Terminus in Bombay to Kurla was the first railway to be opened to electric traction in India on February 3, 1925. Then came lean years following the worldwide slump in the 1930s, and the 1939-45 war which brought in its wake tremendous wear and tear.

The railways were called upon to release large numbers of locomotives, coaches, wagons and track material for the Middle East. Many railway workshops were diverted to the manufacture of ammunition, leading to heavy arrears of renewals and maintenance which virtually crippled the railways. The India / Pakistan partition which followed in 1947 made the situation worse. At the same time, the volume of passenger and goods traffic increased tremendously. It was against this background of excess demand over supply of transport

Left: Class CS 2-4-0T No 774 on the 2ft 6in-gauge Shantipur-Nabadwip Ghat line at Shantipur in November 1970.
L G Marshall

Below: Modern Indian-built steel wagons and Indian-built ac electric locomotive on a trunk coal haul from a coalfield.
N Viswanath

Bottom: Class WP Pacific No 7060 on the Coalfield Express (Howrah-Dhanban Junction) leaving Calcutta Howrah in February 1968. *T B Owen*

that Indian railways entered the final phase of development under the complete control and management of the government.

The very first problem that the national government had to tackle was the inadequacy of rolling stock and other equipment. As the railways were mostly dependent on imports of several essential items, steps were taken to broaden domestic production to make the country self-sufficient. The Chittaranjan Locomotive Works, the first of the three railway production units set up in 1950, has exceeded its targets and also diversified its products. It has so far turned out 3,000 steam locomotives and nearly 300 electric locomotives.

Manufacture of diesel locomotives was established in 1963 at Varanasi and the plant has produced over 300 diesel-electric locomotives. Its production target is aimed at over 150 units a year. The Integral Coach Factory opened at Perambur, Madras, in 1955 is now producing large numbers of passenger coaches of modern design. Wagon building has been left to private industry to develop. The railways themselves have been purchasing wagons costing Rs 50 crores per annum (a crore is ten million) and wagons are also being exported.

Indian railways today run about 11,000 trains daily, carrying 6.6 million passengers and half a million tonnes of goods. During 1970-71 (April to March) the net tonne-kilometrage of freight moved was 125,700 million. In other words, about 210 million tonnes of goods were moved through an average distance of about 600km.

For moving this large volume of traffic, the railways maintain 9,500 steam, 1,250 diesel and 620 electric locomotives, 387,000 goods wagons, 24,500 passenger coaches, and 1,830 electric multiple-unit coaches. Gross revenue receipts in 1970-71 were about Rs 1,002 crores and working expenses, including contribution to depreciation fund, came to Rs 860 crores. While most of the railways' costs have risen by 100 per cent or more during the past 20 years, passenger fares and freight rates have been raised by 69 per cent only.

The Chittaranjan works started manufacturing in 1950 steam locomotives of the WG heavy freight type for the broad gauge. The initial capacity was eight WG engines a month, which was increased to 14 units a month in 1956. In 1959 production was diversified to include WP locomotives for fast passenger traffic on main lines, YTs (tanks) for suburban and shunting services, and WLs (light passenger) for branch lines. In addition, a variety of spares such as boilers, fire boxes, cylinders, wheel sets and so on have been produced.

In 1961 the manufacture of straight electric locomotives was started at Chittaranjan, with a first batch of 21 units for the 1,500-volt dc system in the Bombay region. They were mixed-traffic locomotives of 3,600hp and used electric equipment supplied by the UK English Electric Company.

In 1963 the European 50-cycle group's

25kV ac design, with mono-motor bogies, was taken up for production and a separate project was sanctioned for the domestic manufacture of traction equipment, heavy steel castings and so on to save foreign exchange. During the current fourth Five Year Plan, the Chittaranjan works has a production target of 340 electric locomotives, providing self-sufficiency for Indian Railways and a surplus for export.

Since it was set up in 1963 the Varanasi Diesel Locomotive Works has produced 300-plus diesel locomotives of 5ft 6in and metre gauges, with an indigenous content of about 80 per cent. The production target of 150 locomotives a year is fully adhered to. The Integral Coach Factory since 1955 has produced about 7,500 broad-gauge and metre-gauge coaches, and furnished about 5,000 of them. Production now includes diesel railcars and electric multiple units. Progress has also been made in domestic production of signalling, telecommunication and overhead electrification equipment and track components.

Construction of wagons for Indian Railways is undertaken at 16 privately owned concerns with a total capacity of 38,500 four-wheel wagons a year, and in the railways' own shops with a capacity for about 5,000 wagons a year. Capacity is considerably greater than the domestic requirement and during the past five years export orders, including one from Yugoslavia for 3,600 wagons valued at Rs 37.45 crores, have absorbed some of the surplus.

The railways in India are running about 10,800 trains daily, serving over 7,000 railway stations and covering distances aggregating 1.3 million kilometres per day. The railways carried about 200 million tonnes of freight in 1971. About 90 per cent of the country's coal moves by rail. The bulk commodities moved are coal, iron and other ores, cement, foodgrains, fertilisers and petroleum products. There is a fleet of 25,000 special type petrol tank wagons in use.

Since 1950 there has been good progress with railway electrification; more than 3,600 route-kilometres of electrified line are in service and a further 664 route-kilometres is in course of electrification. The electrified lines now cover 12.5 per cent of the total route-kilometrage on the broad-gauge lines and handle 25 per cent of the total volume of goods traffic moved. Electric traction on 1,500V dc system was introduced on the Great Indian Peninsular Railway (now Central Railway) in 1925, on the suburban section between Bombay and Thana. Electric working was progressively extended to Igatpuri on the Bombay-Calcutta route and Poona on the Bombay-Madras route. In the Madras area, the metre-gauge section of the South Indian Railway (now Southern Railway) was electrified in 1931. Electrification of the Calcutta - Burdwan main line between 1954 and 1958 was the first scheme designed, planned and executed by Indian Railways engineers.

In 1957 Indian Railways formed a

technical association with French National Railways and embarked on an ambitious and large-scale programme of electrification on 25kV single-phase ac traction system, which was adopted as the future standard for main lines. So far, electrification has been introduced over the entire length from Howrah (Calcutta) to Kanpur on the Howrah-Delhi route, Howrah-Durg on the Howrah-Bombay route, Bombay to Bhusaval on the Bombay-Calcutta route and Madras to Villupuram on the Madras-Trivandrum route.

Power for the electric railways is drawn from the 132kV grids of the various regional electricity supply authorities. Design of traction overhead equipment is generally based on French practice adapted to suit Indian conditions.

A pertinent—but by no means unique—facet of Indian railway history was the ancient controversy over railway gauges, which dragged on for about two decades before final settlement. Naturally, when the construction of railways in India was proposed in the middle of the nineteenth century, the English experts thought of adopting their standard gauge. Paragraph 13 of the despatch No 27 dated November 14, 1849, of the Court of Directors of the East India Company to the Government of India runs thus: '. . . with respect to the weight of rails and gauge of line to be employed on these railways, we are disposed to recommend a gauge of 4 feet 8½ inches and a weight of rails of 84lb to the yard as combining the greatest utility and economy . . .'

But they had reckoned without Mr Simms, Consulting Engineer to the Government of India for Railways, for he strongly opposed the standard gauge and advocated 5 feet 6 inches. His reasons were that the wider gauge would give space for better arrangements of the working parts of a locomotive and would lower the centre of gravity for greater stability from the 'fearful storms of wind so frequent in India'. But Lord Dalhousie went one step further. In his lengthy minute on the subject, he strongly recommended a gauge of 6 feet.

In reply, the Court of Directors wrote that they were disposed to think that the gauge of 5 feet 6 inches was the most suitable. Although Lord Dalhousie pressed

again for a 6 foot gauge stating . . . 'I think that those who come after us will see cause to lament that the originators of this great system in the East did not profit so much as they might have done by the errors of their predecessors in Europe . . .', the 5-foot 6-inch gauge was finally adopted as standard for the trunk lines in India.

The controversy was even more bitter in the 1870s over choice of the narrow gauge for secondary lines. The success of the gauge of 3 feet 6 inches in Norway and other countries, and financial considerations encouraged a proposal for its adoption. But of a panel of four railway engineers asked by the Secretary of State in London to give an opinion, three voted for 2 feet 9 inches and only one for 3 feet 6 inches.

In the meantime, the military authorities were pressing for the standard gauge of 5 feet 6 inches for a line to the North West Frontier because of its strategic importance. The Duke of Argyll, then Secretary of State, agreed, but gave no opinion on gauge. So, the choice fell on the Viceroy, Lord Mayo, and he finally suggested 3 feet 3 inches as a via media, and that was adopted.

Even so, fresh controversy arose for every new line proposed. After careful consideration of the subject, in the course of which the relative merits of the standard and the metre gauges were freely discussed, the Government of India in 1884, laid the matter before the Secretary of State. He referred the matter to a Select Committee of the House of Commons, who recommended on a broad principle (a) that the leading trunk lines with their more important feeders should be on the (Indian) standard gauge and (b) that the metre gauge, as far as possible, should be confined to districts where traffic was unlikely to be heavy.

Top: Turning W-class 0-6-2 No 569 on the 2ft 6in-gauge line at Nadiad.
L G Marshall

Above: Another Indian product, a two-car multiple-unit set from Integral coach factory on the Indian Southern Railway.
N Viswanath

Left: A full load for B-class 0-4-0ST No 788 locomotive and coaches at Jalpaiguri on the roadside track of the Darjeeling Himalayan light railway. L G Marshall

**Top: 0-4-0ST engine blasting its train out of
Tindaria on the roadside Darjeeling Himalayan
line.** *E Talbot*

**Above: Number and manufacturer's plates on
one of the Darjeeling Himalayan 0-4-0STs.**
E Talbot
**Right: Another view of the roadside line,
showing No 737 and supercargo.** *E Talbot*

ASIAN
Railways in Pictures

Above: Typically overworked 0-4-0ST No 797 of the Darjeeling Himalayan Light Railway near Sukuo in February 1968. *T B Owen*

Below: Indonesian 4-4-0 No B5308 near Madiun in Java (Ponogoro branch) in August 1972. *C J Gammell*

Right: Indian Railways SER No 26244 leaving Calcutta Howrah with a passenger train in February 1968. *T B Owen*

Below centre: Beyer Peacock tram engine (early 1900s) at work on Indonesian State Railways near Surabaya, Java, in August 1972. *C J Gammell*

Below far right: Japanese-built diesel locomotive of Thailand State Railways at Bangkok in May 1972. *J V Cadiz*

Above: Indian Railways Vulcan Foundry-built
4-6-0 No 24259 at Mughan Sarai shed, on the
Calcutta-Delhi main line, in February 1968.
T B Owen

Below: Indonesian State Railways 0-4-0
No B5226 awaiting a turn at Maos in August
1972. *C J Gammell*

JAPAN'S NEW TOKAIDO LINE

Above: A New Tokaido Line train crosses one of the long viaducts over river estuaries found to be necessary in constructing the high-speed line. *Japanese Embassy, London*

NTL train winds through Yurakuchi station where tracks are brought alongside old narrow-gauge lines for passenger interchange. *Japanese National Railways*

Aerodynamic nose for 130mph maximum speed, soon to go up to 156mph. *JNR*

NO OTHER TRANSPORT route in the world, whether rail, road or air, can show anything in daily inter-city mass movement to compare with the Japanese New Tokaido Line. On the basis of speed alone the NTL, as it is generally known, has become a world symbol of modern railroading; more than that, its dazzling performance has proved to the world a 'shop window' on which Japanese industry has been able handsomely to capitalise. Moreover, its daily high-speed running, at sustained speeds up to 130mph, has been no mere technological gimmick; with its combined speed, frequency and comfort the new service has been able to produce a very substantial dividend on a total expenditure of nearly £400m.

Perhaps the most remarkable feature of what has been done, which is so greatly to the credit both of the Japanese National Railways and of Japanese manufacturers, is that the whole scheme has been thought out practically from zero, for until the opening of the NTL all the Japanese railways had been operated on a gauge no wider than 3ft 6in, on which the speed of the fastest trains had reached the extreme limit of 75mph. At one stroke the 4ft 8½in gauge of the NTL made possible an increase of 66 per cent in maximum speed, which later will be more than doubled.

The most populous area of Japan is that known as Tokaido, which stretches for 320 miles along the shore of the main island of Honshu, from Tokyo to Osaka; in this narrow strip is concentrated 40 per cent of Japan's population, with 71 per cent of its industry. Tokaido's population is growing constantly; it is calculated that by 1985 the three great population centres of this coastal strip—Tokyo and Yokohama; Nagoya; and Kyoto-Osaka-Kobe—will have about 64 million inhabitants. The original Tokaido main line, laid to the 3ft 6in gauge, was the first long-distance railway in Japan, and it was in the spectacular resurgence of the country after World War II that its limitations first began to be seriously felt. Electrification, completed in 1956, proved to be no more than a temporary palliative, for traffic over it was increasing at the rate of $7\frac{1}{2}$ per cent per annum, or twice the highest figure among European railways at that time. It therefore appeared probable that by the 1970s the Tokaido Line would no longer be able to cope with its vastly increased traffic.

In 1957, therefore, the Japanese Ministry of Transport set up a committee to study the problem, and its report was issued a year later. This ruled out any attempt to increase the capacity of the existing line, over which curvature, 1,060 level crossings, and above all the limitations of the 3ft 6in gauge, ruled out the possibility of higher speeds. The only alternative, therefore, was to build an entirely new railway on the wider gauge

of 4ft 8½in from Tokyo to Osaka, 320 miles in length. It was realised that the difference in gauge would make impossible any through running between the new line and the rest of the Japanese system, but as the traffic over the existing line was mainly passenger, it was felt that this would not be a serious disadvantage. Freight traffic and stopping passenger trains could continue to use the old line, while the new line would be used exclusively by high-speed inter-city trains serving a limited number of stations only.

Electrification already carried out in Japan had been at 1.5kV dc, but the development by the French of railway electrification at 25kV ac had been so successful that the adoption of the same current for the NTL was seen to offer considerable economic advantages. So the latter was decided on, with the only difference from European standards that it would be at 60Hz (cycles per second), the national industrial frequency, rather than the 50Hz of Europe. A further decision was that the new line should be operated by multiple-unit rather than locomotive-hauled trains. These would make possible simpler terminal layouts and quicker turn-rounds at terminals, and more uniform standards of performance irrespective of train length, so leading to maximum operating efficiency. Also with lower axle-loads than those of locomotives and more uniform weight distribution there could be economies in the

Top: Although of different gauges, NTL and old lines are brought together at all stations on the new line. *Japanese Embassy, London*

Left: Typical coastal belt country through which the 320-mile new railway was built. *Japanese Embassy, London*

Left below: Line-up of 'bullet-train' noses at the NTL maintenance depot. *JNR*

Above: Buffet car service on one of the NTL expresses. *Japan National Tourist Organisation*

Above right: NTL Tokyo passenger station foyer. *Japan National Tourist Organisation*

Right: Pressure effects at tunnel entrances at the high NTL speeds has been the subject of considerable study. *JNR*

construction of bridges and viaducts.

A vast amount of study then began, of the standards which would be required for high-speed track design, motive power, braking, overhead current collection at speed, signalling and traffic control. For this wide-ranging enquiry the Japanese National Railways not only had at their disposal their own highly developed Railway Technical Research Institute, but also the ample research facilities of the industries of Japan, a country in which co-operation between the railways, industry and the universities had long been a characteristic of Japanese railway development.

The first sod of the New Tokaido Line was cut on April 20, 1959, no more than two years after the project was first launched, and few could have foreseen that this remarkable enterprise would be brought to completion in as short a time as five years. The new line was to be more direct than the old, 25½ miles less in length, and its directness made necessary some major engineering works. These included some lengthy tunnels, in particular Tanna, all but 5 miles long, and Otoyahama, 4½ miles, and also some long viaducts across river estuaries. The 1,320yd Fujigawa viaduct near Shizuoka posed some problems; its twenty 196ft spans are carried on pneumatic caissons which had to be sunk to depths of from 45 to 55ft to find a firm foundation, and the task took 2½ years.

The NTL has ten intermediate stations only. Except at Yokohama, Hajima and Osaka, the new line was brought into stations in each city adjacent to the former main line stations, for purposes of interchange. At Tokyo the two island platforms of the NTL are in an annexe to the previously existing terminal, to facilitate transfer of passengers between the suburban lines and the NTL trains. But at Osaka the new terminal, known as Shin-Osaka ('Shin' simply means 'new'), is two miles from the former station. From Osaka a 101-mile extension, known as the New San-yo line, designed for an even higher top speed of 156mph, will soon be opened to Kobe and Okayama; this is proving very expensive, with one 10-mile and two 5-mile tunnels, and five viaducts ranging in length from 656yd to 1,094yd.

The track suitable for the high speeds contemplated was the subject of intensive study. For an ample margin of safety the minimum radius of curvature (except where sharper curves were unavoidable and speed has to be reduced) was settled at 2,734yd, or just over 1½ miles; the maximum cant was fixed at 7in. The type of rail installed is the JNR 50T flat-bottom section, weighing 106½lb per yd, on concrete sleepers spaced at 2,770 to the mile. The rails are continuously welded, in 4,920ft lengths, with two-sided tongue-rail-type expansion joints between them.

Between the track centres on ordinary double line a space of 13ft 9½in has been left, but on the New San-yo line extension,

over which higher speeds are in contemplation, this will be increased. The track strength on the NTL is roughly 1½ times that of the highest class of JNR main line on the 3ft 6in gauge. In the whole length of the NTL there are 230 turnouts, and in order to ensure that at each turnout the straight line shall have a solid rail bearing throughout, 80 movable crossing noses have been installed. Non-stopping trains can therefore take all these turnouts at full speed; trains being diverted must reduce speed to 43mph.

We come now to the trains. As previously mentioned, it was decided that they should be multiple-unit rather than locomotive-hauled formations, and the final decision was that every coach should be motor-driven. Every axle is driven by a motor with a continuous rating of 248hp, and a standard 12-coach train therefore has a total of no less than 11,900hp available for traction. Each coach measures 82ft overall, except the end coaches, which with their streamlined noses are 6in longer; a complete train therefore measures 985ft overall. The coaches are 11ft 1in wide and have a maximum height of 13ft 1in above rail. By ingenious design and the use of special materials the weight of the trains has been kept down to the extremely low figure of 325 tons. The coaches are assembled in self-contained pairs, with the auxiliary equipment of both coaches divided between them; each pair weighs no more than 54 tons. Six manufacturers were invited to submit designs for the bogies, and out of eight designs submitted the Kawasaki design was adopted, with diaphragm-type air springs helping to ensure smooth riding.

Braking presented some unusual problems, due in part to the high speeds that had to be allowed for, and in part to the light weight of the stock, with no more than 7 tons imposed on each axle. With the high horsepower there would be a tendency for the wheels to slip on starting, and for the trains to skid on the brakes being applied. After a good deal of experiment, it was found that the most efficient resistance to the intense heat generated by emergency braking from high speeds was by a combination of cast-iron discs (which did not distort after overheating as did cast-steel discs) with bronze-based metallic pad linings. Anti-skid devices also are installed.

It was realised that an intolerable strain would be imposed on motormen if they had to rely on the observation of lineside signals at the speeds contemplated; the New Tokaido Line therefore has no signals, but the movement of the trains is regulated by a completely automated control system, with continuous cab signalling. The motorman starts his train by opening his controller. If the line is clear, the electric traction equipment automatically accelerates the train at a rate of 0.56mph per sec until the maximum permitted speed of 130mph is reached.

quakes, and for this reason seismographs are installed at all the 25 NTL sub-stations. When the intensity of an earthquake exceeds a predetermined limit, a device in the sub-station affected cuts off power in the section of line fed from that station, and so brings all the trains in the section to a stop. The track staff must then patrol the section to see if any damage has been done, and if not they report as quickly as possible to Tokyo by lineside telephone so that normal running can be resumed. Similarly anemometers are installed at 24 different points where the track is exposed to high winds, and the information that these transmit to Tokyo enables the control staff to decide what action, if any, to take. There are also special arrangements for dealing with abnormal snowfalls.

From the opening of the New Tokaido Line with a stock of 360 motorcoaches, made up into 30 12-coach trains, traffic increased with such rapidity that in no more than three years the stock had been increased to 684 coaches, sufficient for 57 trains. At first the fastest time over the new line was fixed at 4hr for the 320 miles, until the earthworks had consolidated, but by November 1965, 16 months after opening, the time had come down to 3hr 10min, including stops at Nagoya and Kyoto, requiring an overall average of 101.1mph.

The fastest point-to-point timings are between Nagoya and Kyoto, 83.4 miles covered by a number of Hikari expresses in 47min, at a start-to-stop average of 106.5mph—a world record—while among other Hikari bookings are those over the 212.4 miles between Tokyo and Nagoya, the fastest in 120min at 106.2mph. In tests the highest speed attained has been 156.5mph. The ultimate aim is to cut the Tokyo-Shin Osaka time to 3hr flat, with speeds up to 155mph, which is also to be the maximum speed on the San-yo Line extension. The high-speed Hikari trains run at hourly intervals throughout the day, and at 20min intervals in the morning and evening peak periods. The present NTL overall times compare with a minimum of 5hr by the former 3ft 6in gauge Tokaido line.

From 60,000 passengers daily over the New Tokaido Line at the time of opening the number had grown to 113,000 two years later and 151,000 three years later, while by the beginning of 1969 no fewer than 348,168 passengers had been carried on a single day. First class has now been abolished, and each 12-coach train, which also includes two buffets and ample lavatory accommodation, can seat just over 1,000 passengers. So the New Tokaido Line has been one of the greatest railway success stories of all time. It was established in the perhaps unique conditions of rather poor rail and very poor road and air transport services between the two principal cities linked by the new service. Whether similar high-speed rail services can similarly succeed against established modern motorway and airline competition remains to be seen.

Meantime the Centralised Traffic Control Office at Tokyo has taken over. There, on a panel 60ft long, are displayed the signal aspects of all block sections throughout the 320-mile route, with the precise position and number of each train, and the conditions at each of the current feeder sub-stations; on the panel also are 200 control switches and about 1,300 indicating lights.

Experience has proved that at least 3,900yd is needed to bring a train to rest from a speed of 120mph; if a train enters a section where speed has to be reduced (either because a preceding train is being overtaken or because of a speed restriction), the signalling aspect in the driving cab changes, and automatic braking begins. This is in six stages, from 130mph down to 100, 68, 44 and 18mph and stop. The motorman actually brings the train to a stand at the various scheduled stops; otherwise his duties are to keep a sharp look-out for any obstacle on the track ahead, and to watch all the indications on the driving panel to note how the complex equipment on his train is functioning.

In order to minimise the need to move switches on the Tokyo central panel, the

Mount Fuji forms a backdrop to NTL train on elevated section.
Japan National Tourist Organisation

Coaches are over 11ft wide and provide for comfortable three-and-two seating with gangway. *Japan National Tourist Organisation*

Kodama trains, which stop at the few intermediate stations, are themselves equipped to actuate ahead of them the points leading to the station loops and those from the loops back to the main line. On approaching one of the loops each train emits a signal indicating whether it is a stopping Kodama train or one of the Hikari expresses, which call intermediately only at Nagoya and Kyoto; the signals actuate the points accordingly.

Japan is a country subject to earth-

II
The Railways of Africa

Big Steam in Southern Africa

CECIL RHODES had many dreams, but one which became almost legendary was the proposal of a continuous line of railway from the Cape to Cairo. It was never to come true. Certainly, when the eastern portion of Africa was coloured red it could have been technically possible, but political and economic circumstances decided otherwise.

But a large part of the dream was fulfilled—it became possible to travel by train from Durban and the Cape up through the Union of South Africa and on through the (then) two Rhodesias. World War I was a further staging point for, after the defeat of Germany, British influence over the whole of Africa south of the Nile became very strong indeed. A glance at the map will show that horizons were opened east and west from the borders of Rhodesia, in that the ex-German East African territory of Tanganyika with its main line from Kigoma on Lake Tanganyika to Dar-es-Salaam gave opportunities east and north to Kenya and Uganda, while the British-owned Benguela Railway in Portuguese West Africa (Angola) made connections via the Belgian Congo.

Political boundaries today have removed any thoughts of through running, but freight still operates through from Zambia (Northern Rhodesia that was) into Rhodesia, which in turn runs through services into the Union. A very large proportion of the traffic is steam-hauled—indeed that part of the world is, for the moment, one of steam's strongholds. The gauge is 3ft 6in and to carry the loads, a policy of big steam power has been necessary—including the use of articulated Garratt-type locomotives in profusion.

There is so much of interest, as far as steam goes, from the equator through Kenya southwards, including East African Railways and the Benguela line in Angola with its wood-burning Garratts, that one could fill a book. Consequently, we must limit ourselves to an area, which is the continuous line of railway from the now Rhodesian border at Victoria Falls southwards through South Africa to Cape Town and Durban. This is the railway student's

'tourist route' as far as steam is concerned.

The Rhodesian-Zambian border cuts the rail line between the two countries high over the Zambesi River halfway across the Victoria Falls Bridge. Rhodesian motive power works through into Zambia and engines are changed in a loop in Zambian territory between the border and Livingstone. Traffic is relatively heavy, with long trains, usually headed by the huge 20th-class 4-8-2+2-8-4 Garratts introduced in 1953. One can sit happily on the terrace of the comfortable Victoria Falls hotel and watch the trains crossing the bridge with this odd international traffic.

Rhodesia is very much a Garratt country with locomotives in the form of 2-6-2+2-6-2, 4-6-4+4-6-4, 2-8-2+2-8-2, and 4-8-2+2-8-4 classes plus numerous standard 4-8-2s and a few 4-8-0s. The Northern section from Victoria Falls through to Bulawayo uses three main classes—the 20th class of 4-8-2+2-8-4 for through freight, the 15th class of 4-6-4+4-6-4 for the daily through sleeping car express named The Mail, and the 4-8-2s of Class 12 based on Thompson Junction (there

Top: Number plate of South African Railways Class 24 2-8-4 locomotive No 3628. *D T Rowe*

Above: Rhodesia Railways Class 12 4-8-2 shunting coaches from The Mail train at Victoria Falls. *P B Whitehouse*

Below: On the Garden route, a Class GEA Garratt 4-8-2+2-8-4 hauls the Cape Town-Port Elizabeth train up Montague Pass between George and Topping. *P B Whitehouse*

Above: South African Railways Class 15 Garratt taking water at George, between Mossel Bay and Port Elizabeth. *P B Whitehouse*

Left: Rhodesia Railways Victoria Falls station with a Class 20 Garratt on a freight train from Zambia. *P B Whitehouse*

Bottom left and below: Two views of Garratt-hauled SAR Cape Town-Port Elizabeth express, that below taken from the dining car on Montague Pass. *Both P B Whitehouse*

Right: SAR Class 15F 4-8-2 heading a Bloemfontein-Johannesburg train in 1969. *J B Snell*

is no locomotive depot at Victoria Falls).

There is no better way to consider steam in Southern Africa than by making a journey southwards, having relaxed at Victoria Falls for a few days. The train is the evening Mail, which would be headed as far as Thompson Junction either by a 4-8-2 or one of the larger 20th-class Garratts. The make-up of the train, which arrived from Bulawayo the night before, will have coaches for first, second, third and fourth classes of travel, including sleepers and a dining car. Engine and crew are changed at Thompson Junction, where a 15th-class Garratt comes on and the load is increased to about 450 tons to Bulawayo. There is one further crew change at Sawmills. Speeds are not high, 45mph being the normal maximum.

Bulawayo is very much a steam centre with a large locomotive shed containing as many Garratt classes in one place as can be found in any country today, several classes of 4-8-2s, including the 19D class purchased from South Africa in 1966, and a few of the older 4-8-0s on shunting duties. The Rhodesia Railways workshops are also situated at Bulawayo and it is a fascinating sight, and one becoming increasingly rare in the world, to see large works undertaking heavy general repairs to steam locomotives—including, until very recently, those from Zambian Railways.

Bulawayo is the junction for the Salisbury line and is a terminus, but a connection with the Victoria Falls Mail train is made by the daily train south to the Union of South Africa; it is due to leave at 10.30 headed by a 15th-class 4-6-4+4-6-4. The trip of just under 500 miles to Mafeking runs through Bechuanaland, and since 1966 Rhodesia Railways has operated the section throughout. This has brought in the 19th-class 4-8-2 locomotives purchased from South African Railways specially for operating the line; they have large tenders carrying about 6,500 gallons of water—ideal for this arid country. The journey by the two trains, steam-hauled throughout, could entail the use of at least four different classes of engine, and provides a degree of comfort and service not found in many places in the 1970s.

South Africa can produce the largest locomotives of traditional design operating on the 3ft 6in gauge, down to some of the last steam engines constructed for the narrow gauge (2ft) in the form of 2-6-2+2-6-2 Garratts built as recently as 1968. Electrification is proceeding apace and the diesel is coming in, but steam areas are large, and some tremendous journeys can still be made by steam power behind the incredible 4-8-4s and 4-8-2s, as well as a considerable mileage behind Garratts. Big engines has been the policy of South African Railways since 1929, with the introduction of the 15CA-class 4-8-2s, followed by the large 15F and 23 classes, in addition to the huge 25-class 4-8-4s.

Bloemfontein, De Aar, and Kimberley are the homes of South African big steam. It is the width rather than the height of the engines which makes them seem so huge. In both Britain and South Africa the height of a locomotive can be 13 feet, but South African engines can be, and are, up to 10 feet wide, compared with the British 8 feet 9 inches. The impression of size becomes more obvious when one compares the South African gauge of 3ft 6in with the British 4ft 8½in.

Heading south from Mafeking, the nearest point of South African steam will be Kimberley, where the Mail arrives at seven in the morning, electric-hauled from Mafeking. There one can pick up either a through Johannesburg-Cape Town express, the Blue Train, or perhaps the Orange Express running from Durban to Cape Town via Bloemfontein. Both will be headed by 4-8-4s to Beaufort West. To travel on either train is to find comfort and courtesy which have to be experienced to be believed. At Beaufort West electricity takes over to Cape Town.

Cape Town itself, like Johannesburg, has a superb all-electric station, and apart from freight trains and shunting locomotives the steam shed at Paarl Eiland is little used. But a train runs out of Cape Town for Port Elizabeth at four o'clock each afternoon and is steam-hauled for two nights and a day once Worcester, 108 miles out, has been left behind. The journey between the two cities, in a direct line, is only 400 miles, but such are the gradients to be climbed that the distance by rail is 675 miles, taking 39 hours, giving an overall speed of 17 miles an hour. It is in fact, quicker to do the trip by Union Castle mail boat! This run is known as the Garden Route and the scenery is extremely fine. The *piece de resistance* however, is around 20 hours of 4-8-2+2-8-4 Garratt steam haulage, including several notable climbs, the greatest being the ascent of the Montague Pass from George to Topping where the gradient is as steep as 1 in 38. The train is luxurious, with full sleeping and restaurant facilities, and loads to just over 500 tons.

The first Garratt (Class GMAM) comes on at Worcester and runs through the night to Riversdale where another of the lighter 4-8-2+2-8-4 GEA class, takes charge and heads the train through to Mossel Bay, which is reached soon after breakfast. There the train is reversed and re-marshalled and makes the short journey to Hartenbos junction where a new GEA class engine is added, running bunker first because of the tunnels to come. At Hartenbos the train is crossed by yet another Garratt-hauled express which has come down from Johannesburg via Kroonstad and Bloemfontein.

From Hartenbos (reached at 10.32) the line runs close to the sea—so close that whales can be seen quite frequently, and at George (shortly after noon) the GEA takes water for the climb ahead. The Montague Pass section with its gradients and tight curves limits speed severely—twelve coaches is the maximum permissible load—

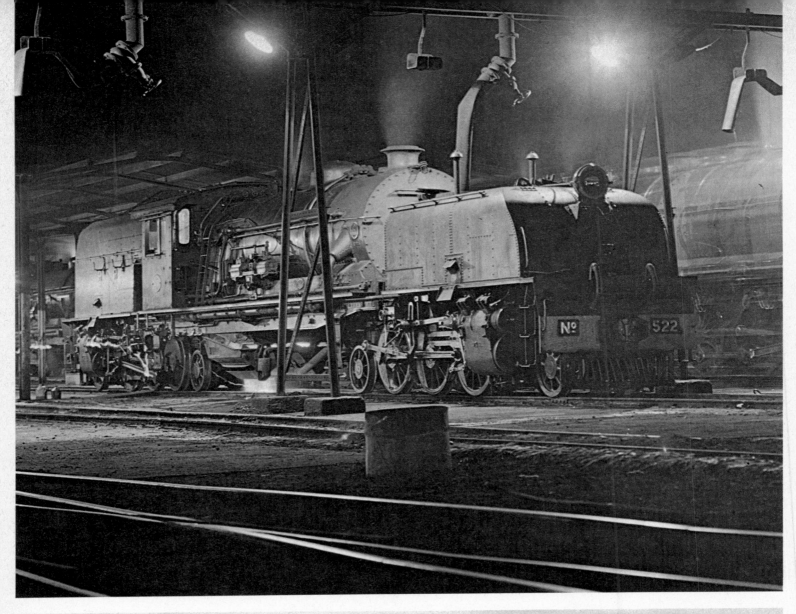

Above: A SAR Class 10C 4-6-2, normally used as a shed pilot, on a Bloemfontein local train in October 1969. *J B Snell*

Below: A Class NG15 2ft-gauge 2-8-2 being serviced at Loerie, near Port Elizabeth. *P B Whitehouse*

Left: Night work preparing steam locomotives for next day's traffic, at Bulawayo motive power depot. *Rhodesia Railways*

Below left: Class 24 2-8-4 with a goods train at Wilderness, beside the Indian Ocean, in July 1972. *J Hunt*

and the Garratt has to work hard. Beyond Power, a water stop, the train travels the most spectacular section, where the line hugs the cliffside and passes through some very smoky tunnels until the summit is reached at Topping—1,700 feet higher than George—climbed in fifteen miles and with the exhaust shooting 40 feet up into the air.

The descent is less steep and by four in the afternoon the train is at Oudtshoorn, with its ostrich farms, where engines change from the GEA Garratt to a Class 19D 4-8-2 for the journey through the dusk and early night to Klipplaat. (The 19D engines carry 12 tons of coal and 6,500 gallons of water). On this section the character of the line seems to alter, taking on more of a narrow-gauge atmosphere, and the train runs alongside the road into the foothills before another long series of climbs begins. Curves are sharp, and riding on a rocking and rolling engine panting uphill and running fast down, means holding on tight. As the clear South African night comes on, one gets a dramatic effect on looking back at the twisting well-lit train of red and brown coaches with the pulsating engine belching out fire and smoke under one's feet. During the night locomotives are changed again, the journey from Kliplaat to Port Elizabeth (reached at 07.00) being made behind a Class 15AR 4-8-2.

At Port Elizabeth a completely new factor in the range of South African steam emerges, in the 2ft gauge line to Avontur, 177 miles away. The Avontur Railway, with other 2ft lines, is fully described in Sydney Moir's excellent book *Twenty Four Inches Apart*. It is worked by Class NG15 2-8-2 locomotives originally built for German South West Africa, and by 2-6-2+2-6-2 Garratts. It is a well-constructed line, and speeds of 35mph are sometimes reached with the occasional special passenger trains, though the normal freight-only service is much slower. Traffic is heavy to Loerie, about 45 miles out of Port Elizabeth, for this is the route of the frequent stone trains working to the Port Elizabeth cement works. Gradients are steep, needing double-heading by the 2-8-2s when loads are heavy, which is often for 250-ton trains are common. The summit of this section of the line is 29 miles out and there are frequent passing loops. One interesting feature both of the 2-8-2s and the Garratts is the small padded seat for each crew member pivoted on the cab handrail, so that the men can be inside or outside according to the weather.

The 2ft-gauge lines become more frequent in Natal and in the general direction of Durban all are worked with Garratt engines of varying age and manufacture, the last having come from the workshops of Hunslet Taylor in 1968. The new Garratts were completed at Germiston works and were hauled on flat wagons 500 miles over SAR tracks to Port Shepstone.

So, even on the 2ft gauge, South African steam is large and modern. Its engines are mostly Garratts and there is even a regular (daily) passenger service behind one—from Mid Illovo to Umlaas Road in Natal. For real hard work though, they must be seen on the Port Shepstone to Harding or Esperanza to Umzinto and Donnybrook branches. They, like all South African steam, are still there to be savoured —but perhaps only for the next decade.

Rhodesian Railways in Pictures

Left: East African Railways Class 87 (old 90) 1,840hp 1Co-Co1 diesel-electric No 8737, just out of the paintshop, at Nairobi in August 1971. *C M Whitehouse*

Below left: East African Railways 2-8-2 No 2506 (Vulcan 1929), at Tabora, Tanzania, in January 1971. *C J Gammell*

Above: Rhodesia Railways diesel-electric locomotive at a level crossing on the outskirts of Salisbury. *Rhodesia Railways*

Right: Rhodesia Railways Class DE4 Brush 1,875hp Co-Co diesel-electric locomotive at Salisbury. *C M Whitehouse*

Below: One of the 1955 English Electric DE2 2,000hp diesel-electric engines heading a goods train in the eastern district of Rhodesia. *Rhodesia Railways*

Above: SAR Class 19B 4-8-2 climbing the Lootsberg pass, near Middelburg, in August 1967. *D Huntriss*

Above right: SAR electric express passenger train on the Indian Ocean coast near Durban. *Courtesy South African Railways*

Below: SAR Class 24 2-8-4 near Aprilskraal on the Jamestown branch in July 1972. *J Hunt*

Right: A Garratt taking water (and stoking up!) on the Umtata branch in eastern Cape Province in July 1972. *J Hunt*

South African Railways
IN PICTURES

Above: Garratt 4-6-2 + 2-6-4 climbing from
Franklin towards Donnybrook in June 1969.
T B Owen

Below: The last-serving SAR 6J 4-6-0 and a
Class 8 4-8-0 on a Bethlehem-Frankfort goods
train in September 1969.   *J B Snell*

Above: EAR 4-8-0 No 2412 on the shore of
Lake Victoria at Kisumu, Kenya, with a Butere
train in January 1971. *C J Gammell*

Below: Mozambique Harbours Railways &
Transport Class 304 Pacific (Baldwin 1923) at
Lourenço Marques in July 1967. *T B Owen*

Above: Class 15AR 4-8-2 shunting at Molteno in July 1972. *A G Bowles*

Below: Class 14CRB 4-8-2 taking water at Toleni on the Umtata line with a northbound freight train in July 1972. *A G Bowles*

12
The Railways of Australasia

Overleaf: First standard-gauge train through Avon yard (near Northam) from Merredin to North Fremantle in November 1966.
Western Australian Government Railways

RAILWAYS OF AUSTRALIA

AUSTRALIA, the 'Island Continent', has an area of nearly three million square miles —almost as great as that of the United States of America, nearly three-quarters of the area of the whole of Europe and about 25 times as large as Great Britain and Ireland. Its government powers are vested in six sovereign States, plus a Commonwealth Parliament, to which certain specified powers were transferred when the states agreed to form a Federation in 1901.

All these facts are important when we come to study the history of railway development in Australia. For, in this large country with a comparatively small population (under 13 million in 1972), there are not one, but seven independently operated railway systems and three main gauges of rail track—3ft 6in, 4ft 8½in and 5ft 3in. One state railway system, the South Australian Railways, operates significant mileages of all three gauges. Two others—Victoria and Western Australia—operate on two gauges, and there are remnants of former narrower-gauge (2ft 6in and 2ft) lines in Victoria and Queensland. The problem of differing gauges in Australia has become well-known throughout the world, and it is only in the years following the 1939-45 war that any material change has occurred. It has plagued railway operations ever since the lines of two adjoining systems met, in 1883.

But at the time when railway communication was first established in the Australian states, each was a self-governing independent colony of Great Britain, free to make its own choice on transport policy. Right at the start of railway construction, in Victoria and New South Wales almost simultaneously, an unsuccessful attempt was made to achieve uniformity of rail gauge, but could the problem of its lack be truly appreciated? After all, the population of the entire continent was just over half a million European settlers; the closest of any two major settlements (Sydney and Melbourne) were over 500 miles apart, and passenger-carrying railways had been in existence in England for less than 20 years. The story of railway progress in Australia, therefore, can best be told by looking at each system in turn, and drawing the threads together at the end, as has been done, almost literally, with new construction since 1945.

In the early 1830s, coal companies in New South Wales drew on English practice by using horse-operated railed ways for moving coal to loading staiths in the Hunter river. Convicts provided 'push power' for a five-mile line on the notorious Tasman peninsula in Tasmania for a period after 1836. In May 1854, a horse-worked railway was opened between Goolwa and Port Elliott in South Australia —it was lengthened a little but remained isolated and horse-worked for 31 years. So that the honour of opening the first steam-operated railway on the continent, the first of the lines which became railways as we know them today, went to Victoria—a separate colony since 1851.

Australia's first railway was built to link Melbourne, capital of Victoria, with its port of Sandridge (now Port Melbourne), 3½ miles away. The Melbourne and Hobson's Bay Railway Company was incorporated in 1853. Engines, rails, rolling stock and machinery were ordered from England. Construction was completed well in advance of the expected arrival of the engines. To avoid a delay in the start of the service, a local contractor was commissioned to build an engine—which he did, in the space of 10 weeks at a cost of £2,500.

The opening took place on September 12, 1854. Passenger carriages and goods

Top left: Opening in February 1902 at Beech forest, Victoria (devastated by fire) of the 2ft 6in-gauge line through the Otway ranges. *M C G Schrader*

Top right: VR A2 4-6-0 on a passenger train at Melbourne Spencer Street station in November 1963. *M C G Schrader*

Centre: S-class three-cylinder Pacific heading the air-conditioned Spirit of Progress Melbourne-Albury train introduced in 1937. *Victorian Railways*

Above: A South Australian Rx 4-6-0 on the shores of St Vincents Gulf near Adelaide. *M C G Shrader*

Below: The Jet interstate (Victoria-South Australia) express goods train headed by two VR diesel-electric locos—one S class and one T class. *D Doubleday*

Left: R-class 4-6-4 on a special passenger train in northern Victoria in April 1971. The blue coach in the middle is air conditioned.
M C G Schrader

Bottom left: AA-class 4-4-0 with a Sydney express near Melbourne in 1902.
Victorian Railways

Above: New South Wales Railways Alco-designed diesel-electric Co-Co and a Daylight express on the northern line out of Sydney. *M C G Schrader*

Right: A (c) 36-class 4-6-0 pilots a Beyer-Garratt on a heavy freight climbing 1 in 40 at Borenore, NSW, Sydney bound.
M C G Schrader

Bottom right: No 3813 Pacific, one of the most renowned of Australian steam locos, hurries the air-conditioned Newcastle Flyer towards Sydney, before diesels took over the turn in 1971. *M C G Schrader*

wagons followed typical English practice of the period and the locomotives were also of English design. The gauge of the line was 5ft 3in, which was adopted by other companies building lines to other Melbourne suburbs and became the 'standard' gauge for Victoria. The early Melbourne suburban railways operated profitably and were taken over by the Victorian government only when it became necessary to integrate their operation with longer-distance country lines.

Similar financial success was not achieved by companies building those country lines. The Geelong and Melbourne Railway Company, which opened Victoria's first long-distance line connecting the two settlements in 1857, failed, and was taken over by the government in 1860. Another company intent on building lines to suburban Williamstown and the goldfields at Bendigo, was taken over during the construction phase in 1856—and with that purchase, the Victorian Government Railways really originated. From then on, prime responsibility for development of railways in Victoria was vested in the state parliament.

By 1864, railways linked Melbourne with the important centres of Geelong, Ballarat, and Bendigo, forming 200 miles of main trunk route. The line to the New South Wales state border on the Murray river at Wodonga was completed in 1873; ten years later, the NSW line reached Albury on the northern shore, and a connection was made. For the first time, Australia's break-of-gauge problem manifested itself—passengers and goods had to change trains at the border.

Following the gold boom of the 1850s, settlement became widespread, land values rose rapidly, and a vast programme of railway construction was authorised by the Victorian parliament in the early 1880s. About 70 new lines at an estimated cost of over £50 million were planned. Most were purely developmental and it required the collapse of the boom to slow construction down. When the collapse did occur, experiments were made with cheaper forms of railways—four isolated lines of 2ft 6in gauge were built. They were never viable and today only a truncated remnant of one line survives as a very popular enthusiast-sponsored excursion route: Victoria's 'Puffing Billy' railway.

Early Victorian locomotives, mainly of the 0-6-0 wheel arrangement for goods working and 2-4-0 for passenger, were built in England. By 1873, the Phoenix Foundry at Ballarat was producing engines locally, sometimes to a 'pattern' engine from overseas. With the expansionist boom of the '80s, the Railway Commissioners introduced a degree of standardisation and five new classes containing some interchangeable parts, and design features needed for Victorian operation, were introduced, and the locomotives developed a distinctive appearance. The Railway workshops at Newport built their first locomotive in 1893, and were largely instrumental in providing heavier and more modern power after 1900. The DD and A2 classes, both 4-6-0s, preceded heavier Consolidation and Mikado types for goods working, while four three-cylinder Pacifics were the pride of the passenger fleet up to the outbreak of war in 1939.

The 180 or so modern steam engines built after the war, including 70 R-class 4-6-4s of new design, had a comparatively short life; when dollar funds became available, Victoria embarked on dieselisation. Various of the American General Motors designs with components built in Australia under licence form the back-

bone of the present fleet of about 300 locomotives. Apart from a small fleet of reserve and special-use steam engines, all of Victoria's traffic is now handled by diesel or electric power.

Passenger rolling stock in Victoria has tended to blend English and American design features. Four- and six-wheel carriages were replaced by bogie vehicles, the first of which appeared in service in 1862, and which became more widespread after 1874. Longevity has been a feature—some suburban carriages built in 1880 were lengthened in 1910-15, adapted for electric traction, and are still running today. The Melbourne suburban railways were electrified, after wartime delays, from 1919 onwards, when the first electric train in Australia left Melbourne for the suburbs of Essendon and Sandringham. Electrification to the heart of the brown-coal-producing areas in the Latrobe valley, 110 miles from Melbourne, was inaugurated in 1954-55.

Air-conditioning of passenger carriages was introduced experimentally in 1935, and in 1937, a new all-steel air-conditioned train named Spirit of Progress started running non-stop between Melbourne and Albury, 190 miles. Spirit of Progress is now support to Southern Aurora, an all-sleeping-car train running through from Melbourne to Sydney on 4ft 8½in gauge. On January 3, 1962, after nearly 80 years of wasteful changeover at Albury, a new line parallel to the existing broad-gauge track was brought into use southwards to Melbourne. It was the first of the major developments in through connections in Australia which have been a feature of railway growth since 1945. They will be described later.

The honour of opening the first steam railway in Australia nearly belonged to New South Wales. Before any decisive move was made in Victoria, the Sydney Railway Company was formed by an Act of 1849 to build a line of railway south and west from Sydney. A series of financial

difficulties hampered construction for five years and, in the event, the government acquired the undertaking on September 3, 1855, 23 days before the official first train ran over the 13½-mile 4ft 8½in-gauge line. Thus, the first NSW railway became the first state-owned steam railway in the British Empire. In practice, the constructing contractor, a Mr William Randle, operated the line under licence from a newly appointed board of commissioners for the first 12 months. Service was started with four 0-4-2 locomotives supplied by Robert Stephenson, and 32 carriages and 57 goods wagons, all from England.

As the oldest of the railway constructing bodies in Australia, the Sydney Railway Company accepted the advice of its Irish engineer, a Mr Shields, to adopt the Irish 'standard' gauge of 5ft 3in. for its Sydney-Parramatta line. The Victorian and South Australian governments agreed to the proposal and rolling stock for the Melbourne-Sandridge and Goolwa-Port Elliott lines was ordered accordingly. Shields resigned; a Scot—James Wallace—was appointed to replace him and persuaded the Sydney Railway to adopt 4ft 8½in for its track. As no rolling stock had been ordered, the directors agreed, and from that small beginning, Australia's rail gauge muddle began.

After its acquisition of the Sydney Railway Company, the NSW government assumed responsibility for most railway construction in that state, where early builders faced tremendous problems. The city of Sydney is surrounded by rocky plateaux and mountain ranges, the ascent of which required great engineering skill. Chiefly responsible for overcoming those problems was Mr John Whitton, appointed engineer-in-chief in 1857. He fought and won a battle to build full-scale railways instead of narrow-gauge horse-worked tramways and even today, many of his engineering works are in constant use. He was responsible for the design and construction of 2,100 miles of railway

during his 33 years of office.

Jointly with development out of Sydney, the NSW government provided rail connections inland from Newcastle, 100 miles to the north and a port on the Hunter river. The first 20-mile section of what became known as the Great Northern Railway opened in 1857; it was gradually extended towards the Queensland border, which was reached at Wallangarra in 1888. The Queensland Railways had built their line south from Brisbane to Wallangarra in 1887.

Meanwhile, progress out of Sydney was slow. The escarpment of the Blue Mountains presented a barrier to the settlement of the rich Bathurst/Orange area which was finally broken when Whitton designed two zig-zags for carrying the line over the range. The more spectacular, the Great Zig-zag near Lithgow, achieved world fame when it came into use in 1869; its three graceful sweeps carried the line down into the valley on a grade of 1 in 42. Increasing traffic forced major expenditure on tunnelling and re-grading to eliminate the zig-zag in 1910, but its stonework is preserved today as a national monument.

Because the route to be followed was somewhat easier, progress on the main line south from Sydney proceeded quite rapidly. Long stretches of 1 in 40 gradient were, however, common on the route through Goulburn (reached 1869), and Wagga Wagga (1879) to Albury (1881). There the matter rested until 1883, when the two state governments had decided on how the bridge across the Murray river was to be financed, and inter-colonial communication was established.

The years 1880-1885 saw great progress in the railway network, with 1,000 miles of new lines constructed. But Sydney and Newcastle remained unconnected by rail, although the gap had been narrowed to a four-mile ferry journey along the Hawkesbury river. At last, in May 1889, a 2,900ft rail bridge over that river was opened,

linking Sydney and Newcastle, and making possible a through rail journey from Adelaide to Melbourne, Sydney and Brisbane—albeit with two gauge changes en route. NSW resisted the temptation to cheapen rail construction costs by changing to a narrower gauge for feeder lines. Instead, they remained standard-gauge 'light' lines, built as cheaply as possible for a designed speed of 15mph, to be improved when funds permitted.

Long distances are a feature of travel in NSW, and at an early stage night-time mail passenger trains became an established pattern of service. In consequence, sleeping cars were introduced quite early, in 1877, and eventually formed a large fleet for the inter-colonial expresses and other night trains. Only in the years since the 1939-45 war have higher-speed day trains tended to supplant night trains on premier passenger services. The NSWGR system has for many years been the busiest of all seven in Australia. Route mileage at peak was only slightly below that of Queensland, but the density of traffic warranted construction of double track over many hundreds of miles and, in later years, electrification to handle rapidly growing tonnages.

As with most other Australian railways, the NSWGR relied mainly on English sources for early locomotives, but by the 1870s, local builders were at work, including the railways' own workshops. Clyde Engineering later became a prominent supplier and the American Baldwin company a continuing supplier. Continuing capacity for hard work, longevity, and success have characterised a number of

NSW locomotive types, and some must be mentioned. The P6 (later C32) class 4-6-0s, designed by newly appointed locomotive engineer W Thow, in conjunction with Beyer Peacock in England, were first introduced in 1892. Over a period of 19 years, a total of 191 was supplied by four different builders. They were extremely successful and versatile, handling express, goods and mixed trains with ease. One of them hauled the last regularly steam-hauled passenger train in NSW in 1971, not specially selected but on regular roster. For goods working, Thow introduced the T524 (later D50) class 2-8-0s in 1896. The 280 engines of this class, complemented by 190 of the improved D53 and 120 of the D55 class, became standard goods engines of NSW, and some are still at work in 1972.

In 1925, the first of 25 D57 three-cylinder 4-8-2s was brought into service for heavy goods working. Their tractive effort was 67 per cent greater than the standard goods engines, but high axle loads restricted availability. The increasing weight of passenger expresses brought about the displacement of the C32s, firstly by two successful classes of 4-6-0 C35s and C36s. For the heaviest long-distance trains, the C38 class 4-6-2s entered service from 1943. Of the 30 engines, the first five were streamlined, and the entire group gained the respect of professional railwaymen and enthusiasts throughout Australia. In 1971, class leader No 3801 ran from Sydney to Perth over the new standard-gauge lines hauling an enthusiast special, and became the first locomotive ever to cross the continent in steam. In 1952, the NSWGR placed in service the first of 42 AD60-class 4-8-4 + 4-8-4 Beyer-Garratts, the most powerful steam locomotives in Australia, and among the largest of their type in the world. The last examples are still at work in 1972.

Mainstay of the present locomotive fleet are Alco-designed diesel-electrics of various classes. The twenty 40-class units introduced in 1951 are now all out of service in NSW, although some were reconditioned and sold to a mining railway in Western Australia. As such, they are the first class of Australian diesels to be fully withdrawn from service. General Motors locomotives, locally built by Clyde Engineering, are also represented on the NSWGR. Notable straight electric engines are the 46-class main-line general-purpose units rated at 3,400hp, supplied by Metropolitan-Vickers, which are designed to haul trains of 400 tons up continuous 1 in 33 gradients at a speed of 35mph.

We have already noted that a horse-worked railway commenced operation in South Australia in 1854. The first steam-operated line in the state linked the capital, Adelaide, with its port, and opened for traffic on April 21, 1856. Construction took place under government control, after private enterprise had failed in an earlier attempt to build the line. Three 2-4-0 engines named *Adelaide*, *Victoria* and *Albert* were imported from the Fairbairn company in England to begin the service. Originally, the track was laid with bridge rails, screwed and bolted to longitudinal sleepers, on the Great Western or Brunel system, but it proved unsuitable for the climatic conditions and the track was relaid with conventional cross-ties (sleepers) in 1868-69.

In South Australia, railway development first proceeded northwards from Adelaide. The copper-mining town of Burra was reached in 1870 by a 5ft 3in-gauge line, which was extended to Terowie by 1880. The first section of what is now the main interstate line to Melbourne was opened as far as Aldgate, 22 miles, in 1883, and continued to the Victorian border by 1885. The Victorian Railways reached that point in 1887, and a through rail service over the one gauge from Melbourne to Adelaide became possible. The Intercolonial Express, as it was termed, included examples of the first rolling stock to be jointly owned by two Australian railway systems, and to this day the same practice is followed. The modern Overland express, with its sleeping, sitting, cafeteria and lounge cars, is jointly owned by the two state governments.

In the late 1860s, the South Australian government made a momentous and unfortunate decision that future rail expansion in light-traffic areas would be built on the 3ft 6in gauge, allegedly cheaper to build and operate. No fewer than eight such separate railways originated at ports on the state coastline. They finally merged into four major systems, the first of which, later known as the Western system, opened with a horse-operated line from Port Wakefield in 1870. Steam replaced horses in 1876. The Northern division originated at Port Pirie in 1875, and was built in stages to Petersburg (now Peterborough) in 1881.

Following the discovery of minerals at Broken Hill, the South Australian government built a line from Petersburg to the NSW border at Cockburn, whence a privately owned 'tramway' ran on to Broken Hill. This line was destined to carry millions of tons of ore concentrates from Broken Hill to smelters established at Port Pirie. The South Eastern narrow-gauge system based on Kingston opened in 1877, and the Port Lincoln division started operations in 1907. The government built and operated a line south from Darwin to Pine Creek, 146 miles, in 1889 and pushed a line of rail northwards through the desert to Oodnadatta by 1890. These two sections were intended to meet ultimately as a north-south link.

South Australia, therefore, faced major

break-of-gauge problems within her own state borders. It eventually converted the Western system to 5ft 3in gauge, by 1927, and the South-East division by 1959. The Port Lincoln division remains an isolated 450-mile 3ft 6in-gauge stronghold, but the busy Cockburn - Peterborough - Port Pirie line was converted to 4ft 8½in gauge in 1970. So South Australia today operates major segments of railway on three different gauges.

Locomotive development on the South Australian Railways was characterised until the 1920s by a proliferation of types and classes. Most notable on the 5ft 3in-gauge lines were the 84 Rx-class 4-6-0s, built by English and Australian builders in the period 1886 (as R-class) to 1915. The 3ft 6in-gauge lines employed a series of 2-6-0 locomotives of increasing size and power as their mainstay of operation until 1903, when the first of 77 T-class 4-8-0s made their appearance. These originally handsome machines were used on both freight and passenger workings; in a less aesthetic modified form they survived in regular service until 1970.

Motive power—and indeed the whole operating practice of the SAR—underwent a major change from 1923 with the appointment of Mr W A Webb as Commissioner for Railways. Webb had had extensive experience in the USA and the SAR became largely Americanised. A big-engine policy produced some powerful machines on the 5ft 3in gauge; notable were ten 500-class 4-8-2s for express working through the extremely difficult Hills section of the Interstate line; ten 600-class Pacifics for passenger work on flatter terrain; a series of 2-8-2s of the 700 and 710 classes for heavy freight working; and latterly a group of 2-8-4s for the same purpose. A lighter series of Pacifics, the 620-class, were built from 1936.

But motive power was only part of the plan. Bogie freight rolling stock and caboose-type brakevans were purchased.

Large-capacity high-speed coaling plants were installed at the main depots. Central train control was introduced on the main South line in 1924, and later extended. On light-traffic lines, train orders replaced the British-based staff-and-ticket system of safeworking common throughout the rest of Australia. Automatic signalling on both double and single lines replaced block working and electric staff where traffic was heavier. American-built railcars provided passenger services on both suburban and country lines.

It was an exciting, visually rewarding, and worthwhile change which has continued to influence South Australian thinking through to the present day. The SAR introduced its first diesel-electric locomotive—an Alco-based unit in 1951, and the system is now totally dieselised. Of interest is the fact that one class of diesel-electric, the 830-class Goodwin-Alco 900 hp locomotive, operates on all three gauges in South Australia—3ft 6in, 4ft 8½in and 5ft 3in.

Above: A pair of 830-class 3ft 6in-gauge Goodwin-Alco 900hp diesel-electrics leaving Cockburn yard with an ore train for Peterborough and Port Pirie. *M C G Schrader*

Below: SAR Class 400 (No 406) 4-8-2+2-8-4 Beyer-Garratt with a mixed bag of wagons near Crystal Brook in February 1969. *M C G Schrader*

Bottom: Rx-class No 20 and R-class No 103 at the head of the Melbourne Express at Adelaide station in the 1920s. *South Australian Railways*

Above: A PB15 4-6-0 takes a passenger train over Stoney Creek on the Cairns Railway in North Queensland; the coaches ('grandstand cars') originally had deep windows on one side and seats tiered up from the windows so that passengers could enjoy the view.
M C G Schrader

The pattern of railway development in Queensland differs somewhat from that in other states, and reflects the manner in which settlement itself grew along the Queensland eastern seaboard. Self-government of the colony in 1859 was followed by a demand for rail transport; the first line was designed to connect Ipswich with the fertile Darling Downs district. Political pressure influenced the choice of Ipswich, about 20 miles upstream from the capital, Brisbane, as the starting point rather than the capital itself. Through connection to Brisbane awaited the building of a river bridge in 1876.

On the recommendation of an Irish engineer, Abram Fitzgibbon, the gauge of 3ft 6in was adopted for the new line, which opened as far as Bigge's Camp (now Grandchester), 21 miles, on July 31, 1865. Surmounting two significant climbs, the Liverpool range and the Main range, the line reached Toowoomba, principal city of the Darling Downs, on May 1, 1867. Settlers in the southern part of the colony thereby had access to the sea, albeit with transhipment from the small steamers reaching Ipswich to larger ones at Brisbane.

There followed a period when unconnected railways developed along the east coast. The hinterland from Rockhampton was tapped with a 30-mile line of 3ft 6in gauge in 1867. Construction of the Great Northern Railway westwards from Townsville began in 1880 and the line reached the mining centre of Charters Towers in 1882. From Maryborough and Bundaberg, small sections of line opened in 1888; Cooktown and Mackay followed in 1885.

In 1887, work started on the Cairns railway. Construction of the 15-mile Barron Gorge section proved to be the most arduous in all of Queensland, and even today, a journey over the line is one of the most spectacular in all Australia. There are 15 tunnels ranging from 56 yards to 470 yards in length; the longest is approached on a $7\frac{1}{2}$-chain radius curve, has a 5-chain curve in the middle and a 15-chain curve at the other end. Six steel bridges and 59 wooden trestles complete part of the story. From the top of the range, about 300 miles of 3ft 6in-gauge line was built by the Chillagoe Company to serve its mining interests on the Atherton tableland; it was later absorbed into the government system.

The joining of these independent coastal rail systems was a gradual process. Rockhampton was linked with the southern system in 1903, and a special Act of 1910 authorised the building of a north coast line through to Cairns, completed in 1924. Vast distances and a relatively small population have contributed to the operating problems of the Queensland Railways over the years. The system had the greatest route-mileage (approximately 6,600) of any state, and although the total has been reduced somewhat by closures in the years since the 1939-45 war, many lines are still laid in very light rail (42lb/yd). The light-line policy, to an extent forced upon the state by the need for development at low cost, brought with it small locomotives, light rolling stock, minimum services, and a reputation for slow speeds and discomfort. The image has changed dramatically in the last 10 years.

For use on the first section of line, the Queensland government ordered four 2-4-0 engines from the English firm of Slaughter Grunning (which became the Avonside Engine Company soon afterwards). The diminutive machines weighed only 22 tons and produced a tractive effort of 4,500lb. They were soon joined by a later group of 22-ton 0-4-2 Neilson engines, one of which was later sold to a private sugar milling firm and saw out almost a full

century of service. It was returned to the QGR for participation in its Centenary and eventual preservation. Not so successful were three double-Fairlie 0-6-6-0s brought out in 1867, and returned to their builders as unsatisfactory.

In earlier years, the QGR purchased locomotives from Baldwin in America and various English sources. For light lines, the 4-6-0 type ultimately found favour; 112 Class B13s were built from 1883 onwards and 98 Class B15s introduced for goods working in 1889. Even more ubiquitous were the 202 Class PB15 passenger 4-6-0s with 4ft driving wheels introduced in 1900 and a further 30 of similar class developed in 1924. Kitson, of Leeds, built 20 of the originals; all the others came from Queensland firms, including the QGR's Ipswich workshops. The PB15s remained in service until 1969, when all steam traction finished on the QGR (except for special workings). An extremely successful 4-8-0 for goods working, the C17 class, was introduced in 1920 and totalled 227 engines; the last were built after 1945. For heavier passenger trains, the $B18\frac{1}{4}$ class 4-6-2s were introduced in 1926 and 83 were completed. An improved $BB18\frac{1}{4}$ was first built in 1951. Other recent steam locomotives included 30 4-8-2+2-8-4 Beyer-Garratts, and 12 4-6-4Ts to augment the fleet of suburban tank engines in Brisbane.

Diesel-electric traction first came to Queensland in 1952 and spearheaded moves to increase the system's capacity and operating performance. Today the fleet comprises nearly 400 diesel-electrics ranging up to 2,000hp, and 70 diesel-hydraulics which have taken over much of the work of the PB15s on light lines.

For long-distance country services, nine air-conditioned all steel trains have been built since 1953. The QGR developed railcar services more extensively than any other system, and eventually replaced many of them with modern stainless-steel units in 1956; where secondary passenger services survive, they are railcar operated. In the Brisbane suburban area, 112 stainless-steel coaches suitable for conversion to electric traction if required have been built in the last 10 years.

Above: One of the 30 QGR Beyer-Garratts of 1951, No 1006 at Rockhampton shed in 1964. *M C G Schrader*

Right: First train out of Kalgoorlie for Port Augusta on the 4ft 8½in-gauge 1,051-mile Trans-Australian line on October 25, 1917. *WAGR/Commonwealth Railways*

Below: Break-of-gauge station at Marree on the Central Australian line; at left a 3ft 6in-gauge Class NM 4-8-0 with a northbound train for Alberrie Creek and at right a Commonwealth Clyde-GM diesel-electric and passenger train from Port Augusta. *M C G Schrader*

Bottom: A WAGR G-class 4-6-0 No 123 (one of 22 built by Dübs and Beyer Peacock from 1895) on a train of vintage carriages crossing the Capel river in 1968. *M C G Schrader*

Top: Tasmanian Government Railways Centenary in 1971 brought out a train of restored coaches, seen near Deloraine, headed by a CCS 2-6-0 and MA Pacific. *M C G Schrader*

Above: An Emu Bay Railway Standard Australian Garratt on a special train in 1964, with Tasmania's rugged mountains as a backdrop. *M C G Schrader*

Three major projects to assist the minerals industry in Queensland have recently been undertaken by the QGR. In the first, completed in 1965, the 600-mile track from Townsville to Mount Isa was upgraded and strengthened to cater for the vastly increased output from the Mount Isa copper mines. A new 112-mile line was completed from the Moura coalfield to the port of Gladstone in 1968, and another 125-mile line connecting the Goonyella coalfield with a port at Hay Point, near Mackay, opened in 1971. New track standards permit the operation of trains of 70 hopper wagons grossing 5,200 tons.

The QGR also owns trackage of two other gauges — the 2ft Innisfail Tramway, formerly a passenger and general cargo carrier which now serves only the sugar milling interests in the area, as do many private 2ft-gauge lines in other parts of Queensland. A 69-mile 4ft 8½in-gauge line runs direct to Brisbane from the New South Wales border, but rolling stock is provided by the NSWGR. This line was an early successful attempt to minimise break-of-gauge problems.

Australia's smallest state, the island of Tasmania, also has the smallest route-mileage of railway, but there are fascinating aspects to its history. Private enterprise built the first line, from Launceston to Deloraine, to a gauge of 5ft 3in; it opened in February 1871. The Launceston & Western Railway Company, however, ran into financial difficulties and was taken over by the government in 1872. The Tasmanian Main Line Railway Company,

another private venture, built and operated a 3ft 6in-gauge line from Launceston to the capital, Hobart, opening throughout for traffic in 1876. For the last nine miles into Launceston, a third rail was laid on the Launceston & Western's track and dual-gauge operation continued until 1888, when the latter was narrowed to 3ft 6in. The government built branch lines from the Hobart - Launceston line and acquired the assets of the Main Line Company in 1890.

On the island's west coast, the Van Diemen's Land Company had laid a 44-mile 3ft-gauge wooden-railed horse tramway inland from the port of Burnie on Emu bay to the tin mines of Waratah. In 1884, the Emu Bay and Mount Bischoff Railway Company took over the line and relaid it with steel rails to 3ft 6in gauge. The Emu Bay Railway Company, formed in 1897, extended the line 50 miles to the important mining centre of Zeehan. The Zeehan-Queenstown area, rich in minerals, abounded in small railways and tramways, both government and private, built to serve the mining communities.

The government - operated 2ft-gauge North - East Dundas Tramway was notable both for its spectacular scenery and for its contribution to world locomotive development. Over its metals from 1910 were operated the world's first Beyer - Garratt locomotives; they were diminutive 33-ton machines with 0-4-0+0-4-0 wheel arrangement, designed to negotiate curves of 1½ chains radius and to climb gradients of 1 in 25. The two engines continued in service, intermittently from 1929, until 1938-39, when the tramway closed. Number 1 was restored in 1947 and shipped back to the works of Beyer Peacock in Manchester, England; when the works closed the relic passed into the care of the Festiniog Railway.

From Queenstown to Regatta point, the Mount Lyell Mining and Railway Company operated a spectacular 21-mile line, including 4½ miles of Abt-system rack. The line was opened throughout in 1899 but closed as a result of high costs in 1963.

The Emu Bay Railway operated large Beyer - Garratts, each using two firemen to maintain steam on the continuous heavy

gradients. The company was the last stronghold in Australia of a far-from-successful machine known as the Australian Standard Garratt. In an attempt to increase quickly the locomotive power available to meet wartime needs on Australia's 3ft 6in-gauge lines, 65 4-8-2+2-8-4 119-ton Garratts were built to a new and unproved design in railway workshops throughout Australia. The locomotives operated for varying periods in Queensland, South Australia, Western Australia and Tasmania. The Emu Bay bought two in 1948 and two more from Tasmania in 1961; they lasted until diesel-hydraulic locomotives replaced steam on the line.

Settlement in Western Australia came more slowly than in the eastern states, and it was the development of the state's natural resources which first created a demand for rail transport.

Timber milling led to the building of the first lines from Lockeville to Yokonup in 1871, and from Rockingham to Jarrahdale, near Perth, in 1872. The former used the first steam locomotive in Western Australia. Named *Ballaarat*, it was in fact built by the Phoenix Foundry in Ballarat, Victoria. Today, it is preserved in Busselton. The second line became part of a large network of timber - getting railways throughout the south-west of WA. Some of the lines were incorporated into the government system and carried general traffic as well. All have now been replaced by other forms of transport, or have been abandoned. The right - of - way of the Rockingham-Jarrahdale line is now partly used by some of the heaviest block trains in WA conveying bauxite from the mine site to a coastal aluminium smelter.

The first government railway in the state was built to assist industry, this time lead and copper mining. Opened in 1879, the line ran from Geraldton, a mid - northern port, to Northampton. The gauge finally adopted was 3ft 6in, which was adopted as standard. Perth, the state capital, was connected by rail with its port of Fremantle, 10 miles away, in 1881 and the line continued inland to Guildford. It formed the first section of the Eastern railway, which continued through the Darling ranges to York by 1885. The range itself provided a formidable barrier—the main line was relocated completely on easier grades in 1896. It was again relocated in 1968 on another new route in conjunction with the introduction of the 4ft 8½in gauge to the state railways.

Two major railways in WA were built under the Land Grant system, by which private investors were granted ownership of land in return for building a railway through it. A London syndicate built a 243-mile line from Beverley (extension of the York line) to Albany on the south coast, opening in 1889. The Great Southern Land Company worked the line until 1891, when it was taken over by the government for £1,100,000. The venture had had mixed fortunes; public opinion led to the government takeover. While construction of the

Great Southern Railway (as it became known) was in progress, another agreement was signed for a line from Midland junction (near Perth) to Walkaway (near Geraldton), a distance of 277 miles. Lack of capital on the part of the original grantee brought about formation of the Midland Railway Company of WA, which took over and opened the line in 1894 and continued to operate it until 1964, when the state took over.

In the late 1800s and early 1900s, WA was in the midst of exciting gold discoveries. The Eastern Goldfields Railway was opened by the government to Kalgoorlie in 1897. Another main line was pushed inland from Geraldton to the Murchison goldfields, and in a five-year period from 1894 to 1899, over 1,000 miles of line were added to the state network. The link with the verdant southwest of the state came with connection to Bubbury in 1893, and the framework of the system was well in sight by 1914.

The pattern of locomotive development in WA is complex—a striking mixture of the conventional and the experimental which has persisted to the present era. The first WAGR engines, two M-class 2-6-0s built by Kitson, of Leeds, epitomised English narrow - gauge locomotive practice of the time, and were used in building the Geraldton - Northampton railway. For work on the completed line, the government imported two double-Fairlie articulated locomotives from the Avonside Engine Company, of Bristol, one of which was later converted to a 2-4-2 tank engine. Three single-Fairlie 0-6-4Ts were purchased from New Zealand Railways in 1891, but did not achieve the success hoped for in surmounting the grades of the Eastern Railway. In their place, a series of small-wheeled K-class 2-8-4T engines was designed. For general purposes, WAGR utilised 2-6-0 and 4-6-0 engines in the early stages, typical of many such locomotives throughout the Australian 3ft 6in-gauge systems.

In 1912, six 2-6-0+0-6-2 Beyer - Garratt locomotives (class M), the first 3ft 6in-gauge Garratts in the world, were ordered from Beyer Peacock, of Manchester; they were joined by six superheated engines of the same wheel arrangement in 1913. So successful were they that the WAGR Midland workshops produced 10 more, to a slightly modified design (Moa class), in 1930. Notable conventional locomotives were the F-class 4-8-0s (goods) and the E-class 4-6-2s (passenger) introduced in 1902; Baldwin Locomotive Works supplied 32 locomotives, 20 of them compounds, in 1901-2. The 4-6-2 wheel arrangement was favoured for main-line engines up to and after the 1939-45 war, largely stemming from the P-class supplied initially by North British Locomotive Works in 1924.

Western Australia was the first state to introduce diesel - electric railcars to Australia in 1937. Although quite successful, they were gradually replaced in common with most mixed and passenger services by a fleet of railway-owned buses from 1945. Today, country passenger services in WA are minimal. The diesel-electric locomotive was introduced to the WAGR with an order for 18 400hp shunters from BTH, England, closely followed by 48 X-class 1,100hp 2-Do-2 units from Metropolitan - Vickers, England. More recently, GM and English Electric have supplied units to complete the dieselisation.

The state has benefited greatly from the construction of a 4ft 8½in-gauge line between Kalgoorlie and Perth (mentioned later). Since 1965, there have been tremendous developments in iron ore-carrying privately owned railways in the north-west of the state. Four separate companies operate over 500 miles of heavy - duty 4ft 8½in track between mine sites and coastal ports, and another 200 miles are under construction in 1972. Diesel - electric 3,600hp locomotives in multiple haul 16,000-ton trains, a level of operation unknown elsewhere in Australia.

The federation of the six Australian states into the Commonwealth of Australia in 1901 brought with it a promise that east and west Australia would be linked by rail. Subsequent agreements between the Commonwealth and South Australian governments brought about the transfer of the North Australia Railway and the Central Australia Railway to Commonwealth control and formation of the Commonwealth Railways as a separate entity. In 1911, an Act authorised construction of a 1,051-mile 4ft 8½in-gauge line from Port Augusta, South Australia, to Kalgoorlie, Western Australia. Active construction started in 1911 and, despite wartime supply problems and the treeless Nullarbor plain which the line crossed, it was completed in 1917.

From the outset, passenger rolling stock on the Trans-Australian Railway has been of a high standard, including such features as on-board showers for all first-class passengers after 1918. The tradition has been maintained over the years, and today's air - conditioned stainless - steel carriages are Australia's finest. Steam locomotives were of designs proved elsewhere, but the problems of water and coal supply were such that the Trans-Australian was a logical choice for diesel-electric traction. The first General Motors units were introduced in 1951 and steam became extinct on the line within 10 years.

When first acquired by the Commonwealth in 1911, the Palmerston (Darwin) to Pine Creek railway was administered by the Northern Territory Administration. It became part of Commonwealth Railways in 1918 and was extended as far south as Birdum by 1929. Now known as the North Australia Railway, it has been upgraded to handle ore traffic into Darwin for export and rail - road - rail traffic from the south.

The line from Port Augusta to Oodnadatta, also acquired by the Commonwealth in 1911, was leased back to South Australia for operation by the state system.

Prior to an extension north to Alice Springs, Commonwealth Railways took over full operation in 1926. Alice Springs was reached in 1929, but the 640-mile gap between that point and Birdum is unlikely ever to be bridged by rail. To cater for heavy coal traffic from Leigh Creek in South Australia, a new line of 4ft 8½in gauge was built on quite a different route from Port Augusta to Marree in 1957. The old formation of the so-called Central Australian Railway was abandoned except for a 40-mile section of 3ft 6in gauge, isolated from the remainder of Commonwealth Railways, but linked to the South Australian system. Commonwealth also owns a five-mile section of track between Queanbeyan and Canberra, the capital, but the NSWR provides all its rolling stock.

Problems of gauge differences were foreseen even before the first meeting of two systems of different gauge (at Albury in 1883). One notable step to reduce the problem took place in 1930 when a 4ft 8½in-gauge line from Grafton NSW to Brisbane was opened, obviating the need for transhipment at Wallangarra. Then, in 1937 Commonwealth Railways extended its 4ft 8½in-gauge line southwards from Port Augusta to Port Pirie, there to meet a new 5ft 3in-gauge line built from Red Hill, which was already connected to Adelaide; thus one other transhipment was eliminated. Finally, as a result of a Commonwealth Government committee report of 1956, three major traffic routes have been constructed or reconstructed. They are:

Albury (Wodonga, Victoria) to Melbourne — a new 4ft 8½in line paralleling the existing 5ft 3in track, opened for traffic in January 1962.

Kalgoorlie to Fremantle and Perth—a new 4ft 8½in 450-mile line, deviating from the former 3ft 6in route at the ends, opened throughout in 1968.

Broken Hill to Port Pirie—a 4ft 8½in line, largely parallel to the 3ft 6in line, opened at the beginning of 1970, completing a trans - continental route of one gauge. Linked projects were upgrading work on the Parkes - Broken Hill line of the NSWGR and further rehabilitation on the Trans-Australian line.

The future for the Australian railways looks bright under a new image created in the name Railways of Australia, an organisation sponsored by all systems. Jointly owned passenger rolling stock is already in service between Sydney and Perth on the Indian-Pacific Express and lettered accordingly. At principal remaining break - of - gauge points, (Melbourne, Peterborough and Port Pirie) mechanised bogie changing equipment allows most bogie wagons of 5ft 3in and 4ft 8½in gauge to be freely interchanged. It is expected that a 4ft 8½in-gauge line will be built to link Adelaide with Broken Hill (and thus Perth, Sydney and Brisbane). Western Australia is considering further extensions to its 4ft 8½in network. Another substantial state - owned mineral line is planned for Queensland.

Above: Preserved streamlined Pacific in steam in 1970 to take part in a commemorative run across the continent on the completed Trans-Australian line. *T B Owen*

Left: NSW six-car air-conditioned stainless-steel double-deck train for long-distance services at Gosford. *J C Dunn*

Below: Commonwealth Railways GM Class Co-Co 1,750hp diesel-electric locomotive with Indian Pacific stainless-steel train. *J C Dunn*

Previous page: Commonwealth Railways Trans-Australian inter-state train in the Avon Valley. *Commonwealth Railways*

RAILWAYS OF NEW ZEALAND

LONG AGO there was a wooden railway. Aptly, it was in New Zealand, a country of trees even to this day, despite all the early settlers burnt in the name of agriculture or used for building houses and just about everything else. The railway was not a toy either, but an attempt by the Provincial Government of Southland, New Zealand's most southerly province, to open up the hinterland north-west of Invercargill. The Oreti Railway, as this strange concept was named, ran in a nearly straight line for about eight miles from Invercargill. The effect of rain and sun on the wooden rails might well have been catastrophic, but in fact fire got there first and wooden railways departed rather abruptly from New Zealand's railway history.

If there was one thing that the Oreti Railway owned that was not made of wood it was its locomotive—a splendid machine, by Crampton out of Stephenson. It was a 2-2-0 well-tank called *Lady Barkly* after the wife of the Governor of the State of Victoria in Australia where the strange engine was made. It was kept on the track by two additional pairs of small wheels bearing on the inside of the wooden rails at an angle; the concept was known as Prossers Patent. Strange to say, this prodigy actually worked; for two or three years from 1864 running an erratic service between Invercargill and the bush town of Makarewa seven miles to the north. But on the whole the wooden railway was not a success and by 1866 the

railways of New Zealand were set on a more conventional course.

In a newly settled country like New Zealand, railways were laid not for linking existing centres of population, but to establish some means of communication between small towns clustering round natural harbours and to aid the opening up of the interior. The two main islands of New Zealand are about 1,000 miles long and then the North was totally covered by forest, but much of the South Island was only lightly forested and much of the east coast was open plains. By the 1850s, when railways were becoming a practicable proposition, the pattern of settlement in the South Island was developing into three main districts—Southland with its main town at Invercargill fed by the port of Bluff, Dunedin in Otago on a splendid natural harbour and Christchurch with the port of Lyttleton as the main town of the Canterbury plains. The North Island was little settled.

The fact that two out of the three main towns in the South Island were not ports in their own right gave an early stimulus to railway development. But in fact it was in another centre of South Island settlement, at Nelson in the NW corner, that in 1862 the first railway was opened. It was the Dun Mountain Railway, which ran for a short distance inland from Nelson and was used for bringing timber and minerals down from the hills to the embryo port. It was 3ft gauge worked by

horses and did not survive very long, but for all that it has the honour of being the first.

The port of Lyttleton was on a splendid natural deep-water harbour but was cut off from Christchurch and the Canterbury plains by the volcanic Port hills. The intention was for the railway to tunnel through the hills, but it proved a tall order with the primitive methods available and so the first railway to use steam locomotives in New Zealand ran from Christchurch to a temporary wharf at Ferrymead. The line was opened in November 1863 and was built to the 'Irish' gauge of 5ft 3in. From Christchurch the terrain was easy in all directions, apart from several big rivers to be bridged, so tentative starts were made with lines to both north and south of the city That to the north got only a few miles, and that to the south exhausted itself getting across the Selwyn River, a relatively small stream by Canterbury standards. These lines had been financed by the Canterbury Provincial Government, backed by some capital from the various settlement companies who were sending emigrants out from Britain, but in no sense were they private railway companies.

In Southland the position was much the same, some form of all-weather communication between Invercargill and its port at Bluff, again on a splendid deep-water harbour, was needed urgently. The trouble there was not hills but swamps and to this day the Invercargill-Bluff line floats,

405

rather than runs, over much of its length. Various officials fought and wrangled and some tentative starts were made before the discovery of gold in Central Otago stimulated a lot of projects and a lot of people. The wooden Oreti Railway was born, and the more conventional Invercargill-Bluff line was completed in December 1866. Unlike the Christchurch schemes, both the Bluff and the Oreti lines were laid to the British standard gauge of 4ft 8½in.

So by 1870 there were two isolated sections of railway in the South Island operating on three different gauges, for in Canterbury some 3ft 6in gauge track had been laid 'on the cheap' to feed into the stunted branches of the 5ft 3in-gauge lines leading to Christchurch and Lyttleton. The North Island, apart from a coal line in the far north of 4ft 8½in gauge, was not in the running, for settlement was sparse and Maoris and earthquakes rather frequent.

In 1870 there came on the New Zealand

railway scene a positive Brunel of a man. A man of vision, and with the personality to carry it through against the petty wranglings of provincial politicians. Mr (later Sir) Julius Vogel, at one time a newspaper editor, had the vision to see that what the infant country needed more than anything else was a system of railways to open up the hinterland and ultimately to link the established centres of population on the coast. He also saw, as the Australians did not, that there had to be one gauge throughout the country; the fact that he opted for 3ft 6in in retrospect might seem wrong, but it had advantages—relatively cheap to build and able to take sharper curves than the standard gauge.

Where he did score was in realising that track gauge and loading gauge were not the same thing, and that it was loading gauge that was critical. How true this is was brought vividly to the author's notice one evening in 1956 when riding in the cab of an oil-fired Ka-class 4-8-4 we ran

for mile after mile at 70mph on 3ft 6in-gauge track, in a locomotive as long, as large and nearly as heavy as a Duchess. Certainly this was an exception as the line maximum was 55mph and the driver got an almighty rocket afterwards for his trouble in showing the 'Pommie' just how hard they could go.

Under Vogel's Public Works Acts after 1870 the New Zealand Railways really got under way, of 3ft 6in gauge but supported with government capital and at last free of the wrangling of local politicians. Once the question of gauges and so on was decided the development of railways in South Island was fairly rapid and logical. Lines were pushed into the interior, generally speaking following the great river valleys, the main trunk line along the East Coast was completed linking Invercargill with Dunedin and Christchurch and finally with Picton and Blenheim in the north-east corner, though it was into the 1960s before the two main islands were

linked by the Picton-Wellington train ferry. One part of South Island remains to be dealt with—the West Coast, which is wet, very mountainous and isolated; one might wonder why it should have been settled at all and the answer is in one word—coal.

New Zealand to date has been found to be very lacking in minerals. There is some coal in the Waikato valley about 60 miles south of Auckland in the North Island but the coal found in a crescent between Westport, Reefton and Greymouth in the South is of superb quality and relatively easily mined. Where you get coal you get railways and a network of local lines grew up in this area relatively early in NZ railway history, taking coal from the mines to the ports of Westport and Greymouth. Both the ports were bedevilled by tides and shifting sand bars and for a long time a rail link between the West Coast and the more populous and wealthy Canterbury Plains was considered to be a very desirable thing. Various abortive moves were made towards this ideal, including a privately financed Midland Railway Company pushing westward from the Canterbury plains at Rollieston towards Arthur pass; the line did not get far as the country was too vast for it, with great river gorges and formidable grades.

Only in 1923 did the completion of the Otira tunnel under the axial range between Arthur pass and Otira make the linking of the east and west coasts of the South Island an established fact. It is a breathtaking line scenically and of interest in that the Otira tunnel has been worked by electricity from its opening; the steam locomotives work up to each end, where they are replaced for the five steeply graded miles through the tunnel by small electric engines working in multiple from locally generated water power. Before leaving

the South Island two more lines have to be mentioned. The first is an isolated section running southwards into the hills from Nelson that was destined to link up with the coal lines of the west coast, but never did. Indeed the Glenhope branch never did anything very much and became better known for the manner of its dying than for its life, for it died amid a blaze of publicity with people sitting on the track in protest and the civic dignitaries left behind in the rain after the train had to be divided on the last steep grade back into Nelson.

By contrast the Otago Central, among the last built of the South Island branches, is incomparably the finest of all New Zealands railways, a Southern Hemisphere Denver & Rio Grande, 146 glorious miles of great hills and rocky gorges. In fact, it was more than a branch; it was a secondary main line built between 1889 and 1921 in stages to open up the lovely intermountain basin of Central Otago. The political bickerings that dogged its construction in no way detract from its spectacular nature. It runs from Dunedin by devious routes to Cromwell, and within eight miles of staid Dunedin's back door plunges for nearly twenty miles through the gorge of the Tieri river with steep rock faces cut through by narrow tunnels and tributaries crossed and recrossed by stone and lattice girder viaducts. It is a fitting start to a glorious line which in so many ways resembles the railways of the Andes without the latter's discomforting altitude.

Railways came to the North Island later than to the South and as such avoided much of the bickering, gauge wars and other odd forms of experimentation of the provincial railways in the south. Apart from the short coal-carrying line near Opua in the far north and one or two short lines round Auckland, the northern lines were all spawned by Vogel's 1870 Public Works policies and as a result were laid down to the standard 3ft 6in gauge. As with most of the NZ railways they basically were opened up to develop the interior and with one exception built by Colonial Government money. By 1870 the North Island had polarised into zones of influence based on Wellington in the south and Auckland in the north; again the sites for the cities were governed by good natural harbours. Auckland tapped the rich agricultural valley of the Waikato and its coal, the timber lands of the Rotorua Highlands to the south, and the goldfields round Waikato and the Bay of Plenty in the north-east.

To the north a long single line wound up towards Whangarei and the Far North, opening up sub-tropical country which for some reason has never fulfilled its early promise. While many of the lines based on Auckland were steeply graded, none of them posed abnormal constructional difficulties. It was a very different story with the first line built to link Wellington with the interior to the north and east—the Wairarapa. At the time it was built it must have been one of the most remarkable in the world. For six miles along the side of

Wellington harbour it ran on a raised beach thrown up by an earthquake in 1855—an embankment raised by nature. Then, after ten relatively placid miles wandering through the lower reaches of the Hutt valley, densely populated at an early date, the nature of the country changes and the railway has to twist and claw its way up heavily wooded ridges on gradients as steep as 1 in 40 for long stretches to the 2,000ft top of a narrow pass through the Rimutaka ranges. There, at the isolated passing loop called simply Summit, there started that remarkable 3½ miles of Fell-worked Rimutaka incline where the line dropped down the precipitous eastern scarp of the mountains to Cross creek on the edge of the Wairarapa plains.

Rimutaka incline was probably New Zealand's best-known railway institution; it closed with the opening of the 5½-mile Rimutaka tunnel in October 1955. The Fell system of working mountain railways was conceived by an Englishman, Colonel Fell, and had its first successful application on the original railway over the Mont Cenis pass between France and Italy. It employed a double-headed rail raised horizontally between the two running rails and, on the locomotives, an extra set or sets of horizontal driving wheels engaging the raised centre rail. The horizontal wheels could be wound into and out of contact with the centre rail while the locomotive was in motion. It was a slow slow process and from a railway operating point of view must have been an expensive nuisance, but to an observer it was a splendid thing. Three or four little tank engines working flat out at 4mph up a 1 in 13 grade, through precipitous hills with little rat-holes of tunnels and the chance of the violent Rimutaka winds—which on one occasion blew a whole train clean off the track. Nobody who ever saw the Rimutaka incline in action would ever forget it—nobody who travelled through one of the rat-holes on the footplate of the third loco in a four-engine train could ever forget it, much as he would like to!

Yet for many years this extraordinary line worked all the rail traffic between Wellington and the north. Not without delays, however, and the delays got so bad that a private company, the Wellington & Manawatu Railway Company, built a rival line from Wellington to Palmerston North up the west side of the spine of the Rimutaka ranges following the Tasman sea coastline. The line was pure early American with American type stock and locomotives and its influence was destined to have a long and lasting effect on NZ railway practice down the years. It was also a very efficient railway, so much so that in 1907 it was 'amalgamated' with the State system ending the career of the one and only major privately owned railway in New Zealand.

Gradually the lines based on Wellington extended fanwise to serve Napier and the Hawkes Bay area on the east coast and Taranaki and New Plymouth on the west.

The lines south of Auckland likewise fanned out across the Waikato and Bay of Plenty, but it was not until November 1908 that the great Main Trunk line was completed linking Auckland and Wellington. Its central section was a triumph of engineering, with steep grades, great viaducts and remarkably few tunnels (the rock is soft and unstable for the most part). With one exception it is also a very conventional line for all the mountain country it traverses—no racks, no zig-zags and no grade steeper than 1 in 50, but a lot of miles at this inclination. The one oddity is the Raurimu spiral used to gain height abruptly from the head of a deep valley at Raurimu to the high windy volcanic uplands at National Park. The line makes a long hair-pin bend followed by a complete circle with only two tunnels, both of them very short. The grade is a steady 1 in 50 but uncompensated for the very sharp curvature.

With the completion of the Main Trunk in 1908 the railway map of New Zealand was almost finished, apart from the inland sections of the Otago Central, and the extension of the line from Hawkes Bay to Gisborne finally pushed through as a strategic measure in 1942. As recently as 1955 a high-speed logging line has been built to serve the great pulp mill at Kawerau in the Bay of Plenty and work is currently proceeding on a tunnel through the Kaiamai hills to avoid some strenuous grades around Waihi in the same area.

Alas, the closure of branch lines is now taking place in New Zealand . . . the railways opened up the hinterlands, the farmers and traders prospered, bought motor-cars, had roads made and killed the railways that gave them their start: Britain is not alone in this.

Locomotive development in New Zealand differed from that elsewhere because there were no competing lines and the early engines were designed generally by one man to cover the whole country. On the whole it was remarkably successful, though in the early days there were some very strange oddities let loose on the embryo railways. But local eccentricities, built often as not with very good reason, gave way to standard late-nineteenth-century British practice, which in turn was found wanting, being considered unsuited for tight curves and steep grades coupled with rather limited and primitive maintenance. Then the Wellington & Manawatu Americanisation proved more suitable for the local conditions.

The New Zealanders were, and still are for that matter, the most British of all the Commonwealth countries and they could not accept that Yankee locomotives were better for their conditions than English ones. At that time they undoubtedly were, but the refusal to face facts gave birth to one of the most remarkable steam locomotive phenomena of all times, the native NZ locomotive, forged out of the English versus American schools of locomotive engineering, than which there have been few more effective compromises. My Ka Class 4-8-4

doing its 70mph between Feilding and Terrace End near Palmerston North was the mightiest of the breed, but other classes frequently do just as well without the stimulus of a visiting 'Pommie' to show off to !

Once the gauge question was out of the way in New Zealand there arose a series of remarkably sturdy tank engines, some to Fairlie patents but the most of them strictly conventional, small rugged and very easily maintained. Of them, the F class, an Avonside design, was also remarkably long lived, some survivors working coalfield lines as late as the mid-1950s. Once the bare bones of the main lines were constructed something more was needed ; it was then that the American influence first became apparent, with some very pretty 2-4-2s from Rogers coming for the South Island main line. For a long time various classes of 2-4-2s, 2-8-0s and 4-6-0s were supplied by both American and British manufacturers.

In most respects the honours were even, though the American engines showed up favourably in ease of maintenance. The success of the Wellington & Manawatu Railway in the 1890s with its nearly 100-per cent stud of American engines had two very important and far-reaching effects. The first, and in retrospective the more important, was what might be called a big-engine policy ; the second was that compounding became respectable. To take the big engine concept first, its immediate outcome was the immortal Q-class 4-6-2s. They were the first *class* of conventional Pacifics in the world. Odd single examples had been built in America a few years before, but they had not been standardised.

In 1901 Qs were ordered off the drawing-board from Baldwins for the South Island main line and the reason is interesting. At the time they were ordered only soft lignite coal from South Otago was available ; Baldwins had developed the Wooten firebox

native designs were built as compounds. That influence did not last, as it happened, though the big-engine policy did. Between 1906 and 1910 four-cylinder compound Pacifics emerged from various New Zealand engineering works; designed by A L Beattie, the A class, as they came to be known, were a success from the word go. So much so that in 1915 he designed a modified two-cylinder version, the Ab class, that were destined to become the 'Black Fives' of New Zealand. Latterly the As themselves were rebuilt as two-cylinder simples.

The other big compound was the mighty X-class 4-8-2, which emerged in 1906 and was probably the first Mountain wheel arrangement in the world. The X's were massive and very impressive machines designed for working over the newly opened Wellington-Auckland main line. They were strong but very very slow, they survived as compounds on secondary freight duties until 1940, when ten were converted to four-cylinder simples, but on account of their appetite for coal and rather dilatory speed they were never popular and the last two departed in 1957. While the As and the Xs were the last gasp of compounding, a series of rugged and simple big engines led, in 1930, to the massive coal-fired 4-8-4s of the K class, followed in the early 1940s by the Ka oil-fired version.

In 1939 a lighter variant, the J class 4-8-2, was developed for secondary main lines, which in turn spawned an oil-fired version, the Ja, for the North Island services in 1950. Coal-fired Js were being built for the South Island as late as 1956 and some of the locos were destined to be the last steam locomotives in regular service on the NZR.

This summary of NZ motive power has only traced the main stream of development, and there is no space to enlarge on such things as the three imposing Garratts tried on the North Island main line with limited results, then rebuilt as three-cylinder Pacifics for the South Island with a positively catastrophic outcome. The diesel era has resulted in a similar mixture of British and American—and Japanese—practice, while the limited application of electric working so far has been a British monopoly, and a very effective one at that. Indeed one wonders why a country like New Zealand with cheap hydro-electric power bothered with diesels at all.

One last feature of the railways of New Zealand remains to be mentioned and that is the civil engineering structures. One of the claims for adopting the 3ft 6in gauge was the minimising of major civil engineering works in the mountainous and broken terrain of the country. Curvature has replaced the deep cuttings and high embankments of the railways of Britain and Europe. Tunnels up till a few years ago were few, and in the main short, but since the piercing of the Southern Alps at Otira in 1923 the fear of such things has been lost and the Rimutaka tunnel in the North Island and the one

which could burn lignite efficiently, but it was a rather wide firebox and to carry it on 3ft 6in gauge a trailing truck on a 4-6-0 was essential. This rather prosaic reason gave birth to the Pacific type and no other. The Qs were simple, fast and rugged and a great success from the outset. They were also very long lived and some of them were still working passenger trains between Invercargill and the Bluff as late as 1956-57. The success of the Qs gave rise to other Pacifics in NZ but, strange to say, it was their success that sounded the death knell of American locomotives, for out of them came the native type. Rather a case of anything they can do, we can do better.

The other influence from the Wellington & Manawatu's Americanisation was that of the chief engineer at Baldwins. Samuel Vauclain was one of the very few locomotive engineers to succeed with the pipe-dream of compounding and it was through his influence that the first two true NZ

Top: Timber trestle bridge over Firewood Creek on the North Island mining branch in the Waikato coalfield, with Bb 4-8-0 No 635 and a single car-van (brake composite), one of the two daily 'mixed' trains, in autumn 1956.
D Cross

Above: Two ex-NZR Fa 0-6-0 tanks of 1897 build of the Whakatane Board Mills on the company's private railway in April 1957.
D Cross

presently being bored at Kaiamai in the Bay of Plenty are massive undertakings. Stations in the main have been simple functional things apart from the superb Scots Baronial structure at Dunedin which is somehow very much in keeping with the city as a whole.

To an outsider the great engineering feature of the NZ Railways is the bridges and viaducts, in number, size and variety. In this country we can have no concept of the great rivers, many of them snow-fed, that dissect the plains of the South Island, or the ravines that gash their way down to the coasts from the volcanic mountains of the central massif in the North. Add a climate of extremes and sudden floods and it is easy to see why viaduct building in New Zealand has risen to a very high art indeed. The railways of New Zealand challenged nature in some of its most primitive and unstable forms, and on the whole won. Not without reverses though, as the main line between Palmerston and Napier has had one major bridge knocked down by earthquakes twice and much minor damage from the same cause besides. Earthquakes have proved a major hazard on several occasions and it is an interesting sideline that the early wooden trestle bridges proved to be more resilient to such nasty freaks of nature than newer and theoretically stronger steel ones.

Top: The Rimutaka incline in action in November 1953 showing the raised central rail, with two H-class Fell 0-4-2Ts, Nos 203 and 199, each pulling 90 tons in view and a third just out of the picture. *D Cross*

Above: Typical of the very scenic Otago Central line, with railway and main road sharing the gorge of the Clutha River between Clyde and Cromwell; here Ab Pacific No 812 takes a short goods train towards Cromwell in January 1956. *D Cross*

Left: Typical of the great viaducts on the Wellington-Auckland main line, the Makatote viaduct in the heart of 'King Country', with a Ka oil-burning 4-8-4 at the head of the Northbound Daylight Limited in January 1956. *D Cross*

13
The Railways of America

⋉ BURLINGTON NORTHERN

Top: Ex-Great Northern GP diesel-electric locomotive No 1521 in July 1970. *V Goldberg*

Above centre: Head end of a Burlington Route train of the Chicago Burlington & Quincy RR at Colorado Springs in June 1964. *V Goldberg*

Above: A caboose of the Spokane, Portland & Seattle Railway at Pasco in July 1970. *V Goldberg*

Facing page: During World War II, American loco builders produced large numbers of engines for use by the Allies in Europe. Many stayed there after the war, including this Vulcan Ironworks 0-6-0T, which was bought by the Southern Railway and later preserved on the Worth Valley line in Yorkshire. *J Benton-Harris*

THE NAME BURLINGTON NORTHERN is a newcomer to the American railway scene. It dates only from March 2, 1970, when three major railways, and certain other lines, were merged. The railways involved were the Chicago, Burlington & Quincy Railroad (Burlington Route—8,500 miles), the Great Northern Railway (route of the Empire Builder—8,260 miles) and the Northern Pacific Railway ('Main Street of the North-West'—6,780 miles). Also included were the Spokane, Portland & Seattle Railway—950 miles) and the Pacific Coast Railroad—32 miles.

The merger had been proposed more than once over the years and was finally approved only after prolonged inquiry by the Interstate Commerce Commission—the United States Federal regulatory body for transport. There had, however, for many years been interlinking ownership between the various companies involved. The GN and NP owned jointly the CB&Q, although the latter was larger than either of its parents. The GN and NP also owned jointly the SP&S, which was geographically quite separate from the CB&Q. The CB&Q and the SP&S were also operated quite separately, with their own individual managements.

With over 24,500 miles of route, Burlington Northern is second only to Canadian National Railways in size of system in North America, with Penn Central a poor (literally!) third.

Each of the three major components of BN included numerous short, local, or bigger constituents, but the first to achieve major system status was the Northern Pacific. After the choice for the first

transcontinental railroad fell to the central route, that is, the one followed by the Union Pacific and Central Pacific to San Francisco, for which a charter was granted in 1862, pressure continued for the alternative route to be built. A further charter was granted in 1864, in the midst of the American Civil War, but construction of the Northern Pacific route, from both ends, began only in 1870. The eastern end started at Carlton, near Duluth, Minnesota, and the western end started, northwards initially, from the Columbia river, near Portland, Oregon.

Bismark, ND, and Tacoma, Wash, had been reached from east and west respectively when a national financial crisis caused suspension of construction in 1873. Work resumed in 1879, and the transcontinental route of the NP of 2,260 miles was finally completed in 1883. New construction and acquisition brought the NP route mileage to about 6,780 at the time of the BN merger. The main line, one that is still largely (and unusually) signalled by semaphores, runs from the Twin Cities of St Paul—Minneapolis via Fargo, Bismark, Mandon and Billings to Butte. At Butte is one of the world's largest open-pit copper mines, served by the Butte, Anaconda & Pacific Railway, which until recently had electric traction. In the same area there is an alternative more-northerly loop of the NP serving Helena, state capital of Montana. The two routes rejoin at Garrison, Mont, and the main line continues west to Spokane, Wash. A south-westerly course takes the route on to Pasco, Wash, through much of Washington State's fertile country, and so to the Puget Sound at Tacoma. From there tracks fork north to Seattle and south to Portland.

The NP had several important secondary routes. From the Twin Cities, a line led up to the two lakehead ports, Duluth and Superior, which also had a direct route to the west via Brainerd to link with the main transcontinental route at Staples. A little to the west of Staples, and still in Minnesota, the NP had a route via Grand Forks to Winnipeg, in Canada. North Dakota was served by a number of branch lines. In Montana, a huge state ('Big Sky Country') which takes a whole day to cross (the rail mileage is about 760), Livingston acts as gateway to the Yellowstone National Park. Westward from there, the main line follows a scenic route through the Big Belt and Bitter Root ranges of the Rocky Mountains. Much of the route west follows the trail of the Lewis and Clark expedition of 1804, particularly up the Yellowstone river in Montana.

The NP's 'herald', or crest, was unusual. An annular ring containing the words Northern Pacific surrounded a monad—a Chinese mystical symbol formed by a circle split into two equal parts by an S-shaped line. One half was black, the other red. The symbol appears to date from the inauguration of NP's crack train, the North Coast Limited, in 1900. The eight-car train had electric lighting and represented the peak of wooden carriage construction.

The North Coast Limited required six sets of equipment to maintain service and some new stock was acquired in 1909 and 1930, but the first major delivery of streamlined cars did not appear until 1947-8. In 1954 20 dome cars, both coaches (second-class) and sleepers, were acquired, to be followed by buffet-lounge cars in 1955 and six new diners in 1958. Finally, in 1959 slumber coaches (each named after a Scottish loch) were added, to make economy-class sleeping accommodation available. The various additions to stock during the 1950s permitted the second-line transcontinental train, the Mainstreeter, to be re-equipped, although latterly this train was formed of only five or six cars.

Northern Pacific passenger services were almost entirely dropped when the government-financed organisation AMTRAK took over responsibility, but political pressures soon brought back service over the NP main line, three days a week, on a 'trial' basis.

The Great Northern Railway had its beginnings in the St Paul & Pacific Railway, which had become moribund, after starting to build north-westward out of St Paul. A young Ontario-born man, James Jerome Hill, moved to the west in 1856, intent on trading with the Orient. Instead, he became involved in river transport on the Mississippi, and later gained control of the St Paul & Pacific. With vigour he extended the line up to the Canadian border at Pembina, to which point the Canadian Pacific built a link

south from Winnipeg. Incidentally, until 1883, Jim Hill was also associated with the Canadian Pacific Railway.

The St Paul-Winnipeg link prospered, and Hill resolved to extend westward to the Pacific Ocean. The new line followed a route between the Canadian border and the line of the Northern Pacific and was well engineered. The title Great Northern was adopted in 1890. In 1893, the line reached the Puget sound at Everett, Wash, 33 miles north of Seattle. The route reached a summit of 5,213ft above sea level, 12 miles west of Glacier Park station, and only 55 miles of route was higher than 4,000, an important consideration when winter snows are remembered.

The GN crossing of the Cascade mountains was greatly improved in 1929 when the original Cascade tunnel ($2\frac{2}{3}$ miles) was replaced with one $7\frac{3}{4}$ miles long. The new tunnel formed part of a new 73-mile electrification at 11,500-volt 25-Herz alternating current, which replaced an earlier three-phase system. The later electrification was in turn discontinued in 1956 when diesel traction took over. Another major new tunnel and lengthy re-alignment of the GN route (by then, in fact, Burlington Northern) took place in 1970 with the construction of the Libby dam, in Western Montana.

On the west coast, the GN had its main line from Seattle through Everett to the Canadian border at Blaine, and thence into Canada, partly over tracks shared with Canadian National, to its own station in Vancouver. The GN station was demolished in the late 1960s, after GN trains had been transferred to the CNR station. After a year (1971/2) during which the line was without passenger trains, international service was reintroduced under AMTRAK sponsorship in July 1972.

At its easterly end, the GN reached Chicago over tracks of the CB&QRR (as did the NP). Between St Paul and Minot, ND (almost 500 miles), the GN possessed two separate routes, and its branch-line coverage in northern North Dakota was particularly complete, with over a dozen separate lines to the north, but all of them stopping short of the Canadian border. The representation of these on a map has given rise to the term 'picket fence country'. As with the NP, the GN had links from the twin lakehead ports both to the Twin Cities and to Crookston, Minn, on the Winnipeg line, and Grand Forks on the transcontinental route.

Above left: Like most US railways, Burlington Northern's traffic is mostly freight, and increasingly in containers as shown in this huge road-rail interchange depot.
Burlington Northern Inc

Above: Powerful line-up of four ex-CB & Q diesels (two E8s and two E9s) at St Paul in July 1970. *V Goldberg*

Top: Ex-Northern Pacific East Coast Limited at Billings in July 1970. *V Goldberg*

Right: Restaurant car named 'Lake Michigan' in BN livery at Grand Forks in July 1972. *V Goldberg*

Jim Hill's construction of the GN without Federal land grants (in contrast to the NP), and his vigour in encouraging settlement of immigrants in the country through which the GN passed, earned him the title of Empire Builder—the name also given to the principal transcontinental GN train in 1929, when it was refurbished. The Empire Builder was successor to the Oriental Limited, dating from 1905, which had a maritime extension in the form of the GN steamship *Minnesota* (20,000

Winnipeg train making connections with the Western Star at Grand Forks.

Although we have given prominence to the passenger services of both GN and NP, population along both lines has been relatively sparse, and both roads have been predominantly freight carriers, with freight revenue far outstripping that from passengers. Forest products, agriculture and mines are the main sources of freight traffic, while NP was also a major landowner.

to the Texas-New Mexico state line form part of a cross-country link from Denver to the Gulf of Mexico at Galveston, Tex. The 792 miles from Texline to Galveston are part of the 1,362-mile Fort Worth & Denver Railway, owned by the C&S. The C&S, in turn has been controlled by the CB&Q since 1909. An interesting part, for a time, of the C&S system was the narrow-gauge (3ft) Denver, South Park & Pacific Railroad, built through rugged scenic country, south-west from Denver, as a rival to the D&RGW to tap Colorado's mines. Apart from one short spur, which was converted to standard gauge during the 1939-45 war, the last leg of the DSP&PRR, between Denver and Leadville, closed in 1937. The C&S and FW&D are controlled by—but not part of—BN.

Above: Ex-GN sleeping car of Empire Builder stock at the GN Fargo station in July 1970.
V Goldberg

tons) linking Seattle with Japan and China. A further marine venture was the Great Northern Pacific Steamship Co (jointly owned by the GN and NP), which in 1915 inaugurated a service between Portland and San Francisco. The voyage took 30 hours, three hours less than the competing Southern Pacific's train !

The Empire Builder train joined the ranks of the streamliners in 1947, when five new train sets (four owned by GN, one by the CB&Q) entered service, having been ordered in 1943, but delayed by the war. The schedule of the new trains was 45 hours between Chicago and the Pacific Northwest, $13\frac{1}{2}$ hours less than former timings. A further five new 15-car trains entered service in 1951, at which time the 1947 equipment and one further new train made up another revised and slightly slower schedule by the Western Star. In 1955, 22 dome cars (six of them full-length Great Dome lounge cars) were added to the fleet. Both trains continued until the advent of AMTRAK, which maintained operation of the Empire Builder, but via Milwaukee in the East and rerouted over the former NP line to Seattle, west of Spokane.

The first Empire Builder streamlined trains introduced a colourful livery of bands of orange and green, separated by gold striping. In the 1960s the GN introduced its Big Sky Blue livery, but it had by no means been fully applied by the time of the BN merger, when a green livery was adopted.

Other GN passenger services operated until the formation of AMTRAK included the picturesquely named Badger and Gopher trains linking the Twin Cities with Duluth-Superior, and a Grand Forks-

The Chicago, Burlington & Quincy Railroad, or Burlington Lines as it was known with its subsidiaries, was rather different. Although its mileage was greater than either of its parents—GN and NP acquired joint control in 1908—it did not reach the Pacific. It did, however, form a latter-day link in the transcontinental route followed by the famed California Zephyr train, which, west of Denver, used the Denver & Rio Grande Western's short line to Salt Lake City. West from the Mormon capital, the tracks of the johnny-come-lately Western Pacific, completed only in 1909, were used to reach the Pacific Ocean, or rather, the San Francisco Bay area at Oakland.

The CB&Q had its beginnings in the Aurora Branch Railroad, a spur off the short Galena & Chicago Union, which became the foundation of the CB&Qs rival, the Chicago & North Western Railway. The Aurora built west first to the Mississippi river (it adopted the title Chicago, Burlington & Quincy Railroad in 1855), forming a link with the Missouri river at St Joseph, via a ferry at Quincy, Ill, and thence the Hannibal & St Joseph Railroad. A more northerly crossing of the Missouri was later made at Council Bluffs, Ia (reached in 1870), whence the main line stretched west to Denver, 1,034 miles from Chicago. Other routes reached south to St Louis and to Kansas City; north from Aurora to the Twin Cities of Minneapolis-St Paul; and two lines to the north-west—one from Lincoln, Neb, the other from Denver, to reach Billings, Mont, on the NP main line, where a GN branch was also met.

Of the Denver-Billings route, the 238 miles from Denver to Wendover, Wyo, form the northern end of the Colorado & Southern Railway. Of the Southern's 718 miles, the 589 miles south from Wendover

Although the Burlington (as the CB&Q was often called) was a leader in the western railroad passenger field, it, too, derived most of its income from freight. The Burlington's best-known contribution to the passenger market is probably the Zephyr title, afterwards carried by a whole fleet of high-speed trains. The pioneer Zephyr introduced in 1934 brought stainless steel car-body construction, and successful diesel-electric traction, to the railroads. While the early articulated trains became an embarrassment due to their limited capacity, the basic designs were developed, and today's General Motors diesel locomotives and Budd stainless-steel passenger cars are the consequences of those early efforts.

Zephyrs raced in all directions, from Chicago to the Twin Cities, from Denver to Dallas (Texas Zephyr) and on many other routes. The Denver Zephyr, with two full-length train sets built in 1936, was one of the most successful. In 1956 the two 12-car trains were replaced by new stock, the last completely new trainsets to be built for US service until the advent of the Metroliners and experimental Turbotrains. Today, the route of the Denver Zephyr is still served by AMTRAK's San Francisco Zephyr which proceeds from Denver over the Union Pacific to Ogden, and then over the Southern Pacific to Oakland.

The original trackage of the CB&Q between Chicago and Aurora is, in addition, served by double-deck Gallery cars in commuter service, over a three-track section of the line.

The Spokane Portland & Seattle Railway provides a 380-mile short cut, via the north bank of the Columbia river, for the GN and NP, from Spokane, Wash, to Portland, Ore. The latter-day twice-daily (in each direction) passenger train service provided connections with both transcontinental trains of both the NP and the GN. The SP&S itself owns two subsidiaries, the Oregon Trunk Railway from Wishram, Wash, to Bend, Ore, and the Oregon Electric Railway (no longer electrified) from Portland to Eugene, Ore. One small line, the Pacific Coast Railroad serving industries in the Seattle area, rounds off the Burlington Northern system.

UNION PACIFIC SOUTHERN PACIFIC SANTE FE

THE CENTENARY of the completion of the first transcontinental railway across the United States of America has but recently been celebrated by the **Union Pacific Railroad** and its guests—the Golden Spike was driven at Promontory Point, west of Ogden, Utah, on May 10, 1869. Much has been written of the original construction of that most important main line. Suffice it to say here that today's route from Omaha, Neb, or rather Council Bluffs, Iowa, on the east bank of the Missouri river, to Ogden (about 994 miles) is a very different property from the pioneer route of 1869. Among the busiest of any main lines west of Chicago, it is the core of the Union Pacific system; over the years it has been constantly improved, with double tracks throughout (often on separate formations to follow flatter gradients), easier curves, and several generations of mammoth motive power units of different types.

The Union Pacific, despite its ideal geographical position, does not, on its own, meet the definition transcontinental, nor does it extend from Chicago to the Pacific coast—not, that is, on this 'central' route. Chicago is reached over the tracks of the Milwaukee Road, which is a transcontinental route in its own right, and the Pacific, at San Francisco bay, is reached over Southern Pacific tracks west of Ogden. The whole forms the famed Overland Route, once served by such popular trains as the City of San Francisco, the Overland Limited, the Pacific Limited and the San Francisco Challenger. Until 1955, the Chicago & North Western Railway was used between Chicago and Omaha; possible merger plans at present being considered could transfer UP traffic to the Rock Island Lines between those two points.

Union Pacific's 9,000 miles of route include many other main lines. Among the

Top: Eastbound City of San Francisco train near Ragan, Wyoming, en route for Chicago.
Union Pacific RR

Above middle: Typical Consolidation goods engine of the Union Pacific built in the 1890s.
V Goldberg collection

Above: Union Pacific 2-8-0 No 6051 on display at Riverside, California, in June 1969.
V Goldberg

Right: Sketch from an 1869 issue of 'The Illustrated London News' showing the Union Pacific running along the floor of Weber Canyon with the Weber river on the left.
Illustrated London News

earliest of them was the Denver Pacific, a relatively short branch from the main line at Cheyenne to the then burgeoning city of Denver, 106 miles away, and completed in 1870. Later, Denver was to have a more direct UP route to the east, joining the original transcontinental route at Julesburg, 197 miles from Denver, in the extreme north-east corner of Colorado. This was the route taken by the streamliner City of Denver, which competed with Burlington's Denver Zephyr for Chicago-Denver traffic. Another early component was the Kansas Pacific, a 640-mile route from Denver to Kansas City and thence east to St Louis over the Wabash Railway (now part of the Norfolk & Western). Over this route ran the streamliner City of St Louis, later the City of Kansas City.

Subsequently, UP put out its own links to reach the Pacific coast. First came the Oregon Short Line, leaving the main transcontinental route at Granger, Wyoming, and heading north-west through Pocatello (214 miles) and Hinkle (756 miles) to Portland (940 miles). From Portland, UP tracks head north a further 183 miles to Seattle, via Tacoma. Both Portland and Seattle are important ports, and also interchange points with other railroads serving the north-west Pacific area. Union Pacific reaches other major sources of traffic by major branch lines. From Pocaletto, the mines at Butte (263 miles) are served, as well as West Yellowstone, while from Hinkle, the city of Spokane (191 miles) and Washington's agricultural area are reached, as well as Yakima, centre of a fruit-growing belt.

Last of UP's major links is the Los Angeles & Salt Lake, which brought UP service to Southern California. From Ogden, the route serves the Utah state capital of Salt Lake City, only 36 miles south of Ogden, before crossing the great deserts of Utah and Nevada as it runs south-west via Las Vegas—the gambling city of Southern Nevada. It reaches the Los Angeles area after crossing the spectacular Cajon pass. This 821-mile extension brought UP to tidewater on its own tracks, and also gave access to the industries and major fruit and vegetable growing areas around Los Angeles.

The early years of Union Pacific were

WILL'S CIGARETTES.

(15) 1ST RAILWAY TRAIN TO CROSS THE ROCKY MOUNTAINS.

somewhat chequered. The scandals of the Credit Mobilier—the original construction company—are long since passed, but by no means forgotten. Then the UP went into receivership in 1893, but by the turn of the century, many physical improvements were in hand. UP became part of the Harriman empire. With its strategically located trunk main line, the railroad could hardly avoid being profitable; lengthy freight trains of 100 vehicles, 10,000 tons in weight and a mile or more long can today be seen at half-hourly or hourly intervals between Omaha and Ogden.

Notwithstanding the heavy and profitable freight traffic, a fleet of streamlined passenger trains developed from modest beginnings in the mid-nineteen-thirties. Named City trains linked Chicago with Denver, Portland, San Francisco and Los Angeles. Sporting a bright yellow livery, with bold red lettering, the UP passenger train was a striking sight. As costs rose and passenger service contracted, the four city trains were consolidated one by one, until finally a single combined train was operated with through cars to each city. In summer, the City could load to 23 cars, with five diesel locomotives providing 12,000hp for a train nearly half-a-mile long. High standards were maintained by UP until service passed to AMTRAK, which has largely concentrated on other routes. The current San Francisco Zephyr, which uses UP tracks only between Denver, Cheyenne and Ogden, is now the only passenger train over UP rails.

Left top to bottom:
Pacific type 4-6-2 locomotive of the Oregon Short Line later absorbed in the Union Pacific. *V Goldberg collection*

Atlantic-type 4-4-2 of the Oregon Short Line with a Vanderbilt tender. *V Goldberg collection*

Wills cigarette card depicting early American-type 4-4-0 wood-burning locomotive circa 1870, labelled 'The first railway train to cross the Rocky Mountains'.

Diesel-hauled City of San Francisco in Echo Canyon. *Union Pacific RR*

Above: The Cascade overnight streamlined train of Southern Pacific linking Portland (Oregon) and San Francisco southbound at Eugene (Oregon). *Southern Pacific*

Southern Pacific Lines extend over about 14,000 route miles, a figure which exceeded that of the Santa Fe only as a result of its recent acquisition of control of the Cotton Belt line—the St Louis-Southwestern Railway, in which SP has had a majority holding since 1932. Southern Pacific Lines is the title used by the Southern Pacific Transportation Company for its railway operations; SPT Co also operates pipelines and highway freight services. SP is already well past its centenary, having had its origins in the Sacramento Valley RR, which extended 21 miles East from Sacramento, California, and was opened in 1855 to serve the gold camps in the foothills of the Sierra Nevada mountains.

The first major segment of the SP was the Central Pacific RR. Chartered originally only to build that portion of the first transcontinental railway within the State of California, CP built east from Sacramento, climbed the Sierra Nevada rising to the rim of the canyon of the American river, surmounted Donner pass, then crossed into Nevada, following the Humboldt river. It passed into Utah and finally met the Union Pacific to the north of the Great Salt Lake at Promontory. The four main financial backers of the Central Pacific—Charles Crocker, Mark Hopkins, Collis P Huntington and Leland Stanford —turned to building and acquiring other lines in California, and so built up the SP, which leased the CP in 1885.

The Southern Pacific forms part of two other transcontinental routes. The most southerly, the Sunset route, extends from New Orleans via El Paso, Tucson and Phoenix to Los Angeles, 2,033 miles. In 1894, SP inaugurated the Sunset Limited over the route, and the train took 58 hours from New Orleans to Los Angeles. In contrast to the high altitudes of the other transcontinental lines, the Sunset route skirts the Salton sea in Southern California, 202 feet *below* sea level. West of El Paso, the Sunset route is shared by trains of the Golden State route, which use the SP line north-east out of El Paso to Tucumcari (331 miles) in north-east New Mexico, where an end-on junction is made with the Rock Island Lines from Chicago via Kansas City.

South of the San Francisco Bay area,

Southern Pacific has two quite separate routes to Los Angeles. From the city itself, the coast route goes south via San Jose (47 miles), to which point commuter service is operated, over Paso Robles and then via San Luis Obispo and Santa Barbara to Los Angeles, 470 miles. For over 100 miles, the line is within sight of the Pacific ocean. The alternative route starts from Oakland, across the bay from San Francisco, and proceeds east, skirting San Pablo bay and Suisun bay before turning south into the San Joaquin valley, via Merced and Fresno to Bakersfield (313 miles). There, the easy grades end and the line climbs to the summit loop built around a cone-shaped hill, to gain height in the Tehachapi mountains (3,967 ft) before crossing the western end of the Mojave Desert, and descending to Los Angeles (479 miles). The last few miles from Burbank are shared with the coastal route.

North from San Francisco, or rather Oakland, SP has its Shasta route (parallel to the coast, but well inland) which takes it through the Redwood forests of Northern California and Oregon to Portland, 712 miles. The Shasta route included an important alternative route to the east of the original line over Grants pass—the Cascade line via Klamath Falls, completed in 1927. The new line is about 25 miles shorter than the old Siskiyou line.

Across the Golden Gate and north from Marin county up the Northern Californian coast is another member of the SP family, the Northwestern Pacific Railroad. It is an amalgam of a number of small companies, some of which operated commuter services in the bay area, with ferry links to San Francisco, until the opening of the Golden Gate bridge killed off the traffic. The SP gained control of the NWP in 1929, and maintained passenger service over the northern end of the line, between Willits and Eureka, until the advent of AMTRAK in May 1971. Latterly, the service was but twice weekly, worked by a solitary railcar, but it provided access to the isolated Eel River valley.

The SP had a number of other rail interests, including certain electrically operated lines. Two branch lines south-west of Portland were electrified in 1912-14, but electric services there ceased in 1929. In the San Francisco bay area, some of the NWP commuter lines were electrified in 1903, and discontinued in 1941 while in the east bay area, around Oakland, several lines electrified in 1911-12 were also abandoned in 1941. Much the largest of the electrified systems was the Pacific Electric Railway, extending over 520 miles of route. The SP gained control in 1911, by which time the PER was already changing from an inter-urban to a suburban operation, as the area it served rapidly developed. Its value to SP was largely as a freight feeder from all over the greater Los Angeles area. Cut-backs in PER passenger service began before the 1939-45 war. Very heavy wartime traffic stemmed the decline, but contraction continued

after the war, the last passenger service having closed in 1963.

Perhaps the early opting out of local passenger traffic was a portent of the future of long-distance trains, for by the early nineteen-sixties, SP's disenchantment with passengers had become very evident. And that despite its fleet of streamlined named trains—the Coast and Valley Daylights, the Shasta, the Cascade and others—on which standards had once been very high. Service was deliberately downgraded; restaurant and sleeping cars were withdrawn even from trains with journeys extending over two nights. The wanton behaviour eventually attracted official notice and permission for further discontinuances was refused by the regulatory bodies on the ground that substantial traffic had been deliberately discouraged by the deterioration of standards.

Today AMTRAK provides service over four different SP routes. The Coast Daylight is operated daily between Los Angeles and Oakland (for San Francisco and via San Jose). Thrice-weekly service is offered on the other routes—the Sunset between Los Angeles and New Orleans, the Coast Starlight between Portland and Oakland,

and the San Francisco Zephyr, between Oakland and Chicago, the last-named train operating daily in summer.

The Atchison, Topeka & Santa Fe Railway had its beginnings in Kansas, which state granted it a charter to build to the Colorado state line in 1859. Only with the spur of a substantial land grant —with a time limit of 10 years—did construction get under way in 1868. Starting from the state capital, Topeka, (66 miles west of Kansas City), Dodge City became end-of-line in 1871, and the Colorado state line was reached in 1872. The Atchison & Topeka, as the line was then known, played a major part in the settlement of Kansas, and its colonisation agents sought potential farmers in the Mennonites, a Russian religious sect, among others.

Although the town of Santa Fe, capital of New Mexico, became the next goal, the main line bypassed it, as construction proceeded across South-east Colorado to Albuquerque, and the capital was served by a short branch line from Lamy. To reach Albuquerque, the Raton pass near the New Mexico-Colorado state line, had to be surmounted. The physical

Above: Santa Fe diesel-electric locomotives 106 and 108 backing on to train 17 at Dearborn station, Chicago. *J K Hayward*

Left: Colorado Springs station on the Santa Fe in August, 1966. *C J Gammell*

Below left: Southern Pacific 4-4-2 No 3025 on display at Traveltown, Los Angeles. *V Goldberg*

Above right: The Super Chief rounds the last curve of the double horseshoe near Ribera, New Mexico. *Santa Fe RR*

problems there, however, were second to those presented by the young and expanding Denver & Rio Grande, which at that period was still aiming south from Denver; later, it was to head west, into the Rockies.

Battles, both physical and legal, ensued; the Sante Fe won and its first train surmounted Raton at the end of 1878. With its title extended to Atchison, Topeka & Santa Fe, the railway looked even farther west. The Southern Pacific, however, considered New Mexico to be its own territory, and opposed the expansion plans. The Sante Fe parried by obtaining an interest in a charter owned by the St Louis and San Francisco RR. Further legal exercises ensued, but finally the Santa Fe was able to build through to the Pacific coast, completing its line to Los Angeles in 1887.

At its eastern end, acquisitions and new construction brought the Santa Fe to Chicago. Included there was the Chicago & St Louis RR, whose line from Chicago to Streator, Illinois, 90 miles, provided the entry link to the big city. The Santa Fe stretched 2,224 miles from Chicago to Los Angeles. Later construction brought the Santa Fe to San Francisco bay, at Oakland. From Barstow, the line ran to Bakersfield and thence down the San Joaquin valley via Stockton and Richmond, to a terminal at Oakland, 454 miles from Barstow.

From Chicago to Los Angeles, the main line today is double track throughout, except where an alternative route is available, that is, between Newton, Kansas, and the Albuquerque area, and between Los Angeles and San Bernardino, California. The original main line has summits at Raton (7,622ft), Glorietta (7,421ft), Continental Divide (7,247ft) and Arizona Divide (7,313ft). The alternative main line via Amarillo, Texas, 46 miles longer, has a summit level of only 6,470ft at Mountainair. The majority of passenger trains used the old main line via La Junta, which initially had been built to Pueblo, Colorado, before the extensions into New Mexico had left Pueblo on a 64-mile-long branch from La Junta. Pueblo gave con-

nections to the Colorado mining areas, and eventually by joint trackage and running agreements to Denver. Other western extensions took the Santa Fe to San Diego and to El Paso, both points with Mexican connections.

Apart from its coverage in the far south-west, the Santa Fe also served much of Texas, and reached the Gulf of Mexico. From Newton, Kansas, on the main line, a 200-mile-long extension leads to Oklahoma City, and from there (over the rails of the subsidiary Gulf, Colorado & Santa Fe Railway) Fort Worth, Dallas, Houston and the port of Galveston are reached. Western Texas is served by another subsidiary, the Panhandle and Santa Fe Railway. Together, the Santa Fe system covers 13,000 miles of route; until the recent advent of Penn Central and Burlington Northern, it was the longest rail system in the USA. Serving areas which are economically still expanding, and with a high proportion of long-haul and high-rated traffic, the Santa Fe is a prosperous and well-kept railway.

In the middle nineteen-fifties, freight revenue outstripped that from passengers in the ratio of 12 to 1. Even so, its passenger trains were for many years among the very best in the country. The fleet name of -Chief was widely used, having its origin in a train advertised as 'The Chief —extra fast, extra fine, and extra fare', which entered service towards the end of 1926 on the Chicago-Los Angeles route. Prior to that, the Santa Fe De Luxe had been a companion of the California Limited on the run, both of them crack trains.

Closely associated with passenger service on the Santa Fe from as early as 1876 was 'Fred Harvey' service. Harvey was a Scot who built up a chain of railway station restaurants on Santa Fe lines, prior to the advent of dining cars. He set high standards at a time when train meal stops were a prime subject for jokes. The Harvey Houses made a name for themselves, and expanded to become a big hotel group; for a time Harvey was also a dining car contractor.

History was made in 1937 when the Santa Fe placed in service the first diesel-powered all-first-class streamliner in the USA. The Super Chief was a beautifully appointed train, built by Budd, and it ran from Chicago to Los Angeles in under 40 hours. In 1938, it was joined by a second similar train, built by Pullman-Standard. Dome cars and more new equipment were added after the war, and in 1956, the fast all-coach (second class) economy train, the El Capitan, was equipped with so-called high-level coaches. Other crack trains of the Santa Fe included the Texas Chief and the Kansas Cityan. Today, under AMTRAK, service over Santa Fe rails is provided between Chicago and Los Angeles by the combined Super Chief/El Capitan (as well as by the Chief during the summer only), the Texas Chief to Houston and by three round trips daily between Los Angeles and San Diego.

THE PENN CENTRAL

PENN CENTRAL, to give the Penn Central Transportation Company its popular title, is, like Burlington Northern, a new name in the railway field. Third in size (based on route mileage) of railways in North America, it just comes over the 20,000 miles mark, with BN and Canadian National. There, any comparison with the other two giants ceases, for, while BN appears quickly and easily to have consummated its recent merger, and CN has likewise in its half-century of existence become a well-run property, Penn Central in 1976 is a very, very sick railroad.

Before we consider today's situation, it is best to look at the historical development of Penn Central's components—the New York Central Railroad System (NYC) and the Pennsylvania Railroad (PRR), whose merger took place on February 1, 1968. Both constituents were themselves the result of the combination, over the years, of many smaller companies.

The name New York Central dates from 1853, when a number of short lines were linked up and consolidated to provide a through route between Albany, capital of New York State, and Buffalo, a gateway city, opposite Canada's Niagara peninsular. Two links with New York city, the New York & Harlem and the more-direct New York & Hudson, were acquired by Commodore Cornelius Vanderbilt, who had made a fortune from real estate and ferryboat operation. In 1867, the commodore consolidated the lines to Albany with the NYC to form what was to become the New York Central & Hudson River RR from NY City through to Buffalo. A couple of years later, he acquired the Lake Shore & Michigan Southern, which linked Buffalo with Chicago via the south shore of Lake Erie, Cleveland and Toledo, on an easily graded route.

Another Vanderbilt component was the Michigan Central—from Detroit in Kalamazoo to Chicago—and the associated Canada Southern, a geographically direct link between Detroit and Buffalo across south-western Ontario, and north of Lake Erie. A further accretion at the western end of the developing system was the

'Big Four' route—the Cleveland, Cincinnati, Chicago & St Louis. By then the cities served included not only those named in the last title, but also Columbus and Indianapolis. All of them were also to be served by the Pennsylvania RR. The Michigan Central also had a long rambling secondary main line from Detroit up the east side of the upper Michigan peninsula, via Bay City to Mackinan City. The latter was also served by a similar offshoot of the Pennsylvania, the Grand Rapids & Indiana RR, up the west side of the peninsula, from Fort Wayne.

A further important link gave the NYC access to Boston—the Boston & Albany, which facilitated passenger traffic between Boston and points west of Albany and made many important freight connections to New England. The NYC also acquired erstwhile rivals. The New York, West Shore

& Buffalo was built up the western bank of the Hudson river, from Weehawken, New Jersey, opposite New York city. A rate war ensued, the West Shore went bankrupt, and the NYC acquired it. Today, the West Shore line, singled, is still an important supplementary freight route to and from the New York metropolitan area; cross-river connection was by ferry and car float.

Two major constituents remain to be mentioned. Much the busier is the Pittsburgh & Lake Erie; its importance is quite out of proportion to its small mileage, for it serves the competitive Pittsburgh industrial area, with its many steel plants and heavy coal traffic. The P & LE is one prosperous corner of PC. The last line to mention is the Rome, Watertown & Ogdensburg; it linked the Niagara Falls area, Syracuse and Utica with Massena in northern New York state,

where connection was made with the Grand Trunk (now CN) so providing a through route to Montreal.

So much for the New York Central, which extensively served Ohio, Indiana, Michigan and Illinois as well as its name state. The Pennsylvania also grew to serve *its* name-state and the four other states just mentioned, and the Philadelphia–Baltimore–Washington so-called corridor as well. Although the corridor is the busiest of PRR's passenger routes, the system's main line is the route that leaves the New York-Washington line at North Philadelphia and heads west via Paoli, Harrisburg and Pittsburgh (for Chicago and St Louis). Dating as a through rail route from 1858, the main line is heavily graded as it climbs the Allegheny mountains, and includes the spectacular Horseshoe curve.

The PRR was conceived and financed from Philadelphia, at one time the largest and most important American city. It was the threat of either New York or Baltimore becoming a rival port for traffic to and from the developing American West that made finance available for the building of the PRR. The line expanded to the west of Pittsburgh through several subsidiaries. The Pittsburgh, Fort Wayne & Chicago, again a consolidation of several small lines, provided the western link in an alternative (to the NYC) New York–Chicago route. The Vandalia Line—the Terre Haute & Indianapolis RR—gave access to St Louis. Another major western constituent was the Pittsburgh, Cincinnati, Chicago & St Louis Railway; with yet others, they provided the PRR, with a comprehensive network of lines west of Pittsburgh, thoroughly intertwined with NYC routes in the same area.

In the east, the picture, at least viz-a-viz the NYC, was rather different, for the NYC served only to a small degree the states of Pennsylvania and New Jersey. The PRR had other competitors—the Reading System, and the Baltimore & Ohio. It, too, acquired a number of smaller eastern roads. Among these were the United RRs of New Jersey (in the Philadelphia area), the Northern Central with a north-south route out of Baltimore which penetrated the NYC's territory to reach the shores of Lake Ontario at Sodus Point, the West Jersey RR (to Cape May), and the Camden & Atlantic—Philadelphian's short route to the seaside (and, in the heyday of steam, site of some very smart running with Atlantic-type locomotives).

The route to Atlantic City has other features of interest. It forms the core of a relatively rare American phenomenon, a joint railway—the Pennsylvania–Reading Seashore Lines. The Camden–Atlantic City–Cape May area was served by parallel overlapping lines of both the PRR and the Reading System. In the aftermath of the economic depression, the two groups of lines were placed under common management and much of the duplication was eliminated. Even today, services in the

Above: High-speed electric Metroliner on the Penn Central system at Washington Union station in February 1972. *B W Mouat*

Left: Ex-PRR Silverliner leaving Chestnut Hill for Philadelphia in June 1971. *V Goldberg*

Below: A westbound freight train passing an eastbound passenger train on the PRR main line between New York and St Louis at Steubenville on the Ohio river. *V Goldberg collection*

Bottom: Early PRR 2-8-0 freight locomotive No 2813. *V Goldberg collection*

area are provided by Budd diesel railcars lettered 'Pennsylvania Reading Seashore Lines'.

The PRR and the NYC brought just under 10,000 route miles each to the new Penn Central system. A third, important but smaller, constituent included from the start of 1969 was the New York, New Haven & Hartford RR. The New Haven was already bankrupt, having been so since the early nineteen-sixties, but a condition of the P-C merger, imposed by the Interstate Commerce Commission (ICC) was that PC took responsibility for it. The New Haven brought over 1,600 additional route-miles to the system, including the 230-mile-long main line—the so-called shore line—between New York and Boston, as well as a number of branches of varying importance in Southern New England. In addition there was the important freight-only route between the Maybrook, NY, gateway (with links to the south and west) and New Haven, Conn.

The New York, New Haven & Hartford RR, in addition to serving the area indicated by its title, expanded in the decades from 1890, by taking over a number of other fairly small systems. Its shore line extended beyond New Haven to New London, whence the New York, Providence & Boston RR continued to Providence, RI, to connect with the Old Colony RR. The Old Colony linked Providence with Boston and had a small network east of that route serving Cape Cod. Another important constituent was the New York & New England RR, extending from Fishkill (on the Hudson, 60 miles above New York) via Hartford, Willimantic and Readville, to Boston. Other sectors of the New Haven include the Housatonic System from Bridgeport

Below: Early NYC Atlantic express locomotive No 3889, from the Locomotive Publishing Co series. *V Goldberg collection*

Facing page: Old suburban electric stock of the Pennsylvania RR at Washington Union station in February 1972. *B W Mouat*

Above: Mixed bag of Penn Central rolling stock, including diesel loco No 4266 on the Admiral train, at Chicago in July 1970. *V Goldberg*

Left: Triple-headed PRR freight train on the famed Horseshoe curve, Altoona. *J M Jarvis*

Below: Another from the Locomotive Publishing Co series, PRR loco No 4060 on a mixed freight. *V Goldberg collection*

north to Pittsfield, and the Connecticut River RR, north from Springfield with connections to Canada.

The sub-components of the three PC constituents had largely, by the turn of the century, become consolidated in varying degrees to the three major systems. The New York Central and the Pennsylvania became great rivals. Serving the most developed areas of the United States, their train services and frequencies were more akin to those in Europe than those of the railroads which served the west, where sparse population, vast distances and limitations on capital meant infrequent service and rough tracks. (Later, the position was to be reversed.)

The Central and the Pennsylvania vied with each other in many fields, quality of rolling stock, competitive trains between common points, in particular New York and Chicago, and in presenting a public image which spoke for itself. Both railways carried out many improvements and consolidated their positions. Even by 1891, the Central had a four-track main line between Albany and Buffalo, and indeed, by the combination of routes, there were four tracks all the way from New York City to Chicago, about 960 miles.

Much of the Central's consolidation, after Commodore Vanderbilt's death in 1877, was carried out by his son, William H Vanderbilt. It was William who first used the phrase 'the public be damned', when being questioned by a reporter over services to Chicago. The expression still has a familiar ring today!

In Edwardian times, the Central invested heavily in a great new terminal—Grand Central—in New York city. Train operations were on two levels, both underground, and were served by a sizeable suburban electrification scheme, using the protected third-rail dc system. Harmon, 33 miles from New York city, was the changeover point between steam and electric traction for long-distance trains; suburban services have mainly been worked by multiple-unit trains. The Central built many fine stations (sometimes jointly) in the twentieth century. Albany, Cleveland, Buffalo and Cincinatti come to mind, each a different expression of the importance of passenger service.

Grand Central was also the New York terminal for all New Haven suburban services, and for most of its long-distance trains, but the spectacular Hell Gate bridge high-level route to Penn station in Manhattan was used to give connections to points south and west. The New Haven also embraced electrification in the Edwardian era, but selected an overhead-wire 11,000V ac system, making it necessary to dual-equip electric mus and locomotives since the approach to Grand Central, being NYC owned, was electrified third-rail dc. The electrification extended as far as New Haven, 72 miles. The branches to New Canaan and Danbury were also electrified. The New Haven intended to extend its electrification beyond the end of its four-track main line at New Haven

through to Boston, but its finances did not permit it.

The Pennsylvania also carried out substantial improvements in Edwardian times. In place of its ferry-served terminal in Jersey City, opposite Manhattan, it extended under the Hudson river in tunnel to a 28-acre site in mid-town New York, the new Penn station. The extension did not stop there, but continued on in tunnels under the East River to Long Island. There, connection was made with the Hell Gate bridge route, and hence to the New Haven, permitting through services from the south to Boston. Sunnyside PRR car storage yard in the borough of Queens was also served, and the PRR obtained control of the Long Island RR, many of whose trains were extended to Penn station, much more convenient than its own terminals east of the East River.

The initial Pennsylvania river tunnel electrification was third-rail dc, but a few years later, suburban electrification in the Philadelphia area was carried out at 11,000V ac 25Hz, with overhead contact. The same system was later adopted for main-line work, and by the late nineteen-thirties, it was in use between New York and Washington, and west as far as Harrisburg on the main line. Eventually, about 660 route-miles were electrified and are still in use today. The famous GGI streamline locomotive class was developed in the 'thirties for the electrified lines.

Many of the express trains on Penn Central's constituents carried famous names. Between New York and Chicago, the New York Central had the longer, but easier route — indeed the term 'Water Level Route' was much used in advertising. The Pennsylvania had tough grades west of Philadelphia, but measured only 908 miles to Chicago, compared with the Central's 960 miles. Running time between the two cities was reduced from 28 hours to 20 hours in 1902. The Twentieth Century Limited (of the Central) and the Pennsylvania Special (from 1912, the Broadway Limited) were the rivals, and the schedule was reduced to 18 hours for both in 1905. At intervals, each train was re-equipped with the finest and latest in rolling stock. In the 'twenties and 'thirties, the Central's famous Hudsons and the Pennsy's Class K4 Pacifics, were mainstays of express passenger motive power while steam was king. In 1938, streamlined equipment was introduced on both trains, both on a new 16-hour schedule. Diesel traction followed in post-war years, together with more new train sets.

The New Haven, too, had its crack expresses, the Merchants Limited, the Yankee Clipper and the Bay State; all (at one time) were all-parlour car trains, ie all first-class day accommodation for the main New York–Boston run.

During the 1939-45 war, all railroads carried phenomenal passenger loads, and large orders for streamlined equipment were placed after the war, to meet the hoped-for continuation of the boom. Air competition (and new highways) decreed

otherwise. The railroads appeared to be slow to appreciate the erosion of their traffic. Certainly, it was *not* the case that no traffic survived; rather, the railroads failed to act to hold traffic in those fields—the shorter distances—where they could continue to compete effectively. Losses on long-distance services seemed to lead to a lack of faith in all services, and during the 'sixties, there was a rapid decline in punctuality, cleanliness, staff courtesy and maintenance. Management appeared to have completely lost heart.

It is on Penn Central's constituents that most of the blame for the bad image nationally of all railroad passenger service in recent years must fall, serving as they did, New York, nerve-centre of the country's communications. To the writer of these words, albeit a visitor from abroad, it was clear in the 'sixties that all three component railroads were in a serious decline, with major deficiencies in management and maintenance. It is all the more surprising that the ICC should approve the merger of such obviously ailing operations, and accept the specious arguments in support of it put forward by the railroads' managements.

The outcome was a shock more to the financial world than to the serious student of railways—bankruptcy from June 21, 1970. The subsequent disclosures of corruption and incompetence in management have been dealt with in the book *Wreck of the Penn Central*. The story revealed is not a creditable one. Inter-company strife, incompetence, personality clashes, trade

union intransigence, job feather-bedding, plain corruption in the financial field—all were to be found in Penn Central.

At the time of writing, it would be a brave man who would predict the future for Penn Central. Nationalisation has been mentioned; the writer, in his innocence, asked an American legal friend if the bankruptcy trustees also looked after the public interest. The answer was 'no, only the creditors'. Once again, 'the public be damned'. Times have not changed!

Above: Pacific Great Eastern (now British Columbia) Railway diesel railcars at Squamish, BC, in May 1964. *V Goldberg*

Right: CP's eastbound Dominion transcontinental train leaving Rogers pass in the Selkirk range, summit of the line, in February 1963. *J G Tawse*

Below: CN's Ocean express headed by four diesel locos through the rock cutting at Halifax, Nova Scotia, in September 1972. *J G Tawse*

Bottom: Aerial shot of CN's Supercontinental in the Jasper area. *Canadian National Railways*

Railways of Canada

SEVERAL PARALLELS with the story of British Railways can be found in the history of Canadian National Railways. CN, as it is known colloquially, is an amalgamation of many predecessor companies, as is British Railways. In contrast with Canadian Pacific, it was not conceived as a nationwide system, although some of its principal components eventually grew to meet that description. The formation of CNR took place in stages in the period 1918-1923. The new system included three major components (and several minor constituents), namely, the Canadian Northern Railway (CNoR), a Canadian enterprise; the Canadian Government Railways (CGR), in public ownership; and the Grand Trunk Railway (GTR), an English-owned system.

The Grand Trunk was the oldest established of the three, and included Canada's first railway, the Champlain & St Lawrence, a portage railway linking the St Lawrence river, opposite Montreal, with the Lake Champlain river system at St Johns. Built to a gauge of 5ft 6in, it opened on July 21, 1836, with an English locomotive, *Dorchester,* four American coaches and Montreal-built wagons. For several decades, the 5ft 6in gauge was widely used in Canada, and it was adopted by the Grand Trunk when it opened in 1856. The GTR was conceived as a main line linking Upper and Lower Canada (Ontario and Quebec), and was built to high standards. Extensions to its main line between Toronto and Montreal, and the take-over of other companies eventually brought it west to Chicago in the USA, and east to Quebec and beyond. All its track was converted to standard gauge by 1874. However, the railway was far from being an unqualified success financially, despite its 4,800 route-miles.

Two late-Victorian Canadian entrepreneurs, William MacKenzie and Donald Mann, fathered the Canadian Northern Railway. From a small group of lines in Manitoba, the CNoR expanded, in less than two decades, to an 8,000-mile transcontinental system, most of it new construction, but incorporating some existing local lines. Booming immigration spurred the growth, but it was supported also by public and government desires that transcontinental traffic should not be wholly dependent on the Canadian Pacific.

Canada is unique in the railway field in possessing, side by side, two major railway systems, one publicly owned, the other in private hands. Early examples of public ownership (and, indeed, construction) were found in the maritime colonies of Nova Scotia and New Brunswick. A rail link with Canada East and West (i e Lower and Upper Canada) was a requirement for the inclusion of those colonies in the Dominion of Canada, just as British Columbia needed the construction of the Canadian Pacific.

The Intercolonial Railway, (ICR) as the eastern link became, was finally completed in 1875 as a standard-gauge line, although certain of its components had earlier been built to the 5ft 6in gauge. Its route lay close to the shore of the St Lawrence, well away from the US border. The ICR was a sizeable unit of the Canadian Government Railways, but the National Transcontinental Railway (NTR) was longer. Its route—deliberately circuitous to open up formerly untapped areas—ran through Northern Ontario and Quebec, linking Winnipeg with Quebec City, and on east to Moncton, New Brunswick.

A subsidiary of the Grand Trunk, the Grand Trunk Pacific (GTP) was built west from Winnipeg, to reach the Pacific at the new port of Prince Rupert, through country much of which was ready for immediate development. The completion in 1915 of this new transcontinental route (which was built from the start to main-line standards) followed the outbreak of the 1914-18 war. In consequence, the tide of immigrants upon which the newly-opened railways depended, ceased, with dire consequences for much of Canada's railway network. The war-time traffic boom came only in already developed areas; Halifax, Nova Scotia, for example, became a vital port in the route to Europe.

The new lines, the CNoR, the NTR, and the GTP, quickly experienced financial problems, such that the CNoR passed to the control of the CGR late in 1918. The combined system started to be called Canadian National Railways early in 1919, and the GTP, after being placed in receivership in that year, came under CNR management in 1920. Management of the GTR itself passed in 1922 to the CNR and late the same year the name Canadian National Railways was formally adopted. In January 1923, all the constituents were legally amalgamated.

Most of the CNR components had included smaller secondary railways taken over in a variety of circumstances over the years. Space permits mention only of two of particular interest. Railways in the then colony of Prince Edward Island were sponsored by the island's government, and a 3ft 6in-gauge system developed there from 1874 had reached a mileage of 278 by 1912. In an island only 120 miles long, and never more than 25 miles wide, financial problems were in evidence from the start, and a condition of the entry of Prince Edward Island to the dominion in 1873 was that the dominion assumed responsibility for the PEI Railway. It was placed in ICR hands, so eventually becoming part of the CN system. Conversion to standard gauge was spread over the period 1919-1930. Today, train ferries link the island with the mainland, and although, alas, passenger services have recently ceased, the aura of the narrow gauge lingers on in the island.

Newfoundland is an island the size of England. It claims to be Britain's oldest colony and Canada's newest province. The railway came late to "Newfie"—1884, but eventually over 900 miles of 3ft 6in-gauge track crossed the island, and branched out to some of the coastal communities. Of narrow gauge to this day, the system, after a chequered career, first in private hands and then under the Newfoundland government, passed to CN when Newfoundland joined the confederation in 1949. Although mileage has shrunk to 700 and passenger service is confined now to mixed trains, CN's nearest approach to Britain is an area of great interest. Train ferries provide a link with the island's increasing freight traffic, and freight can be transhipped at Port aux Basques, the island ferry terminal, or trucks (bogies) can be changed on dual-gauge sidings.

A few other lines of local interest also passed to CN hands after 1923, but we must now look at CN's major traffic centres. Focal points of the system are Moncton (for the Maritime provinces), Montreal and Toronto (for Quebec and Ontario respectively) and Winnipeg, for the Prairie provinces. Major freight marshalling yards are located at these four points—with many other yards elsewhere.

In the passenger field, CN has had the best-filled timetable folder in N America for many years. With a system route-mileage now of 25,000, and many hundreds of miles of new lines built since the war, this is, perhaps, not surprising. In addition to transcontinental service linking Montreal and Toronto with Vancouver, CN serves the "trunk" corridor Quebec-Montreal - Toronto - SW Ontario, where much of Canada's population, industry and agriculture are located.

System headquarters is in Montreal, where the modern Central station offers appropriate facilities for the traveller. There, also, is the only electrified part of the system, an 18-mile suburban line, with a 3-mile-long tunnel under Mount Royal, equipped with a 2,400V dc overhead system.

Toronto has some surburban rail service along the lake shore, provided by CN over its tracks under contract to the Government of Ontario, with the title GO Transit. On its own account, CN operates just a handful of local trains around Toronto.

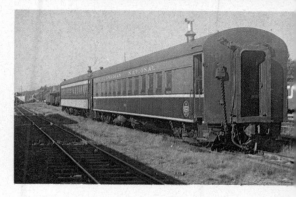

Other areas of passenger activity include the Maritimes, served by the well-known Ocean Limited and the Scotian trains, and northern areas where highways are lacking.

Rolling stock on Canadian National Railways has followed North American practice for many years, although a number of English features were in evidence in early days. With so many different constituents, the steam locomotive fleet was quite varied. At its peak it numbered 3,260 locomotives, but the figure later settled down to about 2,500. Perhaps best known were upwards of 200 4-8-4s, half of which dated from the 1940s, and most of which survived to the end of steam in 1960. In order of totals, 2-8-0s (850), 2-8-2s (500), 4-6-0s (600) and Pacifics (330) filled out the fleet, with other types less in evidence. A particularly Canadian feature in more recent construction was the fully enclosed cab to provide protection against the northern winter. Dieselisation took place late (compared with the US) and quickly, in the period 1951-1960.

Passenger stock also followed conventional N American practice. A change from an all-over dark green livery to an attractive green-gold-black livery coincided with an extensive order for over 350 modern streamlined passenger coaches in the mid-1950s. A few years later, a modern corporate image was adopted, with a new CN device and passenger coaches finished in black and white, with bright reds and blues internally.

A large fleet (105,000) of freight wagons, all of bogie type, rounds off CN's rolling stock. The fleet includes many with carrying capacity up to 100 tons, and specialised types to deal with particular traffics. Diesel locomotives number over 2,000 and are of standard North American builders' designs, although incorporating some internal modifications to cater for the extremes of Canadian weather.

CN's activities are not confined to rails. Again, like British Railways, there is a railway-owned hotel chain in principal cities, and coastal shipping activities are extensive, particularly in the east. Newfoundland's coast is well served, and several ferry services are operated elsewhere on the Atlantic seaboard. The SS "*Prince George*" provides a link to Alaska on the Pacific, as well as barge service to link up with CN's isolated freight lines on Vancouver Island. CN is also active in the telecommunications field, and until recently, "fathered" the national airline Air Canada.

In its earlier days, CN had a conservative reputation, but it was an instrument of government social policy. Today, the federal regulatory body, the Canadian Transportation Commission, is studying the role of each mode in the field of transport. One can rest assured that this well-run railway, today a leader in the North American railway field, will continue to be a vital part of Canada's

economy. Its courageous stand in the 1960s in respect of passenger service, and its (qualified) intentions to continue to serve the passenger market, is an object lesson which might well be noted elsewhere.

The activities of the CPR now extend far beyond the original concept, for the company operates international air and shipping services, has vast mining and property interests and provides telecommunications, road haulage and hotel services, in addition to its railways. Even so, CP railways today extend to over 21,000 miles of route. The title CP Rail and a new CP device have been adopted for most of the company's rail activities in Canada.

From its headquarters at Windsor station in Montreal, a main line extending through Toronto to Windsor (for Detroit) is now a freight-only route competing with CNR. Until the last decade, Toronto-Montreal/ Ottawa passenger train services of CNR and CPR were co-ordinated and operated in pool. Also, in Canada's main corridor, CPR extends to Quebec City, again in competition with CNR, but there passenger trains still run, three times daily, to Quebec's ornate Palais station. From Montreal also there is passenger service along the North Shore (of the Ottawa River) to Ottawa, in addition to that via Vankleek Hill on the transcontinental route. There is also suburban service on the Vankleek Hill route as far as Vaudrevil

(40 miles from Montreal). Base service is operated by diesel railcars helped out in the peaks by conventional hauled stock, and by a handful of double-deck coaches worked push-pull.

East from Montreal there is overnight service to and from Saint John, NB, by the Atlantic Limited and a CP route which is about 260 miles shorter than CN's route via the ex-Intercolonial line along the Gulf of St Lawrence. At Saint John, service continues to Digby, NS (48 miles), across the Bay of Fundy with its 40ft tides, by the MV *Princess of Acadia*. (This vessel and the Pacific Coast coastal steamers are operated by CP Rail and not CP Steamships.)

At Digby Wharf connection is made with the CP-owned, but separate (both physically and operationally) Dominion Atlantic Railway, which extends 217 miles from Yarmouth to Halifax. The branch line from Windsor to Truro sees one of the very few surviving mixed passenger and freight trains in North America. The mainline DAR passenger service is operated by two intensively worked diesel mu trains, lettered Dominion Atlantic Railway.

Another independently operated member of the CP Rail family in the east is the Quebec Central Railway, which links Quebec City with Sherbrooke (148 miles) on the Montreal-Saint John line. The QCR serves the vast asbestos mines which provide it with much of its traffic.

In SW Ontario, two further members of the CP family are the Grand River Railway and the Lake Erie & Northern Railway, which both run out of the city of Galt, respectively north to Waterloo (14 miles) and south to Brantford (21 miles). The former frequent electric inter-urban (express tramcar) passenger services are long gone and the remaining freight trains have been dieselised for a decade. In the same area is the branch to Owen Sound (129 miles), once the narrow-gauge (3ft 6in) Toronto, Grey & Bruce Railway; it became part of CPR in 1884. Traces of the old narrow-gauge formation can still be found, where they were discarded after conversion to standard gauge at the end of 1881.

Farther west, beyond the grain-shipping lake-head ports at Thunder Bay, CP Rail operates a complex network of branch lines in the Prairie provinces. Some of them now see little more than seasonal use after the grain harvest. Branch-line passenger services there are now confined to twice-daily trips between Calgary and Edmonton (194 miles). From Edmonton, the Northern Alberta Railways stretch farther north over several routes, totalling 923 miles, into an area with much mineral and agricultural promise. The NAR is owned jointly by CP Rail and CNR.

In the South of Alberta, west from Medicine Hat and over Crow's Nest pass, extends the Kettle Valley route of CP Rail. It crosses the Rocky Mountains close to

Left: CP Rail freight train at the Lower Spiral tunnel in 1968. *CP Rail*

Top: GO (Government of Ontario) transit train in Toronto suburban service at Oakville in May 1968. *J K Hayward*

Above: CP Rail diesel railcar on Toronto-Windsor service at West Toronto in May 1971. *V Goldberg*

Right: On CP in 1959, Pacific No 2470 leaving Montreal Windsor Street station. *J N Westwood*

the US border. Since its completion at the turn of the century, it has provided an alternative to the original transcontinental route, which it rejoins at Spence's Bridge. Freight only now, it serves the fruit-growing and mining areas in southern British Columbia. In the heart of this mountainous area, there still survives an isolated railway to Nakusp, linked to the rest of the system by car floats on Slocan lake.

In 1971, CP Rail was seriously considering electrification of its main line through the Rockies west of Calgary. Coal, bound for Japan from British Columbia mines is the reason behind the proposal; a supplementary new port, Roberts Bank, near Vancouver, is already under construction.

Vancouver is the terminus of the transcontinental route, and is home base to the Pacific Coastal steamer services, now much reduced in extent. However, year-round ferry service links Vancouver with Nanaimo, on Vancouver Island. Nanaimo is situated at about mid-point on CP Rail's most westerly outpost, the Esquimalt & Nanaimo Railway, which links Victoria with Courtenay (140 miles); a single diesel railcar provides daily passenger service.

The foregoing has summarised CP's railway activities over 16,000 miles of route in Canada, but brief mention should be made of CP's 57 per cent interest in the 4,700-mile SOO Line Railroad, a US-based company which covers an area between Chicago and Winnipeg, and east to Sault Ste Marie, between Lake Superior and Lake Huron.

In the matter of equipment, CP was unusual in North America in building its own steam locomotives and passenger coaches. Its Delorimier and, later, the Angus shops, both in Montreal, built quality products of traditional designs. Of the steam locomotive fleet (which numbered 1,962 in 1937) the large Selkirks (2-10-4s) and Royal Hudsons (4-6-4s) are well recorded, but numerous workaday 2-8-2s and 2-8-0s provided the backbone for freight service. For secondary lines, a large fleet of 4-6-0s, of Class D10 and others powered trains across the system. Much of the passenger equipment was of conventional heavyweight construction, but forward-looking smooth-sided coaches were introduced in the 1930s; regrettably, much of the fine coach fleet has recently been sold, although the 173 stainless-steel cars purchased in 1954-5 cover most of the surviving loco-hauled services. There is also a fleet of 54 diesel railcars and over 1,100 diesel locomotives.

Freight stock totals about 80,000 wagons of conventional North American design, with a high proportion of specialised and high-capacity types. Forest products, grain, coal, ores and manufactured goods all provide traffic for CP Rail's nationwide system, on which freight provides about 90 per cent of the revenue.

Below: arly Canadian Pacific poster. *CP Rail*

SOUTH AMERICAN RAILWAYS

Left: Chilean State Railways Alco 2-8-2 locomotive at Antilhue, near the southern end of the South system, in March 1972. *R M Quinn*

Bottom left: Diesel locomotive of Argentine Railways General San Martin Railway, at Palmira in March 1972. *R M Quinn*

Above: A 2-8-2 engine of Argentine Railways General Roca Railway taking water at Lepa in March 1972. *R M Quinn*

Right: Slogan-covered carriage of Chilean State Railways at Antilhue in March 1972. *R M Quinn*

Below: A two-truck Shay geared locomotive of Bolivian National Railways on shunting duty at La Paz in March 1972. *R M Quinn*

N PICTURES

Above: Diesel-headed train of Southern
Railway of Peruvian Corporation Railways
leaving Cuzco in March 1972.
R M Quinn

Below: Diesel railcar set of Transandine
Railway, partly owned by Chilean State
Railways, at Poluaridas, Argentine, in
March 1972. *R M Quinn*

A READER WHO is not well-informed in railway matters might well receive with incredulity the information that there is a railway which climbs to a greater height than the summit of Mont Blanc, on standard gauge—not narrow gauge, and without any aid from rack-and-pinion traction; and, moreover, that this 15,848ft summit is but one of a number in the same region that top the 14,000ft mark after arduous climbs from their lower terminals at sea level. The region is South America; the countries concerned are Peru, Chile and Bolivia; and the reason for these airy exercises in railway engineering is the towering mountain mass of the Andes, which borders the Pacific coast of South America throughout its entire length.

In the heart of the Andes is considerable mineral wealth, of nitrate, copper and silver, and whereas the coastal side of the mountains is in large measure completely barren, there are high-lying valleys near the equator in which the temperate climate encourages sheep farming and agricultural activity also. It is to connect these sources of revenue with the coast that railways such as the Peruvian Central, the Peruvian Southern, the Antofagasta (Chile) & Bolivia and the Argentine Transandine, to name the most important, have been carried up into the forbidding mountain range.

By far the most difficult of the Transandean lines to operate is the one that reaches the maximum altitude of 15,848ft, the Central Railway of Peru. It owes its planning and construction to an American adventurer named Henry Meiggs, so much so indeed that at the close of last century it was widely known as the Meiggs road in Peru. What he conceived originally was a Central Transandine Railway, which ultimately came into existence as the Callao, Lima & Oroya Railway, but in

1890 became the Central of Peru Division of the Peruvian Corporation Railways. So it is from Callao, the chief Pacific port of Chile, that this remarkable railway starts its 216-mile course towards the interior. From there it is a run of a few miles only to the Peruvian capital, Lima, where, in the Desamparados station, the journey of the two daily trains to Oruro really begins. One, of lightweight stock, is the *Rapido;* the other, which follows, is heavier and slower, and does the roadside work.

From Lima the line makes straight for the great mountain chain of the Andes, the Cordillera. At first the rise up the Rimac valley, to Chosica, is gradual; in the first

Railways on the roof of the world

Top: In the early days of the Central of Peru Railway, locomotive No 13 'Santa Domingo' heading a works train across Verrugas bridge.
Ian Allan library

Above: Puente Ruinas station deep in the Urubamba canyon, near Machu Picchu on the Southern Railway of Peru.
C & D Gannon

Above left: Central railway station at Lima in 1970. *D T Rowe*

Right: A modern diesel railcar and a German-built steam locomotive side-by-side on the Southern line near Cuzco in 1969. *C & D Gannon*

25 miles the average gradient is a little easier than 1 in 100, but climbing then begins in earnest. The ruling gradient steepens officially to 1 in 25, and enginemen at least have little doubt that up some pitches 1 in 20 is nearer the mark. The steeper climb is continuous for 73 miles, until at the Galera tunnel the line crosses the Continental Divide at an altitude of 15,848ft.

On the ground of expense spiral tunnelling to gain height was ruled out; instead, the line climbs up precipitous mountain slopes by an endless succession of zigzags, or V-switches, each of which requires reversal of the train at the two ends, greatly increasing the journey time. Most of the climbing is up deep mountain valleys which are completely barren, though the line runs through a few towns, such as Matucana, and several smelting plants. Of tunnels there are plenty, and great viaducts over gorges joining the main valley.

Also plentiful in such country are hazards to trains, particularly from boulders breaking loose from the mountainsides and falling on to the railway. Trolleys manned by two men, called pilot gravity cars, are run regularly down the grades ahead of the passenger trains to discover and warn if such rock-falls have taken place. For the relief of passengers who might suffer from mountain sickness at the great altitude reached on the climb cylinders of oxygen are carried in the trains.

Before entering the 1,287yd Galera tunnel the train stops at Ticlio, which at 15,610ft above the sea is the highest railway junction in the world—"cold, dismal and lonesome", as one account has it. The junction is for the original Marococha loop, which reaches the record altitude of 15,848ft; the Galera tunnel was bored in later years to provide a shorter and slightly easier route eastwards. Curiously enough, even at this tremendous altitude snow gives little trouble to the operating staff; the reason, of course, is the nearness of the Equator, as a result of which the snowline is as high as 17,000ft. The run from the Galera tunnel down to Oroya brings the level of the railway to 12,220ft, and there giant smelters proclaim one of the principal reasons for the railway's construction.

Oroya is the junction for the independent Cerro de Pasco Railway, which runs for 120 miles northwards along the Cordillera, at no point less than 12,722ft above sea level and, at its maximum (Alcococha), reaching 14,385ft; this line was laid to tap the great Cerro de Pasco copper deposits and other minerals. Meanwhile, the Central of Peru main line continues for 78 miles from Oroya down the Mantaro Valley, finishing at Huancayo, at 10,700ft, in a fertile valley that contrasts totally with the barren mountain gorges through which it has passed to that point. The Peruvian Government owns a metre-gauge line that continues from Huancayo to Huancavelica.

In the southern part of the country there is the Southern Railway of Peru, another property of the Peruvian Corporation. Its starting point is at Mollendo, on the Pacific coast, and like the Peruvian Central it climbs into the interior on the standard 4ft 8½in gauge. The coastal strip there is wider and the climbing, though steep, is less abrupt and zigzag layout was unnecessary. The Peruvian Southern is very up-to-date in its equipment and diesel-electric locomotives are the mainstay of its tractive power.

At La Joya, 55 miles from Mollendo, where the line has climbed to 4,441ft, it is joined by a 39-mile branch from the port of Matarani, which was opened in 1952. Matarani, north of Mollendo, is the safer and better-equipped harbour of the two, and now handles the bulk of the railway's freight traffic. Climbing continues as far as Arequipa, the most important town on the route and the railway's headquarters. Apart from one or two ravines, the line is entirely out in the open in rolling upland country—differing totally from the fearsome gorges threaded by the Peruvian Central—with views for many miles of the graceful snowclad cone of the 19,163ft Mount Misti, an extinct volcano.

At last, 223 miles from the coast, the summit level is reached at Crucero Alto, 14,668ft up. About 72 miles further on is Juliaca, at 12,551ft altitude, a junction from which the line to Cuzco bears away for 210 miles to the north-west, through some of the finest sheep-rearing country in Peru, and finishes in what was formerly the capital of the Inca empire, with its notable megalithic remains. Still more interesting is the continuation of the main line from Juliaca to Puno, at the north-western end of the most astonishing lake

in the world, Titicaca, 130 miles long and up to 41 miles wide, at an altitude of 12,466ft.

At Puno the Peruvian Southern takes to the water, on which it maintains a fleet of five ships. The most interesting of them is the SS *Inca*, which was built at Hull, sailed across the Atlantic, round Cape Horn and up the Pacific coast to Mollendo; there the ship was taken to pieces for transit up the railway to Puno, where it was put together again and finally launched on Titicaca. This ship and the SS *Ollanta* (also built at Hull) both have sleeping accommodation for the overnight journey along the length of the lake, which takes 12 hours.

The lake voyage ends on Bolivian soil, at

Above: A 2-8-2 locomotive heads a freight at Cochabamba on Bolivian National Railways, with which Southern of Peru steamer services on Lake Titicaca connect. *D T Rowe*

Below: A diesel railcar at Cochabamba station in 1970. *D T Rowe*

Bottom: Bolivian 2-8-4T No 553 in bright new paint at Oruro in 1970. *D T Rowe*

Guaqui, the terminus of a 60-mile metre-gauge line which links Lake Titicaca with the Bolivian capital, La Paz, and which by agreement with the Bolivian Government is operated by the Peruvian Southern. About 40 miles out from Guaqui the line reaches Viacha, an unpretentious station which nevertheless is a junction of some note. There it joins the Arica-La Paz Railway, which comes up from the Pacific coast over a 13,963ft summit at Jeneral Lagos, to provide by far the shortest route (293 miles) between La Paz and the sea. However, poor port facilities at Arica and the fact that 26 miles of the climb up from the coast are operated by rack-and-pinion on a 1 in 6 gradient has always limited its usefulness.

The other line coming into Viacha is (or was, for reasons to be described in a moment) the Antofagasta (Chile) & Bolivia, from the Pacific port of Antofagasta, 701 miles to the south. All three metre-gauge lines combine to use the 18½-mile stretch of the Guaqui-La Paz line from Viacha to the Bolivian capital, passing at El Alto, 13,396ft, over the rim of the great basin in which lies La Paz. Down its precipitous side is the 5½-mile drop of 1,370ft, negotiated with electric power on a gradient which at its steepest is 1 in 14½. It was brought into use in 1905 and was the first railway electrification in South America.

The Antofagasta (Chile) & Bolivia Railway, or FCAB, is by far the biggest of the independent Andean lines and formerly had a total route mileage of 1,821. Immediately after the Pacific War of 1879-1882 between Bolivia and Chile had cut Bolivia off from the Pacific coast and pushed the frontier back inland for several hundred miles, a beginning was made with a line on the very narrow gauge of 2ft 6in from the port of Antofagasta north-eastwards, to tap the nitrate deposits. After the war the Chilian Government authorised the railway to extend to the new frontier at Ollague, 274 miles from Antofagasta, passing on its way over a summit level of 12,976ft at Ascotan. A 60-mile branch was thrown off northwards from Ollague to Collahuassi, the centre of an extremely rich copper-mining region, which at Punto Alto reached the world's second highest railway altitude of 15,835ft; this section of the branch has now been abandoned.

Before Ascotan summit the railway enters a stretch of line which for 500 miles continuously is never below the 12,000ft level. In 1889 a Bolivian mining company had extended the line, but on the metre gauge, for 110 miles from Ollague to Uyuni, and in that year a British company not only took over the Antofagasta-Ollague line, but also, by consent of the Bolivian Government, the Uyuni extension, adding further to the latter by 101 miles to reach the important mining centre of Oruro by 1892.

Then in 1903 the Bolivia Railway Company was formed to lay 126 miles of line from Oruro to the junction at Viacha

already mentioned, together with two very important branches, one of 132 miles from Oruro to Cochabamba, and the other of 109 miles from Rio Mulato to Potosi. The latter is distinguished by possessing the highest railway station in the world—Condor, 15,705ft above the sea—and also for tapping what to date has been the world's greatest deposit of silver, a mountain at Potosi which is calculated to have produced about £350 million-worth of the precious metal !

In 1903 the FCAB took over the working of the main line from Uyuni to Viacha. For many years all went well, except for the troublesome change of gauge from 2ft 6in to one metre at Uyuni, which meant transhipment of both passengers and freight. At last the courageous decision was reached to widen the narrower gauge—an immense task, involving 236 miles of track. Before the major operation took place, 56 miles had been converted to mixed gauge by laying a third rail; then, after meticulous preparation like that of the Great Western Railway of England in changing its principal main lines in the 1890s from 7ft to 4ft 8½in gauge, in 1928 the FCAB carried out 180 miles of track widening in only six days, fortunately in fine weather—a remarkable feat at over 12,000ft altitude.

After the widening was completed, the FCAB International Limited at last began to run through from Antofagasta to La Paz, with the journey time cut from 42 to 31 hours. For a long time powerful 2-8-4 steam tank locomotives worked the principal trains, but in more recent years the inevitable diesel-electrics began to make their appearance.

In its efficient management and operation the FCAB has always had a high reputation, but the picture has now changed. Traffic has been lost through the opening of new roads parallel to the railway, and passenger traffic also has been lost to air competition. But the worst trouble has been with the Bolivian Government, notorious for its instability, which by degrees imposed such onerous conditions on the railway that in February 1959 the FCAB entirely suspended its operation in Bolivia, save only over the main line between Ollague and Oruro. While the Chilean section of the FCAB is still efficiently run, the Bolivian lines have gone into a sad decline.

Of many other railways in the Andes, most of them relatively small privately owned concerns, one other, very much farther to the south, deserves mention. It is the 155-mile Transandine Railway proper, which is partly in the Argentine Republic and partly in Chile and has had a chequered history. It was first planned in 1889 but owing to many delays it was not until 1910 that the two sections met in the 3,464yd-long Cumbre tunnel (the summit) at 10,452ft above sea level. At its eastern end the Transandine linked up at the city of Mendoza with the former Buenos Ayres & Pacific Railway (now the Ferrocarril General San Martin), and at

Above: One of the Alco Co-Co 2,150hp diesel-electric locomotives developed for high-altitude work on the Peru Southern line in 1961. *Alco Products Inc*

Left: A Garratt steam locomotive of the Antofagasta line at La Paz-Alta, Bolivia. *D T Rowe*

Below left : A Bolivian 2-8-2 heads a freight at Cochabamba in 1970. *D T Rowe*

Bottom: Bolivian National Japanese-built 1,870hp Bo-Bo-Bo diesel-electric locomotive at Oruro in 1970. *D T Rowe*

its western end, at Los Andes, with the Chilean State Railways, both of 5ft 6in gauge, although the Transandine itself has always been of metre gauge. From Mendoza the gradients up the gorge of the Mendoza river at first are not more severe than 1 in 40, but nearing the summit tunnel the inclination steepens to 1 in 16, with rack-and-pinion traction. On the Chilean side the descent is considerably more abrupt, with a fall of 7,750ft in 44 miles, and the rack-and-pinion sections steepen to 1 in 12. This handicap led to the electrification of the Chilean section in 1923.

In its heyday the Transandine did well, even to the extent of operating a daily Pullman train between Mendoza and Los Andes. The train took 12 hours to complete the journey of 155 miles, and it formed the link in a 38½-hour rail journey between Buenos Ayres and Santiago. Being well south of the Equator, snow caused considerable operating difficulties in winter, but Nature could impose far worse hazards than mere snowfall. In January 1934, in one of the lateral valleys feeding the Mendoza river a large lake formed high up in the mountains due to the formation of a massive dam of ice. When the ice wall gave way a vast mass of water swept down into the Mendoza valley, completely obliterating many miles of the railway.

Ten years elapsed before sufficient finance became available to restore the track, but by then conditions had changed ; the railway had to face air competition and soon afterwards that of a new motor road over the Cumbres pass. As a consequence, the Transandine Railway today, the two halves of which have been taken over by the national systems of Argentine and Chile, is steadily losing its former importance.

14
Railway Architecture

Above: From 'The Illustrated London News' of March 13, 1880, an artist's sketch of the arrival at Airolo of the first train through the Gotthard tunnel. *Illustrated London News*

Below: One entrance of the Loetschberg tunnel built between 1906-1912 on the new main line of the Berne-Loetschberg-Simplon Railway. *BLSR*

Facing page: On the Denver & Rio Grande Western standard-gauge section with a Denver-Salida train in the Royal gorge in August 1966. *C J Gammell*

THE WORLD'S
LARGEST TUNNELS

OF THE SEVEN longest railway tunnels in the world Europe can claim six, including the first five, which are shared by Switzerland and Italy. The two longest of them are in effect the same tunnel—the Simplon, which comprises two parallel bores, one opened to traffic 15 years after the other. Tunnelling techniques are now making such rapid strides, however, that before long existing maximum lengths are likely to be left well in the shade by such projects as the Channel tunnel, the Gotthard Base tunnel in Switzerland, and various tunnels planned for the network of new high-speed lines in Japan.

In the early days of railways the great mountain chain of the Alps was an insuperable barrier to railway communication between France and both Switzerland and Italy. As far back as 1842 the idea had been mooted of a direct line between France and Italy which, it was realised, would involve the boring of a tunnel considerably longer than any previously attempted; the French and Italian authorities eventually agreed on how the costs should be divided, and that the route should be up the valley of the Arc to Modane, and down the valley of the Dorre from Bardonecchia. A start was made in August

1857 on tunnelling between Modane and Bardonecchia, just over $7\frac{1}{2}$ miles apart, under the Pointe de Fréjus, 9,660ft high. Hence, strictly speaking, the name of the bore should be the Fréjus tunnel, and not the Mont Cenis tunnel, as it is commonly known.

Progress at first was very slow, but in 1860 new Sommeiller pneumatic drills were introduced and the rate of boring increased from 15 yards to 81 yards of completed tunnel a month. The tunnel was finally brought into use at the end of December 1870, but no national rejoicing was possible as France was then at grips with Germany in the Franco-Prussian war. However, during the tunnel construction a narrow-gauge railway had been operating over the Col du Mont-Cenis, climbing from 2,330 feet altitude at St Michel du Maurienne to over 6,860 feet on the pass, thence to drop to 1,625 feet at Susa. The railway was worked on the Fell system, with a centre rail engaged by extra wheels on the locomotives for additional adhesion in climbing and braking in descending the gradients as steep as 1 in $12\frac{1}{2}$. Trains took six hours to cover the $48\frac{1}{2}$ miles, but the line soon went out of use after the tunnels were opened.

The Fréjus tunnel has had a chequered history. In 1877 a serious landslip put the Modane entrance out of action; work on a new entrance was started but was abandoned after another slide. Finally a new bore of nearly $1\frac{1}{4}$ miles carried the tunnel to a third entrance, increasing its length from $7\frac{1}{2}$ miles to just over $8\frac{1}{2}$ miles. Reopening took place in 1881 and traffic carried on normally until a further interruption towards the end of the 1939-45 war. Then, before the German forces retreated, they mined and destroyed 300 yards of the French end of the tunnel. Reconstruction took from May 1945 to August 14, 1946, when an ex-PLM 4-8-4T locomotive took the first train through the reopened bore.

Regular passenger traffic was restarted in September of the same year, and has continued without interruption since. The Fréjus tunnel forms part of the main line from Paris to Turin and beyond. It is worked by Italian electric locomotives, the change from and to French power taking place at Modane, on the French side.

Not long after the Fréjus tunnel project was first mooted, another and more important plan came into the limelight— a direct Swiss link between South Germany and North Italy, first discussed as far back as 1848. But more than 20 years elapsed before a conference at Berne in 1869 decided on a route by way of the Swiss Reuss and Ticino valleys, with a tunnel under the Gotthard pass. The French objected, because of possible loss of traffic to their Fréjus route, but France's defeat by the Germans in the 1870-1871 war weakened her opposition, and the

Above left: From 'The Illustrated London News' of September 30, 1871, an engraving depicting the first train through the Mont Cenis tunnel. *Illustrated London News*

Above: A BR Bo-Bo electric locomotive leaves the new Woodhead tunnel with a Sheffield-Manchester train in March 1968. *B Stephenson*

powerful German and Italian interests had their way.

Of the original capital, Italy contributed £2,250,000 and the German and Swiss governments £1,250,000 each, making it possible to start the work from both ends simultaneously in 1872. Construction of the Gotthard Railway through Switzerland was hardly easy, but it was the Gotthard tunnel, nine miles 562 yards in length, that proved the most difficult proposition of the whole project.

After 10 years of continuous work, the tunnel was opened to freight traffic on the first day of 1882 and to passenger traffic the following June. Despite all the difficulties and delays in construction, the surveying and execution were remarkably

accurate; when the bores from opposite ends met they were out of alignment by only a few inches vertically or horizontally.

The Gotthard Railway is the principal artery for passenger and freight traffic between Germany and Italy and consequently one of the busiest and most important main lines in Europe. So that maximum use can be made of its capacity, the $9\frac{1}{4}$-mile length of the main tunnel is divided into 13 block sections, automatically signalled, so that three and even four trains on each track can be in motion in the tunnel simultaneously. Even so, the line is now working to capacity and, with traffic still increasing, a relief route is urgently being sought. Of various possible schemes, the one most likely to be adopted

is the Gotthard Base tunnel, already mentioned, of which the north portal would be at Amsteg and the south at Giornico, with a total length of 28 miles. It would cut out all the toilsome approaches to the present Gotthard tunnel, with their continuous 1 in 38-40 gradients, and provide a straight and practically level run through the heart of the Alps, making possible a closer spacing of trains and very considerable accelerations—but at a staggering cost.

We come now to what until today, apart from sub-surface cut-and-cover and tube tunnels under cities, has been the longest double line railway tunnel in the world— the Simplon tunnel: the original bore measures 12 miles 537 yards and the parallel tunnel is 18 yards longer. By the year 1878 the then Jura-Simplon Railway had pushed its way up the Rhone valley as far as Brigue, and from 1853 onwards its promoters had had in view an extension from there into Italy which would provide a direct route not merely from Lausanne and Geneva, but also from Paris, to Milan. By 1898 the major project had taken shape, and penetration of the mountain barrier by the Simplon tunnel had begun. In 1903 it came under the auspices, on the Swiss side, of the Swiss Federal Railways, which in that year absorbed the Jura-Simplon.

The boring of a tunnel through any mountain range has its uncertainties and its surprises today, when instruments and trial borings can at least give some indication of conditions many hundreds of feet below the surface. It was considerably more uncertain 70 years ago, of which workers in the Simplon tunnel were all too painfully made aware when, $5\frac{1}{4}$ miles from the Swiss end, the temperature in the workings rose to 127 degrees Fahrenheit; work could proceed only by spraying cold water over the rock face and with the use of powerful ventilating fans. From the Italian end also work was held up by the irruption of cascades of hot and cold water from underground streams, which for a time brought the work to a standstill. Through one zone the pressure of the overlying rock became so great as to splinter and break great baulks of timber and to bend out of shape substantial steel reinforcements.

The Simplon tunnel plan was first to bore a pilot tunnel of smaller dimensions than, and with a centre 56 feet away from that of, the main tunnel. The smaller tunnel was used for removal of excavated material from the main tunnel, which was designed to accommodate a single track; soon after its completion the pilot tunnel was to have been enlarged to carry the second track, but 15 years elapsed from the opening in 1906 of the first tunnel before the second came into use in 1921. The 1914-18 war was partly responsible for the delay, but it was partly due also to a repetition in an even more acute form of the difficulties encountered in the first tunnel. Over a distance of 180ft the pressure through a stratum of weak rock was causing cracking of the walls of the first tunnel. Eventually the danger was overcome by the insertion of a massive steel lining, later encased with concrete to a thickness of four feet. A large chamber in the centre of the tunnel houses an emergency crossover road between the two tracks, and for some years signalmen had the unenviable task of manning a subterranean signalbox which controlled it; the crossover is now controlled remotely from Brigue.

Although the Simplon tunnel became a valuable means of communication between southern Switzerland and Italy, it was of less value to the capital, Berne, as a circuit of 151 miles was necessary to reach Brigue from Berne by way of Lausanne. Belfort and Eastern France generally were

also keen on securing a more direct route to Milan. Such was the genesis of the Berne-Lötschberg-Simplon Railway, planned to follow a course which would cut the Berne-Lausanne distance from 151 to 74 miles. Railways were already in existence from Berne to Thun and Spiez, and from Spiez up the Kander valley as far as Frutigen, from which $37\frac{1}{2}$ miles of new line would be needed to reach Brigue. However, the new construction would need a climb of 1,842ft and a lengthy tunnel through the main chain of the Bernese Alps. In 1906, the year of the first Simplon tunnel opening, on the Lötschberg tunnel.

Once again, however, Nature laid a heavy hand on the workers. At a distance of $1\frac{3}{4}$ miles from the north portal, where the tunnel was to run about 600ft below the upper basin of the Kander valley, known as the Gasterntal, there occurred a very deep water-bearing fissure. Suddenly, at 2.30 in the morning of July 24, 1908, a blasting charge was exploded—and it let in a vast mass of water and glacial debris, engulfing the 25 workers, none of whom escaped, and all the boring machinery. Many months were spent in deciding what to do next, but eventually, at a point three-quarters of a mile from the northern entrance, a 33ft masonry wall was erected to block the old working and a new tunnel was built round it to carry the line at a greater depth under the Gasterntal. A similar curve was introduced from the southern end, and the length of the tunnel (nine miles 140 yards) is now half a mile greater than was originally planned. Another disaster occurred in February 1908, when the workers' camp at the southern end of the tunnel, at Goppenstein, was overwhelmed by an avalanche, with the loss of 12 lives.

The main Lötschberg line was opened in 1913, and it was one of the first railways in Switzerland to be electrically operated throughout from the outset, though electric working through the Simplon tunnel between Brigue and Domodossola also began with the opening of the first bore in 1906. It is of interest that the Lötschberg Railway was responsible for the construction and opening in 1915 of an $8\frac{1}{4}$-mile cut-off line, completely detached from its own system, between Moutier and Lengnau. The cut-off shortened by nine miles the circuitous route previously followed by trains from Paris and Eastern France; it involved the boring of the Grenchenberg tunnel (five miles 581 yards) through the final ridge of the Jura range.

Italy's major contribution to tunnelling in Europe, taking second place in length only to the Simplon tunnel, is the Apennine tunnel; it is 11 miles 892 yards in length, under the mountains of the same name between the cities of Bologna and Florence. The Apennine bore formed part of the two important *direttissima* (direct railway lines) built in Italy during the Mussolini regime (the other was between Rome and Naples) and both required

tunnelling on an extensive scale. The former route between Bologna and Florence went, with 1 in 45 gradients and much curvature, via Pistoia over a summit of 2,021ft; the new line cut the maximum altitude down to 1,070ft and reduced the distance by $21\frac{1}{2}$ miles, reducing train times by more than a half.

In boring the tunnel there were difficulties caused by irruptions of water and also of poisonous gases, which at some points caused outbreaks of fire, but there were no serious interruptions of the work. The work was in fact greatly assisted by the cutting of two lateral galleries sloping downwards from the surface to the tunnel workings at intervals along the route. At the tunnel end of one of the galleries a large chamber was blasted out to house sidings into which slow trains can be shunted if necessary to clear the main line for faster traffic. The Apennine tunnel crossovers also have recently been converted to remote control to remove the need to man the underground signalbox. On the same *direttissima*, the Monte Adone tunnel (four miles 760 yards) was also brought into use with the opening of the line in April 1934.

One of the earliest railways under the Alps was the Arlberg tunnel, in Austria, opened in September 1884 to provide a new direct route from Eastern Switzerland to Innsbruck and Vienna. It is six miles 650 yards in length and takes ninth place among the world's longest. There are two lengthy tunnels also on the Austrian Federal Railways main line from Salzburg to Trieste; the Tauern tunnel, just south of Badgastein, opened in 1909, is five miles 551 yards long and the other, farther south through the Karawanken range, was opened in 1906 and is a few yards short of five miles long.

In addition to the tunnels already mentioned, Switzerland has the Lower Hauenstein tunnel (five miles 95 yards), completed in 1916 to provide a new and easier route from Basle to Olten and

beyond than that which until then had carried this important main line up to the shorter but much higher Hauenstein Upper tunnel. Between the Lake of Zurich and the Toggenburg region there is the Ricken tunnel (five miles 608 yards) which some years ago earned a sinister reputation because a steam train stalled on its steep gradient and the engine exhaust asphyxiated the crew.

Switzerland also has the highest tunnel in Europe, which starts at 7,612ft above sea level and ends at 11,333ft, covering the four miles 750 yards between Eigergletscher and Jungfraujoch, on the Jungfrau Railway. The difficulties of working in the rarified air and the low temperature at such high altitude, and extreme hardness of the rock, made the going very slow and 16 years of boring elapsed before the

opening of the line in 1912.

The United States has a high main-line tunnel, six miles 373 yards long, of which the centre is 9,239ft above the sea; it is the Moffat tunnel of the Denver & Rio Grande Western Railroad, opened in 1928. It is not the longest American tunnel, however; that distinction belongs to the Cascade tunnel of the Great Northern Railway, not far from Seattle, which is seven miles 1,397 yards in length and was completed a year later than the Moffat.

The Japanese National Railways has one long tunnel at Hokutiku, which is eight miles 1,089 yards long and was finished as recently as 1962; it will soon be beaten by other lengthy Japanese tunnels now in course of construction on the new high-speed main lines.

Facing page: Austrian Railways IA-Bo-AI electric locomotive leaves the Arlberg tunnel at St Anton with the eastbound Arlberg Express in June 1967. *B Stephenson*

Above: Gotthard tunnel mouth at Göschenen in December 1967 with a car ferry train waiting to depart. *B Stephenson*

Overleaf: A mixed train from Porto to Regua crossing Pala viaduct in Portugal in September 1971 *A G Orchard*

THE WORLD'S GREAT BRIDGES

THE ART OF the railway engineer may be seen at its greatest in some of the remarkable structures he has designed and built to carry railways across deep gorges or wide stretches of water. In the earliest days railway engineers were limited by the building materials available, but one notable example of what could be achieved with masonry may be seen in the 181ft centre span of the Ballochmyle viaduct on the Glasgow & South Western main line in Ayrshire, built in 1850 and generally recognised as the biggest masonry span in the world. Many much longer bridges have been constructed of what might be termed artificial stone—concrete with steel reinforcement — for example, the noteworthy viaduct in the centre of Berne of the Swiss Federal Railways, the Lorraine bridge over the River Aar, has a main span of 492ft, carrying four busy railway tracks. But, of course, steel is the structural material for all the world's biggest railway bridges. Steel bridges are of three principal types. There are first of all the lengthy viaducts comprising a number of straightforward plate girder or lattice girder spans mounted on masonry, concrete or steel piers. Then there are the cantilever bridges, in which the principle of balance has been used in order to cut down the weight of steel needed to bridge a given gap. Last we have the arch bridges, some of such size that the crown of the arch rises high above the railway track that it carries, the bridge floor being suspended from the centre of the arch and passing right

Top and above: Two views of the Forth bridge at Queensferry in Scotland, first of the great cantilever structures; the colour shot was taken in December 1970 *(R Bastin)* **and the other is from 'The Illustrated London News' of October 19, 1899, when the railway track was being laid.** *Illustrated London News*

through the arch to stand on the haunches on both sides.

Before dealing with the steel bridges in more detail, however, it is worth while to mention two British bridges of original design in which the main spans were originally of wrought iron. One was the Britannia tubular bridge by which Robert Stephenson carried the Holyhead main line of the London & North Western Railway across the Menai Strait from North Wales into Anglesey. For each of the two tracks he designed and built a rectangular box girder, 1,510ft long and 4,680 tons in weight; the trains ran inside the tubes, which were carried side by side on three tall masonry towers. From its opening in 1850 the Britannia bridge carried all the Holyhead traffic until, believe it or not, a couple of careless boy trespassers looking one night in 1970 for birds' nests with a naked light set fire to

the timber lining of the tubes, and brought Stephenson's work to ruin. The line has been reopened with a single track on a new steel arch bridge, still using the original masonry piers.

The other early bridge of note was that which the eminent engineer, Brunel, designed to carry the Great Western Railway across the estuary of the Tamar from Devon into Cornwall. The originality was seen in the two elliptical wrought-iron tubes, each 16ft 9in in diameter and 12ft 3in deep, which were arched and strengthened by linked iron plates curved in the opposite direction in such a way as to form trusses 56ft deep at the centre, built up to form two clear spans each 455ft across. From the trusses, the bridge floor carries a single track suspended by eleven pairs of evenly spaced vertical members. With steel at our command today, we should never be likely to imitate Brunel's design, for with modern bridge techniques we can span such a gap with a far lower weight of metal. But the Royal Albert bridge at Saltash was a masterpiece of its time; it still carries the Western Region trains to and from Cornwall, 113 years after its opening in 1859, as a monument to its designer.

The early iron structures were followed by lattice steel viaducts, one of which, Barlow's bridge across the Firth of Tay, achieved a record for length on its opening in 1897. It is 11,653ft long with 85 spans, 13 at the centre of 227ft each, and the remaining 72 from 129ft to 145ft in

Above: From a painting by Terence Cuneo, commissioned by the Western Region of British Railways to commemorate the centenary in 1959 of Brunel's Royal Albert bridge at Saltash, one of the great wrought-iron designs. *British Railways WR*

Below: Quebec bridge, opened in 1917, has the longest span of any cantilever at 1,800ft; the Forth bridge has two spans of 1,710ft each. *Canadian National Railways*

length. Barlow's was in fact the second Tay railway bridge. The first structure, opened in 1878, was designed by Thomas Bouch; it was on the same site and had the same number of spans, but insufficient allowance was made in the design for the effects of high wind; and there was some question of the quality of materials and workmanship. As a result, on one wild night in December 1879, all the centre spans were swept from their piers just as the night mail was crossing the bridge; the middle spans, with the train and all on board, were lost in the waters of the Tay.

Later years have seen the length of the Tay bridge, and the length of individual spans, exceeded. Just as Tay bridge was built to replace a train-ferry across the firth, two bridges have been built in Denmark to perform the same office. One is the Storström bridge between the islands of Zealand and Falster, carrying the principal main line linking Copenhagen with Germany. It incorporates 50 steel spans, with one 452ft centre span flanked by two of 341ft, and the remaining 47 spans alternating between 190ft and 204ft in length. Together they make up a total of 10,437ft. An even longer structure bridges the mouth of the River Zambesi in Portuguese East Africa, with a 40-span steel viaduct 12,064ft long. Such lengths are put completely in the shade by the Huey P Long bridge over the Mississippi in the USA, but as that is partly a cantilever structure it will be mentioned later. One further lattice girder bridge of note needs to be mentioned, as with its maximum height of 435ft above the valley that it spans it is the highest railway bridge in Europe. It is the Fades viaduct in Central France, with a central span of 472ft 6in carried on slender granite piers 330ft high, and two side spans of 380ft 6in—a most impressive structure.

Cantilever bridges, as previously mentioned, depend in part on the principle of balance to reduce their weight of structural steel. One which still ranks high among the engineering wonders of the world, though opened as far back as 1890, is our own Forth railway bridge. Its main feature is the three great diamond-shaped towers, each rising to 360ft above the water level and balanced about the broad base on which it stands foursquare. The centre diamond stretches out arms on each side to grasp the ends of two 361ft lattice girders, of which the opposite ends are held by the similar arms of the side diamonds. The shoreward cantilever diamonds are balanced at the outer ends by 1,000 - ton counterweights. The main structure of the bridge consists of 12ft-diameter steel tubes which form the strongly braced framework of the three towers and of the arms which complete the diamonds on each side. For the foundations, a centre tower was built on Inchgarvie island, but the foundations for the other two towers had to be built below from 70ft to 90ft of water.

Each of the two main spans is 1,710ft across, and provides a headroom of 150ft above high water. Including the approach viaducts, the Forth bridge measures 8,296ft, or 1½ miles, in length. It absorbed 54,160 tons of steel and offers a total surface area of 145 acres which has to be painted to prevent rusting. Repainting is continuously in progress, as it needs three years to complete and directly one painting is finished the next one begins. Other components that went into the vast structure were 6,500,000 rivets, 740,000 cubic feet of granite, 48,400 cubic yards of rubble, and 64,300 cubic yards of concrete.

The world has only one cantilever span that is longer than the 1,710ft spans of the Forth bridge, and that is the 1,800ft of the Quebec bridge, which carries one of the main lines of the Canadian National Railways across the River St Lawrence. The erection of the bridge was attended by two major tragedies. The original construction was well under way when one of the great diamond towers collapsed through overstrain. A new and stronger design was prepared and work on the two towers was completed, leaving only the lifting into position of the 640ft girder span that was to link them together. The linking span had been built in an adjacent creek and floated on scows to the position for lifting. While it was being raised a vital link in the lifting gear broke and the 5,000 tons of steel fell with a mighty splash into the river. A new centre span had to be built and fitted into place, and as a result of the disasters it took 16 years to complete

Top: Eiffel's notable arch structure over the Douro in Porto, Portugal, the Maria Pia bridge, opened in 1877. *C Gammell*

Above: First of the really long bridges was Robert Stephenson's Britannia construction of riveted rectangular wrought-iron tubes across the Menai strait in Wales.
British Transport Museum (B Sharpe)

Left: The elegant Langwies viaduct on the Rhaetian Railway in Switzerland is a notable early reinforced-concrete structure, opened in 1914. *Swiss National Tourist Office*

the construction; it was 1917 before the Quebec bridge was brought into service.

The world's longest railway bridge, already mentioned, crosses the wide Mississippi river just above the city of New Orleans; it was named the Huey P Long bridge after the former Governor of Louisiana. From the flat lands on each side of the river the railway had to be raised sufficiently to provide a headroom of 135ft above the water, and with approach gradients no steeper than 1 in 80. To keep to the specification, the gradients had to start so far back from the river that the total length, with approaches, is no less than 22,235ft, or 4½ miles. That part of the bridge which is actually over the river is a cantilever structure with a centre span of 790ft, flanked by two 530ft spans on one side and one of 530ft on the other. The railways whose trains cross the bridge, including the Southern Pacific, have to pay a rental to the City of New Orleans, which was responsible for its construction.

Of the world's great steel arch bridges, France has two notable examples. Eiffel, of the Paris steel tower fame, was responsible for the Garabit viaduct, in Central France, of which the great central arch, of 541ft span, carries the rails about 400ft above the valley floor. The arch is approached by a lattice steel viaduct of considerable size. Farther south there is the Viaur viaduct, which is really a combination of cantilever and steel arch construction. Two T-shaped cantilevers stand on what seem remarkably small pin joints on both sides of the valley, and meet in another pin joint above the valley floor; their opposite ends are anchored above the valley sides. In the Fades, Garabit and Viaur viaducts the French have three unique bridge designs, all different.

In Central Africa, immediately below the Victoria Falls of the Zambesi river, there is the Victoria Falls bridge of the Rhodesia Railways, with a clear span of 500ft, 400ft above the swirling waters at the bottom of the gorge. It was intended to be a link in Cecil Rhodes's railway from Cairo to the Cape, which was never achieved, but in fact provided the incentive for the big advances in span and load-carrying capacity, epitomised in Lindenthal's Hell Gate bridge opened in New York in 1916, leading eventually to Sydney.

Of the great steel arches, the one that has no comparison is the Sydney Harbour bridge in New South Wales. It is of the type in which the height of the arch, compelled by its 1,650ft span, could not possibly carry a railway over its crown because of the gradients that would be involved. Consequently, the railway track passes through the sides of the arch and with the bridge floor is suspended from the centre of the arch and carried above the haunches.

With a bridge of such size the problems of erection are enormous; during erection some parts of the structure are subjected to greater strains than any that the bridge has to sustain after completion, and calculation of the constructional stresses plays

an essential part in the design. Sydney Harbour bridge was erected in the only way possible, that is, built outwards from both sides of the waterway until the two halves of the arch met. In the final stage of construction, two immense masses of steel, each 825ft long, were projecting towards each other from rock cavities in which were set the bridge bearings, each designed to take a maximum thrust of 19,700 tons; the upper parts of the half-arches were held by 128 steel cables passed through rock tunnels to the top corners of each half-arch.

During construction, the extending structures had to take the weight of the travelling cranes which moved gradually outwards above each half-arch, lifting the steelwork for each panel up from lighters on the water below, and then advancing over each panel as it was completed. So accurate were both the calculations and the workmanship that when at last the two half-arches met, the alignment proved to be perfect.

Sydney Harbour bridge is, of course, far more than a two-track railway crossing. In fact it carried originally four railway tracks, a 60ft-wide roadway and two 10ft footways, requiring between them a bridge

floor 150ft wide. In recent years it has been found that all the railway traffic can be carried by two tracks, and the space previously occupied by the other two has been given over to providing an eight-lane highway for road traffic.

It is interesting to recall that when the designs of the bridge were put out to tender, prominent bridge - building firms in Germany and the United States declared that erection would be impossible; but the British firm of Dorman Long, which was largely responsible for both the design and the erection, triumphantly proved them wrong and provided the citizens of Sydney with a structure which is one of the engineering wonders of the world today.

There are, of course, notable suspension bridges in the world with considerably longer spans than any of those described, as, for example, the 3,000ft span of the Forth road bridge in Scotland, the 4,200ft span of the Golden Gate bridge in San Francisco, the 4,260ft of the Verrazano bridge across the entrance to New York harbour, and now the 4,580ft clear span of the bridge on which construction was recently begun over the Humber estuary, just south of Hull. But none of them carries a railway.

British Stations

Top: Main entrance of the new Waterloo Station when it was opened by Queen Mary in March 1922. *Topical Press*

Above: Business end of the 1922 station in the 1960s. *I Krause*

Facing page top: LNER No 4472 'Flying Scotsman' on the sandstone Lockwood viaduct on the Huddersfield-Penistone line in June 1969. *R Bastin*

Facing page bottom: Mellowed stone-arch viaduct at Sernada, Portugal, in September 1970. *C Gammell*

THE EARLY British railway company directors knew that passenger stations in the larger towns enhanced the company's 'image', and all the more if the premises incorporated the company's headquarters or other offices. Pleasing, dignified and solid buildings also suggested reliability in what was soon to prove an age of mushroom concerns in the Railway Mania of the 1840s.

The station buildings of the first Liverpool & Manchester Railway terminus at Crown Street, Liverpool, were a solid structure and the company lavished money on the celebrated Moorish Arch (shown in so many early prints) across the cutting. The L&MR Manchester terminus at Liverpool Road, part of which remains today, likewise is a solid structure of good design. They were far eclipsed, however, by the Euston terminus (1837) of the London & Birmingham, now, including the world-famous Doric Arch entrance to the forecourt, totally demolished. The site is covered by the new Euston—a structure for which few have much enthusiasm. Although intended to be functional, it is not really modern architecture and many users complain that it is inconvenient.

Largely because of lack of common sense in local planning, British Railways was prevented from building a tower block of offices over the terminus, which would have earned money from letting and at the same time eased London street congestion by affording work-places for many commuters who travel to and from Euston by train.

The original plan for Euston, soon abandoned, was for London & Bristol Railway trains to use a structure to the west of the site, matching the London & Birmingham buildings and trainshed. Other glories of Euston were the Great Hall and the adjacent spacious L&BR (and later London & North Western) headquarters offices. They were—and rightly—believed to epitomise the railway. That did not stop the L&NWR later in the century—and rather uncharacteristically—from blocking the view of the Doric Arch from the Euston Road by building its hotel block—in a bid for extra revenue.

The Euston buildings, like most station buildings of the 1840s and 1850s, were in one or other of the classical styles, or composite of several, or an adaptation of a classical style to the English (or Scottish) idiom. The standard was high. Exploring railways throughout Great Britain, you can still find remnants of 'Early Railway' style station architecture of 1830-60. Some are incorporated in later, often shoddier, buildings; some form parts of freight depots or have been converted into warehouses or offices.

The 1830-60 period was one of good architecture: Southwark (now part of London Bridge), Brighton, Chester Central with its fine frontage, the magnificent Newcastle Central and two London termini —Kings Cross (1852) and Fenchurch Street (as rebuilt in 1853). Kings Cross combines the fine engineering of the twin trainsheds with the splendid facade and the dignified, particularly British, architecture of the station buildings. The facade was long disfigured by a conglomeration of small buildings in front, but work is now well under way in clearing the mess and building a new booking hall which will be pleasing in a modest steel-and-glass way and low enough and positioned to set off the facade to advantage. Fenchurch Street facade is at present marred by a canopy of later date, but one may hope that some day the original elegant canopy over the pavement will be restored. The elegant frontage at Cambridge has been restored (but Oxford station was a mean structure until its recent rebuilding; it is now modest and well-mannered).

The Gothic revival was at first mainly an epidemic affecting ecclesiastical and allied (school, for instance) buildings largely because it was associated with pious and charitable uses. When it caught on with railway stations it did so like wildfire. An early example is Bristol Temple Meads, with its trainshed with Gothic beam roof. The greatest Gothic station of them all is Gilbert Scott's St Pancras, opened in 1869, with associated hotel (now offices) and

Top: London Kings Cross (1852), illustrating particularly British architecture of the period.
British Transport Museum (B Sharpe)

Above centre: World-famous Euston entrance (1837), now no more. *A Wood*

Above: The new Euston (1968). *I Krause*

Below: Fenchurch Street platforms after the rebuilding in 1853, probably about 1900.
Ian Allan library

the great span of the trainshed. St Pancras is a complete monument, even to the wooden panelling in the booking hall, let alone the 'gas-pipe Gothic' marble shafts of pillars in the hotel and the elaborate window tracery. Even Somerstown freight depot, across the road to the west, tries to conform. No wonder that preservationists fear that St Pancras might share the fate of the old Euston. It seems unlikely, for plans for combining St Pancras and Kings Cross have proved to be impracticable from the engineering aspect; the amount of traffic along the old Midland line is increasing, demolition of the trainshed and massive hotel block would be difficult and costly, the Government is aware of the aesthetic significance and there is pressure for retention on environmental grounds.

The latter half of the century saw Gothic station buildings spawning everywhere, mostly in bastard styles much inferior to St Pancras. Even wayside stations, such as an early one in the eighteen-fifties at Battle on the South Eastern line to Hastings, were Gothic in contrast to the dignified yellow-brick architecture of many Great Northern stations, medium and small. As though a complement to St Pancras, Glasgow St Enoch, the Glasgow & South Western terminus of the joint Midland and G&SWR Anglo-Scottish route, has (or had) a Gothic air—but its trainshed, now being demolished, in no

way resembles that of St Pancras, though it is striking in its way. Many other Scottish stations, though not the more recent, have Gothic overtones, and some, like Perth, the former Dundee West and Stirling, suggest 'Scottish Baronial'. Even timber buildings, such as the early wayside station buildings of the South Eastern, can have charm or, at least, good manners. The corrugated iron that began to be used in new stations, especially on light railways in the 1890s, has always been an abomination.

The uninspiring blocks that front Charing Cross and Cannon Street (or what remains of it) date from the 1860s. Also of that era are the London Chatham & Dover's St Pauls (now Blackfriars, being reconstructed, and recently still bearing on its facade the names of Continental destinations that could be reached by LC&DR boat trains and steamers). From that time onwards, architects began to adopt French Renaissance and a variety of styles for stations, although the new trend overlapped the slow decline of the Gothic revival. A heterogeneous variety includes in London, the two Victorias; the London & Brighton terminus and, cheek by jowl, the 'South Eastern & Chatham and Great Western' erection of the early 20th century, monument to an uneasy railway partnership that never came to fruition, apart from a Victoria to Birmingham Snow Hill GWR express and a few local trains.

By the end of the century railway boards had begun to feel that 'there is no money in passenger stations'. That is why the Great Central's turn-of-the-century Marylebone terminus is a mean building, not atoned for by the huge Hotel Great Central, today the headquarters of British Railways. Even so, during the closing years of the last century and the Edwardian era some big (though perhaps not beautiful or even pleasing) buildings for big stations were completed: Glasgow Central for example— a remarkable instance of participation by the Caledonian Railway in urban development—to the benefit of the railway passenger and railwayman, perhaps rather than the generality of citizens and visitors to Glasgow. It was one of the first to include offices and shops for letting.

There were also Birmingham Snow Hill, Cardiff General and Aberdeen Joint, the GCR stations at Leicester and Nottingham and Dover Marine, and the start on the meanest of all big British stations— the rebuilt Waterloo. Only pictures can give an idea of the variety of styles. The architects employed by the railways had lost their ability to design anything distinctive. There is no really outstanding architecture in any large British passenger station designed since St Pancras—which is odd, when one bears in mind many admirable public buildings of the period (or several overlapping periods as far as trends were concerned) built for purposes other than railway.

In fact, St Pancras was the last of the 'great' stations. There were many smaller structures that were distinctive in their way. You need only travel by train over branch lines still open, or walk over or drive to lines that are closed, to see a variety of styles. The habit of lodging the stationmaster (as he then was, however small the station) on the premises gave the architects scope in designing 'station houses'. Unstaffed stations as opposed to the halts and mere platforms that began to be erected in the Edwardian era hardly existed. On many lines in rural Sussex (some long since closed to passenger and some even to freight traffic) there is an enormous variety of station buildings and platform canopies, varying in respect not only of the date of design, but also of the standard practice that varied from time to time on the railway concerned; London & Brighton, South Eastern, London & South Western, even Kent & East Sussex and Hundred of Manhood & Selsey Tramway, and their successors.

Much farther north there are differences even in wayside stations of the old High-land Railway, illustrating the history of its expansion. There are varieties everywhere: stations straddling streets and on piers, and buried in depressions like Edinburgh Waverley. A good setting can add charm even to the straggling buildings of Folkes-tone Harbour station, now being rebuilt, or Wemyss Bay (transfer between train and Clyde steamer), or Aviemore with its mountain background, or the bald little maritime terminus at Kyle of Lochalsh, or Kingswear with its landing stage or the scores of stations in unexciting but lovely settings in East Anglia and Somersetshire, or more striking scenery in Devon.

Emphasis hitherto has been on the architecture of the buildings. In the early days of railways the low platforms—or even simply the ground when there were no platforms—was regarded simply as an adjunct to the buildings. The buildings mattered, rather as the buildings mattered more than the yard in the coaching inn, which was the nearest thing to a station that had previously been known. Then came the high platform of carriage floor level, or a little below. Platforms have been a major factor in the design of stations. They necessitate footbridges and pedestrian subways, and should be roofed at least in part where there is no overall roof. Footbridges and 'umbrella' and other types of platform roof alter almost the whole look of stations. How many country stations are characterised by the type (open or roofed) of footbridge? The designs of platform canopy are legion, and one species of railway connoisseur specialises in classifying and identifying canopy styles.

There are 'split stations' with separate platforms for diverging lines and there was long a 'double-split' at Ashchurch near Cheltenham, where Midland Railway branches to Tewkesbury and Evesham diverged west and east respectively from the Bristol to Birmingham main line in the centre. Ambergate in Derbyshire was once a triangular station, with up and down platforms for each of three double-track

lines forming the triangle where the Midland's former Manchester (now only to Matlock) line branched off from the main line from Derby to Sheffield. Only the Derby to Matlock line platforms are now used, and the others by now are wholly or partially unusable or demolished.

Platforms are solid and therefore expensive to build and remove. This has affected the whole layout of many large stations, where growth has been piecemeal and conditioned by platform layouts. Examples are the old Euston, where the only solution in rebuilding was to make a clean sweep, and Kings Cross, where at least the platform numbering has been rational-ised. The only really rational principle of platform arrangement is in the trainshed at St Pancras, where the strongly-built 'train' floor over the cellars beneath allows the platforms, built largely of timber, to be remodelled relatively easily. The wooden platforms at Charing Cross and Cannon Street were relatively easily altered when those termini were rebuilt.

The type of traction affects the design of a station and the comfort of the passenger. It is perhaps surprising that in steam days more attention was not paid to ventilation, whether in stations underground or adjacent to tunnels. Birmingham New Street, in a depression but conveniently near the centre of the city, with tunnels adjoining, long had a reputation

Top: Gothic-style London St Pancras (1869), last of the really great British stations to be built. *G P Cooper*
Above centre: Elegant frontage at Cambridge (early 1850s), here pictured in 1908. *Ian Allan library*
Above: Victorian Gothic Bristol Temple Meads station in 1967. *P J Fowler*
Below: Typical style of the 1930s, Southampton Central. *Topical Press*

for smokiness; in these days of electric and diesel traction the absence of smoke since rebuilding New Street is no compensation for the low roof, with massive supports and staircases, over the sharply curved platforms, in contrast to the old, more spacious overall roof. New Street, however, sprang from small beginnings, and railway managements of later years are not to be blamed for the site. The same is true of London Liverpool Street, Glasgow Queen Street, Liverpool Lime Street and other big stations in cramped sites below ground level. Even Nottingham Victoria, now closed, a turn-of-the-century creation on the Great Central extension to London, is between two tunnels, although much land was acquired for the many platforms, while traffic never grew to anything approaching the capacity of the station.

Curves, as stated, can be inconvenient. Even so, they have an aesthetic value. There is something magnificent in the curve of the trainshed at York, a fine example of civil engineering, of which the station buildings and hotel are unworthy. Newcastle Central combines such structural beauty with the classical architecture of the buildings and the hotel. The combination of curved platform and Victorian Gothic at Bristol Temple Meads sets off the designs of the diesel locomotives and passenger vehicles as trains run in and out. At Runcorn the sharp curve affords good views of electrically hauled expresses between Euston and Liverpool, with the arch of the girder bridge over the Mersey in the background.

Runcorn is a good example of BR engineers making the best of a bad job. It was necessary to renew the over-age station buildings, but the curve could not be got rid of. This does not matter, for the day expresses stop at Runcorn because it is the railhead not only for the town in its own right, and for part of Cheshire, but also for a large part of South West Lancashire more easily reached by road from Runcorn than by continuing by train into Liverpool Lime Street. Consequently BR has provided a great deal of car parking space.

Apart from Euston, there has not been much building of large stations since the 1939-45 war. What has been done—for instance at Sunderland, Harrogate, Stafford and Manchester Piccadilly and at smaller stations such as Harlow and Chichester and some on the Glasgow electrified suburban lines—is pleasing. A striking example of new techniques is the use of timber at Manchester Oxford Road. The standard has certainly risen since the decade before 1939, which saw some ungainly structures. What an opportunity was missed—not by the architect, whose scope was limited—at the Southampton Ocean Terminal, opened after the war and already starting to outlive its usefulness! Even the architect of the new Euston was restricted. There are plans for a new office block to replace the existing building at Liverpool Lime Street. The local planners would like to have part of the original

trainshed visible from the square in front of the station—and some even would deplore demolition of the existing building because it is a monument of the great age of railways.

Opportunities for creating great new stations are fewer than in the 1940s, but they still occur. One of the next creations is likely to be a London Channel Tunnel Terminal at the White City, and there might yet be in the not too distant future a terminal at Kings Cross for trains to Foulness (or other airport if it is sited elsewhere east or north-east of London). It would adjoin and lie to the west of Kings Cross terminus, and the airport electric trains would approach the terminus at a level above the present tracks and run into platforms on an upper floor of the new structure. Let us hope the opportunities afforded for worthy architecture are not missed.

Top: York station in 1971. *M Esau*

Centre: A suggestion of 'Scottish Baronial' at Stirling. *P J Sharpe*

Bottom: A fine example of expansive Victorian Gothic, Carlisle Citadel. *British Transport Museum (B Sharpe)*

General view of Euston station, looking south. *British Railways LMR*

ITALIAN STATIONS

ALL ROADS LEAD to Rome, and Rome Termini station happens to be aesthetically the best of the Italian State Railways larger passenger stations and functionally one of the most efficient. By far the busiest, however, as regards numbers of both trains and passengers, is Milan Centrale, which is likely to be the first big station seen by travellers entering Italy from Switzerland, that is, by most passengers from Britain. Milan Centrale is a terminus. Its characteristic features are the massive ornate block facing the square in front and the high glass-roofed trainshed beyond. The terminal building was long criticised by opponents of the Fascist regime as an example of Fascist bombast. The station was built under that regime and opened in the 1930s, and those who admired its deplorable architecture and its dimensions gave credit accordingly. It was in fact conceived before the 1914-18 war and its construction was postponed by the war and lack of funds. The design, like that of many public buildings, was chosen by competition at a period when Italian architecture was in a bad way.

Milan Centrale (there are half-a-dozen other busy stations in Milan used by commuters) is a terminus outside the inner area of the city. It replaces a large through station that was nearer the city centre. Relegation from the centre of Milan's main

passenger gateway was due to the desire to rid the city of the smoky station and approach tracks in the steam era, when most Italian locomotives burnt soft coal. At the time the new station was planned the city fathers could think of no way of putting steam-worked lines underground and electrification of all the many approach routes appeared equally impossible. So the station had to be a terminus, and some way out.

Unlike most big Italian stations, most of Milan Centrale is above street level. The several approach lines are on a viaduct, so there are no flying or burrowing junctions and trains are often held up for the departure or arrival of other trains over conflicting tracks. The train shed is austere, and although very few steam-hauled trains

Top: Grandiose exterior of Milan Centrale station. *Italian State Railways*

Above: Class 424 electric locomotive arrives at Alassio with a local train. *J R Batts*

Right: Milan Centrale: Note the two prominent semaphore signals which in Italy are similar to British designs. *J R Batts*

Above right: The exterior of Florence's new station compared with the more elaborate Milanese facade. *Italian State Railways*

Facing page: Another of the modern Italian stations is that at Naples with its extensive use of glass and concrete in the passenger concourse. *Italian State Railways*

now enter the terminus, the glass roof seems grimy and lets through little daylight. The platforms are long enough to accommodate most of the lengthy trains that are made possible by the powerful electric and diesel locomotives of today. The designers showed prescience, although they probably had long troop trains in mind. The concourse that spans the whole area behind the buffer stops is well provided with stands selling periodicals, food and drink. At a lower level is that welcome feature of Italian public places—the *albergo diurno* (day hotel) where one can enjoy all hotel amenities except a bed, besides hairdressing and so on. The booking hall is grandiose and, in fact, grandeur is the keynote everywhere.

Apart from the delays to incoming trains, the handling of passengers is not very efficient. One reason is that many of the long-distance trains dealt with include through vehicles to different destinations, so that there is much uncoupling and recoupling at the station and drawing of vehicles and portions of trains out into the yard and back again.

A great number of long-distance services are dealt with at Milan Centrale. The most famous is the Settebello (pages 242 and 501), the electric multiple-unit first-class express which takes 5¾ hours

each way to and from Rome; although the sets are now in middle age, they afford some of the most comfortable day travel in the world. Equally fast is the Freccio del Vesuvio (Vesuvius Arrow) which continues beyond Rome to Naples. The fastest trains between Italy's first and second cities, however, are the as yet unnamed new high-speed electric mu trains, which cover the 393 miles between Milan and Rome via Bologna and Florence in 5½ hours non-stop. Other notable day trains are the Cisalpin to Lausanne and Paris (equipped to run on the four different voltages used along the route); the Gottardo and Ticino Trans Europ Expresses to Zurich; the Lemano TEE to Geneva; the Mediolanum to Munich via Verona and Innsbruck; and the Roland to Frankfurt, Hanover and Bremen, which includes coaches for the Hook of Holland (for the steamer to Harwich) and Dortmund. The Hook coaches are worked north of Basle in the famous Rheingold Express, enabling a passenger to leave Milan at 9.26 in the morning and reach the Hook at 10.59 the same evening and London Liverpool Street at 9.15 next morning.

Among the night trains dealt with at Milan are the Riviera Express between Amsterdam and Rome and the Italia Express between Rome and Scandinavia,

which conveys a Milan-Stockholm sleeping car of the Wagons-Lits Co and a couchette car for Copenhagen. There are also trains that work the through USSR Railways sleeping cars once a week between Turin and Moscow via Milan, Venice, Trieste, Budapest and Kiev, for the benefit of workers in industrial plants in Italy and Russia. The most famous international service calling at Milan, however, the Simplon Express between Paris and Venice, Trieste and Jugoslavia, calls at Milan Lambrate station and bypasses Centrale. There are of course many other day and night expresses to all parts of Italy of which Milan is the nodal point.

In contrast with Milan Centrale is Rome Termini, the city's main passenger station —although the Ostiense, Tuscolana and Tiburtina stations all deal with fair amounts of traffic. Termini has always been a terminus, but the rebuilt station, brought into full use over 20 years ago, replaces a rather squalid structure of the later nineteenth century. It is centrally situated for long-distance travellers, near many of the hotels, and is the present terminus of Rome's one existing urban underground line, over which trains run as far as Ostia, on the coast. Termini does not handle as much passenger traffic as it might because of the rather devious routes followed by

Above: The high arched roof and platform area of Milan Centrale. The centre platform between tracks is used for parcels and mail movements. *Italian State Railways*

Left: Former station building, now closed, at Nuoro, Sardinia. *J R Batts*

Below left: Mandas, another Sardinian station, with a diesel railcar standing at the platform. *J R Batts*

Below: The magnificent main concourse of Rome's Termini. *J R Batts*

Locomotive No E636.153 on automatic train control demonstration at Florence. *J R Batts*

some approach lines in relation to the suburbs.

The characteristic station frontage, with steel-and-glass canopies and facade of travertine stone, is on the Piazza die Cinquecento, near the remains of the baths of Caracalla. At first glance the impression is one of modernity, but closer inspection shows the facade to be broken by a ruined stone wall running at right-angles; it is the *agger*, one of the ancient city walls, and its incorporation in the modern building is an architectural feat. The *agger* is skilfully used to provide a background to the view from the station's principal restaurant. Booking of tickets and seat reservation are done under the great glass canopy in front of the main block. The booking hall is spacious, and needs to be, for many passengers seem to like to arrive long before train time and despite the many ticket windows there are queues at all hours. In contrast, seat reservation by computer takes a very short time and it is impressive to be handed one's ticket and seat reservation for travel several days ahead within 90 seconds of asking.

Between the main block and the platforms is the glass-roofed concourse, on to which open a variety of shops selling comestibles, newspapers and other travellers' supposed wants. There is a well-equipped *albergo diurno* and refreshment premises of various standards. The whole terminus is at street level and can be entered freely from the street at each end. Its covered expanse and the range of amenities make it one of the Romans' favourite promenades at all hours, but chiefly in the evening.

Termini station today handles a large passenger traffic between the north and Naples and Southern Italy and Sicily, which for geographical reasons must be routed via Rome. However, some trains between Turin and Genoa on the one hand and Naples and Sicily on the other, bypass Termini and call only at Rome Ostiense to the south of the city; also certain trains between the north and Naples and beyond via Florence stop only at Rome Tiburtina, in a northern quarter. There is consequently much less shunting than at Milan, and the yard outside Termini is more extensive.

The obvious train name associated with Rome is Rome Express, which runs to Paris faster than ever before but caters nowadays mostly for traffic between Paris

and Genoa and the coast resorts beyond and Pisa. It conveys through ordinary coaches and couchettes, but no longer any sleeping car, between Rome and Calais. It is surpassed by the Palatino, which covers the 912 miles to Paris via Genoa, Turin and the Mont Cenis tunnel in just under 15 hours (more than a mile a minute) overnight, and just over 14½ hours in the opposite direction. The 736-mile trip from Rome to Vienna via Florence, Bologna, Venice-Mestre (on the mainland, and six miles from Venice Santa Lucia station in Venice proper across the lagoon), Klagenfurt and the Semmering is done in a little over 15 hours by the Romulus. There are many trains to Naples, of which some are high-speed electric mus which run to Naples Mergellina, 130 miles, in 90 minutes non-stop. Sicily is reached by several through services; vehicles are carried by the train ferry over the strait between Villa San Giovanni and Messina. The fastest is the Peloritano, which leaves Rome at 12.15 mid-day with through units for Palermo and Syracuse. Palermo, 552 miles from Rome, is reached at 10.41 at night and Syracuse, 521 miles, at 10.11.

Across the Tiber from Termini is a terminal station unique in the world, serving the Vatican City. A double-track line branches off from the State Railways line to Viterbo, crosses a gully on an arched bridge and enters Vatican territory through a gateway in a wall, beyond which is a two-platform station with a spacious passenger building and a siding. Only on one or two occasions has the station been used by a Pope, to whom the President of Italy lent his special train. The branch has dealt with many wagonloads of clothing and foodstuffs etc distributed by the Vatican to the needy in many countries.

Until the railway was built in 1846 over the lagoon on a viaduct to a terminus in the western part of Venice, everybody and everything had to cross from the mainland by boat. There were comparatively few protests against vandalism when the city's seagirt isolation was ended by the 222-arch structure over two miles long. Then under Austrian domination, Venice was economically much decayed, and the railway, by encouraging tourists in the first flush of the railway age who might otherwise have been in too much of a hurry for a visit by boat, began to enter by train in their thousands and so helped to save Venice from ruin. The railway moreover was extended by sidings to serve the quays of the modern port which grew up. Conscious perhaps of its incongruity the passenger terminus, named Santa Lucia, has always been a modest structure, though the predecessor of the present station was poky. Completed since the end of the 1939-45 war, Santa Lucia today is a well-mannered one-storey building largely of glass, with a frontage on the Grand canal. The passenger can see the 'rank' of gondolas and the piers for the canal passenger boat (*vaporetti*, but now diesel) almost as soon as he reaches the concourse. The yard outside is on re-

claimed land at the end of the viaduct and much skill is needed in shunting in the restricted space. Despite road traffic over the adjacent road viaduct, built under the Fascist regime, Santa Lucia's traffic is growing. Apart from tourists, there is a brisk commuter traffic between Venice and Mestre and other stations on the mainland; the morning peak of commuters arriving by train and crowding on to the *vaporetti* is skilfully handled. To increase capacity, the viaduct over the lagoon is being duplicated by a modern steel and concrete bridge that will carry two more tracks.

Two of the largest Italian stations, in Genoa and Turin, incorporate some notable architecture of the last century. One of the frontages of Genoa Piazza Principe is a pleasing Renaissance structure in the corner of a square. Turin Porta Nuova, with its high roof over the concourse, has conserved a 19th-century layout and aspect but is nevertheless convenient for the passenger, and efficiently worked. Like other passenger stations in large Italian cities—Rome, for instance, and Florence—it is in a central area with hotels near at hand, and contributes to a good image of the city. In contrast is Trieste Centrale. Although Trieste is a thriving port, the number of passenger trains using the station is small, and Centrale is tucked away at the north end of the city, and recently was still the modest structure built late last century by the Austrians, who were still busy creating grandiose buildings along the waterfront.

Since the war many new stations, some designed under Fascism, have been opened. If Rome Termini is the most notable, Venice Santa Lucia and Florence Santa Maria Novella terminus are some of the most successful. Florence SMN is boldly sited near the heart of the city, but contrives to harmonise even with the adjoining great church after which it is named. War damage has necessitated the reconstruction not only of stations but also of whole lengths of line—including that between Genoa and La Spezia, along the Riviera di Levante, part of which was damaged by naval gunfire. The opportunity was taken to realign the tracks to cater for higher speeds. One result is a whole range of pleasing new and rebuilt wayside stations. The same has happened south of Naples on the route to the Straits of Messina train ferry at Villa San Giovanni, where the line has been widened to cater for the growing Sicilian traffic. The station designs combine modernity with the ability to tone in with the local architecture and landscape.

The fact that the vast majority of trains are now electric or diesel contributes to cleanliness. Several more realignments and railway widenings are in progress or about to begin in Italy, and many passenger stations are being or are to be rebuilt or re-sited. To judge by what has been done to date, the railways—not only the State, but some of the smaller undertakings also —are making positive contributions to the beauty of city and countryside.

FOR OVER A century, from the 1840s to the 1950s, most wayfarers from Britain to Paris arrived by train at the Gare du Nord, terminus of the Chemin de Fer du Nord, now the Northern Region of the French National Railways (SNCF). Like the travellers—in carriages, mounted or afoot—along Route Nationale 1, Napoleon's highway from the Straits of Dover, they had come from Calais, probably, or Boulogne. Travellers entering Paris from the north can see to their right the hill of Montmartre, which however has been crowned only for less than a century by the white basilica that looks down on the Gare du Nord and other stations.

Until it was rebuilt in the 1880s with its present facade, the Gare du Nord was not an imposing building. The early French railway builders were less confident than their British counterparts and did not invest heavily in passenger stations. The earlier terminals in cities were little more than a few sidings with modest structures for passenger and freight traffics. The word gare originally meant siding, with a connotation of keeping the running track (or main canal waterway) clear; nevertheless, among the various French words for station, gare is used today for the largest installations. Only as railways prospered, or were hoped to, and as civic pride demanded it, were grandiose structures erected. Most things in France are concentrated on Paris, whose rebuilding under the direction of Baron Haussmann was an opportunity for some striking railway architecture, but there are many notable stations elsewhere, including some in local styles to accord with the environment.

The characteristic feature of the Gare du Nord is its frontage decorated with female statues representing cities reached from the terminus, and there is a not unpleasing late nineteenth - century air about the architecture and decor. It is the second biggest in Paris after the Gare St Lazare as regards the number of passengers handled. There are 28 tracks served by platforms. It is a gateway for Britain, Belgium, Holland, North Germany, Northern Europe generally and Russia. The traffic includes electric Trans-Europ Express (TEE) day trains to Brussels, Amsterdam, Cologne and Hamburg. Some of them are hauled by SNCF four-voltage locomotives that can run over the lines of the SNCF Northern Region (25kV), Belgian (3kV), German Federal (15kV) and Netherlands (1·5kV). There are also longer-distance trains, such as the Scandinavian with a couchette car for Stockholm (taking 26 hours) and the Ost-West Express with its daily green-and-white USSR Railways sleeping car for Moscow via Cologne, Berlin and Warsaw, a journey of 1,840 miles taking 46 hours.

Nearly all trains are electric. A chief exception is the comfortable express diesel railcar of the Silver Arrow service to Le Touquet connecting with the half-hour flight to Gatwick and the British Rail train to London Victoria; it affords transits of less than four hours between the Gare du Nord and Victoria—the fastest public service between the central areas of the two capitals. Metro connections at the Gare du Nord are good except, strangely, to the south-west, to the St Lazare area and beyond, though there are buses. The terminus is on a slight eminence and for decades a typical street scene in this part of Paris, the 10th arrondissement, included cabs galloping up the long Rue Lafayette hurrying Britons to their boat trains. Today Britons tend to go by air—but the motor cars and taxis still hurry.

Next, anti-clockwise in the ring of Paris termini, is the Gare St Lazare. Its late nineteenth - century Renaissance frontage is partly masked by the Hotel Terminus St Lazare of the same period. The interior seems unromantic, but it would be unfair to dismiss the huge glass-roofed concourse (salle des pas perdus) spanning almost the whole width of the station and separated from the 26 platforms by a circulating area. Functionally the station is excellent. It is all of a piece, with all the barriers in a row and none of the nooks and corners that characterise stations that have been developed piecemeal.

The terminus is one of the three main stations in Paris of the SNCF Western Region and its predecessor the Chemin de Fer de l'Ouest that was taken over by the State (Etat) Railway in 1909. Apart from electric suburban services carrying well over 300,000 passengers a day and including one of the three routes to Versailles, there are main-line trains to places in Normandy ranging from Dieppe to Rouen, Havre, Deauville, Caen and Cherbourg. The Rouen and Havre expresses are hauled by electric locomotives. Most of the summer Trouville-Deauville and year-round Caen and Cherbourg services are worked by the SNCF's first gas-turbine trains, the yellow-and-white

ETG four-car units. In the heyday of the North Atlantic liner there were many steam-hauled boat expresses between St Lazare and Havre and Cherbourg, and the Hotel Terminus was built largely for the American traffic. There are still a few boat trains including those of the Dieppe-Newhaven service to London.

St Lazare is the only Paris terminus on its original site. The first station of the Paris to St Germain railway was opened in 1838. No trace remains of the first structure and the two most drastic of several rebuildings and enlargements were completed in 1886 and 1938; from the latter date five pairs of tracks have been available through the Batignolles cutting in the flank of Montmartre. Paris stations have often been mentioned in French and other literature, but the railway itself figures prominently in Zola's La Bête Humaine.

The Seine is crossed to Invalides, another Ouest terminus, on the rive gauche, near the famous building indicated by its name Invalides. A spacious structure, mostly below street level, and incorporating skilful use of steel and glass, it was opened at the turn of the century as the terminus of a new electrified line to Versailles and for some years also dealt with long-distance trains on the line to Granville in Normandy.

Most of the Invalides station now forms the Paris Invalides Aerogare (air terminal) but a few platforms are used by Versailles trains. Another Western Region terminus is Montparnasse in the well-known Left Bank district of that name. It is the object of intensive property development. In front of the station the only skyscraper in the inner area of Paris is nearing completion. The architecture of the station and associated office blocks is functional and nondescript. There is a fair commuter traffic by electric train, and the long-distance services to Nantes and Brittany coast resorts are greatly augmented in the summer season, the only time when Montparnasse approaches capacity. Most expresses are hauled by electric locomotives to Le Mans or Rennes where electrification ends but the diesel locomotives of some Nantes expresses are shortly to work into Montparnasse to save time changing engines at Le Mans (130 miles). The rebuilt station is several hundred feet farther south (at the 'country end', in railway parlance) of its original site. Some of the Metro station platforms constructed many years ago consequently are a longish walk away, so that the long flat moving pavement is a boon.

Near the Paris Zoo, oddly called the Jardin des Plantes (it is partly botanical) is the Gare d'Austerlitz, also on the *rive gauche*. It is the terminus of the SNCF South West Region, successor of the former Paris Orleans Railway. The vaguely Renaissance style resembles that of many French public buildings of the last century. From Austerlitz there is a growing electric suburban service that includes trains to Rungis, whence buses ply to the Rungis market complex, a super Covent Garden which has replaced the former Halles in the heart of Paris, and to Orly Airport; because of Paris street congestion, the latter service is claimed to provide the only reliable transport to the airport. Main-line trains from Austerlitz, all electrically hauled, run to Bordeaux (361 miles in exactly four hours non-stop by the Aquitaine), Toulouse, the Pyrenees and the Spanish frontiers. The Puerta del Sol through train reaches Madrid overnight in just under 15 hours. The Gare d'Austerlitz is spanned by a high-level line of the Metro, which continues on a viaduct over the Seine. Before suburban trains reach Austerlitz they dip down below ground level and enter the new brightly decorated and spacious low-level station. From there a double-track line runs under the Seine embankment downstream, almost entirely in tunnel, past the busy little Pont St Michel station that serves the Latin Quarter, $2\frac{1}{2}$ miles to the Quai d'Orsay terminus, near the French Ministry of Foreign Affairs and near the Pont de la Concorde, in the very heart of the city.

The Gare d'Orsay and the extension from Austerlitz were opened in 1900, in a bid by the PO Railway to reach the central area, for before the development of the internal combustion engine and of the Paris Metro, Austerlitz seemed too remote. The Gare d'Orsay is a magnificent structure fronting the Seine. Efforts to preserve it as a historic monument have been in vain and it is being demolished to make room for a hotel and/or offices. The platforms and tracks are below ground level. After serving as the terminus of nearly all PO trains (and certainly the expresses) from 1900 to 1939, when all trains used the two tracks from Austerlitz, the platforms proved too short for the longer main-line trains which traffic requirements demanded and development of electric traction made possible. In 1939 Austerlitz became once more the terminus of South West Region expresses. Some of the platforms at the Gare d'Orsay have been abandoned and those that remain form the terminus for suburban trains. There are plans for an extension under the Seine embankment to link the South West Region and Western Region lines at Invalides, but it will be necessary eventually to convert the Invalides - Versailles 750V lines to the 1.5kV supply system of the Region Sud Ouest.

From the Gare d'Austerlitz it is not far, back across the Seine, to the Gare de Lyon, whose clocktower is a Paris landmark. The terminus dates from 1900, but there has been a station there since 1855, when the Paris to Lyons Railway opened its new station. The Paris - Lyons eventually became the Paris, Lyons & Mediterranean (PLM) and remained France's premier railway until nationalisation in 1938. At first, it constituted the South Eastern Region of the SNCF, but it was later divided into the SE and Mediterranean regions. Now the two (or most of the lines which constituted them plus a few others), have been reunited as the Réseau Sud Est. (Réseau means system; the former Eastern Region is now the Réseau Est and the Northern, Western and South Western Regions are to be re-designated Réseaux on January 1, 1973. All the Réseaux embrace or will embrace a number of smaller regions.)

The Gare de Lyon is the long-distance passenger terminal par excellence of Paris. It was built at a time when there was little suburban traffic along the PLM, running south-east out of Paris; the situation has changed since and there is a growing commuter traffic by electric trains. The station remains, however, primarily a long-distance terminus. There are plans for a low-level suburban station, similar to that at Austerlitz, which would eventually allow connection with other lines and a physical connection with the Gare du Nord and possibly the Gare de l'Est. The plans are complex and at present remote.

The PLM paid great attention to its winter traffic to the French Riviera, and Italy (via the Mont Cenis and, later, Simplon tunnels), and also to summer traffic to fashionable spas such as Vichy, Aix-les-Bains and Evian and mountain resorts such as Chamonix. Much of it was first-class, or in the days of three classes, second-class. It is not surprising that the booking hall at the Gare de Lyon, whose ceiling now forms that of the restaurant that was later constructed as a mezzanine, is lavishly decorated with landscapes (with female figures) representing the beauty and elegance of the places reached by PLM. Development of the terminus over the years, including a nine-platform annexe on the down side for main-line departures, means much walking — especially as many trains are made up to 18 vehicles and often more. There is an enormous winter sports traffic to the French Alps, especially at weekends, for many young people think nothing of travelling 350 miles overnight in a couchette or even sitting up, for a few days' skiing.

The destinations reached from the Gare de Lyon are legion: Lyons, Marseilles, Nice, Monte Carlo, large parts of Switzerland, the whole of Italy, Jugoslavia, Greece, the Balkans, and Central and all the South of France. Famous trains include the Mistral TEE by day to Lyons, Marseilles and Nice (676 miles in nine hours) and the Paris-Côte d'Azur and Blue Train overnight to Riviera resorts. The Palatino reaches Rome overnight in $14\frac{1}{2}$ hours; the Rome Express, also overnight, is rather slower. The Simplon Express runs overnight to Venice and Trieste and on to Jugoslavia. The Direct Orient follows the same route and includes through vehicles

for Athens and Istanbul on certain days of the week. Some of the trains convey through vehicles from Boulogne, Calais or Amsterdam, which are worked round Paris from the Gare du Nord by a diesel locomotive on the Petite Ceinture inner-belt line.

There are also expresses to Vichy, Clermont - Ferrand and other parts of Central France, but unlike the other trains in and out of the Gare de Lyon they are diesel powered, as they diverge from the electrified lines at Moret, only 42 miles from Paris. The cleaning and maintenance of a great quantity and variety of passenger stock, including that of foreign railways which is worked on an exchange - compensation basis, requires enormous installations that can be seen from the train soon after leaving the Gare de Lyon.

Last in the circuit of Paris stations is the Gare de l'Est terminus of the Réseau Est (the former Chemin de Fer de l'Est) and only a few hundred yards from the Gare du Nord. It is the largest as regards the number of its platforms (30) and third in the number of passengers. The present buildings date from 1931, and include the original train-shed (now a booking hall) built in 1850. The station largely reflects the ideas of the 1920s, and was designed in the steam age. Nevertheless it incorporates all manner of amenities for passengers, including one of the best restaurants in Paris. Some of the suburban trains are electric, and electric locomotives haul expresses to Nancy, Metz, Strasbourg (and Germany and beyond), Rheims and Luxembourg. Those to Belfort and Basle (and Italy, Austria and beyond) are worked by diesel locomotives. Among the many long-distance services are the Stanislas TEE to Nancy and Strasbourg, the Goethe TEE to Metz and Frankfurt, the Orient Express to Vienna, Budapest and Bucharest, the Arbalète TEE to Basle and Zurich, and the Arlberg Express to Chur (for the Engadine), the Tyrol, Salzburg and Vienna.

Just as French provincial cities are small in relation to Paris, so are their stations

Above: Business end of Nice station, an example of voluptuous nineteenth-century chic. *J R Batts*

Below: Bold structures of early twentieth-century architecture at Limoges Bénédictins. *SNCF*

smaller. Architecturally there are some outstanding structures; voluptuous nineteenth century *chic* at Nice, Marseilles St Charles boldly perched on a bluff overlooking the city and harbour, the great train-shed at Metz built under the German occupation of Alsace - Lorraine for troop movements (in the age before aerial bombardments) bold structures of the earlier decades of the present century at Limoges Bénédictins, Bordeaux St Jean, Toulouse Matabiau, and Rouen Rive Droite, and the striking terminus at Havre. Many of the larger stations in the provinces tend to be Second Empire Renaissance in style.

One of the pleasing characteristics of the architects employed by the French railways is the effort made to harmonise with the environment. Thus in Normandy

there are stations, some successful, in the indigenous domestic style; in Béarn there are charming wayside stations in Basque farmhouse style. Between the wars an attempt was made when rebuilding the regions in the North devastated in 1914-18 to create designs in red brick that would accord with the rising forest of red-brick structures; many stations in the French Alps are Savoyard in style, and so on. So far, however, there seems to be no outstanding structure in a style purporting to be Provençal. Meanwhile modern architects are being given their heads when the SNCF can afford new stations which tend to be suburban, to cater for housing developments; but there are striking new structures at Grenoble (built to cater for the winter sports Olympics) and elsewhere.

German Stations

Above: Working view, from the Hohenzollernbrüke, of Köln-Hbf in the shadow of Cologne Cathedral. *DB Film Archiv*

Right: One of the entrances to Köln-Hbf, with restaurant to the right. *DB Film Archiv*

Below: Main concourse of Köln-Hbf. *DB (Umbrecht)*

DURING THE GREAT AGE (1840-65) of railway building in Europe, 'Germany' was a geographical expression, not a unified State. Consequently, despite a leaning towards Baroque everywhere from the Baltic to the Alps, architectural styles in the two Germanys of today, the Federal Republic (Western) and the Democratic Republic (Eastern Germany), railway architects have long resorted to local styles, more particularly for wayside stations such as the little Alpine stations in Bavaria. Until long after the establishment of the German Empire in 1871, there was a preference in northern regions for red or yellow brick structures. The Gothic revival is (or in many cases was, before the 1939-45 war) apparent throughout the German railway systems. After 1871 ponderous debased Baroque and Renaissance styles were adopted for stations in big cities. There was and is much civic pride throughout Germany, and even in Prussia, the biggest state of the empire and of the subsequent Weimar Republic and Third Reich of 1918-39, with its tradition of centralised government, the city fathers voted contributions towards grandiose stations in varying styles.

Another reason for variety is that until after the 1914-18 war there were a number of railways in Germany, namely, the separate main-line railways of the eight kingdoms and grand-duchies of the empire, and innumerable minor railways. The main-line systems were amalgamated in 1920 to form the Deutsche Reichsbahn (German State Railway, or DR); on partition of Germany in 1945 the system in the Federal Republic was designated Deutsche Bundesbahn (Federal Railway, or DB) and that in the Democratic Republic retained the title of Reichsbahn. Hence there is great variety of station design, though neither the DB nor the DR has attempted to impose uniformity in post-war rebuilding.

If there is one common German characteristic, it is the use of the steel-and-glass overall roof, in the design and construction of which German engineers and contractors continue to excel. Such roofs began to be erected on a big scale under the Empire. One reason was to facilitate entrainment of troops in an age when aerial bombardment was undreamt of and it was inconceivable that German cities could ever be within range of enemy artillery. Overall glass roofs continued to be built after 1918 largely to pre-1914 designs. Between the wars, but not for any strategic reason before rearmament began in the 1930s, the opportunity was taken to dismantle glass roofing, but even the glazed platform canopies that were substituted extended over a greater length than in any other country, to shelter passengers, baggage and parcels. The concern for passengers and parcels is typical. From the passenger viewpoint, German stations are some of the most convenient (but not always the most sumptuous or best decorated) anywhere. Modern practice is to provide platforms that are not quite as high as in Britain; but many low platforms of the usual Continental type remain at smaller stations.

Whether you arrive in Germany from the Hook of Holland or Ostend, Cologne (Köln) Hauptbahnhof (main station) is the first one that you will probably use. If your route is via Ostend your train stops at Aachen and if via the Hook at Duisburg and Düsseldorf, all big but comparatively characterless stations, and perhaps other places en route. Cologne Hauptbahnhof (Hbf for short) is unique. Incidentally, German practice is to name all the stations that serve a large city after that city with a qualifying suffix; the DB timetable (*Kursbuch*) lists more than two-dozen passenger stations under 'Köln', ranging from Köln-Barbarossaplatz through Köln-Hbf to Köln-Worringen. Not all are on the DB; some are on local railways, which makes the *Kursbuch*, with its diagrams of rail routes in and around big cities, a very useful guide.

Environment, as opposed to civic pride and imperial grandeur, did not count for much towards the end of the last century, when Köln-Hbf was built largely in its present form. Many old and slummy but picturesque streets next to the cathedral were demolished when the four-track Hohenzollernbrücke, the city's main railway bridge, was built across the Rhine. Whatever was destroyed, the result is a passenger traffic centre that has only recently begun to be cramped. There are five double-faced island platforms under the overall roof, that is, 10 platforms each served by a

track with each track capable of accommodating one long or two medium-length passenger trains. The platforms are above street level. Tracks converge at one end to cross the Hohenzollernbrücke and at the other to cross the city on bridges and embankment before ramifying into main and branch lines. Apart from some local trains which serve the lower level of Köln-Deutz station on the right bank and do not cross the Rhine, virtually every DB train that stops or terminates at Cologne serves Köln-Hbf and most of them cross the bridge.

Although the number of through vehicles in DB trains has been reduced in recent years and many expresses simply make a brief halt—which needs some smart platform work in loading baggage and so on—shunting of international trains is still necessary, especially at night; shunting has to be done on the tracks south-west of the station, that is, on the Rhine left bank. Most trains are hauled by electric locomotives or are worked by electric multiple units (emus) but big diesel locomotives and occasional diesel multiple units (dmus) are to be seen. Trains which call include the famous Trans Europ Express (TEE) Rheingold (Hook of Holland to Basle and beyond) and the Hanover-Munich Rhine Arrow (Rheinpfeil). These two trains stop for two to five minutes each at Köln-Hbf without shunting; in fact they 'swap' through vehicles in a complex series of shunting movements farther north at Duisburg, where the track layout is more suitable for them than Cologne.

Other trains that call are the TEE Parsifal between Paris and Hamburg; the Paris-Scandinavia Express; the Ost-West Express (Paris-Berlin-Warsaw-Moscow) which includes USSR Railways Paris-Moscow sleeping cars; and the Ostend-Wien (Vienna) Express, which goes on beyond the Iron Curtain to Budapest and Bucharest. Among the variety of stock to be seen are coaches from most of the major railways of Western Europe, sleeping and refreshment cars of the German Sleeping & Dining Car Co and of the Cie Internationale des Wagons-Lits and coaches chartered by tourist organisations. To stand at the bridge end of one of the

platforms is interesting at almost any time of day, although not as diverting as watching the engines puff slowly across the Hohenzollernbrücke in steam days.

Below the platforms and tracks, which are supported on arches and pillars, is the 'crypt' at street level. It contains an excellent restaurant (nearly every big German station has a good restaurant plus a variety of snackbars notably with beer and sausages, café etc), waiting rooms and passenger amenities generally and opens out into the booking office facing the street. The main frontage block includes a comfortable bed-and-breakfast hotel run by the DB. Its ornate late-19th century and rather debased German Renaissance architecture contrast oddly with the 'Wagnerian' medievalism of the towers of the Hohenzollernbrücke. There are good pedestrian connections with urban transport, and the Hauptbahnhof is in fact, the public transport centre of the city in the heart of the business and shopping area, near the cathedral and other sights and hotels, and in easy reach of the Rhine steamer quay.

If Köln-Hbf is the DB's most notable through station, Munich's main station (München-Hbf), only slightly less familiar to thousands of Britons, is the DB terminus (though no longer, as appears below, strictly a terminus) par excellence. Munich is an ancient city, but unlike the 19th-century rebuilders and developers of Cologne, those of Munich spared more of what was by then left of the medieval and 18th-century city and located the terminus of the then Royal Bavarian State Railways at street level west of, but near, the city centre. All DB trains must terminate or reverse in the Hauptbahnhof except for the emu trains that dip down to the new low-level platforms of the München-Hbf Tunnel; they run over the new S-bahn in tunnel under the city and the River Isar, calling at various underground-type stations, to the Ostbahnhof; there they rejoin the main line that has made a long detour around the southern perimeter. This enables emus to run through between stations, on electrified lines radiating west and east of the city calling at S-bahn stations including Marienplatz where there is pedestrian subway connection with the

first north-to-south line of the Munich U (Untergrund)-bahn. S-bahn, which originally meant Schnellbahn (fast line) now means any DB surburban line or group of suburban electrified lines that are operated more or less as a distinct service or group. There are S-bahnen in and around several German cities. Creation of the Munich S-bahn involved building the line under the city (the S-bahn proper) and a similar cut-off line is being constructed under Stuttgart to link the terminus in the north of the city with the suburbs to the south.

The handsome 19th-century, vaguely Renaissance, frontage of München-Hbf, facing one of the city's main thoroughfares is a landmark. The main block, which incorporates a hotel, opens on to a large circulating area and the many terminal platforms. As might be expected in Europe's beer capital, beer is readily obtainable—and its consumption is a major station activity at certain times of day. The station is in three parts, designated (from north to south) Starnbergerbahnhof, Hauptbahnhof and Holzkirchnerbahnhof. The first and third deal with local services. There is a big acreage of glass roof over all their platforms. In addition, there are the Tunnel platforms. Like Köln-Hbf, the terminus deals with trains to and from all parts of Europe. Here the Blauer Enzian, still the DB's fastest train, hauled by an electric locomotive, reverses en route between Hamburg and (according to the season) Klagenfurt or Zell-am-See in Austria; its journey includes runs of 31 minutes northbound and 32 minutes southbound over the 38 miles between Munich and Augsburg. Other visitors are the Orient Express (Paris-Strasbourg-Vienna-Budapest-Bucharest) and the Mozart (Vienna-Paris by day in just over $14\frac{1}{2}$ hours).

Munich is the tourist centre for the Bavarian Alps and a collection and distribution point for traffic to and from South eastern Europe via Salzburg and Vienna and Italy via Innsbruck and the Brenner pass. There is consequently much transfer of through vehicles between long-distance trains. The Mediolanum (Latin for Milan) Trans Europ Express, an Italian train, plies between Munich and Milan via the Brenner and Verona. As the venue of the 1972 Olympic Games, München-Hbf has dealt with bumper traffic over and above its usual summer peak. Among Olympic traffic was a daily special express from and to Moscow via Warsaw, Berlin and Nuremberg, including Russian 'hard-class' coaches for the journeys of about 43 hours. München-Hbf is also the terminus of the Sassnitz Express to Berlin via Nuremberg, which connects in Berlin with its namesake which runs from Berlin to Stockholm via the Sassnitz (GDR) to Trelleborg train ferry.

In contrast with München-Hbf is Hamburg-Hbf, a through station. By reason of an accident of pre-Imperial German history, there are two major stations in the Hamburg-Altona conurbation. Hamburg-Altona is the terminus of most trains to the east, south and west (which call also at Hauptbahnhof) and many that run to Kiel, the German North Sea and Baltic coast resorts north of Hamburg, and to Denmark reverse there. Expresses between Western and Southern Europe on the one hand, and Denmark and Sweden on the 'Birds Flight Route' via Lübeck and the Puttgarden-Rödby train ferry on the other, do not call at Altona.

Facing page: German Federal Railway diesel-hydraulic TEE train at Düsseldorf-Hbf. *DB (H Sauberlich)*

This page top to bottom: Hamburg-Altona station, with a DR (East German) Pacific steam locomotive heading a train for Berlin in 1970. *P B Whitehouse*

Hamburg-Hbf as it was in 1938. *DB Film Archiv*

Entrance to the main block of München-Hbf —a terminus. *DB Film Archiv*

Control tower at München-Hbf affording all-round views of the terminus and shunting movements. *DB Film Archiv*

Overleaf upper: Attractive use of lighting and fountains at the main entrance to Frankfurt-Hbf. *DB (Umbrecht)*

Overleaf lower: Hauptbahnhof at Stuttgart, of vaguely moated castle appearance. *DB Film Archiv*

of the city and dates back many years. The termini proper, going clockwise from the north, were the Stettinerbahnhof, the Görlitzer (in the south-east), the Anhalter and the Potsdamer in the south, and the Lehrter, slightly north-west of centre and north of the Stadtbahn. The main-line stations on the Stadtbahn which are still open are, from the west, Charlottenburg, in the important quarter of that name, and Zooligischer Garten, both in West Berlin; and Friedrichstrasse, near the geographical centre of the city before partition, and Ostbahnhof (formerly Schlesischerbahnhof) in East Berlin. Another large Stadtbahn station, Alexanderplatz, between Friedrichstrasse and Ostbahnhof, is no longer served by expresses. The names of these stations originally denoted the destination served before the lines concerned were developed and the significance largely lost.

Hence, trains from the Stettiner ran not only to the Baltic port of Stettin, but also to Sassnitz and Warnemünde, train ferry ports for Sweden and Denmark respectively. Anhalter was the gateway for a large area of central and southern Germany and places beyond. From the Potsdamer Bahnhof expresses ran far west of the 'Prussian Versailles'. The Fliegender Hamburger and other expresses to Hamburg started from the Lehterbahnhof, which was unique in having virtually no suburban service. Görlitzer was the terminus of a secondary line to the town of Görlitz and beyond. Stadtbahn trains ran west and east over the plains of North Germany to Hanover, Bremen, Holland, the Ruhr, Cologne, Belgium and Paris in the west and Silesia (now part of Poland), Poland and the Russian frontier breaks of gauge in the east; eastbound and westbound trains overlapped to serve all or most Stadtbahn stations. Today all DR main-line trains, including the Ost-West Express, are concentrated on Stadtbahn stations using the many connecting lines to the Ringbahn that has long existed to enable freight—and troop and military supply trains—to avoid the Stadtbahn.

The former termini have been demolished or used for other purposes. None was architecturally outstanding, though the Anhalter and Potsdamer boasted late 19th-century quasi-Baroque frontages. There were some magnificent high arched roofs. The Stadtbahn is on embankment above street level; much of the passenger accommodation at the stations is below the platforms and tracks and the architects were given little scope.

In the GDR, war damage of 1940-45 to many stations is only now being made good, often involving complete rebuilding. It is not easy for Westerners to visit—and unwise to try to photograph—new structures even in Berlin, Leipzig or Dresden. The architects, however, do not seem to have created any notable buildings. One can be sure, however, that the comfort and convenience of the passenger, besides rationalisation of baggage and parcels handling and train working, have been carefully studied.

The nondescript pre-1914 design of the main block of Hamburg-Hbf is unexciting and unworthy of the city, as is the overall glass roofing. The main building is at street level, straddling the platforms and tracks. The approaches are cramped and there is little room for marshalling, much of which as a result is done at Altona. Nor, for some reason, are the passenger amenities quite so attractive as at most other large DB stations, although there is an astonishing variety of shops in the main hall. As you approach Hauptbahnhof from the Bremen and Hanover directions, you get a first glimpse of the Elbe and the busy port, while continuing towards Altona you run over a causeway between the Aussen and Binnen Alster, those sheets of water in the built-up area which contribute so much to the city's charm.

Hamburg has its own S-bahn system worked by emus over several routes. There is also a comprehensive U-bahn network, only partly underground, with which there are DB/U-bahn interchange stations. Besides the expresses already mentioned as serving Cologne and Munich, there are through trains between Hamburg-Altona, Hauptbahnhof and Berlin via the West/East frontier at Schwanheide. The fastest train takes $5\frac{1}{4}$ hours between Hauptbahnhof and Berlin Zoo (in West Berlin) and another 15 minutes to Friedrichstrasse (beyond the Wall). Before 1939, the Fliegender Hamburger (Flying Hamburger) dmu—a pioneer development by the then Reichsbahn—took a little over $2\frac{1}{4}$ hours for the 178 miles. Today, however, there are frontier stops for immigration and customs processing, and the DR track between Schwanheide and Berlin has not yet been restored to pre-war standards.

Like London, Paris and Moscow and other capitals today, and like Vienna and Dublin in living memory, Berlin was served by a ring of passenger termini. Since the partition of Germany most of them have been closed. Those that remain are through stations, some large, on the DR's west-to-east link line (Stadtbahn or City Railway—no direct connection with the Berlin U-bahn) which runs through the centre

15
The Great Expresses

Overleaf: Poster, c1895, advertising joint London-Scotland services of the Great Northern, North Eastern and North British railways, by lithographers, Andrew Reid & Co Ltd. *British Transport Museum (B Sharpe)*

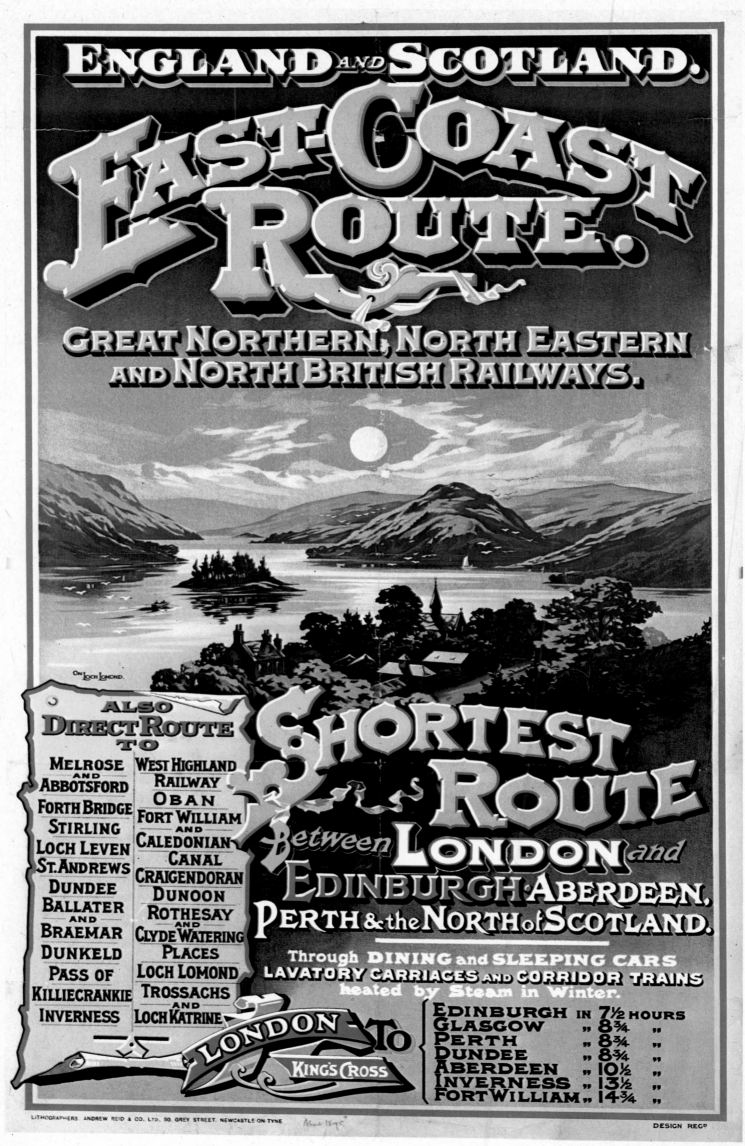

ENGLAND AND SCOTLAND.

EAST COAST ROUTE.

GREAT NORTHERN, NORTH EASTERN AND NORTH BRITISH RAILWAYS.

ON LOCH LOMOND.

ALSO DIRECT ROUTE TO

MELROSE AND ABBOTSFORD	WEST HIGHLAND RAILWAY
FORTH BRIDGE	OBAN
STIRLING	FORT WILLIAM AND
LOCH LEVEN	CALEDONIAN CANAL
ST. ANDREWS	CRAIGENDORAN
DUNDEE	DUNOON
BALLATER AND BRAEMAR	ROTHESAY AND CLYDE WATERING PLACES
DUNKELD	LOCH LOMOND
PASS OF KILLIECRANKIE	TROSSACHS AND LOCH KATRINE
INVERNESS	

SHORTEST ROUTE Between LONDON and EDINBURGH, ABERDEEN, PERTH & the NORTH of SCOTLAND.

Through DINING and SLEEPING CARS LAVATORY CARRIAGES and CORRIDOR TRAINS heated by Steam in Winter.

LONDON TO KING'S CROSS

EDINBURGH	IN	7½	HOURS
GLASGOW	,,	8¾	,,
PERTH	,,	8¾	,,
DUNDEE	,,	8¾	,,
ABERDEEN	,,	10½	,,
INVERNESS	,,	13½	,,
FORT WILLIAM	,,	14¾	,,

LITHOGRAPHERS ANDREW REID & CO. LTD. 50. GREY STREET. NEWCASTLE-ON-TYNE.

About 1895.

DESIGN REGᴰ

468

FLYINC SCOTSMAN

Top: A3 Pacific locomotive 'Flying Scotsman' after restoration by Mr Pegler. *B A Reeves*

Left: No 1 Stirling Single with driving wheels over 8ft in diameter, one of the GNR express locomotives that helped to make the Flying Scotsman famous. *Ian Allan library*

Below: Another locomotive type that hauled the Flying Scotsman north of York in the early years was the R4-4-0 of North Eastern Railway. This one is pictured just south of York Station. *Ian Allan library*

Above: The fast haul to Scotland by the East Coast route was taken over from the Stirling Singles and the R4-4-0s by the Ivatt Atlantic 4-4-2s at about the turn of the century. This one is pictured in new LNER livery after grouping in 1923. *Ian Allan library*

THERE IS ONE British express only which can claim the distinction of having had an unchanged departure time for 110 years, and it is the Flying Scotsman. To be precise, there was a brief period in 1917 and 1918, during World War I, when the start from each terminus, Kings Cross and Edinburgh Waverley, was moved to 09.30, but that hardly counts; otherwise 10.00 always has been, and still remains, the historic starting time. Also the Flying Scotsman was probably the first of all British trains to earn a title, even if for many years it was unofficial. It was not until after the three partners in the East Coast Route, the Great Northern, North Eastern and North British Railways, had

been merged in 1923 into the London & North Eastern Railway that the title appeared in the timetables and was displayed on the carriage headboards.

June 1862 saw the inauguration of what was described as a 'Special Scotch Express', leaving Kings Cross at 10.00 and reaching Edinburgh at 20.30—a journey of 10½ hours. At that date the direct line from Shaftholme Junction, north of Doncaster, and that from Durham to Gateshead, had not been built; in the former case the route was through Knottingley and Church Fenton and in the latter through Penshaw. The Selby line was opened in 1871 and the Team Valley line from Durham a year later; with their help the overall time of the Special Scotch Express had come down to nine hours by 1876. But this included half-an-hour spent at York to enable passengers to bolt a hasty lunch.

In 1887 the East Coast Companies made the momentous decision to admit third-class passengers to the 10.00 from Kings Cross, and this move so excited the competing West Coast Companies as to precipitate the 'Race to Edinburgh' of 1888. Schedules were pared until in just under three weeks the Flying Scotsman had its time from Kings Cross to Edinburgh cut from nine hours to seven and three-quarter hours, and on August 14 of that year the train put in an appearance in Edinburgh Waverley at 17.32, in seven hours 32 minutes from London. Then, by common agreement between the railways concerned, the time was stabilised at eight and a quarter hours, though few could have foreseen that the dead hand of this agreement would cause the journey time of the Flying Scotsman to remain unchanged for 44 years.

It is astonishing also that until 1900, 21 years after the introduction of the first British restaurant cars, the lengthy stop was still being made at York by the Flying Scotsman for passengers to obtain a sketchy lunch. But at last, in 1900 two new trains made their appearance, composed throughout of American-type 12-wheel cars, with clerestory roofs and Pullman vestibules. Each car was 65ft 6in in length—a revolutionary advance on the mixed bogie and six-wheel stock used until then. Needless to say, first- and third-class restaurant cars were included. This meant a considerable increase in train weights, but by then the first Ivatt Atlantics were beginning to replace the famous Stirling 8ft 4-2-2s on the Great Northern main line, and the efficient North Eastern Class R 4-4-0s, soon also to be succeeded by Atlantics, were taking over north of York, so that the heavier trains presented no problem.

For a good many years after that, because of the hampering East Coast-West Coast agreement on journey times, the history of the Flying Scotsman saw few changes. The year 1914 saw the introduction of new train sets, now of eight-wheel vehicles throughout, with elliptical roofs, and each train with one car given over entirely to kitchen and pantry. In that year World War I broke out; before it ended the restaurant cars had been withdrawn and the journey time had been extended to nine hours 50 minutes in each direction. However, after the war ended recovery was rapid, the cars reappearing early in 1919 and the eight and a quarter hour schedule being restored in 1923.

That same year witnessed the merging of the Great Northern, North Eastern and North British Railways into the London &

Top: The restored locomotive 'Flying Scotsman' in June 1969 on one of its periodic appearances on BR before it was shipped to the US. *B A Reeves*

Above: Another shot of an Ivatt Atlantic showing the broad firebox permitted by the use of a carrier axle behind the drivers. *Ian Allan library*

Right: Flying Scotsman behind BR Pacific 60143 'Sir Walter Scott' passing Shaftholme Junction in June 1951. *R E Vincent*

North Eastern Railway; from then on the competition was to be between two more powerful rivals—the LNER and the London Midland & Scottish companies. So it was that in 1924 further new Flying Scotsman train sets took the rails, including triplet restaurant cars with Gresley-type articulation, and equipped for electric cooking. By that time also, Gresley's first Pacific locomotives of the Flying Scotsman type were adding immensely to motive power resources compared with the existing Great Northern and North Eastern Atlantics.

Four years later a notable milestone was reached in Flying Scotsman history. As the LNER and LMSR, still tied by their agreement, could not compete in the matter of time, other forms of competition had to be devised. One of them was in the matter of non-stop running. After an experiment in working the first portion of the Flying Scotsman non-stop between Kings Cross and Newcastle, the LNER decided from May 1928 to inaugurate what was easily the longest non-stop run in the world, over the 392.9 miles between London and Edinburgh. As one engine-crew could not be expected to man the locomotive for eight and a quarter hours at a stretch, arrangements had to be made for a second crew to take over at the mid-point on the journey. For this purpose Gresley devised the only corridor tenders that the world has ever known, providing a passage from a compartment in the leading coach, reserved for the engine-crews, direct to the footplate.

With this bold development there appeared a fourth new pair of Flying Scots-man trains, this time with a cocktail bar, a retiring room for ladies and a hairdressing saloon complete with barber—this last an idea derived from the United States to help passengers to while away long journeys. The only silly feature of the non-stop run was that the engine-crews also had to while away the same length of time because, although all the intermediate stops had been taken out, no reduction in the overall journey time could yet be permitted. But at last, in May 1932, it was realised that acceleration had become imperative.

So 25 minutes was cut from the Flying Scotsman winter schedule, bringing it down to seven hours 50 minutes, with intermediate stops at Grantham, York, Darlington (southbound), Newcastle and Berwick. Later, when the summer non-stop run between Kings Cross and Edinburgh reappeared, it was with the time slashed by no less than 45 minutes, to seven and a half hours. In 1936 the time came down to seven and a quarter hours, and a year later to seven hours, while by 1939 the winter schedule had been pared to seven hours 20 minutes each way. Bit by bit the train had grown very substantially in weight; when in 1938 yet another new pair of trains had been introduced, they were 14-coach sets weighing no less than 504 tons and comprising through portions for Glasgow, Perth and Aberdeen. The main train included a triplet articulated restaurant car set and a full-length buffet car.

In the up direction the booked time over the $105\frac{1}{2}$ miles from Grantham to Kings Cross had come down to $105\frac{1}{2}$ minutes. This mile-a-minute conclusion to the journey, with gross loads which at times rose to 600 tons, was one of the hardest locomotive assignments in the country, even for a Gresley Pacific.

Then came the devastating interruption of World War II. One of the only trains so to do during the war, the Flying Scotsman retained its official name, but passenger and troop demands were on such a scale as to demand two trains each way daily. Nevertheless, during the earlier part of the war the Flying Scotsman seldom loaded to fewer than 20 coaches, even without restaurant cars, and loads up to 21, 22 and even 23 coaches, with a gross weight up to 800 tons, were not unknown, and were worked single-headed by Gresley's highly competent A4 streamlined Pacifics. But eventually such demands were affecting locomotive maintenance so adversely that a limit of 18 coaches had to be placed on train formations, which was again reduced later to 15 coaches.

Arrears of maintenance became so serious during World War II that recovery to pre-war conditions was much slower than after World War I. By 1948, however, non-stop running had been resumed between London and Edinburgh, and it was in September of that year, after a cloudburst had washed away a whole series of bridges on the East Coast main line between Dunbar and Berwick, making temporary diversion of the train necessary via Galashiels and Kelso, that on several occasions competent engine crews succeeded in completing the lengthened route of $408\frac{1}{2}$ miles without any intermediate halt. These were probably the longest non-stop journeys with steam

Above: Bill McAlpine's preserved 'Flying Scotsman' being serviced at Chester.
B A Reeves
Left: 'Flying Scotsman' with a railfans' special at Kings Cross. *B A Reeves*

Below left: A current Flying Scotsman train headed by English Electric Deltic diesel locomotive 9021 'Argyll and Sutherland Highlander' passing Hornsey Station in May 1968. *G S Cocks*

Facing page: No 4472 'Flying Scotsman' climbs Holloway Bank shortly after leaving Kings Cross with a Locomotive Club of Great Britain special. *B A Reeves*

power ever made in world railway history. The main preoccupation of the crews was water; with the hard initial climb from Edinburgh over Falahill summit included, the added distance of the diversion involved running for 86 miles before the first replenishment of the tender supply could be obtained from the Lucker troughs.

In 1949, in order that the 10.00 workings from Kings Cross and Edinburgh should continue to make the normal stops, the non-stop workings were given earlier starting times and a new title—the Capitals Limited. But this arrangement lasted for a short time only, and later the Glasgow portion was split off to form a separate train, following the main train and making some of the stops that the Flying Scotsman proper was now omitting. For by 1949 the latter had settled down to stops at Grantham and Newcastle only, and to a journey time of seven hours 50 minutes, still 30 minutes longer than in 1939. Then, in 1955, the Grantham stop was cut out and a non-stop journey of 268.4 miles between Kings Cross and Newcastle became a daily assignment, with the London-Edinburgh time cut to seven hours each way. Further accelerations followed in succession until the year 1962 saw another milestone of note reached in the history of this famous train.

This was the disappearance of steam from its head end, and the substitution of diesel power in the form of 3,300hp Deltic locomotives, which for several years were the only diesel-electric locomotives of anything like that power. Not only so, but it was decided to cut the journey time to six hours, thus for the first time getting back to the six-hour schedule of the pre-

war Coronation streamliners. But with this difference, that the Coronation trains weighed 312 tons with and 279 tons without their beaver-tail observation cars, whereas the Deltic-hauled 11-coach sets turned the scale at 385 tons apiece.

It may be added that before the non-stop London-Edinburgh steam workings came to an end, their time had been cut to six and a half hours; the Gresley A4 Pacifics were thus maintaining an overall average of just over a mile-a-minute with 400-ton loads, a very notable achievement for steam power.

Since then the Flying Scotsman schedule has been pared still further, until today the Deltics are required to complete the journey of 392.9 miles in five and three-quarter hours. This means that the down express has to cover the 268.4 miles from Kings Cross to Newcastle at an average of 70.9mph; the up train, with a few minutes less from Edinburgh to Newcastle, is allowed three minutes more on to London. But the maximum speeds, of course, are very much higher, as may be realised by reviewing some of the passing times. Going down, for example, the train is booked over the 26.95 miles from Hitchin to Huntingdon in 17 minutes, at 95.1mph, and over the 20 miles from Stoke signal-box to Newark in 13 minutes at 92.3mph. On the up journey 18 minutes only are allowed for the level 28.35 miles from Northallerton to Skelton, the junction just north of York, which works out at an average of 94.5mph. Such bookings demand maximum speeds up to 100mph, which is permitted over a total of 170 of the 268.4 miles between London and Newcastle.

Today's normal loading of the Flying Scotsman is 12 coaches, increased to 13 at weekends and during the summer season. One full-length open coach is devoted to meal service, and an adjoining coach contains the kitchen and some restaurant seats. Elsewhere in the train a miniature buffet takes up part of a second-class coach. Seats are provided for 108 first-class and 379 second-class passengers in the 12-coach train, with 64 more second-class in the extra 13th coach. The weight of the complete train therefore has grown to 411 and 443 tons according to formation—a very substantial tonnage to haul at such high sustained speeds. Yet the Deltic diesels have often proved that they have something in hand, and even when they have suffered out-of-course delays can still succeed in completing their Flying Scotsman journeys on time.

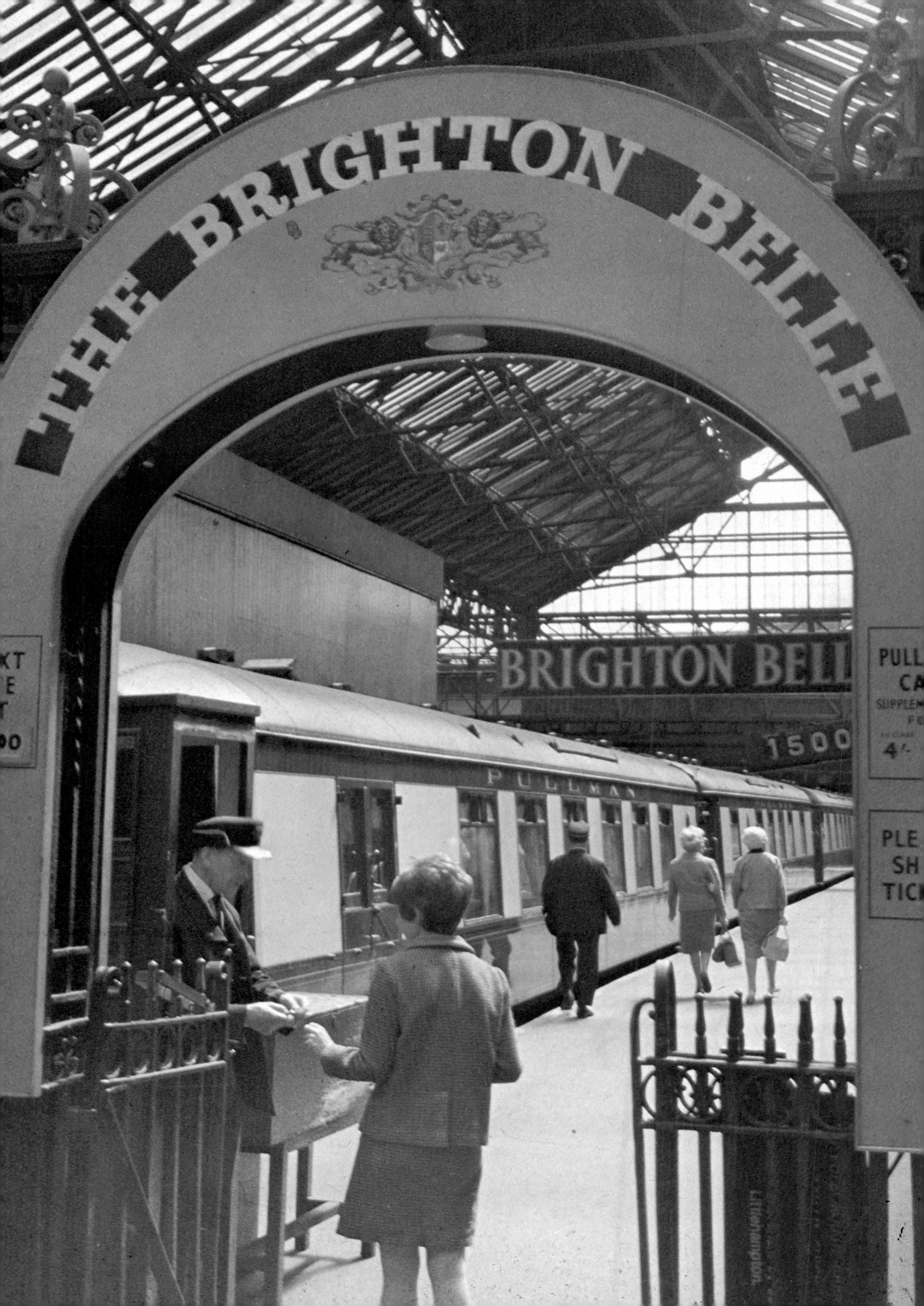
THE BRIGHTON BELLE
BRIGHTON BELL
PULLMAN
1500

IF ONE WAS told that on the last journey of its 39-year history a certain express had been filled with a distinguished party whose members had paid heavily to be entertained on the journey with champagne and other delicacies, and to be welcomed on arrival at midnight by a band playing *Auld Lang Syne,* one might well imagine it was some famous long-distance express that was succumbing to air or other competition. Nothing of the kind. It was a train whose route was no more than a shade under 51 miles in length, short enough, in fact, to be covered four times in each direction daily, and taking no more than 60 minutes, or, in its final years, 55 minutes, for each trip. It was the all-Pullman Brighton Belle, whose demise on April 30, 1972, marked almost the end of Pullman operation on the Southern Region of British Railways; final Pullman eclipse was withdrawal of the Golden Arrow a few months later.

The origin of the Brighton Belle, and of Pullman car facilities in the South of England, dates back to the former London Brighton & South Coast Railway. The LBSCR, however, was not the first railway in Britain to introduce Pullman travel. In 1872 James Allport, general manager of the Midland Railway, crossed the Atlantic to see the luxury cars that George Mortimer Pullman was building for railways in the United States, and he was so impressed that an order was placed for similar cars for Midland use. They were built in Detroit, shipped across the Atlantic in sections and re-erected at a special Pullman works at Derby; the first car, appropriately named *Midland,* was completed in January 1874. By the end of that year 14 cars had entered Midland service, and in June 1874, five cars had been assembled in a single train, which travelled from Bradford to St Pancras in the morning, and left London at midnight on the return journey. The sleeping cars were of the early American type, which were transformed from day to night use by pulling the seats together to form longitudinal lower berths, and letting down the hinged upper berths on both sides of the central gangway; curtains along each side of the gangway provided privacy.

The London Brighton & South Coast Railway acquired its first Pullman car in 1875. Strange to relate, it was a sleeping and not a drawing-room or parlour car, because no journeys on so limited a system as the LBSCR involved any night travel; so *Mars,* the car in question, remained permanently as arranged for day use until in 1884 it was sold to an Italian railway to serve its proper purpose as a sleeper. But in 1877 seven new parlour cars joined *Mars* in the service of the London Brighton & South Coast Railway, to run, at first, exclusively between Victoria and Brighton.

In 1881 the LBSCR tried a new venture. Until then, all its Pullmans carried first-class passengers only, and four Pullmans were marshalled into a single train for service between Victoria and Brighton, the forerunner of the Brighton Belle. One car, the *Beatrice,* made history by being the first railway coach on record to be lighted by electricity—at a time when many homes still had only oil or candle light. Electric current for the coach lighting was from 32 accumulators, which were charged at Victoria by a steam-driven dynamo specially installed there.

By 1888 the first Brighton Pullman train in which vestibules permitted movement between the cars began its service. Also for the first time the whole train was lit by electricity, provided by a dynamo belt-driven from one of the axles and located

Above: End car with cab of the unique Pullman five-car electric sets used on Belle service. *P J Bartlett*

Right Centre: One of the second-class motor coaches, giving an aggregate 1,800hp in a five-car set. *P J Bartlett*

Right below: A first-class coach after repainting in standard BR livery. *B W Mouat*

Overleaf top: Down Belle crossing Balcombe viaduct in April 1972, shortly before the service was withdrawn. *J Bradshaw*

Overleaf centre: Brighton station in April 1972, which lost for ever some of its appeal with the withdrawal of the Belle a month later. *B W Mouat*

Overleaf bottom: This interior shot in a Brighton Belle first-class car reflects an ambience that the economics of rail travel can no longer support. *J C Morgan*

Facing page: The Brighton Belle at Victoria Station in 1967. *P J Bartlett*

in a specially designed six-wheel van shaped and painted to resemble the Pullmans. The new system of train lighting was originated by the versatile William Stroudley, the LBSCR locomotive, carriage and wagon superintendent. The vans, of which two were built, were irreverently known as Pullman Pups. In 1898 a new all-Pullman Victoria-Brighton train took the rails, and outraged the Sabbatarians by starting a Sunday service, named the Sunday Pullman Limited, which soon became so popular that up to seven first-class cars were needed. Early in 1899 the name was changed to Brighton Limited.

Until 1895 the Pullman trains were mostly hauled by Stroudley's unique 0-4-2 express engines, with their striking gamboge livery, of which *Gladstone* is still preserved in York Railway Museum. In 1895 there appeared the first Brighton 4-4-0 locomotives, R J Billinton's B2 class; by 1899 they had been expanded into B4s, one of which, No 70 *Holyrood,* on July 26, 1903, was responsible for the fastest journey ever made with steam power between Victoria and Brighton. At that time the LBSCR was being threatened by a scheme for a new railway between London and Brighton which would have no intermediate stations, and over which fast times would be possible with electric power, and the LBSCR management was out to show that with steam as yet they had far from shot their bolt with 60-minute schedules.

So the Brighton Limited was cut to three Pullman cars and a Pullman Pup weighing 130 tons, and with *Holyrood* driver Tompsett, who had been instructed to run as fast as he could, cut the time for the 50.9 miles to 48 minutes 41 seconds start to stop. The run included a restrained passage through the London area, then a minimum speed of 58mph at Quarry tunnel, followed by 80mph at Horley, 66mph minimum at Balcombe tunnel, no less than 90mph through Haywards Heath,

and 69mph minimum at Clayton tunnel. On the return journey the maximum speed was 85mph and the time 50 minutes 21 seconds. So the electric railway scheme never materialised, and Brighton was destined to wait another 30 years before it welcomed its first electric trains from London.

By 1908 the Brighton Pullman Limited began to run on weekdays as well as Sundays, twice in each direction daily, and with a handsome new train of 12-wheel cars, also the new title Southern Belle; it was still first class only. New locomotives were becoming available for its haulage, including, for the first time, tank instead of tender locomotives. It was argued that for such short runs it was uneconomical to haul about a weighty tender, when side tanks and a rear bunker could hold more than all the supplies necessary. Earle Marsh had proved the argument to the full when in the exchange working with the London & North Western Railway in 1909 of the Sunny South Express his 4-4-2 tank No 23 proved its ability to run from Brighton to Rugby and back on one heaped-up bunkerful of coal, about $3\frac{1}{4}$ tons, and to cover the 90 miles between East Croydon and Rugby without any replenishment from track-troughs of its 2,000-gallon side water tanks.

Later, in 1910, there came the bigger 4-6-2 tanks *Abergavenny* and *Bessborough,* and finally, from 1914 to 1922, Lawson Billinton's magnificent 98-ton 4-6-4 tanks, Nos 327 to 333, all of which took their turn in working the Brighton Limited. But by that time it had become a much heavier train, for to make the time-table paths that it occupied more profitable, the authorities had added ordinary first- and third-class coaches to the four first-class Pullmans.

Eventually, however, it was decided that locomotives with a wider radius of action than the tanks were needed, which led in 1926 to the building of 14 of the famous King Arthur 4-6-0s, of London & South Western Railway origin, for use on the Central Division of what had become the Southern Railway.

The 4-6-0s and the Earle Marsh LBSCR Atlantics were the last steam locomotives to head the Southern Belle, for by the end of 1932 electric conductor rails had reached Brighton from London at long last. So, on the morning of January 1, 1933, there was displayed to an admiring public at Victoria a brand new all-electric Southern Belle. Three new sets of five cars each (two first and three third) had been built, unique in that they incorporated the first and only motor-propelled Pullman cars ever built. Each set had driving cabs at both ends, with 1,800hp at the driver's command. It is doubtful whether all fifteen cars were ever worked in a single formation, but it soon became regular practice to run two sets coupled, making a ten-car formation of 3,600hp. From that time on the Southern Belle carried two classes of passenger, the third-class cars being changed to second class on the abolition of third class in Great Britain.

The speed capabilities of the new Belle were soon demonstrated. On a preliminary trial run the 50.9 miles from Victoria to Brighton were covered in $46\frac{3}{4}$ minutes, but the schedule of the train never dropped below 60 minutes until its final years, when in company with all the hourly trains it became a 55-minute working. It is rumoured that on one occasion, when for some reason one of the down Belle workings left Victoria 15 minutes late, the motorman decided to make up the arrears, and whirled his apprehensive passengers down to Brighton in 45 minutes. There is no confirmation of this feat, and as it would doubtless have involved infringement of speed restrictions it would certainly not have been welcomed by the authorities!

No expense had been spared in furnishing the new train. The inauguration coincided with the publication by the Southern Railway of a new propaganda leaflet called *Southern Weekly News,* which waxed lyrical on the subject. 'A masterpiece of comfort and luxury which will put the *trains-de-luxe* of the Continent definitely in the shade', was how it described the new train. As to those who were privileged to travel in it, we read: 'All were filled with admiration at the beautiful woods used in the panelling of the train, the bright modern tints of the upholstery, the perfection of the lighting, and the devices for expelling foul air and tobacco fumes, which are just a few points of interest in this triumph of modern railway coach building'. Indeed, the Pullman Car Company expressed considerable pride in its new photo-electric-controlled ventilation system. So cheering crowds saw the first Southern Belle away from Victoria, and there was an equally enthusiastic reception at Brighton. On the journey the first passengers were entertained vocally by the London Madrigal Group, whose renderings aroused appreciative comments as to the Belle's acoustics.

So began the career of a train whose cars had become the oldest passenger stock in regular service in Great Britain when the time came, at the end of April 1930, just short of its fortieth birthday, to terminate its career. Because of the intervention of the 1939-1945 war, the service of what in 1934 had been renamed the Brighton Belle (no doubt because of the introduction in 1931 of the Bournemouth Belle) was not continuous throughout the period. For a time during the early part

Above: Still in the standard Pullman 'chocolate-and cream' livery, the Belle at Victoria in 1967. *P J Bartlett*

Below: And at Brighton in the summer of 1967. *P J Bartlett*

of the war, one five-car set continued to run, with a four-coach set of ordinary stock, but after 18 months all Pullman cars were withdrawn, and not until October 1947 was the whole train in service once again. It restarted with three double journeys daily, and then the fourth was added; so the sequence became 9.25, 13.25, 17.25 and 21.25 up from Brighton, and 11.00, 15.00, 19.00 and 23.00 down from Victoria. Many stage and other celebrities live at Brighton, and with them the Brighton Belle was always highly popular, especially the last daily run down from London at 23.00, which they could catch after the end of their theatre shows, take a late meal en route and arrive in Brighton on the stroke of midnight.

Talking of meals is a reminder of the 'club breakfast' which used to be served on the 09.25 working up from Brighton. The meal could include grilled bacon and egg which oddly enough was always described on the Pullman menu as 'pan fried' (unless one preferred 'two eggs styled to choice'), or, as alternatives, grilled sausage, bacon and tomato, or grilled 'royal kippers'—the whole for the modest sum of five shillings. After 10.00 the price of all the eatables went up; after 1960 the price of the special breakfast went up also. At one time in the 1960s kippers were withdrawn from the menu; their disappearance aroused such a mass of complaint, including letters to the national press from the afore-mentioned theatrical notabilities and others, that before long the succulent fish had to make its appearance on the Belle once again.

As is customary in Pullman practice, all the six first-class Pullmans, two in each five-car set, received feminine names; they were *Doris, Hazel, Audrey, Gwen, Vera* and *Mona,* and were preserved until the Belle's withdrawal. In the course of their lengthy lives they were re-upholstered with typical British Railways materials, and there were some modifications of the internal arrangements, more particularly of lighting, but in general their interiors showed very little variation from 1933 to 1972. Externally they were painted in standard Pullman chocolate-and-cream colours during the life of the Pullman Car Company, but in their final years the three sets received the standard blue-and-grey BR livery, with the words Brighton Belle in large letters on both sides of each car. In the course of years the riding of the sets was distinctly rough, though the fact hardly seemed to affect the patronage of the most popular workings, such as the morning 9.25 up, which usually ran filled to capacity, even though the consumption of tea and coffee could be a somewhat hazardous business.

Eventually, however, the service was bound to come to an end. The cars were life-expired, and for the Brighton Belle to continue would have entailed building three new Pullman sets at a time when other Pullman cars on the Southern Region had been or were about to be withdrawn. It would have continued the uneconomic non-interchangeability of the Belle and the standard SR stock used on the Brighton and other workings. Above all, manning the Brighton Belle required a pool of 36 attendants and chefs, of whom at any one time 14 had to be on duty; the average number of breakfasts served in any one day was 44 and there were still fewer other meals served on such a short journey and even with the supplementary Pullman fares the Belle was losing a good deal of money.

So it was that the strains of a band and

the singing of *Auld Lang Syne* were heard at midnight on April 30, 1972, as the Brighton Belle drew into Brighton station for the last time. But not, fortunately, to be broken up; the train was too famous for that. Instead British Railways invited tenders for the purchase of the fifteen Pullmans, and public response was immediate. The cars will now be dispersed all over the country, serving a variety of purposes. First-class kitchen car *Doris* is on a siding at Finsbury Park acting as a reception lounge for a firm of display designers and shopfitters. Innkeepers in Cheshire, Yorkshire and Surrey have purchased first-class cars *Hazel* and *Mona* and a second-class car to use as restaurants. A large firm of brewers has acquired three of the second-class cars, for a purpose which has not been disclosed. One first-class kitchen car, *Audrey,* has been bought by an Eton College master for permanent exhibition at Ashford. So although the Brighton Belle has ceased to run to and fro over the 51-mile course that it has covered for over 39 years, and ultimately eight times every day, this world-famous train is not going to be forgotten for a long time ahead.

Top: The last down run of the Brighton Belle on May 9, 1972, crossing the Ouse viaduct north of Haywards Heath. *J C Morgan*

Above: An up Belle train emerging from Clayton tunnel in August 1963. *J C Morgan*

The Settebello

Italian State Railways ETR300 electric rolling stock forming the luxurious Settebello Rome-Milan express.
Italian State Railways

IN 1939, shortly before the outbreak of the second European war, two very remarkable railway runs were made in Italy. It was at a time when railways in various countries were becoming conscious of their speed potentialities. In both Great Britain and the United States it had been demonstrated that steam locomotives were capable of 100mph speeds. In Germany the Flying Hamburger had become the first of a number of diesel-driven streamlined trains which for the first time required 100mph speeds for timekeeping; and the diesel lead had been followed up extensively in the United States. The Italians, under the Fascist regime had witnessed something like a rejuvenation of their railways and wanted to demonstrate the fact to the world. They now set out to show that they could equal these feats with electric traction.

In 1927 the Italians had opened a new direct line, or *direttissima*, between Rome and Naples, which cut the distance between the two cities from $154\frac{1}{2}$ to $130\frac{1}{2}$ miles, reduced the summit of the line by 676ft and had a vastly better alignment, with many straight stretches and a general minimum curve radius of 50 chains. The

costly construction project involved the boring of two tunnels, both just over $4\frac{1}{2}$ miles long, and a number of shorter tunnels. From the opening of the new line the shortest time between Rome and Naples was reduced immediately from four hours 25 minutes to two hours 50 minutes; before the outbreak of war in 1939 electric traction had cut the fastest time to one hour 48 minutes.

In 1934 a second and even more costly *direttissima* was brought into operation between Florence and Bologna, on the Rome - Milan main line. The original line went over a 2,021ft summit at Pracchia, in the Apennine mountains, approached by 1 in 45 gradients and much sharp curvature. Reducing the maximum altitude to 1,070ft and cutting out the curvature and steep inclinations involved the boring of the 11.9-mile Apennine tunnel—the second longest railway tunnel, after the pair of Simplon tunnels, in the world—as well as the $4\frac{1}{2}$-mile Monte Adone tunnel and 26 others totalling 23 miles in length, and many viaducts and bridges. With the shortening of the Florence - Bologna distance from 82 to $60\frac{1}{2}$ miles the fastest schedule time between the two cities was

brought down from two hours 26 minutes to 66 minutes only, and before the outbreak of war electric traction had permitted a further reduction to 51 minutes.

Over the two realigned main lines high-speed demonstration runs were made by three-car streamlined train sets of the ETR200 type, which had been introduced in 1937. Each set was 203ft 6in in length overall, weighed $115\frac{1}{2}$ tons and was operated with current at 3,000V dc. On July 27, 1938, one of the trains covered the $130\frac{1}{2}$ miles from Rome to the Mergellina station in Naples in 83 minutes, at an average speed of 94.3mph. The achievement was handsomely beaten a year later by the run of 195.8 miles from Florence to Milan, beginning with the Florence-Bologna *direttissima,* in $115\frac{1}{4}$ minutes, at an average of 102mph for the entire distance.

For $123\frac{3}{4}$ miles continuously, from Lavino to Rogoredo, a mean speed of 109.2mph was maintained, with a maximum of 126mph, and even up the 1 in 106 gradient leading to the Apennine tunnel the lowest speed was 82mph. Though much had been done in the immediately preceding years to improve both track

Below, left and above: Three interior views of the Settebello, respectively restaurant, bar and a compartment. *All Italian State Railways*

Right: The Settebello at work in 1967. *Italian State Railways*

and signalling between Bologna and Milan, the journey probably was not without an element of risk, especially with so many level crossings along the route, but fortunately it was completed without accident.

What might have been the immediate upshot of these convincing demonstrations we do not know, for within a matter of weeks after the Florence-Milan run war had broken out, and all railway progress was halted. As in all the other countries of Western Europe that had been involved in the hostilities, and in most of which the railways had been badly damaged by bombing, many years elapsed before the tracks had been restored once again to high-speed standards. So it was not until 1953 that a new streamlined express began its career between Rome, Florence, Bologna and Milan. In the matter of luxury the new train left the record-breaking ETR200 three-car streamlined units far behind, although its six-hour timing in each direction over the $393\frac{1}{2}$ miles between Rome and Milan did not require anything like as high speeds as those of the demonstration runs already described.

But the new train offered a standard of speed and luxury far in excess of anything

previously known on Italian rails. It received the name Settebello (literally Beautiful Seven) from the fact that the formation was, and still is, seven coaches. A previous article has described a journey by the German Rheingold Express as not merely a means of getting from one place to another, but as in itself a unique travel experience. A journey in the Settebello is even more so for, although now 19 years old, the Settebello has a good claim to be regarded as the most luxurious train in Europe. And in order that the passenger might fully appreciate what he or she is being offered, the Italian State Railways exact a Settebello supplement that all but doubles the first-class fare!

The seven coaches of the Settebello are divided into three units articulated in much the same way as the high-quality stock introduced by Sir Nigel Gresley on the former London & North Eastern Railway in Britain. The Italian train has two pairs of coaches at the outer ends, each pair carried on three bogies, and one triple set in the centre on four bogies, making ten bogies in all. All axles of the outer pairs are motored, providing a total power output of 3,040hp, for 364 tons of train. The

driving cabs at both ends of the train are mounted above the coach roofs, giving an excellent view ahead.

The reason for the massive scale of the supplementary fare is evident from the moment of entering the train. The semi-circular outer end of each twin coach set, underneath the cab, is an observation lounge with individual swivelling armchairs for eight passengers ranged round the curved windows, and a settee seating four at the back of the compartment. Because the driving compartment is above the coach end, the view from the lounge is completely unobstructed. There are five compartments in each coach, each of them unusually spacious and measuring 13ft in length; against each wall is a settee seating three, and between them are four armchairs; the whole is not unlike an intimate private lounge in a four-star hotel. Occasional tables are provided, and small lockers for passengers' hand luggage. In the inner car of each unit there are toilets with showers, and a retiring room for ladies. Needless to say the coaches are soundproofed, and it is a pleasant surprise for British travellers to discover that the highly efficient air-conditioning plant was

supplied by the British firm of J Stone of Deptford (now Stone-Platt Crawley Ltd).

The group of three coaches in the middle of the train does not provide any seating, other than 56 seats in the restaurant car. The coach at one end of the set is largely occupied by a baggage room, where luggage is deposited and checks are given to passengers in similar fashion to those in a cloak room. There are also a bookstall and a souvenir shop, and an office from which one can telephone any subscriber in Italy. From the office also radio programmes or records can be broadcast throughout the train, as well as announcements of approaching stops, meal times and so on, in Italian, French, German and English.

The centre coach of the triple set accommodates an all-electric kitchen, accommodation for the train staff, a train office and a mails compartment. The third vehicle contains the restaurant and a bar flanked by pedestal seats. As in the German Rheingold, the vestibule doors in the Settebello vehicles open automatically in response to the step on a treadleplate of anyone approaching, and close automatically after the passenger or crew member

has passed through. With regular seats only in the end pairs of coaches, and some of the space in them occupied by the luxurious observation rooms, the entire seven-coach train has seating for 160 passengers only, which is another factor in the high supplementary fare.

Internal décor of the train is striking, even by Italian standards, with polished wood finishes, elegant murals, and seat, table and floor coverings in deep tan and green shades. Walls and ceilings are in restful shades of blue and grey. Externally the sleek exteriors of the coaches are in blue-and-grey livery; rubber fairings between coach and coach, like those of the former British streamlined trains of the LNER, help to present a smooth surface from end to end of the train. This is further assisted by steps to each door which are let down at stops but are folded flush into the sides while the train is running. Actually the word bello which forms a part of the train's title can also mean lucky, and this is illustrated by a motif of playing cards painted on the train sides alongside the name Settebello.

The task of driving the Settebello is much sought after by motormen, who in fact

take turns in manning it. Three of them ride with the train, the driver proper with his helper in the leading cab, and a third man in the rear cab, where he has to keep his eye on the electrical and mechanical equipment and is in telephonic communication with his two companions. Training for Settebello duties takes three months.

It is surprising that until quite recently the running times of the Settebello remained unchanged since its inception in 1953. Indeed, for quite a few years the standard six-hour timing for the journey was increased by five minutes. Now at last the overall time for the $393\frac{1}{2}$ miles has come down to $5\frac{3}{4}$ hours southbound and a minute longer northbound. Departure from Rome is at 10.50 and arrival in Milan at 16.36, and the return journey starts at 17.40 for a Rome arrival at 23.25. Stops in both directions are at Florence and Bologna, with the addition of Piacenza going north; the fastest start-to-stop run is over the 91.2 miles from Bologna to Piacenza, which has to be covered in 65 minutes, at 84.2mph average. Southbound, the Settebello is booked from Milan to Bologna, 135.5 miles, in 98 minutes at 83mph.

Above: The Settebello at Florence station, showing the driver's cab above the passengers' observation lounge.   *Italian State Railways*

Left, right and bottom right: More interior views, respectively end observation lounge, a compartment and the restaurant car.
All Italian State Railways

Below: Another view of the train on its daily Rome-Milan run.   *Italian State Railways*

The Settebello is no longer the fastest train between Milan and Rome, however. There is now a *Superrapido* two-way service which covers the whole distance without any intermediate stop in 5½ hours, leaving Rome at 08.15 and Milan at 07.55. In addition, for some time past the Settebello has had a rival in speed in the Freccia del Vesuvio (Vesuvius Arrow), which provides service in the reverse direction, starting at 09.55 from Milan and 17.40 from Rome, in the same running times as the Settebello. The *Superrapido* and the Vesuvius Arrow, though first-class only and with supplementary fares, do not equal the Settebello in luxury. A point of interest is that the Vesuvius Arrow runs non-stop between Rome and Naples to make the fastest scheduled run in Italy, of 130.3 miles in 90 minutes at 86.9mph.

Hitherto the weak link in the Rome-Milan journey has been the 195 miles between Rome and Florence, over which much curvature and steep gradients have limited speed and pulled down the average speed of the Milan-Rome run. The handicap is in process of being eased considerably by the construction, at immense cost, of four new direct sections of line totalling 75 miles in length, which will reduce the 195 miles to 157 miles. The new sections are being laid out for high speed and could make it possible to pare the Rome-Florence time to 100 minutes or less, compared with the present fastest time of about three hours. Completion of the scheme is expected in 1974, when it might become possible to cut the Rome-Milan journey of the Settebello to 4½ hours—two-thirds only of the time taken when the train began to run in 1953.

THE TALGOS

AT THE BEGINNING of 1942 railway rolling stock history was made when Lieutenant-Colonel Alejandro Goicoechea, of the Spanish Army, introduced an entirely new type of train and demonstrated it on the Madrid - Leganes section of the National Western Andaluces Railway. The new rolling stock formed a type of articulated train in which all the vehicles except the first, which had two axles, were carried on a single pair of wheels only, and the wheels were independently suspended with no solid rotating axles linking each pair. The leading end of each coach was supported by the rear end of the vehicle ahead; inter-coach couplings in the form of long underframes extended from the outer ends of each axle to the centre of the axle ahead. The demonstration was attended by representatives of the technical departments of various Spanish railways and of the Spanish Government.

The experimental train comprised a four-wheel diesel motorcoach with seven trailers, and was of considerably lower height above rail than conventional trains. However, the major advantage claimed by the inventor was drastically reduced weight, and although war conditions had prevented use of all the lightweight constructional materials intended, the weight of the prototype train amounted to a mere 220lb for each passenger seat, compared with 1,000lb and sometimes considerably more for an ordinary passenger coach. A further advantage foreseen by the designer was that the use of independently mounted wheels, which could be shifted on the axles more readily than normal wheels, might permit running through break-of-gauge stations between the Spanish 5ft 6in gauge and neighbouring 4ft 8½in-gauge lines without changing trains or changing bogies. In the event, it was not until fairly recently that the automatic gauge-adjustment facility became actual fact. A serious objection to the new type of train was that it could run in reverse only at very low speeds, so that terminals had to incorporate an extensive Y-shaped layout to enable the train to be turned.

In the year following the first appearance of the train there were more extended trials over the main lines of the Madrid Zaragoza & Alicante Railway and the Northern Railway between Madrid and Barcelona and Bilbao respectively. On one of the test runs, it is recorded, the 132 miles from Valladolid to Miranda del Ebro were covered at an average speed of 62mph, and a maximum speed of 81mph was reached.

Doubtless because of conditions prevailing during and immediately after the 1939-45 war, several years passed before anything more was heard of the Spanish articulated lightweight train. Attention became focused on it once again in 1948, however, in the United States, when a full-size model of a train of this type was exhibited at the 1948 Railroad Fair in Chicago. The trade fair presentation was followed in April 1949 by a demonstration run of one of the new-type trains, by then named 'Talgo', over the lines of the

Below: Wheelset of the dual-gauge Talgo train showing the wheels in broad-gauge setting.
Patentes Talgo SA

Right: Bar scene in the Catalan Talgo.
Patentes Talgo SA

Delaware, Lackawanna & Western Railroad.

'Talgo' is derived from **T**ren **A**rticulado **L**igero—lightweight articulated train, **Goi**coechea—the inventor, and **O**riol—the family which underwrote the initial development. The demonstration American train was built by the American Car & Foundry Company, which later received from the Spanish National Railways an order for two complete Talgo trains.

The American train was exhibited at a time when lightweight trains of various types were being developed in the USA for fast and frequent inter-city services. After the first American Talgo train entered service on the Delaware, Lackawanna & Western RR, another was built for the Rock Island Railroad, but it finished its career on the Chicago-Joliet suburban service. A still later advanced version of the Talgo, named *John Quincy Adams*, was operated over the New York, New Haven & Hartford Railroad; it was powered by two Fairbanks-Morse 1,200hp diesel-electric locomotives, one at each end of the train, which partly overcame the difficulty of non-reversibility. The push - and - pull version is said to have provided even rougher riding than the other American Talgos.

Rough riding over relatively poorly maintained track was probably a major reason why the Talgo principle never found acceptance in the USA. Another, undoubtedly, was the difficulty of altering the formation of a Talgo train to meet varying traffic demands. There was similar lack of response in several other countries which tried out the new type of rolling stock, notably Germany, Sweden and Argentina, and only in Spain was the Talgo system developed for regular, though limited, commercial service.

The first production version of the Spanish Talgo train was made up of a number of standard single-axle units arranged as passenger saloons, baggage vans, kitchen / service units and observation lounges, with the necessary motive power unit(s). The small-diameter wheels, at the rear end of each coach unit revolved independently on roller bearings on the stubs of a drop-centre axle, giving the exceptionally low coach floor height of only 2ft 9in above rail level. The front end of each coach unit is supported by two pin-and-socket bearers above the axle of the unit ahead and a third pin-and-socket arrangement provides inter-unit coupling, with traction loads taken through a central drawbar. Each two-wheel unit has a front dolly axle, which can be lowered to support the front end when necessary for uncoupling the unit for shunting and other purposes. Coil springs and hydraulic dampers comprise vertical suspension and lateral movements are controlled by damped torsion bars. As conventional railway braking is inadmissible on Talgo stock, the continuous air-brakes follow road vehicle practice, with brake drums and internal - expanding shoes. Air conditioning is provided throughout each train.

Although production trains are heavier than the early experimental sets, the Talgo still ranks as a very lightweight train. A standard passenger unit with 16 airline-type reclining seats measures just over 20ft long and weighs a fraction under 3 tons. The service trailer section containing kitchen, lavatories and air-conditiong plant weighs about 4½ tons and the baggage-van section weighs 2¾ tons. An observation section designed to run at the rear of each train provides 14 seats in a length of 27½ft and a weight of 3.7 tons. Hence, the original Spanish Talgo trains for revenue service, comprising two five-unit sections and an observation unit accommodating 142 passengers, their baggage and kitchen service, had a tare weight of about 40 tons, or about 102½ tons with 800hp (later 900hp) diesel-electric locomotive.

Above: The Catalan Talgo headed by SNCF diesel-electric locomotive BB 67400, with the Alps as a backdrop. *'La Vie du Rail'*

Left & left lower: Train staff compartment and a coach interior on the Catalan Talgo. *Both Patentes Talgo SA*

Below: Demonstration Talgo train built in America in 1949 by American Car & Foundry company, which also built two trains for RENFE in Spain. *ACF Industries Inc*

The very low height (9ft) of the Talgo stock was not matched by the locomotives used to haul the earliest trains. The result was a rather incongruous appearance because locomotives towered above the rest of the train. In later sets, however, locomotives were produced to the same profile as the coaches, to the great benefit of general appearance. Various other developments during the 20-odd years since the first Talgos entered service, including the substitution of disc for drum brakes, increased motive power, and variable track gauge, have left the basic Talgo concept very much intact.

The Mark III stock introduced in 1965 provides considerably improved train make-up flexibility, with a standard train of 15 vehicles (including two kitchen/bar units and one luggage van) taking 96 first-class and 256 second-class passengers in a tare weight of about 135 tons. The 2,400hp Bo-Bo locomotive adds about 73 tons.

The first two Talgo trains in Spain went into regular revenue service in 1950, running three times weekly in each direction between Madrid and the French frontier at Irun, where they connected with the French Pyrenees-Cote d'Argent Express to and from Paris. Accommodation was in open saloons, and the service was classed train-de-luxe, accessible only to first-class passengers at supplementary fares. It took the earlier route via Valladolid between Madrid and Burgos, covering the 396 miles between Madrid and Irun in just under $8\frac{1}{2}$ hours, which was considerably faster than any other train at that time; it provided a service between Madrid and Paris six hours quicker than previously by night train through Spain connecting with the daytime SNCF Sud Express between Hendaye and Paris. After the opening in 1968 of the 175-mile direct line between Madrid and Burgos, which shortened the distance by 61 miles, there were further substantial accelerations. By 1960 a third Talgo train had been brought into service to link Madrid with Zaragoza and Barcelona.

The success of the new luxury trains influenced the Spanish National Railways (RENFE) decision to establish a network of similar services throughout Spain. Orders were placed for 100 Talgo units and ten diesel-hydraulic locomotives, half from the German firm Krauss-Maffei and half from Spanish Babcock & Wilcox in Bilbao. The original trains were altered to carry both first- and second-class passengers, and transferred to the Madrid-Valencia line via Cuenca. The later Talgo sets are fully reversible, though the locomotives still require to be turned and transferred to the opposite end of the train at terminals.

The latest Talgo development is of great interest, as for the first time it brings one of the trains across the frontier into France, and in fact even beyond into Switzerland. The train is Le Catalan, which runs between Barcelona and Port Bou, Cerbere, Narbonne, Avignon, Grenoble, Chambéry, Aix-les-Bains and Geneva. The unusual feature of the 533-mile journey is that, as mentioned earlier, as far as the Spanish frontier at Port Bou it is over the Spanish gauge of 5ft 6in, and between Port Bou and Geneva it is over the general European gauge of 4ft 8½in. Between the two, the wheel spacing on the axles of the coaches is altered to adjust to the new gauge, as the train runs over a special equipment in a building at Port Bou.

On arrival at Port Bou, the wide-gauge diesel locomotive which has brought the nine-unit Le Catalan from Barcelona is uncoupled and run into a siding and a Spanish shunter is attached to the back of the train to push it slowly through the wheel - adjusting equipment. The apparatus is arranged automatically to make the adjustment as each coach passes, first easing the weight off the wheels, then releasing locks that hold the wheels in position on the axles, sliding the wheels on the axles to the narrower gauge, and locking them in the new position. A waiting standard - gauge diesel is attached to the head of the train and draws it through the frontier tunnel into the French station at Cerbére. The process is reversed in the opposite direction. The Talgo locomotives used on the standard-gauge section of the service are unique in that, like the train, they are RENFE property, yet they spend their whole working lives outside Spain.

The gauge - changing process is smooth and some passengers probably remain unaware of what is happening. Frontier arrangements generally are expeditious, the time taken between arrival and departure, including customs, passport examination and the gauge adjustment, totals less than half an hour. In the northbound direction, Le Catalan leaves Barcelona at 09.45 and reaches the Cornavin station in Geneva at 19.38; southbound, the Geneva departure is at 10.40 and the Barcelona arrival at 20.30.

Le Catalan is first-class only and is now in the Trans - Europe - Express (TEE) network, warranting appropriate fare supplements. There have been proposals for a similar Talgo service between Madrid and Paris, with gauge - changing at Irun or Hendaye, but now that a speed of 125mph is being reached by the SNCF on some sections between Bordeaux and Paris, the very lightweight Talgo stock, which is generally limited to a maximum of well under 100mph, would no longer be competitive in speed.

In Spain, in addition to the first-class-only Le Catalan, there are six daily Talgo services, all over considerable distances, and now admitting second-class as well as first-class passengers; in both classes supplementary fares are charged. There are two Talgos in each direction daily between Madrid and Irun, (saving more than two hours over the standard timing of about 8½ hours), one between Madrid and Cadiz (452 miles) one between Madrid and Barcelona (429 miles), one between Madrid and Malaga (394 miles) and one between Madrid and Valencia.

Overall speeds of most of the Talgo services, stops included, are generally over 50mph and they are considerably faster than all other expresses over the same routes, except the TER trains—the 1,700hp four - car diesel - hydraulic multiple units first introduced in 1965, which are now fairly numerous. But the Talgo trains for the first time have introduced into Spanish timetables lengthy runs timed at over a mile - a - minute from start to stop; for example, Madrid - Zaragoza, 211 miles in 193 minutes (65.7mph); Madrid-Burgos, 178 miles in 165 minutes (64.7mph); and Madrid-Linares, 196 miles in 193 minutes (61mph). The Talgo train thus has helped to transform long-distance Spanish travel both in speed and quality of service.

Above: The Catalan Talgo on the standard-gauge track alongside the gauge-change shed at Port Bou. *Patentes Talgo SA*

Right: RENFE standard-gauge diesel-hydraulic locomotive heads the Catalan Talgo out of Geneva. *'La Vie du Rail'*

Top right & below right: Stainless steel kitchen and restaurant of the Catalan Talgo. *Both Patentes Talgo SA*

Centre right: Internal network of RENFE Talgo services. *Patentes Talgo SA*

Overleaf: West German Class 38 (ex-Prussian Railways P8) No 038-039-4 leaving Horb for Eutingen in August 1970. *R Bastin*

BAO

IRUN

SAN SEBASTIAN

VITORIA

BARCELONA

MIRANDA

BURGOS

TARRAGONA

VALLADOLID

ZARAGOZA

AVILA

GUADALAJARA

MADRID

CORDOBA

CUENCA

SEVILLA

VALENCIA

CADIZ

**PRESENT DAY ITINERARIES OF TALGO
ON THE SPANISH TRACKS**

THE ORIENT EXPRESS

IN THESE DAYS of package holidays by air and coach and the ever-present motor car, one wonders why people still travel long distances by train. Yet, in Europe proper the railways are still crowded and especially in the more easterly countries the trains are so full that the population seems to be continually on the move. Mainly, people travel by rail for the purely practical reasons of speed, cost and convenience. The business man wanting to get from city to city in comfort knows that the luxury trains of Europe will enable him to do this to time and that his schedule will not be disturbed by bad weather, while the student moving on to discover new worlds finds travel cheaper. Certainly for the inhabitants of the more socialistic countries with their lack of other means of transport and the advantage of fantastically cheap fares, trains are essential. Good trains in Europe are good, others are often crowded and grubby with long waits at stations which can be exasperating (or exhilarating if you are an enthusiast)—and some combine the two.

What is left of the old Orient Express combines all these factors and today's train survives in two forms—the Orient Express provides a fast luxurious service to Munich overnight from Paris and then on to Vienna with a slower ride on to Budapest and Bucharest, while the Direct Orient gives a similar service to Milan and then to Belgrade, Athens or Istanbul. It is the latter which is the poor relation but still remains the romantic remnant of the once-fabulous luxury train of fact and fiction.

The original Orient Express—and indeed an entirely new concept of Continental

Top: Gare de Lyon in Paris, western starting point of the Simplon Orient. *P B Whitehouse*

Above: Sleeping car for Athens on the Direct Orient. *P B Whitehouse*

Right: The Orient Express passing a local freight train in Turkey. *P B Whitehouse*

Below: Turkish locomotive from the Direct Orient Express at Halkali shed, Istanbul. *P B Whitehouse*

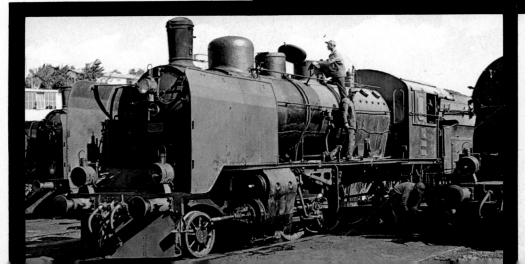

travel—was born on June 5, 1883. The train left the Gare de l'Est in Paris as the first of the great fleet of international expresses operated by the Wagons-Lits Company set out in the direction of Constantinople (now Istanbul). At that time there was no continuous rail route to Constantinople and the fast Orient Express (quite short, being made up of two or three sleepers and a dining car, plus two luggage-cum-mail vans) ran twice a week to Giurgin, a small Roumanian port on the Danube. It ran via Munich, Vienna and Budapest. From Giurgin steamers took passengers over to the Bulgarian port of Ruse where they embarked in another train for a seven-hour journey to Varna on the Black Sea; there they found yet another steamer to take them on their 15-hour trip to Constantinople. The running time, Paris to Constantinople was 81 hours 40 minutes.

Looking back at that period of history and remembering that it *was* luxurious travel and that servants and service were the norm, it conjures up an atmosphere of spice and adventure. The quality of food and drink was superb, even if according to contemporary reports the port of Varna left something to be desired. It is said that facilities there, for embarking passengers and the transfer to the ship, were made 'by means of rough boats steered by boisterous boat-men who waited at the foot of a muddy bank in open country'.

It took only two years more to bring in another and even more adventurous route when a new line from Budapest to Constantinople via Belgrade was completed as far as Nis in Serbia. The Wagons-Lits Company signed an agreement with the Serbian government to allow a weekly service to operate to Nis with trains limited in weight to 100 tonnes normally and 80 tonnes in bad weather or temperatures six degrees below zero. (The reduction was made by omitting the sleeping car!) As the rails terminated at Nis the journey through the fantastic gorge and onwards over the hills to the far side of Bulgaria was made by horse and carriage. The next station was Philippopolis (now Plovdiv) where trains ran through to Constantinople.

On June 5, 1889 the new Orient Express made its first through journey, taking 67 hours and 35 minutes. It ran over the original route via Bulgaria, and the author George D Behrend in his excellent history of the Wagons-Lits Company tells us that before arrangements could be completed an audience with Prince Ferdinand was necessary. Strict court etiquette required that one should be in uniform to be received by the Prince and the Wagons Lits representative lacking any kind of uniform borrowed that of a captain of the Prince's own police. At this the Prince is said to have remarked—'What a ridiculous country!'

In 1895 a new bridge was completed on the Danube at Fatesti in Roumania, which allowed a through route to that country's Black Sea port of Constantza and gave the Orient Express a new rail/steamer service to Constantinople with only one change. The train continued to run over the two routes until 1914—four times a week over the rail line via Belgrade and Sofia and three times on the 'maritime' route via Bucharest and Constantza. The Fatesti

FROM THE THAMES TO THE BLACK SEA
SIMPLON-ORIENT EXPRESS 1938–1939 TRAINS Magazine – Bob Wegner

Based upon information furnished by Cie Internationale des Wagons-Lits et des Grands Express Europeens

route gave a long sea voyage, taking twenty seven hours against fifteen.

Those days prior to the outbreak of the first world war were the halcyon days of the Orient Express and certainly of the Wagons-Lits trains. Princes, aristocrats, statesmen and other celebrities travelled on the services and tourism for the rich was on its way. It cost £58 to make the trip out by Belgrade and Sofia and back via Constantza, or from London via Ostend or Paris at proportionate rates. This was all-in except for transport between stations and hotels and the transport of luggage.

In 1898 when the Wagons-Lits Company celebrated its Silver Jubilee the Orient Express was rejuvenated and for the first time 'cabinets de toilettes' were installed between each pair of compartments with the exception of the two at one end, and the restaurant car had twelve armchairs in a lounge next to the restaurant saloon. The coaches were constructed of varnished teak with mahogany interiors and seats were upholstered in thick plush. All floors in the passenger vehicles were heavily carpeted and, as might be expected, the quality of the food and service was still excellent.

In 1906 Europe provided one of the World's New Wonders in the opening of the Simplon Tunnel—a length of $12\frac{1}{4}$ miles through the mountains between Brig in Switzerland and Domodossola in Italy and immediately afterwards a new sleeping-car train from Calais and Paris began running through to Milan; in 1907 it was extended to Venice and in 1912 to Trieste. It began as a tri-weekly train, becoming daily by

the time the Trieste portion came into service. As this route shortened the best of the existing Orient Express routes by 263 miles, it was an obvious way to travel, but although the idea was put forward at the June 1906 International Timetable Convention at Bremen it had to be shelved due to the refusal of the Austrian-Hungarian Government to open the Italian-Croatian frontier post at Cormons. This situation was remedied at Versailles when the victorious Allies laid down, among other momentous matters, the routes for the de luxe trains of the new era. They were determined that adequate and suitable communication should exist between western and central or eastern Europe without passing through Germany or Austria. Thus, strange as it might seem, it was the politicians and not the Wagons-Lits Company who created the new Simplon Orient Express.

The new service was inaugurated in 1919, running through to Bucharest and the next year to Constantinople. The train took 96 hours 30 minutes, of which over 15 hours were taken up with frontier and customs formalities. In 1920 a further new service came into operation—the section to Athens which had been made possible by the completion of the Greek railway system between Larissa and Thessaloniki during the Macedonian campaign in 1916.

The aftermath of the war of 1914-18 brought operational problems and it was 1932 before the old route was reopened via the Arlburg Tunnel in Switzerland and renamed the Arlburg-Orient Express. But it was the faster Simplon-Orient Express

Above: An evening stop at Sirkeci station in Istanbul, Turkey. *P B Whitehouse*

Left: Another view of Sirkeci station as the arrival of the Direct Orient Express is due. *P B Whitehouse*

Left below: Crest of Cie Internationale des Wagons-Lits from Orient Express sleeping car. *P B Whitehouse*

which caught both the practical and fanciful minds of the post-war generation and the train prospered, running in the later days composed entirely of Wagons-Lits stock. There was even a through coach from Boulogne to Istanbul with a cross-channel connection from London. In addition to the daily through sleepers between Paris-Athens and Paris-Istanbul, a daily Paris-Bucharest sleeper was the rule and by 1930 this latter service was once again extended to Constantza, where a connection was made with the steam packet boat as before. This service was short lived and operations ceased again with the coming of the war in 1939.

Although not strictly part of the story of the Orient Express, it is of interest that the train from 1930 onwards had (and still has) an inter-continental extension, or connection running east from Haydarpasa station across the Bosphorus in Istanbul. In the 1930s a special boat in charge of a Wagons-Lits/Cook interpreter carried through passengers between the two terminal points. The eastward-running train carried (and still carries) the romantic name of the Taurus Express taking through sleepers to Iraq and the Lebanon. This route has now been improved in that there are now through rail connections as far as Baghdad. Connections also were (and are) available to Tehran in Persia.

There is no doubt that both in fact and fiction the Orient Express grew into an institution—it was the civilised gateway to the Near East and provided a business link between two totally different forms of life and civilisation, giving the traveller time to acclimatise en route. Because of the air of excitement and mystery the train has always attracted thriller writers and their leading characters, including such well-known figures as Agatha Christie's Hercule Poirot, Flemming's James Bond and of course Graham Greene's novel itself entitled *Orient Express*. Film makers also used the train—usually full of spies—the two epics probably being the pre-war *The Lady Vanishes* and, a quarter of a century later, the James Bond film *From Russia with Love* in which a considerable part of the action takes place on the Orient Express between Istanbul Sirkeci station and Italy.

As a matter of fact no-one has ever been known to have been murdered on the train, although people *have* disappeared under mysterious circumstances. It certainly is not difficult to understand *that,* for, with the number of diplomats and couriers using the train, a great deal of intrigue must have taken place. This is certainly so when one remembers that even during the winter of 1939 in the period of the 'Phoney War' the Simplon Orient ran for a while with through sleepers coming on as usual for Berlin at Belgrade! George Behrend tells us that the first world war notice 'les Orielles de l'Ennemi vous ecoutant' was once more posted up in French trains and that maybe this was a little unnerving in the Paris Simplon Orient Express cars when it was possible to *see* the enemies' ears wagging! These fantastic arrangements came to an end in 1940.

After a gap of about five and a half years the trains began to run again, but with East/West tension things could never be the same as in the past. It took more than ten years for things to settle down, but the palmy days had gone—what was once an imperious express became a stopping service once the border with Jugoslavia had been reached. By 1947 there was a service through from Paris to Istanbul again, with a running time almost double that of 1939—105 hours—but it was not possible to get through to Athens before 1950. The delay was due in the main to the Communist rebellion and the destruction of the railway between Athens and Saloniki. The Istanbul service suffered badly between 1948 and the early 1950s due mainly to Bulgarian/Turkish border troubles and it was not until 1957 that the Simplon Orient resumed a thrice-weekly service—and even then under orders to have the blinds down running through Bulgaria.

By the early 1960s the trains were becoming what is now known as rationalised—that is, cut back and giving a poorer service. This was almost inevitable, for suspicion was still the by-word at the East/West frontiers. No longer did the Wagons-Lits cars from Berlin connect with the Simplon Orient at Belgrade; as it was entirely within the Communist orbit this section of the train—though still called the Balt Orient Express—had nothing to do with Wagons-Lits, using only coaches from the various countries through which it passed. There were also problems between Varna and Bucharest. This period was perhaps even better for the thriller writers and there were certainly plenty of real incidents—mainly concerning refugees trying to get out to the west. One typical instance was that of a Hungarian refugee travelling from Budapest to Austria on the spring plank of a bogie only to be sniffed out by Hungarian police dogs at the border.

In 1962 the once-proud Simplon-Orient Express disappeared from the time tables and was replaced by the new Direct Orient Express on a slower schedule with through Wagons-Lits cars Paris (Gare de Lyon) to Athens (three days a week) and Istanbul (two days a week). Today the Direct Orient Express runs daily to Belgrade where it joins the Tauern Orient Express from Munich plus coaches from the Eastern bloc. This combined train runs as the Athens Express or the Marmara Express, according to destination, but in each case the through Paris to Athens or Paris to Istanbul vehicles carry the proud boast, Direct Orient Express.

Today's Direct Orient Express is only supposed to carry sleeping passengers beyond Belgrade; the Simplon Express, which also carries Wagons-Lits cars, caters for a daily Paris-Belgrade service. The Direct Orient is a fast train as far as Milan and semi-fast from there on, with a restaurant car (Wagons-Lits) running only from Paris to Milan and from the Turkish border to Istanbul. Wagons-Lits sleeping car attendants are French to Venice, Jugoslavian to Belgrade and Bulgarian to Istanbul.

As East-West relations tempered, 1965 saw the return of the Paris-Budapest service—now entitled the Orient Express. It is an excellent and fast overnight train from Paris to Vienna, leaving Paris (Gare

de l'Est) at 22.15 and arriving at Vienna West at 14.40 the next day. The train then continues on to Budapest, arriving at 19.41, then overnight to Bucharest. The Wagons-Lits company uses some of its very best sleepers on this train, as it now ranks as a European Inter-City express.

But what of the old thrill and romance is left? In many ways a great deal, for Vienna, Budapest and Istanbul are still fine cities with hospitable people and Central Europe is still Central Europe. On the route of the Orient Express there is really first-class comfort in Wagons-Lits vehicles and the Direct Orient is certainly comfortable enough. The former train goes thoroughly into the Iron Curtain with its barbed wire and watch towers at the Hungarian frontier, and the latter travels via Jugoslavia and Bulgaria, where the frontier officials still visit compartments by night. The Direct Orient also poses the problem of foraging for oneself in Italy, Jugoslavia and Bulgaria (quite easy if one plans ahead) but compensates with a glorious Turkish Wagons-Lits diner, built in Birmingham in 1924, still with its leather armchairs and solid-fuel cooking range. In both cases the clean, smart and courteous Wagons-Lits attendants are on hand, which means—'bon voyage'.

One final word for those contemplating the journey or journeys; read it up well beforehand—particularly in Behrend's 'Grand European Expresses' and 'Turkish Steam Travel'—you won't regret it.

Top: Direct Orient Express double-headed by two French-built 2-8-0s on the electrified Turkish section near Istanbul. *P B Whitehouse*

Above: Outside Belgrade loco shed in Jugoslavia, with Pacifics from the Direct Orient in foreground. *P B Whitehouse*

Left: Eastern terminus of the Direct Orient Express, Istanbul Sirkeci station, with suburban emu on right. *P B Whitehouse*

Below: Ex Serbian Railways 2-6-2 outside the Belgrade loco shed. *P B Whitehouse*

TRANS EUROPE EXPRESS

Inset: Coach-side nameboard of the DB Rheingold Hook of Holland-Milan TEE.
J Topham

The SNCF Mistral Paris-Marseilles TEE in the Rhone Valley somewhere south of Lyons.
French National Railways

THE SIGHT OF a train of red-and-cream coaches inscribed 'Trans Europ Express' speeding through Western European countryside has romantic associations. To the uninformed it might mean exciting journeys to the far corners of Europe in the company of La Madonna des Sleepings, beautiful women spies, international crooks or at least Queen's Messengers, all travelling by *wagon-lits* in a *grand express européen* operated or managed by the Compagnie Internationale des Wagons-Lits. Trans Europ Expresses (the absence of final e in Europ emphasises their truly international character) are quite different. They might still occasionally convey spies but they do not include *wagons-lits* as they are day trains mostly making only a few hours' journey, and they run between big cities in Western Europe, remote from the countries where most rail travellers' adventures are supposed to have taken place. (Their biggest thrill must have been in 1929 when the Paris-Istanbul Simplon Orient Express was snowbound for several days in Turkey.)

The *grand express européen* (or *train-de-luxe* in its most exclusive form) with two or three exceptions is no longer particularly grand nor luxurious and usually includes ordinary sit-up-all-night coaches as well as sleeping cars. That is mainly because those who can afford it find air

travel more convenient—but not more comfortable—than by sleeping-car over long distances, say over 900 miles. But for day travel over shorter distances, when the train can compete with air and road, the Trans Europ Express (TEE for short) is the most luxurious, comfortable and safe way.

While European air services began to develop soon after the 1939-45 war ended, for various reasons the attractiveness of long-distance rail travel did not increase. For economic reasons railways tended to concentrate on increasing train loads; there were still too few powerful diesel locomotives in service; and funds for electrification were hard to obtain—even when managements were convinced of the overall advantages of electric traction. Express, and more particularly international, trains tended to become longer and slower than in 1939. Meanwhile, roads generally were improved, motorways were being built and motorcars were increasing in power and comfort. The railways were losing an important part of their international customers for both night and day travel.

By 1950 the war damage to the French National Railways (SNCF) system had been made good and the electrified lines extended far enough for a start in earnest on wholesale long-distance passenger

accelerations (then mostly of internal services); the process has continued ever since. One of the earliest results was the Paris-Lyons-Marseilles Mistral, which has since become a TEE. The German Federal (DB), Italian State (FS), Belgian National (SNCB) and Netherlands (NS) systems also were recovering fast. Because of their longer distances the DB and FS introduced expresses that ran at creditably high speeds in view of the recent damage to track and structures. But the international train services for the first-class passenger—the growing market of businessmen, diplomatists and functionaries of the new supra-national organisations—were still not prospering.

About that time Dr F Q den Hollander, chairman and formerly general manager of the NS and president of the Office for Research & Experiments of the International Union of Railways (UIC), identified himself with the concept of the high-speed international long-distance day train for travel on business—the Trans Europ Express, of which he is the founder. Den Hollander appreciated before his contemporaries the advantages of speed and good connections at nodal points, and the possibilities of diesel traction. The NS had already led the way in these matters, although its speeds are restricted by local conditions and its traffic density has since justified replacement of diesel by electric traction.

The characteristics of the TEE are high speed, short stops at commercially important stations, passage of frontier stations without stopping (or with minimal stops to enable frontier control staffs to entrain or alight) and formalities conducted in the train, maximum comfort, meal and other refreshment service at passengers' seats, limited accommodation and obligatory seat reservation, with reservation fee included in a fare supplement. TEE trains have their own livery of red below and cream above the waist and are symbolised by their own logotype. TEE services are listed separately in all European railway timetables.

The first TEEs started to run in the summer of 1957. The size of the network in the 1957-58 winter service is seen in the table. Comparison with the table of winter 1971-72 services shows not only growth but also the trend to replace diesel multiple-units by trains hauled by electric locomotives. Electrification of DB, SNCB and SNCF main lines has been rapid during the past fifteen years. The fixed-formation multiple-unit train has the disadvantage of being inelastic, that is, it cannot be 'strengthened' by adding another coach or two when there is a sudden traffic demand. All that is possible is to couple up another full unit and work them together, as has been done with the Cisalpin (Paris-Milan) six-car electric multiple-unit train, for example. Each six-car unit accommodates 168 passengers.

A longer TEE mu of smaller capacity is the DB diesel working the Mediolanum between Milan and Munich via Verona and Innsbruck; when made up by inclusion of an extra trailer car to eight vehicles it contains only 155 seats, apart from the 44 in the restaurant. This compares with the 520 seats, apart from those in the two separate restaurant cars, in the full-length, 15-coach Mistral between Paris and Marseilles, beyond which a smaller portion continues to Nice.

The 1974-75 table shows a number of TEEs that run wholly within France and Federal Germany. They afford international service in that seats can be reserved by the TEE telex service, though connections with other TEEs cannot be guaranteed. They also rank as TEEs because the standard of their appointments is that prescribed. Some of the TEEs running within and to and from Germany form part of the DB Intercity Netz of two-hourly services between major German centres. The famous FS Settebello emu from Rome to Milan and back via Florence in a day is fast and luxurious but it does not rank as a TEE because the stock, now ageing, does not achieve TEE standards. The once glamorous and luxurious Paris-Calais Flèche d'Or, the French equivalent of the London-Dover Golden Arrow, has long ceased to attract the TEE class of passenger or to offer appropriate comfort.

Unique among TEEs is the Edelweiss, which runs between Amsterdam and

Zurich via the Hague, Rotterdam, Antwerp, Brussels, Luxembourg, Strasbourg and Basle through five countries and over the NS, SNCB, Luxembourg (CFL), SNCF and Swiss Federal (SBB) railways. The Edelweiss originated before the 1939-45 war as a steam-hauled Pullman train. From its rebirth in 1957 as one of the original TEEs it has been worked by Dutch/Swiss-built diesel push-and-pull trains, the only ones of their kind. Each set consists of a combined power and baggage car and three passenger vehicles seating 114 in side-corridor compartments and open saloons, plus 32 in the restaurant. The power unit remains at one end.

The entire route of the Edelweiss has been electrified since 1957 but at four different voltages: NS 1.5kV, SNCB 3kV, CFL 3kV to Luxembourg City and thereafter 25kV, SNCF 25kV and SBB 15kV. Its four-car sets are ageing; when they are withdrawn they are likely to be succeeded by the six-car electric sets now working the Cisalpin between Paris and Milan and also including in its working roster the Gottardo and Ticino TEEs between Milan and Zurich and Basle. These sets are equipped for the four voltages as they run over SNCF 1.5kV and 25kV lines from Paris to the Swiss frontier at Vallorbe, SBB 15kV onwards through the Simplon Tunnel to Domodossola in Italy and thence FS 3kV to

Milan and 3kV and 15kV on the Gottardo and Ticino trips.

To improve riding over inferior track and on curvaceous routes the Spanish National Railways (RENFE) about 20 years ago adopted for some of its fast services (Talgo trains) the Talgo system of single-axle low-hung vehicles devised by Patentes Talgo SA. The system is claimed to afford better comfort, although improvements in the RENFE track and re-alignment to eliminate curves in the past ten years now allow good riding in conventional vehicles. Talgo trains are light in weight and are hauled in Spain by special Talgo diesel-electric locomotives. Partly to publicise Talgo trains abroad, the Spanish government arranged for a Talgo TEE, the Catalan Talgo, to run between Barcelona and Geneva via the frontier at Port Bou, Narbonne, Avignon, Grenoble and Aix-les-Bains. Because the RENFE track gauge is 5ft 6in the special train-sets are shunted over a Patentes Talgo device adjoining Port Bou station which moves the wheels on their axles inwards to 4ft 8½in gauge when running from the RENFE on to the SNCF standard-gauge track and vice versa. Passengers remain in the train during the change of gauge.

The Catalan Talgo is hauled in France by standard diesel locomotives, and has occasionally been headed by SNCF elec-

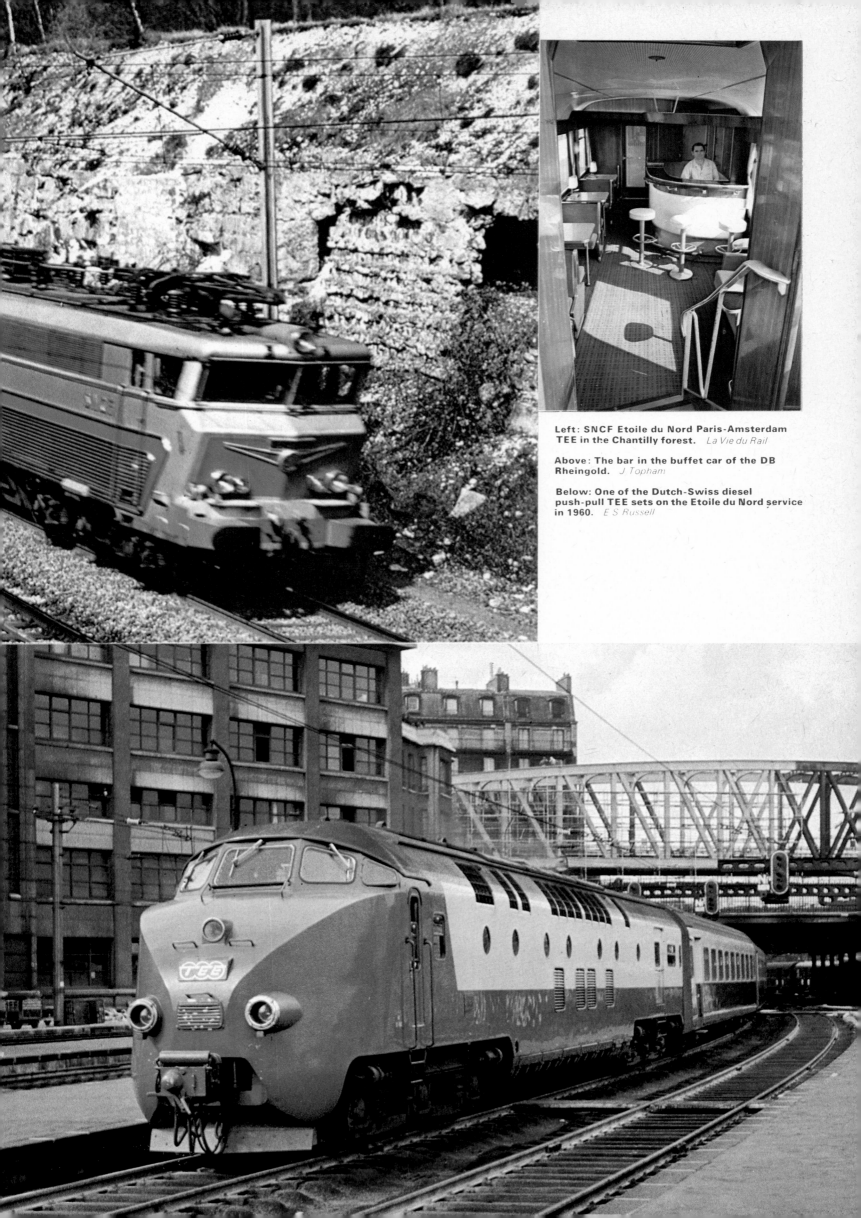

Left: SNCF Etoile du Nord Paris-Amsterdam TEE in the Chantilly forest. *La Vie du Rail*

Above: The bar in the buffet car of the DB Rheingold. *J Topham*

Below: One of the Dutch-Swiss diesel push-pull TEE sets on the Etoile du Nord service in 1960. *E S Russell*

tric locomotives over the electrified part of the route, though for a time it was hauled by a RENFE diesel fitted with standard-gauge bogies. This service provides 10-hour daytime journeys between Barcelona and Geneva without the change of train at the break of gauge that is necessary with other services between Spain and France and beyond. It is doubtful, however, whether the Talgo principle will be applied to other fast trains outside Spain, even if the Talgo trains survive there, largely because there are doubts as to the stability of Talgo vehicles at considerably higher speeds than are attained by the Catalan Talgo in France.

Also the successor of a well-known pre-1939 service is the DB's Rheingold. The main train runs between Amsterdam (with a through portion from and to the Hook of Holland that connects with the Harwich-Hook night sailings) on the one hand, and Geneva on the other. There are through vehicles from Amsterdam, the Hook and Hanover to Munich, Milan and Chur (for Eastern Switzerland). Its route follows the Rhine the whole way via Arnhem, Dusseldorf, Cologne, Mainz, Karlsruhe, etc. The vehicles to/from Munich and Hanover are transferred between the Rheingold and the Rheinpfeil express (not a TEE) at Duisburg, and the Chur and Milan (via the Gotthard line) vehicles are detached from and coupled up with the main train in Basle SBB station. The Rheingold affords a 25-hour journey from London Liverpool Street to Milan, reached at 21.00. It differs from most other TEEs in catering for tourists as well as business travellers, and in consisting of several portions

It runs at high speeds along the Rhine valley, apart from the tortuous section through the Rhine gorge between Bingen and Koblenz. The route is electrified throughout. The 10-minute stops in each direction at Emmerich near the German-Dutch frontier are for changing electric locomotives (NS 1.5kV and DB 15kV); the comparatively long stops at Duisburg are for marshalling and the 16-minute stop at Basle mainly for marshalling; what might be considered the German-Swiss 'frontier' stop is at Basle Badischer (Baden) station, and frontier formalities are undertaken in the train. The Rheingold's principal TEE characteristic is comfort; the rolling stock is all air-conditioned and includes 'vista-dome' cars affording views from high-level glass-roofed saloons. The tradition of luxury in the Rheingold dates from its origin between the wars, when the then German State Railway introduced the steam-hauled Rheingold that consisted of saloon cars between Holland and Switzerland.

Since its reintroduction after World War II and subsequent promotion to TEE rank the Rheingold has increased in comfort and speed. Similar stock used in other DB TEEs is often termed 'Rheingold type' though it does not include vista-dome cars. The current timetable includes the Bremen-Hanover-Frankfurt-Basle-Milan service named Roland, and the

Left: Standard locomotive for DB electrically hauled TEE trains is the Co-Co 103 class which has a continuous output of around 8,000hp. *DB Film Archiv*

Below: The Cisalpin Milan-Paris electric multiple-unit TEE, at Paris Gare de Lyon. *John Adams*

Bottom: Restaurant coach interior of the Rheingold train. *J Topham*

This page far left: Inside the observation coach of the Rheingold. *J Topham*

Left: Inside the cab of the DB Bo-Bo Class 110 electric locomotive the earlier standard TEE engine. *J Topham*

Bottom: Servicing a two-car FS diesel-electric train as used on TEE services that include non-electrified sections of track.
Italian State Railways

TRANS-EUROP EXPRESSES AUTUMN 1957

Name	From	To	Stock provided by
EDELWEISS	AMSTERDAM	ZURICH	SBB/NS
ETOILE DU NORD	PARIS NORD	AMSTERDAM	SNCF
HELVETIA	HAMBURG	ZURICH	DB
ILE DE FRANCE	PARIS NORD	AMSTERDAM	SNCF
LIGURE	MILAN	MARSEILLES	FS
MEDIOLANUM	MUNICH	MILAN	FS
OISEAU BLEU	PARIS NORD	BRUSSELS	SNCF
PARIS-RUHR	PARIS NORD	DORTMUND	DB
PARSIFAL	PARIS NORD	DORTMUND	DB
RHEIN-MAIN	FRANKFURT	AMSTERDAM	DB
SAPHIR	OSTEND	DORTMUND	DB

TRANS-EUROP EXPRESSES WINTER 1971-72

Name	From	To	Stock provided by
AQUITAINE	PARIS AUSTERLITZ	BORDEAUX	SNCF
ARBALETE	PARIS EST	BASLE	SNCF
BAVARIA	MUNICH	ZURICH	DB
BLAUER ENZIAN	HAMBURG	MUNICH AND KLAGENFURT	DB
CAPITOLE	PARIS AUSTERLITZ	TOULOUSE	SNCF
BRABANT	PARIS NORD	BRUSSELS	SNCB SNCF
CATALAN TALGO	BARCELONA	GENEVA	RENFE
CISALPIN	PARIS LYON	MILAN	SBB
DIAMANT	BRUSSELS	HANOVER	DB
EDELWEISS	AMSTERDAM	ZURICH	SBB/NS
ETENDARD	PARIS AUSTERLITZ	BORDEAUX	SNCF
ETOILE DU NORD	PARIS NORD	AMSTERDAM	SNCB SNCF
GOETHE	PARIS EST	FRANKFURT	SNCF
GOTTARDO	MILAN	BASLE/ZURICH	SBB
HELVETIA	HAMBURG	ZURICH	DB
ILE DE FRANCE	PARIS NORD	AMSTERDAM	SNCB SNCF
KLEBER	PARIS EST	STRASBOURG	SNCF
LEMANO	GENEVA	MILAN	FS
LIGURE	MILAN	AVIGNON	FS
LYONNAIS	PARIS LYON	LYONS	SNCF
MEDIOLANUM	MUNICH	MILAN	DB
MISTRAL	PARIS LYON	NICE	SNCF
MONT CENIS	LYONS	MILAN	FS
OISEAU BLEU	PARIS NORD	BRUSSELS	SNCB SNCF
PARIS RUHR	PARIS NORD	DÜSSELDORF	SNCF
PARSIFAL	PARIS NORD	HAMBURG	DB
PRINZ EUGEN	BREMEN	VIENNA	DB
REMBRANDT	AMSTERDAM	MUNICH	DB
RHEINGOLD	AMSTERDAM/ HOOK OF HOLLAND	GENEVA etc.	DB
RHEIN-MAIN	FRANKFURT	AMSTERDAM	DB
ROLAND	BREMEN	MILAN	DB
SAPHIR	BRUSSELS	NUREMBERG	DB
STANISLAS	PARIS EST	STRASBOURG	SNCF
TICINO	MILAN	ZURICH	SBB

DB: German Federal FS: Italian State NS: Netherlands
RENFE: Spanish National SBB: Swiss Federal
SNCB: Belgian National SNCF: French National

Hamburg-Hanover-Munich Blauer Enzian which runs beyond Munich to and from Austrian winter sports and summer resorts.

Eight basic varieties of TEE train composition are shown in the table. They range from the two-car FS diesel multiple-units of the Lyons-Milan Mont Cenis to the 15 coaches of the Mistral. Total distances vary between little less than 193 miles from Paris Nord to Brussels Midi by the Brabant in two hours 23 minutes to 676 miles from Nice to Paris Lyon by the Mistral in nine hours three minutes and 725 miles from Villach to Hamburg-Altona by the Blauer Enzian in 12 hours 23 minutes. Catering arrangements also vary widely. The caterers are the Wagons-Lits Company (CIWLT), the German Sleeping & Dining Car Company (DSG) and the Swiss Restaurant Car Company (CSWR). Meals are served in separate restaurant cars; at passengers' seats in open vehicles adjoining the restaurant cars in SNCF and SNCB locomotive-hauled TEE train-sets; in restaurant compartments which do not take up the whole vehicles, as in the Edelweiss; at passengers' seats only (in the Pullman manner) in the FS two-car diesel trains; and buffet service only in the FS Lemano Geneva-Milan service. The type of facility varies with the length of journey, time of day and number of stops, and with seasonal changes in average passenger complement.

Most TEE stock is fully air-conditioned; the only exception at the time of writing is the FS two-car sets which have a quite effective form of forced-air ventilation. There are agreed standards for lighting, heating and appointments. In several types of vehicle hand baggage is conveyed in special compartments. Among fitments are the outside doors of the vestibules of Mistral coaches which can be opened only when the train is moving below a predetermined low speed. All locomotives that haul TEEs other than multiple units are electric. Schedules are exacting and the most powerful locomotives available are rostered for TEE duties. They include the DB's Class 103 8,000-10,000hp Co-Cos for several TEE's within Germany and the SNCF's Class CC6500 8,000hp Co-Cos for the Mistral, Etendard and other TEEs on 1.5kV electrified lines. Locomotive-hauled TEEs between France, Belgium, the Netherlands and Federal Germany are headed over parts at least of their journeys by SNCF, SNCB or DB three- or four-voltage locomotives. The NS at present does not favour multi-voltage locomotives.

By and large the TEEs have been an economic success, as the increase in their numbers show. Suitably appointed and adequately fast existing services have been promoted to TEE rank, to reap maximum advantage from the growth in traffic that stems from fast, comfortable and punctual rail service. With the general increase in business and tourist travel in Western Europe, reflecting the growing unpleasantness of motoring on crowded roads, the railways have gradually moved away from the fixed-formation multiple-unit to locomotive-hauled TEE trains, particularly as the original TEE trainsets have become too old for exacting TEE service. Even so, the present trend towards locomotive haulage of fast passenger services might not long continue. Most Western European railway managements are developing high-speed multiple units, some electric and some powered by gas turbines, designed for speeds up to 150mph. If successful the new generation of advanced passenger trains will undoubtedly find their way on to the front-line service of the Trans Europ Express network.

FOR MANY YEARS it was claimed that no stay in the United States was complete unless the tourist had had the opportunity of Riding the Century'. Today, alas, the experience is no longer possible, for with the drastic curtailment of American passenger services that has resulted from air and road competition most long-distance trains have ceased any longer to be a paying proposition and many have been withdrawn. Among them is the subject of this article, and one of the world's most famous trains—the Twentieth Century Limited.

The service originated in June 1902 when the then New York Central & Hudson River Railroad and the Lake Shore & Michigan Southern Railroad introduced an express service over their joint 961-mile route between New York and Chicago; the 20-hour schedule cut four hours from the previous best over the course. The new train was named Twentieth Century Limited. As the names of the two railways indicated, for the first 142 miles, to Albany, the NYC&HRR main line, running due north, ran along the left bank of the Hudson River. At Albany the line turned due west through Syracuse

to a course just south of Lakes Ontario and Erie, through Buffalo, where the LS&MSRR took over, to Cleveland and Toledo, after which a cut across country brought the line into Chicago, at the southern end of Lake Michigan.

The proximity of the railway to the water over most of its length prompted the New York Central slogan, 'Water Level Route—You Can Sleep', which the NYC splashed over its timetables and other publicity. The slogan was also a sly dig at the competing Pennsylvania Company, whose Pennsylvania Special (in 1912 renamed the Broadway Limited), was introduced on the same day as the Twentieth Century Limited and on the same 20-hour schedule. The Pennsy train took a shorter 908-mile course through the Allegheny mountains, at the cost of climbing to a summit level of 2,193ft at Gallitzin, west of Altoona, up gradients as steep as 1 in 50, with correspondingly hard effort and noisy exhaust by the locomotives.

Development of the Twentieth Century route was undertaken by the New York Central System, an amalgamation of the New York Central and the Lake Shore

THE TWENTIETH CENTURY LIMITED

lines. In later years the route had the distinction of being the longest four-track main line in the world; there was 474 miles of it continuously from Castleton, just outside New York, to Collinwood, in the suburbs of Cleveland. More recently, however, much of the quadruple trackage has been reduced to ordinary double track, but with frequent crossover roads and suitable signalling to permit either-way working on both lines.

By contrast, in former days when the Twentieth Century Limited and other expresses reached Syracuse, their route to the passenger station lay, like a tramway, through busy city streets at 15mph, until at long last a new main line to a new

an all-Pullman train. In its early days the coaches were of the Pullman convertible type, in the daytime providing ordinary seating on each side of a central corridor, and at night converted to sleeping cars by pulling the seats together to form lower berths and folding down panels in sides under the ceiling to provide upper berths. At both levels beds were thus arranged lengthwise along the coach sides and curtains were drawn along both sides of the central gangway. In their berths behind the curtains passengers had the uncomfortable task of undressing and getting into bed, and in the morning of getting up and dressing. Washing and shaving had to be performed in communal wash rooms at both ends of each car.

Left: Streamlined Hudson-type locomotive introduced in the late 1930s by New York Central for its crack passenger services. *Ian Allan library*

Below: Richly furnished Pullman observation car introduced on the Twentieth Century Limited service in 1929. *Ian Allan library*

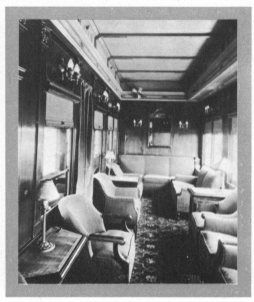

By degrees, however, new Pullman cars were introduced with single and double rooms of various sizes (some oddly described as 'drawing rooms'), and the supplementary Pullman charges were varied according to the size and relative luxury of the accommodation provided. By 1908 wooden coach-bodies were being replaced by all-steel stock, the rear-end observation platforms on the last coach were being replaced by glassed-in observation lounges, and all kinds of other amenities were being introduced.

In the middle 1950s the Twentieth Century Limited had reached the height of its fame. It had become one of a number of 'all-room' trains. The least expensive accommodation was in roomettes, which were tiny single rooms, dovetailed into one another to make the maximum possible use of car space. They provided comfortable seats for daytime travel and a quick-action fold-down ready-made-up bed, with its own toilet facilities. Then there were single bedrooms, similarly with beds folding into the walls, but with rather more space; still larger double bedrooms for couples; and 'master rooms', which were suites with their own shower-baths.

The complete normal formation of the Twentieth Century in its heyday included four drawing rooms, four 'compartments', 79 double bedrooms and 30 roomettes, providing sleeping accommodation for just over 200 passengers in nine coaches. In addition there were two restaurant cars, a club lounge and a rear-end observation lounge, a baggage car with sleeping accommodation for off-duty train staff, and a post office and 'express' (parcels) car. Refreshments could be obtained in a couple of the train lounges as well as in the dining cars.

The size of the staff required to man such a hotel-on-wheels can well be imagined. Including the dining and refreshment car attendants, kitchen crew, a 'porter' for each sleeping car, baggagemen, conductor, barber, lady hostess, even a train secretary, and, of course, the enginemen, it could easily run to a total of 30 or more; the need for a special service charge is thereby explained.

For some years the sleeping cars included two which were transferred in Chicago from the New York Central to the Santa Fe Railroad, and worked by Santa Fe Super-Chief train through to Los Angeles, and thus across the United States from the Atlantic to the Pacific coast. But in time air competition put the Los Angeles sleepers out of business, and also reduced the New York-Chicago *clientèle* until at last, by the middle 1960s, the proud all-Pullman Twentieth Century had been invaded by 'sleeper coaches'. (In the USA the 'coach' has always been the equivalent of European second class.) Also added were reclining-chair cars—that is, open saloons fitted with tilting seats to ease night-time travel—available, like single and double rooms of the sleeper coaches, at second-class fares, with supplementary and the flat service charges added. This democratisation was unable to generate an economic revival and turned out to be only the prelude to the final withdrawal of the Twentieth Century Limited in 1970.

In the earliest days of the Twentieth Century Limited its coaches were all of wooden construction, but in course of time the serious casualties caused by the destruction of coaching stock in American accidents led, first, to the introduction of massive steel underframes, and later to all-steel body construction. Also the length of American vehicles, which grew to 85ft or so, resulted in the almost universal adoption of six-wheel bogies to carry them. With such heavy constituents it was common for American Pullman sleeping and dining cars to grow to weights of 70 or 80 tons apiece, with the result that a long-distance express like the Twentieth Century could easily total upwards of 1,000 tons.

In its earlier years, for that reason, it was not unusual for the train to be operated in three or more sections; indeed, it has been known for as many as eight sections of the one train to follow one another along the 961-mile route. But later on additional named trains with but little

station made it possible to abandon this troublesome practice. Steam haulage throughout of the Twentieth Century for the first five years of its life gave way in 1907 to electric operation between the Grand Central Terminal in New York and Wakefield, extended in 1913 to Harmon, nearly 33 miles out.

The cut of four hours below the previous fastest time between New York and Chicago, initiated with the Twentieth Century Limited, introduced a novel system of fare charging. With the previous 28 hours fixed as the standard time, an extra fare of one dollar (later increased to $1.20) was charged for every hour that the passenger saved with the accelerated service. With every subsequent acceleration the supplement was increased, but with the proviso that for every hour that the Twentieth Century might be late in arriving, the passenger was entitled to a corresponding refund. In later years, however, this flexible fare system was replaced by a flat-rate service charge, in addition to the first-class fare and Pullman supplement.

Mention of Pullman brings its reminder that the Twentieth Century Limited was

longer journey times relieved the pressure on the Century, as also did the splitting off of the Boston portion, attached and detached at Albany, into a separate train called the New England States. By degrees the stops at Albany and Syracuse, going west, became halts to pick up passengers only, and at Buffalo no passenger business was done; the previous stop and reversal at Cleveland Union Terminal was cut out by the use of an avoiding line, reducing the overall journey to 958 miles; and the Toledo and Elkhart stops were restricted to setting down only, with corresponding arrangements in the reverse direction.

From its introductory schedule in 1902 of 20 hours in each direction, the Twentieth Century Limited was accelerated in 1908 for a brief period to 18 hours. It was only a brief improvement however and after a serious accident to the rival Pennsylvania Special, whose time also had been cut to 18 hours, there was a reversion to the 20-hour schedule. So matters continued until April 1932, when an 18-hour booking was again essayed, a year later to be cut to $17\frac{3}{4}$ hours. In June 1938 a further reduction to 16 hours for the first time brought the overall speed of the Twentieth Century up to 60mph, all stops included. In the early part of the 1939-45 war there was a temporary increase to 17 hours, but the 16-hour schedule was restored in the spring of 1946, by which time diesel power had come in to replace the steam locomotives.

Even the 20-hour schedule involved some very fast intermediate times. In the final years the Century was booked in both directions over the 133 miles between Toledo and Elkhart in 111min at 71.9mph start to stop; from Buffalo to Collinwood (a stop outside Cleveland to change engine crews) the time allowed for the 174.7 miles was 147 minutes and in the reverse direction 148 minutes, at start-to-stop averages of 71.3 and 70.9mph respectively. Buffalo-Collinwood was the longest non-stop part of the journey. A later acceleration brought the Toledo-Elkhart time, with diesel traction, down to 108 minutes, boosting the average speed to 74.1mph. Such times demanded speeds of well over 80mph for much of the distance, with a train which, even after the introduction of streamlined lightweight coaches, weighed well over 1,000 tons.

As to Twentieth Century Limited motive power, with the relatively light loads of the early years 4-4-0 locomotives (such as the famous No 999) were able to cope. As weight grew there was a progressive change to the 4-4-2 and 4-6-2 wheel arrangements and then to the highly capable Class J3 4-6-4, or Hudson class. With two $22\frac{1}{2}$in by 29in cylinders, 6ft 7in coupled wheels and 275lb/sq in working pressure, the Hudsons could exert a tractive effort of 43,440lb, to which a booster could add 12,100lb for starting. Ample steam was provided by a boiler with 4,187sq ft of heating surfaces and 1,745sq ft of superheating surface, and a firegrate with an area of 82 sq ft (perhaps

needless to say, mechanically fired).

A Hudson in working order weighed $160\frac{3}{4}$ tons; with a 12-wheel tender carrying nearly 27 tons of coal and 14,000 gallons of water the weight was 300 tons. With the Hudsons the practice began of using the same locomotive unchanged between Harmon, where the changeover from electric haulage took place, and Chicago, a total distance of 925 miles. The water supply was replenished from time to time from track-troughs, and at two points en route the coal supply was topped up from gantries spanning the line. There also, during a brief stop, the engines were given a quick service examination by attendant fitters.

But something bigger and even more imposing came with the advent of the Niagara-class 4-8-4s. These monsters, with $25\frac{1}{2}$in by 32in cylinders but unchanged 6ft 7in coupled wheels and 275lb pressure, had a tractive effort of 61,570lb which needed no boosters; steam was produced in a boiler having 4,827sq ft heating surface, 2,060sq ft superheating surface and a firegrate area of 100sq ft. To provide adequate supplies, a tender carried on 14 wheels was needed, with accommodation for 18,000 gallons of water and 41 tons of coal (which nevertheless required replenishment en route). The tender weighed 188 tons fully loaded and engine and tender together totalled just short of 400 tons. Among unusual fittings, the Niagara had a 'valve pilot indicator', designed to prevent the driver from overtaxing his locomotive by indicating the maximum cut-off that could be used at any moment without causing an excessive drain on the boiler.

Remarkable work was done by the Niagara 4-8-4s during their relatively short life, but as with all other American steam power they were doomed to give way to the all-conquering diesels, and actually did so in 1945, from which time 2,000hp Electro-Motive diesel-electric locomotives in pairs took over the Twentieth Century duty. From that time onwards economies were achieved by a reduction in the cost of fuel and the abolition of the need to refuel or service the locomotives during the journey.

One other contribution to the erstwhile glamour of the Century deserves mention. Most American stations in large cities comprise a spacious entrance hall with the needed passenger facilities grouped round it, from which gates lead to platforms that are no more than passageways to the trains. New York Central's Grand Central station in New York City was no exception. From its concourse, with cathedral-like dimensions of 275ft by 120ft and 125ft high, passengers descended to a 41-track main-line station and, below that, a 39-track suburban station. But from all other main-line departures that of the Twentieth Century Limited was always distinguished. Every day a red carpet was rolled out along the entire length of its platform as a salute to its highly favoured passengers!

Top: New stainless-steel coaches were brought into service by New York Central on its major express services from 1946. *Ian Allan library*

Left: The new stock introduced to the Twentieth Century the roomette, with its own lavatory, individual heating and air-conditioning controls and fluorescent lighting. *Ian Allan library*

Below: Foreshadowing the doom of long-distance rail travel in North America in 1929, a Fokker passenger plane in air-rail joint service flies over the Twentieth Century Limited. *Ian Allan library*

ZEPHYRS, HIAWATHAS AND FLORIDA SPECIALS

Right: The original diesel Burlington Pioneer Zephyr of 1934, as preserved at the Chicago Museum of Science and Industry. *J K Hayward*

Below: Rear end of Southern Pacific diesel steamliner at San Francisco in 1952. *J M Jarvis*

ZEPHYRS AND HIAWATHAS, Chiefs and Rockets, Daylights and 400s, Florida Specials and countless Limiteds—all household names in America in the nineteen-thirties, -forties and -fifties. Each such title, with an appropriate prefix, denoted some crack passenger train, sometimes involving more than one railroad. Space allows us to consider here only three groups of these crack streamlined trains.

Pride of place, and hence first mention, must go to the Zephyrs. As was mentioned in the earlier chapter in this book on the Burlington Northern (pages 413-6), the first Zephyr was a modest affair. It comprised a three-car train set, articulated throughout, and carried on four trucks (bogies). The leading vehicle was a 600hp locomotive whose power unit was a Winton 201A diesel engine mounted integrally with the bogie. Weighing under 100 tons, the three-car train carried just 72 passengers in its two trailer cars. The car bodies were of fluted stainless-steel construction and were built by the Budd Company in Philadelphia. The train was given the name Pioneer Zephyr. It was built early in 1934 and displayed in Chicago at the Century of Progress Exposition that year.

After a series of demonstration runs, towards the end of 1934 the train entered revenue-earning service between Kansas City, Omaha, and Lincoln, Nebraska, a run of 250 miles. A similar train set, but with a coach (second-class) seat section (instead of baggage space) in the rear end of the leading (power) car, went into service between Boston and Portland, Maine, in 1935 for the Boston & Maine and Maine Central railroads. That one was named Flying Yankee; it is now preserved at Edaville, about 40 miles from Boston. The Pioneer Zephyr is also preserved, at the Chicago Museum of Science & Industry.

The Pioneer Zephyr was followed in 1935 by three more train sets. The first two, still of three cars each, seated 88 and entered service as Twin Zephyrs in April between Chicago and the Twin Cities (St Paul and Minneapolis), taking 6½ hours for the 437-mile journey. Their route was markedly longer than the two alternatives, those of the Milwaukee Road (421 miles) and of the Chicago & North Western Railway (407 miles). The third new train was of four passenger cars, seating 92, and an additional baggage/mail car. It became

Milwaukee Road Olympian
Hiawatha at Deer Lodge, Montana, hauled by
electric loco E20 'Little Joe' in 1952. The
engine was built by GE for Russia under
Lease-lend, but not sent and was reduced to
standard gauge for the Milwaukee company.
J M Jarvis

the Mark Twain Zephyr, running between St Louis and Burlington, Iowa, 221 miles, in 5¾ hours with a number of stops. Later, from 1941, this route was also covered by the Zephyr-Rocket, an overnight train between St Louis, Burlington and Minneapolis, using Rock Island tracks north of Burlington on the 585 mile run to the Twin Cities, a 14 hour journey.

More Zephyrs appeared towards the end of 1936, when two 1,800hp locomotive units, named *Pegasus* and *Zephyrus,* entered service on the Chicago-Twin Cities run, with seven-car trains, each set making a round trip daily. The original Twin Zephyr three-car trains were found new fields elsewhere on the Burlington system. One became the Sam Houston Zephyr, running the 283 miles between Fort Worth, Dallas and Houston in five hours. The other set became the Ozark State Zephyr, between St Louis and Kansas City (279 miles).

Also in 1936 came the two train sets which formed the original Denver Zephyrs. Each partly articulated train was hauled by a two-unit locomotive totalling 3,000hp. The pairs of locomotives were named *Silver King*/*Silver Queen* and *Silver Knight*/ *Silver Princess,* respectively. Each of the 12-car trains included coaches, a dining car, four sleepers and an observation car, as well as a crew dormitory/passenger lounge car and a combined power generator/postal/baggage car. The Denver Zephyrs unquestionably provided facilities which set standards for 20 years or more, including such novelties as tightlock couplers, double glazing, foam rubber seats and electric razor power points. The passenger cars were named, using the common prefix Silver—because of the unpainted stainless-steel outer panelling, which was to become a familiar feature of many streamlined trains in years to come. The trains entered daily overnight service with an exciting 16-hour schedule for the

1,034-mile Chicago-Denver run.

In 1939, the 1000hp locomotive *Silver Charger,* the last to be styled in similar fashion to the Pioneer Zephyr (as were all those mentioned so far) entered service with the General Pershing Zephyr on the St Louis-Kansas City run. There are two other pre-war Zephyrs still to be mentioned, the Silver Streak Zephyr between Kansas City and Lincoln (the route of the Pioneer Zephyr) and, later in the year, the Texas Zephyr, running 834 miles, between Denver and Dallas over the Colorado & Southern lines. Not all of the Zephyrs introduced after the 1936 train sets were wholly of stainless steel. Some trains included refurbished sleeping cars of earlier heavyweight pattern.

Eventually the earliest of the epoch-making diesel trains became outdated; by 1942 the Pioneer Zephyr had moved to the secondary Lincoln-Hastings-McCook service, making local stops over part of the Denver Zephyr route. The Chicago Burlington & Quincy RR was first to introduce the now familiar Vista-dome coach, in 1947, in what might be termed the third generation of twin-Zephyr trains. The 1936 train sets so displaced from the Twin Cities run moved to the eastern half of the Chicago-Denver route, providing fast daytime service between Chicago, Omaha and Lincoln, about 557 miles, taking about 11 hours for the run with about 20 stops.

The high point of the Zephyr era came, many observers feel, in 1949 with the introduction of the California Zephyr. This train, often with five dome cars in its formation, ran between Chicago and Oakland (for San Francisco), about 2,525 miles. As far as Denver, Burlington tracks were used. West of Denver the spectacular Moffat tunnel route of the Denver & Rio Grande Western RR was followed, up through the front range of the Rockies and then west via Western Pacific RR

across Utah and Nevada and down the scenic Feather River canyon to Sacramento and on to Oakland. Whereas the other Zephyrs had combined speed and comfort, the schedule of the California Zephyr was arranged so that in each direction, the two most scenic sections were traversed in daylight on the two days and two nights of the run. For years, the train ran completely filled day after day, but rising cost, rather than declining patronage, caused its discontinuance in 1970.

In the early nineteen-fifties still more Zephyrs were introduced, including a new daytime Chicago-Kansas City train (466 miles), the Kansas City Zephyr. It had an overnight counterpart in the American Royal Zephyr. The Ak-Sar-Ben Zephyr (Nebraska spelled backwards) gave overnight service on the Chicago-Omaha-Lincoln run; it received new rolling stock in the early 'fifties. The ultimate Zephyr train sets came in 1956 when two superlative 14-car trains were introduced on the trunk Chicago-Denver route; they displaced the two trains built in 1936, which were then moved to the Texas Zephyr route and the new trains took up the title of Denver Zephyr. Each of the new train sets included three dome cars, one a coach, one a buffet car, and at the rear a dome-lounge for first-class (sleeper) passengers. Each train set also included two slumber-coaches, which introduced second-class enclosed sleeping berths.

All the new types of cars from the 1956 trains are now in Amtrak service, but not necessarily on the Denver Zephyr. (Amtrak is the quasi-government USA National Railroad Passenger Corporation.) The Denver Zephyr continues to run daily, and is extended, as the San Francisco Zephyr, via Cheyenne to Ogden (over the Union Pacific RR) and thence over the Southern Pacific RR to San Francisco. West of Denver, the train runs but three days a week, except in the summer season, when it runs daily.

The Hiawathas of the Milwaukee Road, on the Chicago Milwaukee, St Paul & Pacific RR were for many years in the high echelons of American expresses. It is a pleasure to be able to report that subsequently a second daily Hiawatha service has been restored to the Chicago-Twin Cities route by Amtrak. The North Coast Hiawatha, with a morning run northbound, is extended three days a week west from Minneapolis over the former Northern Pacific route of Burlington Northern & Seattle. The afternoon train, now named Empire Builder east of Minneapolis, (as well as over its run west to Seattle over the former Great Northern route) takes seven hours 40 minutes for the Chicago-Minneapolis run, with four fewer stops. There are corresponding runs into Chicago.

An interesting feature of the various Hiawatha trains was that the great majority of passenger cars were built in the railroad's own shops in Milwaukee, which was unusual for American railways. Exceptions to the home-building were the Super Domes, which came from Pullman-Standard. They were built in 1952 and the 10 vehicles, numbered 50-59, were among the heaviest streamlined cars ever built, weighing over 100 short tons. Because of the large glazed area, extra air conditioning had to be installed. Each car had 68 seats in the dome and there were seats for a further 28 in a café/lounge below. Six of the Super Domes were sold to Canadian National in 1964-65 and are now in use on the Supercontinental between Edmonton and Vancouver.

The Super Domes were built for the short-lived Olympian Hiawatha service, for which Pullman-Standard also built the Skytop lounge cars; they had eight bedrooms and a glazed 21-seat lounge observation area, which formed the tail-end of the train. Pullman-Standard also built 10 sleeping cars, each with 10 roomettes and six bedrooms. They, and the Skytops, dated from 1948. All the Skytop lounge cars were sold to Canadian National in 1964, as were five of the sleeping cars in 1967. All the Pullman-built cars lacked the wood finish which was a feature of the railway-built cars; the latter were somewhat lighter in weight than contemporary contractor-built cars and it is significant that none have been purchased by Amtrak.

Under Amtrak auspices, trains between Chicago and the two northern transcontinental rail routes of Burlington Northern (the ex-GN and ex-NP lines) run over Milwaukee Road tracks as far as the Twin Cities, rather than using the traditional Burlington Route (CB & Q) via La Crosse. Apart from the shorter mileage, the present route provides the city of Milwaukee (population 750,000) with through rail service, whereas the Burlington Route lacks any major intermediate centre of population.

The modern re-routeing had a parallel in 1955. Prior to October 30, 1955, the great fleet of Union Pacific streamlined trains

Below: Union Pacific's first streamlined diesel train of its named City series. *Union Pacific Railroad*

Bottom: Super-dome car of Milwaukee Road's Morning Hiawatha train. *J K Hayward*

ran between Chicago and Omaha over Chicago & North Western Railway tracks, but from that date, UP passenger trains used the Milwaukee Road for access to Chicago. The change brought company to the Midwest Hiawatha on its Chicago-Omaha journeys. It also resulted in a change of livery for the Hiawathas; the maroon, grey and orange colours, which had undergone several variations in application over the years, were dropped in favour of UP yellow, for Milwaukee Road passenger cars were included in through services over the UP to the several Pacific coast destinations.

In addition to the four Class A Atlantics, and the six Class F7 Hudsons built for the principal Hiawatha services, half-a-dozen older steam locomotives were rebuilt with streamlined shrouds for use on lesser services. Two 4-6-0s, Nos 10 and 11 of Class G—quite small engines of 94 short tons each, were so modified for the North Woods Hiawathas in 1936 and 1937 respectively. In their new guise, they resembled the Class A Atlantics. Four 4-6-2s were modified as well, but their new styling was more akin to the Class F7 Hudson. Class F2 Pacifics Nos 801 and 812 were altered (from Class F5) for service on the Sioux Falls section of the Midwest Hiawathas; the main train was in the hands of Class A Atlantics from inauguration at the end of 1940 to

1946-47, when diesels began to take over; the Class F5 Pacifics were finally withdrawn in 1950.

Two Class F1 Pacifics, Nos 151 and 152, were allocated to the Chippewa-Hiawatha north of Milwaukee (the train originated in Chicago). The Chip, as it was known, followed the west shore of Lake Michigan for much of its run. Its ultimate terminal was Ontonagon, on the south shore of Lake Superior. From its inauguration in 1937, Nos 151 and 152 were specially painted in Hiawatha colours, and in 1941 they were streamlined, becoming similar in appearance to Nos 801 and 812. Both were withdrawn in 1954, although the Chip was being hauled by diesel by the end of 1950, and finally discontinued running early in 1960.

In sharp contrast to the Hiawatha service to north-western parts of the USA, the Florida Special was one of a number of trains which linked the winter resorts of Florida with New York (and many other northern cities which had chilly winters). The train had its origins in 1888 as the New York and Florida Special with a first-class-only consist making the 1,074-mile run from New York to Jacksonville in 30 hours. The train was routed over the Pennsylvania RR to Washington, thence via the Richmond Fredericksburg & Potomac RR to Richmond, and the Atlantic Coast Line RR to Jacksonville, and finally over the

Florida East Coast Railway to St Augustine.

The new train ran three times a week in each direction. Initially, each train set had but six cars; the baggage-dynamo car was followed by a combination smoker, a dining car and three sleepers. All 12 cars were newly built in Chicago by the Pullman Company and featured electric light, steam (not stove) heating, and vestibules throughout. The run started in Jersey City, for New York's Penn station was still two decades in the future. For its first two years, the train terminated at Jacksonville and passengers took a ferry across the St Johns River, until the latter was bridged early in 1890. Its operation was limited to the winter season.

The success of the train resulted in the thrice-weekly service becoming daily, and in 1912 the train was extended to Key West, on the island-hopping line south of Miami. New equipment was assigned to the train over the years, and in the early 1920s it was renamed, more succinctly, the Florida Special, and was thoroughly modernised. Despite the depression, the train's popularity was sustained, so much so that during the 1939-40 winter season, it ran regularly in three sections each day. Penn station in New York had by then long been its northern terminal, and the running time to Miami was $26\frac{1}{4}$ hours for the 1,388 miles.

Operation of the Florida Special luxury

service was discontinued during the 1939-45 war but it was reinstated after the war. In 1949, a further 65 minutes was cut from the schedule to Miami, with new lightweight streamlined stainless-steel cars and diesel traction. It was a first-class-only train, exclusively with enclosed sleeping quarters in its 12 Pullman cars and two bedroom/lounge cars. The train was further re-equipped for its 75th anniversary during the 1962-63 season. From then, it was no longer exclusively first class, and the schedule to Miami was reduced to 24 hours.

Today, alas, the Florida Special no longer runs, but Amtrak still operates two off-season New York-Florida trains, the Silver Meteor and the Silver Star, and in addition, the Floridian from Chicago. Indeed, the tourist traffic to Florida is probably the most profitable long-distance train service in the USA. The privately run Autotrain (carrying also passengers' motor cars) adds a fourth year-round service to Northern Florida.

The late Lucius Beebe recorded, in one of his several works on American 'Varnish' (express passenger trains), dozens of named trains which served Florida over the years. Apart from the Florida Special, the Atlantic Coast Line RR took part in the operation of an all-coach streamlined train in post-war years, namely, the East Coast Champion for the second-class traffic from New York to Miami, and intermediate points. The companion West Coast Champion carried Pullman (first-class) sleepers as well as coaches (second-class) to Tampa, St Petersburg and other points on the west side of the Florida peninsula. The Atlantic Coast Line RR included a network of short railway lines which had been consolidated by one Henry B Plant, and which served much of the west coast of Florida.

On the east coast, the ACL was dependent on its connection with the Florida East Coast Railway—the relatively small but eventually very prosperous railroad of Henry M Flagler, a partner in the Standard Oil Company. Flagler was one of the very few railroaders to have a train named after him. His enterprise developed many resorts in Florida, and it was he who conceived and carried out the construction of a railway over the sea by bridging a route south of Miami from island to island, to reach Key West, where steamer connection was made with Havana, Cuba. In pre-Castro days, of course, Cuba was a winter resort for Americans. The Key West extension was closed after being severely damaged in a hurricane in 1936. It is now a road.

Mention should perhaps also be made of the Seaboard Airline Railroad. (The Airline in its name refers to straight tracks and not to aeroplane services, and the term has been in use in America for 80 years or more.) The SAL served much of the same area south of Richmond, Virginia, as the ACL, and had the additional advantage of reaching West Palm Beach and Miami over its own tracks. Its crack train was the Orange Blossom Special, at one time a daily all-Pullman run between New York and Miami. Later companions to it were the Silver Meteor, Silver Comet and Silver Star, each with coach as well as Pullman space, and stainless-steel streamliners in the years following the 1939-45 war. In the 'sixties, two major changes occurred in Florida. The Florida East Coast line ceased to handle passenger traffic, after a major strike by its employees, and the ACL and SAL Railroads merged under the new title of Seaboard Coast Line RR.

Still, Florida passenger traffic by rail survives; today, for the time being, Amtrak is operating, over SCL tracks, two additional trains, the Vacationer and the Champion, as well as the Silver Meteor and the Silver Star, in its New York-Florida service.

Facing page: The CB & Q Denver Zephyr leaving Chicago in mid-1952. *J M Jarvis*

Above: A streamlined Hudson of Milwaukee Road fresh out of the shops in August 1938 to take on a Hiawatha service. *J M Jarvis*

Below: GM diesels of the Florida East Coast line pictured at Miami in December 1951. *J M Jarvis*

The CPR Canadian

CANADIAN PACIFIC Railway has a main line of its own 3,363 miles in length which although not unique is still unusual. The CPR main line crosses the continent of North America at its widest from Saint John, New Brunswick, on the Bay of Fundy, to Vancouver, British Columbia, on the Pacific. Actually this immense mileage is beaten by the rival Canadian National Railway, which from Halifax on the Atlantic skirts the head of the Bay of Fundy, and takes a more northerly course across Canada, to become slightly the longer of the two routes between Montreal and Vancouver.

There are no regular through trains between the Atlantic and the Pacific, however; the journey covered by the train indicated in the title to this article runs between Montreal and Vancouver, 2,880 miles, taking not far short of three days in the process. A section of the train starts from Toronto, making a journey shorter by 176 miles, and joins the main train at Sudbury, 435 miles from Montreal.

But first a word or two about the Canadian Pacific Railway, which helped materially in shaping Canadian history. The first proposal for a Canadian trans-continental railway was made by an Imperial Commission as far back as 1857, and a band of explorers spent four years in trying to map out a route. But although they discovered the Kicking Horse Pass (so named humorously because a pack horse kicked a member of the survey party), through which the CPR was eventually to pass, the difficulty posed by the great ranges of the Rockies and the Selkirks caused the leader of the party to report, 'The knowledge of the country as a whole would never lead me to advocate a line of communication from Canada across the continent to the Pacific'. But in 1865 another survey party, organised by the Surveyor - General of British Columbia, carried out a more-detailed exploration, and claimed to have discovered a practicable route.

Six more years passed before any further steps were taken. Until that time, Canada had been no more than a loose association of provinces or colonies, generally acknowledging British rule, but one of them at least — British Columbia — was becoming extremely restive at its lack of communication with the rest of Canada. Indeed, it is not beyond the bounds of possibility that British Columbia might have seceded to the United States had not the building of a trans-continental railway come urgently under review. The task to be faced was immense—first the rocky outcrops, muskegs and swamps in the almost uninhabited country west of Ottawa before Lake Superior could be reached; then some difficult construction round the cliffs bordering the lake; after that hundreds of miles across prairie country to the great chain of the Rockies west of Calgary in Alberta; and finally 500 miles of track location and laying through fearsome mountain country.

How the task was tackled would itself require one or more books adequately to describe, and at one stage the work nearly came to a standstill through lack of money. The Canadian Pacific Railway was incorporated in February 1881 and before the end of the century included in its corporate structure many railways in the provinces of Ontario and Quebec which had been in existence from the 1850s onwards. The new CPR, with the support of the Canadian government, began pushing eastwards and westwards from Winnipeg with such vigour that in no more than four years—five years before the obligatory date of completion of the railway—rail communication was established throughout between Montreal, on the St Lawrence river, and Vancouver, British Columbia.

With the financial assistance of a number of distinguished men, and the driving power of William Van Horne, the laying of the line proceeded apace in both directions, and on November 5, 1885, the two tracks met at Craigellachie, in the heart of the Gold Range, where the last spike was driven. Such was the necessity of completing the railway before funds ran out that in the 18 months from May 1882, no less than 675 miles of track were laid across the undulating prairies to the junction of the Bow and Elbow rivers— the future site of Calgary—with a maximum of 6 miles 660 yards in a single day.

On May 23, 1887, the first Canadian Pacific Railway train from the east ran into Vancouver. The $1\frac{1}{2}$-year interval since completion had been occupied in improving the hastily laid track so that trains could make the throughout journey safely. Because it had been essential to get the service going at the earliest possible moment, a good deal of the original construction, especially through the three ranges of the Rocky Mountains, was of a rather temporary nature. The intention was to replace the temporary structures by others of a permanent character as soon as the railway was earning money and adequate time could be given to the reconstructions. Over many mountain ravines the railway was carried on great timber trestle viaducts, fabricated from timber cut in the adjacent forests. The greatest of the trestle viaducts was across Stoney Creek, later replaced by a massive steel arch.

Some of the improvements were more costly. After the line had dropped from the Kicking Horse Pass down to the gorge of the Columbia River at Golden, it was felt that to follow the river's great bend to the northwards would mean too great a diversion, so a route was taken through the Selkirk Mountains to reach the river again at Revelstoke. It involved a tortuous climb on 1 in 45 gradients to the 4,350ft altitude

Top: Donald Smith (Lord Strathcona) driving the last spike in the Canadian Pacific trans-continental main line at Craigellachie in 1885. *CP Rail*

Left: CPR locomotive No 1, 4-4-0 'Countess of Dufferin' at rest outside Winnipeg CP station. *V Goldberg*

of the Rogers Pass, $4\frac{1}{2}$ miles of which had to be protected by timber snowsheds in order to avoid blockage of the line by snow in the winter months. The bold decision was reached later to cut out the difficult section by tunnelling under Mount Macdonald. This 5-mile bore lowered the railway's summit by 540ft and, for a cost of £1,125,000, vastly improved the operating over the section when the Connaught Tunnel was opened in 1916.

Another costly improvement affected the descent westwards down the Yoho Valley from the 5,329ft altitude of the Great Divide. For speed of construction the original line was carried straight down the valley on a ruling gradient of 1 in 23, which proved a serious handicap to trains having to climb in the eastbound direction, while in the westbound direction care was needed to prevent trains from running away down so steep an inclination. An entirely new location therefore was devised, reducing the gradient from 1 in 23 to 1 in 45, and was brought into use in 1909. On the new route trains starting the descent enter a spiral tunnel from which they emerge at a level lower by 54ft, travelling in the opposite direction. After crossing the river and the former route, which is now a road, they enter a similar tunnel in the opposite mountainside to emerge at a still lower level heading in the original direction. The relocation has added several miles to the distance covered, of course, but halving the steepness of the descent has made all the difference to the operation. The route closely resembles that familiar to European travellers at Wassen on the Gotthard Railway of Switzerland.

Against the general trend of decline, almost to extinction, of inter-city rail passenger travel in North America, the subject of this article, the Canadian (in parallel with the rival Canadian National Super Continental) continues to provide a very high standard of service across the width of Canada between Montreal and Vancouver. Until recently, the Canadian's 'list of equipment' included in the CPR timetable showed that the train consist included scenic - dome lounge sleeper with drawing - room and bedrooms; scenic - dome coffee shop; stainless steel sleepers with drawing rooms, compart-

ments, bedrooms, roomettes, duplex roomettes, and standard berths; stainless steel streamlined coaches with reserved seats; and dining room car.

Drawing rooms, compartments and bedrooms are self - contained sleeping rooms commanding supplements to the first-class fare varying with their size; Duplex roomettes are smaller sleeping compartments dovetailed into one another. Standard berths are of the older type, in which pairs of seats each side of a central gangway are drawn together to form lower berths, and the ceilings on each side are let down to provide upper berths, curtains being drawn along the aisle side of both to provide a measure of privacy. Coaches are the equivalent of British second class, with reclining seats which can be tilted at night to the near horizontal for sleeping comfort.

As to traction, during the days of steam the Canadian Pacific Railway developed locomotives of very considerable power. On a journey of such length locomotives needed, of course, to be changed at a number of division points, and their crews more frequently still. Exceptional power was essential with passenger trains which, in later years, frequently were comprised of as many as 15 coaches of heavy North American stock, perhaps up to 900 tons in weight.

As train weights increased, locomotive design progressed through 4-6-2 and 4-8-2 types to a culmination in two outstanding designs—a 4-6-4 or Hudson type for the flatter sections, capable of working continuously over distances approaching 1,000 miles and, for the mountain section, an extremely powerful 2-10-4 design. The Hudsons worked the Canadian through over the 980-odd miles between Montreal and Fort William, on Lake Superior, and over the 832 miles between Winnipeg and Calgary. They had 6ft 3in coupled wheels, 22in by 30in cylinders, 80.8sq ft firegrate area, 3,861sq ft heating surface and 1,640sq ft superheating surface; working pressure was 275lb per sq in and they weighed 163 tons in working order, or 295 tons with the 12-wheel tenders.

The 2-10-4s, which first appeared in 1929, had 5ft 3in coupled wheels, 25in

by 32in cylinders, a firegrate area of 93.5sq ft, 5,054sq ft heating and 2,032sq ft superheating surface, 285lb pressure, and a weight in working order of almost exactly 200 tons. The 12-wheel tenders, which could carry 12,000 gallons of water and 4,100 gallons of fuel oil (they were oil-fired) weighed 127 tons. Yet even such monsters required to be double-headed when climbing the 1 in 45 gradients from Revelstoke up to the Kicking Horse Pass and a fleet of 30 of them were needed to maintain the service.

Since then, however, the all-conquering diesels have taken over, and two or three diesel - electric locomotives in multiple handle the toughest assignments without difficulty. A great advantage of diesel traction is that the risk of forest fires started by steam power has now been eliminated.

The Canadian today takes a nominal 68 hours 35 minutes on its westbound run, but actually 71 hours 35 minutes because of the three changes of time en route; travelling east the journey is 70 minutes shorter. The speed might seem no more than moderate, but as it is the only daily passenger train over the route, it makes no fewer than 37 regular stops, which are allowed in aggregate five hours 35 minutes, giving a net running time of 66 hours. There are also 30 conditional stops when required. Many of the point-to-point runs are made at start-to-stop speeds well in excess of 50mph.

Westbound, the start from Montreal's Windsor station is at 13.55, and after halts to pick up passengers at Westmount, Montreal West and Dorval, there is some fast running over the first 109 miles to the capital, Ottawa. At 23.40, the train rolls into Sudbury, an important junction 435 miles from Montreal, where it is joined by the through section which has left Toronto, 260 miles away, at 17.15. The Sudbury stop, 50 minutes, is the longest on the journey, and the Canadian is not due to leave until 30 minutes after midnight.

By breakfast time next day the train has reached White River, and at Heron Bay, 791 miles from Montreal, passengers catch their first sight of the great inland sea Lake Superior. After a little less than 24 hours from Montreal, at 14.20, the Canadian stops for 15 minutes at Thunder Bay (987 miles), the present name for the former Fort William-Port Arthur, with its great elevators to which the railway brings the grain for shipment from the prairies of Manitoba. Watches are there set back one hour, from Eastern to Central time. For the next 475 miles, to Portage la Prairie, beyond Winnipeg, the track, up to this point single, becomes double—an unusual feature of any North American transcontinental line.

At the great city of Winnipeg, 1,406 miles from the start, it is again time for bed (22.15 to 22.45), and the second breakfast aboard may coincide with stops at towns with such Red Indian names as Moose Jaw, Swift Current and Medicine Hat; Swift Current sees the second watch

Right: CPR diesel No 1408 heading the eastbound Canadian at Field, BC, in May 1964. *V Goldberg*

Centre right: A CPR business coach alongside the Canadian at Thunder Bay (Fort William), Ontario, in July 1970. *V Goldberg*

Below: The Canadian crossing Stony Creek bridge in British Columbia. *CP Rail*

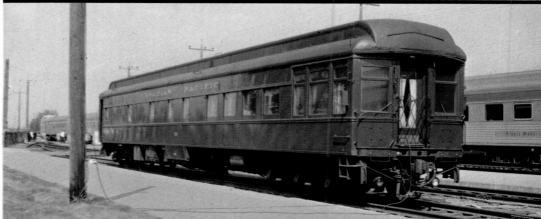

Top: The westbound Canadian making a late evening stop at Chalk River, Ontario, in July 1970. *V Goldberg*

Above: Dining room car 'Acadian', typical of the 1954/5 Budd rolling stock of the Canadian, at the Thunder Bay stop. *V Goldberg*

Below: The main lounge of the scenic dome car of the Canadian. *CP Rail*

adjustment, from Central to Mountain time. At the end of the second complete day, at 14.25, the train reaches Calgary, 2,239 miles from the start, with a 35-minute wait in prospect. Incidentally, the variations in altitude so far have been 110ft at Montreal, 1,412ft at Chapleau, 617ft at Thunder Bay, 1,486ft at Ignace, 772ft at Winnipeg, and then a gradual and almost uninterrupted ascent to 3,439ft at Calgary. But the foothills of the Rockies are now in sight ahead and climbing is to begin in earnest.

The line makes for the Bow River valley, which it mounts until it reaches the important town of Banff (2,322 miles, 4,534ft). Still further climbing lies ahead, past Lake Louise with its famous Canadian Pacific Chateau Lake Louise Hotel in a scenic setting, to the maximum altitude of 5,329ft at the Great Divide in the Kicking Horse Pass. The 'Divide', of course, is between the Atlantic and the Pacific watersheds, and at that point, visible from the train, there is a stream which is divided by concrete channels into two parts, one to flow eastwards so that its waters finish in Hudson's Bay, and the other westwards to be carried by the Columbia River into the Pacific.

Then follows the 1 in 45 descent of the Yoho Valley spirals to Field (4,072ft), an important divisional point (where the third watch adjustment is made, from Mountain to Pacific time) and from there to Golden and on down the Columbia River Valley for 63 miles to Beavermouth, at 2,532ft altitude. There the line turns due west to climb through the Selkirks to the Connaught Tunnel, at 3,800ft altitude, before another very steep descent, over 22 miles to Revelstoke, where the Columbia River is rejoined and crossed after its lengthy bend to the northwards. Through the Eagle Pass alongside various lakes the line proceeds until it reaches the valley of the South Thompson River, which is joined at Kamloops by the North Thompson River.

From the north down the North Thompson River runs the line of the great transcontinental competitor, the Canadian National Railway, which as the former Canadian Northern was carried across Canada by the route formerly proposed for the CPR but rejected as being too circuitous, by way of Edmonton and through the Yellowhead Pass. From Kamloops the two lines continue for 250 miles along opposite mountainsides of the same gorge, with scarcely any connection between them. The final stage, for 156 miles from Lytton, is down the gorge of the swiftly flowing Fraser River, in which, just beyond Lytton at Cisco, the two lines change sides, on big steel bridges, the CPR from then on taking the right bank. Finally, with the comfort of bed sought for the third night aboard for the through passenger, at about Revelstoke, there is ample time for breakfast before the Canadian comes to rest at 10.30 on the third morning, at the end of its memorable journey of 2,880 miles from Montreal.

INDEX